# How to become a successful ANIME-STYLE ARTIST

Tutorials, case studies, and advice from industry professionals

3dtotalPublishing

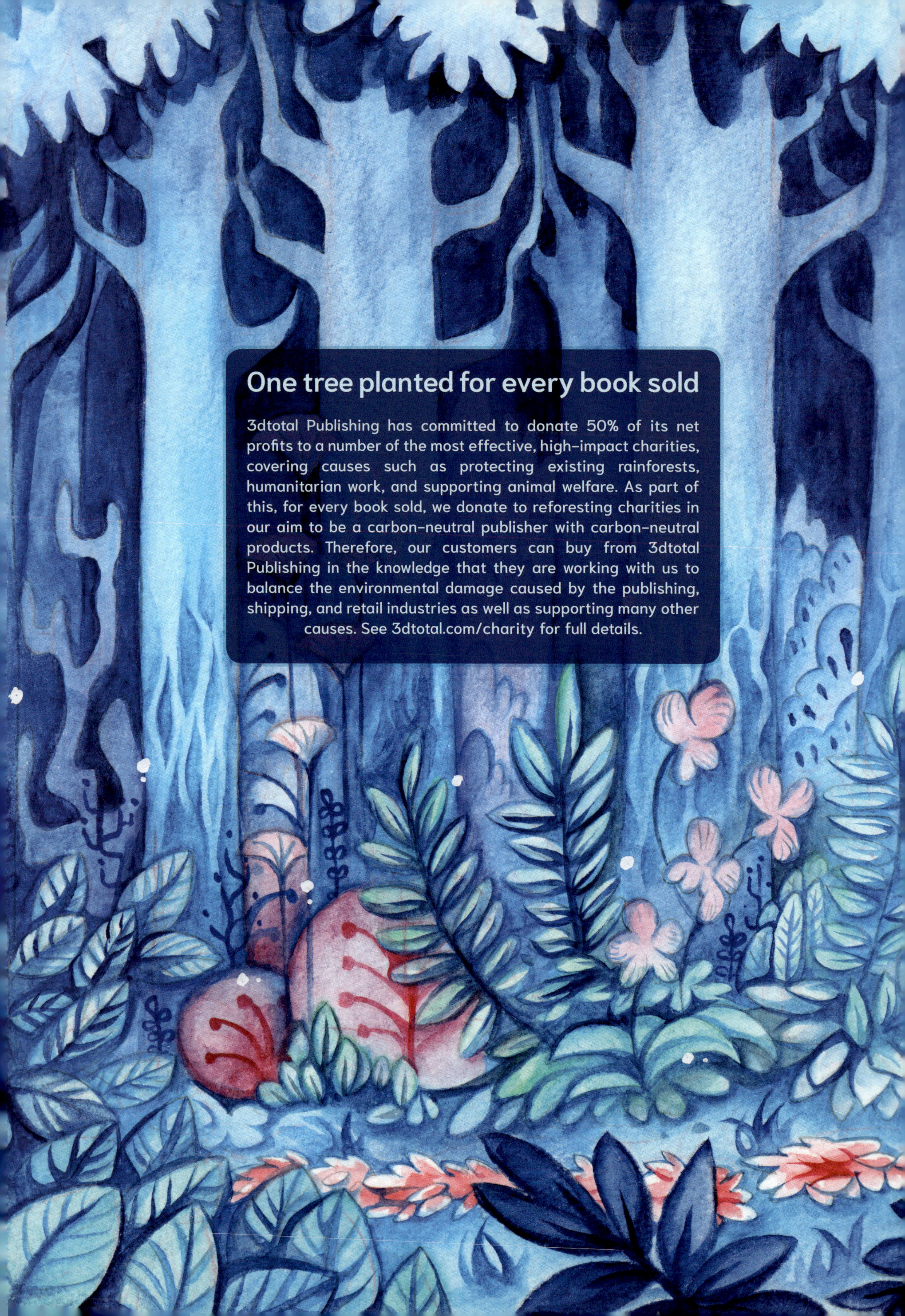

## One tree planted for every book sold

3dtotal Publishing has committed to donate 50% of its net profits to a number of the most effective, high-impact charities, covering causes such as protecting existing rainforests, humanitarian work, and supporting animal welfare. As part of this, for every book sold, we donate to reforesting charities in our aim to be a carbon-neutral publisher with carbon-neutral products. Therefore, our customers can buy from 3dtotal Publishing in the knowledge that they are working with us to balance the environmental damage caused by the publishing, shipping, and retail industries as well as supporting many other causes. See 3dtotal.com/charity for full details.

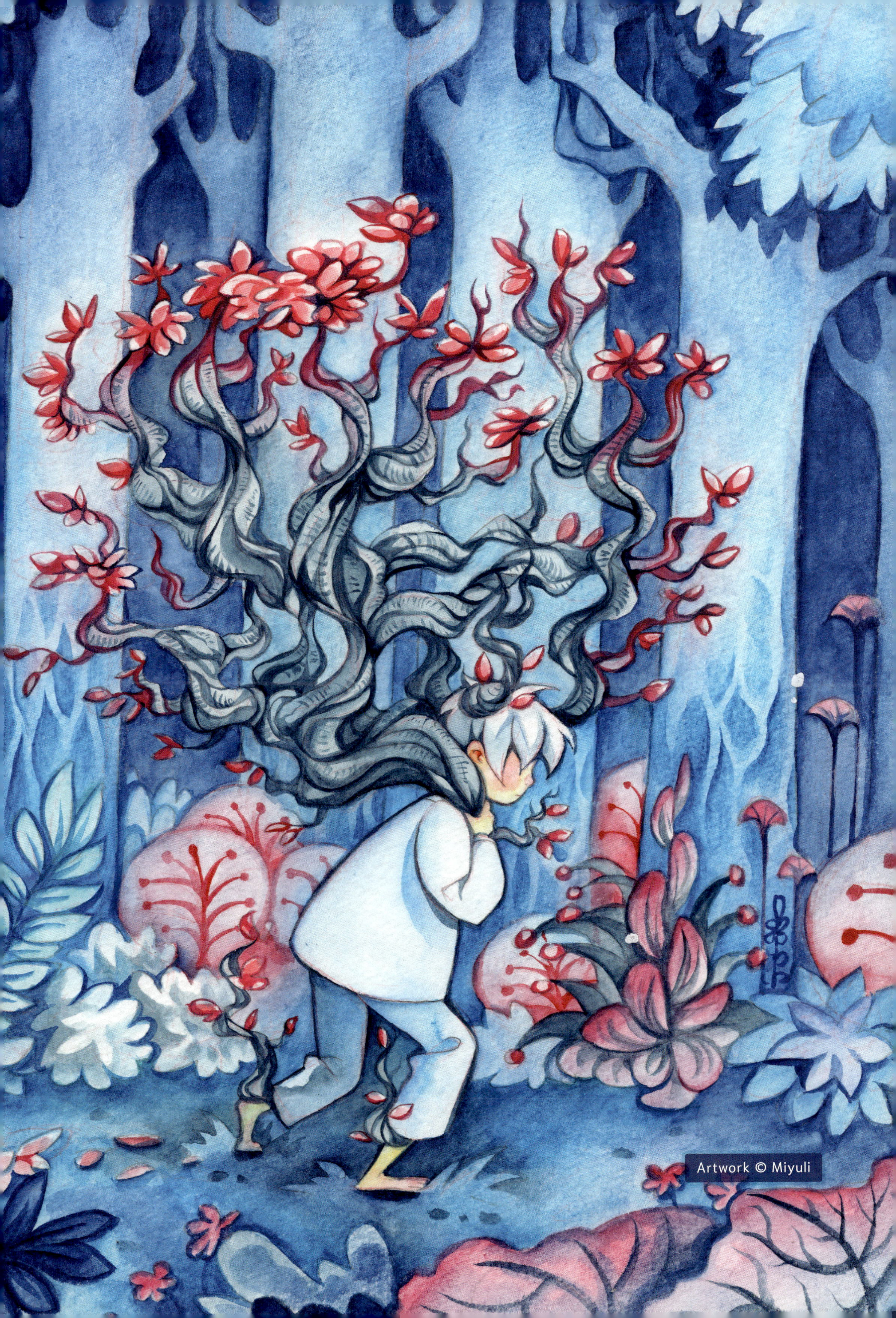

**3dtotal**Publishing

**Correspondence:**
publishing@3dtotal.com
**Website:** www.3dtotal.com



First published in the United Kingdom, 2022, by 3dtotal Publishing.

**Address:** 3dtotal.com Ltd,
29 Foregate Street, Worcester,
WR1 1DS, United Kingdom.

**Soft cover ISBN:** 978-1-912843-49-7
**Printing & binding:**
Gutenberg Press Ltd (Malta)
www.gutenberg.com.mt

Visit www.3dtotalpublishing.com for a complete list of available book titles.

**Managing Director:** Tom Greenway
**Studio Manager:** Simon Morse
**Lead Designer:** Fiona Tarbet
**Lead Editor:** Samantha Rigby
**Editor:** Philippa Barker
**Designer:** Joseph Cartwright

Cover images by individual artists as credited throughout the book.

MIX
Paper from responsible sources
FSC® C022612

*Hideout* © Djamila Knopf

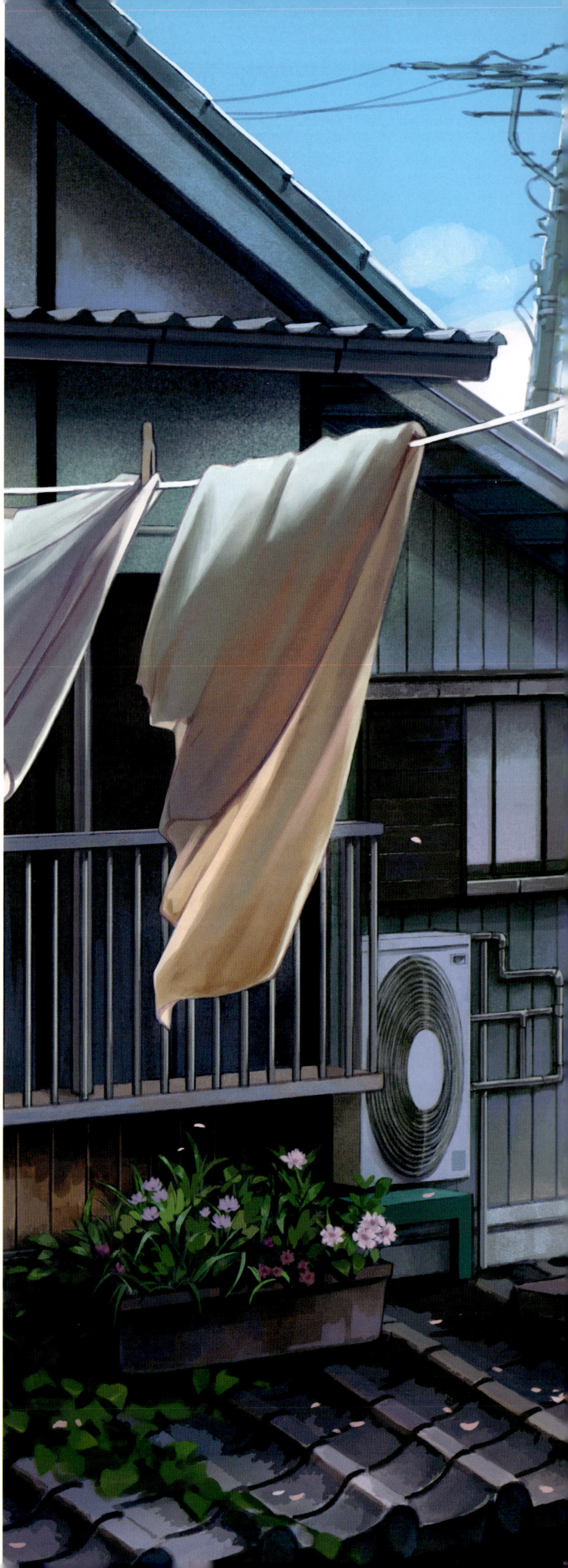

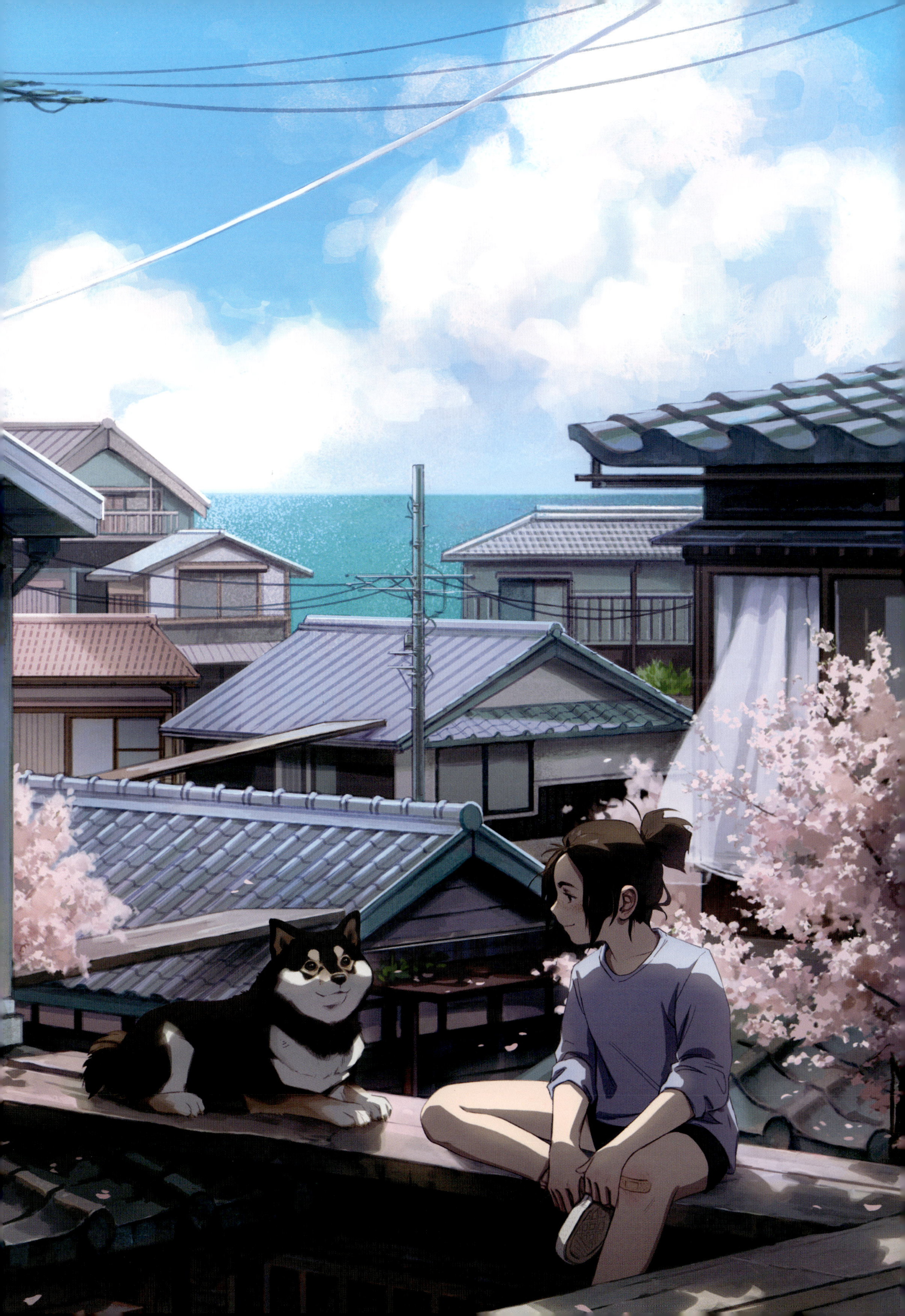

Artwork © Carles Dalmau

# CONTENTS

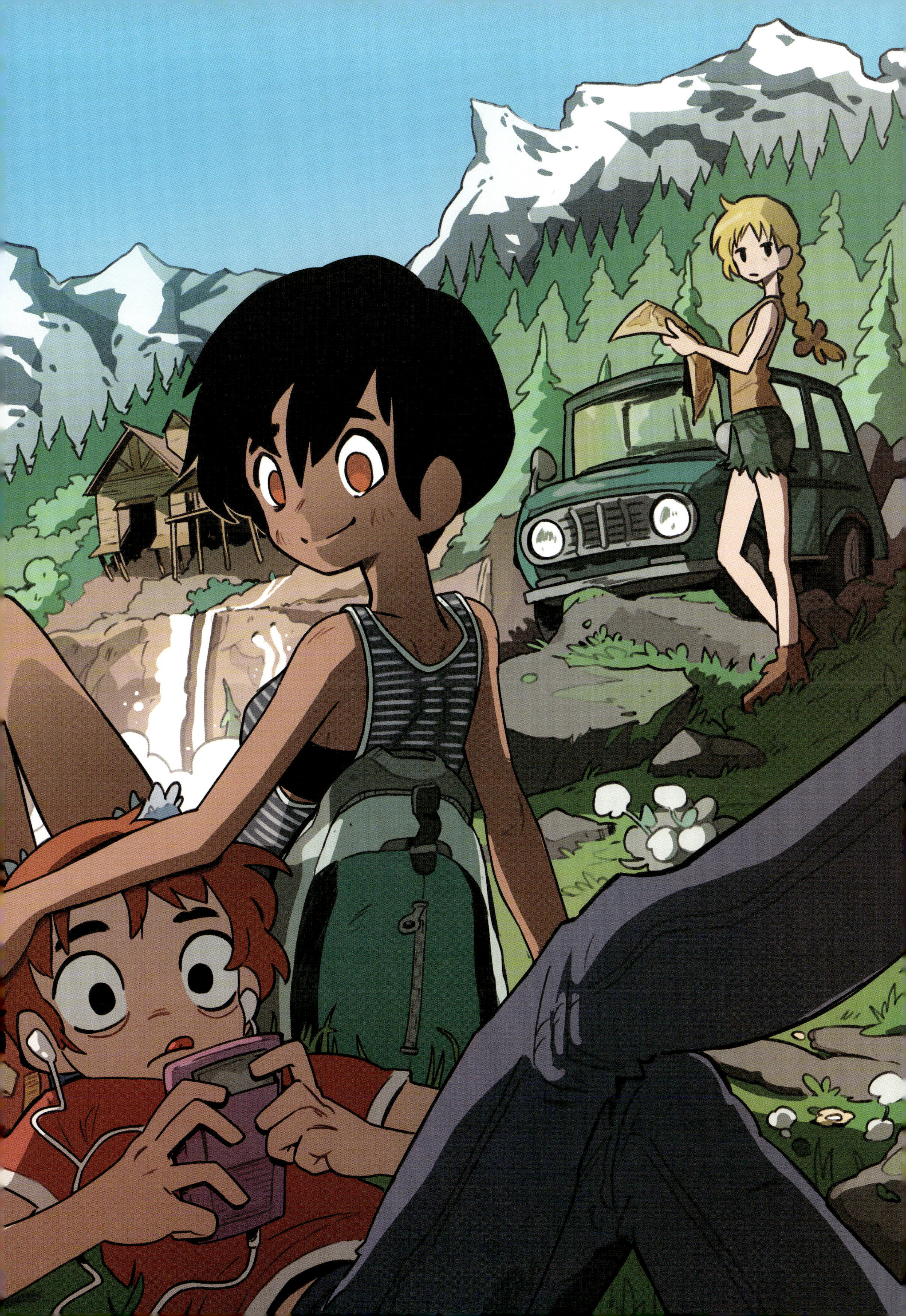

# FOREWORD

Reading this book takes me back to a time when anime was a hugely important part of my life. Every day after school, almost religiously, I would watch my favorite shows, doodle characters, and dream up my own adventures. While these days my relationship with anime no longer borders on obsession, I am still extremely fascinated by it. Anime and manga have the capacity to make you laugh or cry, to pull you to the edge of your seat in suspense, to transport you to different worlds, and to utterly and completely envelop you in the storytelling. Not only is anime a cultural phenomenon and a medium that spans genres and age groups, it is also a much-admired art form.

As a young artist, I owned a series of tutorial books that taught me how to draw in the manga style, covering topics such as character design, anatomy, and stylization. I carried them around with me everywhere I went and learned every page by heart. While the books taught me the basics of drawing that I still rely on today, they didn't teach me what I desperately wanted to know: could I make this my job and, if so, how?

Time and time again, people have told me to "stop with that anime nonsense" and to draw something more sophisticated instead. I was also told that I would need to find a proper job when I grew up, instead of chasing an unrealistic dream. At the time, I had no arguments to prove them wrong. Sure, there were manga and anime artists living in Japan, but that was so far removed from my own life and reality that I didn't even consider it to be a possibility.

*How to become a Successful Anime-Style Artist* is the book I wish I had owned when I was a young aspiring artist. When I felt lost and insecure considering my career goals, this book would have been an absolute game-changer, showing me that my dream of becoming an artist dedicated to creating anime-style illustrations was a possibility. The artists in this book are living, breathing proof that the dream is possible, and I wish I had been able to read these stories of how they achieved their success when I was starting out. The book features a diverse group of anime-inspired artists from all over the world who work in a variety of different styles and mediums. It beautifully illustrates that there is not one single anime style, but shows how each of the featured artists found their own interpretation and creative freedom within the overarching anime genre. The reader is invited to experience each artist's individual philosophies and approaches to making art, and to learn from their experiences – both good and bad.

The book also offers an honest representation of what it means to be a working artist, not glossing over the challenges and obstacles involved. In my opinion, the biggest strength is its heavy focus on the business side of working as an artist. It delves into navigating social media, working with clients, promoting and selling your artwork, making merchandise, pricing, networking, and so much more. The book offers a practical, hands-on approach that provides insight into various business models. It takes the vague notion of "being a successful artist," breaks it down, and transforms it into concrete examples and advice. Combined with the focus on anime-style art, this creates a unique and insightful blend that you will be hard-pressed to find in any other book.

I'm convinced that *How to become a Successful Anime-Style Artist* will open doors for many young and aspiring artists, providing much-needed guidance and direction. The book will encourage readers to keep making the art they love, and drown out any nagging voices that try to discourage them. Most importantly, it will let readers know they are not alone in their endeavor and that others have walked the same path before them, with wildly successful outcomes.

**Djamila Knopf**
**Illustrator & instructor**
**djamilaknopf.com**

*Colorless Streets* © Djamila Knopf

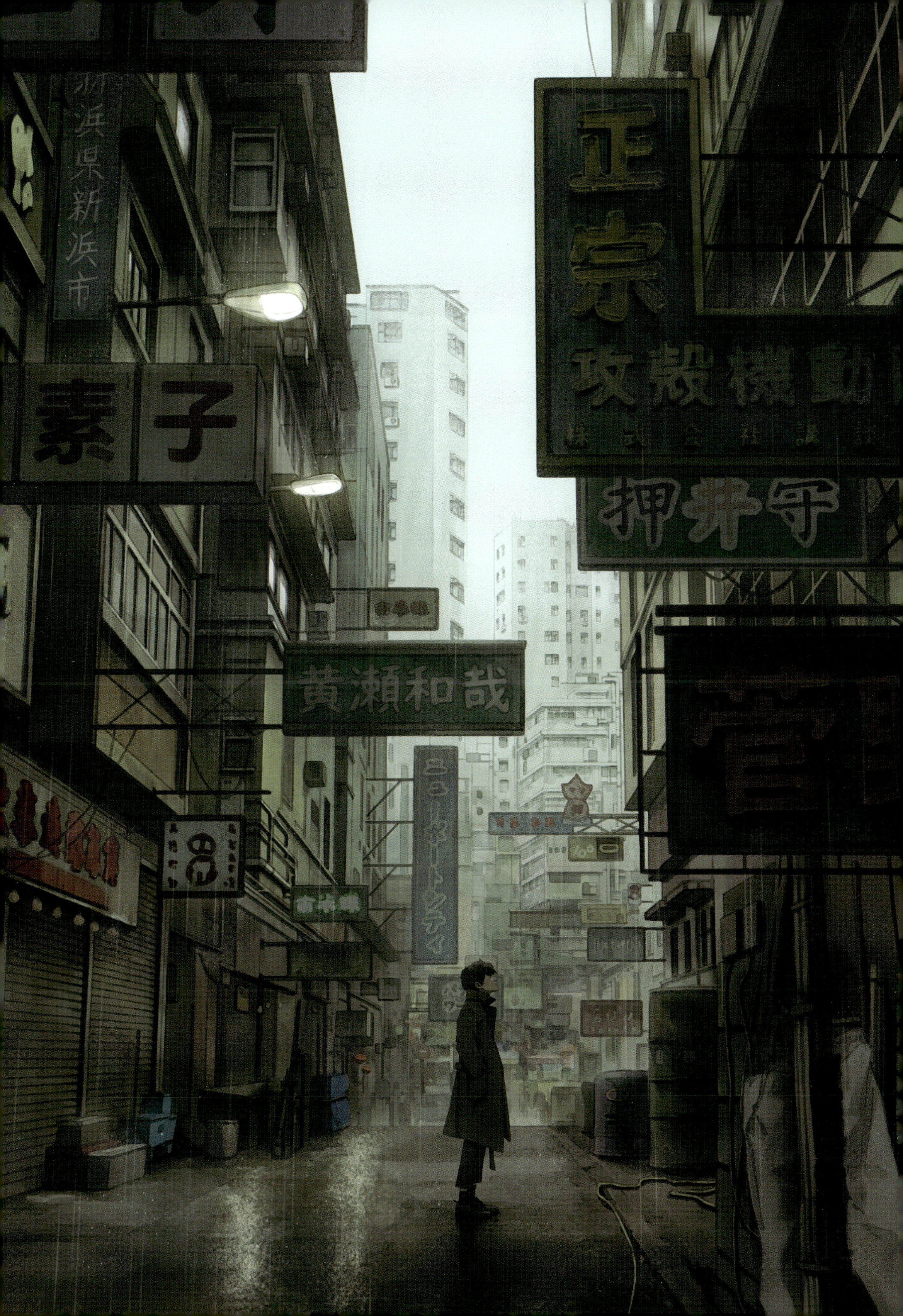
新浜県新浜市
素子
正宗
攻殻機動
押井守
黄瀬和哉

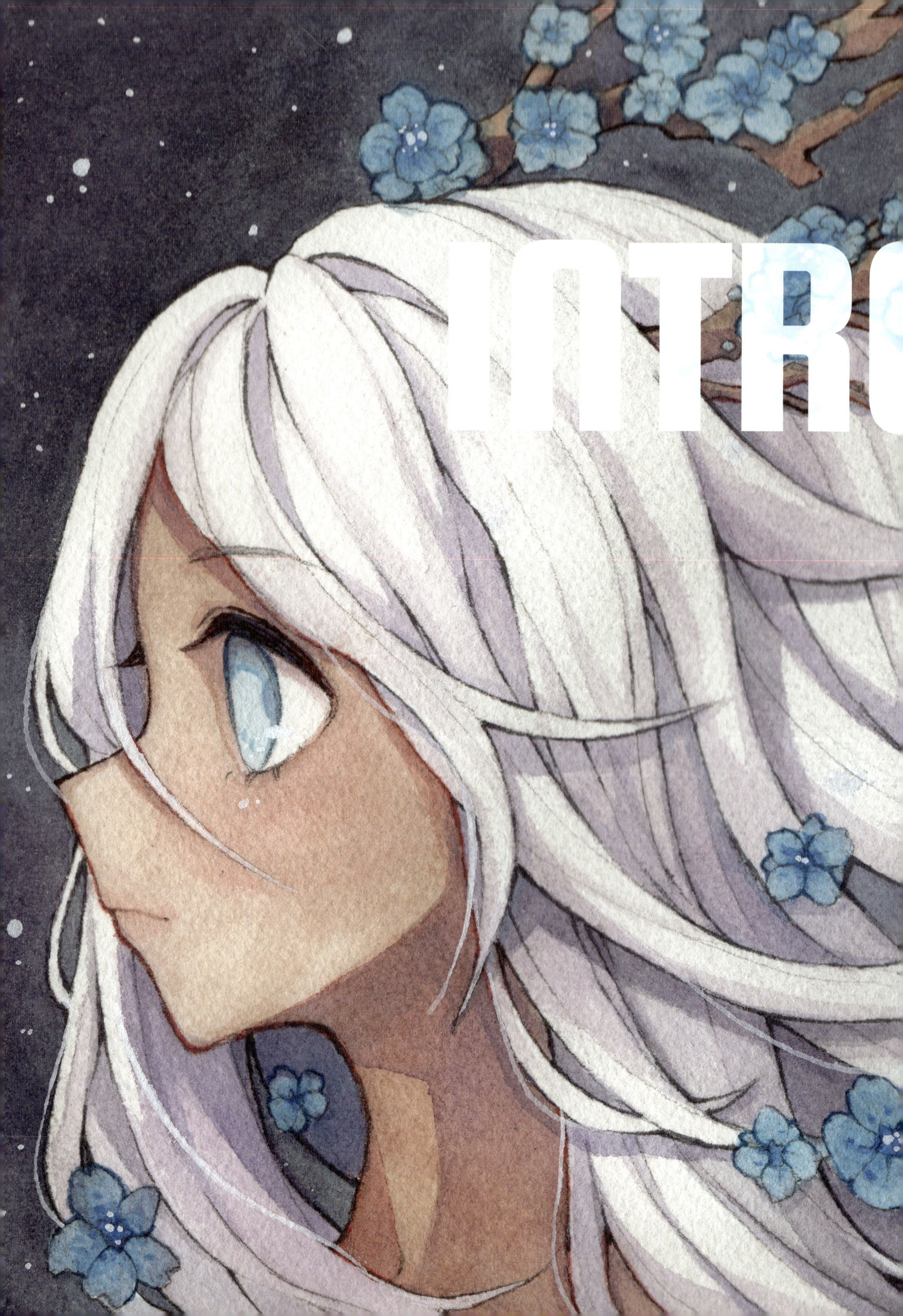

# INTR

# DUCTION

By Anny "Yoai"

## Meet the artist

**yoai.carrd.co | instagram.com/yoaihime**

Anny "Yoai" is a Chinese-Canadian illustrator who likes to design and draw cute characters, sharing them with her large online following. She works in both traditional and digital mediums, but her favorite tools are pens and markers. She has previously worked for Quarto, supplying illustrations for their tutorial books *Chibi Art Class* and *Anime Art Class*.

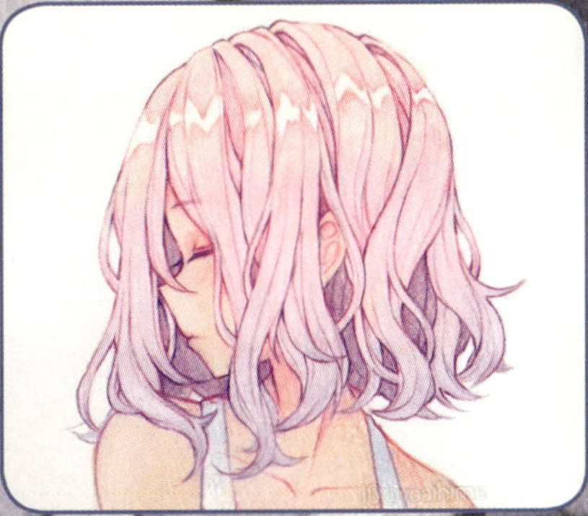

# INTRODUCTION TO ANIME & MANGA

Anime and manga are terms commonly used to refer to Japanese-style cartoons produced in a variety of media, such as animated TV shows and movies, printed comics, video games, and illustrations. Anime refers to animated cartoons, while manga refers to printed comics. The easiest way to explain the difference is you *watch* an anime, whereas you *read* a manga. Manga precedes anime and many popular anime series, such as *One Piece*, were originally a manga before being adapted into an anime TV show.

We can imagine the typical anime and manga style as a halfway point between two popular Western cartoon styles: the non-realistic, highly stylized aesthetic of cartoon shows such as *The Powerpuff Girls*, and characters animated in semi-realism, such as the superheroes in DC comics.

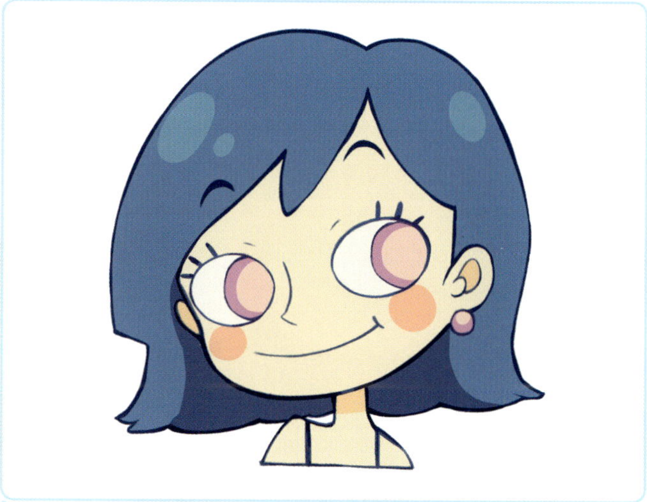

An example of a character drawn in a highly stylized cartoon style; note the obviously unrealistic proportions and facial features, all of which are extremely simplified

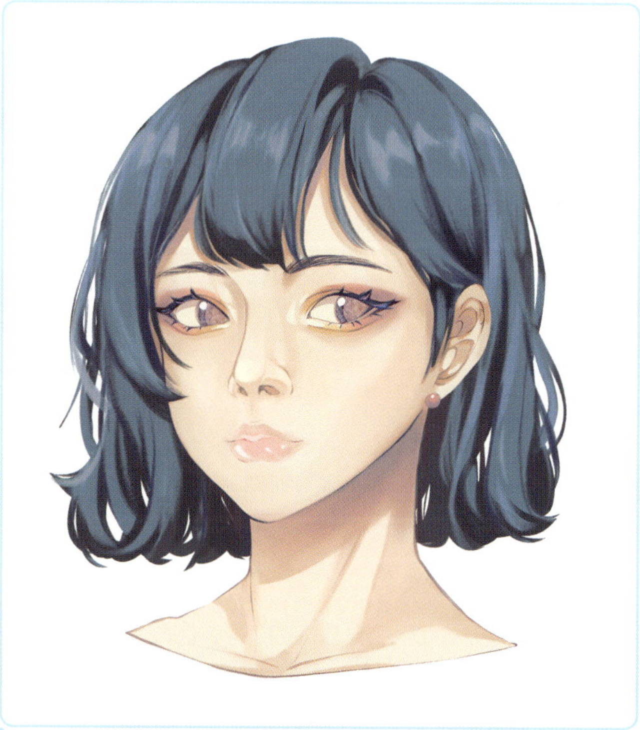

The same character, but drawn in a semi-realistic style; note how her facial features have more realistic shapes, but are still heavily exaggerated

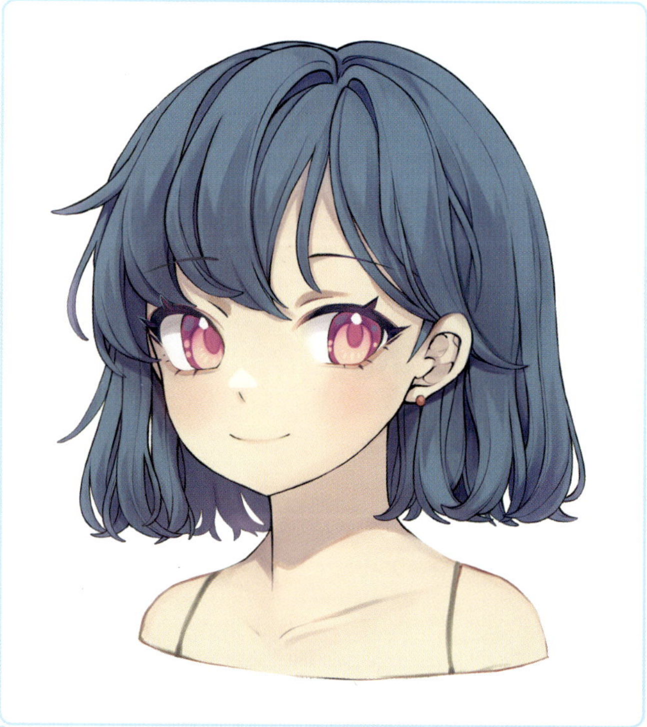

The typical anime-style sits in the middle of semi-realistic and highly stylized cartoonlike styles; note how the obviously exaggerated facial features still bear some resemblance to reality

A fundamental and somewhat iconic aspect of what defines the anime and manga art style – referred to as "anime-style" throughout this book – is how the characters are drawn, specifically their facial features. Minimal line work is used to depict facial features and contours, the eyes are large and highly stylized, the mouth is often extremely simple, and the nose is typically smaller and thinner in proportion to the rest of the face. Details are usually simplified, with a simple line for the mouth and barely any lip or nostril detailing. A character's body proportions are also typically exaggerated, such as being extremely tall or having very long, thin limbs and torso.

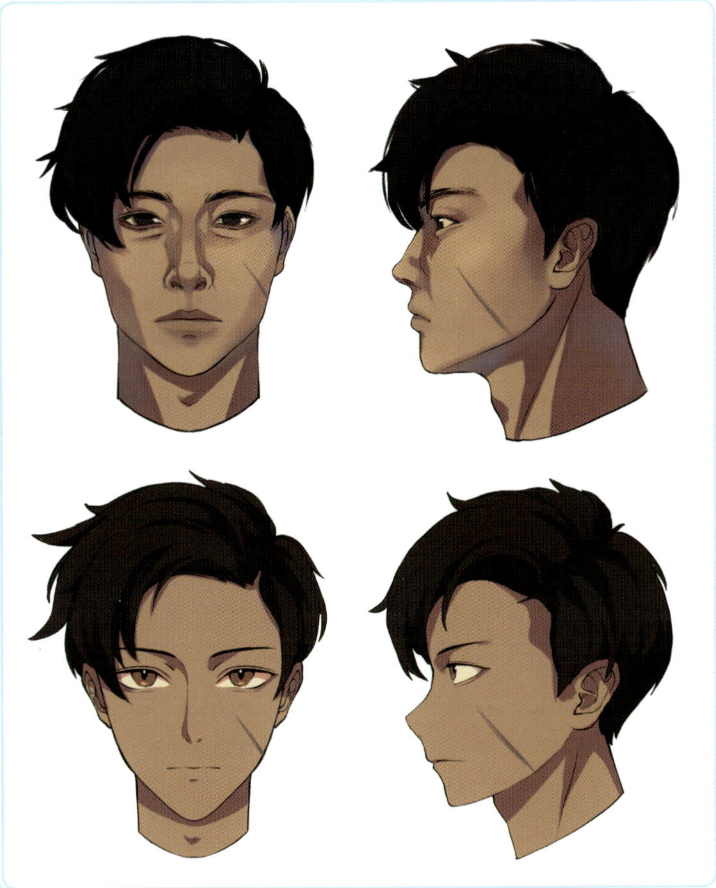

A realistic character (above) and the same head drawn in the anime style (below), showing how the facial features are simplified

## The importance of anime in the art world

The popularity of anime and manga in the online art community has increased dramatically in the last ten years. My experience of anime-style art in the late 2000s and early 2010s was of a very niche online art community. While there were many artists drawing in this style, it was nowhere near as mainstream as it is today. Most of these artists used portfolio websites such as DeviantArt – a platform mainly used by artists, writers, and photographers – to share their work. With the rise of popular social-media apps such as Twitter and Instagram, anime-style art has now been made accessible to a much wider audience.

Anime itself has also become more mainstream around the world. There are now popular streaming services that include numerous anime shows, while others, such as Crunchyroll, are completely dedicated to the genre. Movie theaters around the world are showing an increasing amount of anime, such as the *Pokémon* and *My Hero Academia* movies. The Italian luxury brand Gucci even created an anime-inspired advertisement to launch a new perfume. *Genshin Impact*, made by miHoYo, is one example of an extremely popular anime-style game. Many gamers who previously had no interest in anime and manga media have taken an intense interest in the genre since playing it.

# Turning your anime-style art hobby into a full-time career

From video games to television shows, the market for anime-style art is huge and, as a result, many anime-style artists wish to turn their hobby into a full-time career. Some artists enjoy the flexibility and variety of undertaking freelance commissions for individuals and companies, while others prefer the creativity and entrepreneurial challenge of setting up small businesses to sell products featuring their artwork. Whether it involves designing a cute original character for a keychain or tote bag, or creating a full-color illustration to advertise the next up-and-coming video game for a leading studio, there will always be a demand for anime-style artwork.

For many artists, the attraction of a career in this field is the same as with other art careers: you can continue creating artwork in a style you love and can make money while doing it. As the work is typically freelance, this often provides an element of freedom and flexibility, enabling you to choose your own hours and work from home. There is also versatility within the anime style in general, allowing artists the space to experiment with different looks without worrying about realism and anatomical accuracy. For example, when drawing eyes, you can stylize iris shape and exaggerate eyelashes to create the desired look for your character.

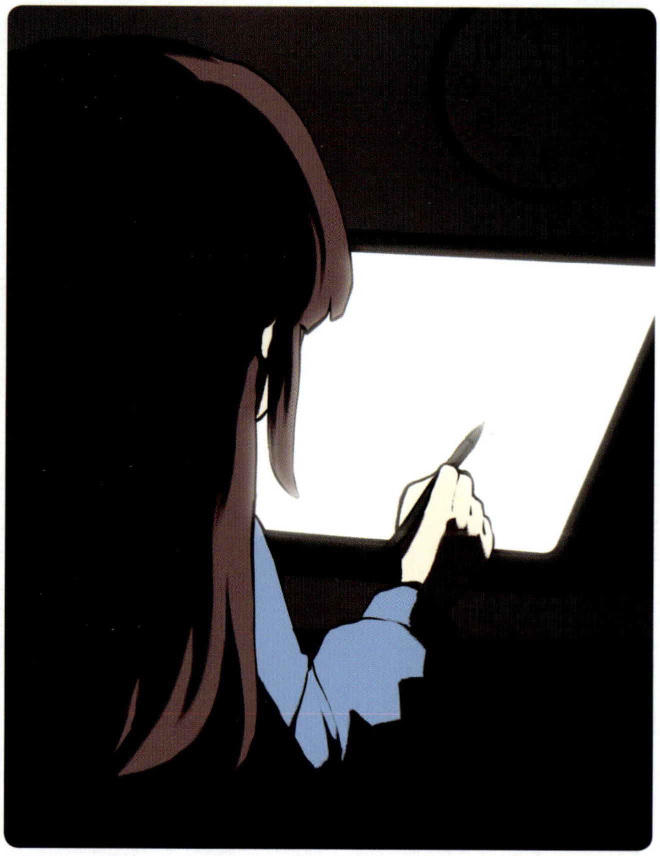

Working as a freelance anime-style artist typically allows for flexible working

Despite the many benefits, working as a freelance artist is not without its challenges. On top of creating your artwork, you are also responsible for your communications, marketing, promotion, admin, and finances, unless you hire a third party to help with these tasks.

In addition, depending on the services you are offering, you may encounter stiff competition until you have established your brand and built up a fan base. For example, if you are designing and selling stickers of original anime-style characters that are similar to others commonly sold online, and you don't already have a loyal following who will buy your stickers first, it may prove hard to find a consistent stream of customers. It may be tempting to sell artwork or products of popular characters from anime and manga due to their existing fan bases, but very few companies allow commercial use of their intellectual property. Selling fan art will infringe on their copyright, which could leave you vulnerable to legal action.

The invention of the internet has vastly improved things for aspiring anime-style artists. Thirty years ago, artists had to physically mail their artwork to an obscure magazine publisher, hoping theirs would be selected out of hundreds of submissions. If their artwork was chosen, it would be published for a small handful of anime and manga enthusiasts to see, perhaps one of whom might be looking for an artist for an upcoming project. Perhaps the artist would have made enough connections over the years to arrange for their work to be exhibited in a gallery, which would then have taken at least fifty percent of any artwork sold.

Twenty years ago, many artists would have spent hours telephoning studios and companies looking for work. They would have lugged around a heavy portfolio they had spent years building, just for an art director to flip through two pages before shooing them out of their office. Copies of the short manga they had spent six arduous months working on could already be sitting in the garbage can of whichever book company they had mailed it to that week in the hopes of getting a book deal.

While social media is not without its downsides, it is an absolutely crucial part of a contemporary artist's business model. It's almost impossible to kick-start an art career in the present day without some kind of online platform and portfolio. Not only does it make it easier than ever to attract an audience and build a fan base to whom you can sell your artwork and products, it also acts as an easily accessible online portfolio for studios and companies who may be looking for an artist for an upcoming project, or even a permanent role. The majority of social-media platforms allow users to post images, and some even allow you to categorize them. This is essentially your own art gallery, without the ridiculous cost. Almost every single job I have been offered was the result of promoting my services on social platforms, or a company rep contacting me after stumbling upon my work online.

## Beginning your journey

Whether you have already begun your journey on the path to becoming a successful anime-style artist, or are tentatively and curiously exploring what this avenue may entail, this book provides a wealth of knowledge and expertise that will help you on your way. The two introductory chapters, *The Business of Anime* and *Developing Your Style*, present an introduction to the profession, covering topics such as: working in the industry, reaching your audience, marketing and promotion, honing your unique style, building your brand, and curating a portfolio.

These are followed by in-depth case studies written by five leading artists with anime-inspired styles, each of whom shares their personal experiences of the industry and passes on invaluable advice. You will learn how they found their signature style, established their well-known brand, grew a loyal following, and built their business. They also share behind-the-scenes insights into their influences, inspirations, training, and failures and successes.

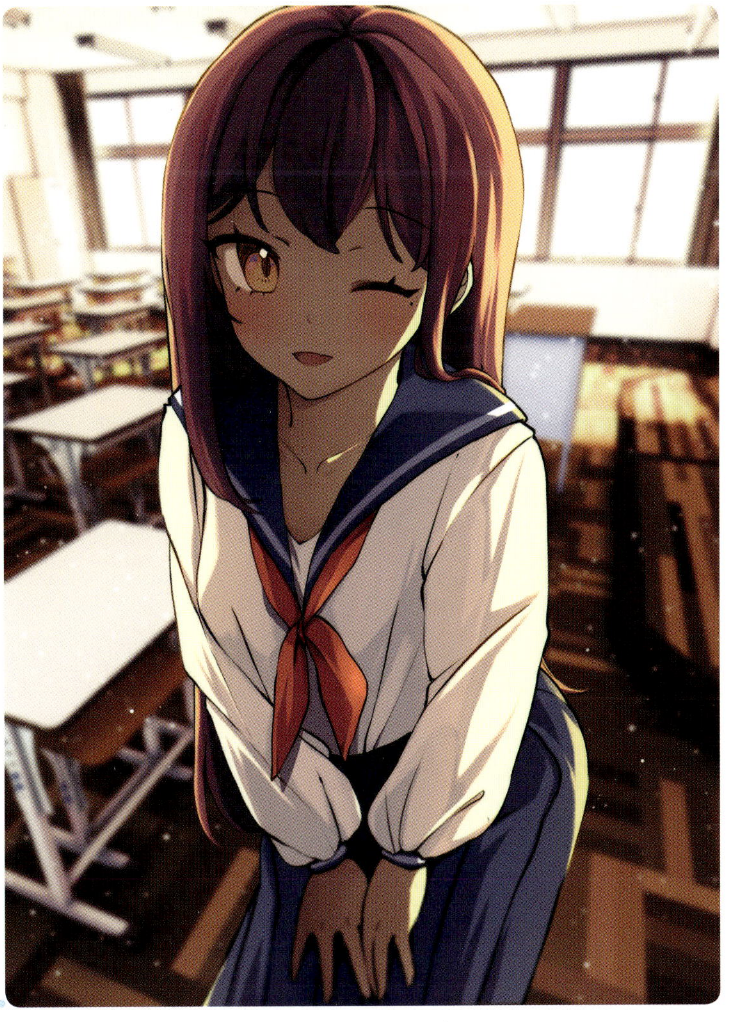

This illustration is typical of my signature anime-style artwork – this book will help you to discover your own individual style

# Advice as you begin your journey...

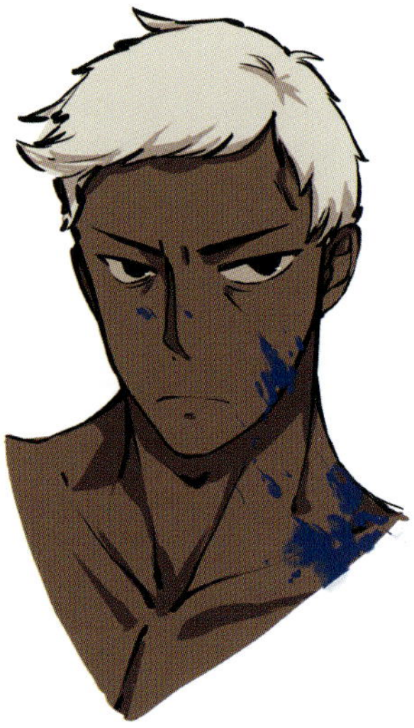

If you are new to anime-style art, or even to drawing in general, don't focus on establishing a unique style until you are at least somewhat familiar with the art fundamentals, such as lighting, color theory, anatomy, composition, and perspective. Not understanding the basics will make for slow progress, as you will find yourself having to pause mid-project to research these subjects. While anime and manga styles allow for variety and stylization, there are still many essential art topics that are worth taking the time to learn.

Consider how you want to brand yourself as an artist. While some artists use their real name, others prefer to come up with an artist name to post under. Don't use a name that is too common or generic, as it should be memorable and easily searchable. Once you have decided on a name, buy the relevant domain name and take the username on all social-media sites and websites you plan to use, even if you haven't started sharing work yet. You would be surprised how quickly people will snag your brand's domain name the moment you start to gain a small following, and then immediately offer to sell it to you.

Even though you are drawing in an anime style, it can be useful to practice some degree of realism. While anime and manga characters are far from realistic-looking, most are still based on the human body. Familiarizing yourself with muscle groups, bone structure, the typical spacing between facial features, how hair falls, and how fabric hangs or gathers will make drawing anime-style characters much easier, while making them more believable, too.

There is a huge variety of anime art styles and genres. Even if you have found the one you want to continue with, it's a good idea to experiment with others and to show those as part of your portfolio. If you are hired alongside other anime-style artists to work together on a project, the project lead will likely want the artwork to look consistent. Showing that you are able to change and adapt how you draw will lead to more job offers.

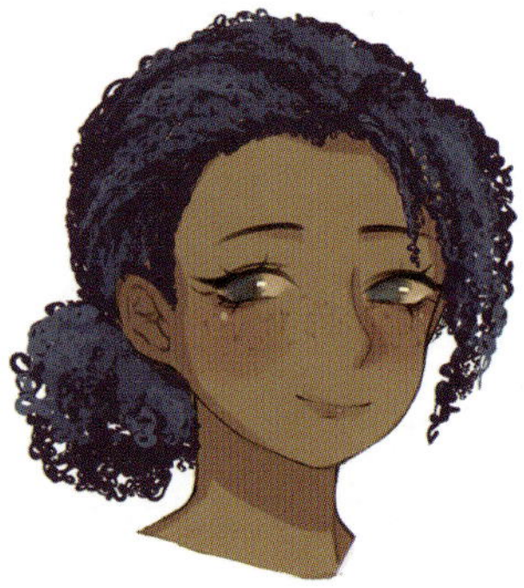

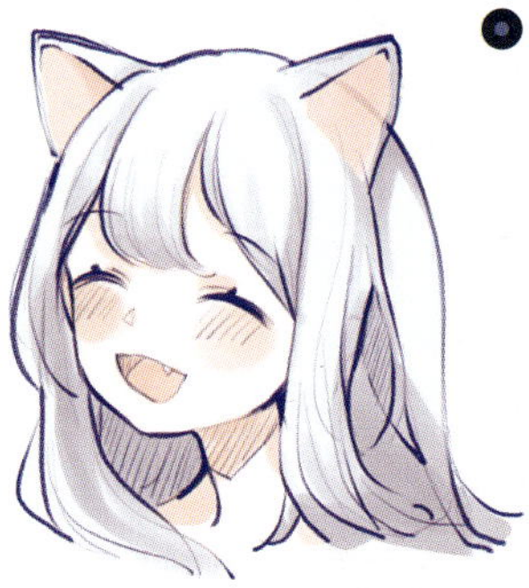

And finally, as a freelancer, you will be responsible for reporting your income and will need to pay taxes on any money you earn from your projects and commissions. While some artists prefer to manage this themselves, others enlist the help of a financial assistant.

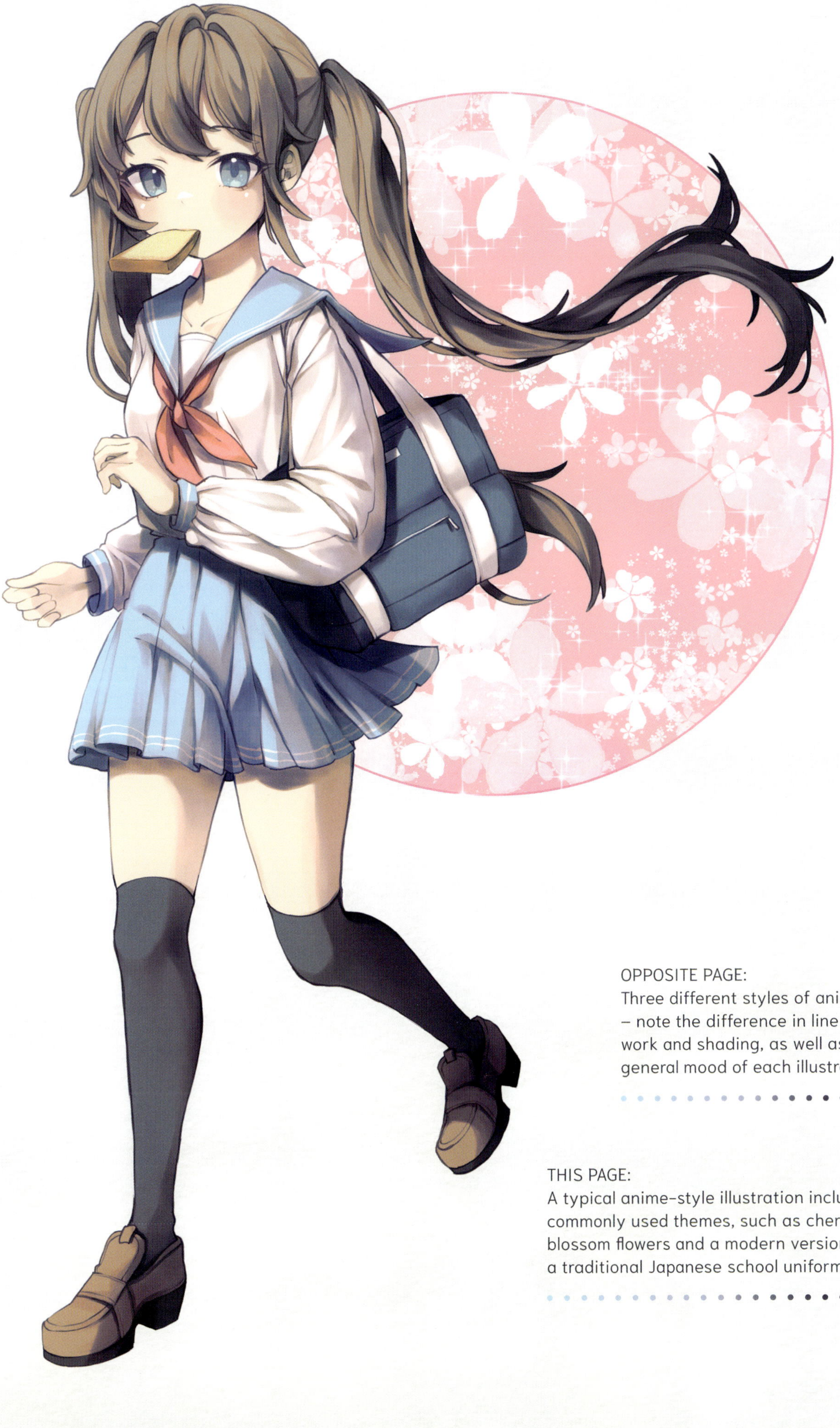

OPPOSITE PAGE:
Three different styles of anime – note the difference in line work and shading, as well as the general mood of each illustration

THIS PAGE:
A typical anime-style illustration including commonly used themes, such as cherry blossom flowers and a modern version of a traditional Japanese school uniform

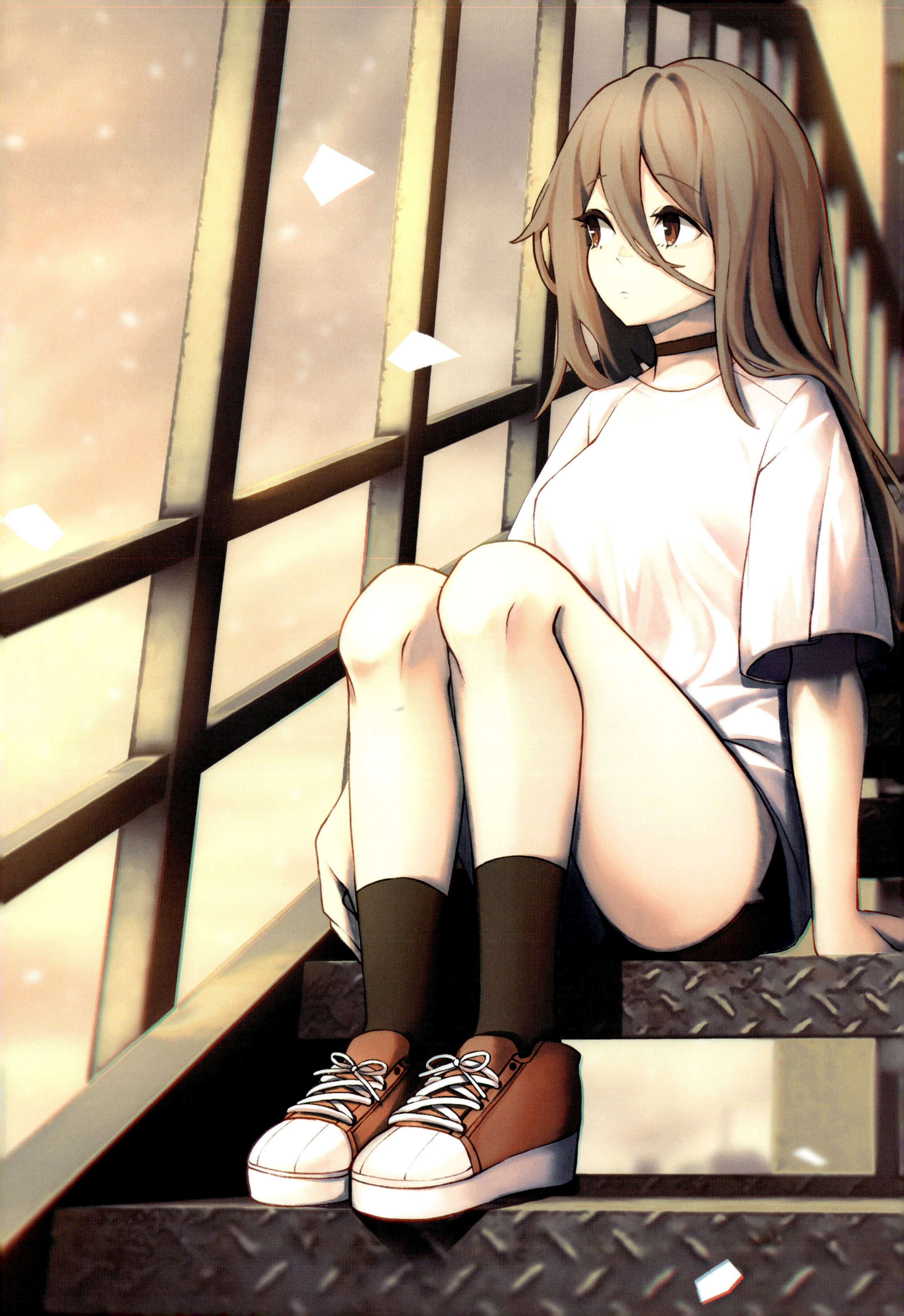

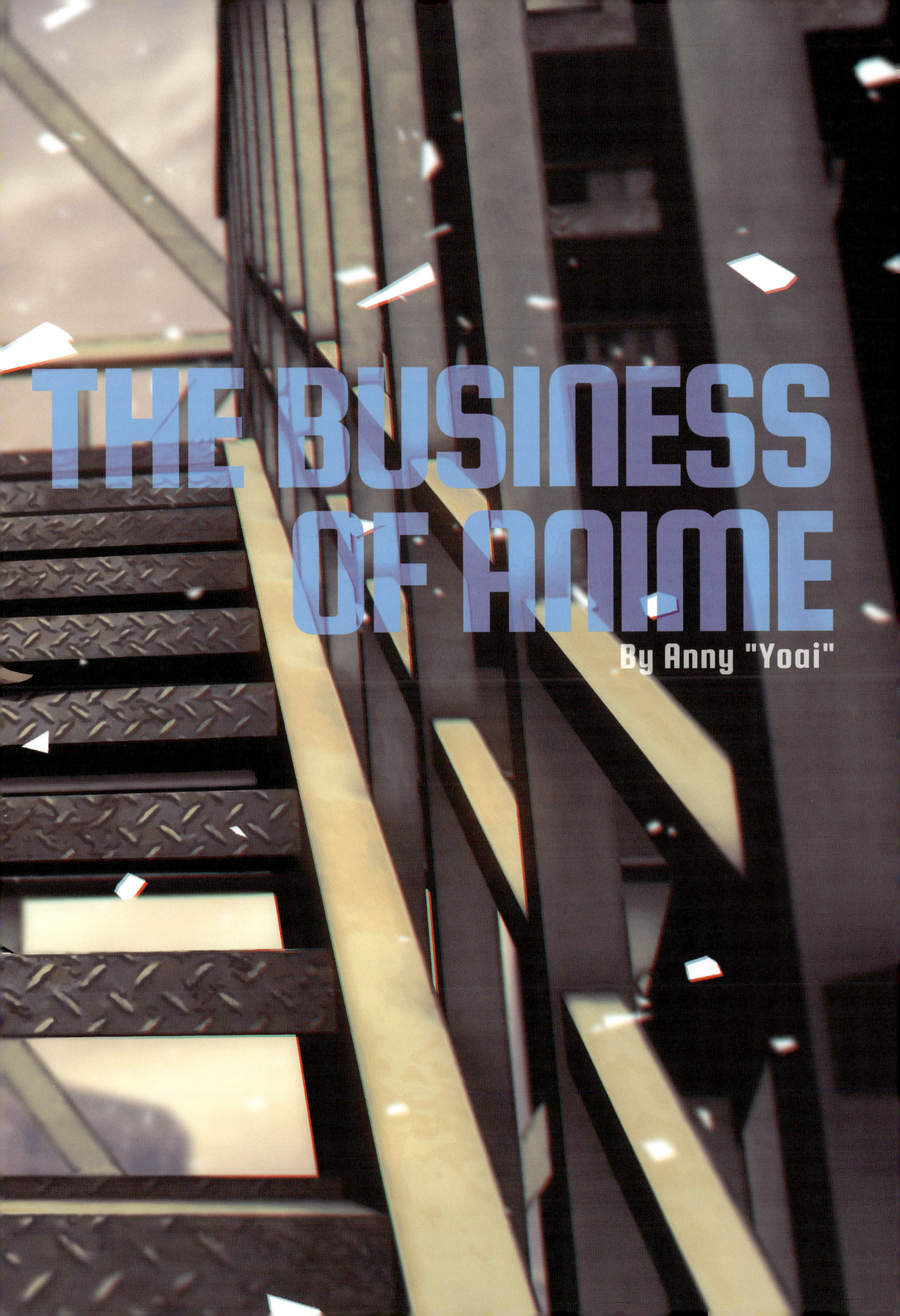

# THE BUSINESS OF ANIME

By Anny "Yoai"

# THE BUSINESS OF ANIME

## GENRE LANDSCAPE

There are many genres and demographics across the various forms of anime and manga literature and media, with new ones popping up all the time. The following five categories are broad headings under which many subgenres exist.

### Shonen

Focused on action, adventure, and sports, the target audience for the shonen genre is young boys and male teenagers. The main character is often a young male aged ten to sixteen, to reflect the target audience. A classic example of shonen manga is the series *One Piece* by Eiichiro Oda.

### Shojo

This genre is similar to shonen, but the target audience is young girls and female teens. The themes align with what younger girls may find appealing, such as romance, music, everyday school life, fantasy, and science fiction. A good example of shojo is *Sailor Moon* by Naoko Takeuchi, which has also gained a mainstream following in the West.

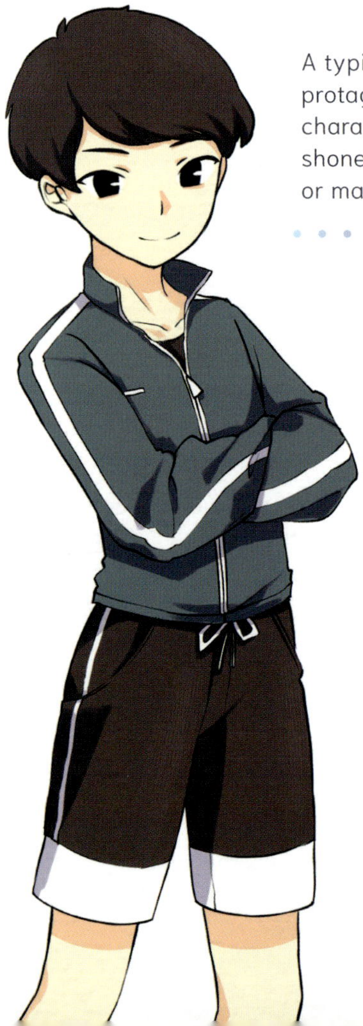

A typical protagonist character in shonen anime or manga

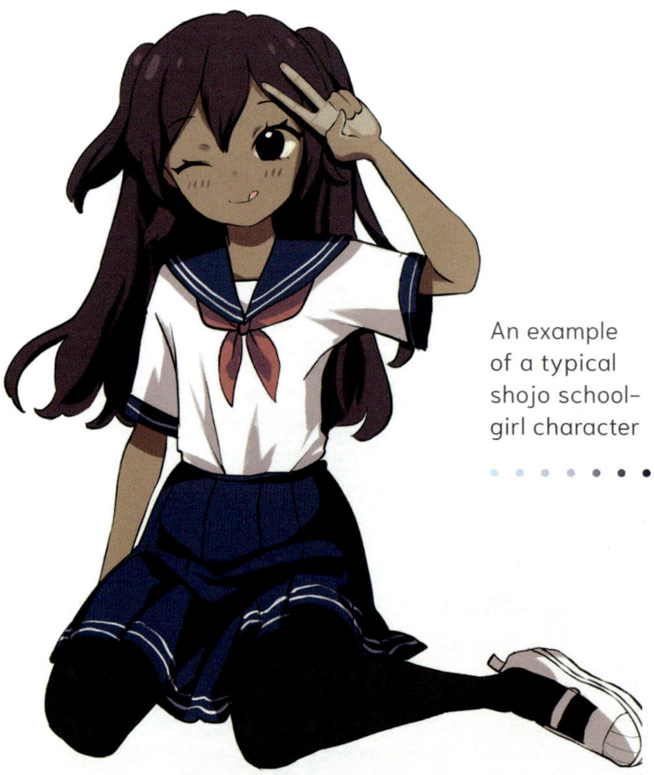

An example of a typical shojo school-girl character

## Seinen

While it is similar to shonen, seinen is aimed at young men, typically eighteen years and older. It has adult characters and can contain themes that may not be suitable for a shonen manga, such as violence (beyond regular fighting), gore, suggestive themes, and comedy not suitable for, or not understood by, younger audiences. The art style and animation can sometimes be darker or even grisly, depending on the theme. A classic example of a seinen manga is *Chobits,* by the Japanese manga collective Clamp.

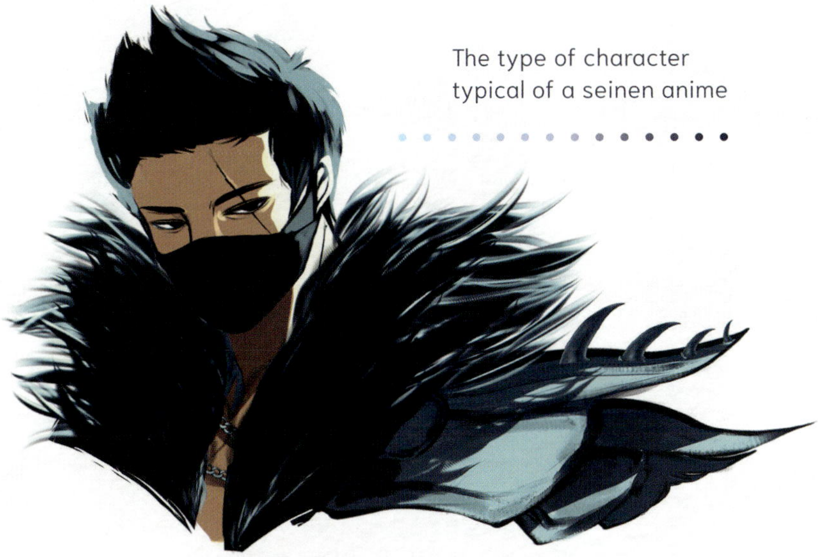

The type of character typical of a seinen anime

## Josei

Though it has similarities to shojo, josei is intended for young women – eighteen and above – as it deals with more serious and mature themes. Romance and love is a common theme; often to an extent that is not suitable for younger audiences. The characters are college-aged young adults, so are older and more mature than in shojo manga. There is exaggeration or more visual focus on human features that are typically considered appealing. An example of a josei is *Chihayafuru* by Yuki Suetsugu.

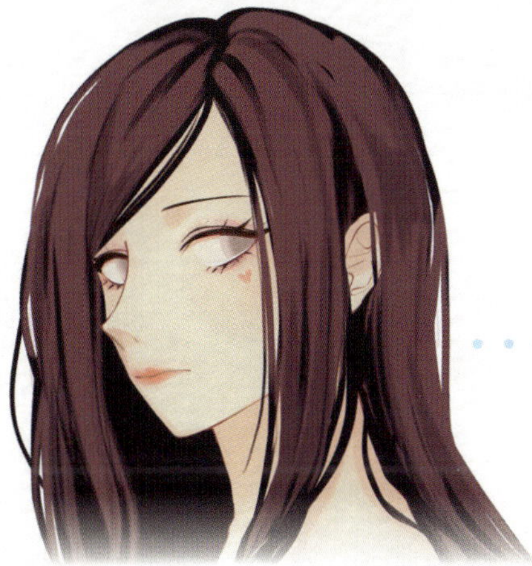

Protagonists in josei anime are usually young female adults between eighteen and thirty years old

## Kodomomuke

This style of anime and manga is aimed at very young children – toddler age and above – and is not marketed toward any specific gender. The art style is similar to highly simplified Western cartoons, but still contains anime-style elements. The themes and styles are always lighthearted and fun, and can be enjoyed by any age. The anime series *Pokémon* is a well-known example of kodomomuke.

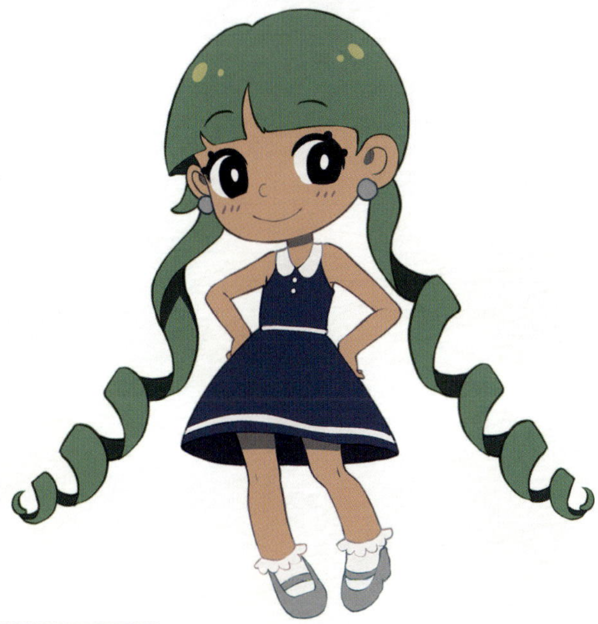

Cartoonlike and cheerful in appearance, this kodomomuke-style character is designed to appeal to young children

**While these definitions are based on the target demographic, the actual audience is not exclusive to that group and often varies widely.**

# Subgenres

There are many subgenres of anime and manga that fall within the five broad categories discussed on the previous pages. Just like with any literature or film, as society's creativity expands, so does the number of subgenres.

## Mahou shojo

Translating as "magical girl," mahou shojo is a shojo manga and anime where magic is the main theme. It typically follows a girl, or group of girls, who have a normal human life, but can transform into "magical girls" when they are ready to fight or adventure, taking on an alternate appearance with a cute design. *Tokyo Mew Mew* by Reiko Yoshida and Mia Ikumi is one such example.

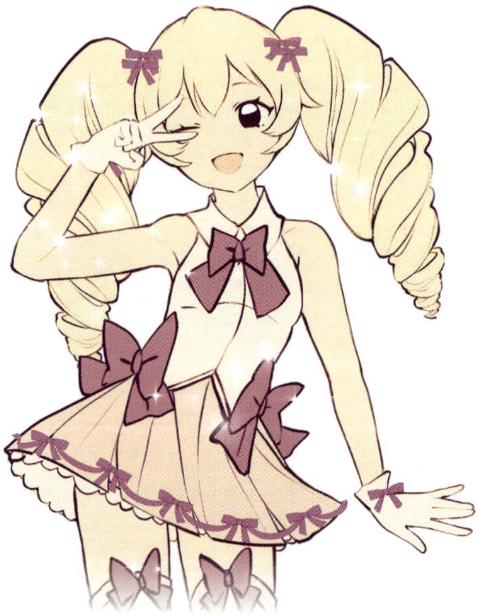

An example of the mahou shojo, "magical girl," subgenre – note the character's cute, magical design

## Mecha

Found under shonen and seinen, this is robot-themed anime and manga that typically involves a lot of action and fighting. The robots are often giant in stature. *Gundam* is both a franchise and sub-subgenre of mecha, featuring a specific type a specific type of giant bipedal robot capable of flight, vaguely humanoid in appearance, and typically piloted and controlled by a human from within.

## Historical

Just as there are historical television dramas, historical anime and manga also exists. Asian countries have a rich history that dates back thousands of years, and it is always interesting to gain insight into how life was back then.

## Horror

The horror subgenre of anime and manga typically features ghosts, demons, psychological horror, and general superstition and folklore. These are often set in everyday life, invoking fear by suggesting that strange, terrifying creatures walk among us. *Yamishibai* is a Japanese horror series that focuses on ghosts, superstitions, and curses.

## Fantasy & sci-fi

This subgenre is commonly set in an alternate reality or universe, though the characters are typically human or humanoid in appearance. Some elements of our world and everyday life may still exist, such as the school system, but the idea is to create a completely different world from the one with which viewers are familiar.

## Kemonomimi

A kemonomimi is a type of humanoid character design that appears in various subgenres of anime and manga. It has mainly human features, but also animal ears and a tail, and sometimes other attributes such as wings.

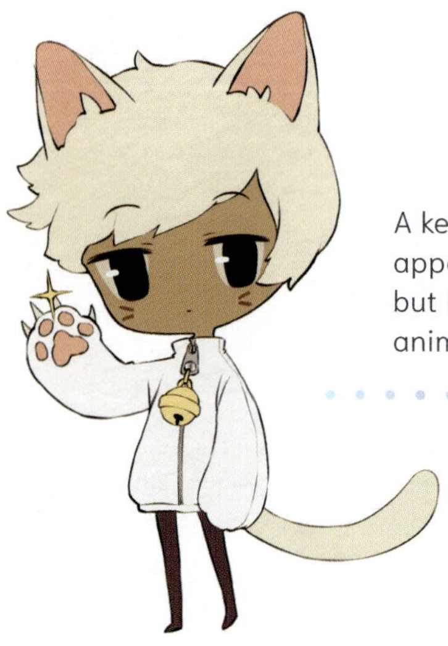

A kemonomimi character appears mostly human, but has distinct animal-like features

# Commercially successful genres

While shonen and shojo anime and manga are extremely successful, ultimately it is seinen and josei that are the most commercially successful. Typically it is adults, rather than children, who have the means to make frequent purchases, whether this is by subscribing to an anime streaming service or buying physical books, DVDs, and anime merchandise such as posters and figures.

Commercial success is also affected by the appeal and relatability of the genre. As seinen and josei typically deal with more realistic themes, the reader can more easily relate to the characters' plight and is therefore more likely to invest in the series.

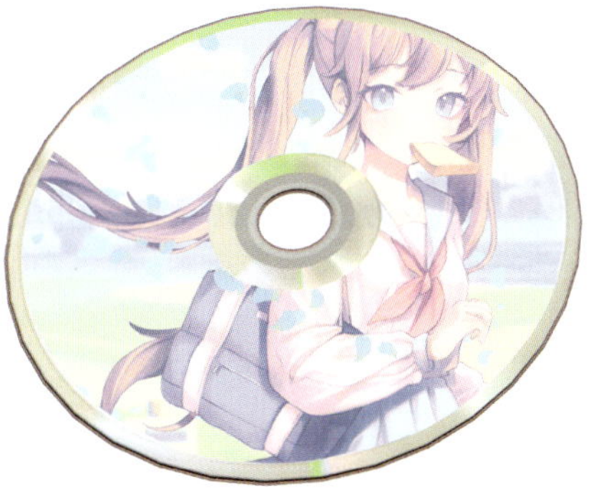

# Finding your genre & audience

When exploring which genre or subgenre you would like your artwork to fall within, consider what you enjoy drawing the most. Sometimes artists experiment with multiple anime styles, themes, and genres, before choosing to pursue the one that proves the most popular with their audience. While this approach may grow your following, your artwork can end up feeling unfulfilling and more like a chore if you end up devoting your time to a genre that does not interest you. Ultimately, it's best to work out what you want to draw first, then build your audience based on that.

Whichever genre or subgenre you choose, there will always be competition. While you will want to stand out and market yourself as new and innovative, this should not be your primary goal. First, focus on establishing yourself in the anime-style art community. Network, build connections, and grow a small audience. Even if you have the most incredible idea, no one will see it if you don't have followers to share it with. It will only show up on the home pages of those who are following you. Connection is key. Spend time getting to know your community and audience, find out why they like your work, and then use this information to further establish your brand and presence within the art community. Over time, as you strengthen your style and establish your brand, your unique appeal will begin to show and resonate with your audience.

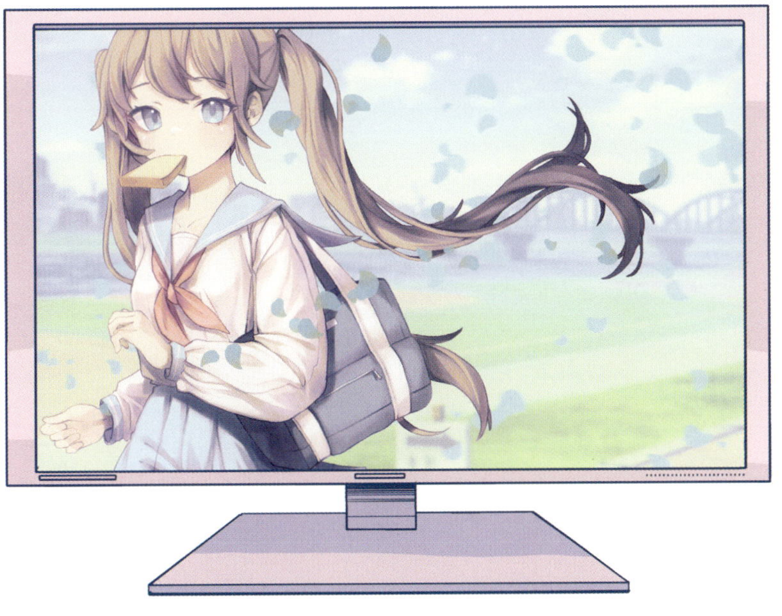

The most successful genres are often dictated by those who have the finances to make frequent purchases, such as buying DVDs or subscribing to an anime streaming service

# AUDIENCE BREAKDOWN

## Demographics

In anime and manga, the subject matter and the style of artwork both play an influential role in the demographic of the audience. The geographical location, language, and gender of the audience are all influenced by these two factors, but it is the age demographic that is perhaps most affected. Anime-style artwork with cute themes and young characters is typically popular with younger audiences, such as teens aged thirteen to eighteen. Conversely, artwork with more mature themes – such as horror, sci-fi, and violence – tends to attract a slightly older audience, such as young adults in their late teens, twenties, and thirties.

As discussed earlier, genre can also dictate the demographic of the audience. While shonen and shojo typically attract a younger audience, classics such as *Sailor Moon* can attract an older audience, likely out of nostalgia. Seinen and josei also attract an older audience. However, while there is no age limit to who can enjoy anime and manga, elderly folks are not the typical target audience.

In terms of geographic location, anime and manga is most popular in East Asian countries, especially Japan. It is increasing in popularity in other countries with a variety of different cultures, however, such as Canada and Australia.

My own anime-style artwork falls mainly in the shojo and josei genres. While I don't specifically tailor my artwork toward a specific gender, analytics indicate that more than half of my audience identify as female. Most are aged between fifteen and thirty-five years old and live predominantly in Asia, North America, Europe, and other English-speaking countries.

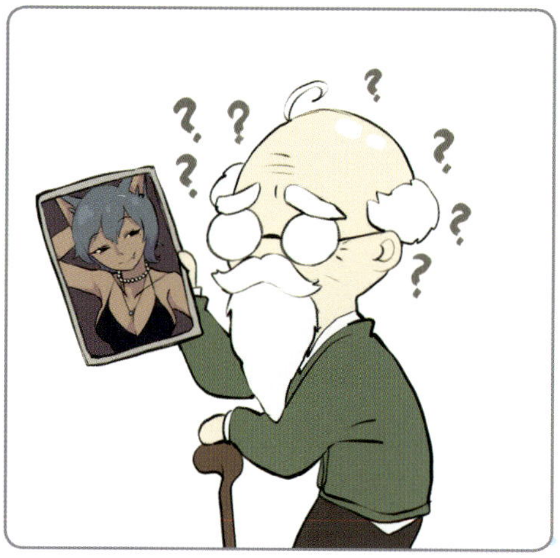

Anime and manga is typically more popular with younger generations than the elderly

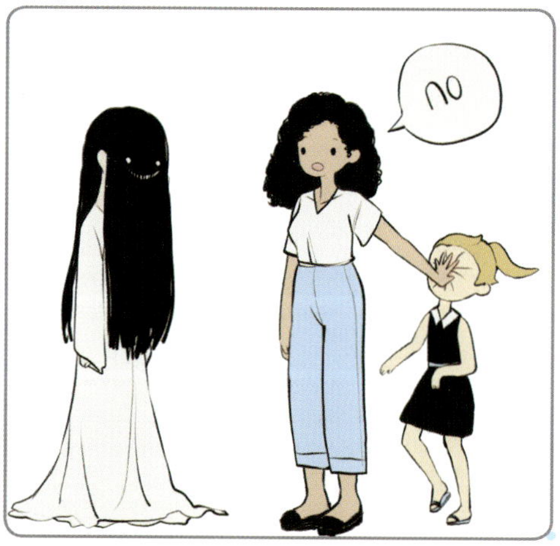


Some types of anime and manga are not appropriate for children and younger audiences, or for those sensitive to mature subject matter

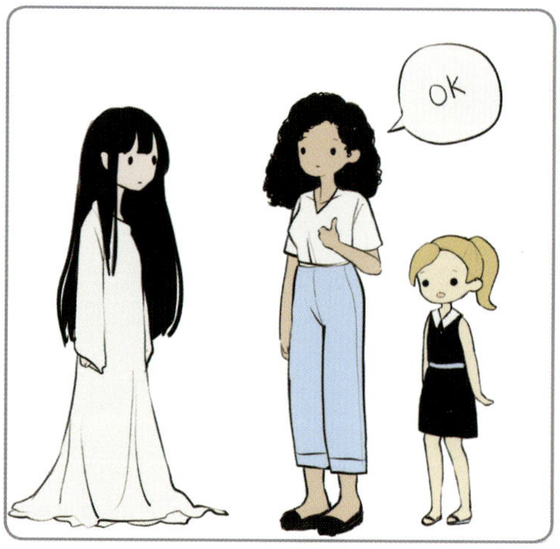


"Family friendly" anime and manga can be enjoyed by audiences of all ages

# Relatability & interest

When examining how well certain anime styles, subject matters, and themes appeal to different audiences, it helps to look at how easily the audience can relate to and identify with the work. For example, if you were to create a short manga strip to raise awareness about a specific societal issue, those facing the same issue would likely resonate with the artwork and its message.

At other times, the popularity of an anime or manga is purely based on what a person enjoys looking at, determined by their own individual interests. If you draw anime-style characters wearing fancy dresses with frills, a dressmaker who also likes fancy dresses with frills may take an interest in your work. Whether consciously or not, we often surround ourselves with people who share similar interests and values. This also means that, if someone likes your artwork, it's likely they will share it with their friends.

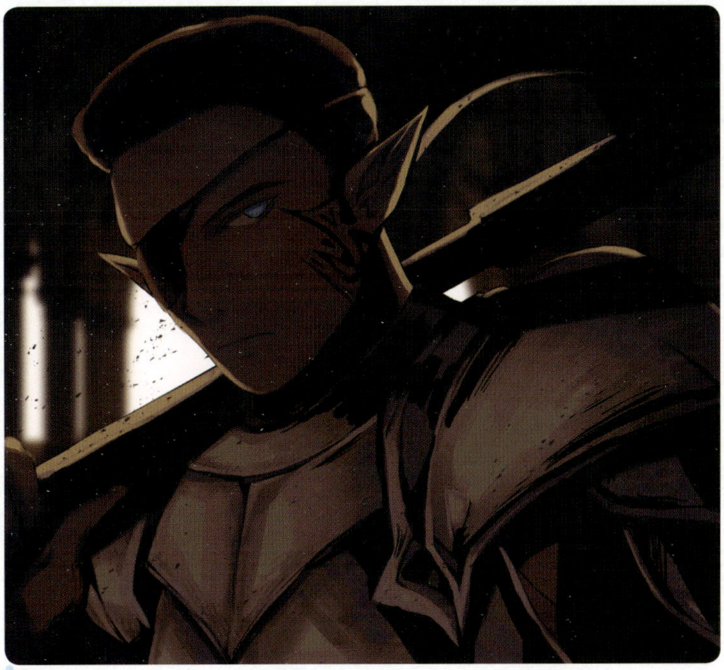

A dark-fantasy elf character that has been created to be admired rather than to be found relatable

# Character design

The demographic for a particular character depends on the purpose of the design. Is this someone fantastical that the audience can root for and admire? Or is the character more like an everyday person to whom the audience can relate?

Characters that are fantastical – such as humanoids, robots, and other non-humans – are often created for the former purpose, while realistic human characters – such as high-school or college students with typical lives – are intended for the latter. Of course, there is always some crossover between the approaches.

Younger people are often more likely to want to emulate or style themselves after characters with whom they can identify, so the realistic approach typically attracts that audience.

When creating my characters, I usually draw for the former purpose: fantastical characters to be admired. However, I focus on relatability when designing clothing, shoes, and hairstyles, as I enjoying drawing clothes I would want to wear myself.

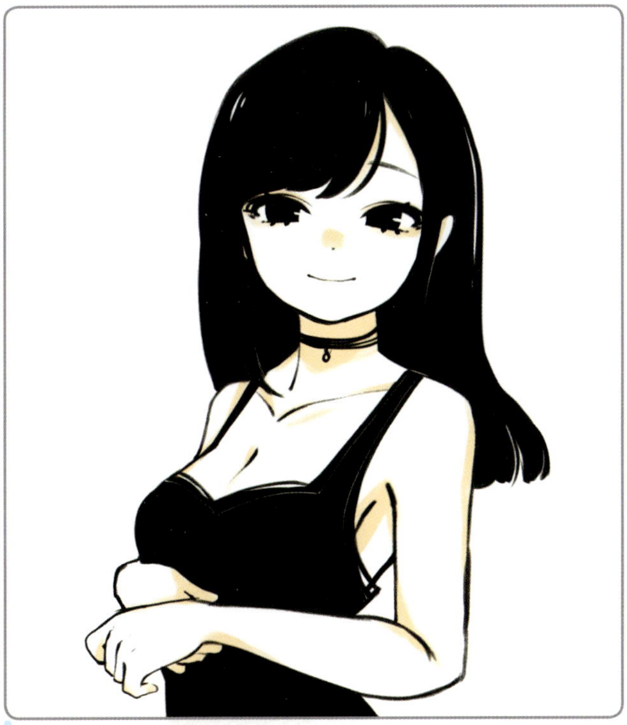

This more realistic female character has been created as someone with whom audiences can identify

## Social media & conventions

Anime and manga conventions have no specific target demographic and the attendees are a mixture of people from many different backgrounds and interests. Social media, however, is slightly different. Unlike conventions, where everything is out in the open, social media only shows a select amount of content at a time, depending on the user's interests. Many social-media platforms have algorithms – based on age, location, and activity, among other factors – that determine what content users are shown. The algorithms use information from artwork people have previously engaged with to show them new artists they may like. If users engage with similar things, they will be grouped together and recommended similar posts on the site.

Familiarize yourself with the different social-media platforms and their algorithms. Does the platform favor likes or shares? Does it prefer video content to still images? Does it favor traditional or digital art? Is your artwork suited to the platform's format? Reflect on the strengths of your artwork and how can you use the available platforms to your advantage.

# REACHING & GROWING YOUR AUDIENCE ONLINE

## Getting noticed

When launching a social-media account for your anime-style artwork, getting noticed and attracting initial engagement can prove challenging. Here are some useful ways to kick-start your online presence:

### Online trends

Study current online art trends and challenges, as well as popular hashtags. Joining in with art challenges and using the official hashtags will allow others to discover your work, and also help you to connect with fellow anime-style artists. For example, in the month of May, many people in the online art community – mostly on Instagram and Twitter – take part in "MerMay." This involves drawing different themed mermaids throughout the month and sharing your artwork using the #mermay hashtag.

A trend that is popular all year round is "Draw This In Your Style," where an artist will create an artwork then invite fellow artists to redraw it in their own signature style. This leads to a huge variety of different interpretations, from which the original artist will typically share a few of their favorites, boosting engagement for all artists selected. If you use the official #DTIYS hashtag – which sometimes includes the artist's name – your work will be viewed by all who browse through the entries.

On specific days, artists and creatives are invited to post their work using the hashtag #portfolioday on Twitter. This is viewed by companies and clients looking to hire an artist, as well as by fellow artists wanting to make connections in the online art community. The format is four of your best artworks, a short bio, and links to your contact pages. Check the official Twitter profile @portfolioday for the upcoming dates. This is a great way to promote your work and get your name out there.

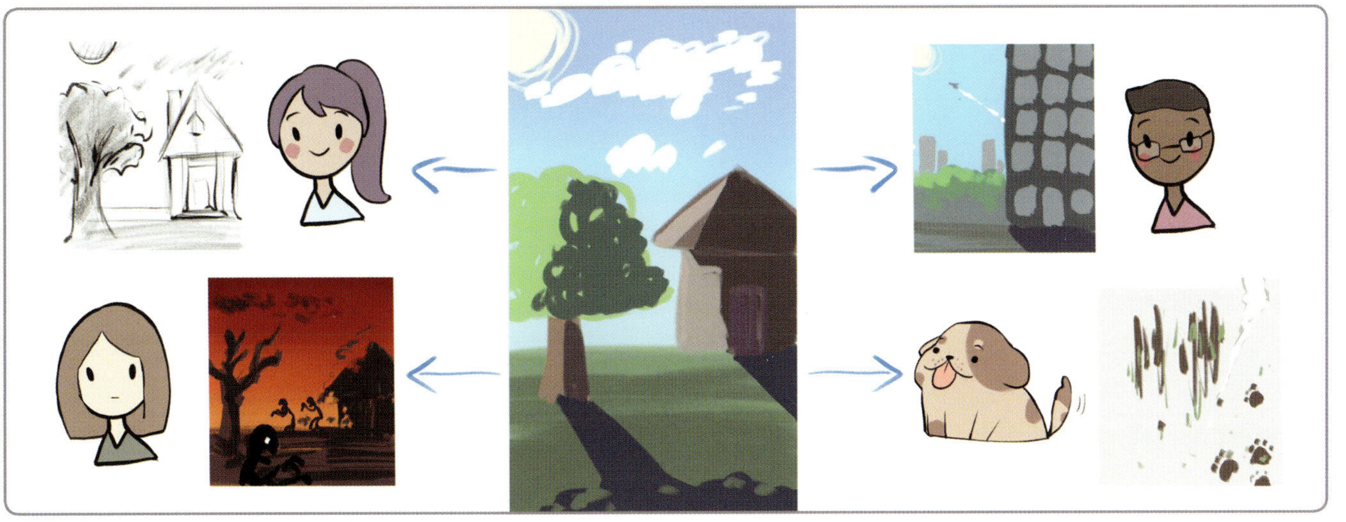

For the "Draw This In Your Style" challenge, each artist reinterprets the original artwork in their own style

## Fan art

A common approach to attract new followers is to draw popular characters from anime movies, TV shows, video games, and comics, posting the artwork with the appropriate hashtag. Fans of a certain show or video game will often search hashtags for posts relating to it, and may decide to follow you as a result. Drawing fan art can also be a useful exercise when you are suffering from artist's block or simply need some inspiration.

## Online forums & groups

Forum websites are now a little dated, except in niche areas, and are typically only used by a slightly older crowd. As a result, these are not particularly valuable platforms through which to promote your anime-style artwork. Reddit is a modern version of classic forums and can be used to create discussion threads and niche communities, called "subreddits," for a specific genre or type of anime. Discussing anime and manga online will enable you to meet people with similar interests, while also allowing them to discover your work.

There are also anime groups on Discord, which is a chat-room application. These are harder to find, however, as some groups are not searchable and some require an invitation. Many artists have their own Discord chat rooms, called "servers," which you can join to network with other artists. As well as sharing your work, you can discuss tips and advice.

## Conventions & events

Another way to grow your audience is to exhibit your work at conventions, on a table from which you can sell prints and merchandise, as well as network with fellow artists. Big conventions, such as Anime North, only happen once a year in major cities, while smaller local conventions are often seasonal. There is usually a charge to have a table and artists have to apply to acquire one. If an artist's application is not successful, sometimes they can opt to share a table with another artist who was accepted. It's also possible for an artist to hire a stand-in to manage their table if they cannot be there in person.

Many artists use the time in the run-up to the convention to make the merchandise they plan to sell. The best way to grow your audience is to include business cards – containing links to your online portfolio and social-media accounts – with all of your purchases, encouraging people to find and follow you online. If they like what they have bought at the convention, they may wish to buy more of it in the future. You should also make your business card obvious and available to everyone walking by your table – you never know who could be passing by.

For a smaller-scale option, some anime-specific art galleries have opened as a way for artists to showcase their work to new and existing audiences. These are mainly in Japan, however. You should also be aware of the cost, as galleries can charge expensive fees.

# Social media

It's fine to only have one social-media account when you are first establishing yourself as an artist, but as you start to grow your following, it can be useful to explore other platforms. Each social-media site has a different media format, and some are more suited to artists than others.

## Instagram

Instagram allows you to post photos (up to ten in a post), videos (of any length), and short-form videos known as "reels" (up to sixty seconds). There is also the option to create a small portfolio using the "guides" feature. The platform is perfect for taking part in art challenges and online trends.

## Own website

Creating a custom website provides a platform tailored to the information and artwork you wish to share in your chosen format. As well as uploading your portfolio, you can create a contact page letting people – particularly potential clients – know what work you are interested in and how they can contact you. Unlike social-media platforms, however, a website cannot be "liked" or "followed," making it impossible to interact with or observe your audience.

## TikTok

Currently the most popular social-media platform, TikTok allows users to post short-form videos (up to 180 seconds) and has proven the best for engagement and growing an audience. This is mainly due to the huge number of active users and how easily content is recommended to others. There are no portfolio features, however.

## DeviantArt

Popular among artists and other creatives, DeviantArt allows users to share image and text posts. While not the best platform for growing a following, due to its niche community and lack of active users, it's ideal for building extensive portfolios. If you don't yet have your own website, you can create a portfolio on DeviantArt and link to it from your other social platforms.

## Twitter

Twitter lets you post a small amount of text, images (up to four per post), and videos. It allows audience interaction and there is an average potential for growth, but there is no portfolio feature.

## Pixiv

Almost solely consisting of anime and manga artwork, Pixiv is a Japanese website with a very high number of users.

| | Active users | Growth potential | Content variety | Portfolio options |
|---|---|---|---|---|
| Own website | N/A | N/A | 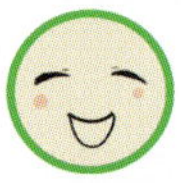 | 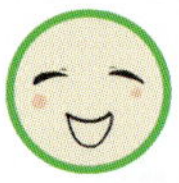 |
| Twitter | 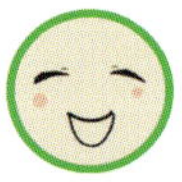 | 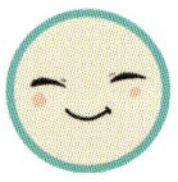 | 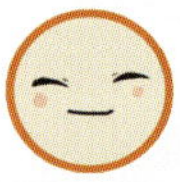 | N/A |
| Instagram | 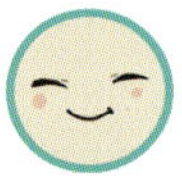 | 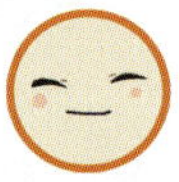 |  | 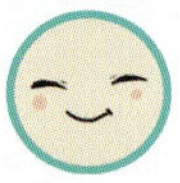 |
| TikTok | 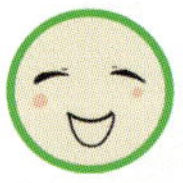 | 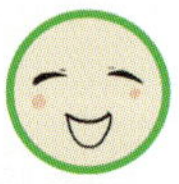 |  | N/A |
| DeviantArt | 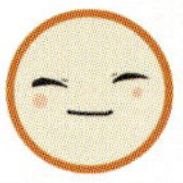 |  | 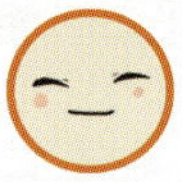 | 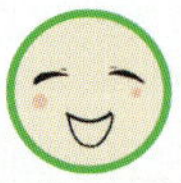 |

My experiences of the strengths and weaknesses of different social-media platforms

# Increasing engagement

The best way to increase your online engagement is to maintain an active presence by posting consistently. While you don't need to draw and post every day, it's important to engage with your followers, as well as with the wider art community, replying to comments on your posts, leaving comments on other artists' posts, and occasionally sharing some of your old artwork for new followers to see.

Your aim is for as many people as possible to interact with your content. It's all too easy to forget about a new artist, so your job is to remind people of who you are and what you do. A good way to encourage engagement from your followers is to ask questions, whether art-related or simply about everyday life. For example, "Should I draw a character with blue or pink hair?" Or, "What is your favorite food?" You could also create a poll asking who their favorite anime or manga character is, or what artwork or merchandise they would be interested in purchasing from you. Communication will not only establish your online presence and keep your artwork present in your audiences' minds, but seemingly simple connections can sometimes lead to bigger opportunities in the future.

## Do

- Engage with other anime-style artists and your followers as much as possible.
- Stay active online. Posting then disappearing for a year will make it difficult to grow a loyal following.
- Try your best to reply to as many comments and messages as you can, especially in the early days of launching your online platform.
- Be open and receptive to suggestions and feedback, especially from more established artists who often have a wealth of experience to share.
- Be willing to adapt your marketing strategy, branding, and format. The prominence of different social-media sites, along with their post formats, is constantly changing. Trends come and go. You must change with them in order to keep up.

## Don't

- Self-advertise your own artwork in the comments section of another artist's post.
- Overload your posts with hashtags, especially on Instagram, as this can flag you as a potential bot account.
- Create fan art for a celebrity or established artist if your sole purpose is expecting them to share or advertise your work to their followers.
- Buy fake followers or likes. Most social-media platforms will find out pretty quickly and you are likely to get banned.
- Obsess over how many comments, likes, or shares your posts receive. Sometimes people are too busy to check social media, or don't see your post because of big news stories or life events, or simply because their minds are elsewhere. Judging the quality of your work or tying your self-worth as an artist to your "numbers" will prove detrimental to your mental health. Online popularity is determined by many different factors and is not always something you can control.

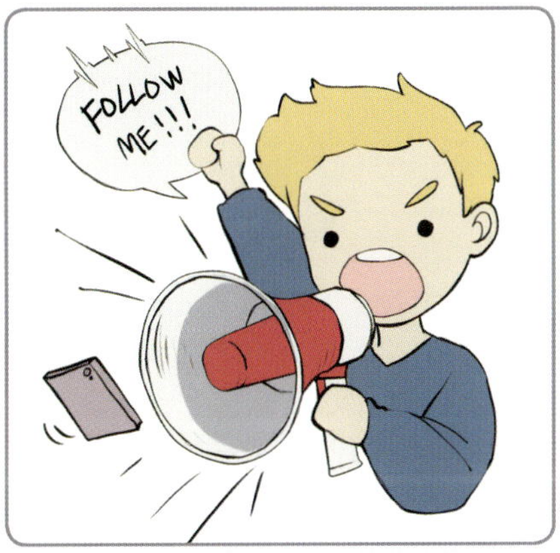

Don't self-advertise your work on other artist's pages

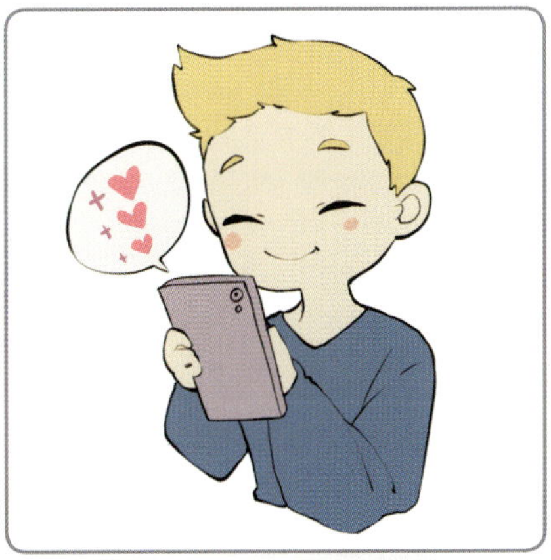
Do your best to support other artists – you may find they return the favor

# Converting followers into income

There are many different ways to earn an income from your anime-style art, depending on the size of your following. Here are some suggestions:

- Undertake commissions – drawing custom artwork for individuals and companies.
- Sell character designs, also known as "adoptables."
- Create exclusive content for subscriptions or memberships, using sites such as Patreon and Ko-Fi.
- Create a donation page, using sites such as Ko-Fi.

After you have built an online presence, you can:

- Livestream your drawing or painting process for donations.
- Create and sell tools and resources, such as brushes for Photoshop or Procreate, or drawing tutorials.
- Take sponsorships, such as paid product reviews or advertisements. That said, try to avoid accepting the common giveaway sponsorships (typically seen on Instagram) if the company is not reputable, or if part of the entry clause is to follow every account that the sponsor company's account is following. It's likely they will be using you as part of a "follower loop" scheme, which further encourages follower-buying and fraud on Instagram. Always do your research before accepting a sponsorship. Also, there is no harm in approaching companies first with a proposal of how you would like to collaborate.

## Merchandise

Once you have built a loyal fan base, or if you have a significant start-up budget, you can sell merchandise featuring your artwork. This could include prints, posters, key chains, stickers, tote bags, clothing, or any other products your followers express an interest in. Prints often prove popular among anime-style artists, as they are easy to make at home or in a print shop. They typically sell well, as people like to collect physical copies of artwork they enjoy. Stickers, acrylic key chains, and charms are also popular, as they are relatively cheap to make and easy to sell. Additionally, you can make art books to showcase your work, or create narrative-driven comics.

If you want to create and sell merchandise but don't have a start-up budget, it's possible to outsource the distribution and production. Many print-on-demand companies, such as Redbubble, offer this service, but they will take a sizable cut of the sale, reducing your profit. You can also explore crowdfunding, on platforms such as Kickstarter or GoFundMe, to fund your project and offer rewards to your backers.

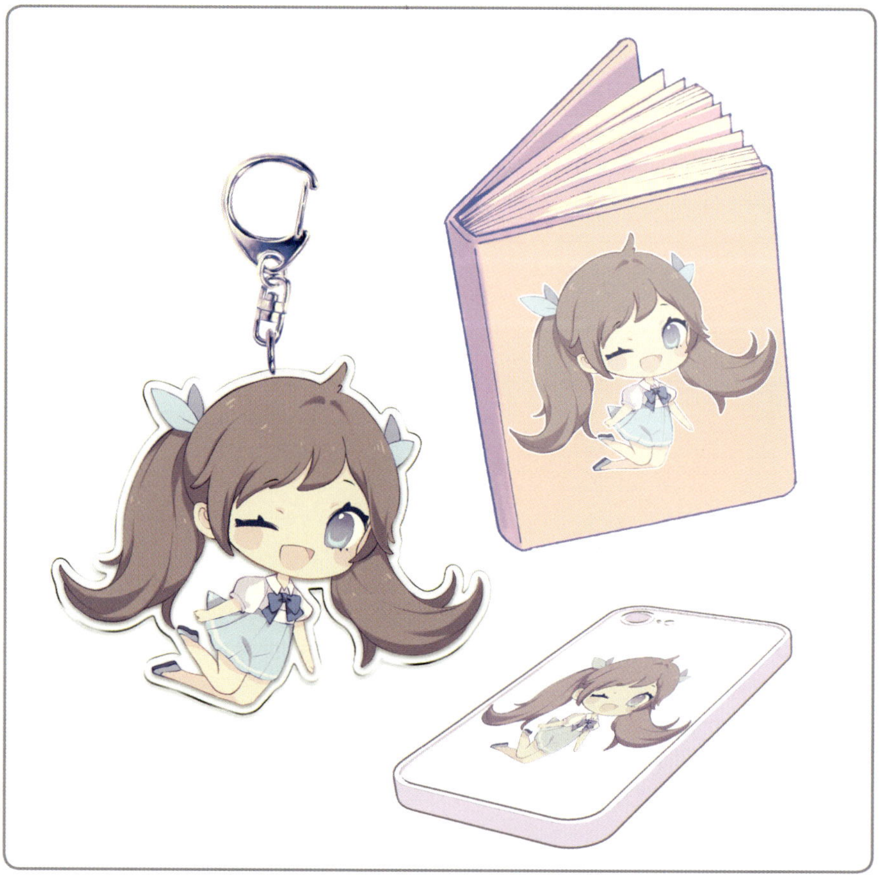

Many anime-style artists like to sell merchandise of their artwork, including phone cases, key chains, or art books

# Investing time & money in marketing

Established brands pay to advertise because tens of thousands of people are already familiar with their company and products. When they launch something new, they are asking their audience, "Hey, remember us?" While a new company will also pay large amounts to advertise, this money is from third-party investors who are convinced the product or service will be a success and make a return on their investment.

It's a different story for individual artists wanting their work to reach a wider audience. In most instances I would avoid investing any money into marketing, specifically advertising. Unless you are already an established company or brand, have investment backers, or possess a significant amount of disposable income, paying to advertise will likely not prove worthwhile. The amount of money you need to spend to reach a significant audience is huge. For example, at the time of writing, if you pay Instagram $100 USD to advertise a post, they estimate the advertisement will be viewed by 8,000 to 28,000 users, though these figures are not guaranteed. Not everyone who sees your post will bother to interact with it or click through to your profile. Many people get annoyed by adverts on social-media platforms, automatically scrolling past them.

# Significant anime trends

If you're active in the online art community and follow other anime-style artists, you will begin to notice popular trends. Getting involved with trends that are currently popular can help to attract new followers, boost engagement, and sell more products. Recent trends include:

- Nineties retro anime-style illustrations. For example, drawing in the style of the classic *Sailor Moon* anime series.
- Character designs with celestial or space themes.
- "Pastel goth" character designs. This trend combines the classic goth style – containing items such as piercings, chains, black fishnet material, and gothic imagery – with cute pastel-colored elements, such as pale pink hair, lilac bows, and girlish clothing.
- Chibi-style characters with large, round heads and small bodies. This style of character design is ideal for merchandise that doesn't work with the typical vertical sizing of character designs, such as stickers and mouse pads. The cute, round shape of chibi-style characters allows artists to draw the full character without adding extra length to the illustration.

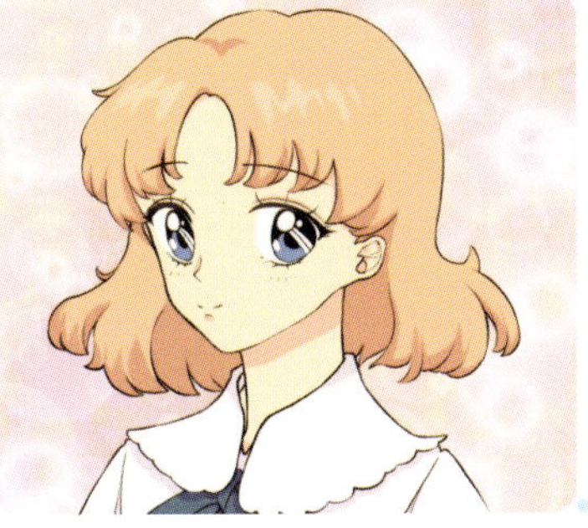

Many anime-style artists have joined the trend of drawing character illustrations in a nostalgic nineties style

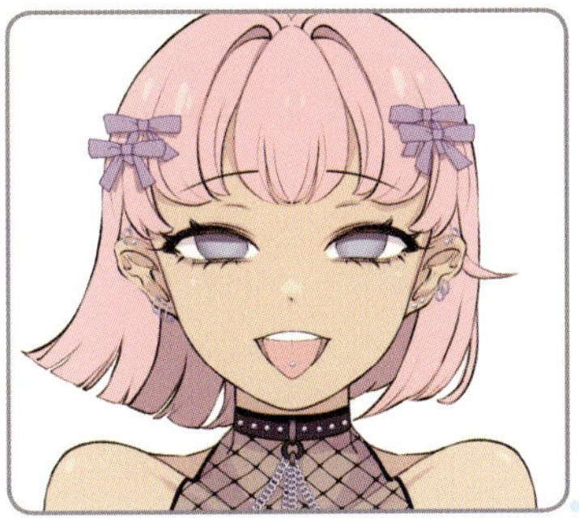

The trend for "pastel goth" anime-style character designs is based on the popular fashion trend

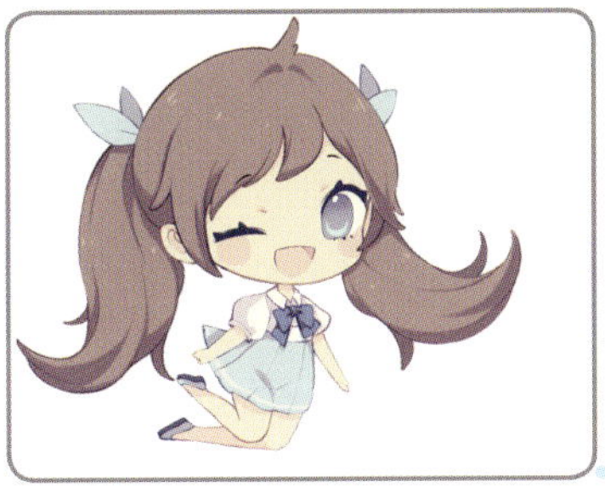

It can be fun to experiment with drawing a regular character as a chibi-style character instead

## Can commercial and creative success coexist?

Not only can commercial and creative success coexist, but for an anime-style artist, they can even complement each other. If anything, it's a positive feedback loop. If you start with good commercial success, knowing how to promote your work and grow a substantial following, you will receive inspiration, ideas, and feedback from your audience in the process. This will motivate you and help improve your work, leading to more creative success. Likewise, if you begin with immediate creative success, perhaps due to having a unique anime art style or video format, you can start to make money from your work, leading to commercial success.

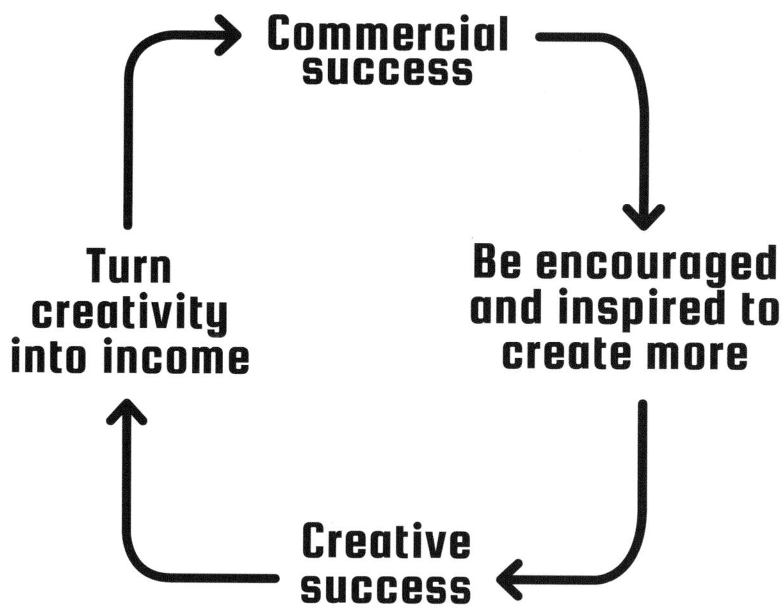


# EDUCATION & TRAINING

## Training for a career as an anime-style artist

While you will struggle to find a college or university-level course focused on anime and manga art, there are many online art courses available that can teach you the knowledge and skills you need to successfully create this type of artwork. Many established anime-style artists have courses on platforms such as Class101 and Skillshare. A quick internet search for "anime art courses" will yield numerous results, all with different price ranges and areas of focus, created by either corporations or individual artists.

Many anime-style artists create online tutorials in the form of images, diagrams, or videos, and lots of these are free. Have a look at the websites and online platforms of your favorite artists to see what they offer in the way of resources and teaching. Sometimes they will offer premium content via platforms such as Patreon, where you can pay to access in-depth lessons for a small monthly fee. Alternatively, some artists will publish tutorial books or post videos where they show their drawing process for a one-time fee. Simply typing "anime drawing tutorial" into an online search engine will provide countless resources that will teach you how to draw something new.

If you want to focus on creating merchandise featuring your anime-style artwork as a business owner, you could consider taking a business or marketing course. If you aim to work for a professional anime studio, however, you will need to study storyboarding and animation at an established art college.

One-to-one mentorships and portfolio reviews can be hugely helpful, but they are rare. Some professional artists do offer such services as part of their online art courses or as a pledge reward on Patreon, but they are usually expensive because they require a lot of time and effort.

# Art fundamentals

You don't need to spend thousands of dollars on a degree or diploma, but you do need to be familiar with the art fundamentals. Color theory is important for all forms of art, including anime and manga. Even if you are working with a solely monochromatic palette, it is still useful to understand the values (light and dark) of different colors and shading. Likewise, knowledge of perspective and composition is necessary for drawing backgrounds and dynamic character angles. Employers will look for these skills in your portfolio.

Figure drawing is another essential skill to learn, especially when designing characters. Even if you plan to stylize your characters to give them an exaggerated anime look, a basic knowledge of anatomy will help you make your designs more believable. Gesture drawing is also key, allowing you to quickly sketch a simplified figure to convey the pose, motion, and gesture of the body. Not only is this crucial for practicing how to capture realistic anatomy, but it will also help you illustrate action and movement. Twenty or even fifteen years ago, in-depth teaching on art fundamentals would have necessitated some kind of art degree or graduate-level training, but thanks to the arrival of the internet, this instruction is now widely available and easily accessible.

I studied independent illustration (freelancing) at Seneca College, Toronto, for two years, where I acquired lots of new knowledge and skills, and made great friends. Academic study does not suit everyone, however, and there are countless resources that can be found online for free. For example, many professional artists share their knowledge at no cost when posting tutorials on their platforms. A simple internet search will provide all you need to get started. Additionally, some of the modules I took were a little outdated, focusing on building a sizable physical portfolio to carry around with you, rather than how to build a more readily accessible portfolio and presence online.

Don't be discouraged if you don't have the money for art college, or if academic institutions don't suit your style of learning. Make full use of the internet to learn the art theory you need. In all of the art jobs I have taken, I was never asked for a degree or diploma. Your portfolio is much more important to employers than a certificate from whichever art course you completed in college. As there are no post-secondary programs specific to anime and manga art, almost all anime-style artists are self-taught.

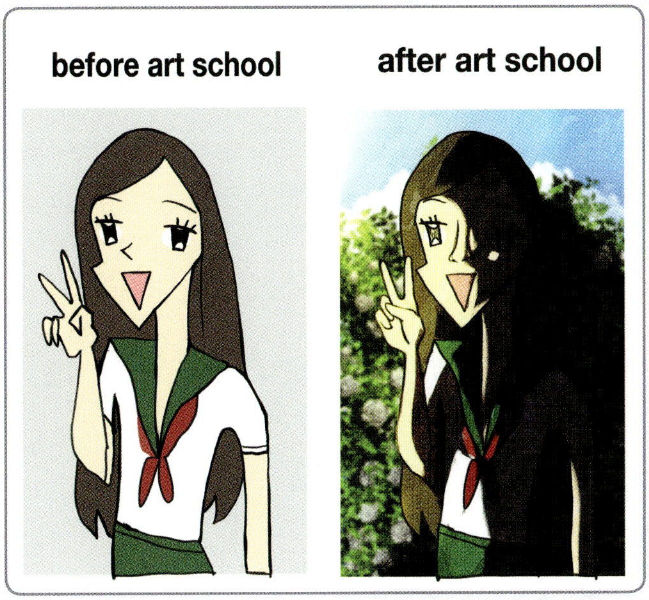


While the art fundamentals teaching I received at college was incredibly useful, the course contained nothing specific to teach me how to draw anime or manga

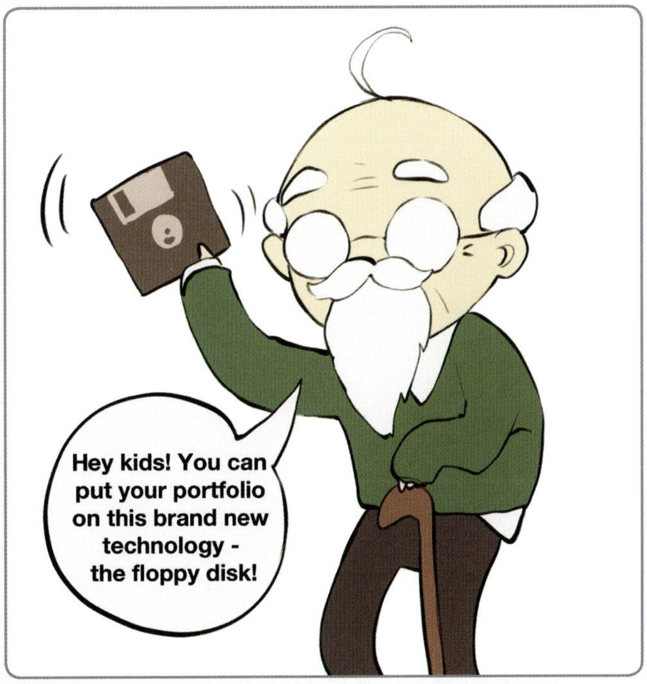


Not all art college programs are up to date – you can learn so much for free online

# WORKING IN THE INDUSTRY

While some artists prefer to remain freelance, taking commissions as and when they can fit them into their schedule, others look for full-time work on a short-term contract. This section will explore the different ways of working and earning an income as an anime-style artist.

## Freelance work

Freelance artists have flexibility in choosing how they wish to earn their income and progress their career in the industry. There are various different career paths and styles of working, allowing each artist to find a way of working that suits them.

### Short-term, one-off commissions

Commissions, whether for commercial or non-commercial clients, can include character design, illustration, concept art, and promotional material, such as album covers or advertisements.

If you are a concept artist, you will be provided with a brief of the required work. This could be a rough sketch or a couple of sentences, such as: "A fantasy world, 3,000 years in the future. There are floating islands, two moons, and the characters have elfin ears." You would then sketch a variety of ideas, from which the company would select one, or several, for you to continue developing. For environmental concept art, you are typically required to create a large landscape painting. For character design, you will usually be asked to create a turnaround, like the one on the right. If the company is creating merchandise for the product, you may also be tasked with creating product mock-ups, providing a preview of what it will look like when manufactured.

Alternatively, studios often require artwork to be created for promotional material, such as posters, book covers, or a digital advert. They will provide you with the concept art for you to use as a reference to draw the necessary illustration. You will often be asked to follow very specific file formats, with a certain canvas size and resolution. For example, most digital media requires at least 300dpi and print media requires 600dpi, especially if your drawing is small and on paper. There will typically be a lot of back-and-forth between the artist and studio. You will need to submit drafts at every stage – sketches, color palette, and line work – and to make the required changes before continuing with the design.

If you are struggling to find work as a freelance artist and want help with finding commissions, you can consider signing up to an art agency. Agencies are regularly approached by companies wanting to outsource some of their art and design work, such as character design or illustration. For example, video-game companies often seek out freelance artists to create the artwork for the promotional material for their latest release. Keep in mind, however, that agencies will take a cut from your fee for each project.

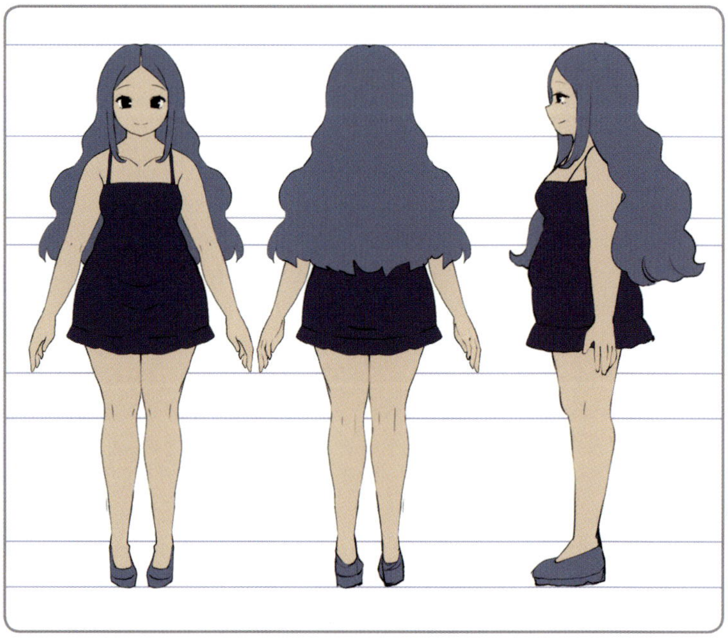

A character turnaround is often required as part of character design work

# Contract work

Contract work is where studios and companies employ artists to create artwork for a specific project, rather than hiring them for a permanent job role at the company. For example, a video-game company may hire a lead artist to work on the game resources, drawing characters, backgrounds, and icons. A publisher may hire an artist to create the cover art for a series of books. Contract work is typically very fast paced. If the project is on a tight schedule, you may only be given a few days to finish a sizable painting or design. If you do not deliver on time, there is always the risk that they will find a replacement.

Unless you require project-specific in-house tools and equipment, or need to work closely with others in person, artists working under contract for a company are typically able to work from home. While there may be meetings you need to attend in person, for the most part you will be required to submit your work online. Traditional artists who own a large quantity of art materials – such as canvases, easels, paints, and printing and cutting machines – may wish to consider renting a studio space. Studio rent can be expensive, however, so it can be worth creating a studio space in your own home.

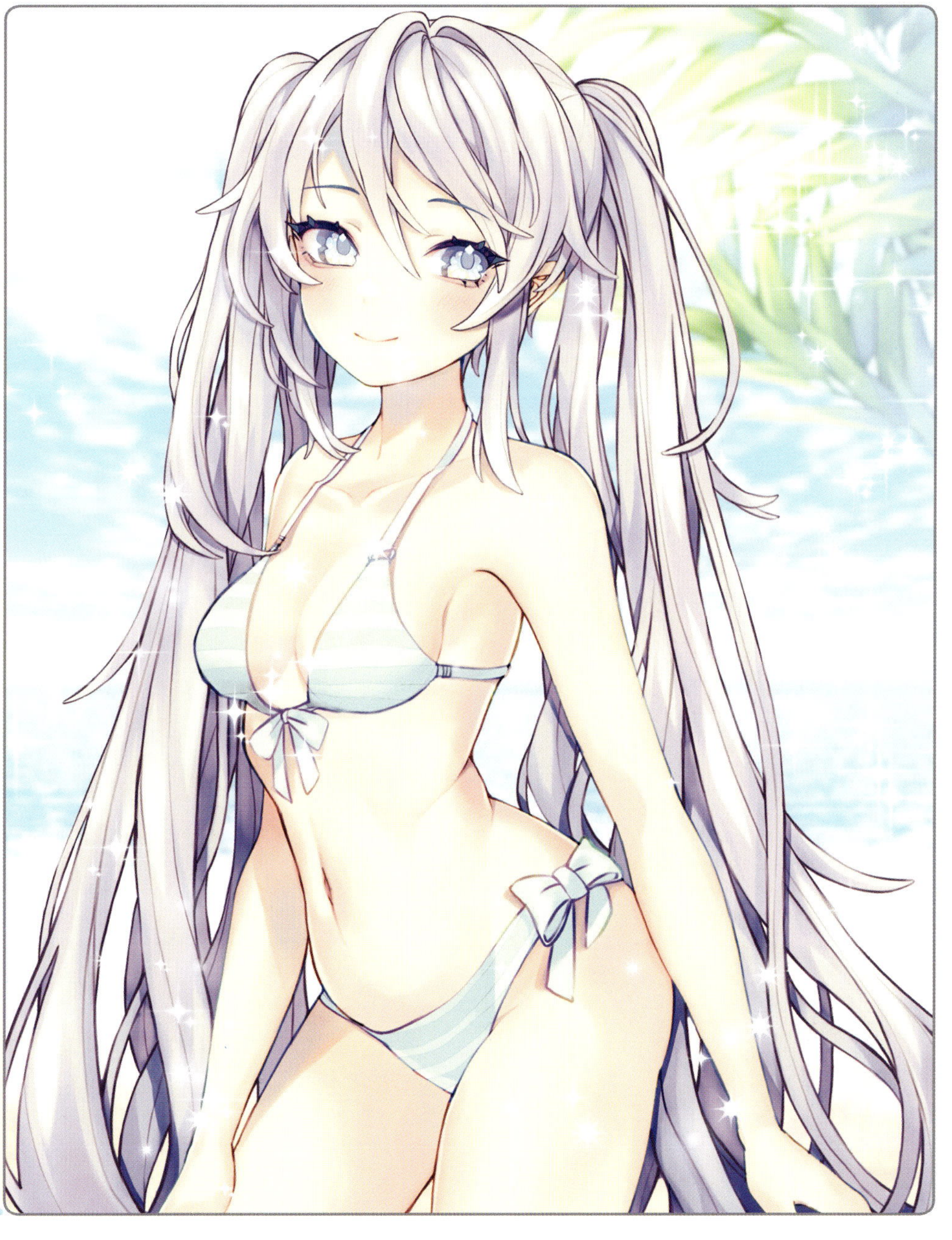

Example of anime-style artwork that could be used for a book cover or promotional poster

# Merchandise business

Many anime-style artists choose to design and make merchandise featuring their artwork to sell online. You will need to consider whether you want to handle the production and distribution yourself, and to what degree, and to keep in mind the additional costs when exploring this route. The alternative is to outsource all of the work to a third-party company, such as Redbubble, that will manufacture your merchandise and mail it to the customer. Third-party companies will take a sizable cut of the profit from each sale, however, so this option might only be viable if you earn your main income from other work, and sell merchandise as a side-gig for additional income.

If you plan to organize the production and shipping of the merchandise yourself, you will need a minimum of around $3,000 USD to get started. As well as covering the cost of manufacturing the products, this will also pay for:

- Shipping materials, such as boxes and envelopes.
- Shipping labels or a postage printer.
- A post-office box for a return address or business address. (Look for PO Box companies that format the box address as a residential or business address, not a PO Box address. Never use your home address.) These rentals are usually renewed annually, so there will be an upfront cost.
- Business registration and license fees, which vary from country to country.
- Creative materials including art supplies, electronic equipment, and any other required materials that you don't already own.
- An online shop, using services such as Wix or Squarespace, with a custom domain name. As you typically pay for these annually, this is another upfront cost to factor in. These sites will help you manage your inventory as well as create a professional storefront.
- Custom business cards to include with every order.
- Product insurance in case of loss or damage during transport, unless you are able to pay out of pocket to cover losses.
- A shipping program for discounted postage fees – this will save you money in the long run.
- Paid-for advertisements.
- Shelving or storage containers in which to store merchandise. You might even want to rent a storage unit if you have a large amount of merchandise, or products that are large in size.

If you plan on manufacturing products yourself, you will likely need to buy equipment, such as a professional printer, ink, and various specialist papers for products like prints and stickers. This may require a few more thousand dollars.

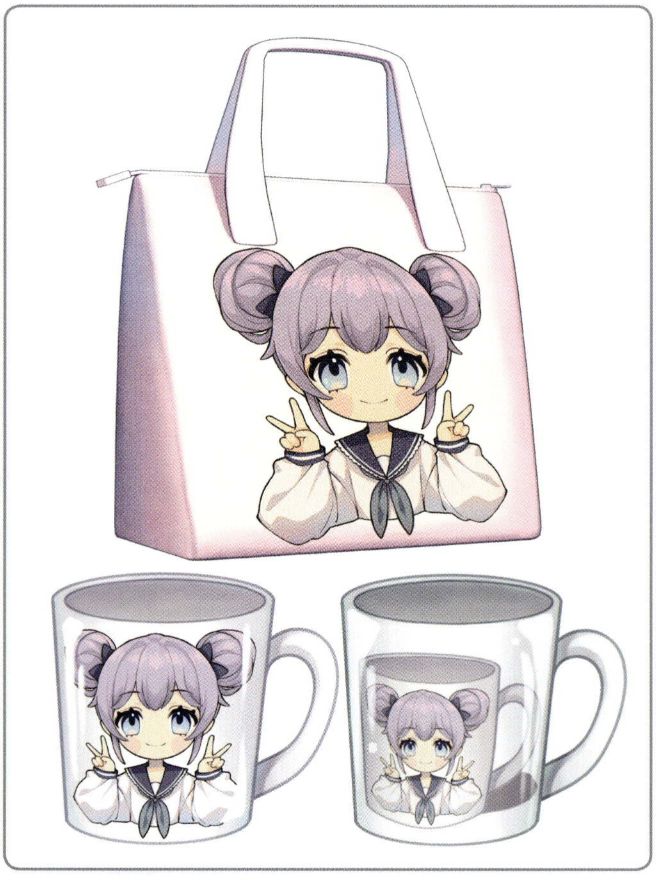

Anime-style artists often ask their followers what artwork they would like to see made into merchandise, or what type of products they would like to buy

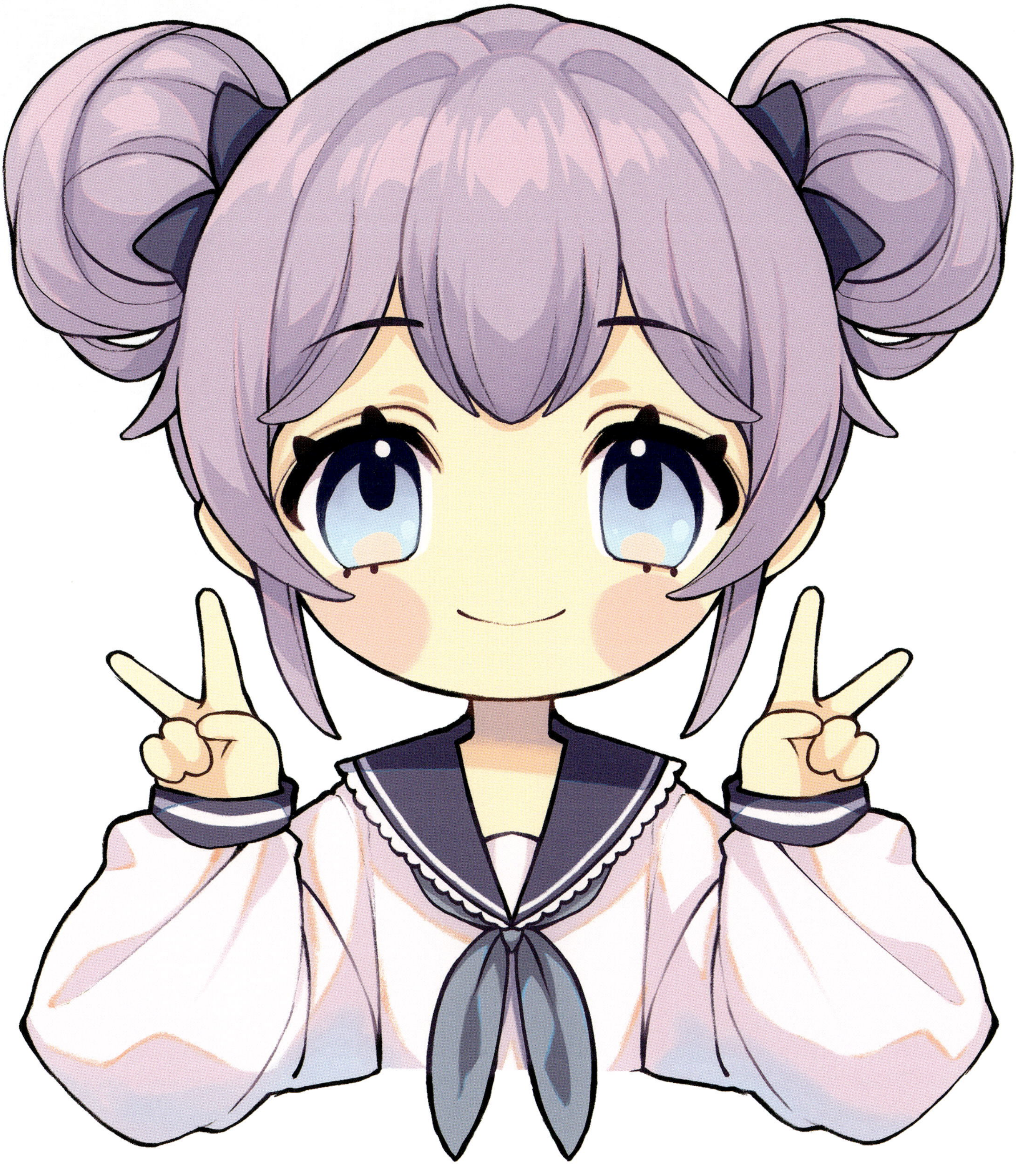

The original artwork

Anny "Yoai"

# Working for anime movie & television studios

Anime studios, where animated movies and shows are produced, have many of the same job roles that are found across the television and movie industry as a whole. The same person can work on multiple roles if they are skilled in several areas.

## Storyboard artist

An invaluable behind-the-scenes role, storyboard artists plan out the shots by sketching panels of each moment and scene – including movement, scene changes, and dialogue – to provide the animators with a visual representation of the narrative.

## Art director

Though not always artists themselves, art directors are in charge of the overall design and direction of the artwork. They provide the artists with guidelines and ideas, based on their vision for the anime.

## Animator

The work of animating a movie or television show is typically shared between a team of animators. Their job is to painstakingly draw each still frame.

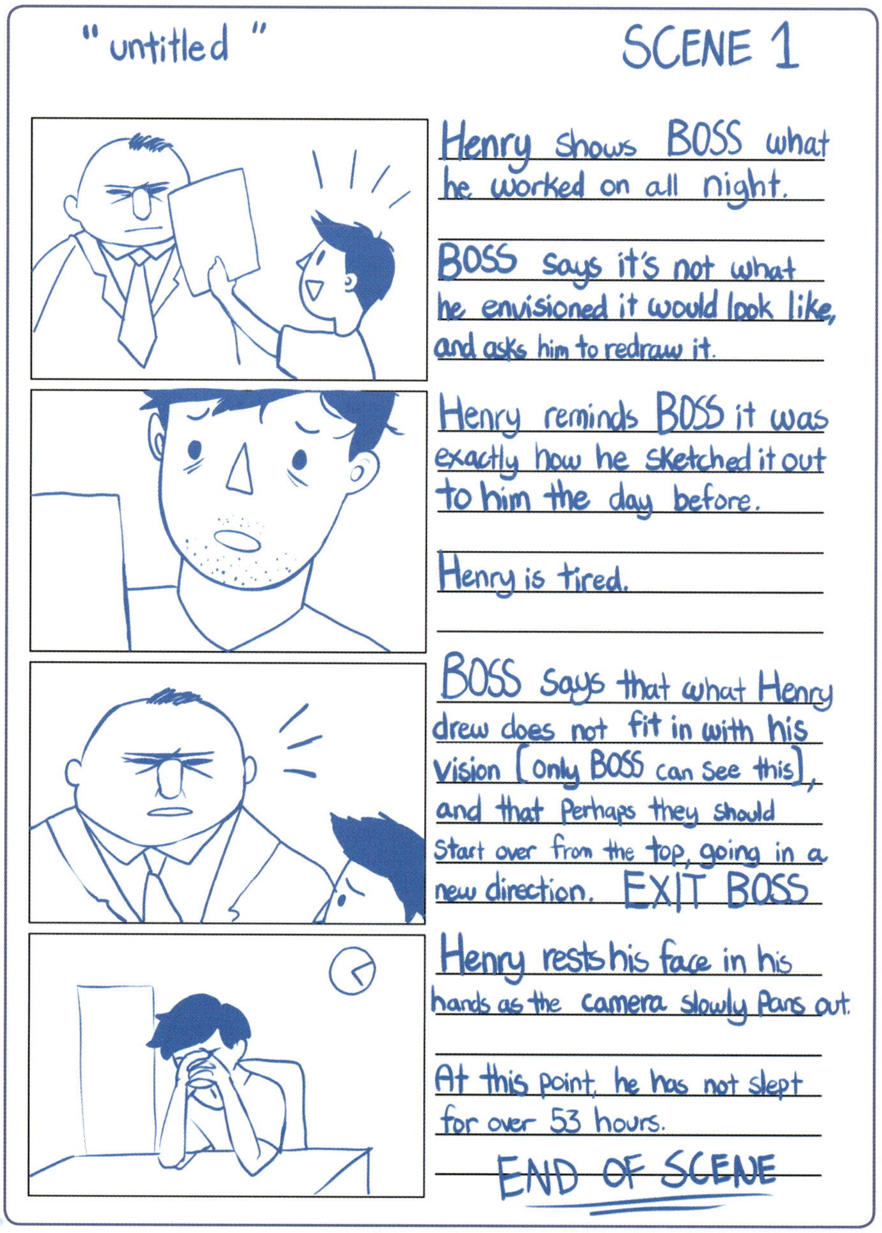


An example of a storyboard

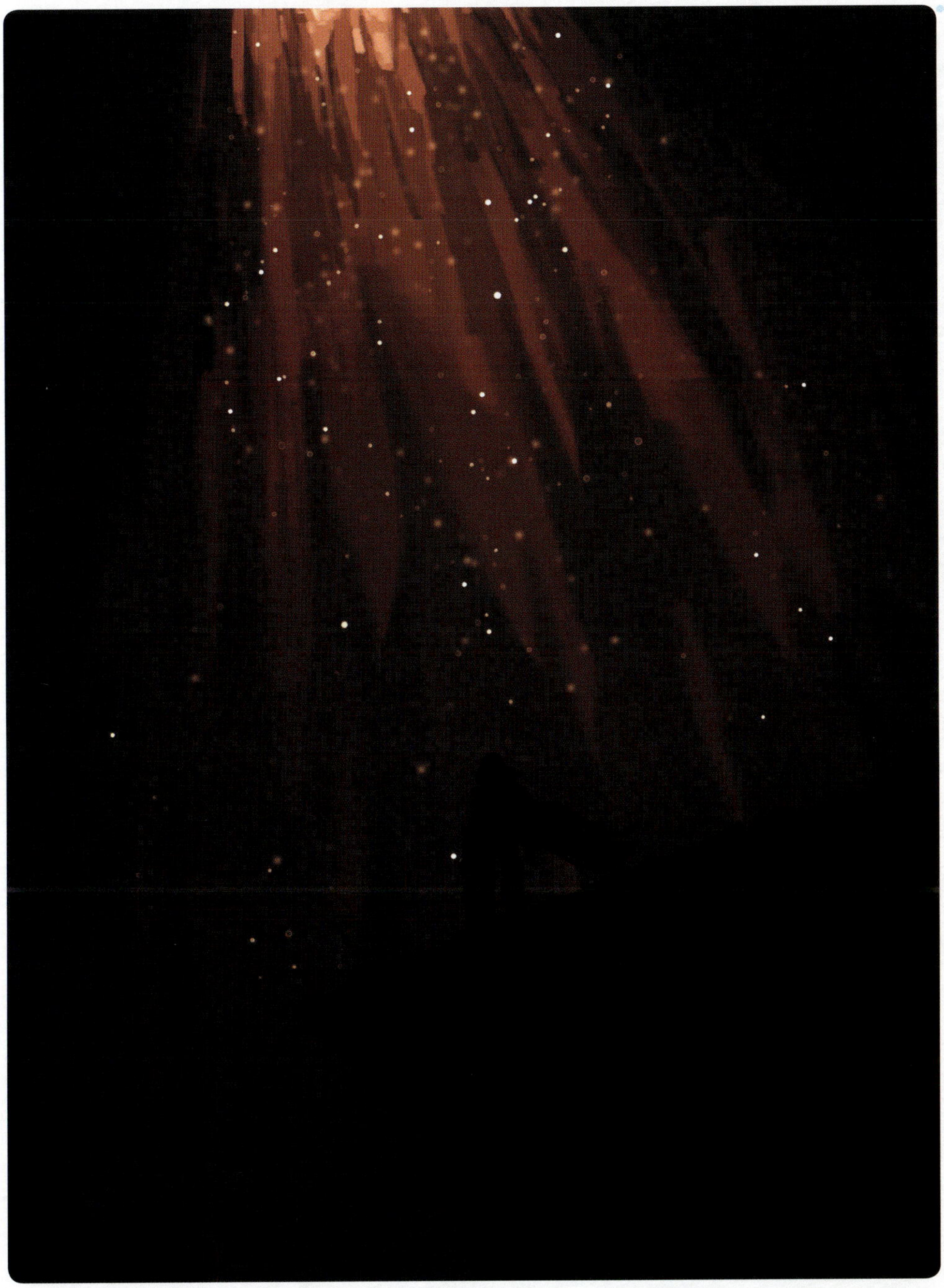

Concept art brings to life the art director's vision for the movie or game, helping to build the world or flesh out the character

## Concept artist

Concept artists take the story and the art director's vision and convert these ideas into a visual form. They work on everything from character designs to environments and world-building. Highly sought after, these roles are mostly filled by freelance anime-style artists.

## Writer

Every anime needs an engaging narrative to drive it forward. Writers come up with the story and its characters.

## Marketing & promotion

Functioning as its own team, the marketing department handles advertising and promotion. The marketing departments of anime studios will often hire freelance artists to create promotional material, such as posters or graphics, to advertise a new movie or video game.

## Editor

Once the story has been written and the characters created, editors polish the narrative to ensure it is consistent and without plot holes.

## Film director

Sometimes known as the animation director, they direct the scenes and dialogue.

# Anime for print & online

The majority of anime-style artists find work designing cover artwork for books and comics; behind-the-scenes concept art and character design for anime movies and television series; illustrations for posters; promotional material for anime movies and television series; or artwork for merchandise and apparel.

While many manga publications are printed in black and white, they typically have a colored illustration for the cover. This may be drawn by the same artist, or artists, who drew the contents of the book, or it could be outsourced to a freelance artist who specializes in cover design. The goal is to create a colorful and eye-catching illustration that makes people want to pick the comic off the shelf.

Some companies will ask you to sign a non-disclosure agreement (NDA) or waive full copyright, meaning you are not permitted to share the work you have created for them or leak any details about the project. Others will encourage you to share the work with your followers on your social-media platforms, as this can be a great source of promotion for them.

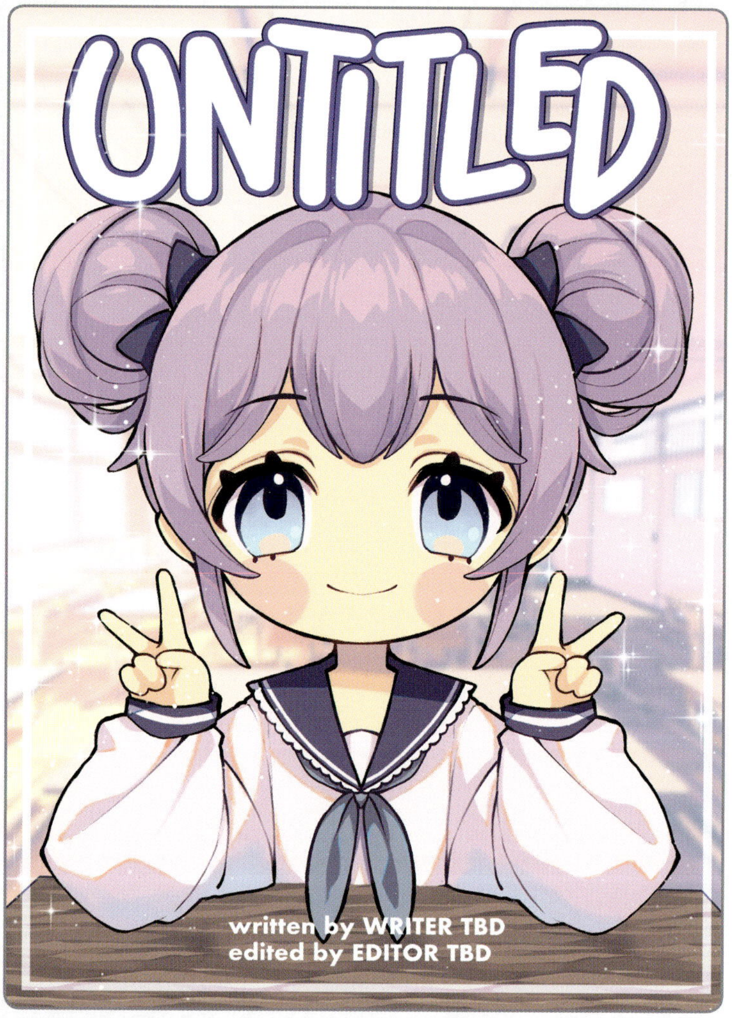


Publishers may approach artists to design covers for books or manga

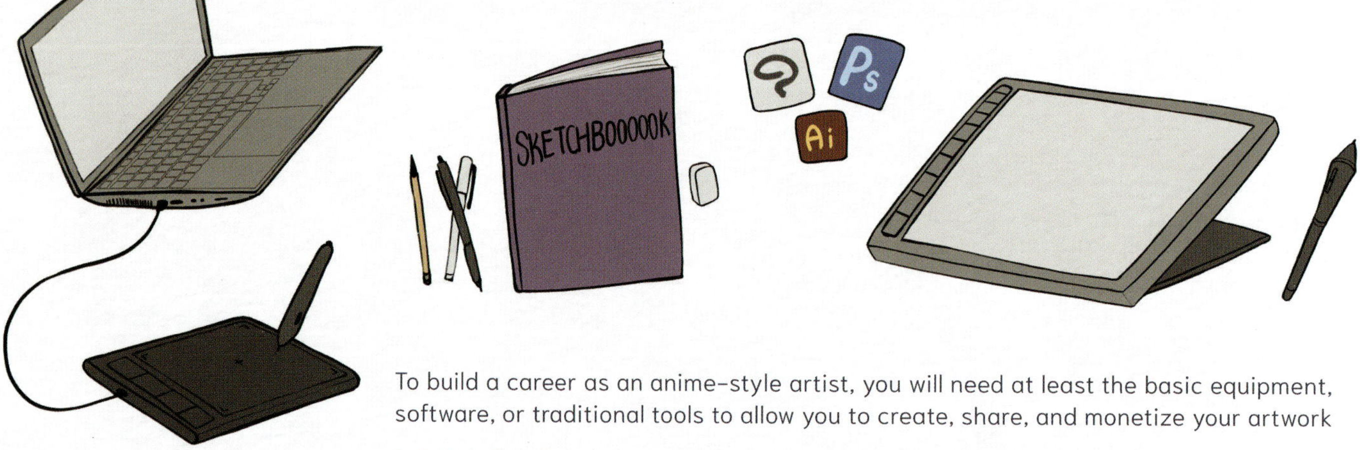


To build a career as an anime-style artist, you will need at least the basic equipment, software, or traditional tools to allow you to create, share, and monetize your artwork

# Comics

Manga exists in physical and online form. Webtoon is one well-known company that allows artists to self-publish their digital comics on their online platform, typically releasing a new chapter each week. As artists can earn an income from this, it has become very popular in recent years.

Artists can also self-publish their own manga, whether in a small section of a zine or an entire book. This can be expensive, however, unless you can collaborate with other artists, receive sponsorship from a publisher, or crowdfund the project on a website such as Kickstarter or GoFundMe. Most artists opt for this third option.

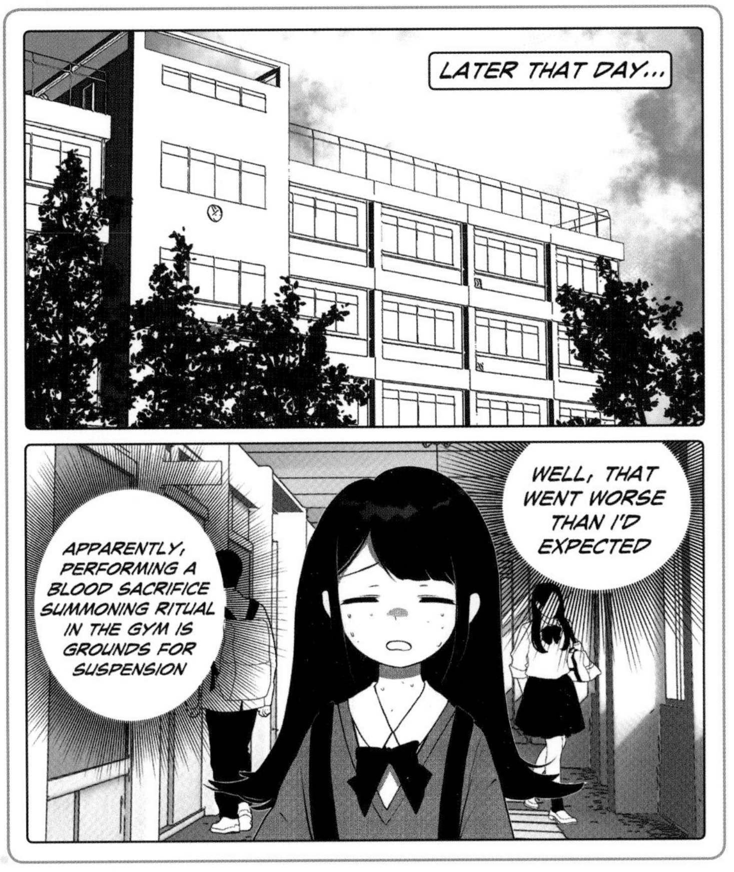


Manga artists often publish on third-party platforms or raise the money to self-publish through crowdfunding sites

# Tools & software

While every anime or manga artist will have their preferred tools and software, there are several key pieces of equipment that are standard across the industry.

Digital artists will typically require a graphics tablet, either with or without a display, such as Wacom Intuos, or a stand-alone tablet with drawing capability, such as the iPad Pro. They will also need some kind of drawing software – such as Adobe Photoshop, Procreate, PaintTool SAI, or Clip Studio Paint – and a computer with decent memory and processing power, if not using a stand-alone tablet. Not only are professional work files often very large, but digital painting programs also require a lot of memory and processing power. In addition, clients will sometimes ask for vector files or illustrations, so you will need software that allows you to create these, such as Adobe Illustrator.

If undertaking work for companies, they usually only require specific software if you are working as part of a team on the same piece of work, or if the company has their own specialist software. As most companies are typically looking for illustrations, it's unlikely you would be required to use a specific program, as long as they can export a file that is readable with their software. Companies normally require specific file formats and sizes, of which a common one is PSD (Photoshop document).

Since the development of the computer and subsequent arrival of digital painting, digital art is now more common across the anime industry than traditional art. While this does not mean there is no place for art created using traditional media, your choice of medium and ability to adapt can dictate the type of jobs you are interested in or simply able to take. That said, almost all of my work from the past six years, which has been largely made up of commissions for individual clients, has been created traditionally.

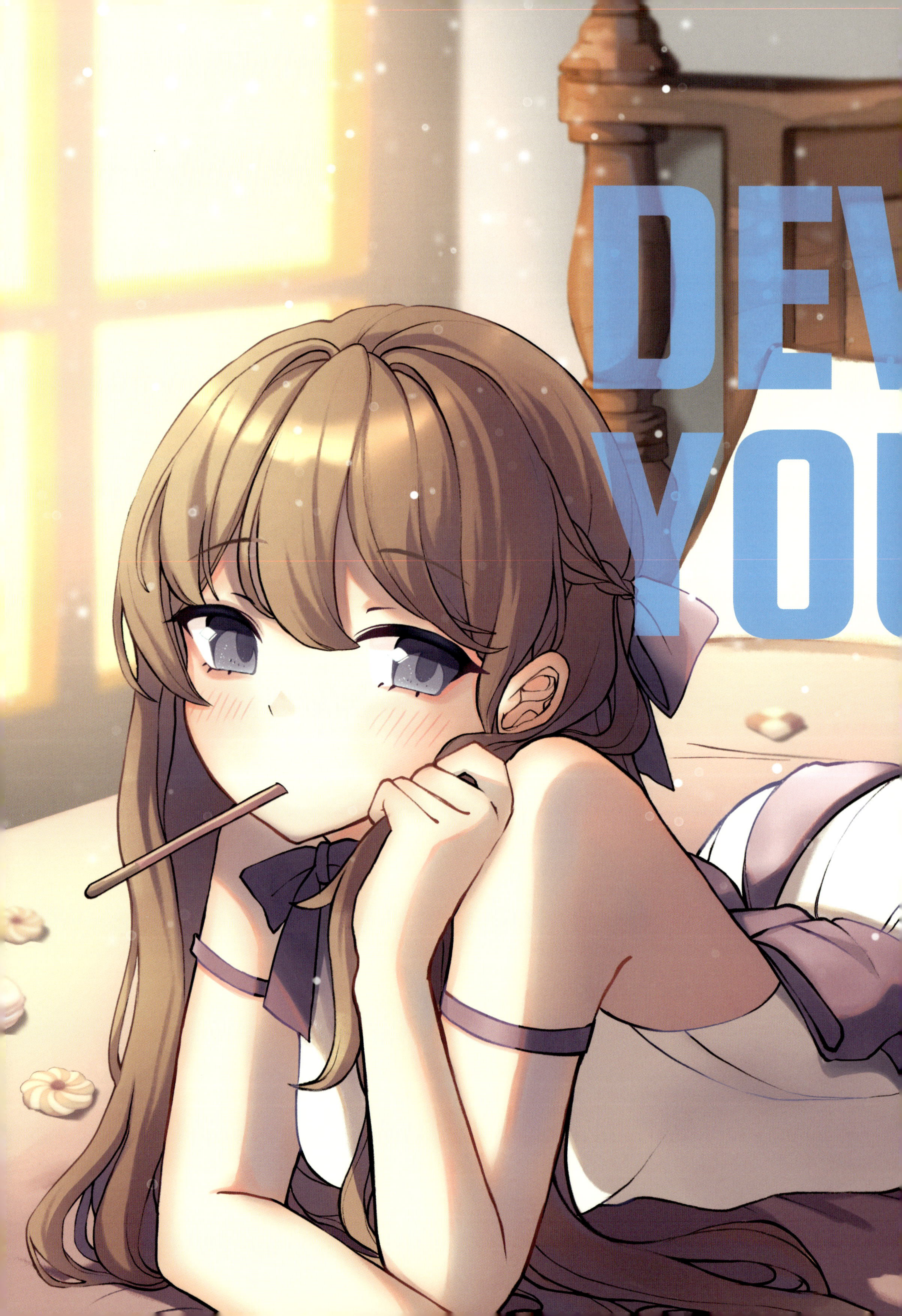
DEV
YOU

# ELOPING
# UR STYLE

By Anny "Yoai"

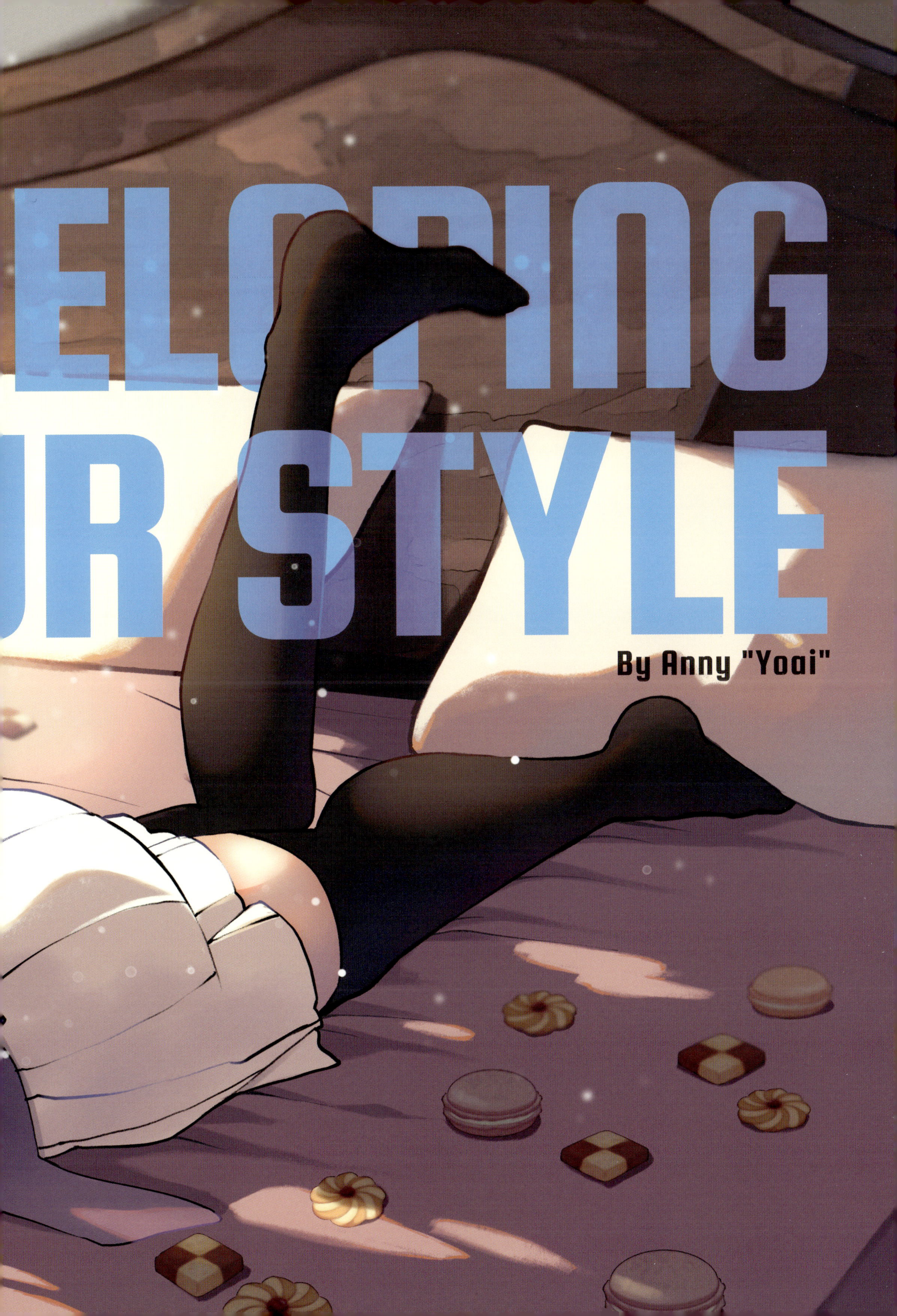

# DEVELOPING YOUR STYLE

## FINDING YOUR INDIVIDUAL STYLE

The different styles of anime art act as general guidelines to follow, but your unique individual style will be achieved by taking those as a base and developing them. Depending on your personal taste and the way you want to express yourself creatively, you might take inspiration from just one anime art style, or you might be influenced by several styles to create your own.

The previous chapter (*The Business of Anime*, see page 20) explored the main anime and manga genres, subgenres, and distinguishing styles of each. If you study two comics or series within the same genre, you will find many similarities specific to genre, but you will also discover just as many differences. For example, *Sailor Moon* and *Mermaid Melody Pichi Pichi Pitch* – both the mangas and the anime adaptations – fall into the shojo genre, specifically mahou shojo ("magical girl"). Both feature a group of girls with their own theme colors, each of which can transform into a "magical girl" outfit in preparation for combat. Yet despite their similarities, the art styles and themes are considerably different.

For example, the *Sailor Moon* characters have short, curly bangs and soft, curly hairstyles, whereas the *Mermaid Melody* characters tend to have long, straight bangs and straight, spiky or choppy hairstyles. Although the eyes of the characters in both are drawn with multiple white highlights, they still look completely different. For example, the eyes of the *Mermaid Melody* characters are always slightly larger in proportion to their face than the eyes of the characters in *Sailor Moon*.

Besides the characters, the atmospheres of the anime adaptations also differ. As with many animes from the nineties, *Sailor Moon* has more of a vintage film-style rendering and a more analog appearance. On the other hand, *Mermaid Melody*, for which the anime was released approximately ten years later, looks completely digitized with smooth, vibrant colors and a bright atmosphere.

The theme of each is also different. In *Sailor Moon*, the characters remain human in appearance and fight with magic, whereas in *Mermaid Melody* the characters are mermaids, fighting and defeating their enemies by singing.

This is one example to show why artists should view an anime genre – in this case, "magical girl" – for its stylistic guidelines, rather than as a strict set of rules to abide by or copy. Individual style allows each artist to put themselves into their work and create their own representation of the anime style. Imagine you are a violinist who plays classical music; there would be some basic rules you would need to follow regarding the instrument and hallmarks of the genre, but over time, with lots of practice, you would develop your own quirks while playing, such as variations in tempo, how you interpret the music, and the overall style of your performance. It's the same with finding your own anime art style.

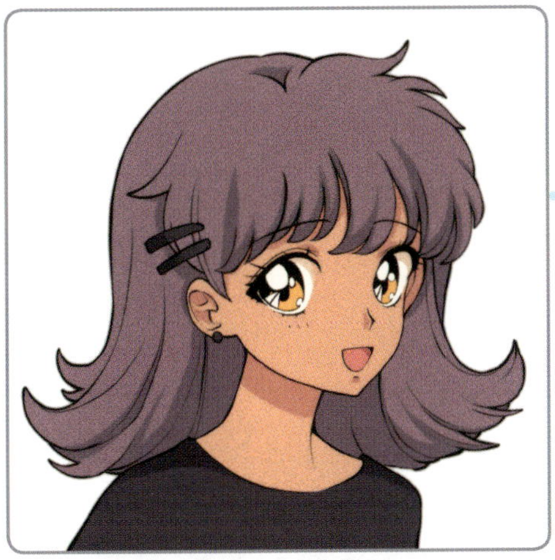

A character drawn in the style of classic anime series *Sailor Moon*

The same character, but instead drawn in the style of *Mermaid Melody* – even though the two animes are the same genre, notice how the art style is different

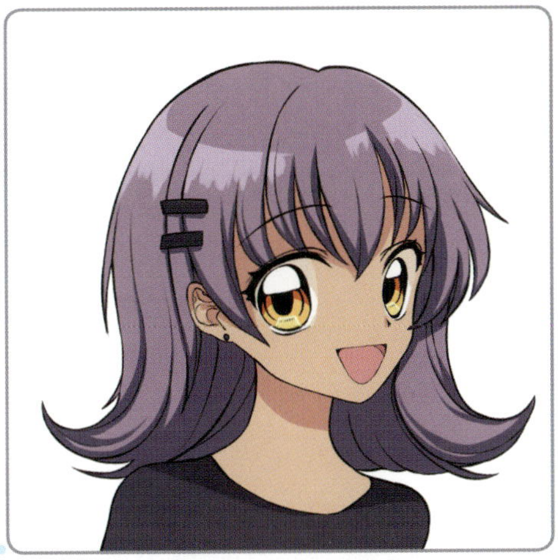

# Experimenting with style

An artist's personal style usually reflects their own interests, the main anime genre they are looking to emulate, and other styles and genres they find inspiring. For example, if you watch a lot of mecha or martial arts anime and practice drawing these types of characters, never taking much interest in shojo, you will likely be able to draw a mecha or fighter character much more easily than you will a cute schoolgirl with pink hair and a frilly dress. If the schoolgirl transforms into a gigantic magma lizard demon, however, and tramples an entire village because someone fed her after midnight, then you may be equipped to draw her after all.

Regardless of what your personal style has been up until this point, it never hurts to experiment with new styles if you are interested in working within different genres of anime. Versatility and adaptability are always selling points in a portfolio and will attract a wider range of clients and employers.

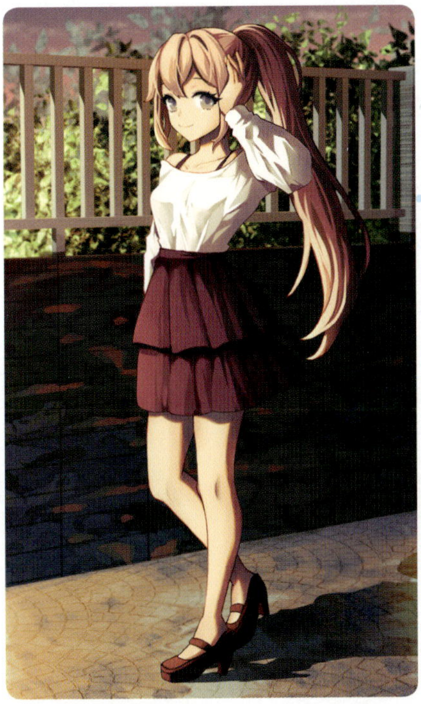

An illustration of a pink-haired girl in a frilly dress, suitable for shojo anime

An illustration of the same pink-haired girl, but in a completely different genre – here she has transformed into a fire-breathing monster, more in line with the seinen anime genre

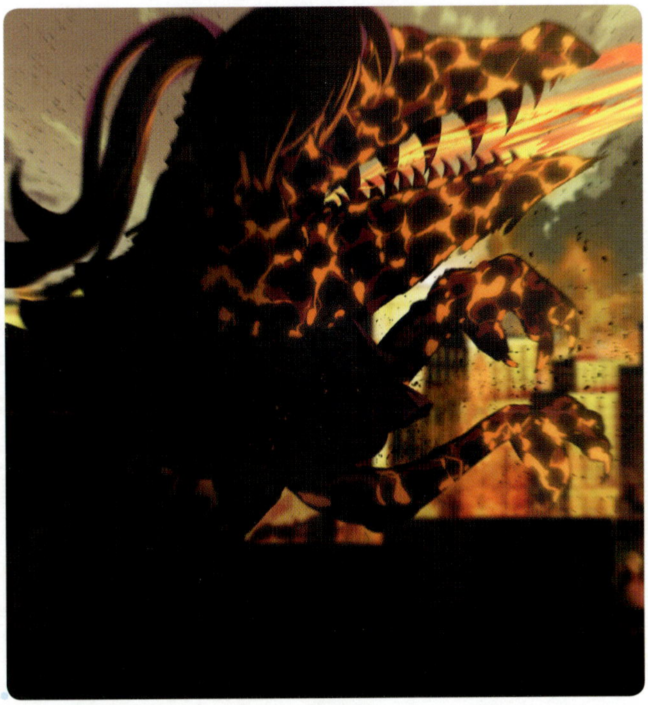

# Stylistic evolution & influences

Every artist's style will evolve over time. Not only does artistic skill improve with months and years of practice, but individual tastes will change over time, as will trends, the preferences of clients, and the anime market in general. As new subgenres are continually popping up, there is no end or limit to the variety of styles you are able to incorporate into your own artwork.

Go to your favorite artist's social-media page and compare the artwork they created recently to artwork they created a few years ago. Chances are, their art style has changed in a noticeable way. Even if the older artwork is still recognizable as their current signature style, there will be many elements that have changed since – whether a stylistic shift or switch up in subject matter or theme. Artists are always developing their style, taking inspiration from elements in other artwork and creative media, anime or otherwise, to incorporate into their own work.

Whether consciously or subconsciously, all artists take inspiration from their surroundings and the media they enjoy, incorporating elements and ideas into their work. Unless you avoid all books, movies, games, comics, and social media, it's impossible not to be inspired by other artists and their creations. It's important to note, however, that you should draw inspiration from many different sources, rather than just one. Your style should stem from your own creative interpretation of the subjects and styles you find inspiring, rather than be a direct copy of anything. Taking inspiration from only one source will limit your creative vision and throttle your ability to improve and develop your own unique style of artwork.

Many anime-style artists imitate the drawing style of their favorite artist or anime series when they are first starting out. While this can help you explore how to stylize your drawings, over time it will be of greater benefit to develop a creative interpretation and execution that is uniquely yours. This is also essential for creating and building your own brand, or simply if want your anime art style to be easily recognizable. However, as explored in *The Business of Anime* (page 33), it's much more important to learn the art fundamentals first – leaving the development of your style for later, once you've mastered the basics.

# Consistency vs. versatility

Many anime and manga artists are known for having a signature style and subject matter. This is what their followers like about their work. For example, an artist may be known for drawing anime-style girls holding flowers, allowing them the freedom to draw a variety of different female characters holding different types of flowers. Though their exact artwork varies, the theme remains the same, reinforcing the consistency of the artist's signature look or brand.

As an artist's style typically stems from what they enjoy drawing, however, it can change over time as their influences change. People may follow your online platforms to see the consistent style of anime art you share, but obsessing over maintaining this consistency can lead to unnecessary stress and make you feel like you have locked yourself into a specific art style forever.

Don't be afraid to experiment and take a versatile approach, evolving and refining your style along the way. If your signature style and subject matter allows for variety, such as fantasy-themed character design, but you choose to draw the same few fantasy characters on repeat, this has the potential to bore your followers, who may then unfollow your platforms. Additionally, while employers like to see that an artist can draw one style, theme, or subject matter really well, they also look for flexibility and the ability to adapt. While it is valuable to maintain your signature style and subjects you specialize in, trying out variations in style and subject will expand your skill and has the potential to attract new followers and clients.

# Does conformity lead to commercial success?

When building a career, many artists wonder if making their artwork fit neatly into a certain anime genre or style will give them a greater chance of commercial success. This depends on what kind of work the artist is hoping to secure, as some clients do seek out specific styles or formats. Generally, however, freelance artists are hired because clients like their signature style, or because they can create art in a variety of styles, rather than because they fit neatly into a specific anime genre.

For example, if a client is working on an anime trading-card game and is looking for multiple artists to create the illustrations, they will likely choose a selection of artists that already use similar mediums and draw similar subject matters to achieve a consistent look across the project. While each artist may be selected because of their penchant for drawing digital anime illustrations featuring brightly colored fantasy characters holding weapons, for example, each artist will have their own unique style. When browsing your portfolio, clients will look to see if you can draw the style and subject matter they are looking for, making it important to include a variety of styles in your portfolio, showing potential clients your confidence and ability to draw many different things.

The only time you will need to make your artwork fit a specific anime style is when working for an agency, or on contract for a company, on a project where some of the illustration work is being outsourced to you. In these instances, you will usually need to draw in an identical style to other artists working on the project to achieve a consistent look. Not many independent anime-style artists go down this career path, however, as the salary is often lower than in other areas, and artists are typically uncredited. But it can be a good way to improve your skills while earning some steady money.

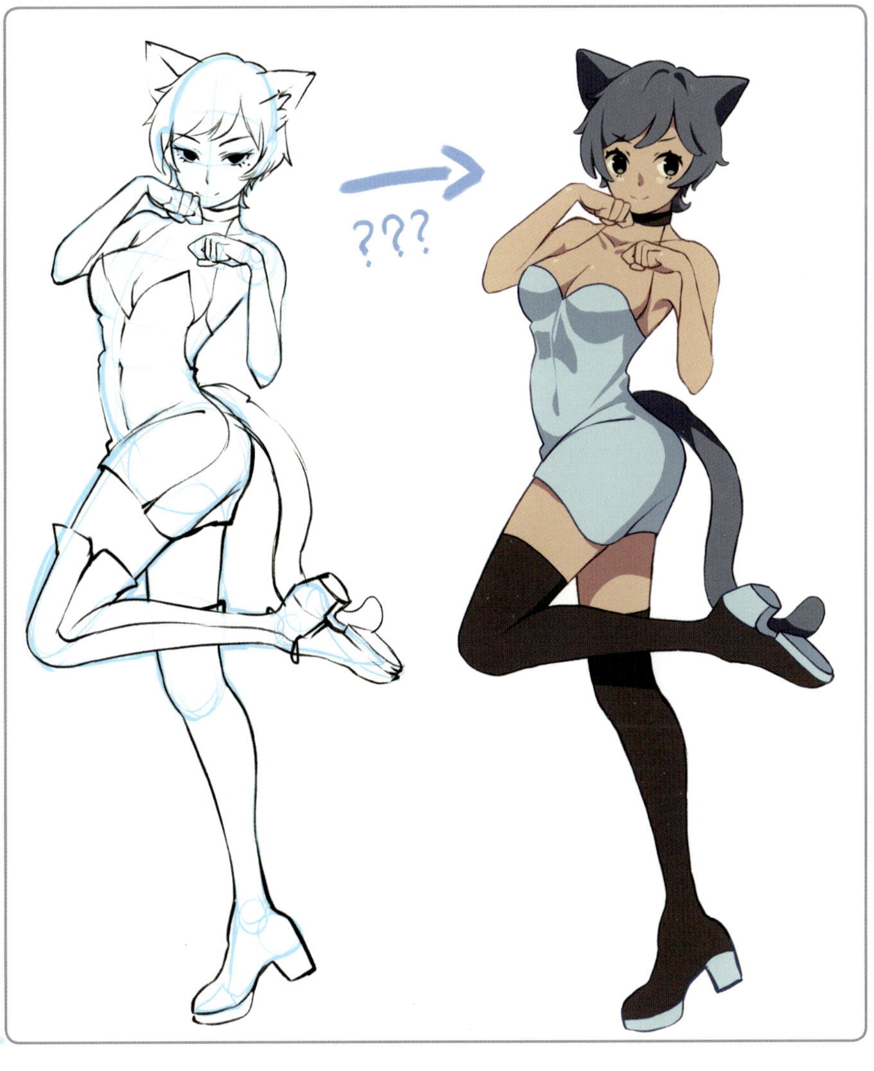


Imagine the sketch on the left was drawn by artist A, then passed on to artist B to finish – even though their styles are compatible, there is still a noticeable difference and the designs don't fully match

# Style & genre

Some styles of anime artwork are more suitable for certain genres, while others may not be a good fit. For example, if you enjoy drawing realistic, gloomy faces and using a monochromatic color palette, then it may prove a challenge to make this style fit into the mahou shojo genre. In contrast, if your signature style is characterized by feminine pastel colors, frills, and bows, it may be hard to translate this into a cover design for a horror manga. This doesn't mean that you can't experiment, however, exploring how to incorporate styles and genres that may not be an obvious pairing at first. For example, shonen and shojo sometimes include an uncanny, realistic-looking face for comedic effect or exaggeration.

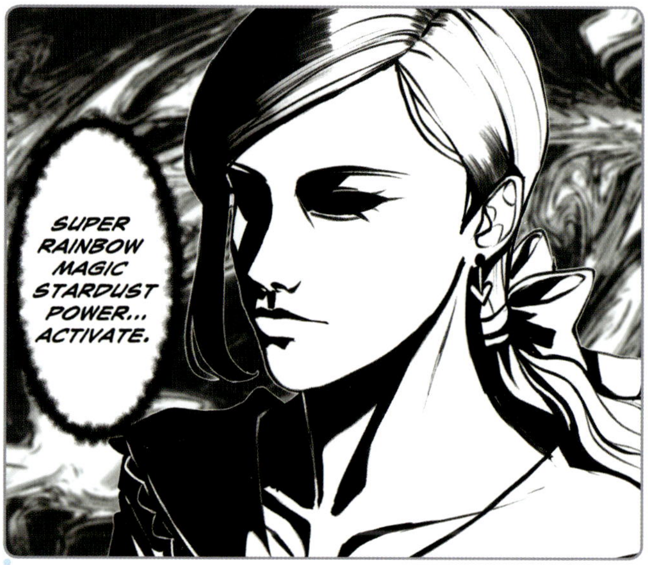


A panel of a mahou shojo ("magical girl") manga, drawn in the monochromatic, realistic style of horror manga

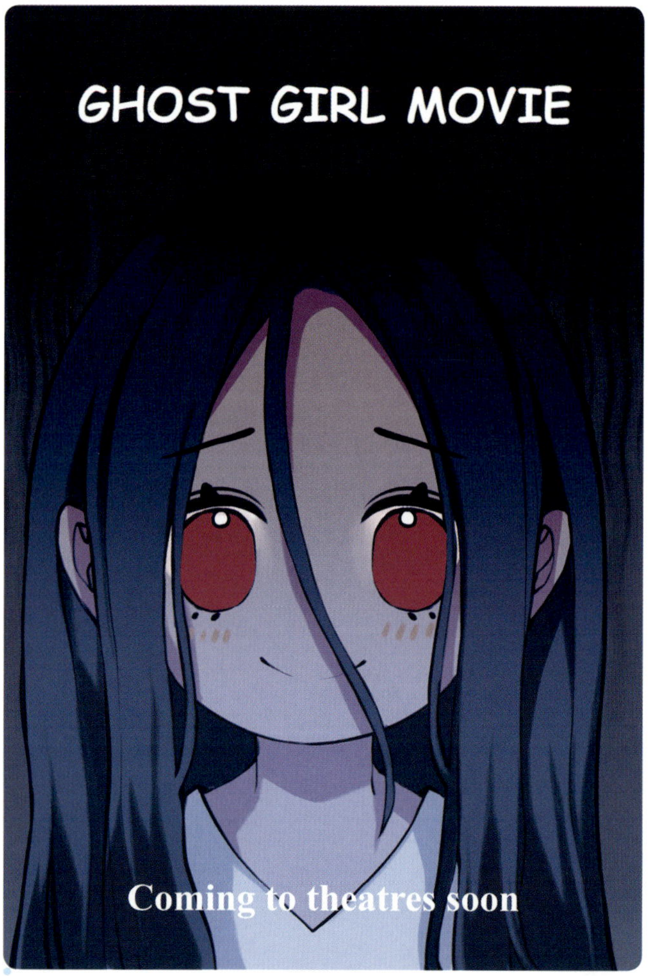


A horror movie poster mock-up showing an example of poor compatibility of art style and subject matter, as well as what happens when an illustrator attempts graphic design with no prior experience!

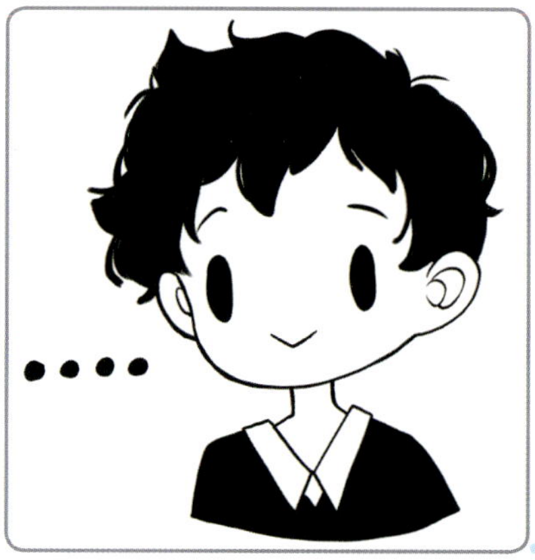


This kind of simplification – chibi style, dot eyes, and blank expression – is often used to express bewilderment or an attempt to process something that just happened

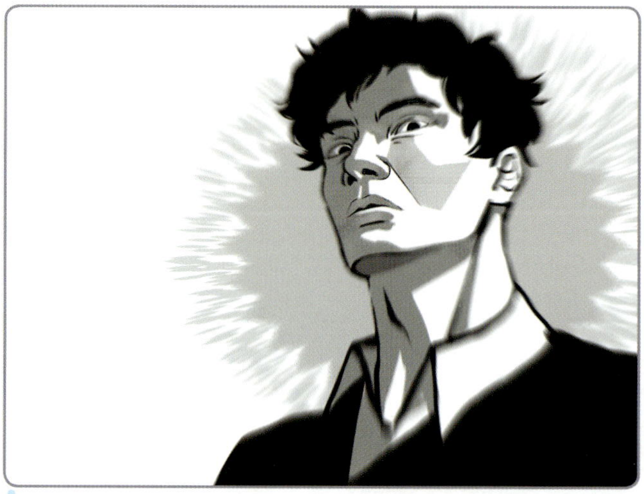

This kind of dramatic semi-realism – with an exaggerated, uncanny expression – is often used as a comedic reaction of surprise or sudden realization

# BUILDING YOUR BRAND

In the context of creating a career as an anime-style artist, your brand is determined by:

- What kind of artwork you are known for creating. For example, pastel-colored mahou shojo characters, or dark, brooding seinen manga.
- The name you go by as an artist, whether this is your real name, a nickname, or an artist name/alias.
- The style of your artwork; what makes it stand out from the work of other artists?

In essence, your brand is the set of characteristics that uniquely identifies the artwork you create and who you are as an artist.

Other factors that can influence your artistic brand include:

- The general mood and theme of your work, such as the type of color palette and imagery you typically use. For example, you may be known for using a rainbow of vibrant colors to convey a magical, whimsical aesthetic.
- The mediums and techniques you use to create your artwork, such as digital painting or drawing traditionally using colored pencils and markers.
- Whether your work is NSFW (18+ mature content) or suitable for all audiences.

Specific to the online art community, some additional factors that can shape your brand include:

- Having one or more mascots or original characters (OCs) unique to your brand that are easily identifiable as yours.
- Having a recognizable and consistent logo or profile picture. Some artists rarely change their profile picture, or opt to use variations of the same character or logo. A recognizable profile picture is especially useful for artists whose username is hard to remember.
- The kind of work that you share and its format. For example, do you post sketches and doodles, works in progress (WIPs), time-lapse drawing videos, or exclusively final artwork?

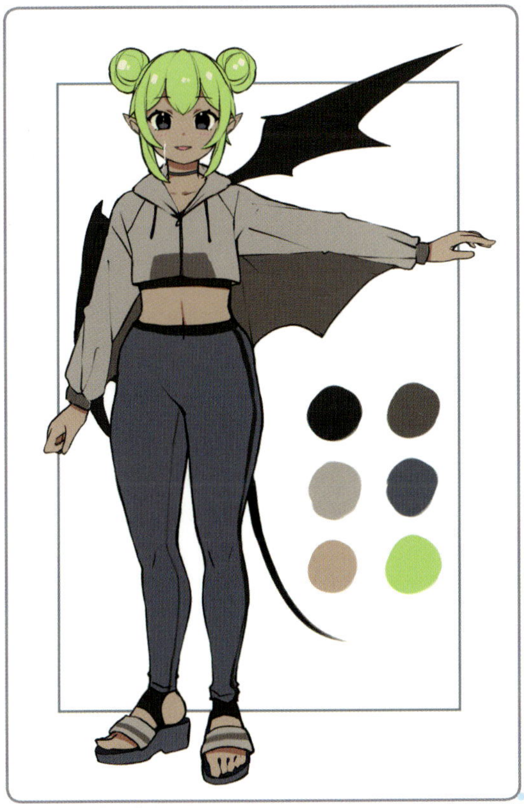

An example of an OC reference sheet, the purpose of which is to show the accurate colors and details of the character design

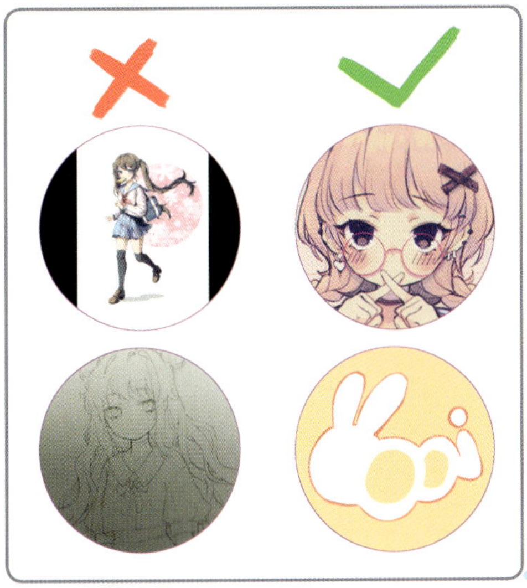

Examples of good versus bad profile pictures. Avoid using awkwardly cropped images or photographs of sketches with poor lighting. Instead, zoom in on one of your artworks so it fills the frame, or create a clear, attention-grabbing logo

# Allowing your brand to grow

While it is important to have a brand as an anime-style artist, don't worry too much about this when you are first starting out. Unless you are also planning to build a business – in which case you need a very clear direction – your initial focus should be on mastering basic art techniques and discovering your individual style. It is, however, a good idea to decide on the kind of artwork you want to create, and to choose a good artist name (unique and memorable). A brand is something that comes later - naturally occurring over time as more people discover your work and identify elements that make it stand out from the work of other artists.

When beginning to share work online, many anime-style artists post under a random name or alias that isn't necessarily the strongest brand name. As they gain more of a following, they slowly begin the process of branding themselves and their work; for example, by changing their artist name or reorganizing their gallery to make it more consistent in theme. So even if you didn't choose the perfect name or theme at the start of your journey, don't panic - you can do this later.

The benefit of having a brand is that it allows people, including your followers and potential clients, to become familiar with your work and what makes it unique. Think about all of the artists you follow online. While you may like all of them, there are likely a few you follow more closely and gravitate toward, perhaps because you admire their artwork, relate to their content, or are influenced by their strong branding. Regardless of whether you have fifty or fifty-thousand followers, you will always be someone's favorite artist – they will always be able to recognize your brand and they are more likely to share your work with others.

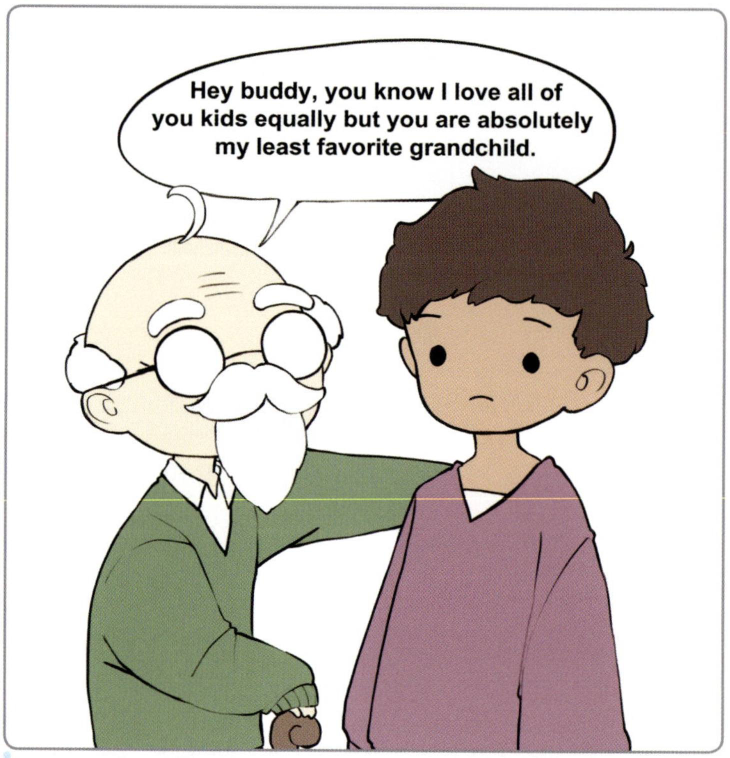


While you may follow lots of anime-style artists online, you likely have a few favorites that you follow more closely

# Recognizable brands

Different anime-related brands are synonymous with certain styles, genres, and mediums. For example:

## Vocaloid

Owned by Yamaha, Vocaloid is a voice-synthesizing software that enables you to purchase different "voice banks." These are collections of different tones and sounds, pre-recorded by voice actors, for the purpose of being remixed and used in software. A unique aspect of Vocaloid is that each of their official voicebanks is associated with a character who serves as the mascot, as an embodiment of the voice. Their most popular voicebank is Hatsune Miku, one of the first Vocaloids. Even if you have never heard of Vocaloid, it's likely you have come across the countless fan artworks of Hatsune Miku, with her iconic teal twin-tail hair and blue-gray-black color scheme. Often regarded as the company's mascot, this character is synonymous with Vocaloid.

## Pastel Girl

Developed by SeyeonSoft, Pastel Girl is an anime-style dress-up game that is popular within the anime-style art community, especially with artists who enjoy cute, colorful art styles. There are a series of dress-up game mobile apps, or avatar-builders, each of which sports their iconic style of light pastel colors, cute designs, and simple line work and coloring. Perhaps the most distinctive feature is the option, in the original Pastel Girl game, to select rainbow hair for your avatar, allowing you to assign a different color to each strand of hair.

A few years ago the "Pastel Girl Challenge" trended in the online art community, inviting artists to create an avatar in the Pastel Girl game, then draw the character in their own style. Many who took part opted for the rainbow hairstyle, as it was challenging yet fun to recreate. While it was not as well-known as other more mainstream art challenges, such as MerMay, it was still fairly popular in the anime-style art community.

# Goals & direction

While a strong brand can prove commercially successful when trying to earn a living as an artist, it's also true that followers are now more aware of marketing tactics and an increasing number are more concerned with authenticity and relatability. When considering what makes a successful brand, you need to reflect on what your goals are as an artist.

Do you plan to start your own small business selling merchandise featuring your anime-style artwork, or do you prefer to take freelance commission work instead? The former career path would require more emphasis on branding and strategic marketing in order to sell your products, whereas with the latter route you could prioritize building an authentic, open, and personal connection with your audience. While it is possible to run a business at the same time as undertaking freelance art commissions, one will inevitably end up taking more of your time and energy, unless you have a separate account for each purpose and hired staff to help you manage the workload. Take the time to consider your goals and plan what you want to achieve over the next few years.

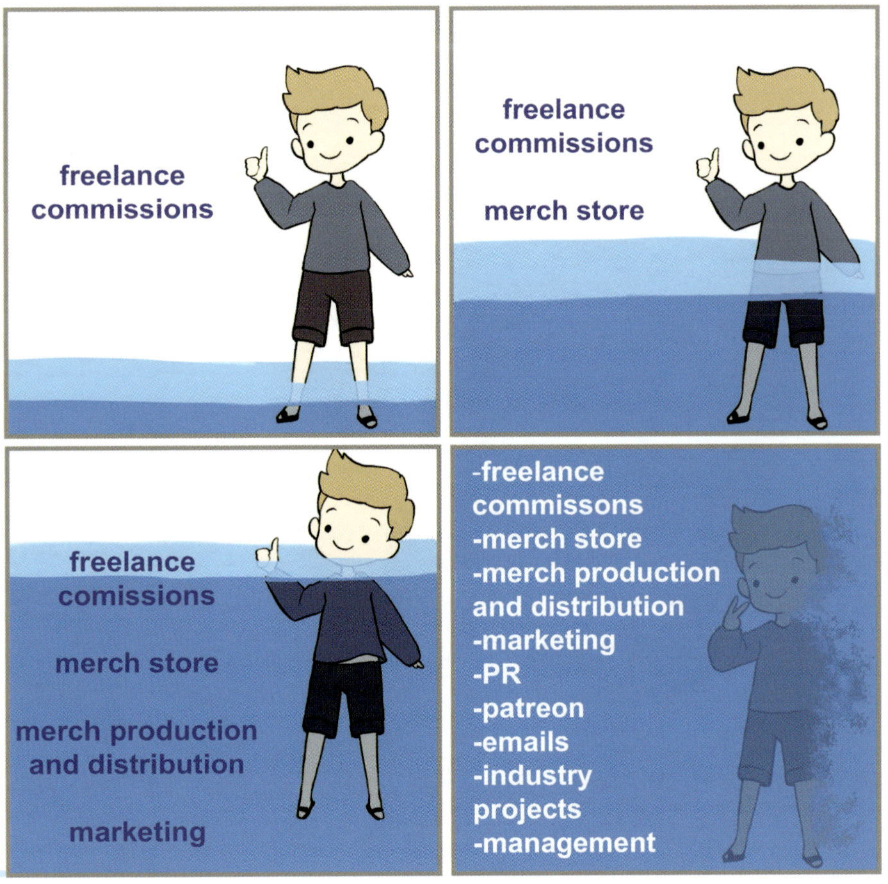


Trying to do everything will lead to burnout – instead, deciding on a limited number of goals will allow you to focus your time and resources

# Choosing your brand name

When coming up with a brand name for yourself, consider the following factors (in order of importance):

- Would you want to keep this name for a significant amount of time, possibly forever? Do you think it will still represent you and your work in ten or twenty years' time?
- Is it unique? Did you make up the word yourself? Will you be the first result if people search the name online, or will they have to scroll down past other results in order to find your online platforms?
- Is it easy to remember? Is it easy to spell and pronounce?
- Does is accurately represent your style of artwork?
- Does it look and sound professional? Does it mean anything offensive in other languages, particularly those your followers might speak?

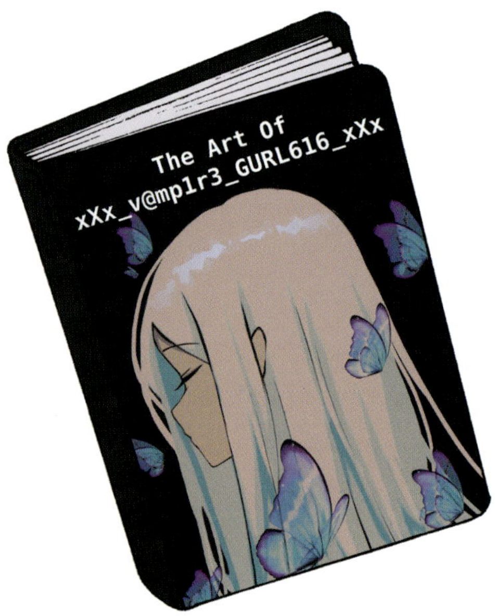


Don't choose a username that's complicated or hard to remember – it should be easy to spell and pronounce

# Brand icon & bio info

Choosing an icon or logo for your brand is optional in the online art community, but it's a good idea to create at least one mascot or original character. This can serve as a visual representation of your brand and as something by which your audience can remember and recognize you. The icon or character can be used consistently across your social-media platforms, as well as on your website.

It is also a good idea to use your social-media bio to briefly sum up your brand, saying who you are, what you do, and how available you are for work. The majority of social-media platforms limit how much you can write in your bio, however, so you should also include a link to your website. As discussed earlier (*The Business of Anime*, page 28), creating your own website will allow you to write a more detailed bio, create a larger portfolio, and let clients know the kind of work you're interested in doing. All of this will contribute to your brand image.

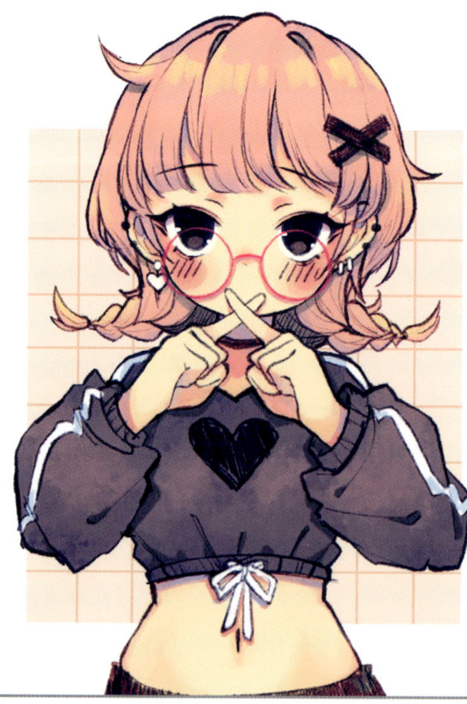

Artwork © Anny "Yoai"

Using the same original character across your social-media accounts will allow people to recognize your brand

# Creating a brand presence

Creating a strong brand presence can be approached in much the same way as growing your audience, (see *The Business of Anime*, page 26), as the two occur side by side. There are some basic things you can do to help grow your brand presence.

Ensure you are active in the art community, engaging with your followers and fellow artists. Reply to comments and direct messages in a kind and encouraging manner, and be open to having discussions. Participate in art challenges, such as "Draw This In Your Style," and take opportunities to market your work. While you should never self-advertise your work on another artist's page, look out for "Artists Support" posts that use the hashtag #artistsupport or #artistssupportartists, or some variation. In these posts, an artist will invite other artists to leave a comment, introducing themselves and the kind of artwork they create, along with details like who their favorite artists are and what inspires them.

It is also important to consider what direction you want your brand to take in the long run. Whether it's drawing concept art, making art books, or creating video tutorials, keep a clear goal in mind. You should also have a plan B, as well as a plan C and D, as it's possible that your goals and preferences will change over time, as will the interests of your target audience and the market as a whole. Trends come and go, as do opportunities for you to increase your presence. Welcome change, whether drastic or gradual, and avoid becoming stuck in the past. Be innovative in the way you market your brand and the formats and platforms you use to share your work. For example, in recent years, short-form video clips have become a key trend across the majority of social-media platforms. Many artists are now utilizing this format to grow their brand and share their work with a wider audience.

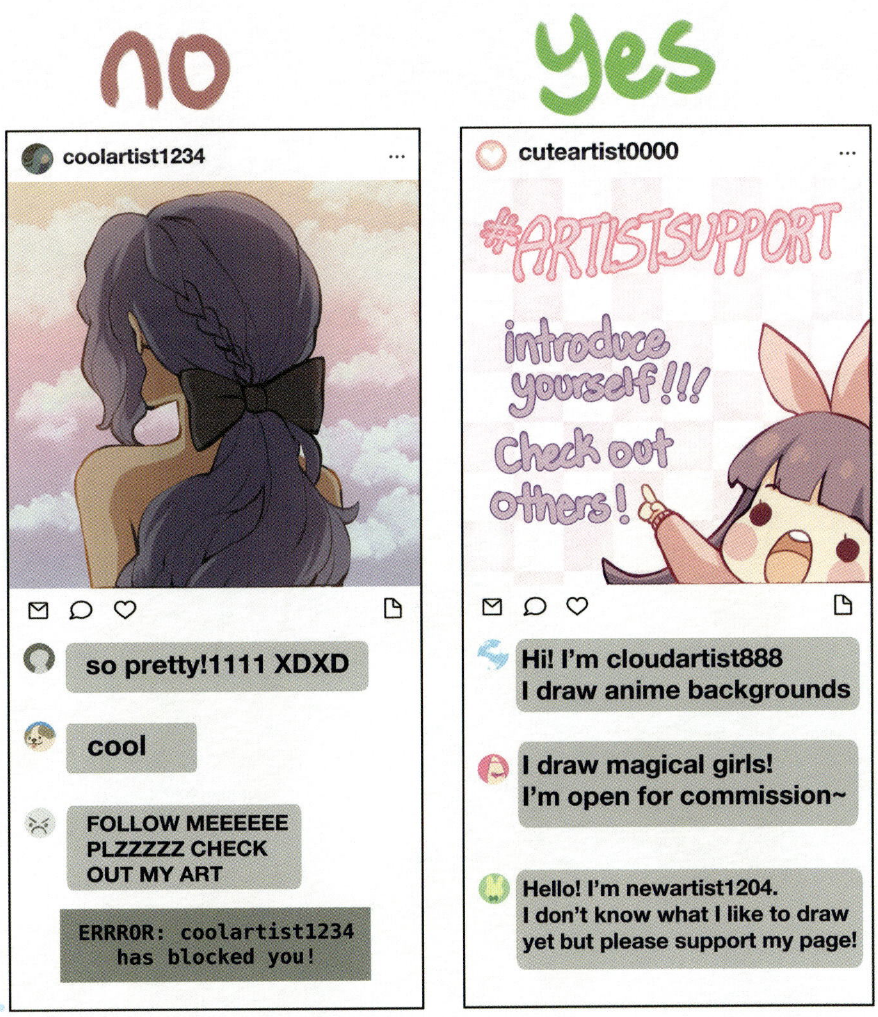


Don't self-advertise your work on other artist's posts – this is bad practice and may get you blocked. Instead, look out for #artistsupport posts that invite artists to introduce themselves and their work – this is the ideal place to share your brand of anime-style art

# Avoiding burnout

Beware of burnout and take care of your mental and physical health. No amount of money or success is worth sacrificing your health and mental wellbeing. Social media and running a brand can become all-consuming, but unless you are a CEO, the owner of a mega corporation, or a significant shareholder in one, you do not need to be consumed in a quest to reach certain numbers on your analytics. While it's good to create goals for your brand and to try your best to reach them, remember why you chose this career in the first place – you want to make money doing what you love.

If you feel overwhelmed, burdened, or stressed by maintaining your brand presence, step away and take a break for as long as you need. Only return when you feel mentally ready to engage with it again. While you may lose some of your active followers, be reassured that every artist experiences high and low points in their career progression. There will be times when you make great progress in the industry, and other times when you see little growth or change. As with any career path, sometimes this is down to factors completely out of your control. Don't be afraid to take a break to reassess your priorities and goals. There will always be opportunities to pick up your brand-building enterprise again, just as there will always be people who love your work and eagerly await your return.

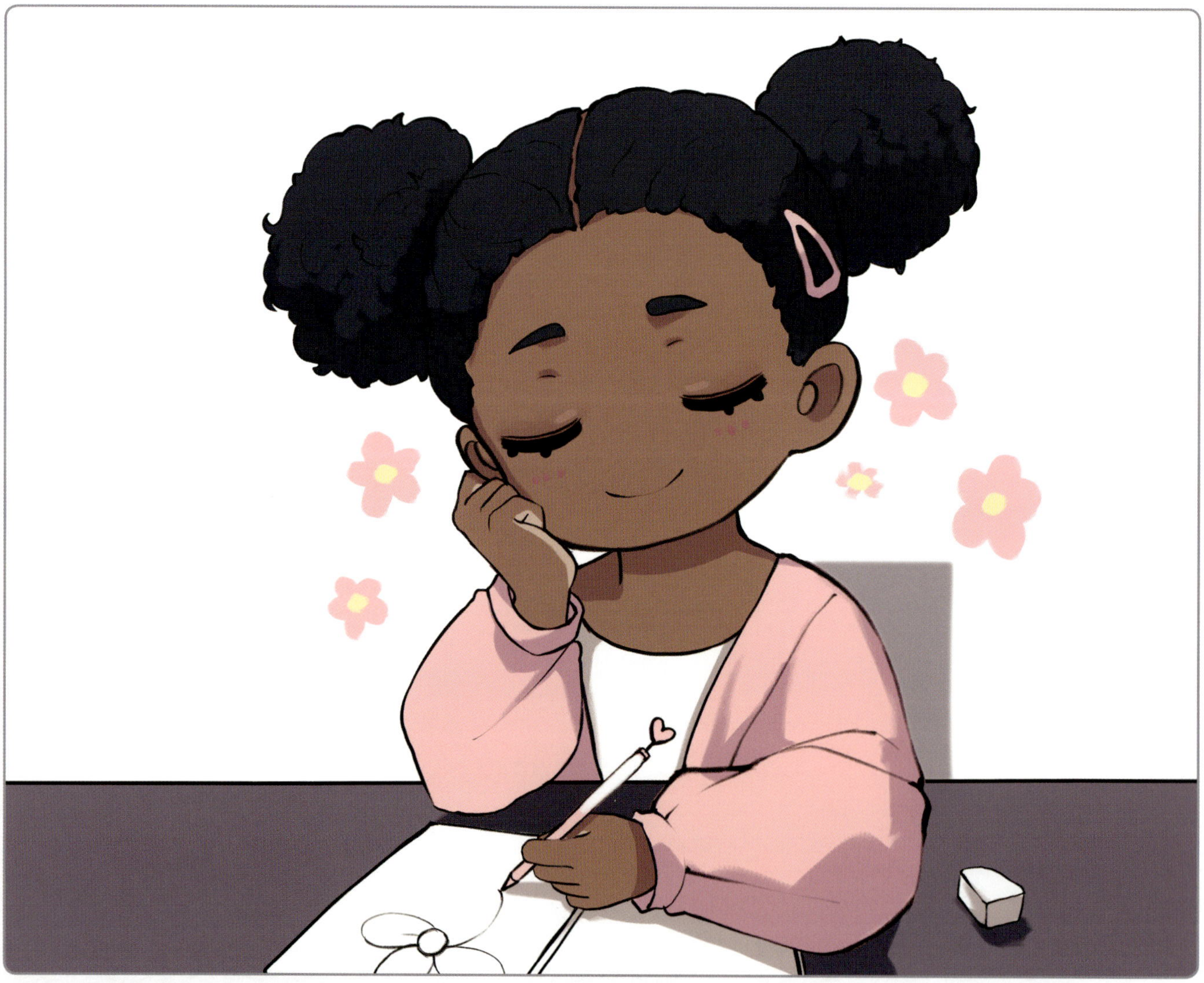

Take regular breaks to avoid burnout – make time to sketch and doodle without a specific project or end goal in mind

# BUILDING YOUR PORTFOLIO

Any creative freelance career – whatever your medium, genre, or style – requires you to have a portfolio of work. This is no different for the anime-style art industry. Employers need to know what you can do, what you have worked on in the past, and to see your skills in practice to determine whether or not you are a good fit for the job. While in some instances an artist won't have the skills or style a studio is looking for, in other cases their qualifications and experience could demand a fee that exceeds the employer's budget.

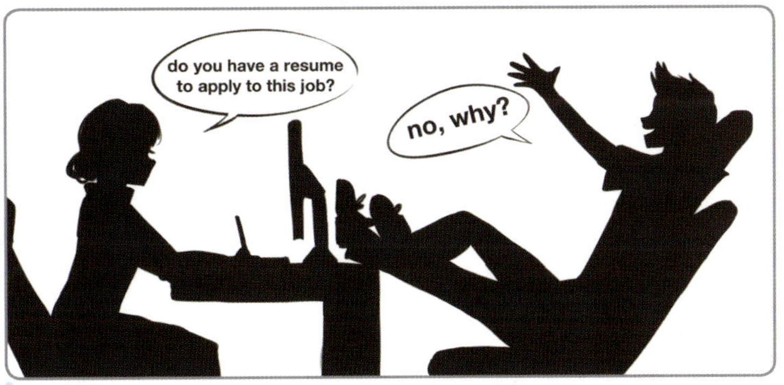


A portfolio acts like a resume, showing potential employers your range of skills and experience

## Physical vs. digital

A traditional portfolio typically consists of original or printed artwork bound in a folder, whereas a digital portfolio is usually a gallery of artwork on an artist's website. Artists can have both digital and physical portfolios, but digital ones are more common. One way to combine the formats is to create postcards or business cards that feature your artwork alongside a link to your online portfolio and contact information. Providing a potential employer with a physical link to a digital portfolio not only allows them to browse it in their own time, but this approach can prove cheaper and more convenient for the artist.

"Commission information" pages are increasingly common. These are pages on your website that list your fees for certain types of commission, along with examples of your work showing a set range of styles. Some artists seeking commercial jobs prefer to use classic portfolio galleries on their websites, however, as commission information pages tend to be aimed at individuals wanting a commission for non-commercial purposes, such as a stylized portrait or custom digital painting to preset dimensions.

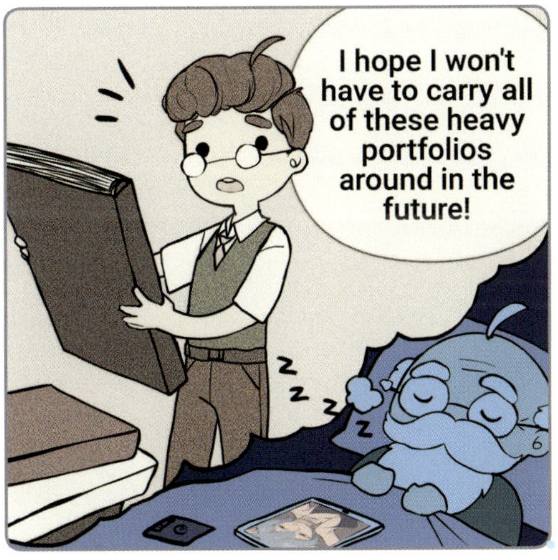


There is nothing wrong with traditional portfolios, but digital portfolios can prove cheaper to create, easier to share, and overall much more accessible and convenient

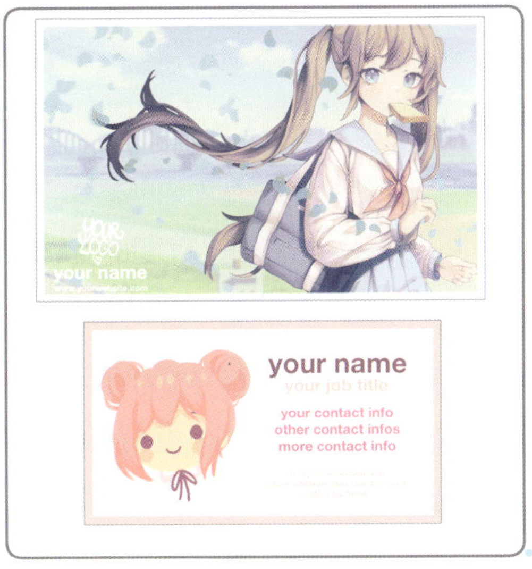


Making postcards and business cards with a link to your online portfolio and contact information combines the physical and digital mediums

# Portfolio & brand

While your brand and online presence are what you are known for, your portfolio's purpose is to showcase your best work, the versatility and extent of your artistic abilities, and, if applicable, previous art jobs and projects you have worked on to show your experience in the commercial art industry. In short, your brand is *what* you do, and your portfolio shows what you *can* do. It's therefore important to experiment with as many different drawing styles, mediums, and genres as possible, even if only a few sketches or paintings deviate from your typical brand. You don't have to share these publicly, since you want your brand to remain consistent, but including them in your portfolio will increase your chances of being hired.

Though most employers will approach and commission you because they like the work you are best known for, if you use your portfolio to display what other styles of work you are also able to create, they will keep this in mind for the future. Once they have seen the range of styles and skills you are confident with, they may come back to you and offer other projects.

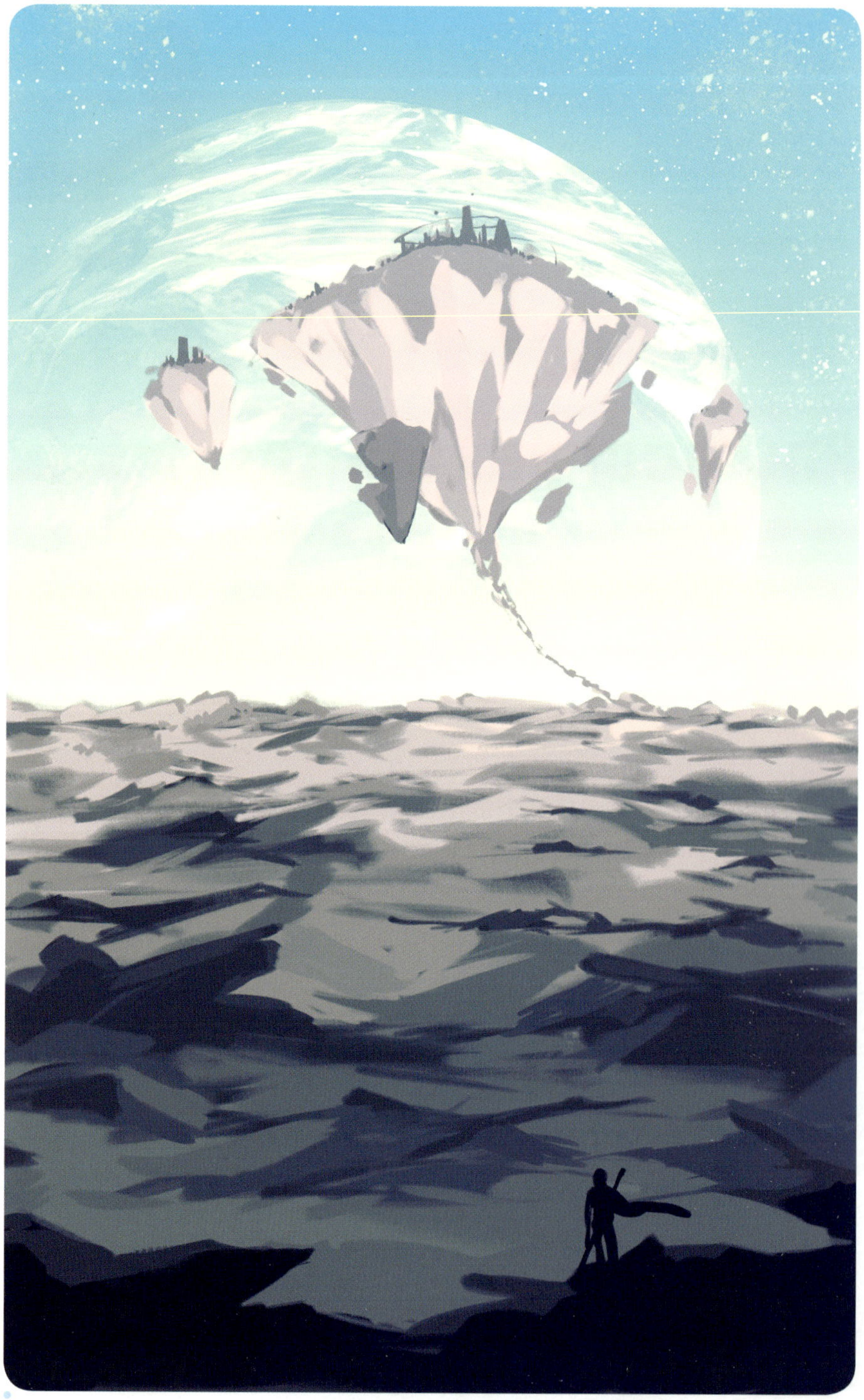

An example of a simple concept-art painting that is different from my usual style of anime art, but shows off my digital painting skills to potential employers

# Different portfolios for different purposes

Take the time to compile separate industry and consumer portfolios, each tailored to the specific audience. As mentioned on page 55, a commission information page can act as a kind of portfolio for non-commercial commissioners, providing a general idea of your style of anime art, the commissions you offer, and the fee for each.

Commercial industry commissions are better suited to a portfolio format that exhibits a wide range of artwork, showcasing your best pieces alongside a variety of different styles and genres to demonstrate your skills. The fee for commercial commissions is typically negotiated, rather than a fixed price, as there are numerous factors to discuss with the employer, such as who retains the copyright, any additional skills needed, how the final artwork will be used, and other contractual obligations, such as promoting the finished product.

There should also be some overlap between the two, however, as you will want to show off your best artwork to both parties.

# Social media as a portfolio

A social-media account, such as your Instagram grid, does not serve as a professional portfolio. Instagram does possess the Guides feature, however, which enables you to create folders or collections of posts from your main grid. This might be satisfactory for an informal portfolio that gives people a general idea of your work, but it is more commonly used to categorize artwork; for example, fan art for a specific character, or artwork you have created in a specific medium, such as oil pastel. This is useful for categorizing your work, but your website will always be the best place for your portfolio. Not only does it look more professional, but you are not limited by size and format.

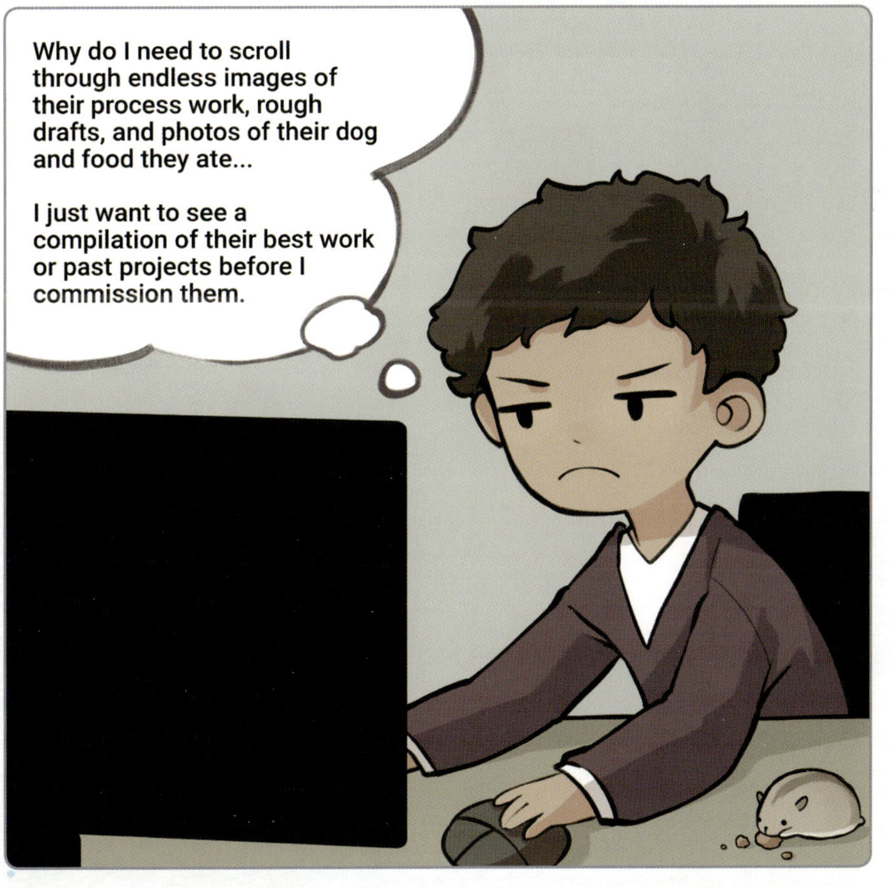


Many potential clients won't enjoy scrolling through your entire social-media feed to look at your work

# CAREER FOCUS

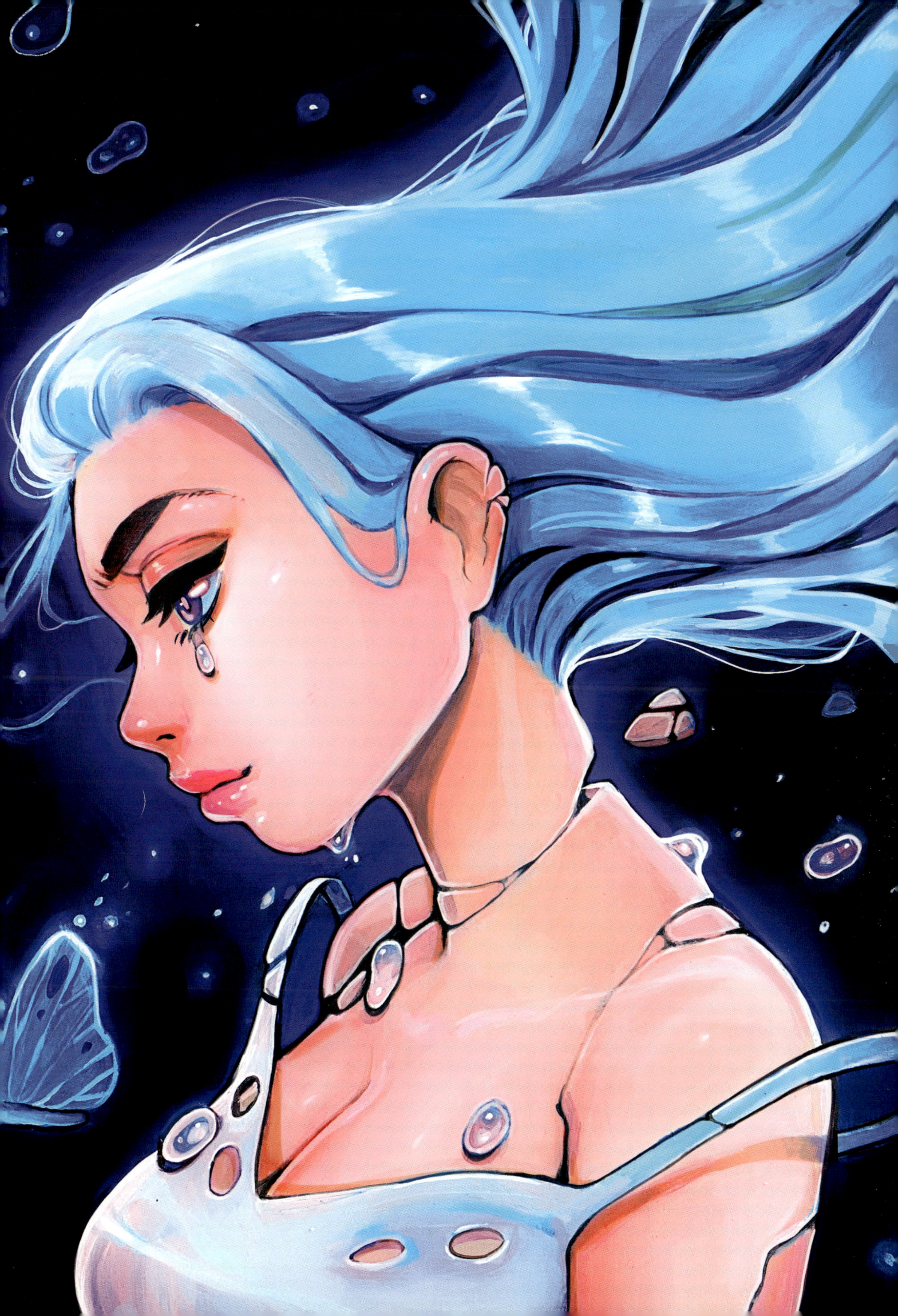

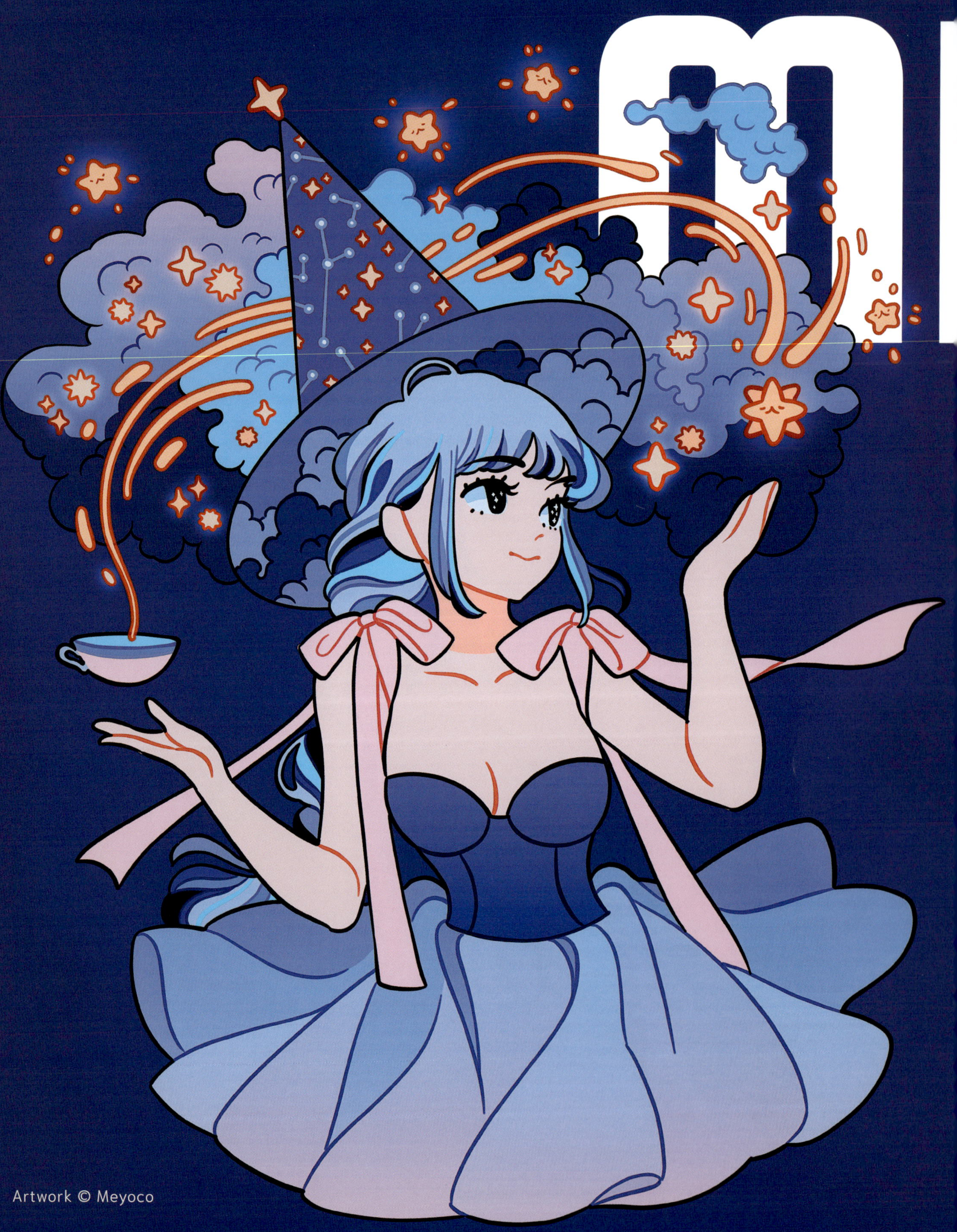

Artwork © Meyoco

# EYOCO

## Meet the artist

**Illustrator & small-business owner**

**meyoco.art | instagram.com/meyoco**

Meyoco "Meyo" is a freelance illustrator and small-business owner from Southeast Asia. Her whimsical artwork has been deeply influenced by anime and manga since childhood. She loves creating products based on her artwork, such as apparel, accessories, and stationery. She has also worked with leading companies including Pixiv, PIE International, BOOM! Studios, Cartoon Network, and more.

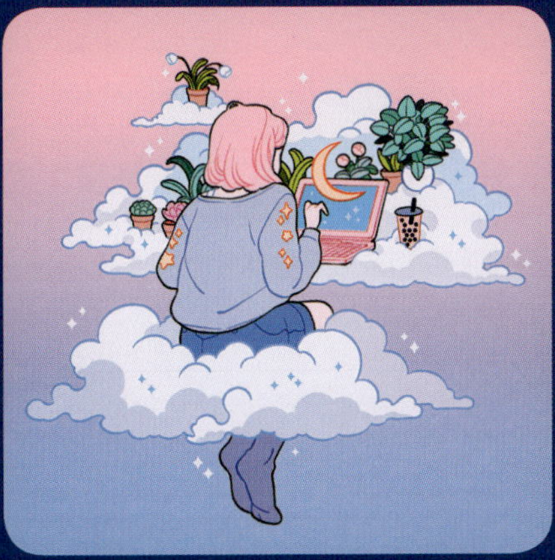

# CASE STUDY



## INFLUENCES, MOTIVATIONS, TRAINING

Art has been an important part of my life since my early years. My parents both have artistic backgrounds; my mother as a watercolorist and my father as an architect. I grew up reading Japanese manga, which are popular in my home country of Indonesia. I've been drawing since I was very young and these comics played an influential role in my artwork. When I was in the third grade of elementary school I wanted to be a comic-book artist, inspired by all of the manga I read.

I have never quite considered myself an anime-style artist, as it's simply the form of art I'm most familiar with. It's extremely common for young artists in my country to be influenced by Japanese manga, anime, and games. Most of us grew up with one or two favorite manga comics or anime TV shows, and those from wealthier families had game consoles on which they played anime-style video games.

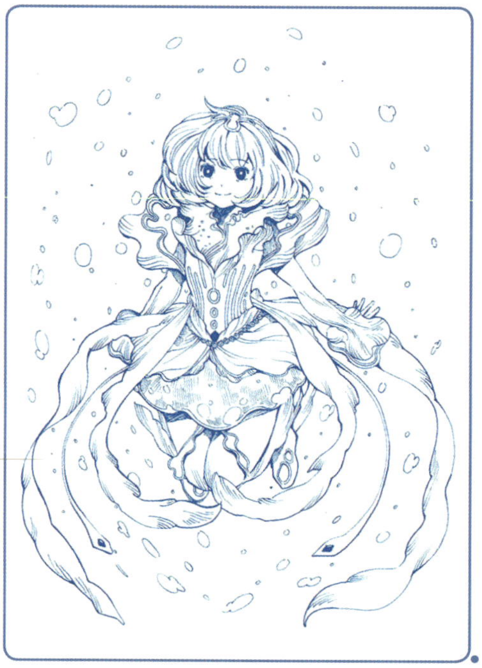

My art prior to 2015 was predominantly uncolored and focused on line art

### Studies & self-taught learning

I kept drawing throughout my early years and started actively posting my artwork online when I was in middle school, although I never took it very seriously. Typical of most kids in Asian countries, I was taught that eventually I would need to find a "serious" academic field in which to study and build a career.

While studying psychology at university, I realized that art was my true passion and I would much rather work in an artistic field. Unfortunately I never had the chance of any formal art education as my parents couldn't afford to pay for art school. Working as an artist and a designer themselves, they wanted me to have a more lucrative career than they had, which is quite a typical mindset in Indonesia. They grew up in a time when social media didn't exist and it was unheard of for artists to make a name for themselves out of nowhere.

I spent most of my university classes daydreaming and drawing, and started regularly posting my artwork on social media. I also began making and selling my own products at anime conventions. Not having the chance to undertake any formal art education made me extremely ambitious. Posting my artwork on social media and selling my products was the only way I could continue pursuing art. I spent the majority of my time between classes drawing, sharing my art online, and creating new products for anime conventions. This was mainly motivated by my frustrations at not being able to go to art school. My dedication paid off when my artwork was noticed by industry professionals and I was given the opportunity to take on multiple freelance jobs while still at university.

Almost everything I learned was self-taught. I did enroll in several online drawing classes, however, which factored hugely into my foundational skills.

I confess to being a bad learner, be it in art or other fields, as I have a short attention span and prefer to learn by doing. I also learn by observing the work of other artists, then trying to emulate what I admire in my own style and media.

During this period of self-taught learning, I was mainly influenced by the manga I grew up reading, as well as by the many artists I followed on social media. The work of Alphonse Mucha was also a visible influence on my work around 2013–2014. I'm often drawn to art styles that have flat colors and intricate line work, which I've tried to replicate in my own work over the years. This is likely a result of the Japanese comics I grew up with, which are mostly in black and white.

I have always been very single-minded and have never loved anything quite as much as I love drawing. My time at university was extremely miserable because I thought I would never get to work in the arts. I graduated in 2017 and, rather than job-hunting like the rest of my peers, I continued to draw, make, and sell my artwork like I'd already been doing for years. Thankfully my parents were never against my pursuing a career in the arts, but they did have their worries when I first started selling my own products, as they were concerned the business could get me into debt. Through hard work, I proved to them, and myself, that I could build a career doing what I love – working in the creative industries.

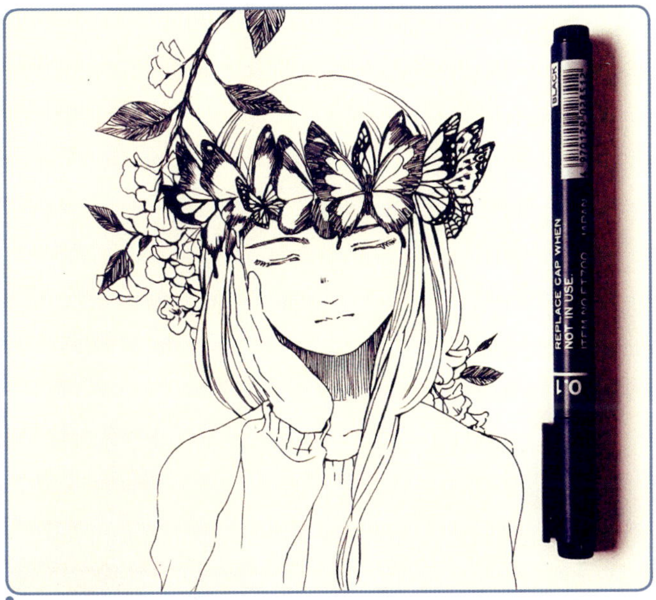

I used to doodle black-and-white sketches between classes

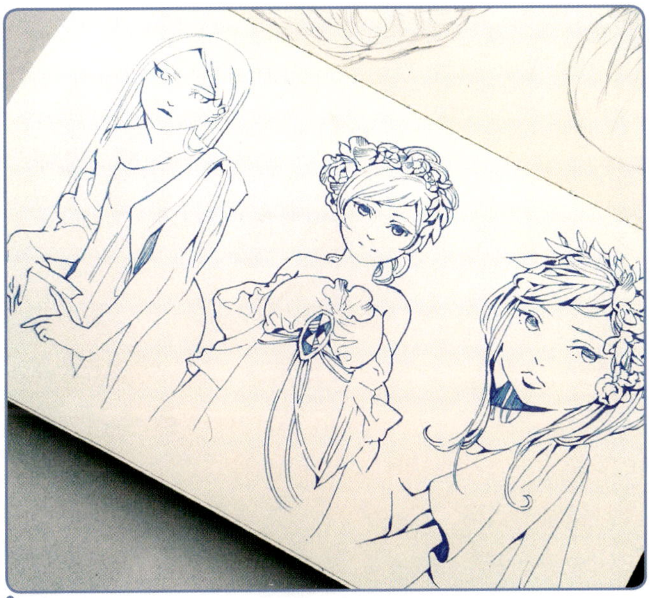

Doodles drawn during university classes

## Finding inspiration

I spend a lot of time on social media and find much of my inspiration there. Over the years I have accumulated a large collection of artwork and photos that I scroll through when searching for inspiration. I also browse platforms such as Pinterest or Instagram to find particular moods or aesthetics I want to capture in my art.

Searching for reference material when I need to draw something specific is a helpful practice, particularly when I am working on a paid job. It's important to research your subject matter before putting pencil to paper to ensure your portrayal is respectful and accurate. However, I rarely study particular techniques unless it's necessary.

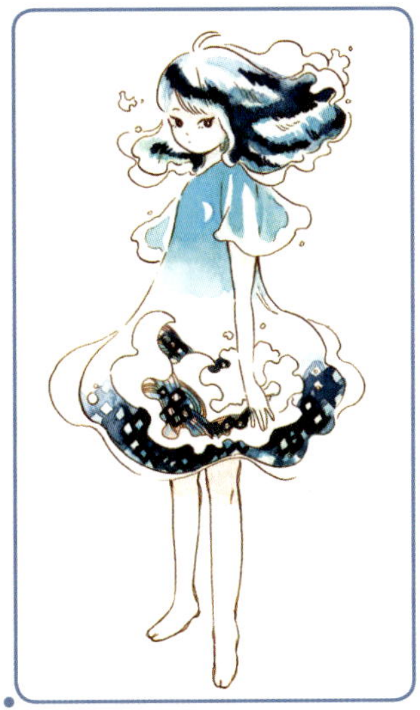

When at university, my goal was to draw as simply and quickly as possible, and to finish one colored artwork a day

## Creative decisions

Ever since I was young, I've never put too much thought into the subjects I draw, nor do I pretend my artwork is particularly meaningful. There aren't any philosophies or deep messages in my work. Unless I'm working on a paid job, I usually draw subjects I'm familiar with or simply enjoy drawing. I find it difficult to draw something I have no interest in. For me, art needs to be enjoyable and relaxing. I often return to floral and celestial themes, as I have always found these to be very comforting and dreamy. Over the years, many of my followers have told me that my art is relaxing to look at, which is a huge compliment.

I started drawing ocean themes several years ago because I hadn't visited the beach in a long time and didn't have the money or time to go. Drawing ocean-themed artwork helped to channel my frustrations. I also drew celestial-themed artwork, because as a child I'd wanted to study astronomy and was fascinated by outer space.

My art represents who I am, particularly what I love and what I know. I'm exceptionally bad at trying to be someone or something I'm not. If I don't have a genuine interest in the subject matter, this will show in the end result. I also struggle to hide my emotions, which translates into my drawing. My artwork is one-hundred percent me.

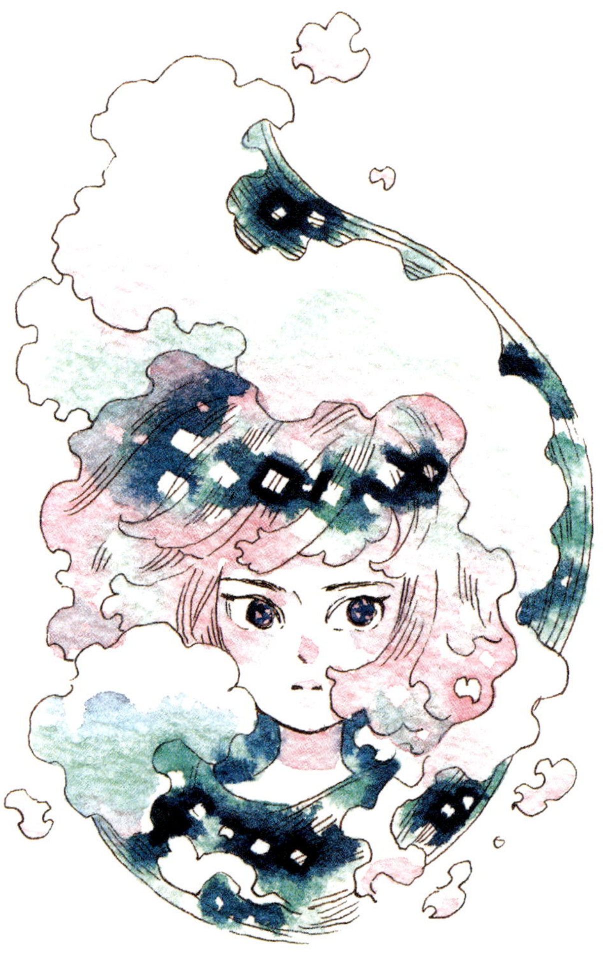

One of my early ocean-themed artworks from 2016

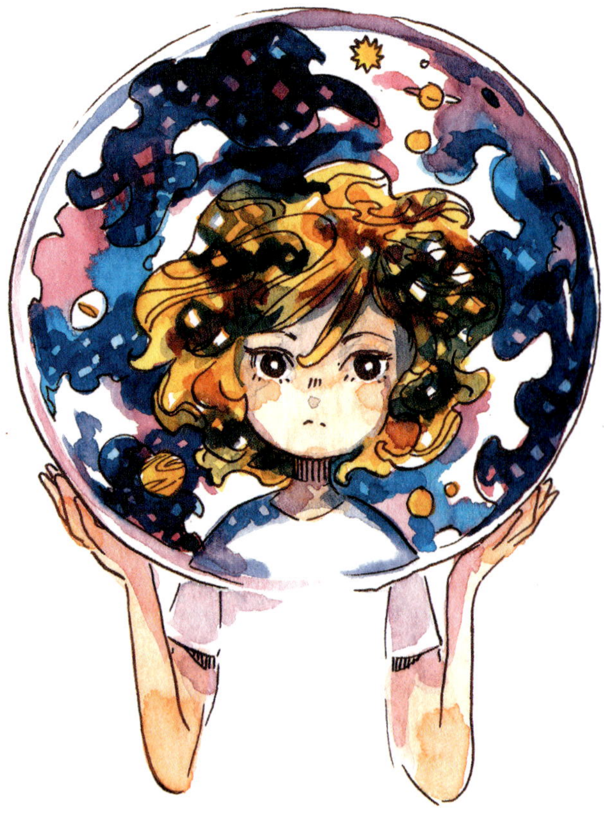

One of my first celestial-themed paintings

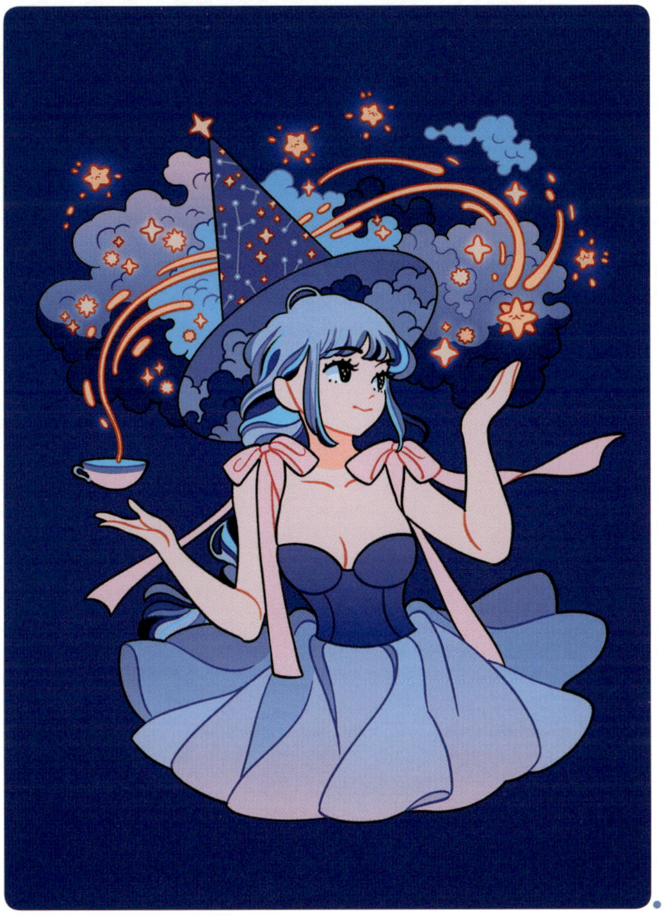

## Tools & media

My current favorite tool for creating artwork is Procreate on the iPad Pro. I love how portable and flexible the setup is, allowing me to carry my work around with me to paint on the go. When I have time, I enjoy painting with traditional media such as watercolors and acrylic gouache. I used to paint solely in watercolor; such was my love of the medium. I also like the simplicity of sketching using drawing pens.

I've always been a slow learner and prefer to stick to one software or technique at a time. The key to my progress is practice and consistency. For example, I will repeatedly use the same software until I feel confident using it. When it comes to creating art for my products and social media, this consistency is important to ensure a high quality. I do, however, enjoy trying new techniques and media from time to time.

It took me three to four years to become comfortable drawing line art in Photoshop

# INDUSTRY EXPERIENCE

I started taking commissions and selling my art products around the same time I began university in 2013. At the time I was thrilled at the prospect of earning money from my artwork, which I'd never imagined would be possible. I found I enjoyed planning, designing, and selling my products. While it started out as a project purely for my own enjoyment, it gradually became routine and a steady source of income.

My family was never very well-off and I had to use the money I earned from commissions and product sales to buy books for my university classes. Over time, I managed to not only earn enough money to cover my school supplies, but also to pay for my phone, clothing, and other daily needs. I continued to sell my products at anime conventions and started to create my own original products and books. Eventually I found myself earning more than I would by working a corporate job in Indonesia. With this realization, I knew I would continue with my art business instead of looking for a conventional job once I graduated.

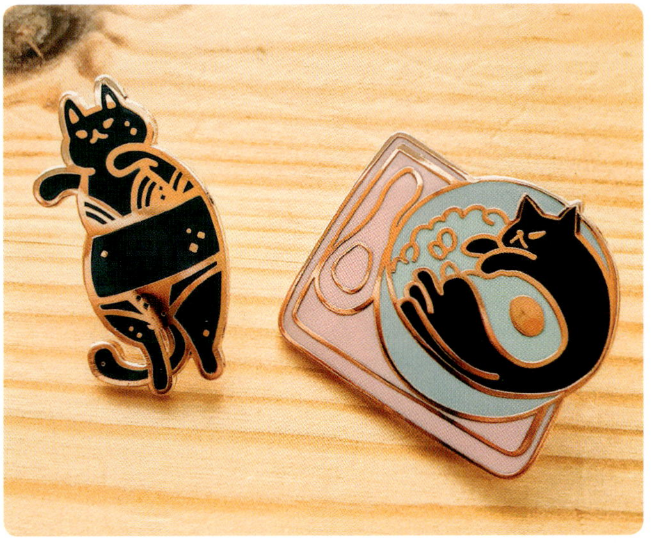

Two of my very early enamel pins, created a few months after I graduated from university in 2017

## Freelance work

I've been commissioned by companies on multiple occasions and always find it to be both fun and slightly jarring. As I consistently draw the same kind of subject matter, I'm fortunate that my clients typically commission a task within my scope and style. It's not uncommon, however, for them to ask me to draw one or two subjects I'm not familiar with. Though this can be challenging at times, it can also be a fun change from my usual work.

It's refreshing to work on freelance projects that have clear guidelines I'm required to follow, both administratively and artistically. When it comes to the artwork I create for my own business, I manage everything on my own and don't always have set guidelines in place.

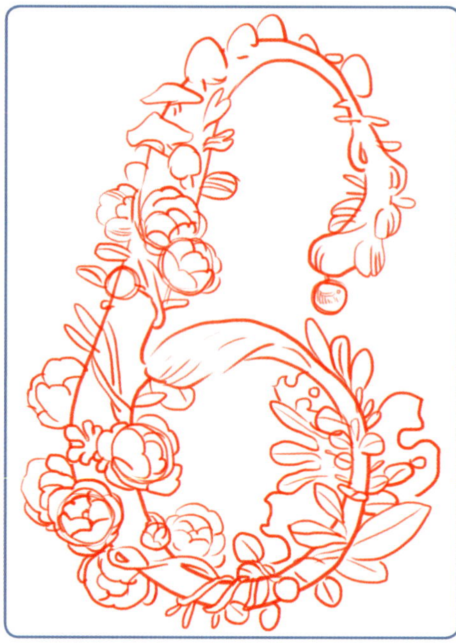

A mock-up created for a typography exhibition in 2017

## Recognition

Sometime after I graduated, I began to feel a little stuck with my art. Drawing wasn't as fun as it used to be and my followers began noticing this from the artwork I was posting. This frustration led me to do a complete overhaul of my artwork. I stopped drawing human subjects and fan art, and almost gave up traditional media to focus on digital paintings instead. I began drawing more objects, particularly food and drink items. It was around this time that I started painting the transparent food and drink artwork I am now well known for.

Anyone who follows me today will recognize my food and drink artwork, particularly those with transparent designs. One of my earliest and most popular designs in this style was a painting of milk cartons with ocean waves. I was surprised at how much attention and positive feedback this artwork received, and it inspired me to explore the ocean theme more in my work. My paintings of transparent objects have since been used in collaboration products with various brands, and were also featured a great deal in my official art book.

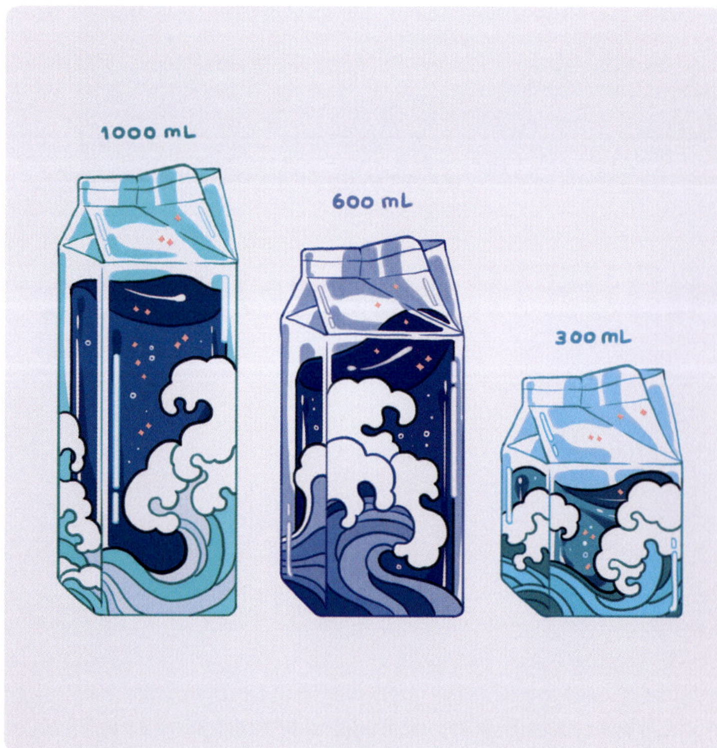


My first painting combining ocean waves and transparent containers

# DEVELOPING YOUR STYLE

Anime and manga were the art forms I was most familiar with growing up, as I began reading Japanese comics and watching anime on television when I was very young. I often copied drawings of my favorite characters and eventually started drawing my own versions. My initial style was influenced by shojo manga – Japanese comics aimed at young girls. I loved reading romance comics and especially loved comics featuring magical girls, both of which defined my early style. I'm still drawn to more "feminine" themes, a sign I never truly left these early stylistic influences behind.

There was a period during my middle and high school years where I read many shonen manga – comics aimed at young boys – particularly those from *Shonen Jump* magazine. While feminine shojo manga was the main influence on my early style, these shonen comics cemented my love for manga as a storytelling medium.

When I began posting my artwork on social media, I started to connect with other artists who also loved manga and anime. I had never communicated with artists on an international platform before, and the experience hugely impacted how I approach my artistic practice. I met people who were extremely passionate about creating art, all because of their love for manga and anime. Their passion inspired me to become even better at drawing.

Following the work of these artists has also allowed me to keep up to date with what's going on in the anime and manga industry and wider art community. While I don't engage in much active research into subject matter or techniques, I do consume a lot of artists' work through social media.

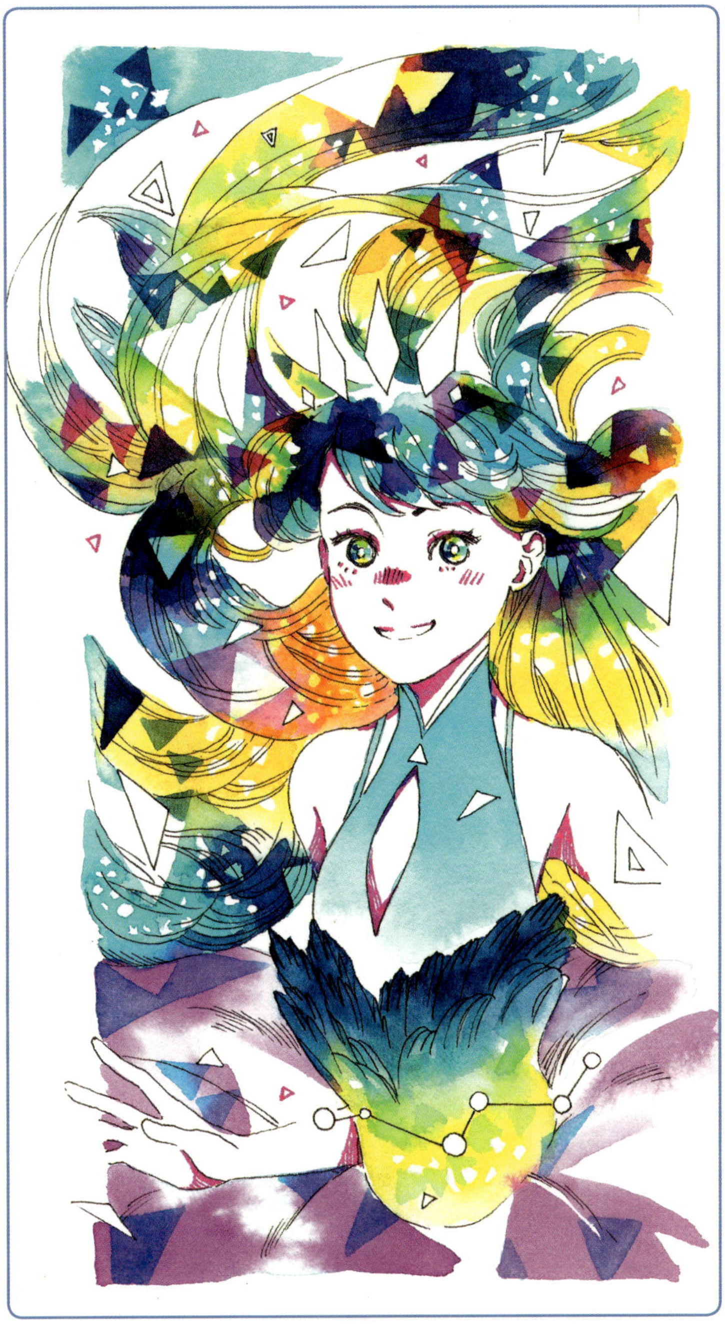

Artwork from my first original art zine in 2016

## Style success

When I started to achieve commercial success, particularly through making my own products, my style was characterized by flat pastel colors, transparent objects, and natural and celestial themes such as ocean waves and stars. I consciously maintained this style due to its popularity with my followers, but also because I enjoy drawing it. Additionally, the style translates well onto products, which not only sell well, but I enjoy making too.

Sometimes my followers will compare my artwork to that of other artists, though I don't mind this at all. I recognize that my work fits into the currently popular aesthetic of pastel colors, feminine witches, and nature-themed ornamentation.

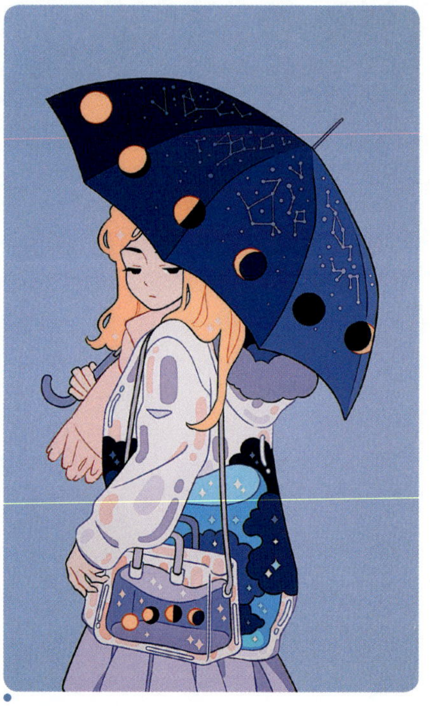

My style has been fairly consistent over the past few years, characterized by natural themes and transparent objects

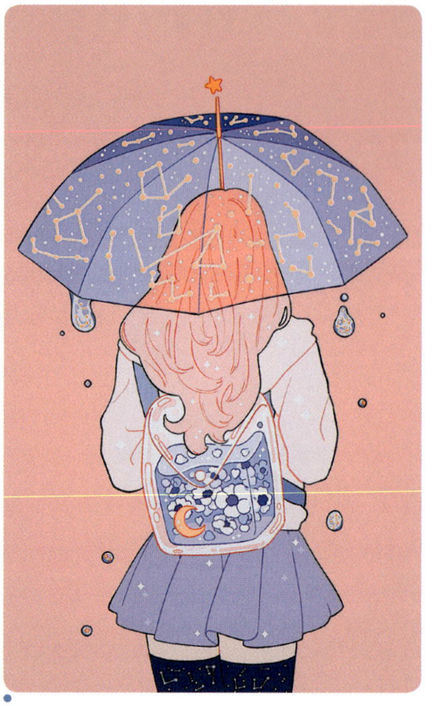

There was a period where I used a lot of pastel pinks, which fit with the popular aesthetic at the time

## Personal style in the commercial world

While there is pressure to be authentic and unique as an artist, there is also pressure to continue innovating, while simultaneously churning out as much new artwork as possible. In the age of social media, art is treated as content. It can be hard to know whether artists are supposed to maintain their signature anime style, or constantly attempt to reinvent themselves for the sake of creating new content to share with their followers.

I prefer to continue with my current style, as it's what I enjoy creating and has proved popular with my following so far. However, some have expressed dislike of my work because I draw the same themes over and over.

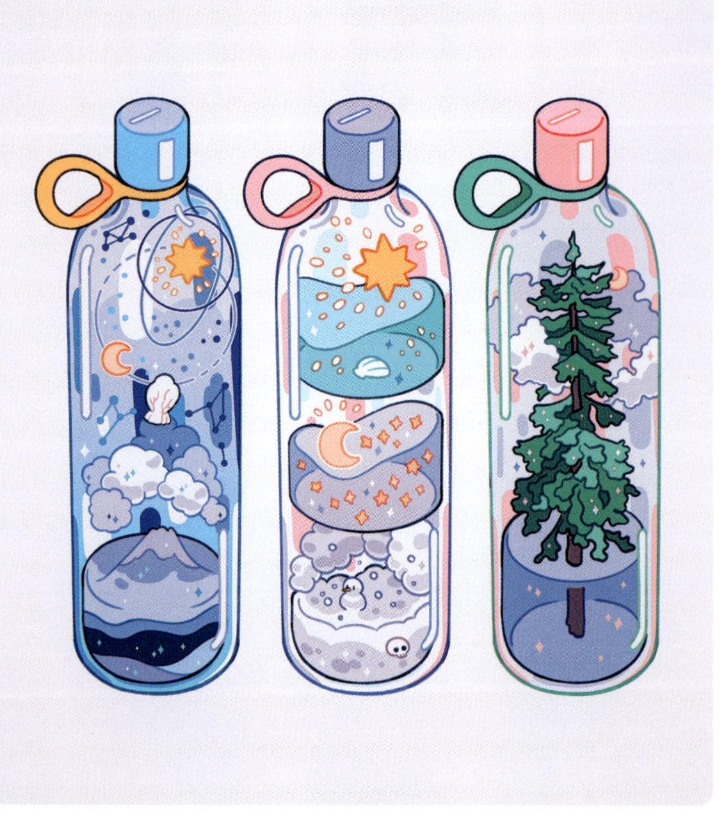

I enjoy drawing containers, such as bottles and food packaging, which has now become my signature theme and what I am known for

# Pivotal stylistic moments

2015–2016 was extremely pivotal in the growth of my anime style. I began watching the TV shows *Steven Universe* and *Haikyuu!!* around this time, both of which influenced the direction of my anime art style. Though *Steven Universe* is an American show, it is heavily inspired by anime and manga, and its art style greatly influenced how I use colors in my own artwork. It inspired me to begin incorporating sparkles and to use more pinks and blues, which are now my signature colors.

*Haikyuu!!* is a Japanese anime that introduced me to a huge community of artists who are extremely passionate about their art. I made three different art zines containing my fan art of the series and it was during this period that I began to solidify my coloring style. The community inspired me to practice drawing a lot more and, as a result, my art became more distinctive without my realizing it.

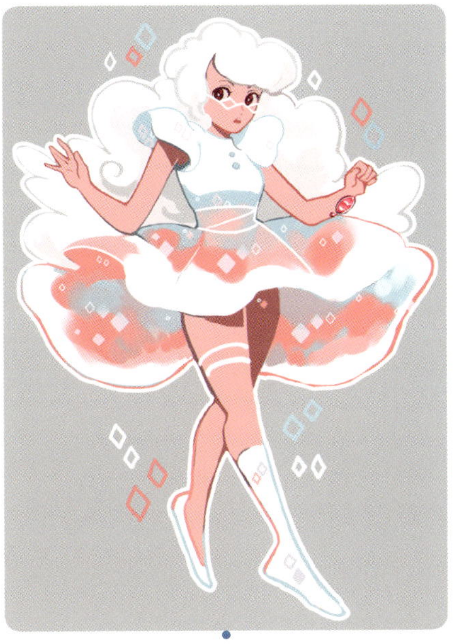

*Gemsona*, 2015

One of my early paintings influenced by the *Steven Universe* art style

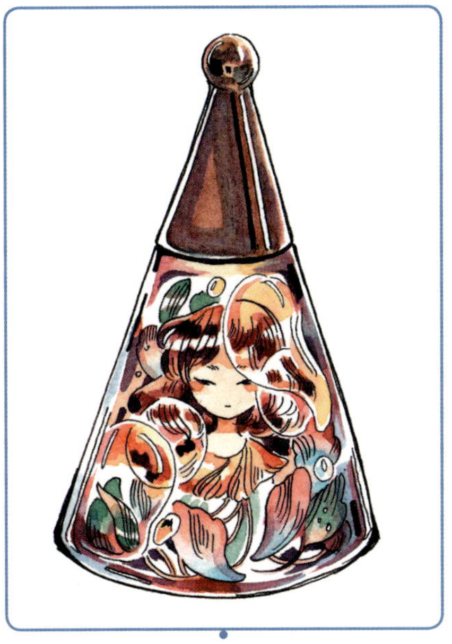

*Perfume*, early 2016

I was inspired to use more pink in my artwork

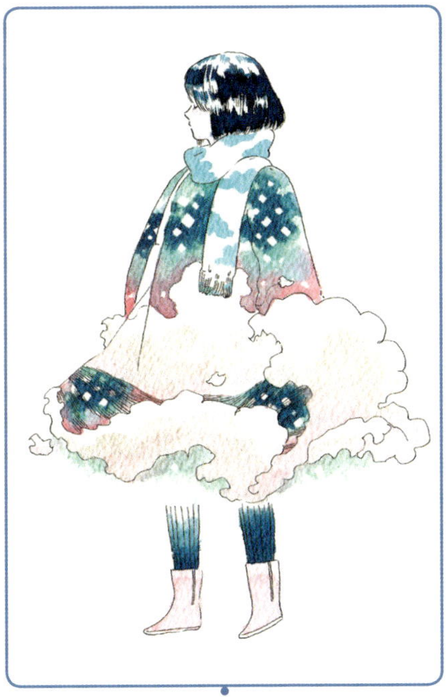

*Wave dress*, June 2016

I started to introduce more pinks and blues, as well as more sparkles

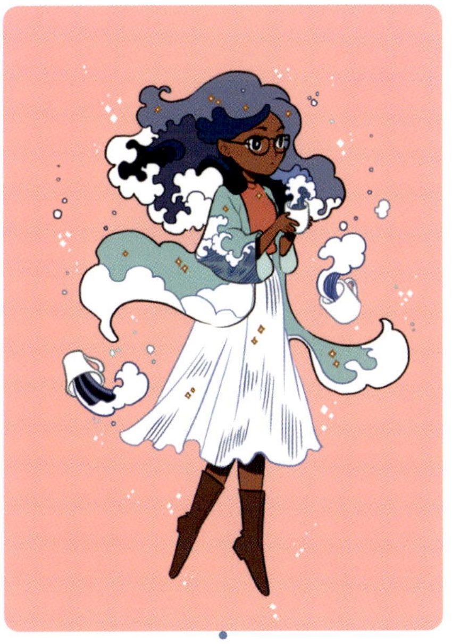

*Witchsona*, mid 2016

After drawing fan art digitally, I became more comfortable with drawing original artwork digitally too

## External influences

I am comfortable working in my own creative bubble with my preferred practices and tried-and-tested workflow. I don't enjoy the process of making art when I'm too influenced by external factors. Social media can prove a bad influence on my art, as it's all too easy to compare myself to other artists and become frustrated that I'm unable to create certain kinds of art that are different from my own. Whenever I doubt my decision-making, I end up creating something I don't like. Last year I took a step back and stopped my constant browsing of social media, which helped to put an end to my self-destructive way of thinking. Now when I need inspiration, I read the many art books I've collected over the years or play video games.

I sometimes feel limited by my style and wish I could draw realistic art or intricate backgrounds. I also wish I had more time and put more effort into learning new skills; however, I have slowly accepted that I don't need to be able to draw every kind of art style there is. There is a place for my anime art style in the world and many people who enjoy my work. I am simply not the kind of artist who has the time and energy to keep reinventing my work or showcasing new styles and techniques. I'm trying to accept rather than resent myself for this, while also staying open to future possibilities.

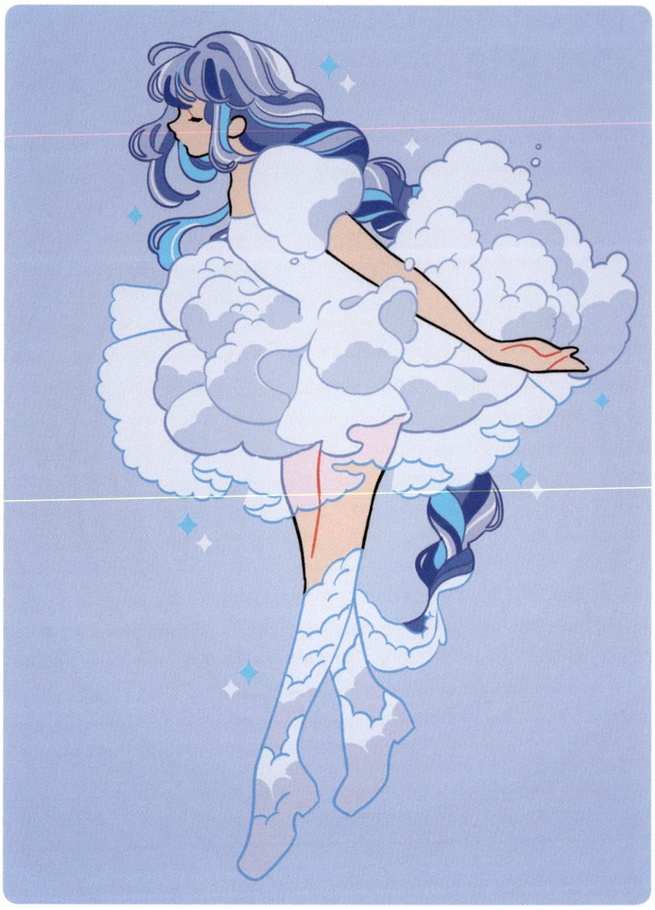

Clouds are one of my favorite subjects to draw and I always return to them when I feel stuck

# BUILDING YOUR BRAND

I think of Meyoco as my brand and consciously keep it separate from my real-life identity. My focus has always been on creating artwork and I see my brand as simply the culmination of my art style, turned into products.

Though the Meyoco brand has evolved over the years, my tendency never to stray too far from my signature anime style has meant it has also remained relatively consistent. I used to create fan art products, but these days I prefer to create my own original products to avoid potential copyright issues. As my style has been identifiable throughout the change in subject matter, this has kept my brand consistent. This process has been both organic and intentional.

I've never consulted a third party, such as a brand consultant, as I prefer to retain full control and manage the business myself. Since the Meyoco brand was born from my identity as an artist, I wouldn't be comfortable with someone telling me how to present myself as an artist. My strategy is simply to create my signature artwork and products that my followers know and love.

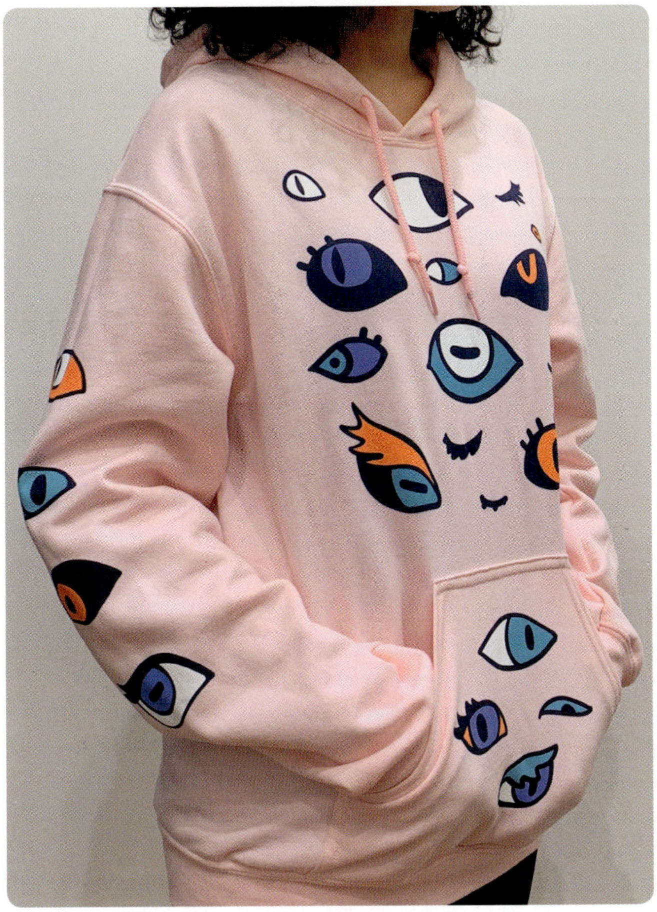

My brand is an amalgamation of various aspects of my art style, including my color palettes, line work, and style of coloring

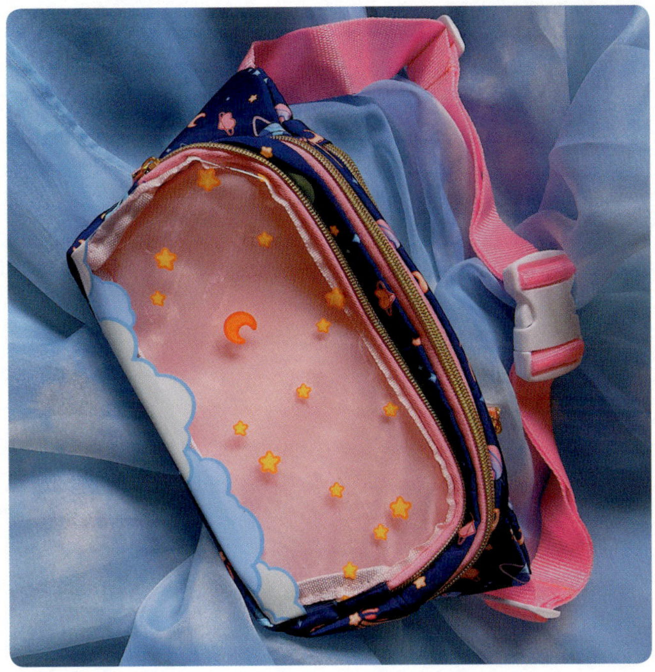

My brand has always been very closely related to my art style, which has stayed consistent over the years

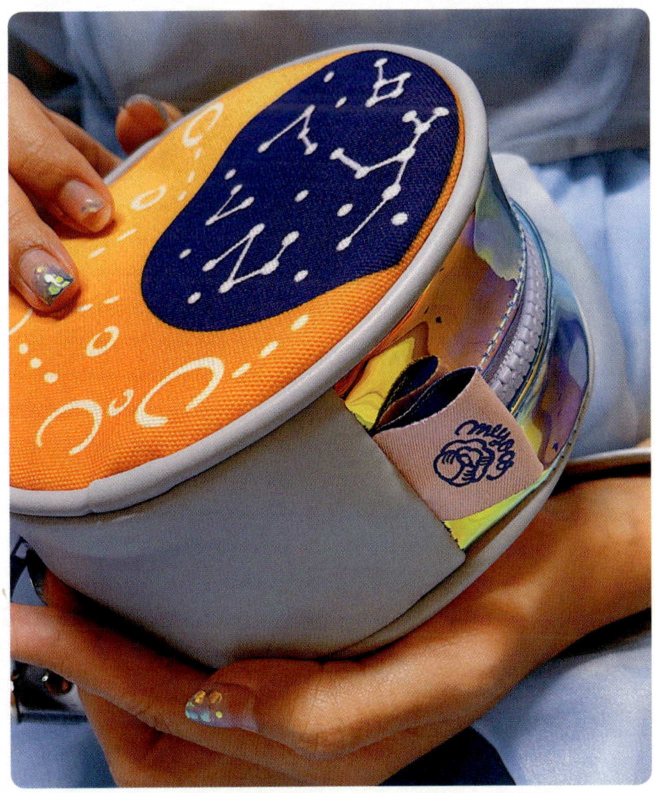

Aside from small details such as using the Meyoco logo on my products, I don't make a conscious effort to manage my branding

## Artist name

When creating my social-media platforms in 2013, I chose a cute, memorable artist name to post work under, rather than using my real name. I came up with Meyoco after experimenting with stringing several sounds and syllables together. Having a professional artist name helps me to separate my work life from my personal life. As much as my art shows who I am and what I like, it can be detrimental to confuse Meyoco with my personal identity.

Over the years I finally began to view the artwork I shared under Meyoco as a brand, rather than simply my artist persona. This helped me to further separate my work life from my personal life, while also helping my followers to associate both my artwork and products with the Meyoco name. I haven't changed my username or social media handle in the past eight years, which also helps to ensure my work and name is recognized.

## Online presence

I use the Meyoco brand name as consistently as possible, including across all of my social-media accounts and in the domain name of any websites I make. When approaching how to communicate my brand, I view social media as more relaxed and organic than a website and talk in a much less formal manner. I also don't write as much on social-media platforms due to the lack of space. On my website, however, I intentionally include more information about my products and my store.

While I occasionally use Tumblr, my main social-media platforms are Instagram and Twitter. These have a higher number of users, as well as a good-sized art community. I find it easier to gain organic engagement from these two platforms and I get a lot of sales from my Twitter posts particularly. Though I like Instagram because it's more graphic-oriented than Twitter, and is therefore easier to showcase artwork on, it's harder to gain sales from Instagram.

I do occasionally invest in paid-for marketing on Instagram, but this hasn't resulted in an increase in sales.

Marketing is more of an organic process for me, and while I do set aside some budget for occasional paid advertising and a newsletter platform, I prefer to keep my followers updated via social media. Sharing posts on Twitter or through newsletters has proven much more effective for selling products.

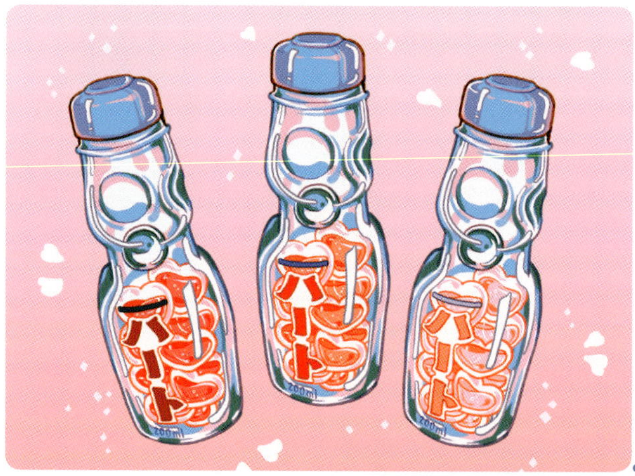

I use the same profile image across all online platforms and haven't changed it in years, making it easier for people to recognize my brand

## Networking & cross-promotion

I've never engaged in any intentional networking. I'm a little socially awkward and got scared even just replying to comments when I first started posting my artwork on social media. It didn't help that English isn't my first language and I wasn't used to conversing in English. With time and practice I became more comfortable talking to my followers and fellow artists online.

I don't currently offer my products out for review. Occasionally I do find the names of fellow artists among my customer list and sometimes I get tagged on social media when they show off products they have bought from me. Not only is this really encouraging, but these posts promote my products to a wider audience. While this kind of promotion is always helpful in growing my brand, I prefer to avoid networking for the sake of networking. My strategy has always been simply to make products that people will want to buy.

I don't have a portfolio, simply because my focus is on building my product business rather than acquiring freelance jobs. Most of my best artwork is showcased on my social media, particularly Instagram and Twitter, which allows potential employers to see it.

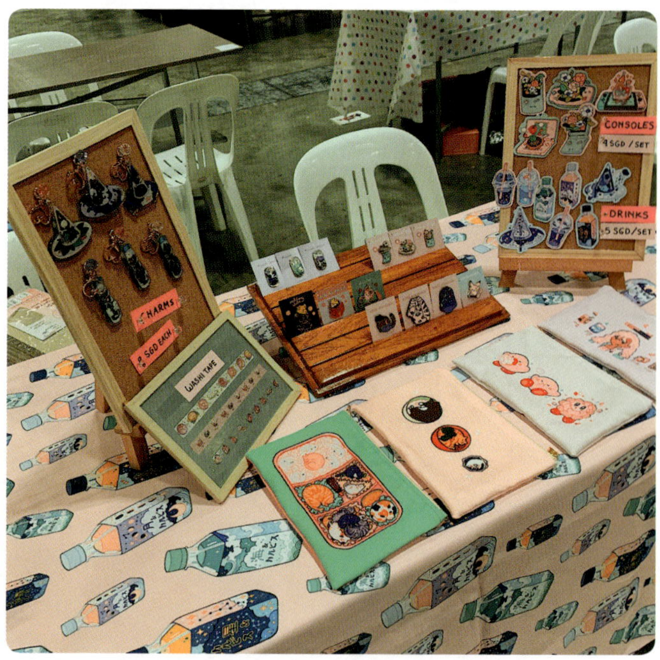

My table display from the last art convention I attended in 2019

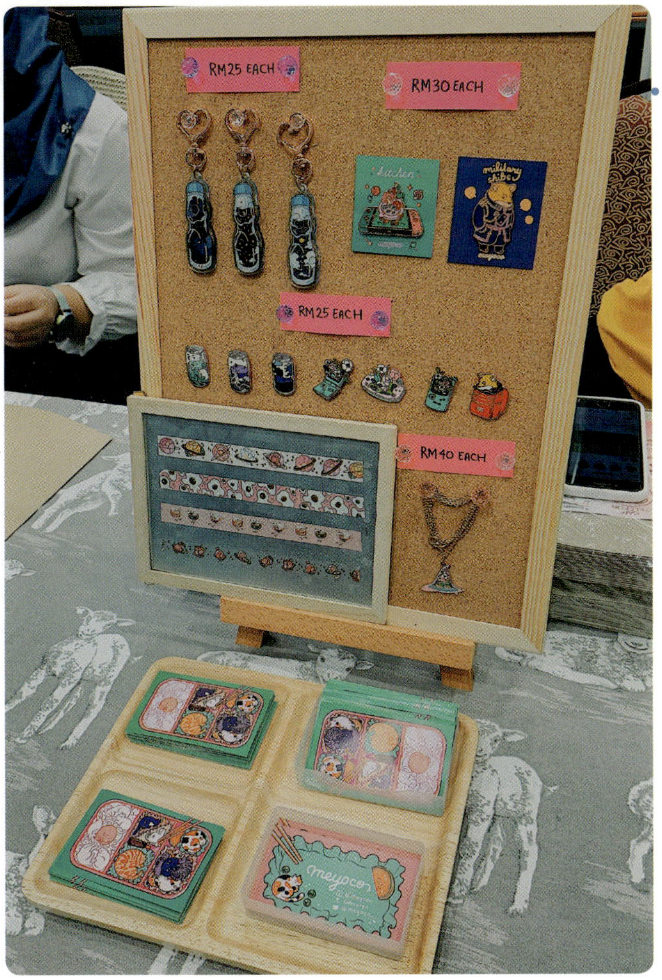


I like to reuse the same display to maintain my signature color scheme

## Promoting & pricing products

I enjoy reinterpreting my 2D illustrations into products my followers can use in everyday life, such as pins and decals (decorative stickers), as well as mini rugs, plushies, and washi tapes. My style of artwork can easily be turned into products like enamel pins, which are typically comprised of flat lines and colors. I price my products based on market price and manufacturing costs, as well as the time and difficulty involved in creating the artwork. As more intricate products typically cost more to make, I will price them higher than market price.

As well as posting regular store updates on my social-media platforms, it has also been useful to create a newsletter in which to share store updates, new products, and discounts. I aim to offer discounts every few months to attract new customers and encourage more sales. While I have tried using paid advertisements on Facebook and Instagram, these have not proved as effective as organic engagement and I have found I acquire more sales through sharing my own posts and newsletter.

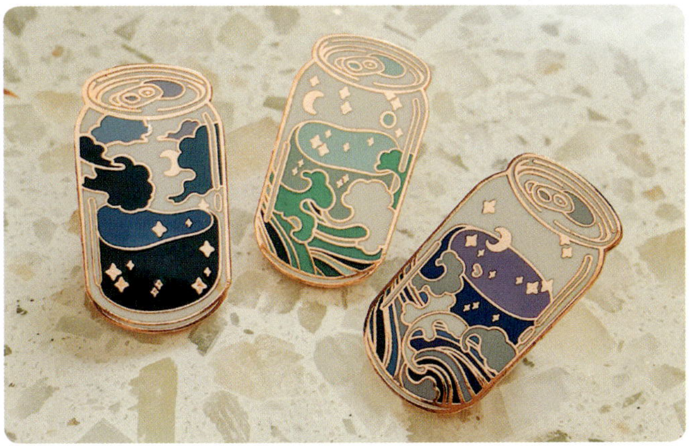

Enamel pins were some of the first products I created, as they are very compatible with my art style

This three-dimensional plushie was created from a flat rug design

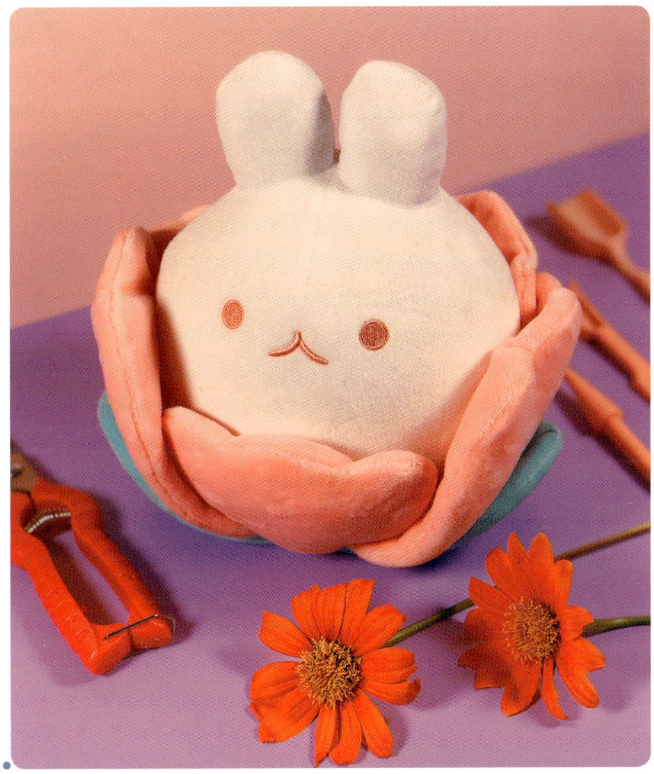

## Commercial & creative decision-making

The products I decide to offer depend on four factors:

1. Manufacturing costs
2. Shipping costs
3. Customer interest
4. Personal interest

Manufacturing and shipping costs are always my number one priority when it comes to making and selling products. Due to limited resources in my country, I almost always source my products abroad, which requires me to factor in manufacturing prices, shipping costs from suppliers, and customs fees, among other expenses. In addition, I need to consider shipping costs from me to the customers. Products that are particularly heavy or big require further care when budgeting, to calculate whether the production is worth the cost.

While these commercial factors are essential, it's also important to gauge if customers are interested in the product. When I have a new product idea, I usually sketch it, post it on social media, and then see how my followers react to it, including if they have any suggestions. To avoid being wasteful, I don't create the product if engagement is low.

My own enjoyment in making a product also plays a key part in whether I decide to pursue it. If I'm not interested in a particular product concept, it's unlikely I will have any appealing ideas for it. Additionally, I consider whether I would want to use the product myself. I usually avoid making anything I can't see myself using.

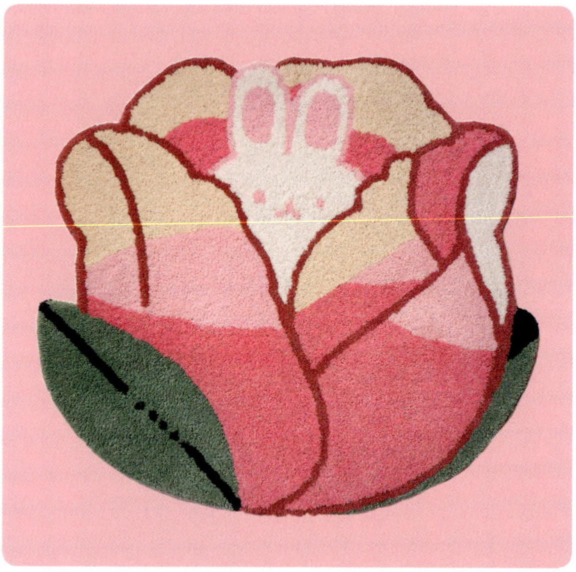

Despite being one of the most expensive products I've ever made, my mini rugs gained a high level of interest, so I decided to continue making them

## Time management

I'm sometimes asked if building a brand and running the business takes me away from creating as much art as I'd like. On the contrary, running the business side of my work allows me a welcome break from routinely churning out new artwork to post online. It can be suffocating to feel like I should always be creating a new painting that will gain likes or can be turned into new products. When I'm running the business side of my brand, however, I'm able to focus on logistics, manufacturers, admin, and inventory, which can be strangely therapeutic.

I manage my time by keeping a physical weekly schedule book. Rather than trying to cram as much as possible into each day, I try to focus on two or three tasks instead. As I find it hard to memorize my schedule, I write down everything I need to do in advance. This act of writing helps to commit my daily schedule to memory. I will also check my schedule book a few times throughout the day to make sure I'm on track.

When you're growing an art brand or working as a freelance artist, set yourself a daily schedule and avoid packing too many tasks into each day. Having a work diary or schedule book for writing down your tasks will help you to identify and prioritize what needs to be done. Organize these into small, manageable tasks, rather than huge assignments. For example, with my online store, I would rather pack a hundred packages over two or three days, than cram this into one day. Breaking it down allows me more time to work on freelance jobs, as well as my hobbies.

When starting work as an artist, begin with small projects rather than overcommitting to very ambitious projects. When I first began selling my products, I would only create one or two new products every few months. This helped me to focus and break my project down into manageable tasks, so much so that I still use this technique now.

## Brand inspiration

I have always admired Maruti Bitamin and her anime-style art brand. She was one of the first artists I followed on social media and her work was hugely inspirational for me during my early years. Watching as she created new products on a regular basis, I dreamed of being as prolific as her when I was younger. Her work has kept me constantly motivated.

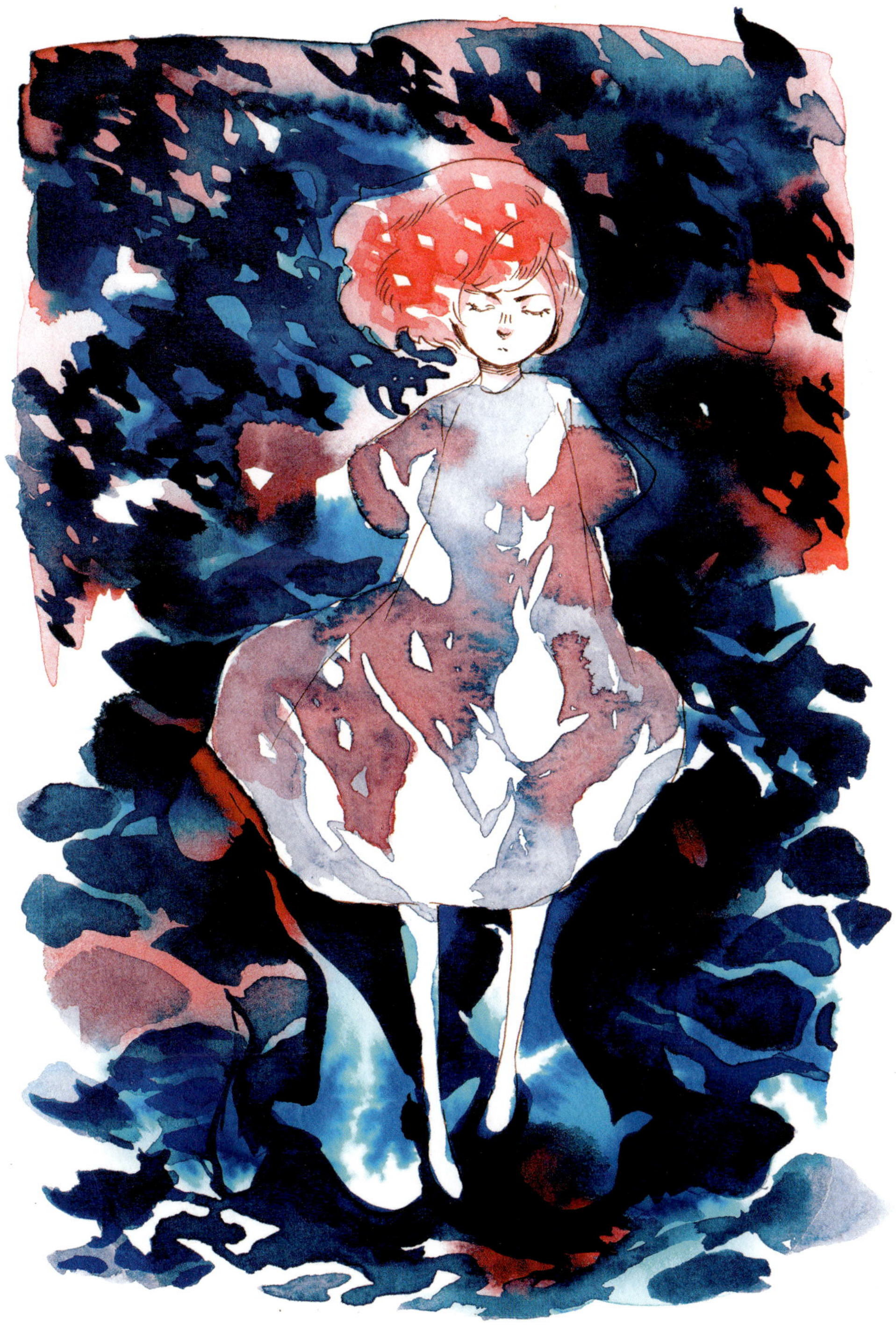

One of my early paintings, influenced by Maruti Bitamin's work

# FUTURE AMBITIONS

Product design is my favorite part of my work and I would love to be able to create a wider range of products in the future. It's fun to translate my illustrations into merchandise and I feel like there are still so many designs and types of product to explore.

I am always looking to improve and develop my work, and would love to learn how to draw intricate backgrounds, such as cityscapes and landscapes. Learning how to draw more varied backgrounds would hugely expand the range of things I could draw, which would allow me to create more varied products as well.

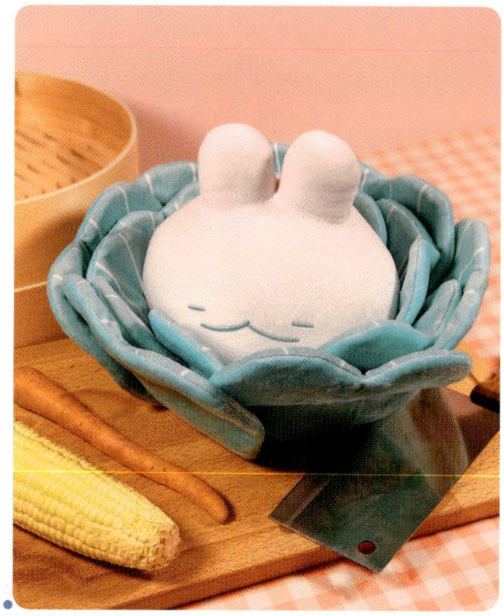

I would love to create more plushies as they are immensely fun, albeit challenging, to design and produce

# ADVICE

## Self-doubt

Artists are often encouraged to try new things and push out of their comfort zone, but I enjoy revisiting familiar topics and honing my signature style. I feel self-doubt almost all of the time, as if I'm being judged for not being creative enough, adventurous enough, or good enough. When I succumb to this pressure and begin to question my own ideals, my artwork always suffers as my heart isn't in it. Trust your gut and create the type of artwork you want to create.

## Artist's block

Artist's block occurs when I force myself to draw too much. While I had the energy and ideas to draw all the time when I was younger, I find myself feeling less inspired and getting stuck in artist's block more often as I get older. I tackle this by changing task and not forcing myself to draw. There was a time where I viewed drawing as a duty, as it was my only source of income, but I've since realized that the more I force myself to churn out painting after painting, the less likely it becomes that I will create good art. Nowadays, if I don't feel like drawing, I simply work on managing my store, playing my favorite video games, or spending time with friends and family. When I am inspired to draw again, I return to my art feeling refreshed.

I rarely encounter artist's block when working on paid client work, as I'm usually given a strict deadline and guidance. I find it easier to draw when I know what's expected of me.

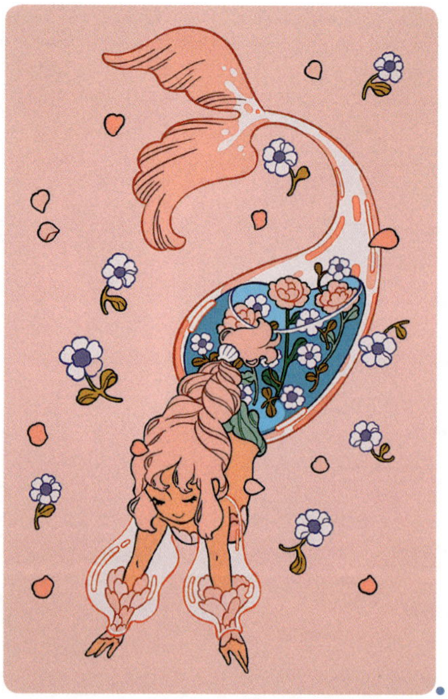

When I encounter artist's block, I either take a break from drawing or return to familiar subjects I know I can draw well

## Dealing with criticism

Criticism can be challenging. Most of my followers know the kind of subject matter I create and that I often draw the same types of themes, so I rarely get any criticism for this. However, I'm also aware that there are people who dislike my art for this very reason. I choose to ignore this criticism, as I'm not forcing anyone to look at my artwork, nor do I charge people to view it. I'm content to continue creating the artwork I like to create.

Of course, it's entirely different when I'm working for paying clients. I'm always open to feedback from clients if the criticism is concrete, constructive, and includes pointers on which parts I need to fix.

## Taking your hobby to a professional level

Find your niche and stay true to what you love to draw. While it's important to know what people like about your work, it's even more important to like your *own* work, to ensure your career is sustainable and you want to do it for years to come. When art becomes a job, rather than a hobby, it's extremely easy to become burned out. From my own experience, it's hard to work in the art industry if you don't like what you're making.

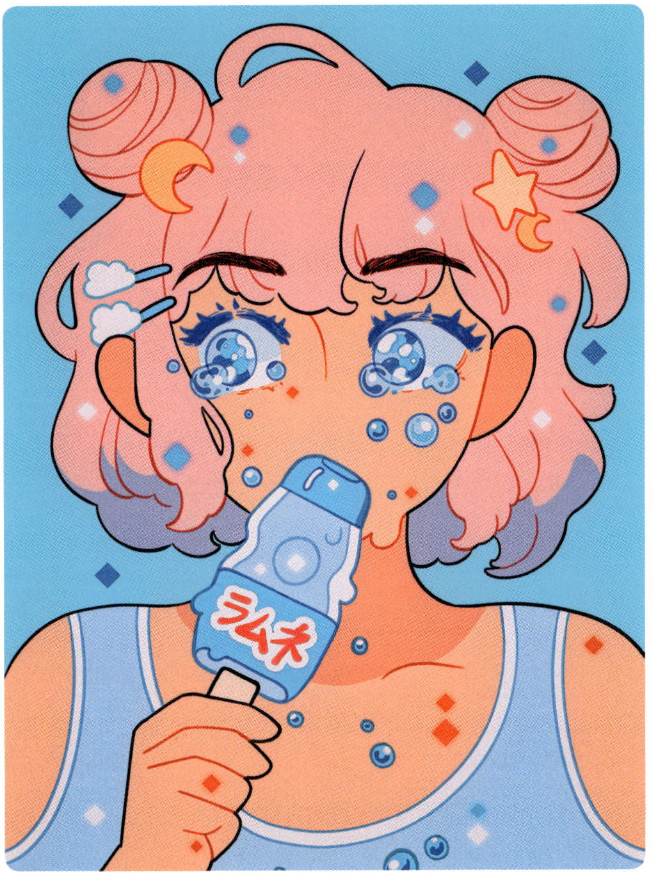


I mainly create paintings in a certain style or color palette, concentrating on it looking good rather than any deeper meaning

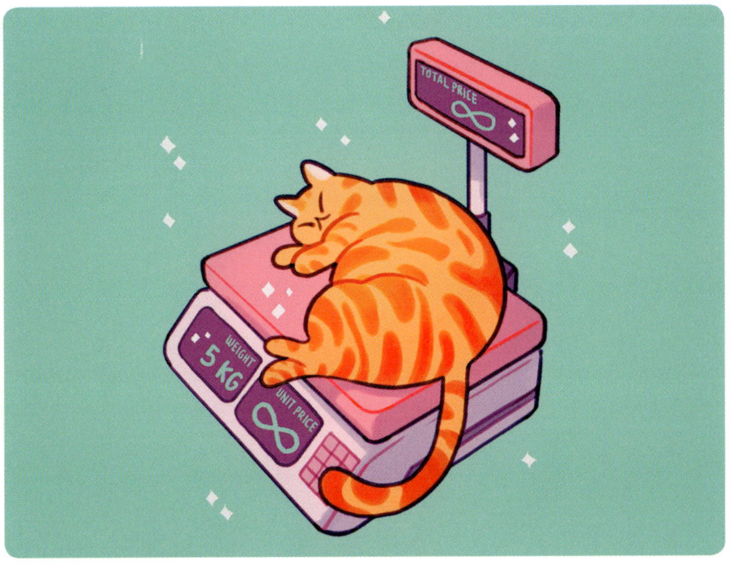


When I look back at my old artworks, I find I'm genuinely still fond of them

## Social media

Aim to create a healthy separation between work and your personal life. Monitor your social-media usage and only use it for specific tasks, such as creating an online portfolio or promoting your work. When you're a professional artist with an online presence, it can be hard not to value your art based on the amount of likes or engagement. While popularity can be a good way to obtain more recognition, confusing your popularity with the quality of your work can easily lead to burnout. It's easy to think your art career is failing or that your art isn't good enough if you don't generate enough likes.

# TIMELINE

**2013**

I started drawing more seriously when attending university, spending all of my classes doodling in my sketchbook.

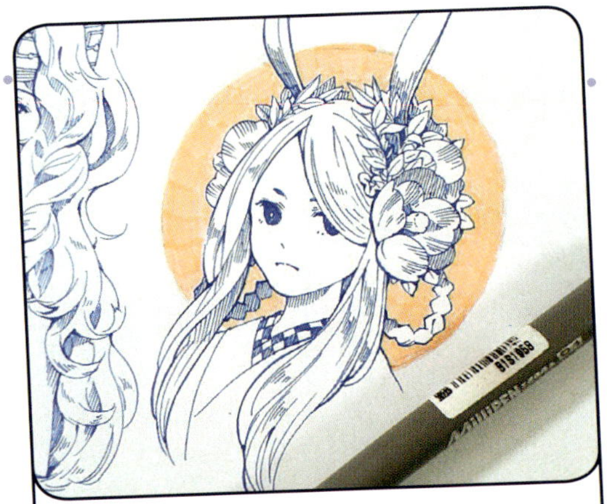

A doodle drawn during university classes.

**Mid 2014**

I started learning watercolors by studying the work of my favorite artists.

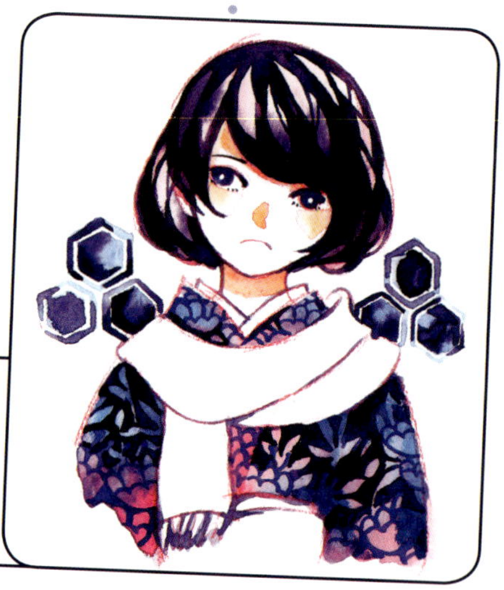

One of my earliest watercolor paintings.

**2015**

I was invited to participate in a charity art book, which was the first invitation I had received of this kind.

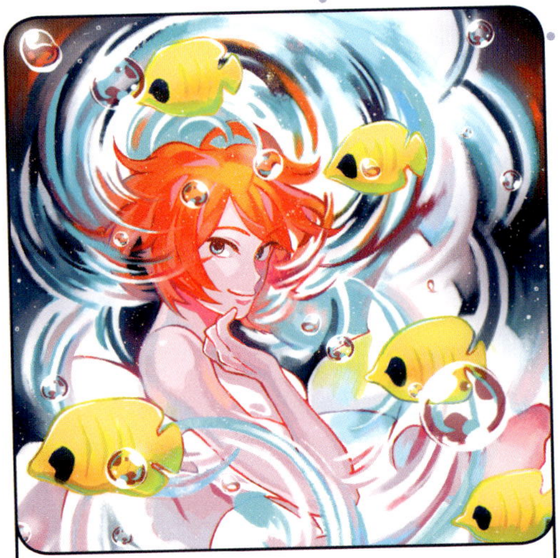

My artwork for the charity art book. I was honored to participate alongside other notable artists.

**2016**

I began drawing more original artwork and compiled my work into several zines.

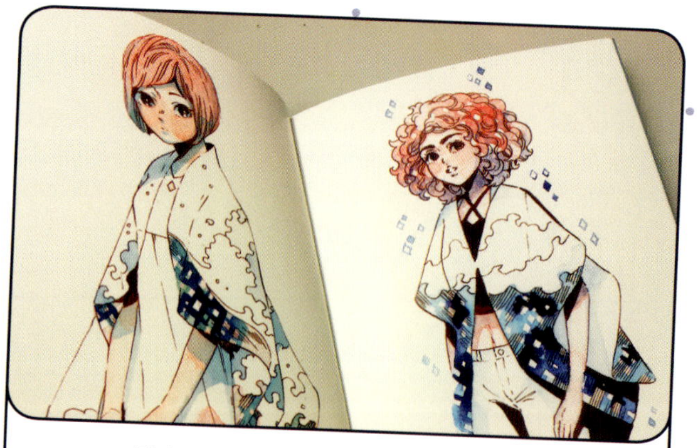

This spread was from one of my original zines, *Bodies of Water*.

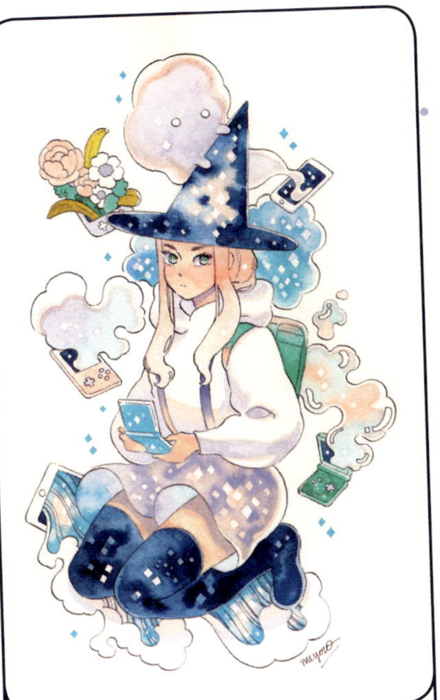

Work submitted for the group exhibition at Gallery Nucleus.

**2018**

I had an idea to make a button-up shirt featuring a full-print illustration. It is still my most popular apparel product to date.

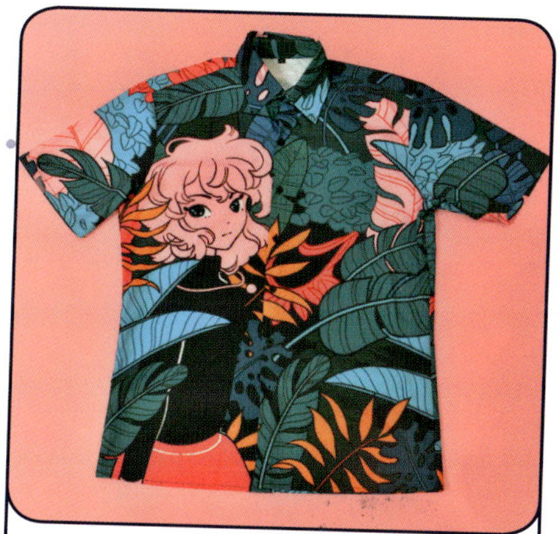

One of my most popular apparel products.

**2018**

I was invited by Gallery Nucleus to join a group exhibition with two incredible artists, Sibylline Meynet and Heikala.

My first product attempt was key chains that could be produced in smaller quantities, in case sales were low.

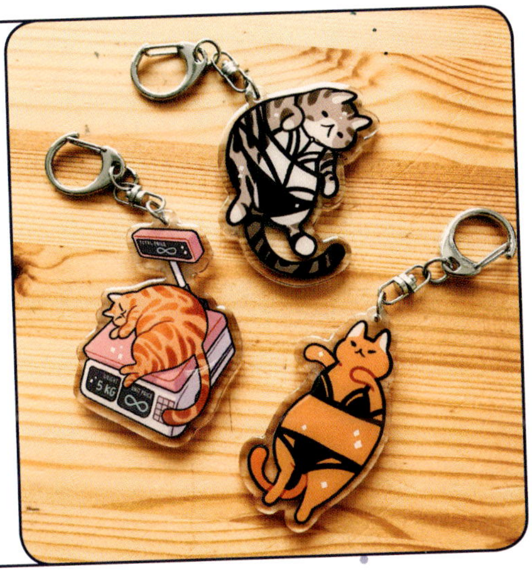

**2018**

I began to create more original products.

**2017**

After graduating from university, I enrolled in a dynamic sketching art class online that focused on foundational drawing skills.

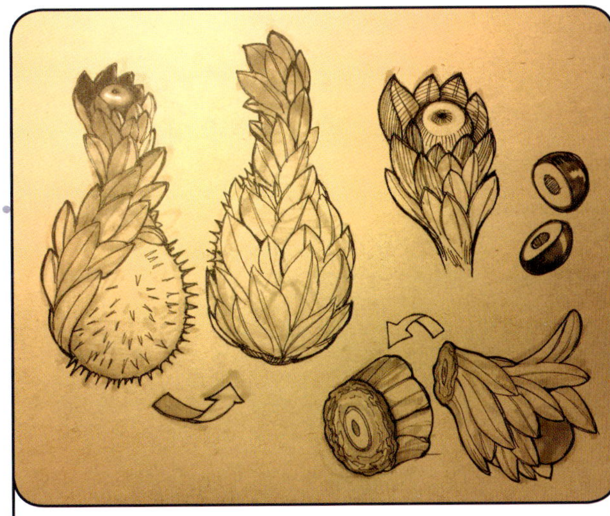

One of my assignments was to redesign a perfume bottle into a plant.

# GALLERY

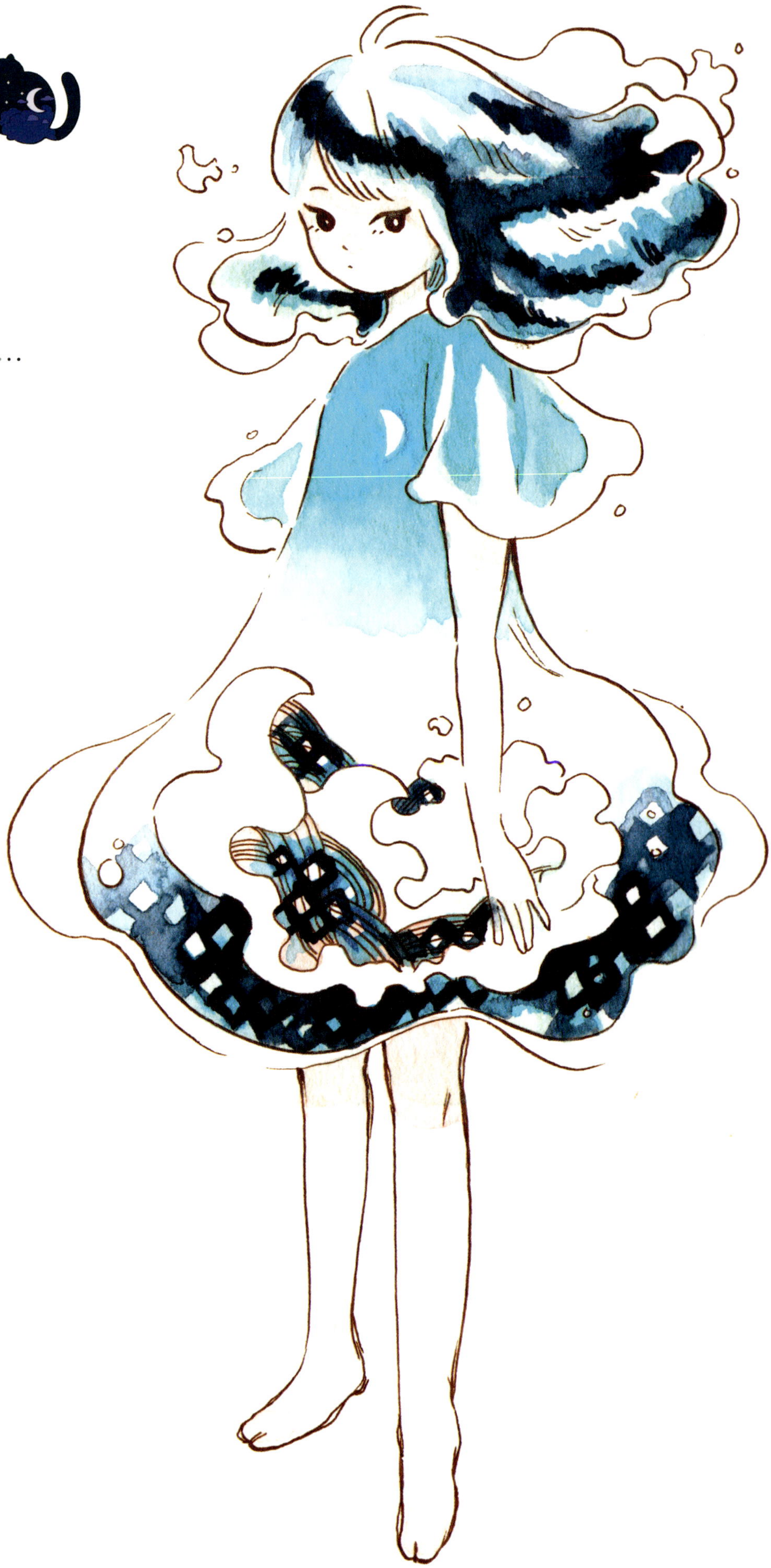

## *Bodies of Water*

My favorite subjects to draw are female characters blended with nature elements, particularly water. This is one of my first artworks featuring a girl combined with a wave motif. It gained a high level of engagement on social media, and I wanted to explore the subject further. I went on to draw many iterations of girls imbued with water and wave motifs, and it became one of my signature art styles.

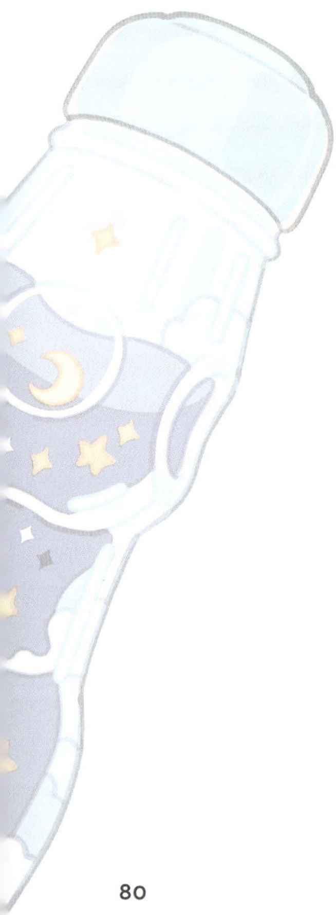

## *Glass Bottles*

Many people associate my art with transparent objects, such as glasses and bottles. This is one of my earliest artworks containing these. At the time I was inspired by terrariums and wanted to try drawing other things encased within them. It was fantastic that the artwork gained a lot of engagement on social media, but even better, I realized I really enjoyed drawing and painting transparent objects.

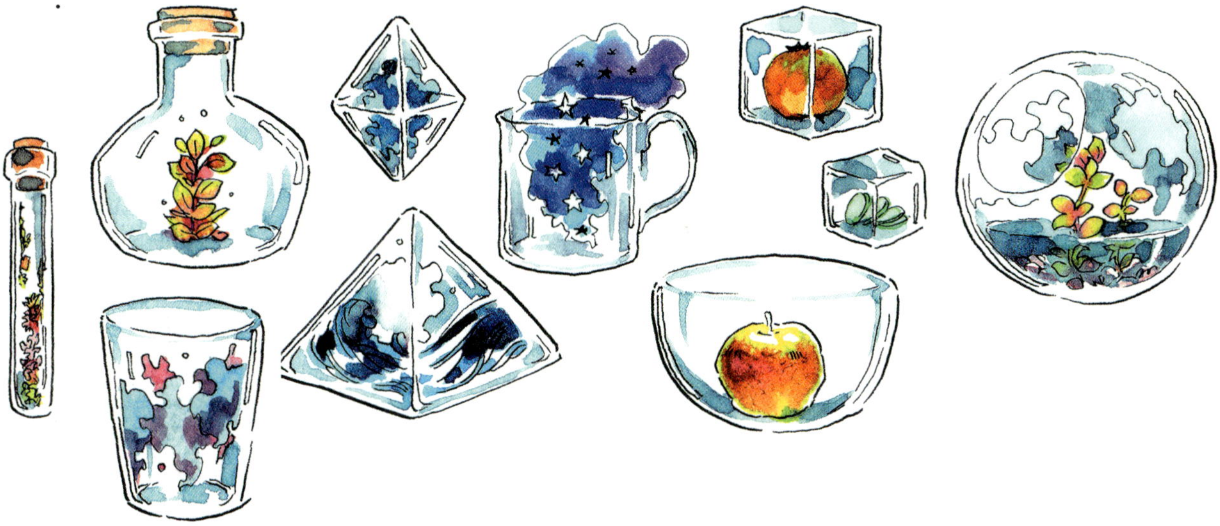

## *Weather Ramune*

This artwork gained a huge number of likes, particularly on Twitter. It was unlike anything I'd ever posted there before. I turned this artwork into a series of acrylic key chains where the water parts were transparent and the bottle sections were opaque. It was the first time I'd experimented with translating a 2D artwork into a product. The key chains were very popular and were bestsellers in my online store for quite some time.

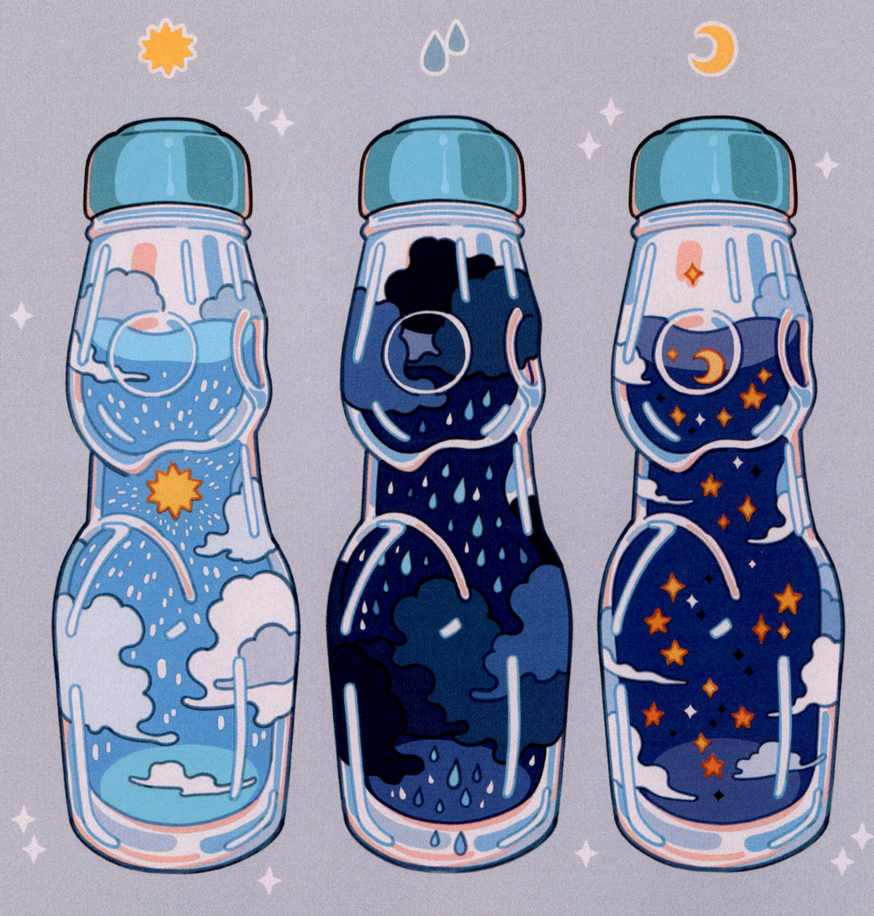

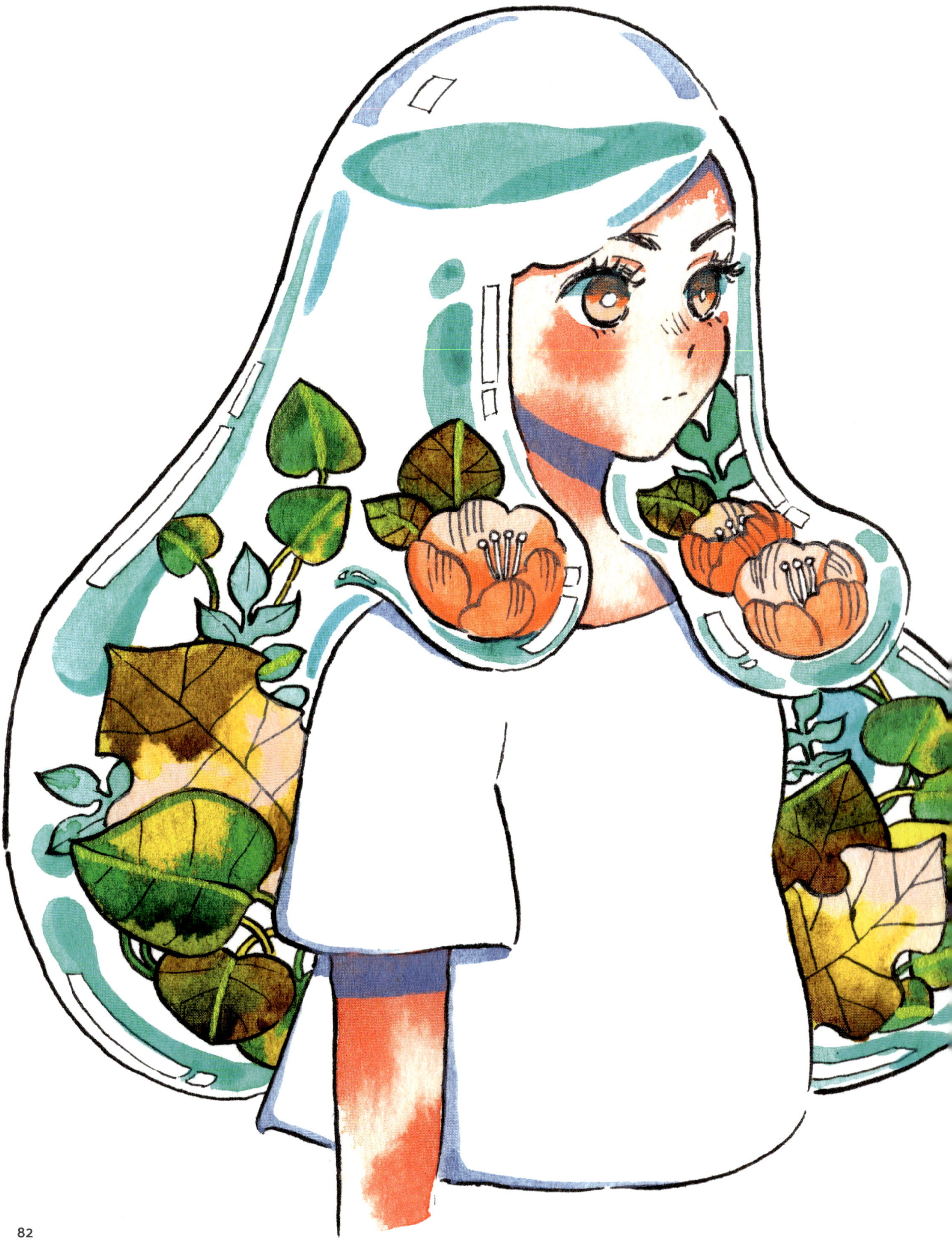

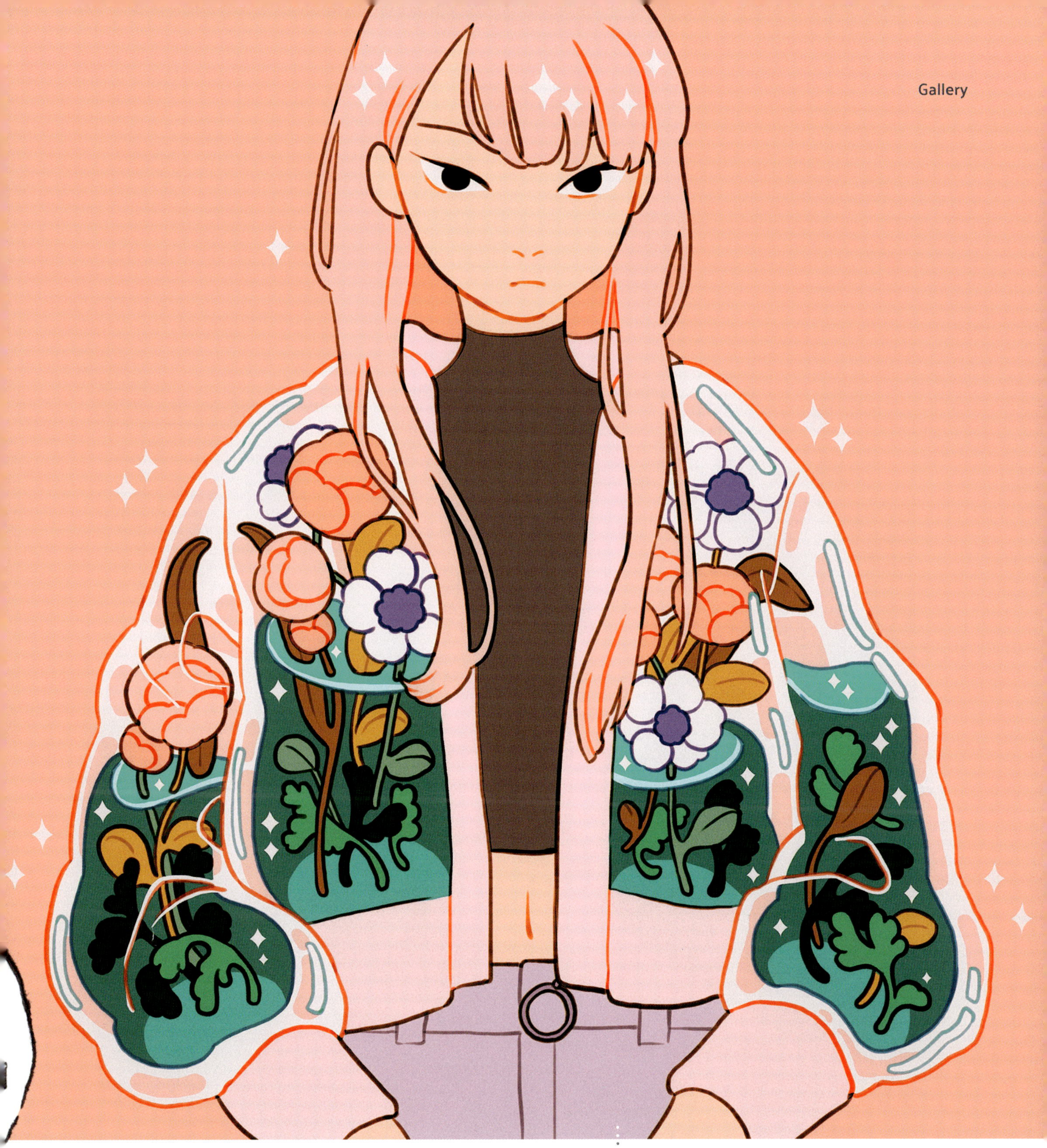

## *Transparent*

This artwork marked a shift toward my current style of drawing transparent objects. It was used as a design for a collaboration with an independent art publisher, where it was turned into a limited edition t-shirt.

## *Transparent Jacket*

This artwork marked my transition to drawing more fashion-inspired artworks. I once wanted to be a fashion designer, as I have always loved enchanting feminine costumes, and this has translated into my current love of drawing magical-themed clothing.

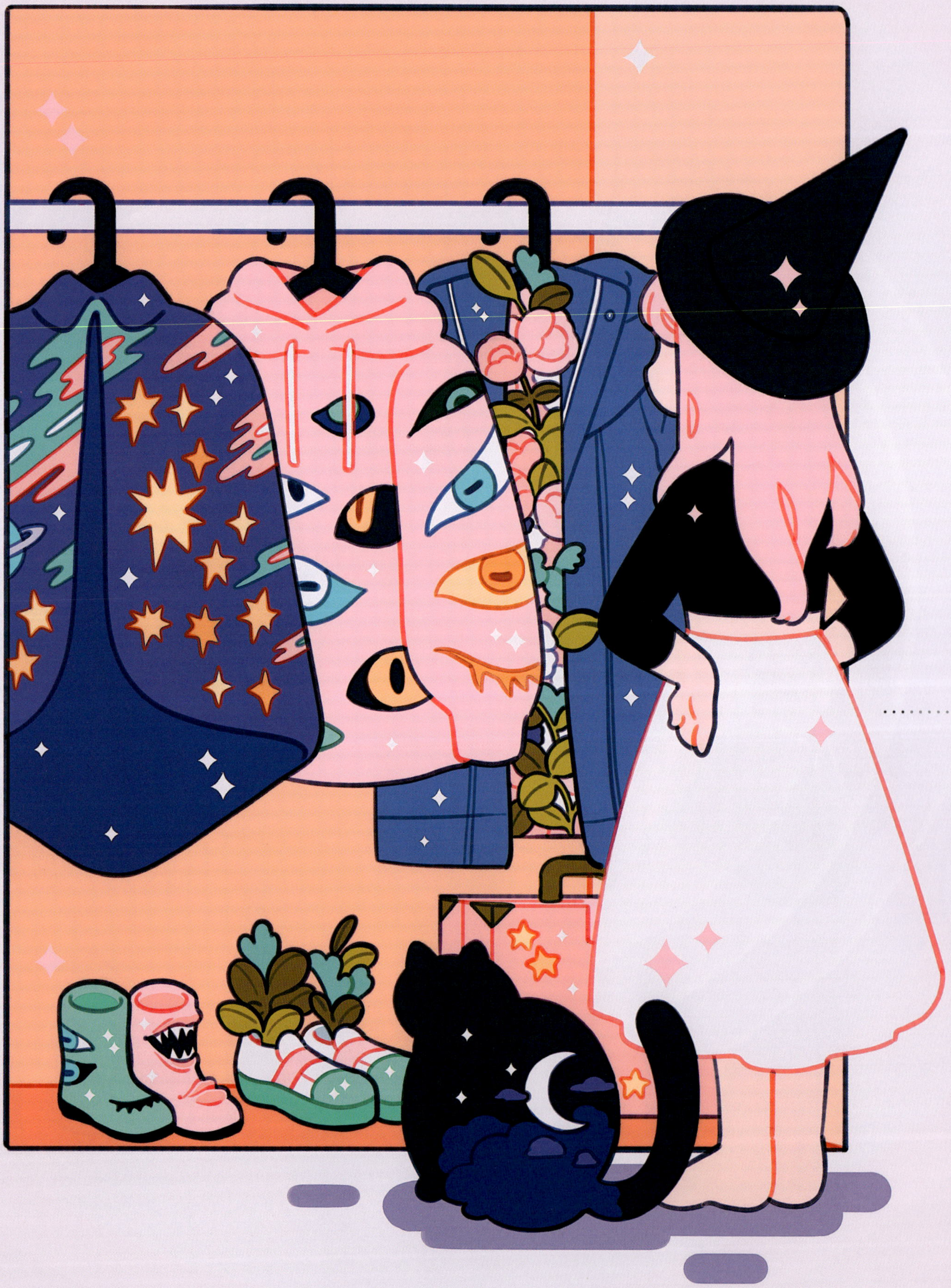

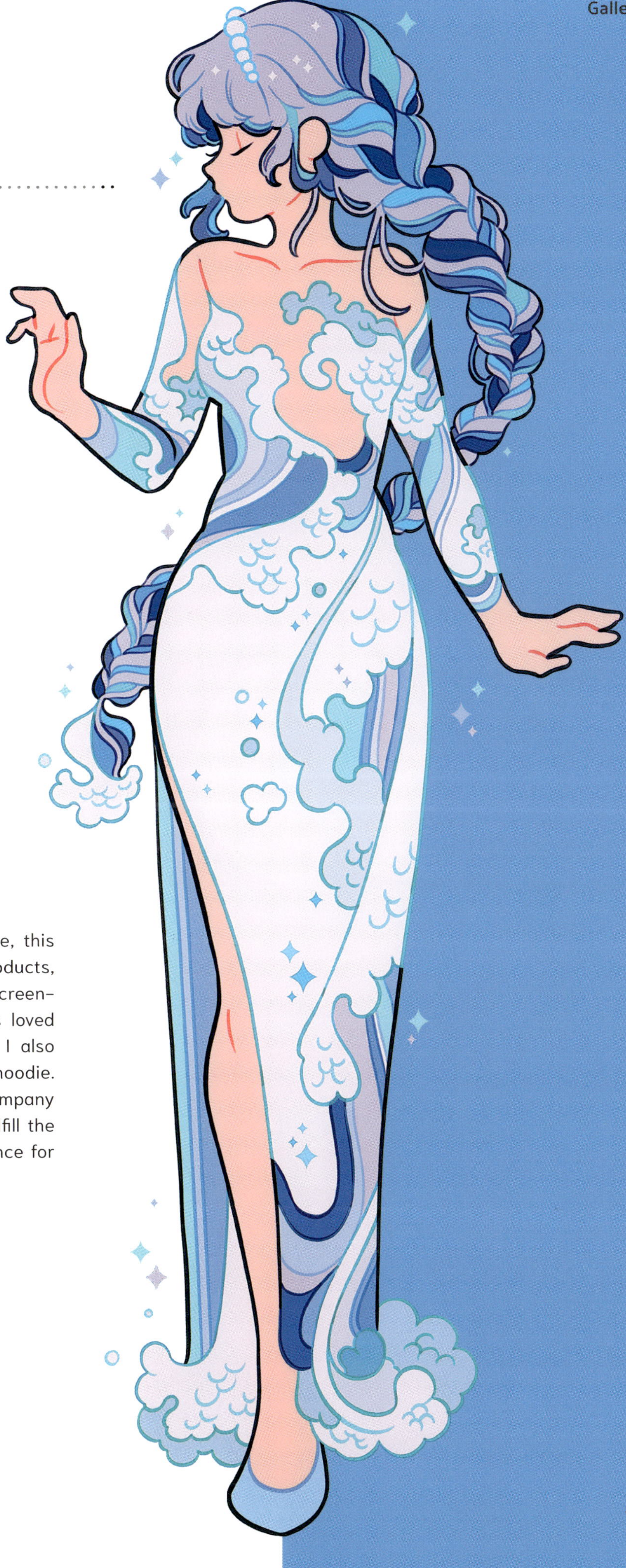

## *Waterfall Dress*

In 2020 I became even more interested in fashion and began looking at notable fashion designers for inspiration. I was particularly fond of drawing dresses and loved browsing the creations of famous designers, such as Teuta Matoshi and the Selkie brand. I mainly drew outfits I wanted to wear myself, which made drawing them even more enjoyable. Experimenting with motifs and shapes allowed me to create magical dresses.

## *The Cat, the Witch, and the Wardrobe*

One of my most popular artworks to date, this piece led to my creation of apparel products, when I turned the artwork into a screen-printed sweatshirt. Many of my followers loved the clothing in the witch's wardrobe, so I also turned the "eyes" hoodie into an actual hoodie. I worked with a store management company based in the US, White Squirrel Co., to fulfill the orders. That was a huge learning experience for me and I still work with them today.

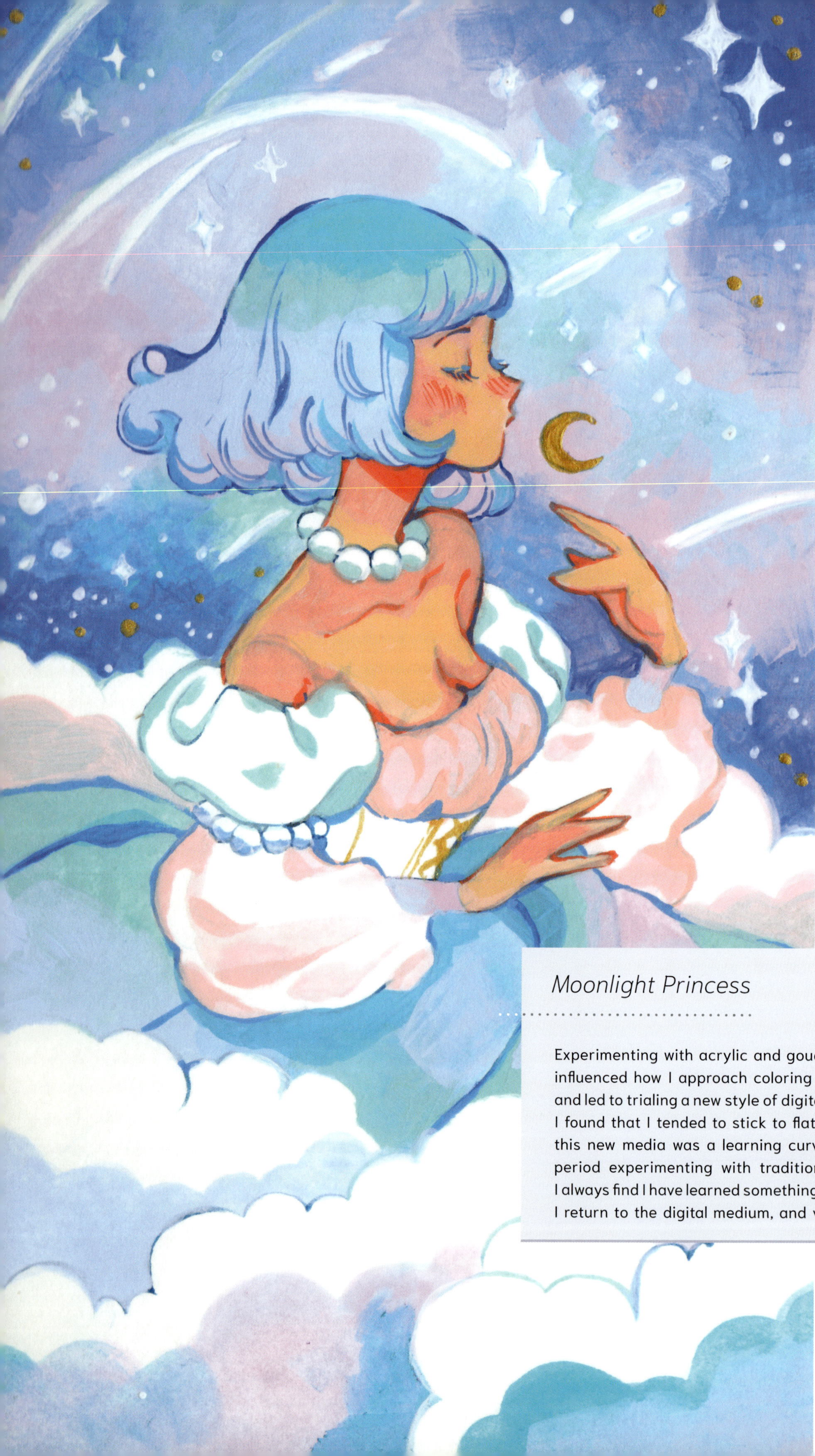

*Moonlight Princess*

Experimenting with acrylic and gouache paint influenced how I approach coloring in general and led to trialing a new style of digital coloring. I found that I tended to stick to flat colors, so this new media was a learning curve. After a period experimenting with traditional media, I always find I have learned something new when I return to the digital medium, and vice versa.

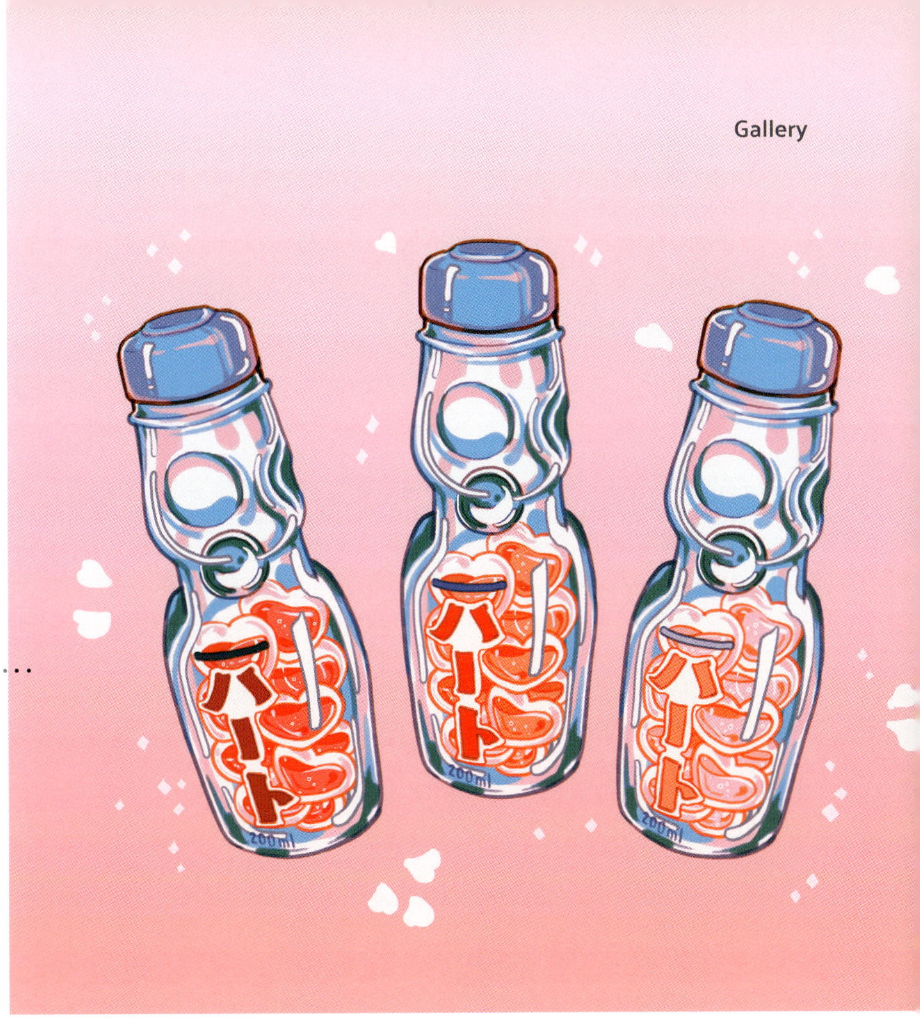


## *Heart Ramune*

This was the first time I drew transparent objects digitally. It gained a significant amount of engagement and drastically increased my social-media following. I started drawing using digital media more often afterward, which was also due to the ease in turning digital artworks into products.

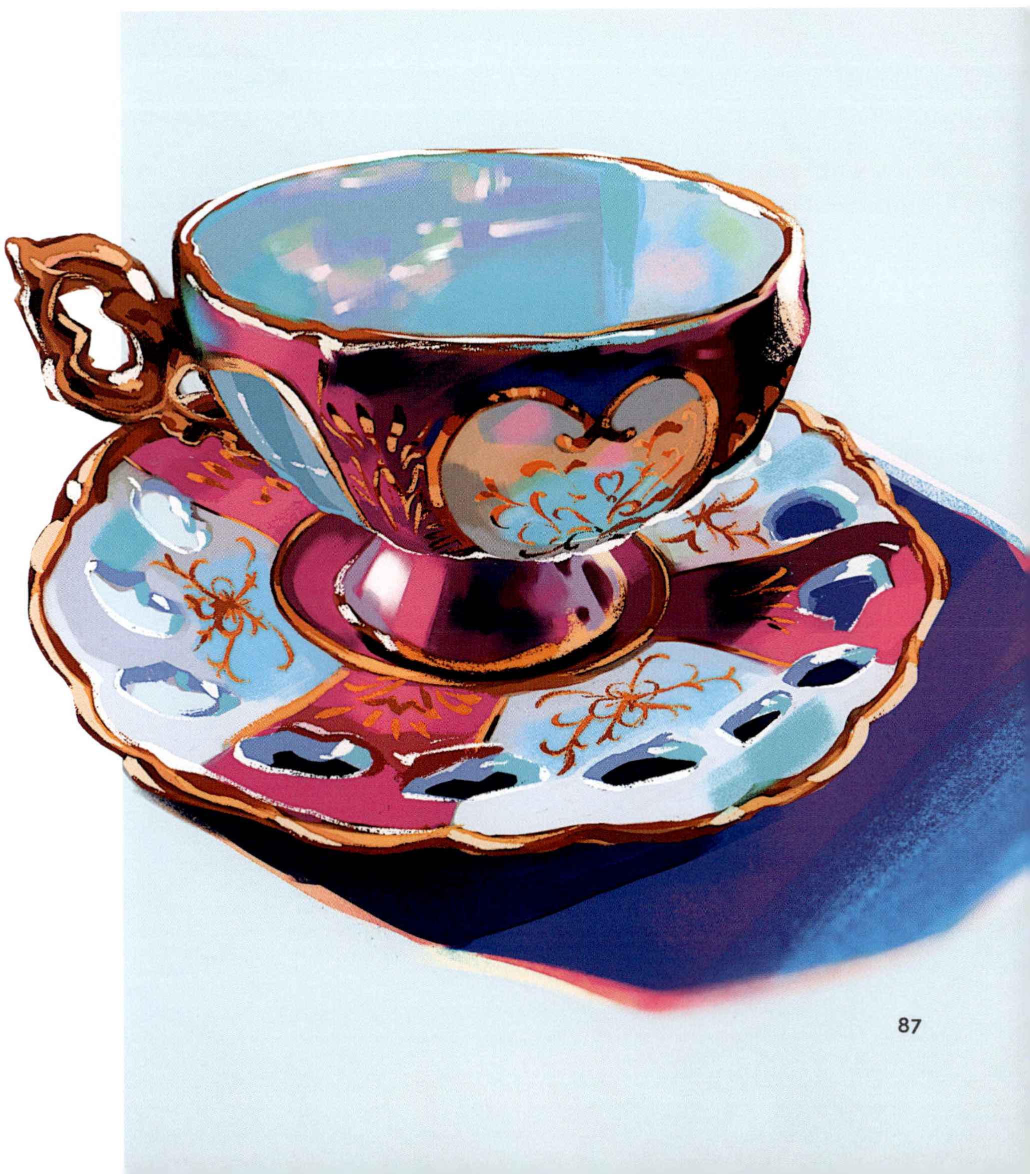

## *Teacup*

This artwork marked a pivotal change in how I approach coloring. I was stuck in a rut and thought I should try drawing studies of real-life objects. I took photos of this vintage lusterware teacup and tried painting it in Procreate. This taught me a lot about how to color this type of painting and I ended up creating several more studies in the same style. Afterward, I tried applying what I had learned in my usual artworks.

# TUTORIAL

This tutorial will guide you through how I create one of my signature anime-style characters. When devising ideas for a new artwork, I often return to subjects I am already familiar with and slightly alter something within the design. For example, I might revisit a theme, such as ocean waves or celestial bodies, but change the overall image with a new pose or clothing style. Using themes you are already familiar with as inspiration for new artwork can help you to focus on the new aspects you want to explore. I also like to look for inspiration in fashion, everyday objects, or the work of other artists, before considering how I could reinterpret or take inspiration from my findings. For instance, I may feel inspired by the silhouette of a particular dress, colors from a still life photo, or the theme or mood of another artist's work.

The tutorial will also explore how I use my audience's preferences to inform my design decisions. My followers typically enjoy fashion-inspired artworks combined with magical natural elements, such as ocean waves. Pay attention to what elements of your artwork your audience engages with and continue to incorporate these in future work. Of course, that isn't to say that you should completely copy your previous work or stick exclusively to popular themes. Experiment with elements that have previously proved successful, as well as ideas you wish to explore or expand on further.

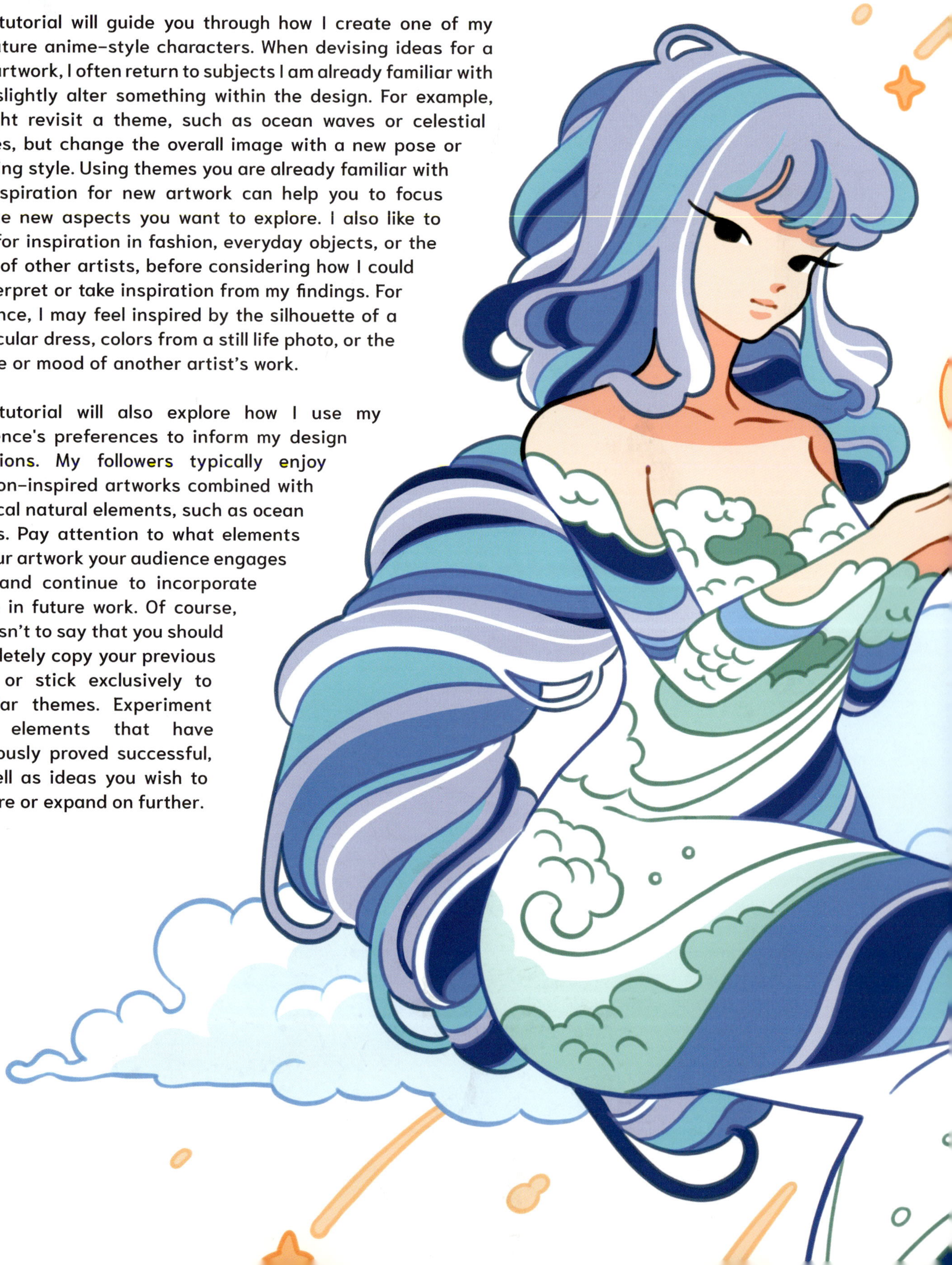

**01** Begin with a rough sketch of your idea. I typically start with the character's face and hair, as I love drawing this focal area the most. Starting your sketch with your favorite element can help to generate further inspiration and ideas. Your rough sketch does not need to be neat or detailed. Instead, focus on capturing the character's silhouette and main shape. It can also help to loosely depict the expression in this early sketch stage, as this will help determine the body pose and the overall mood of the artwork.

I prefer to use a bright color for the first sketch, as this makes the line work process easier

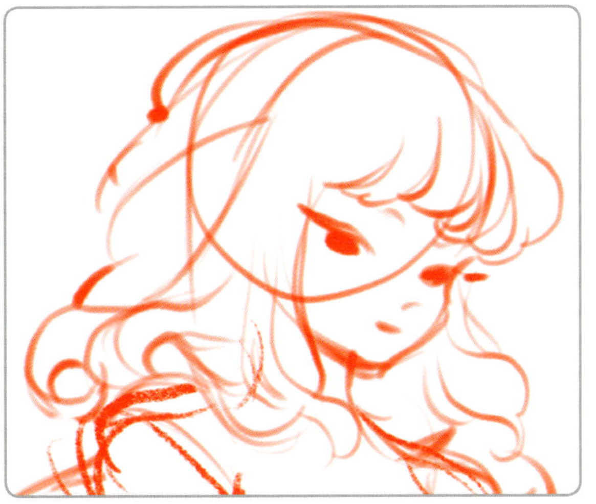

**02** After loosely sketching the character's face and hair, start to draw her body and the dress. Keeping your lines loose and flowing will help in making her body appear graceful and fluid, rather than stiff. Use soft, curved lines and try to avoid sharp, angular corners. Next, draw small curves to create fluffy, cloudlike shapes for the wave crests. To make the artwork more cohesive, use the same style to draw wave crest motifs on the dress and hair. Repeating certain shapes throughout the design like this can create a more unified look. Drawing with soft, fluid lines is part of my signature style and is consistent across my characters.

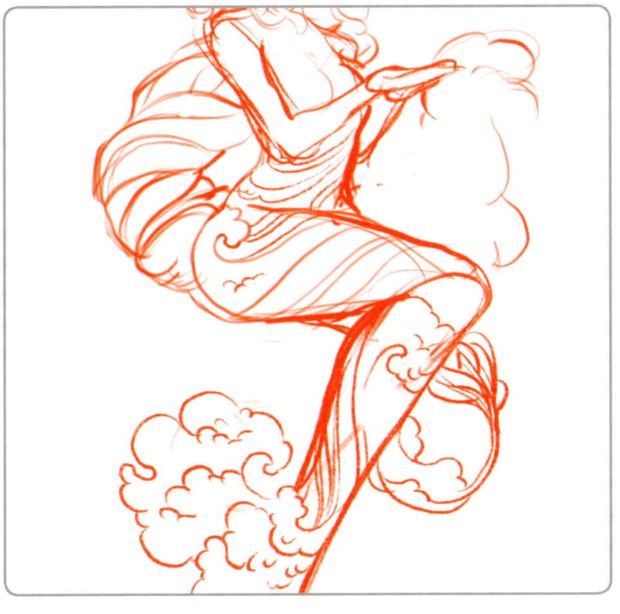

Aim to keep the character's body graceful and fluid, and the anatomy believable

**03** When drawing details, such as waves or strands of hair, ensure they complement the contours and flow of the artwork. The wave detail on the dress should follow the contour of the thigh, while also imitating falling water. Likewise, the detail of the plaited hair should follow the twists and turns of the plait, while still flowing gracefully downward. This will help to maintain the fluidity of the artwork. Again, it's important to observe and maintain the character of the lines throughout the overall design. Do you want your lines to flow together in a cohesive manner? Or would you prefer visible contrast between harsh, straight lines and softer, curved lines?

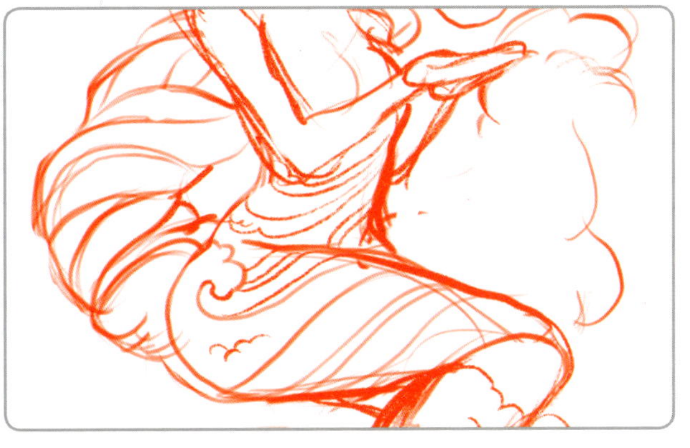

Understand the contours of each item you are drawing, whether hair, fabric, or the human body

**04** After finishing the character sketch, it's time to start work on the background. If your character is very detailed and is the focal point of the artwork, as is the case here, you may wish to keep the background fairly simple. I often use celestial-themed objects in my backgrounds, and in this artwork the background elements will include the moon, clouds, and shooting stars. Don't be afraid to combine seemingly unrelated elements! Ocean waves and celestial objects may not appear to go together at first, but try sketching them collectively and see how they work visually.

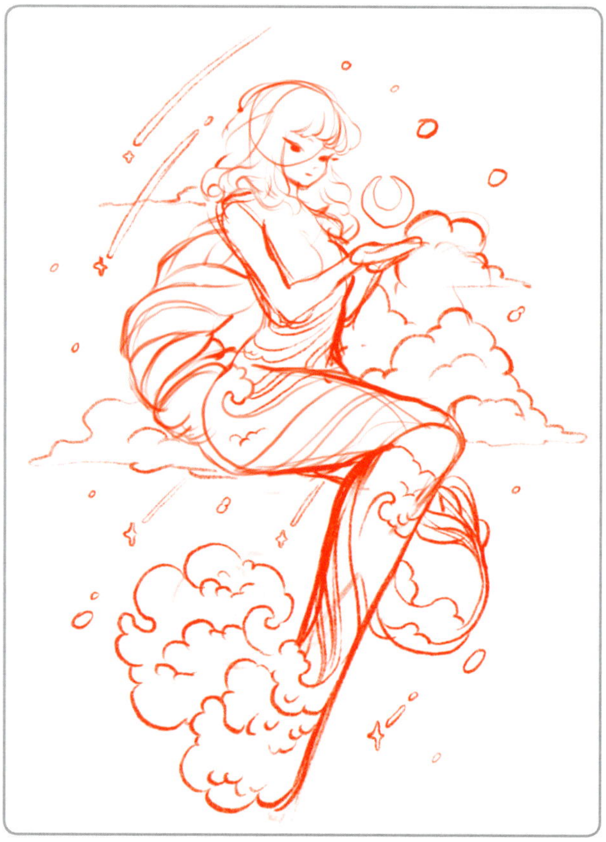

Experiment with combining different elements and details to create the intended mood and atmosphere

## ARTIST TIP

Make a habit of drawing something simple every day. When I started making art, I used to take a sketchbook with me wherever I went and doodle multiple times a day. My sketches were small, not very detailed, and far from perfect. Often I drew the same subjects repeatedly. Regardless, this practice helped me to polish my line work, anatomy, and overall drawing habits, bringing out and shaping my style.

**05** To sketch the clouds, use the same technique used when drawing the wave crests. This will create a sense of cohesion. Use curved lines, but this time try to make the shape look even more soft and rounded than before. The clouds should be sketched using fewer lines than the waves, while still maintaining the fluffy look. As curved lines are a key part of my signature style, I incorporate them into as many different parts of the illustration as possible.

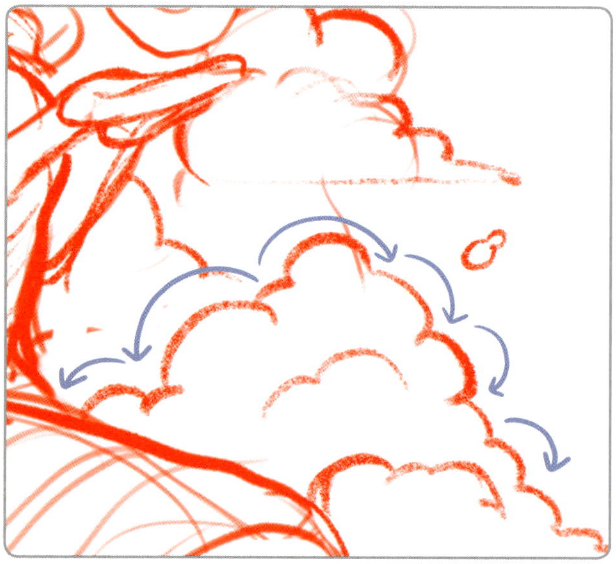

Sketch clouds that appear soft and fluffy to the touch

**06** Sketch in the shooting stars, paying attention to how they complement the detail on the dress. The tails of the shooting stars should follow the same direction and flow of the ocean waves. When drawing a background, ensure it complements the central character instead of distracting from it. Cohesion is key.

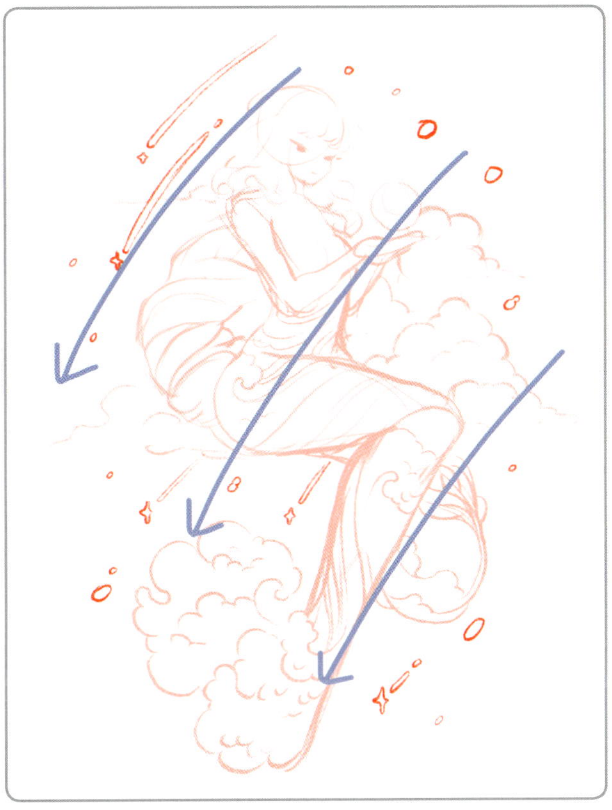

Use background details to complement the existing flow of the design

**07** Once you have finished a rough sketch of the whole design, draw a cleaner sketch on top to check the silhouette and details. Use smooth, clean lines for this, paying close attention to how the outlines and details work together. Erase any lines that are unnecessary and make the remaining curved lines smoother and neater than before. This will provide a neat sketch on which to draw the line art in the next step.

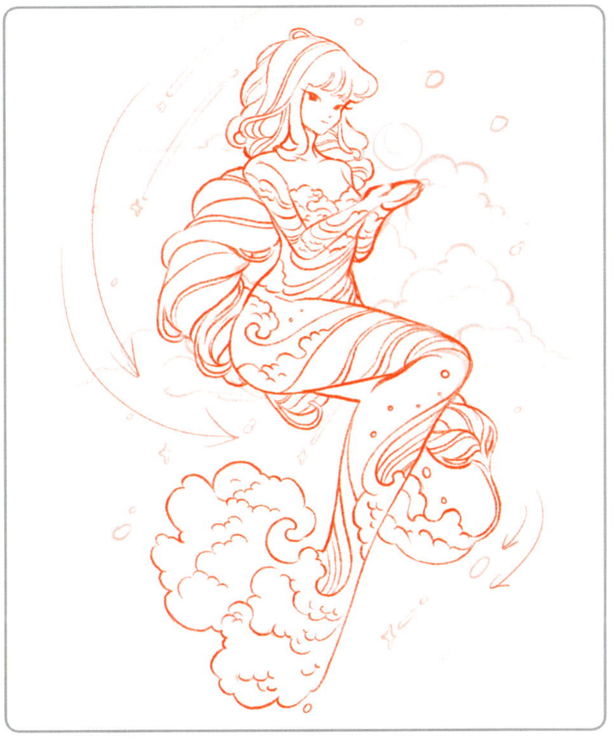

Drawing a clean sketch allows you to correct any major mistakes before solidifying the line work

**08** It's important to draw your line art in an organized manner, especially if your style is quite intricate. I usually separate each element into sets of layers, creating separate layer groups for the hair, body, background elements, and so on. I also always separate my outline layer from the finer details. This method will help you to keep track of your lines, which in turn will help if you need to change or fix something. Separating outlines from detail also helps when checking the overall shapes and silhouette. You can simply turn off the visibility of the detail layers, allowing you to view the main shapes on their own.

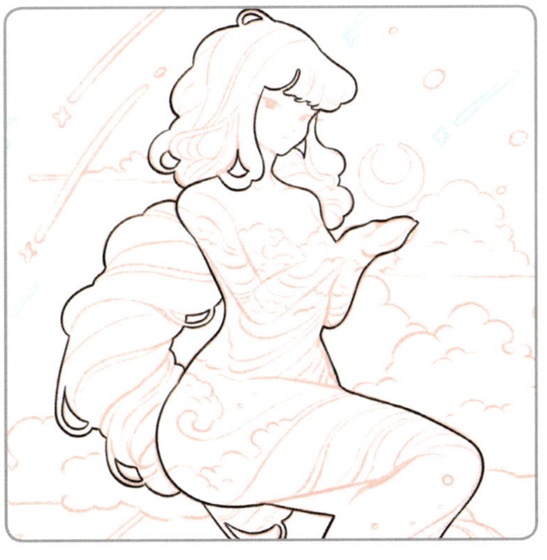

If working digitally, get into the habit of naming and grouping your line work

**09** Once you are finished with the outlines, check the silhouette once more. Are you satisfied with the shape of the main object? Is the composition too convoluted? It's always important to take a step back and analyze your work before continuing.

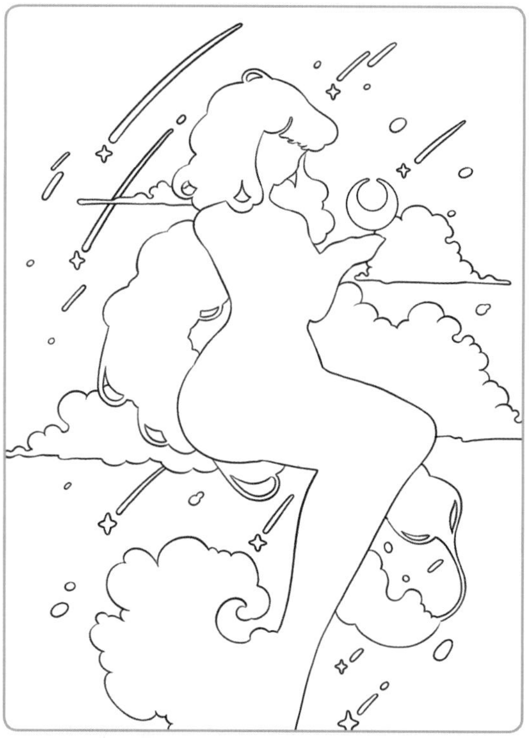

The silhouette we are aiming for in this artwork should be smooth, with lots of curving lines to complement the "ocean wave" theme

**10** When you are happy with the silhouette of artwork as a whole, it's time to start lining the details. Just as you did when first drawing the rough sketch, begin with the details of the character's face and hair, before detailing the rest of the body. Line the body before the wave patterns to ensure you spot any mistakes with the character's anatomy.

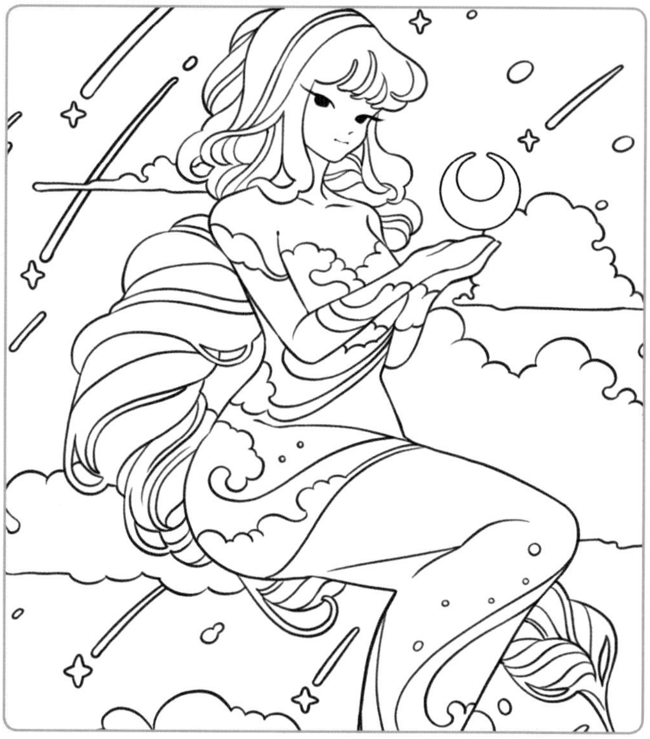

When drawing the line art, focus on the larger shapes first and save the most detailed elements until last

**11** After you have finished lining the general anatomy, start to line the detailing on the dress. When drawing repetitive patterns like ocean waves, alter the line dynamics and how the pattern repeats to give the design more variation. Here I use fluid lines to depict the flow of water and vary the spaces between the lines. Make sure your brushstrokes are smooth to avoid a patchy look.

It's important to maintain a similar line weight to ensure the waves appear cohesive

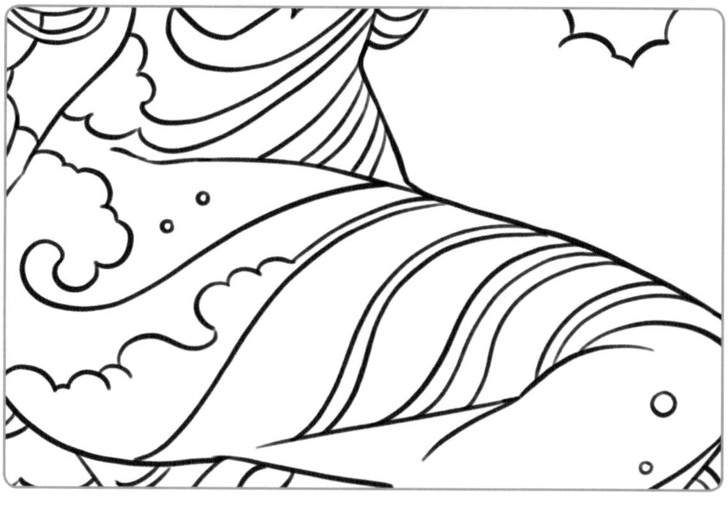

**12** Continue to line the details of the wave crests and clouds, using small, curved lines to illustrate the soft, almost fluffy look. The wave crests should be soft but also frothy, so draw using smaller lines. In contrast, the clouds should look smoother and fluffier, which can be created using longer strokes.

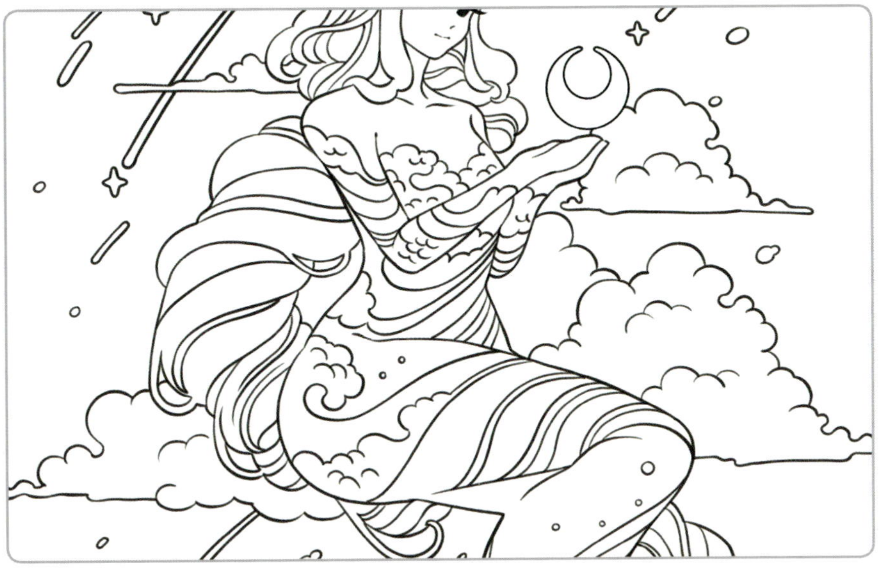

Consider what kind of look you wish to achieve with the line art, making use of references

**13** Begin to paint in the base colors of the artwork one section at a time. True to my signature anime style, I use flat colors with minimal shading. Keep your base-color layers organized to allow you to easily add or remove details later. All subsequent color details should be painted on new layers and clipped to the corresponding base-color layer with the clipping mask function.

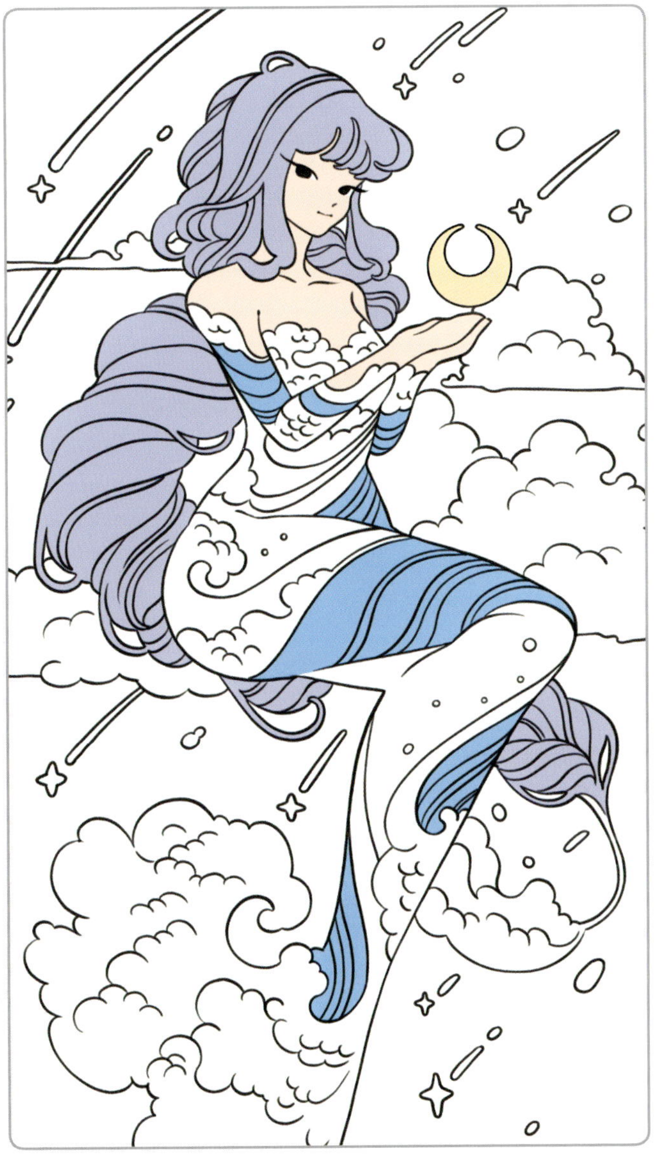

Focus on adding the flat colors of the main subject first

## ARTIST TIP

Style comes out of consistency. Instead of worrying about finding your style, focus on finding a way to draw that you can consciously and consistently apply over time. If you like drawing in a certain way, continue to practice this. The first time I genuinely found my personal style was when I stopped thinking about finding one at all. I made a practice of drawing every day, trying to find a way to sketch, line, and color with which I was most comfortable.

**14** Start to paint in the colors of the wave pattern using several shades of blue, ranging from cool to slightly warmer shades, to add depth. You can also achieve more depth by varying the saturation and darkness of the colors. Here I use four different blues and one shade of purple, and will use this same purple color for the hair. Avoid introducing too many colors, as this can make the artwork look overly busy or complex.

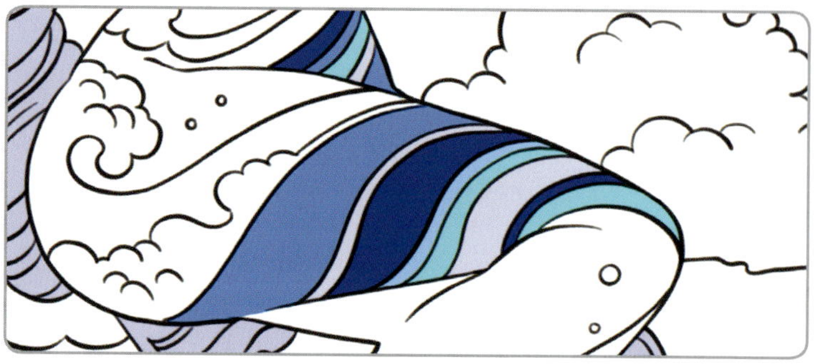

Experiment with different levels of saturation and hue, as well as varying the degrees of darkness and light, to add depth

**15** Paint each strand of hair, selecting colors from the palette used for the wave pattern on the dress. This will create a visually pleasing harmony between the hair and dress, as well as making it look as though the character's hair is also made of waves. Paint thin white streaks on top of the purple strands to suggest fluidity and detail.

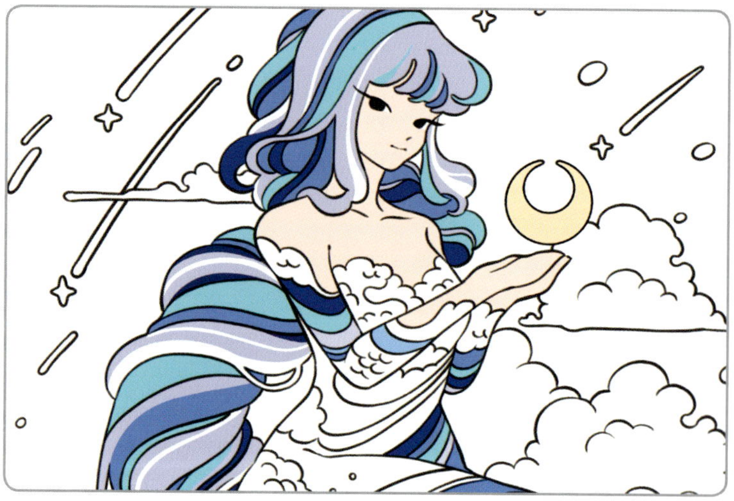

Using the same colors throughout your artwork will create a more cohesive appearance

**16** Start painting the wave crests with color, using three different shades of blue to create a sense of depth. Feel free to vary both the saturation and darkness of your chosen colors. Keep the top parts of the wave crests uncolored to show where the light hits at the top of the foam.

Using as few as three different shades of the same hue can suggest depth

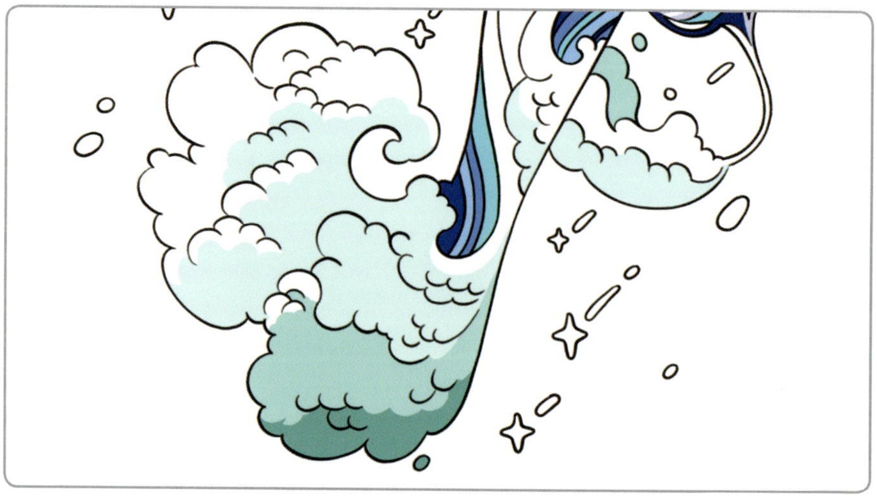

**17** Using minimal colors in the background will help to keep the focus on the character. Color the clouds using one shade of pale blue, leaving the tops white to show where the light hits – this will make them look soft and light. Use slightly different pastel colors for the stars and the character's tail to add variety.

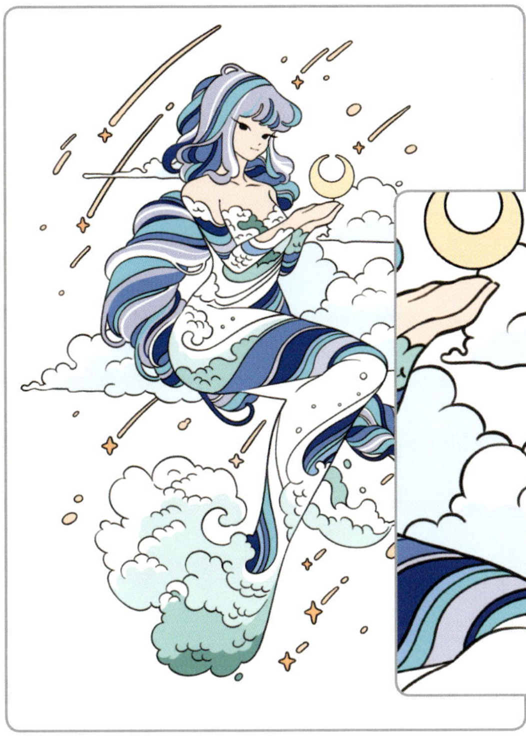

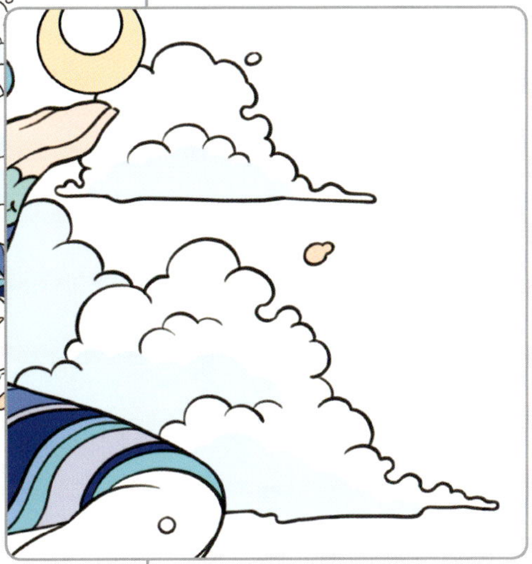

Using soft pastel colors for the background will match the overall color scheme and won't distract from the character

**18** Once you have finished painting the flat colors, look at the artwork as a whole and decide if there's any shading you would like to add. Occasional shading can draw more focus to certain parts of the artwork, or create balance to the entire color composition. Here, I add pink shading to the face, shoulder, and hands to balance the color composition.

The pink shading complements the darker orange stars in the background

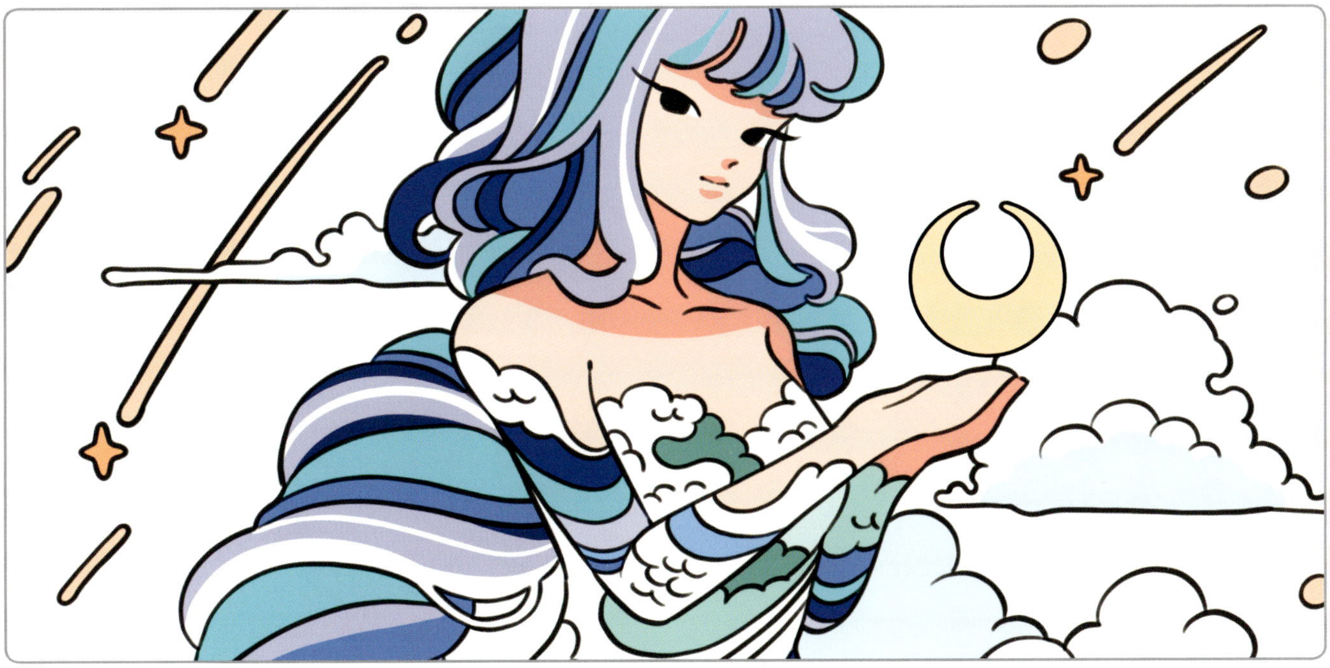

**19** The next step is to color the line work, keeping the outlines darker than the inside lines. Here I use a darker shade of blue for the outline of the hair, followed by a brighter, more saturated shade of blue for the individual strands. If working digitally you can use the eyedropper tool to select the base color of each area, and then make the corresponding lines slightly darker and less saturated. For the background, use light colors to ensure the lines appear softer than those used for the character. When creating my signature anime-style artwork, I typically use darker, less saturated colors for outlines, and lighter, more saturated colors for details.

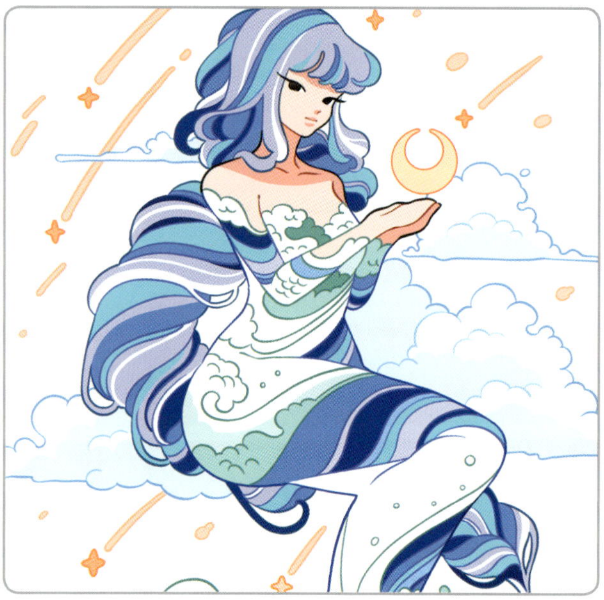

Coloring the line work will make the lines look softer and add to the color harmony

**20** Add a flat background color to the artwork. As the character and celestial background elements are largely made up of light pastel tones, choosing a slightly darker color for the background will make these stand out. Here I choose a darker purple-blue color to suit the monochromatic palette of the main subject.

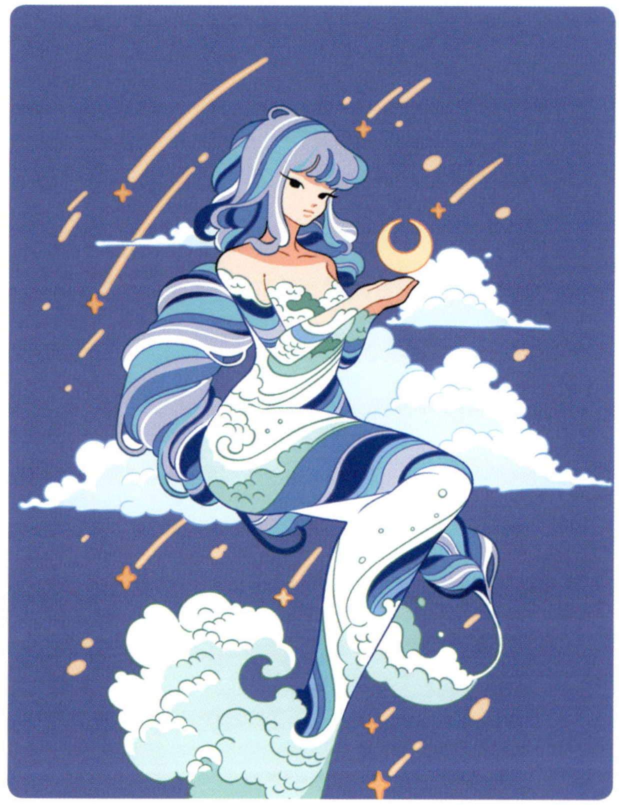

A darker background helps to make the character and pastel background elements stand out

**21** Adding a soft, glowing effect to the moon will create visual interest and a touch of magic. Do this by duplicating the layer containing the color of the moon, then applying a Gaussian blur effect to the duplicate layer. Use a large radius for this to ensure the glow effect is soft and diffused. When adding effects to your artwork, consider whether they suit the atmosphere you wish to create.

Creating a glowing effect on the moon will enhance the magical mood

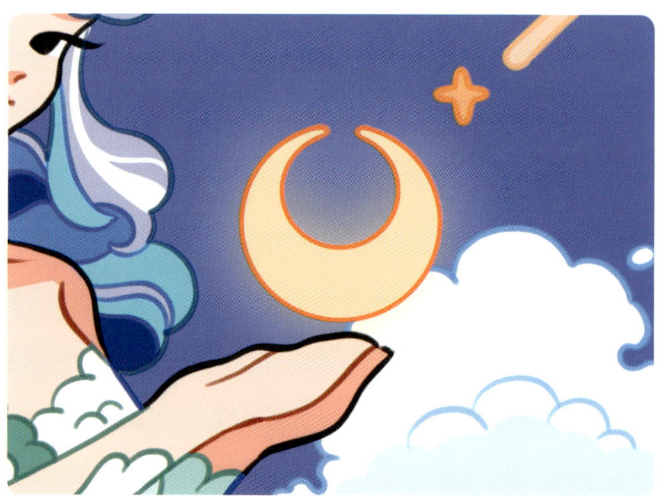

**22** Add this same glow effect to the stars using the method outlined in the previous step. To ensure the glow of the stars doesn't overshadow that of the moon, reduce the opacity of their glow effect layer. This will keep the effect subtle, while still adding to the celestial atmosphere.

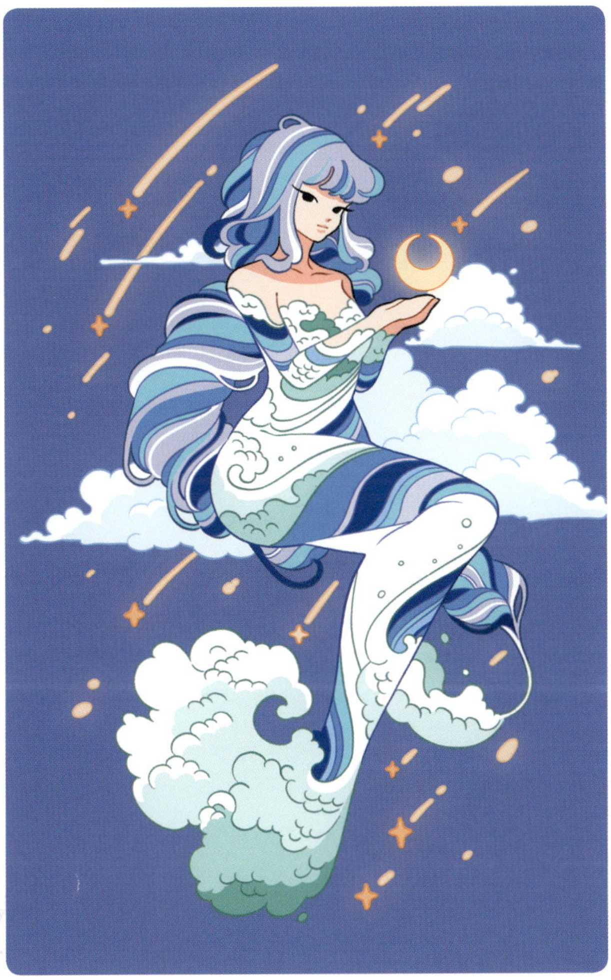

Creating a soft glow effect can bring extra dimension to an artwork

**23** Take a step back and review the artwork as a whole, making any final tweaks and corrections. Once you are happy with the final artwork, consider where you wish to share it and export the file into your preferred image format. I usually use JPEG or PNG, with maximum image quality, to ensure the artwork comes out as smooth as possible. I typically resize or reduce the quality of the image before posting it on social media.

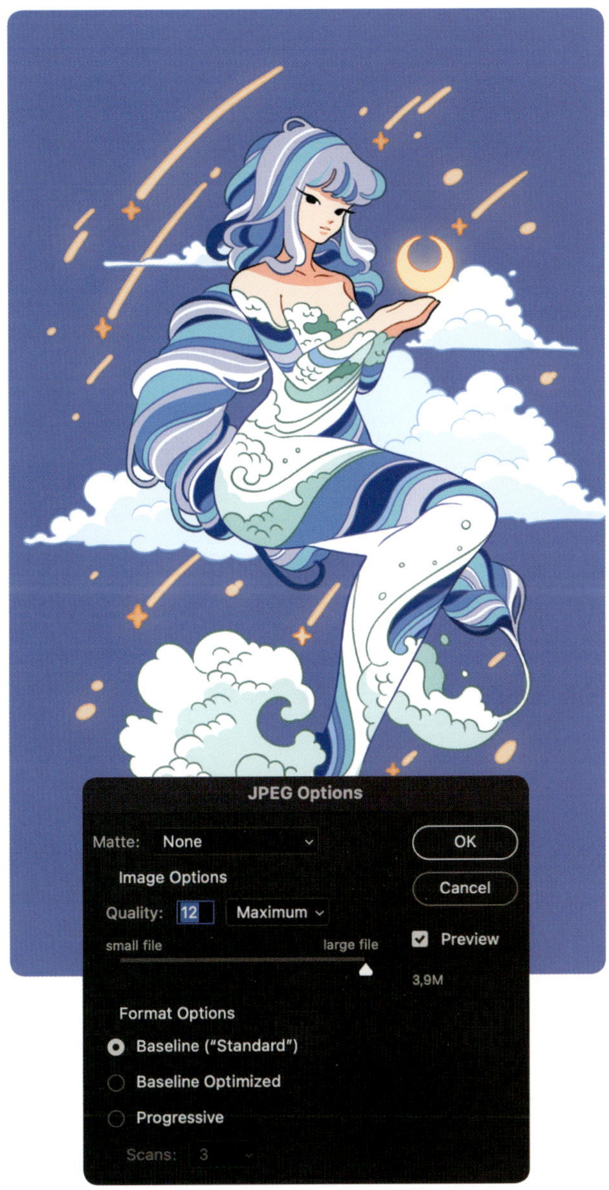


After you have saved your artwork at the highest possible quality, you will also need to make a copy and resize this before posting online

**24** If you plan to post your artwork on social media, experiment with editing the final colors on your phone first. Don't be afraid to increase the saturation and play around with the hues. Try tweaking the exposure, contrast, and saturation until you find a result you like. I like to increase the sharpness of my artwork to ensure all of the details are visible when viewed on a phone. The final image often looks quite different from how it looked on my computer.

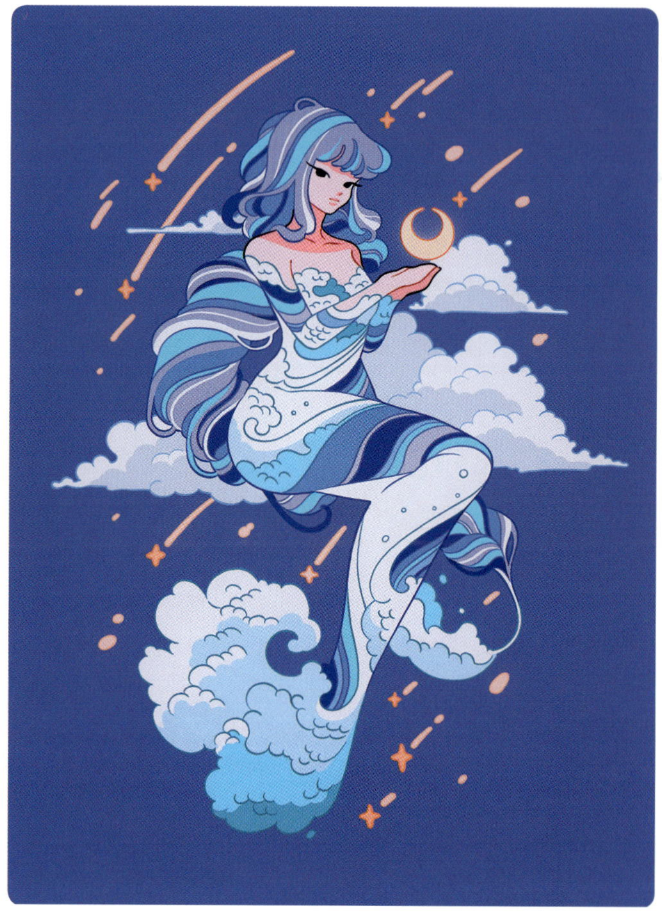

Editing your artwork on your phone will allow you to control how the colors will appear once posted on social media

# CONCLUSION

This final piece is a good representation of my signature style, due to its dreamy mood, subject, and colors. The use of celestial and ocean-themed details that flow into one another complements this feeling of dreaminess. When creating a new artwork, I focus on forming a cohesive overall image. While I keep my steps organized to make the workflow easier and faster, I also try to step away and look at my work from a bird's eye view, observing the entire process at once.

When you work as a professional artist, you need to be comfortable with imperfection and learn to focus on your long-term goals. Pay attention to how you draw, to what you like drawing, and to your preferred way of drawing. All of this will shape your style, as well as a drawing habit that suits it. If what you feel comfortable with differs from other artists, don't feel pressured to follow their style or method. Listening to yourself will create more authentic, unique artwork.

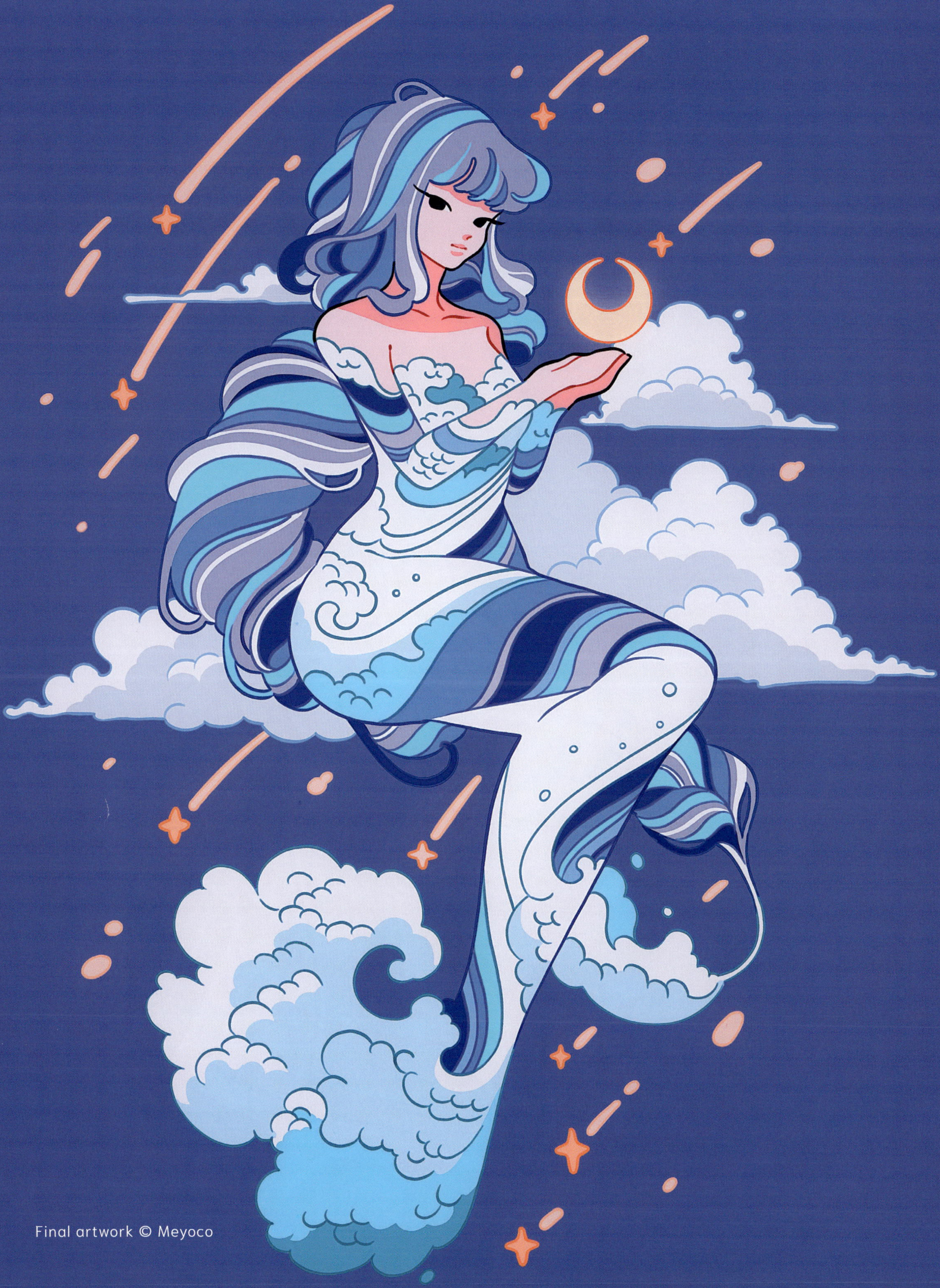

Final artwork © Meyoco

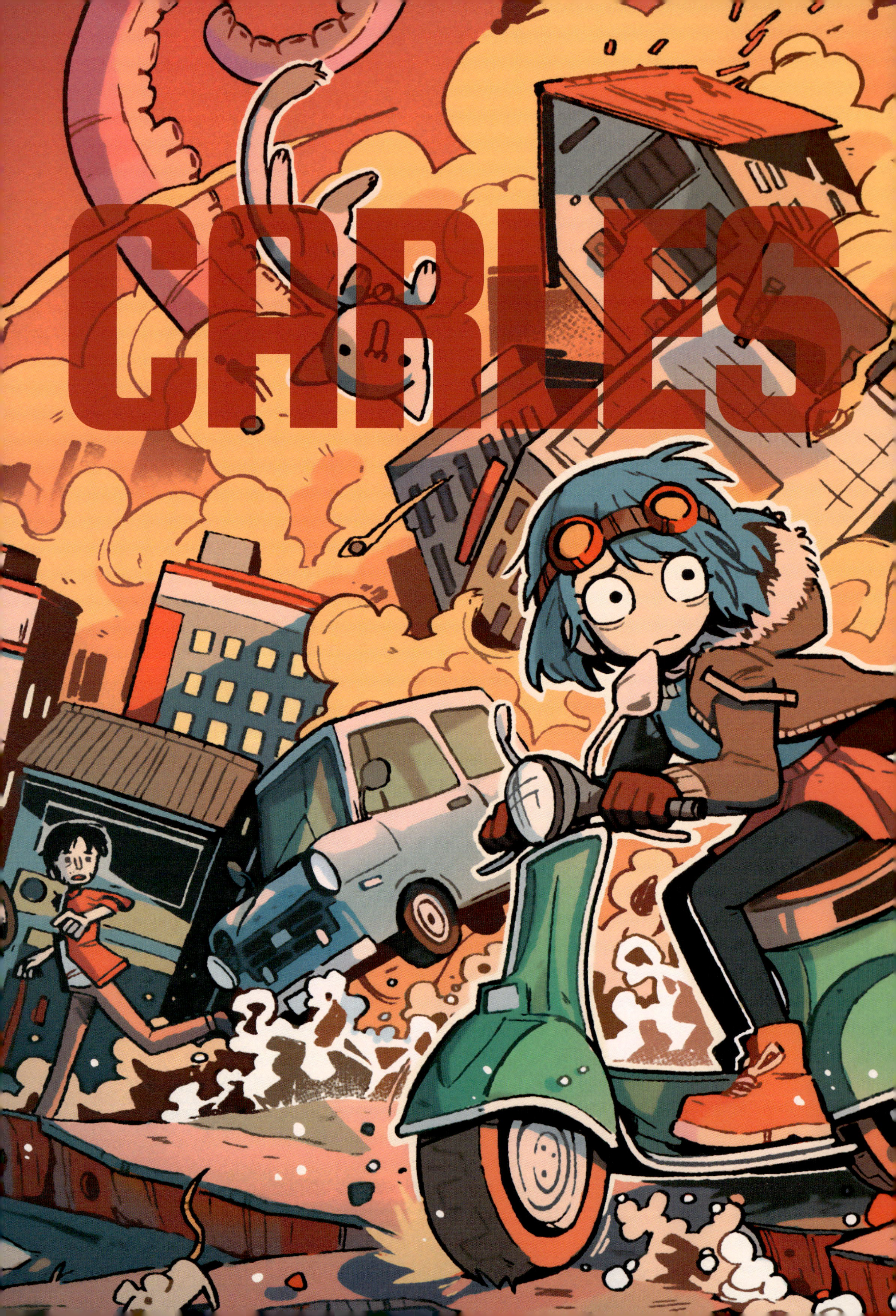
CARLES

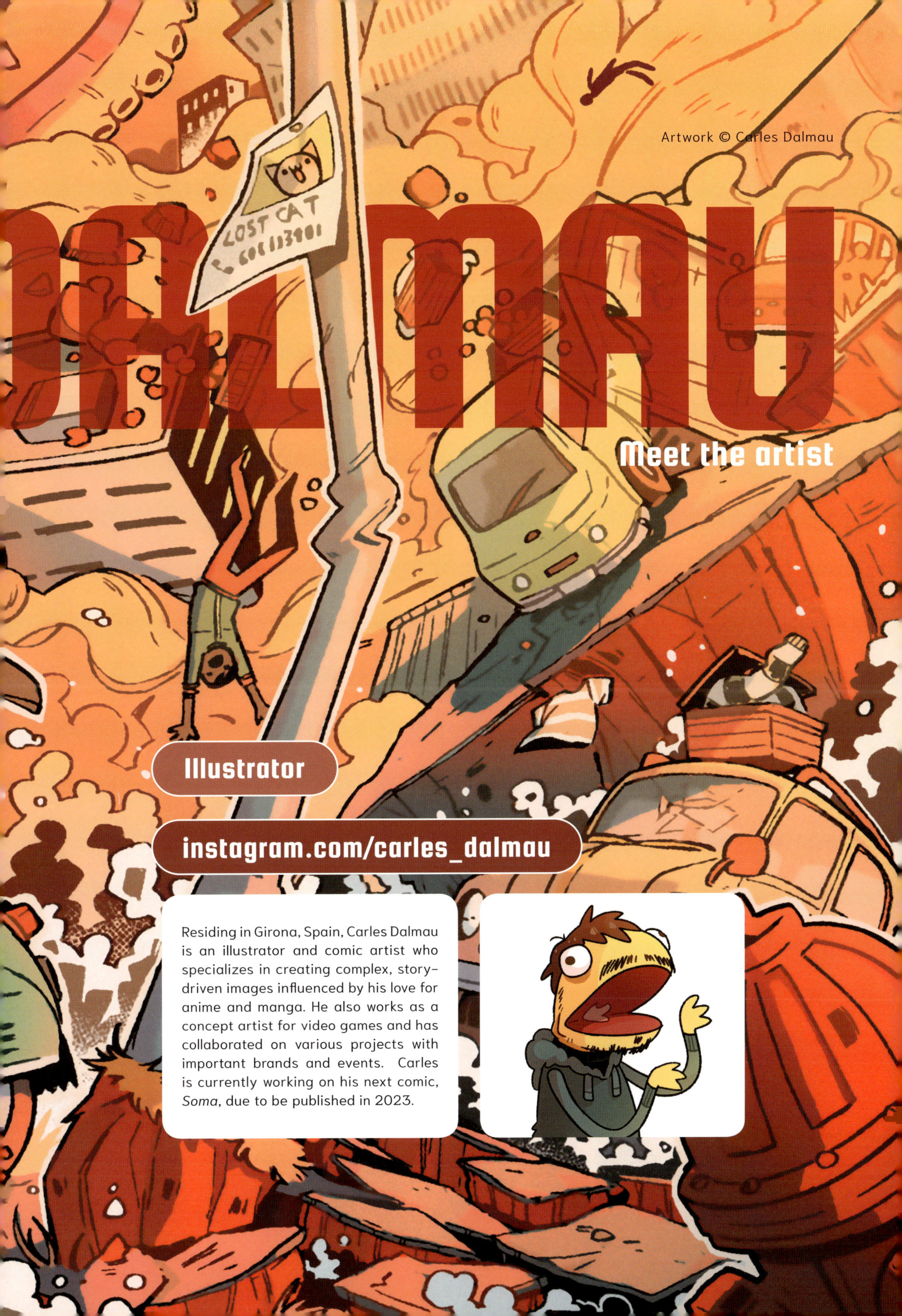


Artwork © Carles Dalmau

# DALMAU

## Meet the artist

**Illustrator**

**instagram.com/carles_dalmau**

Residing in Girona, Spain, Carles Dalmau is an illustrator and comic artist who specializes in creating complex, story-driven images influenced by his love for anime and manga. He also works as a concept artist for video games and has collaborated on various projects with important brands and events. Carles is currently working on his next comic, *Soma*, due to be published in 2023.

# CASE STUDY

All artwork © Carles Dalmau

## INFLUENCES, MOTIVATIONS, TRAINING

I've been interested in comics, manga, and the anime industry from a young age. My favorite childhood anime was *Sgt. Frog* and I always dreamed of one day being able to create something similar. I was the kid in class who was always drawing on tables and schoolbooks. As I grew older and began to think realistically about my future, I gradually stopped drawing and decided to pursue a standard career path instead. I thought trying to make a living as an artist would be impossible as I didn't consider my illustrations to be good enough, or have any connections in the art world to ask for advice. I ended up applying to study an audiovisual and multimedia degree in my hometown in Spain.

In the third year of my degree I realized I wasn't enjoying any of the college work, nor was I looking forward to a career in the field I was specializing in. It was at this time that I began to draw again. I didn't have enough motivation to draw solely for myself, so created an Instagram account to share my anime-inspired artwork with my friends. Over time my drawings began to improve and my online following grew. Though it has been a strange journey, and exhausting at times, the hard work has been worth it. All these years later, my main goal is still to create a comic and adapt it into a cartoon.

One of my favorite artworks from 2021

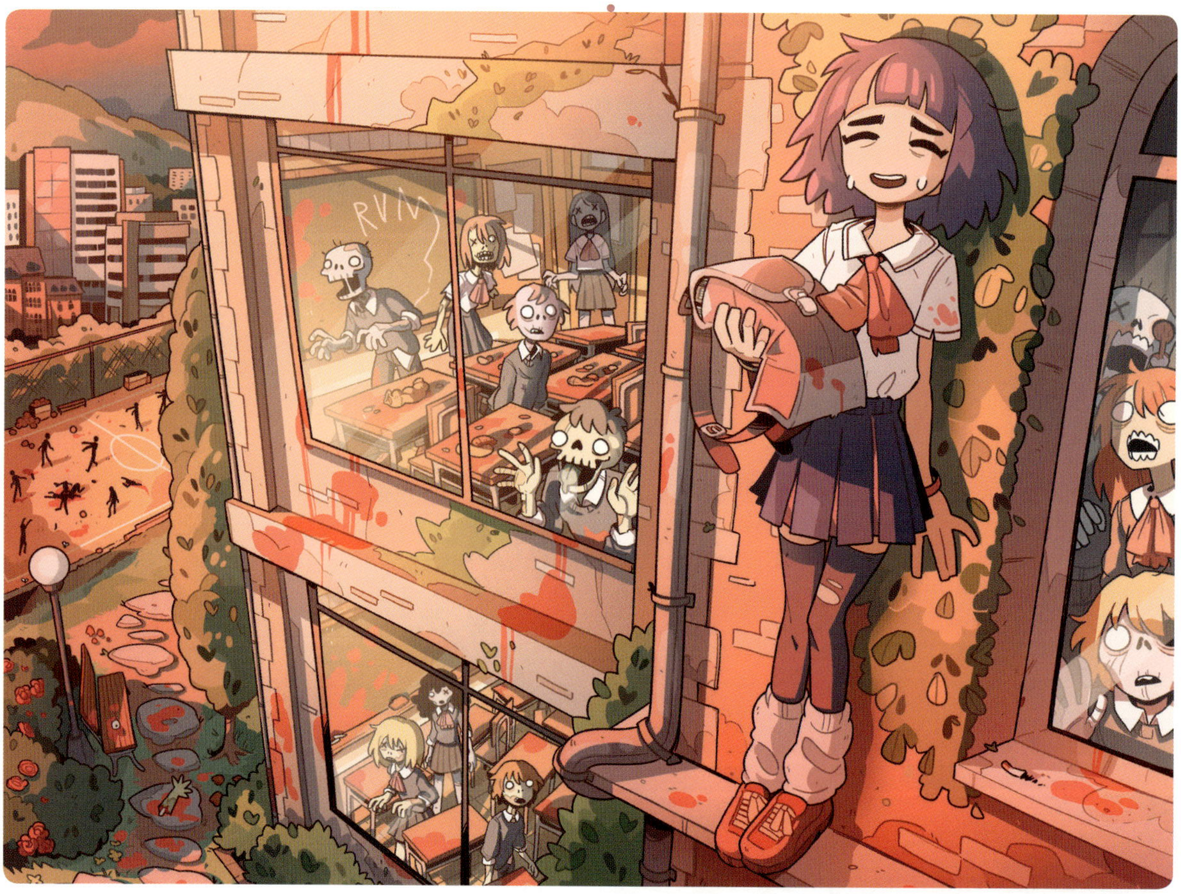

## Education & self-taught studies

Though my audiovisual and multimedia degree specialized in cinema and design, it never covered anything related to illustration. My frustrations with university were my main motivator to pursue an artistic career once I graduated. Even though I didn't enjoy the course, it was an important step on the journey to helping me realize what I wanted to do.

I never applied to an art school as I hate bureaucracy, preferring to focus on exactly what I want to learn instead of entering another institution. While I attended a couple of master classes, for the most part I am self-taught and my learning has been a journey of trial and error. In my experience, illustration is ten percent theory and ninety percent practice. After learning the basics, I spent many hours practicing. There is still much to improve in my illustrations, but with more time and practice, I hope my artistic skill will keep improving.

Two of my main inspirations were the art of Bryan Lee O'Malley (*Scott Pilgrim, Seconds*) and Inio Asano (*Oyasumi Punpun*). When I started sketching, I was frustrated that I couldn't draw as well as my favorite artists. Over time I learned that everyone has their own art style and trying to mimic a particular style will never come entirely naturally. If you put in the drawing practice, your personal art style will slowly start to emerge and will evolve over time as your skill improves.

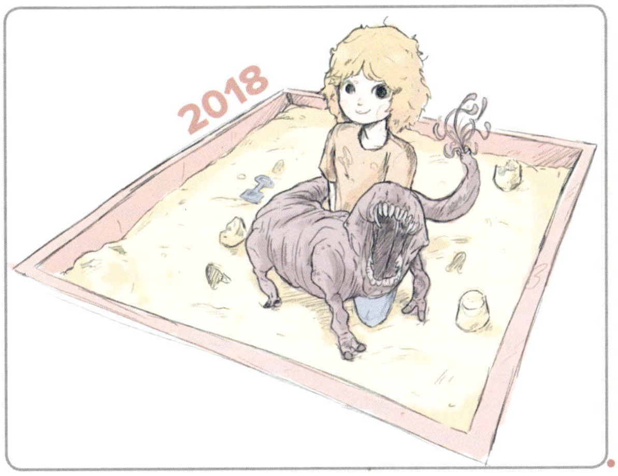


January 2018: This is my first digital drawing that I was truly pleased with

## Finding inspiration

When I'm working on an illustration, I like to hide myself away from the world as much as possible. I'm often impatient when I have an idea, and while I know it's not the optimal way to work, I prefer to capture it as quickly as I can, rather than spending too much time on research and practice studies.

I have a selective memory and my brain is a sponge for concepts and topics that interest me. As I read a lot and enjoy watching reports on the internet, this provides me with a wide-ranging assortment of stories, themes, and thoughts to draw on when searching for ideas for a new illustration. When you experience artist's block, looking at Pinterest, Twitter, and Instagram will always provide plenty of inspiration.

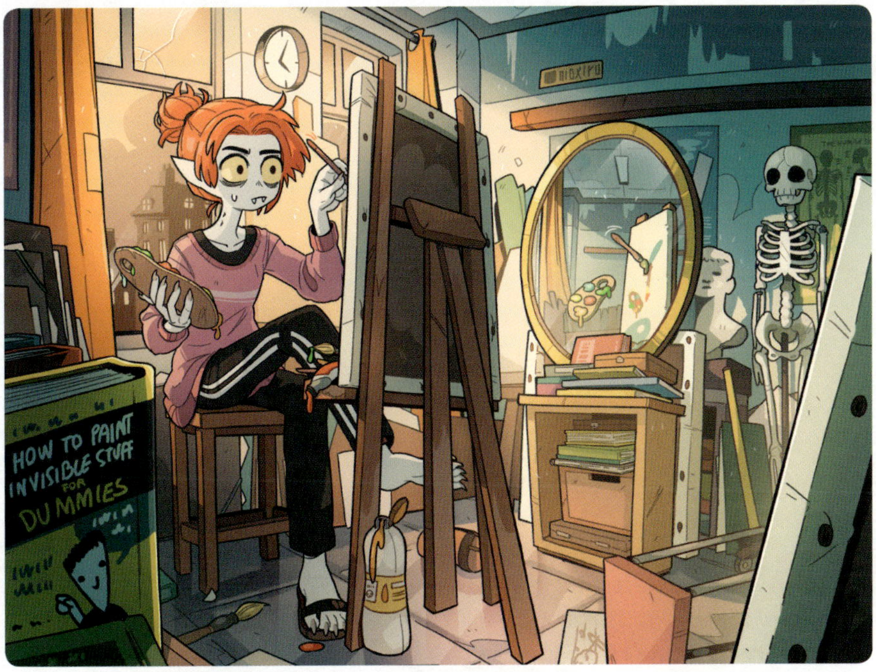


I had an idea for an illustration of a vampire attempting to paint a self-portrait and used my high school art classroom as inspiration for the background

## Representation & expression

I don't use art as a medium through which to express myself as a human being, but rather as an outlet at which to throw all of the random thoughts and ideas swirling around my mind. To make these somewhat cohesive, I like to create original characters and the strange worlds in which they live where fantastical things can happen. When creating comics, such as *Lucid Lucy*, the main idea typically comes from a drawing I have already done. It's almost like working backward; I draw an illustration, then explore a backstory for the character and the world in which they exist.

I'm on the autistic spectrum and have always struggled with knowing who I am and what defines me as a person. I never thought about whether I could represent myself some way in my artwork until my early twenties. My illustrations are usually the result of random concepts and imaginings, yet I think there's a deeper meaning in some of them. While I wouldn't say they represent me, they are still a part of me in some way.

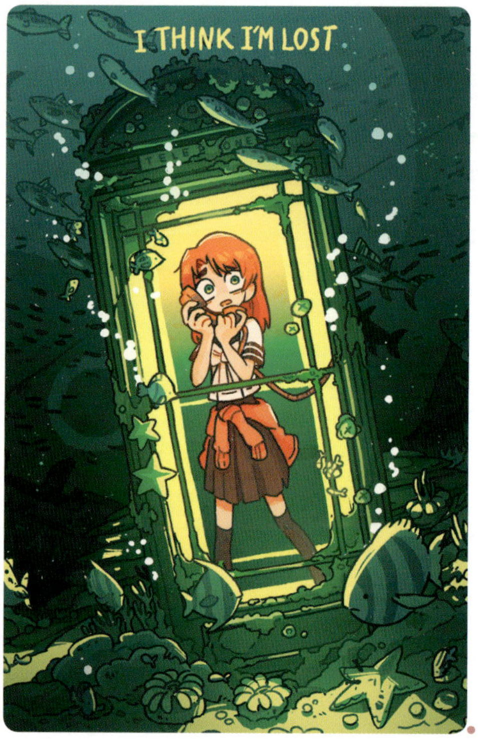


*Lucid Lucy* – I drew this illustration before I had even thought of creating a webtoon for her story

## Tools & media

When I started to take art seriously, I wanted to improve my skills as fast as I could. I wasn't keen on traditional media, so right from the start I drew digitally on a tablet using Clip Studio Paint and Photoshop. While I now know the smartest approach is to take the time to learn core art fundamentals before attempting to apply this knowledge to the digital medium, in the early days I just wanted to get better quickly and didn't have the patience for studying the basics.

It's important to actively set aside time to experiment with different mediums and styles. Pushing out of your comfort zone to explore a variety of avenues before settling on one medium or style can help you to discover what you like to create. Once you have chosen a direction, putting in the practice will gradually lead to visible improvement and your personal anime style will begin to emerge.

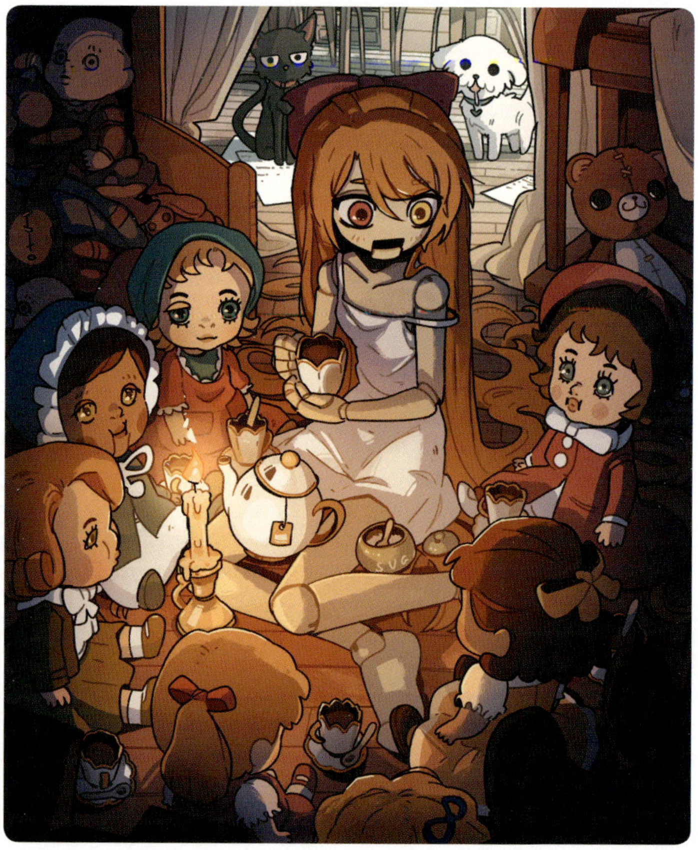

Working digitally allows me to work faster and quickly correct any mistakes

# INDUSTRY EXPERIENCE

Although my main goal is to pursue a career in the anime-style comic and animation industry, I try to gain experience from a variety of different mediums and fields. When you like what you do, it's always fun to learn new skills. Over the past couple of years I have taken on a substantial amount of freelance work from various companies around the world, including Clip Studio Paint and Netflix. At the time of writing, I'm currently working with Devolver Digital as a concept artist for the *Cult of the Lamb* video game. While I'm somewhat of a workaholic and work for around eleven hours each day, this allows me to balance my personal projects as well as my freelance work for companies.

The main differences between creating my own content and working with companies is the content itself and the style of the drawings. I have total creative freedom when creating my own anime-style artwork, but when working for a company I have to take their approach into account, both thematically and stylistically. When working on a video game, for example, I have to adapt my style to the one the company has already established. For this reason I try to work on projects that don't differ too much from my own personal style.

I use Instagram as my main portfolio, which allows interested clients to see the type of artwork I create. If I'm applying for a specific job, however, I create a portfolio tailored to the particular company or job role.

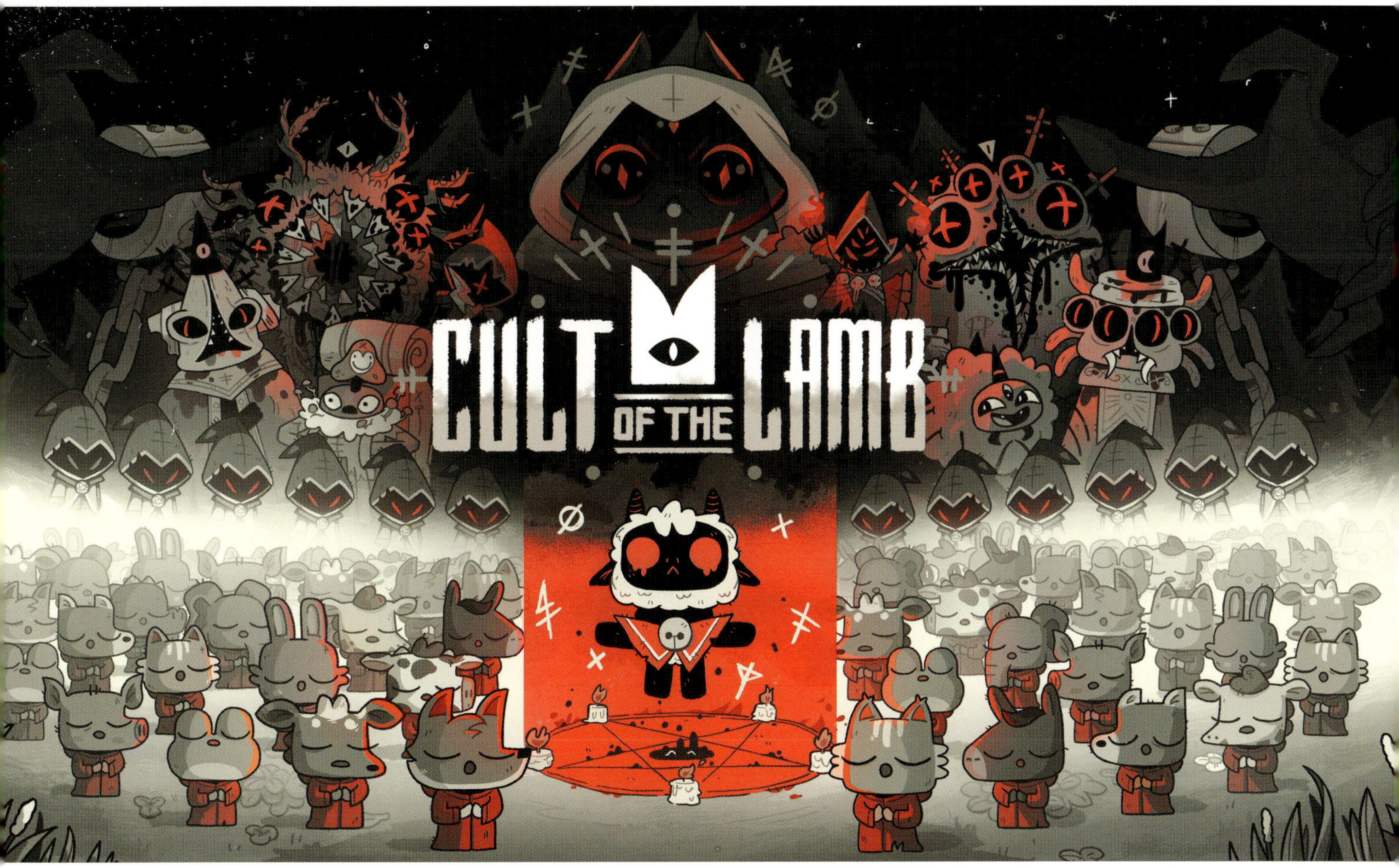


Cover art I created for the *Cult of the Lamb* video game

## Income from art

I made very little income from my first commissions. Over time more people wanted to pay for my artwork, and then companies and publishers started to contact me for work. Now my artwork is my sole source of income.

I prefer to focus on projects week by week, rather than forming a ten-year plan for what I want to achieve or how much profit I wish to generate. This mentality helps me to focus on the present and ensure I give my best to everything I do, instead of stressing about upcoming projects or whether I will find work. The fewer expectations and plans you have, the more everything that comes to you will be a surprise. Focus on creating artwork with your own unique anime style. Once you have built a good portfolio, clients and companies will start to notice you.

## Recognition

There was a period in 2019 when I felt burned out with my artwork and considered quitting. I've always struggled with self-esteem, but when this began to carry over into my artwork I questioned whether I was good enough to make it. That same month, Frederator Studios reached out and invited me to meet with them to pitch cartoon ideas to the company. While they didn't end up selecting my cartoon pitch, their recognition of my talent boosted my self-confidence and motivation, instilling me with hope for the future. I decided not to give up, but to work even harder to pursue my dreams as an artist.

That same month, an artwork featuring two of my original characters reached over 100k likes on Instagram. The fact that my following loved the content I was creating boosted my self-esteem. I will always be incredibly grateful to my audience for their encouragement, pushing me to become a better artist.

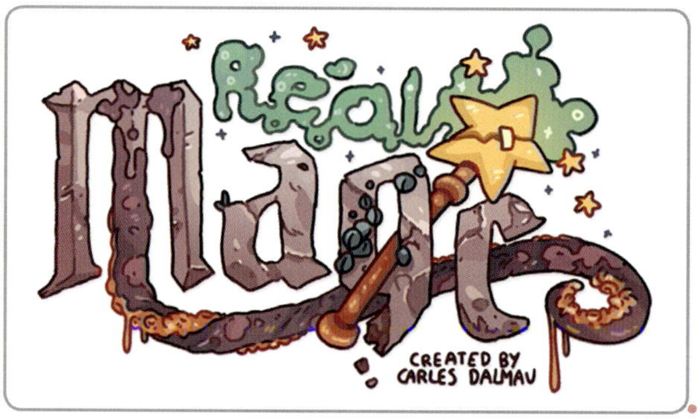


The logo for *Real Magic*, the cartoon pitch I created for Frederator Studios

# DEVELOPING YOUR STYLE

I started drawing because I wanted to create my own comics and TV shows like the ones I admired growing up, though my early drawing style is a long way off what it is today. While imagining original concepts and ideas has always come easily to me, I didn't experience the same ease when representing those ideas graphically. When I began to achieve commercial success, my style was similar to what it is now, but much less polished. I knew little about anatomy and my perspective was full of mistakes. I didn't know much about color, relying on Photoshop filters to make the artwork look better than it was. Learning artistic skill and developing my own individual anime style required a lot of hard work.

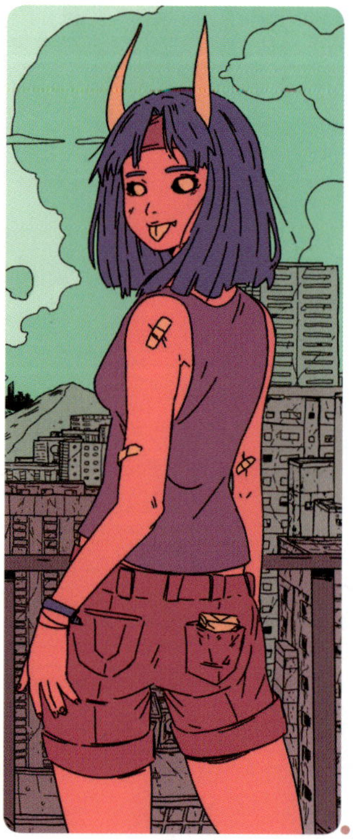

2018 – my first drawing of my original character, Coco

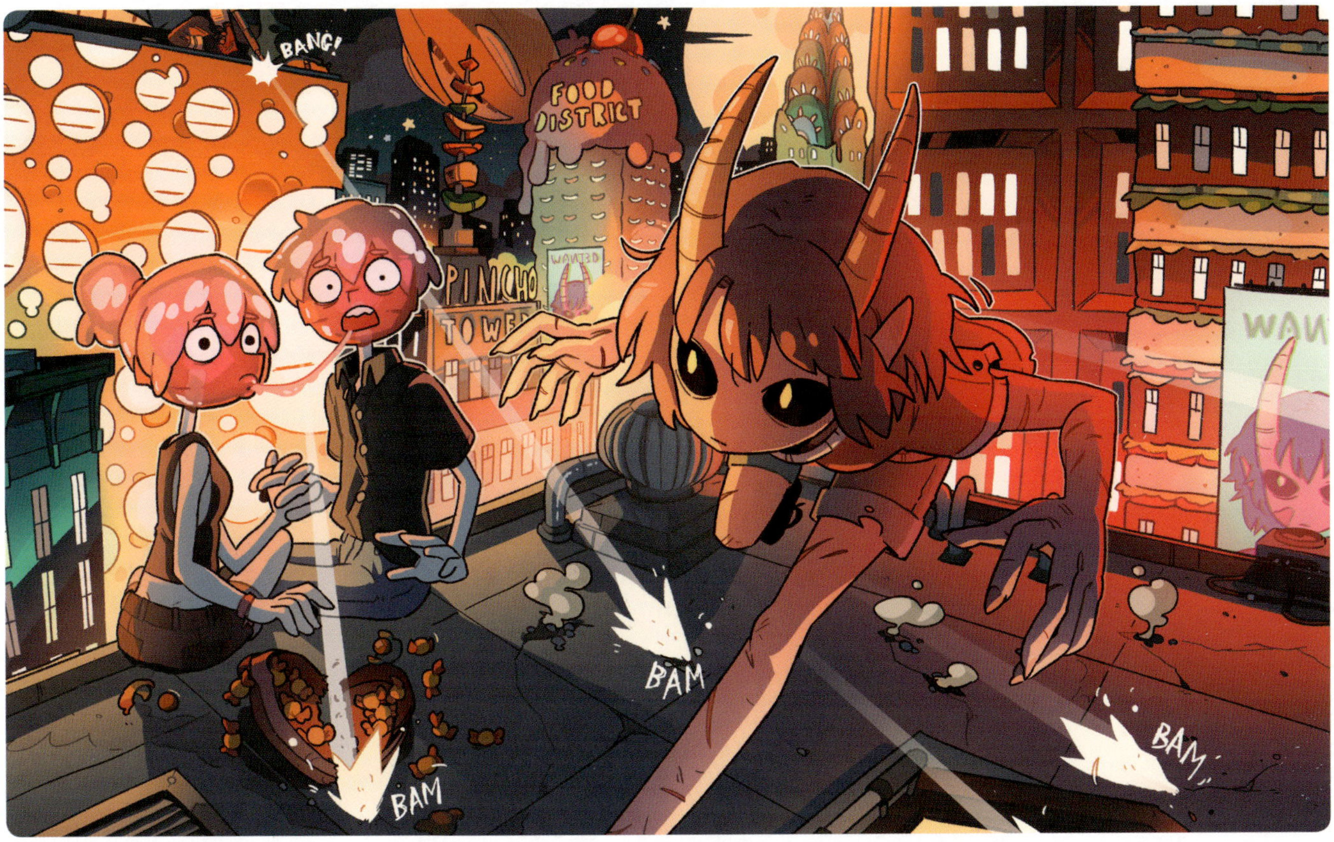


2021 – the most recent drawing of Coco, showing how my style has evolved over the years

I was initially inspired by Spanish comics, such as *Mortadelo & Filemón*, where the characters were more cartoonlike than realistic, yet each panel still contained lots of little secret details. On discovering anime, I wanted my artwork to take this style instead, but my understanding of anatomy was poor and consequently my characters looked very deformed. After reading the graphic novel *Scott Pilgrim*, I attempted to make my drawings similar to that in style. While it was a huge compliment when people said my artwork looked like this, I also wanted my style to be recognized as mine and no one else's.

Over time all three artistic phases combined into one and, with practice and study, my artwork began to look more polished. I define it as a quirky mix of Japanese, American, and European art styles.

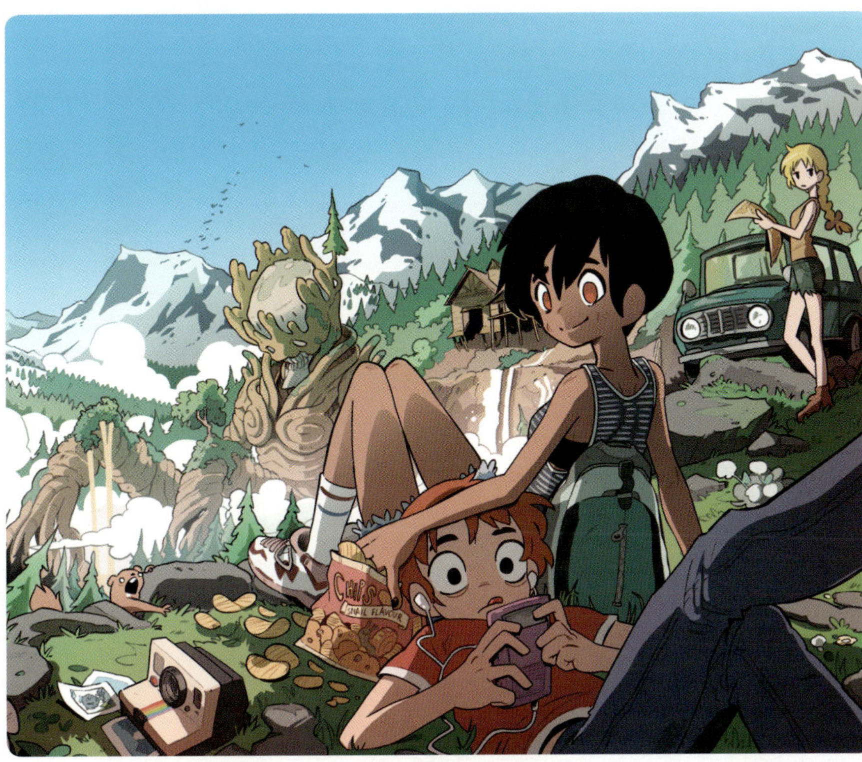

Looking at the boy's face, you can see the influence of Bryan Lee O'Malley's art

I improved by spending time overanalyzing my artwork to find the mistakes. My ability to capture realistic anatomy progressed when I began to practice gesture drawing for half an hour every day. I also worked on inking, coloring, and composition, trying to find a way to simplify the more complex elements.

Nowadays, while I like to look at what other artists are sharing on Instagram, Pinterest, and Twitter, I don't try to copy their style. If I see something I like in another artist's work, I may try to introduce a similar feeling or idea in my own illustrations if it fits with my pre-established style. Discovering your own unique anime style is something that comes naturally with time if you are dedicated to putting in the practice.

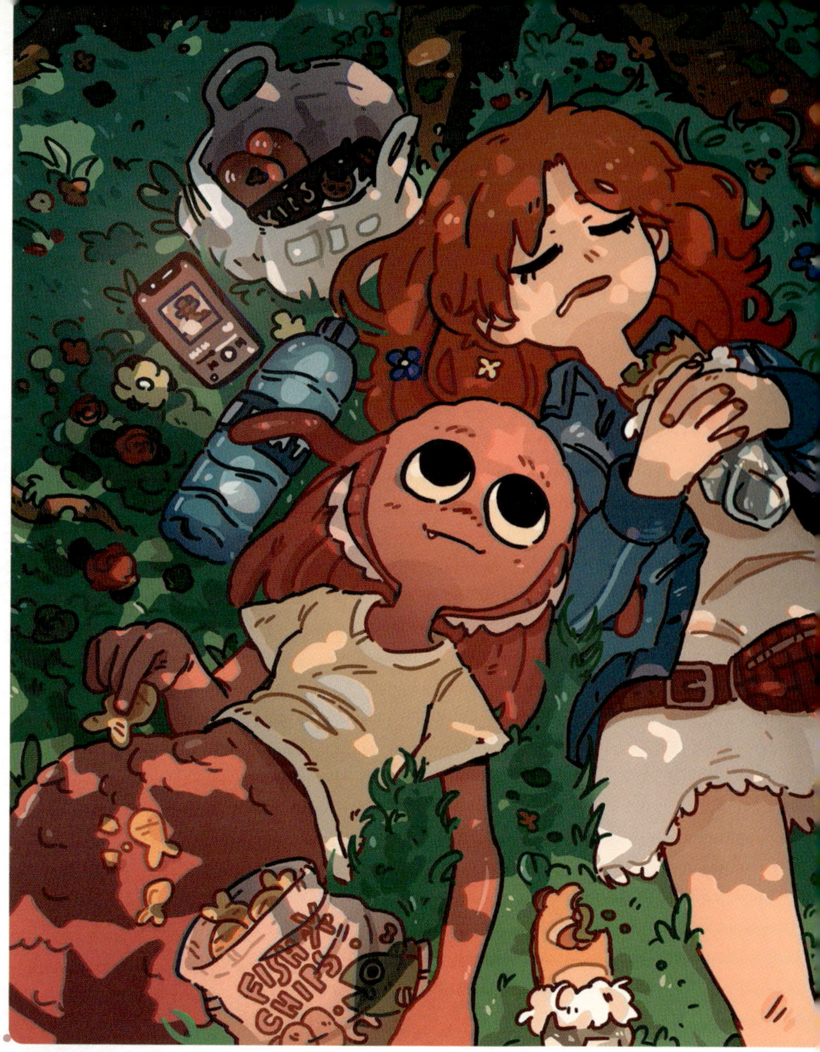


2019 – two original characters, drawn around the time I was starting to experience commercial success

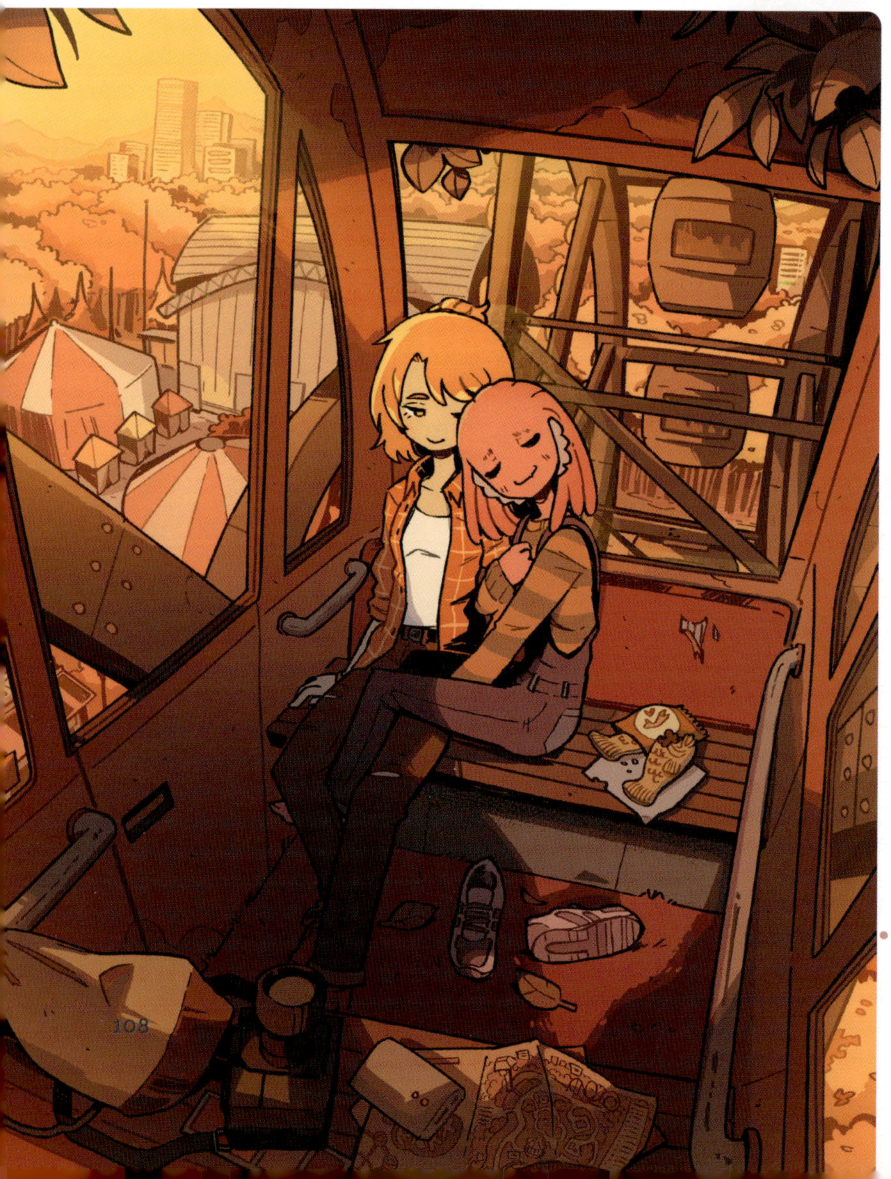

2021 – the same characters, redrawn in my current style

# Stylistic evolution

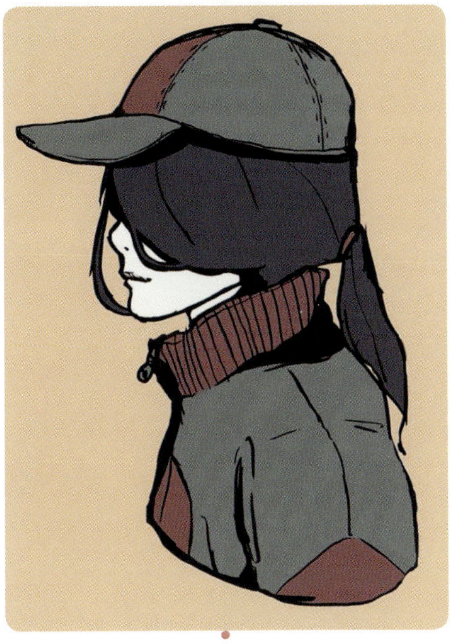

*Head*, September 2017

This was the first drawing I created without reference

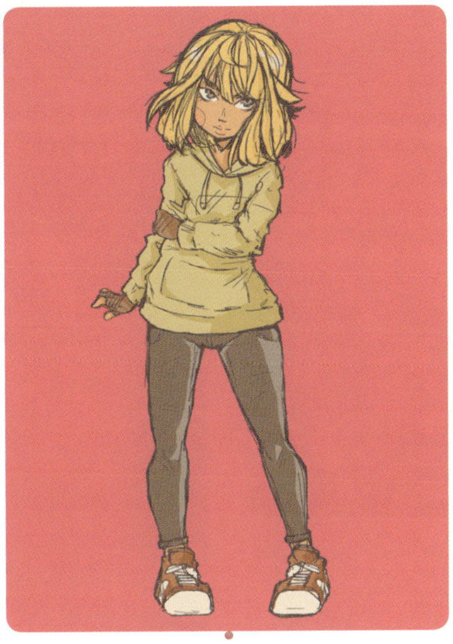

*Body*, February 2018

The first full-body drawing I created when working on improving my understanding of human anatomy

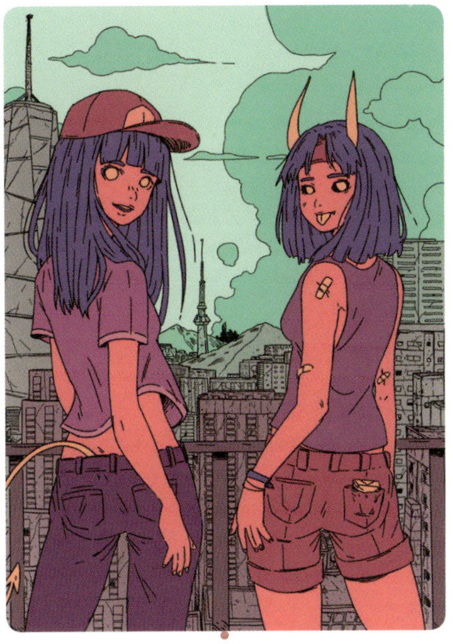

*Coco and Mei*, June 2018

My first drawing of my two favorite original characters

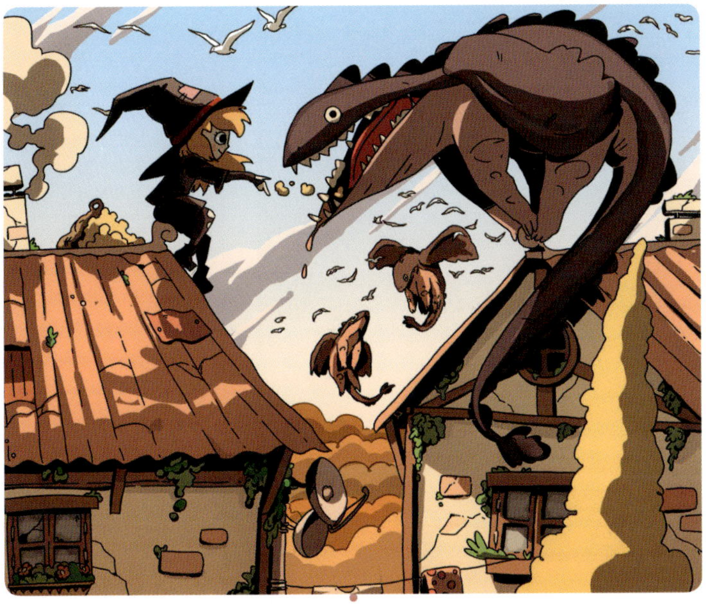

*Witch Feeding Dragon*, November 2018

This artwork attempts to tell a story, a characteristic of my current style of illustration

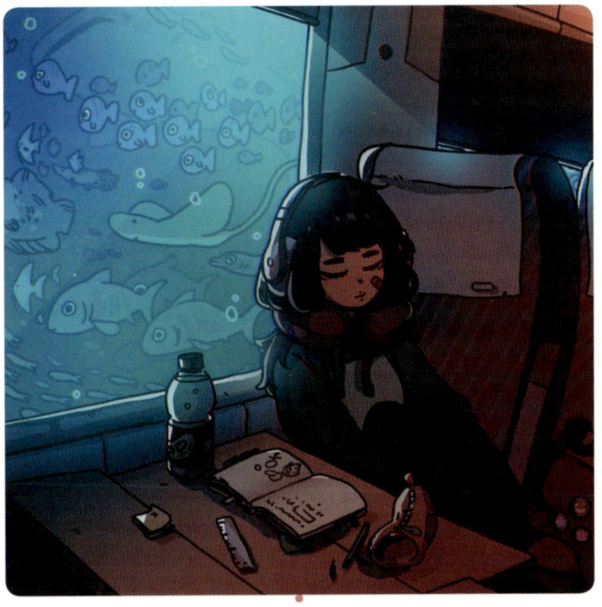

*Underwater Train*, May 2019

After studying color theory and Photoshop, I was able to refine my painting skills

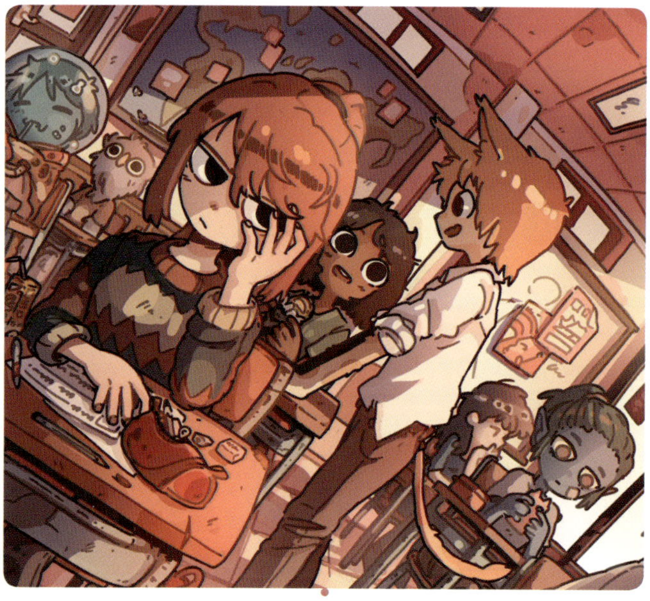

*Class*, November 2019

One of my first attempts at a more complex background

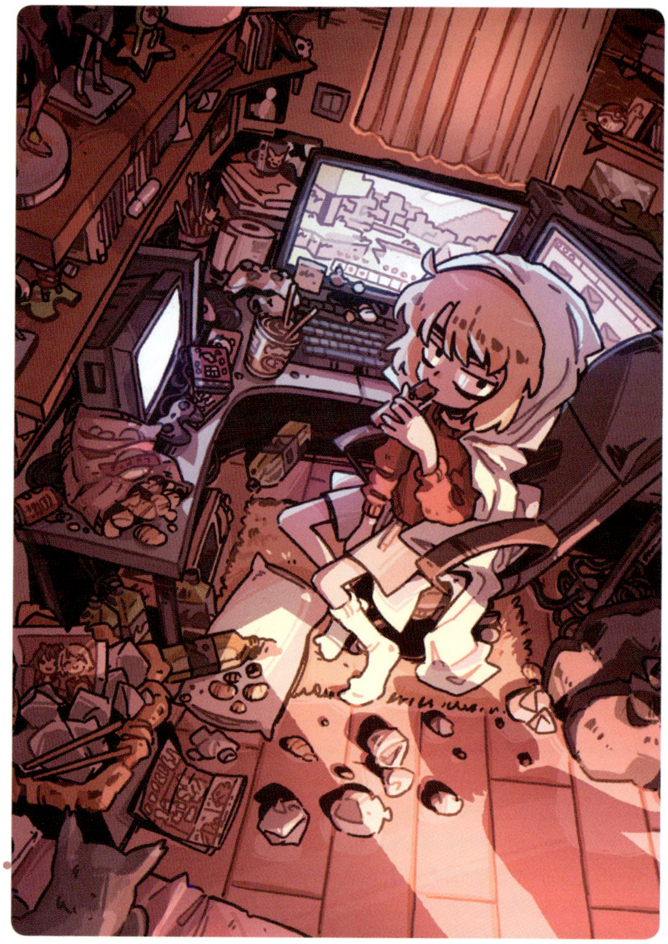

*Hikikomori*, March 2020

In this artwork I attempted to use cleaner line work

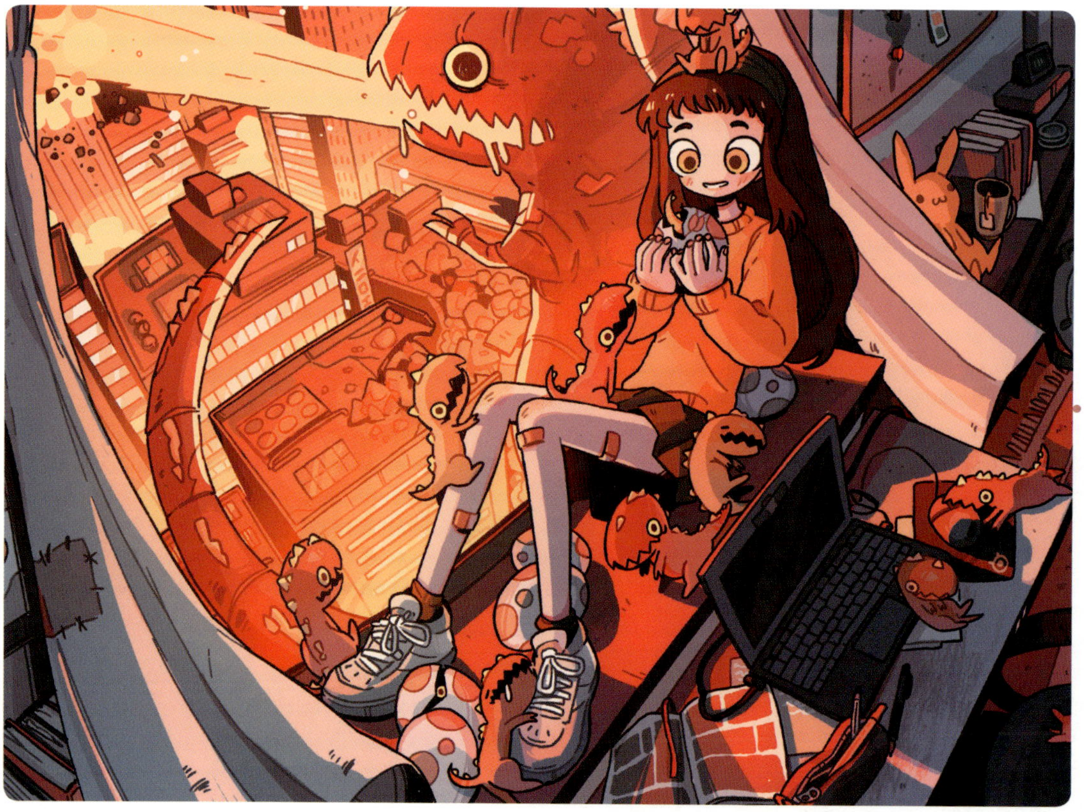

*Monster City Burnout*, August 2020

I was happy with the general improvement in the neatness of my art style, but acknowledged I still needed to improve my ability to capture character anatomy

*Coco and Mei, childhood scene,* November 2020

Comparing this artwork of Coco and Mei to my first drawing of the pair, I noticed the improvement of my style as a whole, as well as the development of the atmosphere elements of the illustration

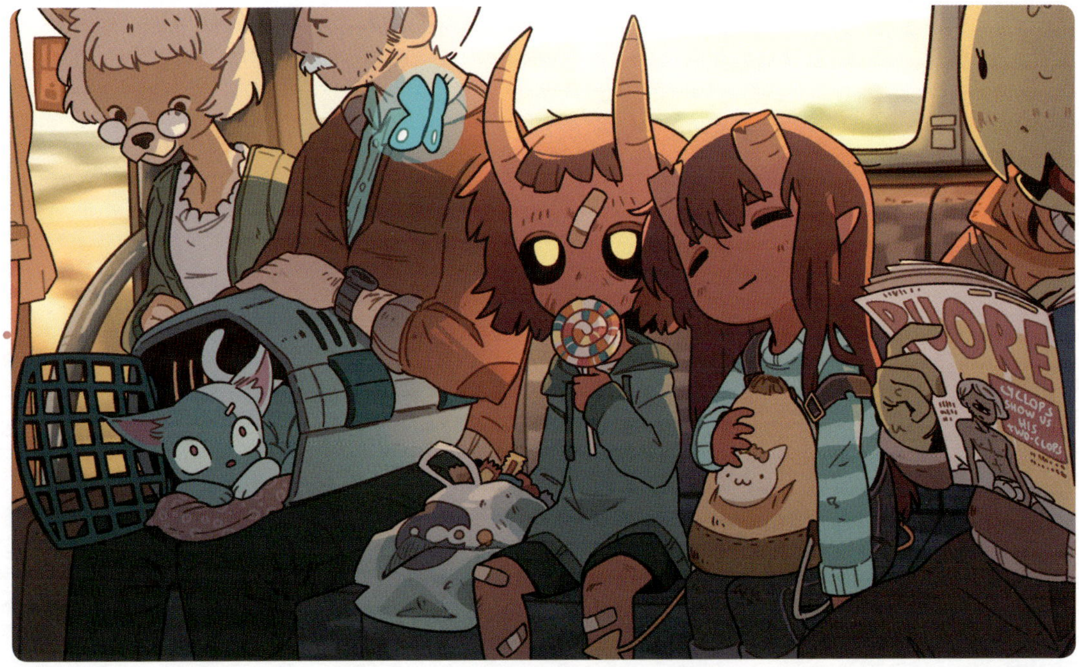

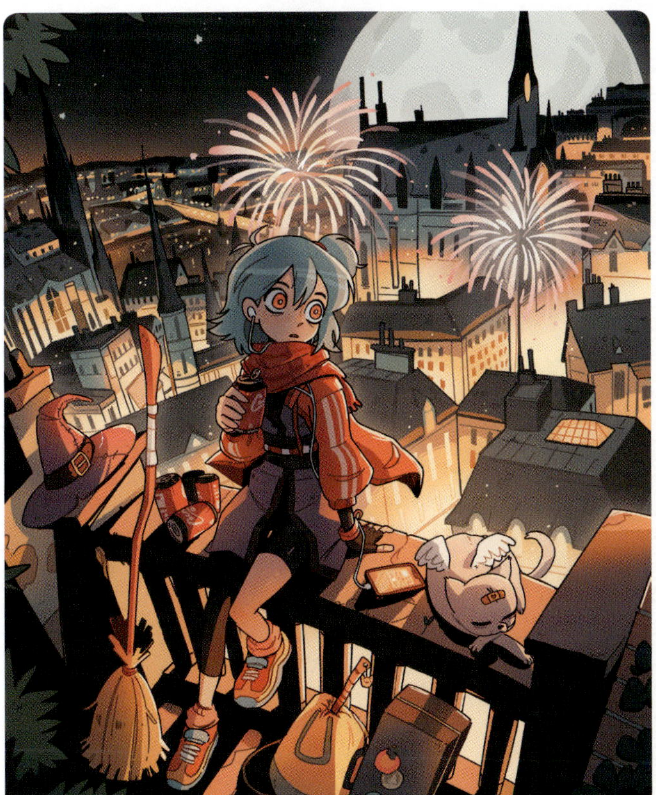

*Witch View,* February 2021

I practiced how to create a complex composition by simplifying different elements, with the style of character beginning to evolve into its current form

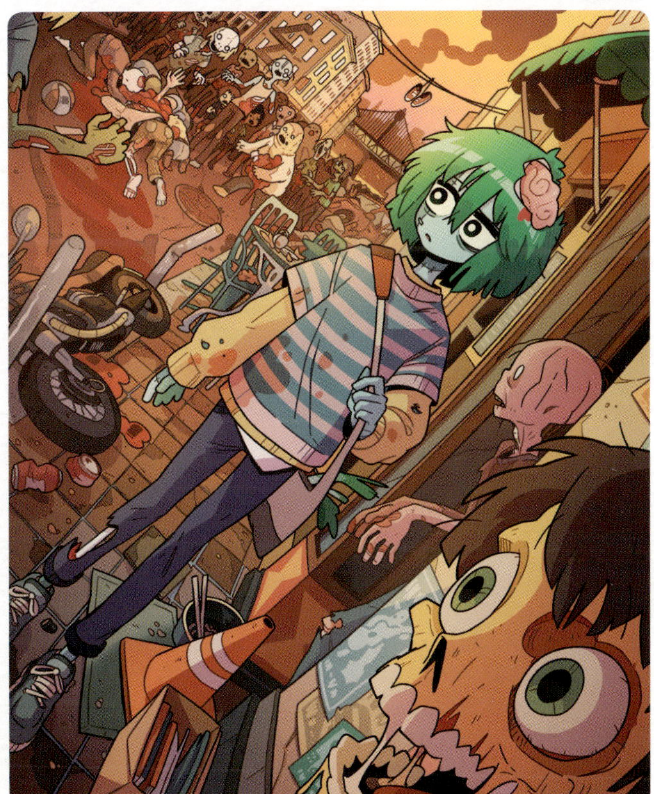

*Vegan Zombie,* December 2021

While I used to struggle with creating such complex compositions, I can now navigate them confidently and the style is identifiable as mine

# External influences

Even after you have put in the practice and developed your own anime style, it's natural to want to continue improving on this. It can be fun to take elements from external influences – whether movies, TV, comics, or even real life – and try to recreate them in your personal style. Experiment with what works in your anime style and what doesn't.

When creating my character's clothing, I was inspired by the *Bloodborne* video game

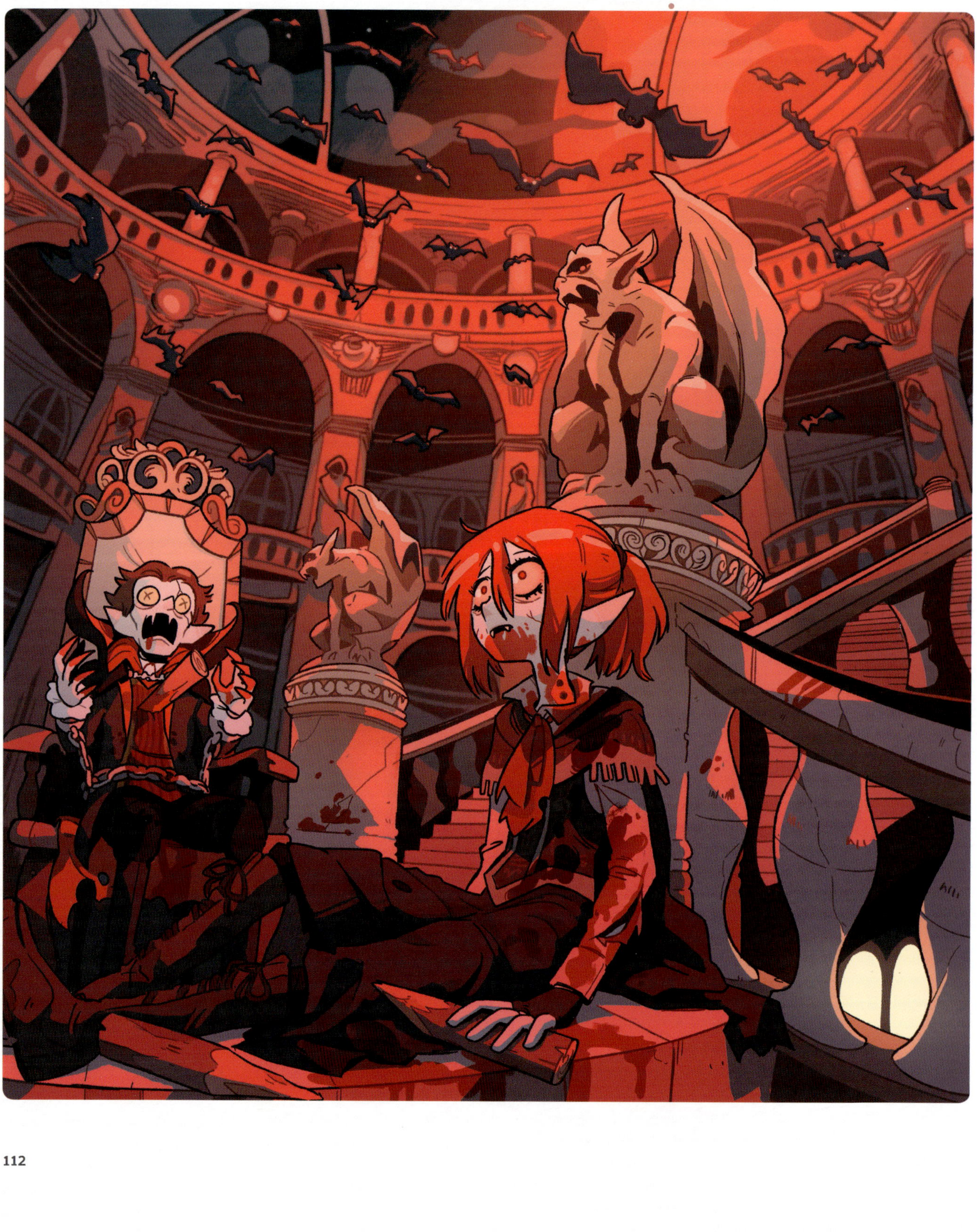

## Personal art in the commercial world

Sharing your personal art in the commercial world allows you to showcase a unique product only you can make, setting you apart from the crowd and shining a light on your talent. However, it's also important to be able to deviate a little from your signature anime style to enable you to find work. For example, if you are lucky enough to be the creative director of a cartoon, you will typically be given full creative freedom and can create the cartoon in your own personal art style. If you are a background artist, however, you need to be able to adapt your style to meet the creative director's style and vision for the project. The more you are able to adapt and show flexibility, the more work you are likely to get.

# BUILDING YOUR BRAND

My focus is on working as an anime-style comic artist, rather than building a brand. That said, in the age of social media, being able to create a brand for your artwork can help establish a name for yourself online and in the art industry. Additionally, it can allow you more artistic freedom when working on bigger projects, instead of having to adapt your signature style to fit with someone else's vision.

I consider my artwork and characters to be my brand, as this is what I am known for. One of the qualities that makes my artwork stand out is the weird little stories and quirky concepts that feature in my illustrations. When reading the comments and messages I am sent on social media, I see my followers trying to figure out the little situations, each offering a different imaginative narrative.

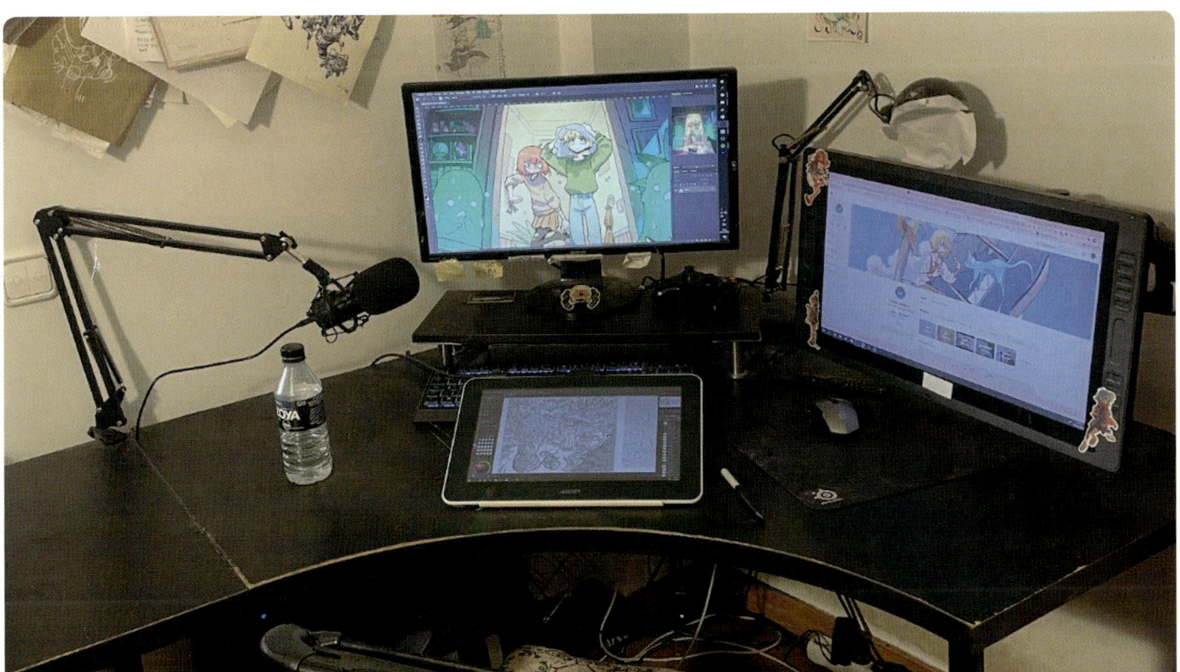

My workspace consists of only the tools and equipment I need – a tablet and two screens – to speed up my workflow and avoid distraction

## Growing your brand & online presence

The growth of my online following and brand has been fairly organic. I have been very active on Instagram ever since I first started sharing my work online and have seen a consistent increase in the number of followers over the years. I regularly post artwork and try to respond to as many messages as I can. I did try to pay for a promotion on Instagram once, but it didn't perform as well as when I simply share a post myself.

I use Instagram, Patreon, and Twitter to build my online presence. Instagram is my main account, as it works well as an online portfolio and I have the biggest following and engagement on there, however I also use Twitter to share drawings and details of what I'm working on. I post a behind-the-scenes look at my illustration process for my subscribers on Patreon, including speedpaints, tutorials, early projects, and any exclusive content I am allowed to share. Patreon allows for semi-consistent earnings each month, which is useful to have no matter how successful or far you are into your art career.

I'm not very good at delegating work to others regarding my brand, preferring to oversee and manage everything myself. However, as my focus is always on creating comics and growing my skills as an artist, I would one day like to have a third party to assist me with branding to allow me to fully concentrate on my artwork. When you work as a freelance artist and are trying to grow your brand and online presence, around half of your day is spent creating your artwork, and the other half is spent replying to emails and messages, as well as managing your multiple projects and commissions.

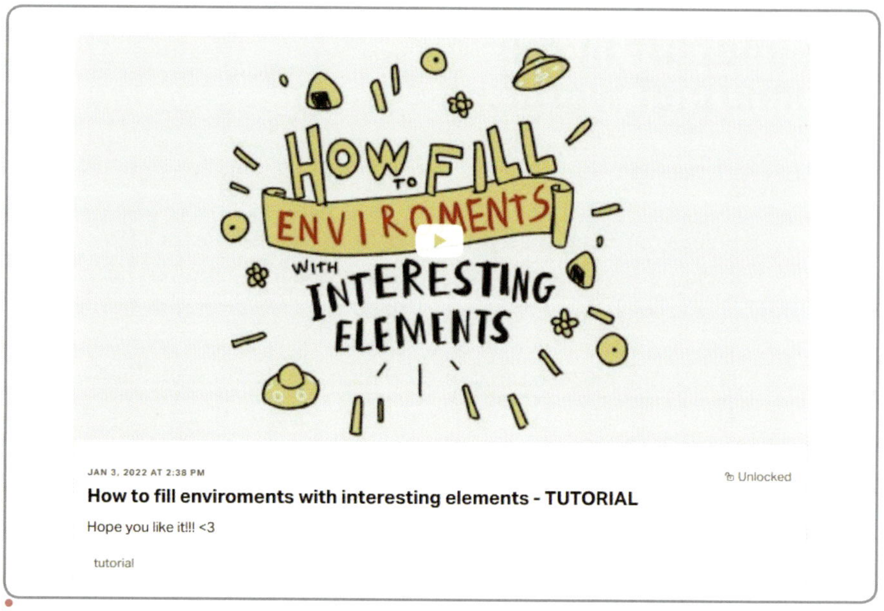


A tutorial post I shared with my patreons

## Influential brands

Hanabushi, Kim Jung Gi, Rinotuna, and Malbeni are just some of the artists whose visual brands I admire. Not only do I adore their fantastical styles, but I also respect their ability to maintain their signature styles and themes throughout their commercial success. Many artists have to sacrifice what they want to create in order to achieve greater success in the industry, which is a pitfall I wish to avoid. These artists inspire me to grow as a professional artist and brand without sacrificing the characters, themes, and style I love to create.

## Networking & cross-promotion

Networking is one of the most important things to focus on if you want to grow as an artist and brand. Connecting with other anime-style artists, as well artists from other fields and professions, will help you to find collaborations and freelance work.

As I sometimes find social situations challenging, I have mainly used social media as a platform through which to network and connect with other artists. The more my following has grown, the more that interesting artists and brands have begun to notice me. I started to talk to them, without even considering it as networking; I simply wanted to meet other artists working in the industry. Many of them are still good friends to this day. Don't feel like you need to force this contact, just be open to it. The best connections grow naturally from a mutual interest in the art you're making.

Attending anime and manga art conventions to sell your merchandise is another way to network with other professionals. While I can struggle with the social side of this, it's a great opportunity to talk with fellow artists in real life. One of the reasons I use my real name, rather than an art alias or brand name, is because it makes it easier to connect with other professionals.

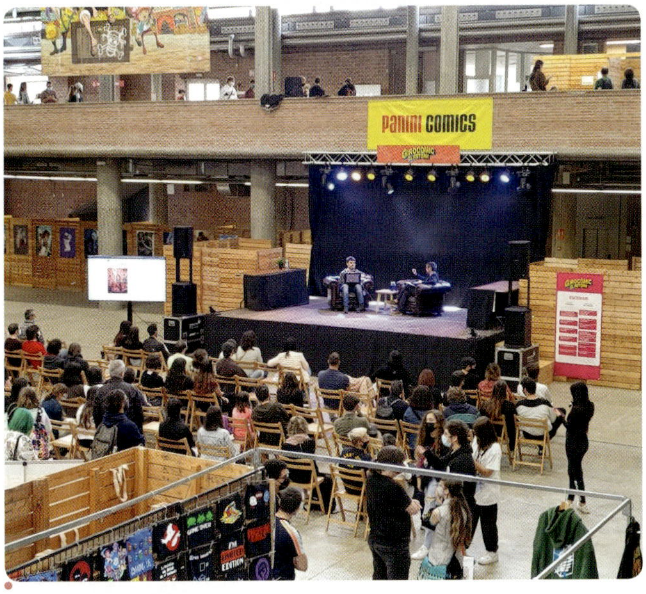


My first public speech at the 2021 Girocomic fair

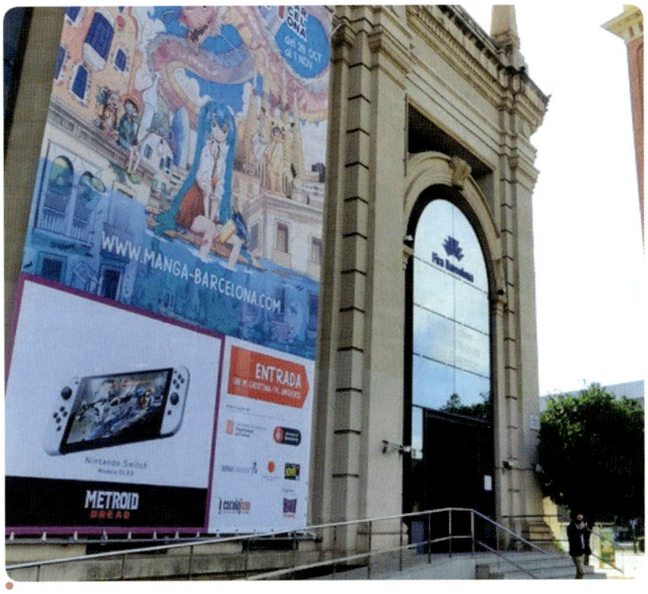


A photograph of the poster I created for the 2021 Manga Con in Barcelona

## Merchandise

When planning what prints, tutorials, or merchandise to offer, I try to commercialize the artwork I like most and would pay money for as a customer. The best marketing I can offer is to make my customers excited by what I sell.

At present my focus is on collaborating with brands. When a company approaches me with an attractive collaboration, I enjoy investing my time and skills creating artwork for the project. I collaborated with Clip Studio Paint to create a tutorial and a webinar, as well as creating courses for the Spanish art schools Ilumina and Paper Monsters. These collaborations were a good investment and I received really positive feedback. I also like to work on merchandise collaborations, such as designing personalized caps with CityCaps and creating t-shirt and print designs for TeePublic and Redbubble. These platforms allow you to make an income from your artwork.

Recently I worked with Norma Editorial to create a 2022 calendar, as well as collaborating with Magpie Cards on a personalized card deck. At the time of writing, I am talking to more art schools about creating courses for them and plan to sell an art book later this year. I am always developing exciting projects behind the scenes.

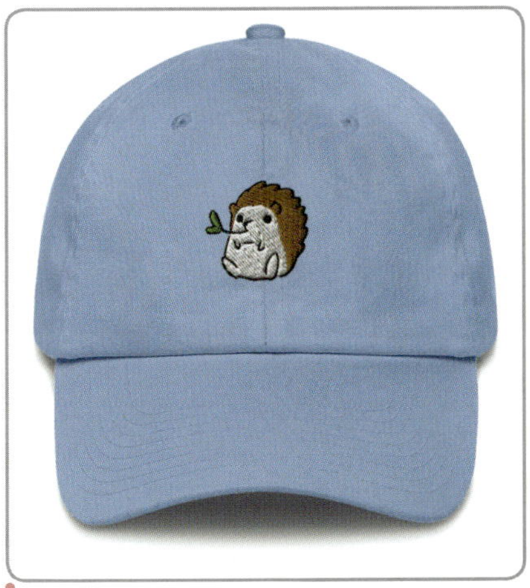

A cap I created with CityCaps

## Pricing

I aim to make my illustrations as polished and engaging as possible, in the hope that my followers will like them enough to invest money in what I do. When you have a social media presence, you are sharing free content with your following on a daily basis. If you succeed in capturing your audience's interest and admiration this way, they are more likely to want to buy your art products and help you in generating income from your work.

When working with external companies to make or sell your products, you will need to adapt to their base pricing to ensure you can both make money from the collaboration. I like to work on collaborations with brands whose products aren't overly expensive, so they are accessible to the largest amount of people. I prefer to sell products cheaply with low revenue, rather than expensively with a higher revenue, as more people are likely to buy the cheaper product, resulting in a greater profit.

# FUTURE AMBITIONS

My biggest goal is to succeed as a comic artist and adapt my work into an animated TV show, movie, or video game. While I try to keep my expectations fairly low, I plan to keep making new connections and improving my artistic skill in the hope of one day making this dream a reality. I am always looking to grow and develop as an artist. I like to draw detailed illustrations with different themes, characters, backgrounds, perspectives, and colors, as this allows me to practice all of these different elements every time I create an illustration. The more you practice and study a skill, the faster you will improve.

At the time of writing I am working with Fernando Llor, one of the best scriptwriters in Spain, on *Soma*, my first physical comic, due to be published with the Spanish publisher Planeta. If I am happy with the result, I plan to send this to the animation producers I know to explore if an animated adaptation would be possible.

# ADVICE

## Self-doubt & artist's block

I struggle with artist's block more than I would like, but as I have so many deadlines, I aim to make these episodes as short as possible by utilizing a number of tools to kick-start my creativity. One exercise that always works is practicing gesture drawing from references. Sketching poses is not only relaxing, but it can help to lift any blocks in creativity and spark new ideas.

Similarly, self-doubt is always present and I experienced this a lot when I began sharing my illustrations on Instagram. These days I'm more confident and even welcome constructive criticism that I can learn from to correct mistakes and improve my technique for future artwork. Any self-doubt I still have motivates me to push myself to improve artistically and learn new skills.

## Final tips

- If you struggle with networking and socializing, practice this in the same way you practice your artwork. Just like drawing, the more you practice, the better you will become at it. You will need to socialize a lot when working as a professional artist, whether messaging customers, arranging video calls with clients, or attending events. If you're not used to this, it could prove a little stressful. Another option is to find an agent and allow them to represent you to companies and clients.
- Be patient. Spend time honing your craft and putting in the practice.
- Learn how to create artwork that is consistent in style and skill. You want people to be able to recognize your signature anime style and brand.
- Stay humble and remember, there's always something you can improve on.
- Build a high-quality portfolio, tailored to the company or general field you wish to work in.

I like to use post-apocalyptic themes in my drawings and I am recognized for this dystopian style

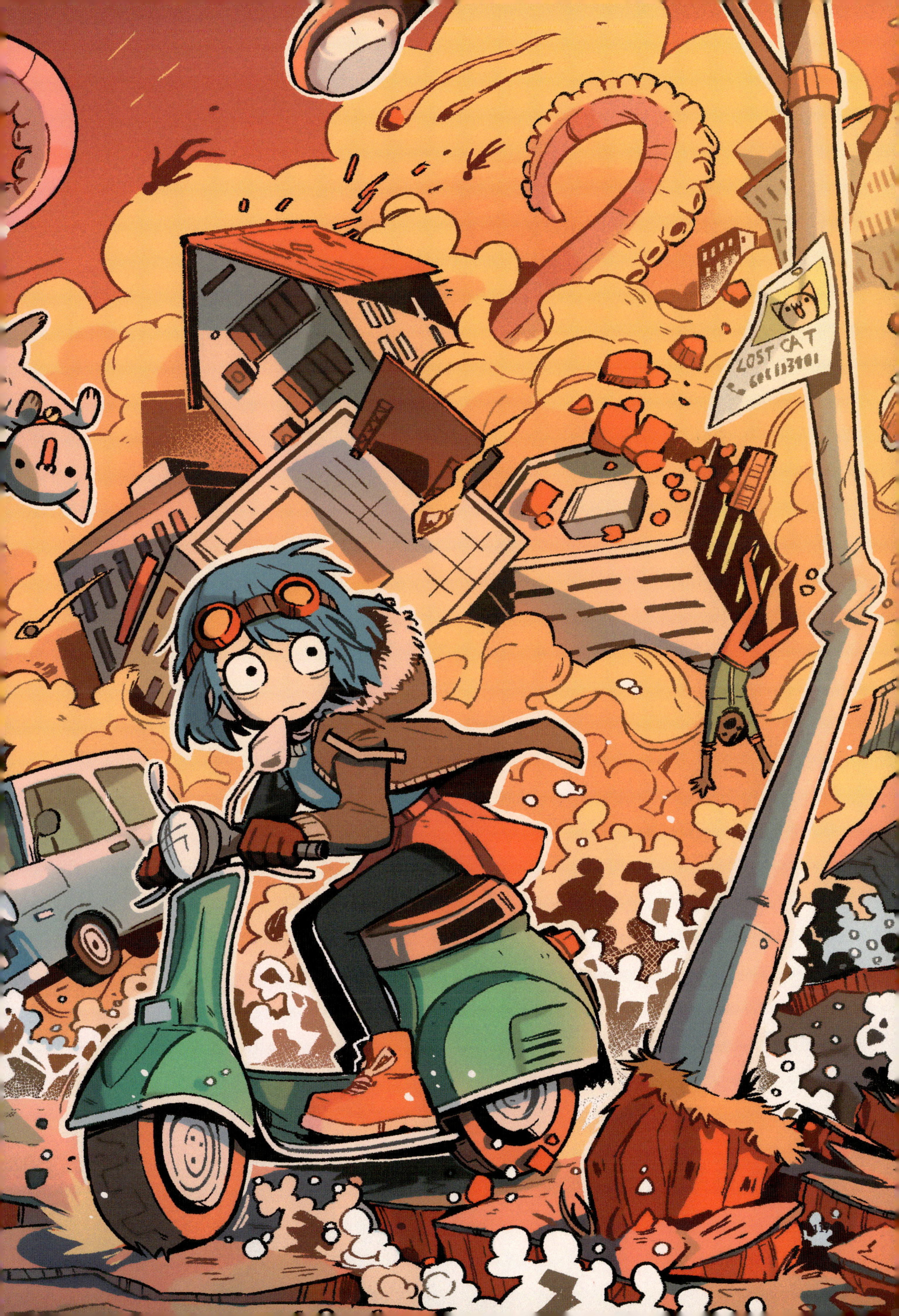
LOST CAT

# TIMELINE

**2007**
Discovered anime and manga.

**2015**
Began studying art, which helped me realize I wanted to work as an artist.

**Summer 2017**
Started to post drawings on Instagram.

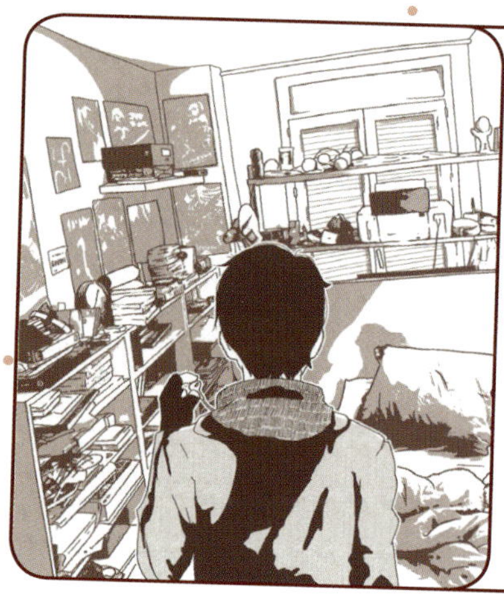

The first ever drawing I shared online. I had no idea what I was doing and practically traced a photo then gave it a manga-style look. While I'm not especially proud of this piece, it was a start.

**2018**
Created my first original characters and began to define my anime-style art brand.

**2019**
Started taking commissions.

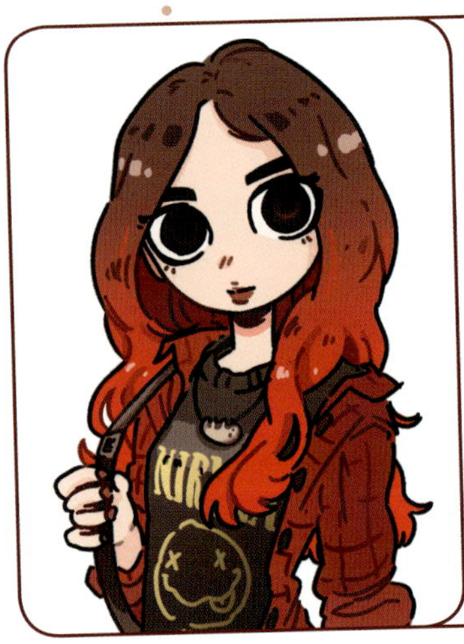

One of my first commissions. The client had followed me since I'd first started posting my artwork on Instagram.

**July 2019**
Reached my first 100k likes for a drawing I posted online.

**August 2019**
Frederator Studios asked to meet with me.

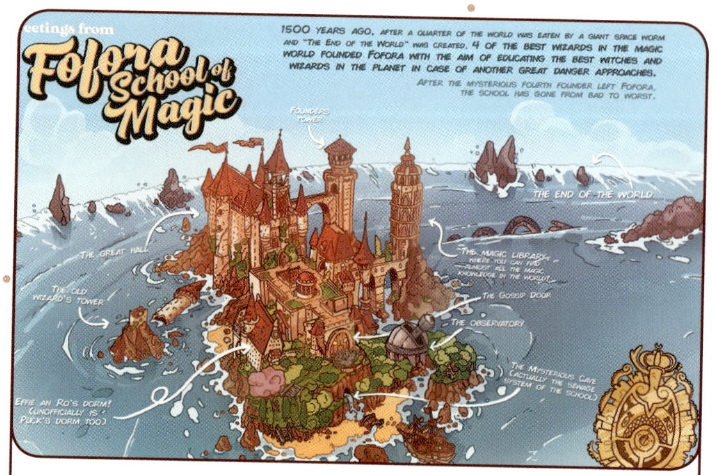


A page from the pitch I prepared for Frederator Studios.

**January 2020**
Created my first short manga for a Spanish Magazine.

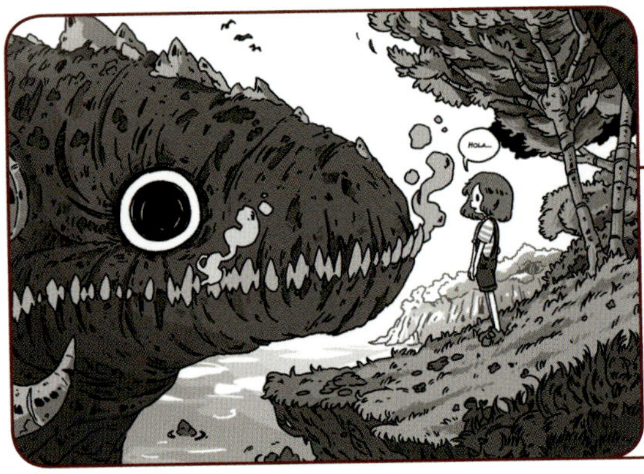

A double-page spread from *My Guardian Angel*. It tells the story of a young girl who befriends a giant monster, and together they decide to destroy the world.

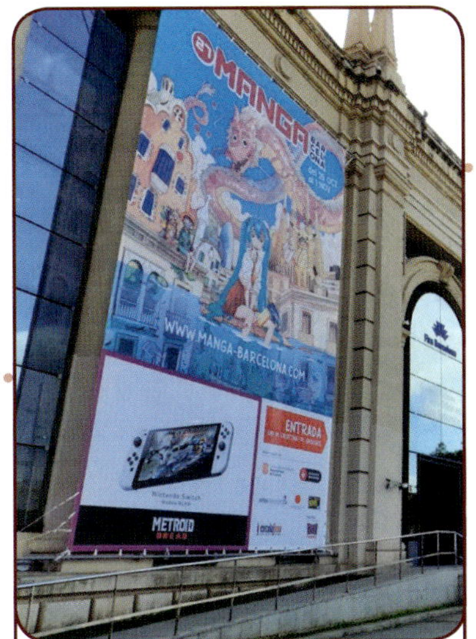


My poster displayed in Plaça Espanya, one of the main squares in Barcelona.

**October 2021**

Created the poster for one of the biggest anime events in Spain, Manga Barcelona 2021.

**October 2021**

Collaborated with Netflix for the *Maya and the Three* TV series.

**December 2021**

Signed a deal to publish my first physical comic, *Soma*, in Spanish- and English-speaking countries.

**September 2021**

Started working as a freelance concept artist for the *Cult of the Lamb* video game.

**September 2021**

Reached 500k followers on Instagram.

The calendar featured artwork I had previously shared on Instagram and had proved popular.

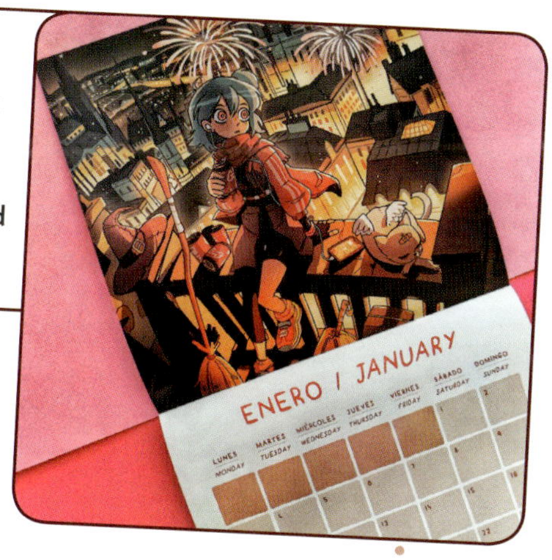


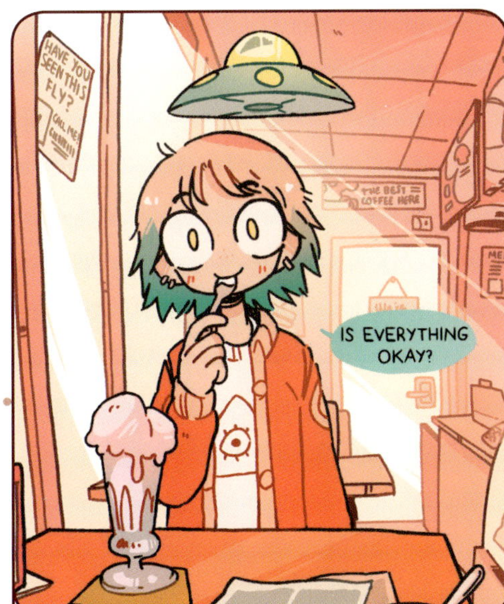


A panel from *Lucid Lucy*, episode 03.

**June 2020**

Created the webtoon *Lucid Lucy* for Webtoon's international short story contest and won second prize.

**November 2020**

Created my first official tutorial for Clip Studio Paint.

**August 2021**

Announced my first calendar with a Spanish publisher.

# GALLERY

## *Magic Train*, 2020

This was the first time I created an artwork that I truly liked. Comparing it to my very early drawings helped me recognize my progress and improvement. Even when I notice the mistakes, it's still one of my favorites.

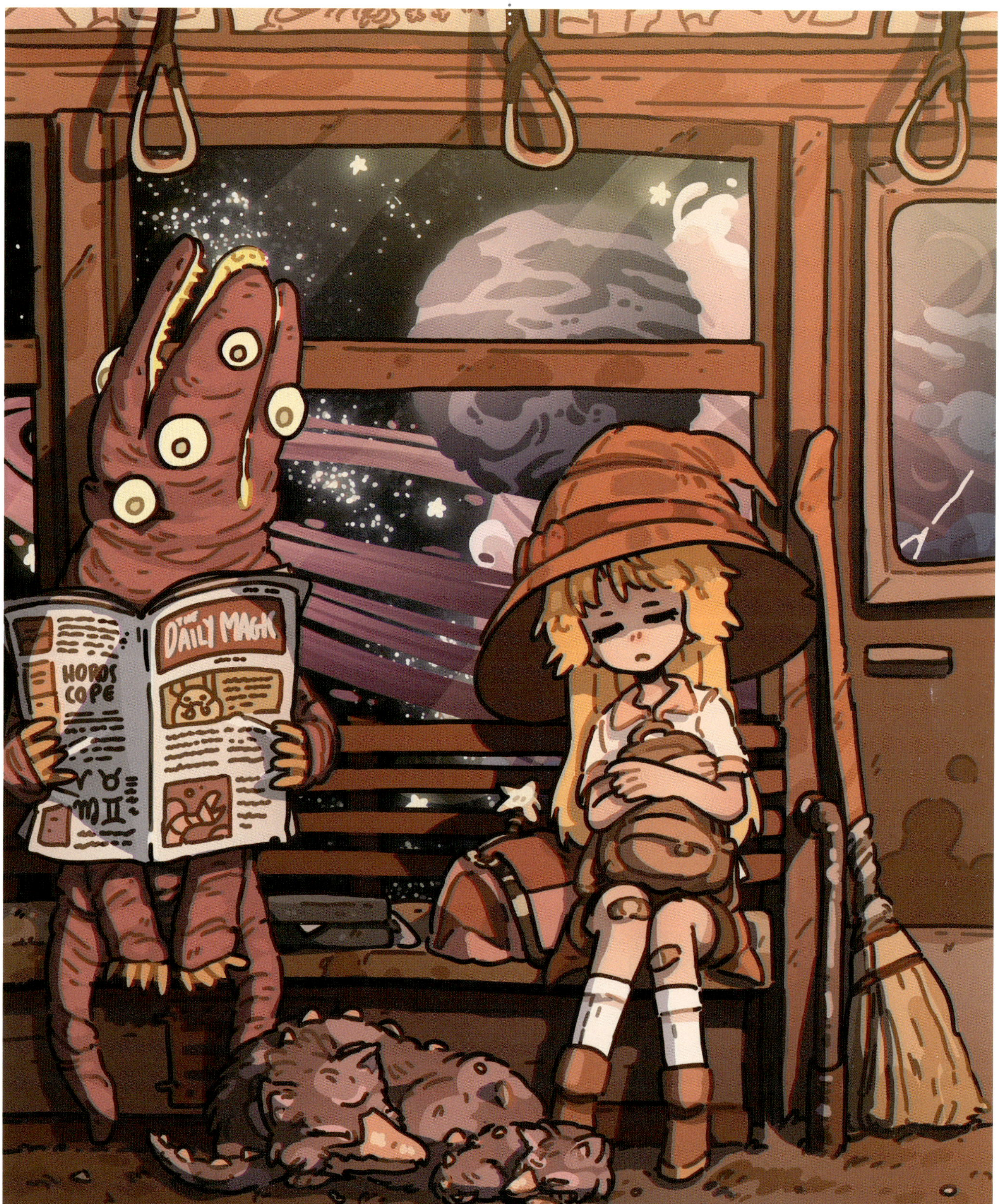

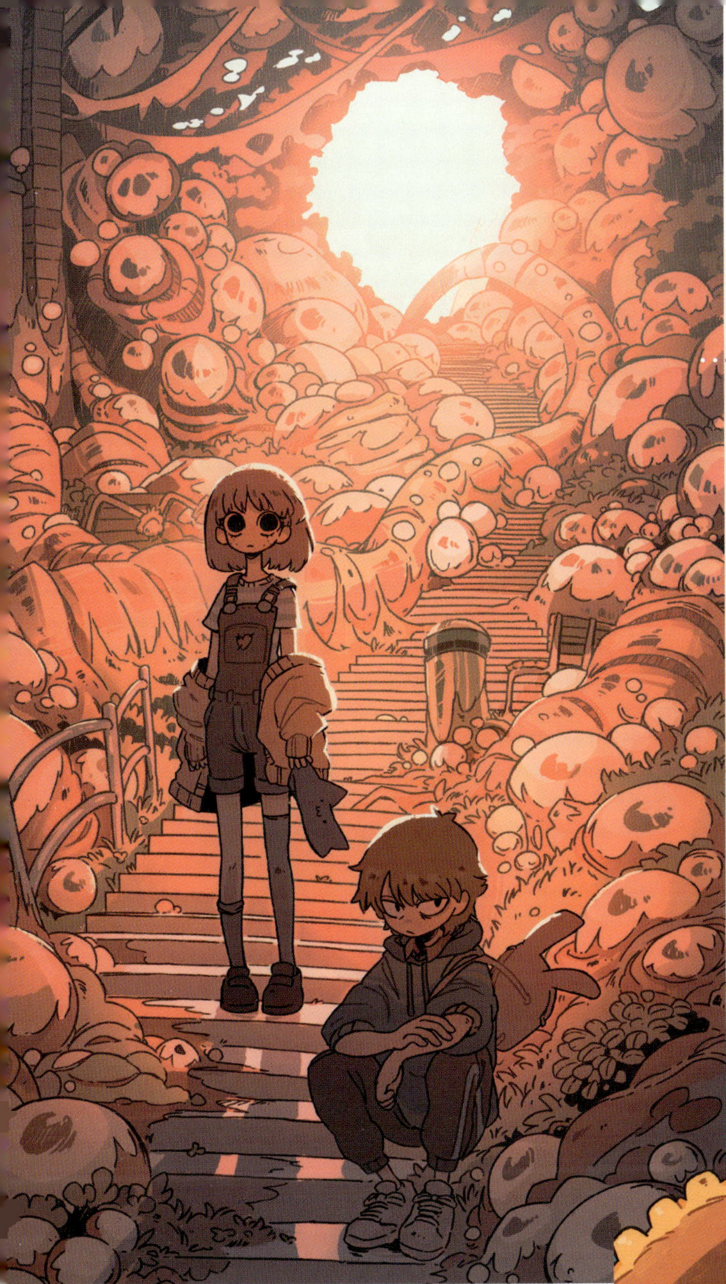

## *The Breach*, 2020

I drew this piece when I was starting to create comics. While I didn't like my first short manga, this artwork became the cover of my second project. I didn't finish the comic due to starting work on my webtoon, *Lucid Lucy*, but it made me realize that I could create cool comic concepts. Without this artwork I don't know if I would have started taking my journey into comics seriously.

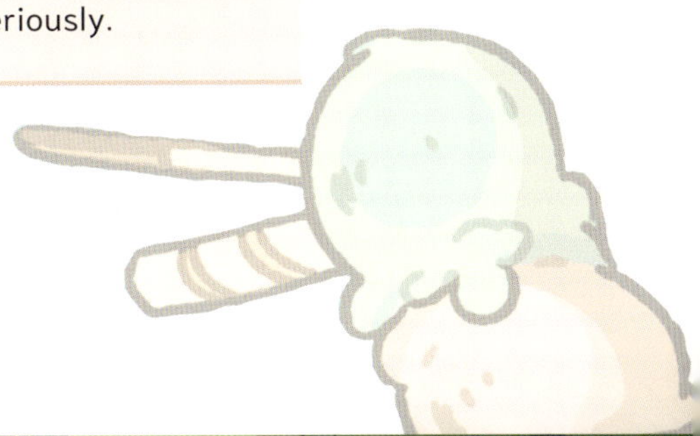

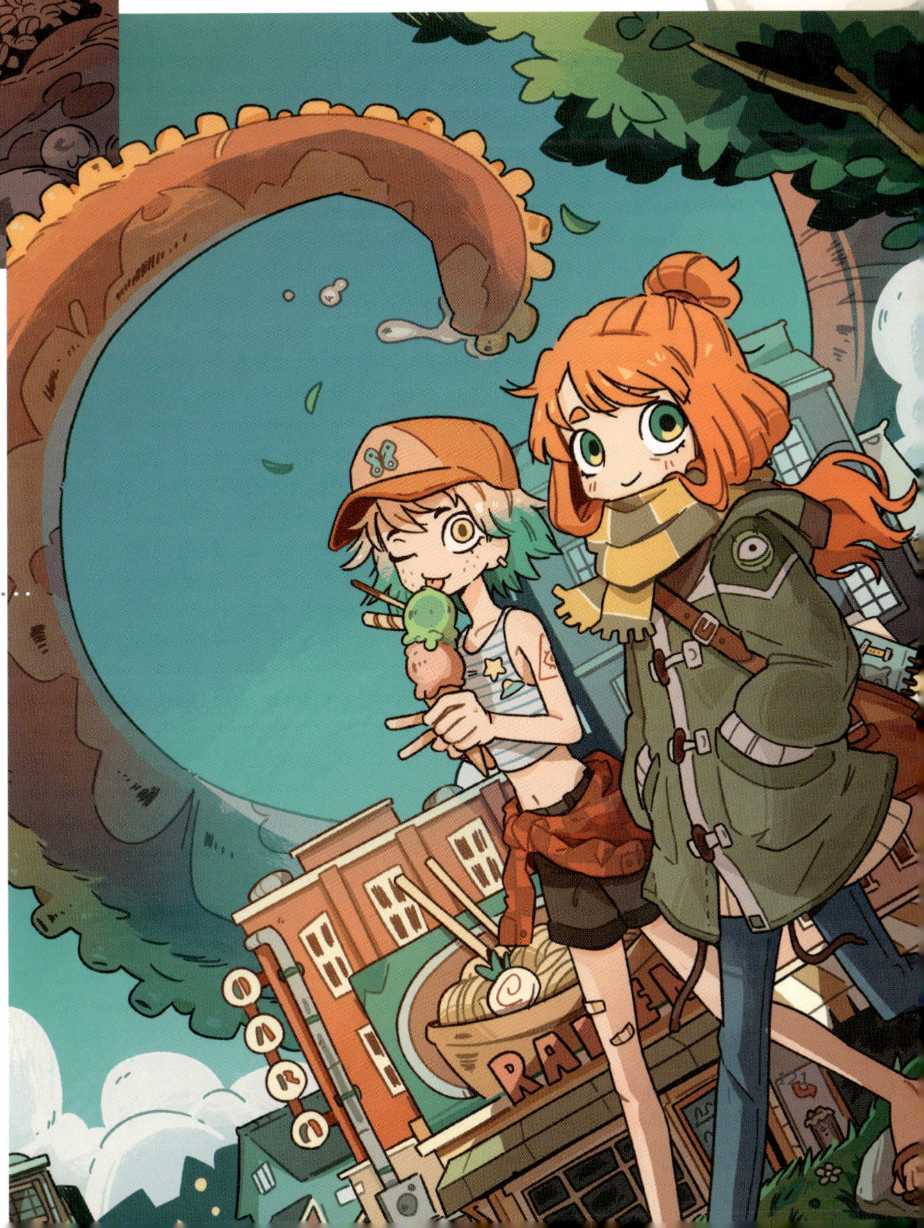

## *Lucy and May*, 2020

My first webtoon, *Lucid Lucy*, won second prize in the 2020 Webtoon Short Story Contest and became a Webtoon Original. It is one of my proudest achievements.

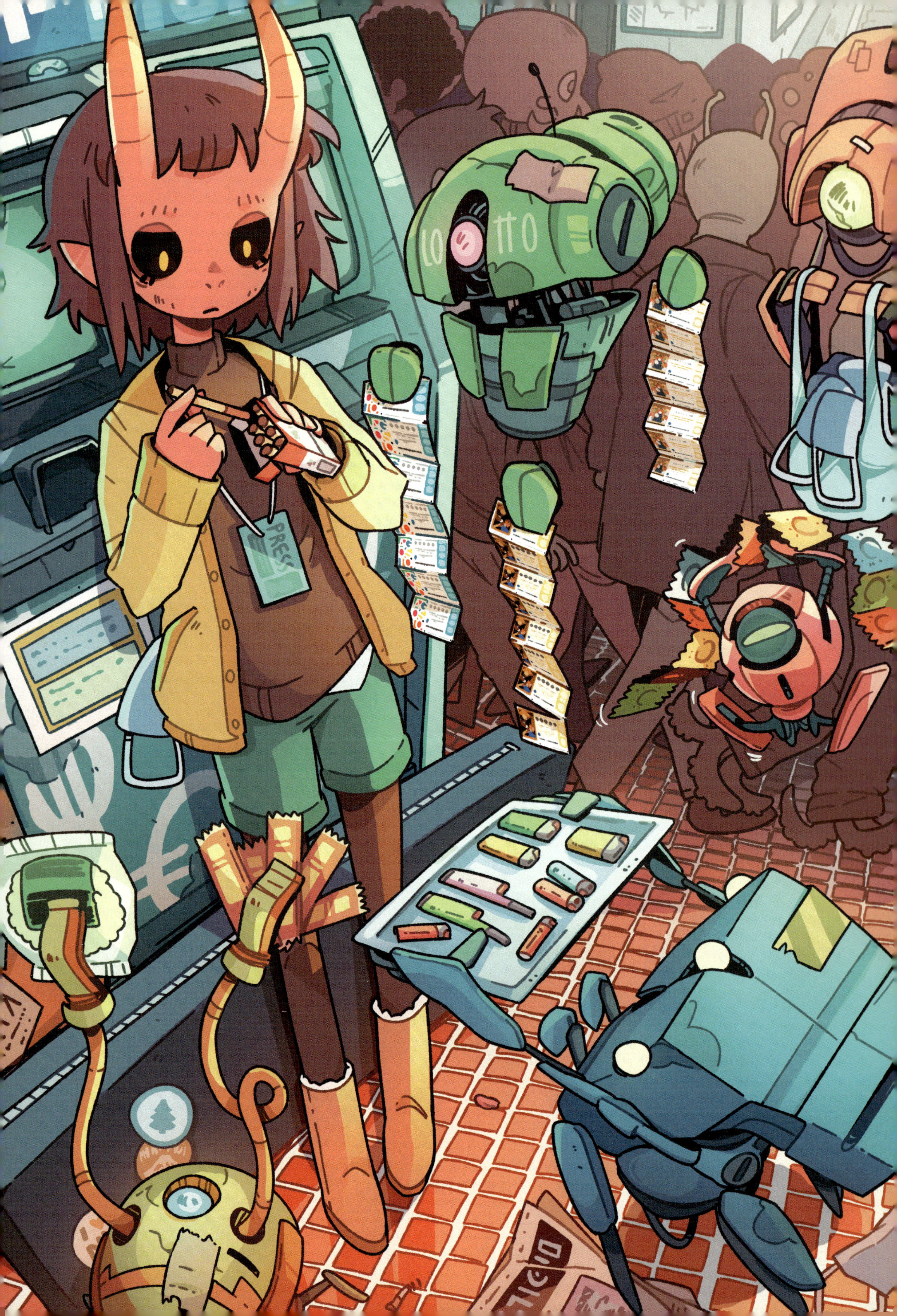
PRESS

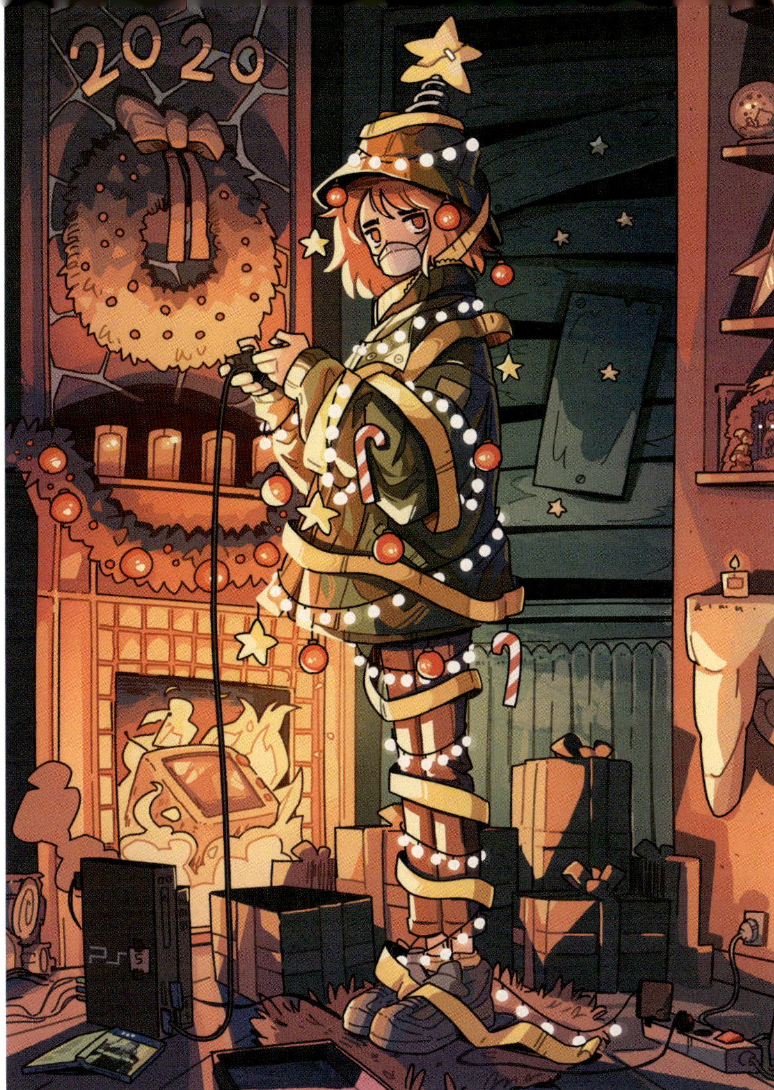


*Happy Holidays*, 2020

2020 was the year in which my art evolved the most, possibly because of the Covid-19 lockdowns. Comparing this artwork to my last drawing from 2019 was one of the best feelings I had experienced as an artist at that time. Seeing the progress over the course of a year meant a lot to me.

*Coco in a Metro*, 2020

Drawing multiple characters in one illustration was always something that scared me a little. I tried to overcome that in this artwork and love the fun result.

*Bird Girl*, 2020

I always found drawing cities really hard. When capturing nature, the different natural elements could be drawn less accurately and it would still look good, but I found that the architecture of cities required more precise perspective and size. This artwork was an experiment and I was very pleased with the result.

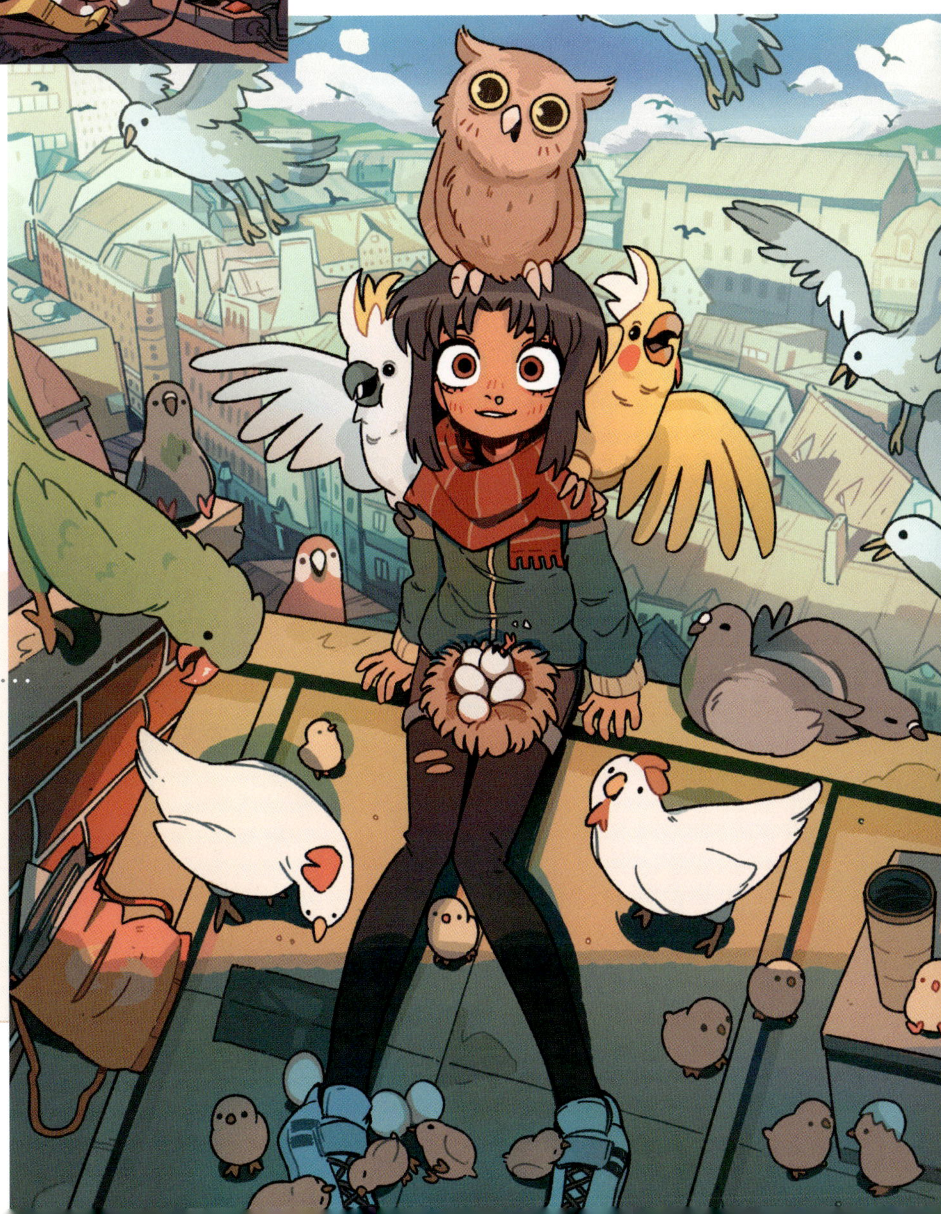

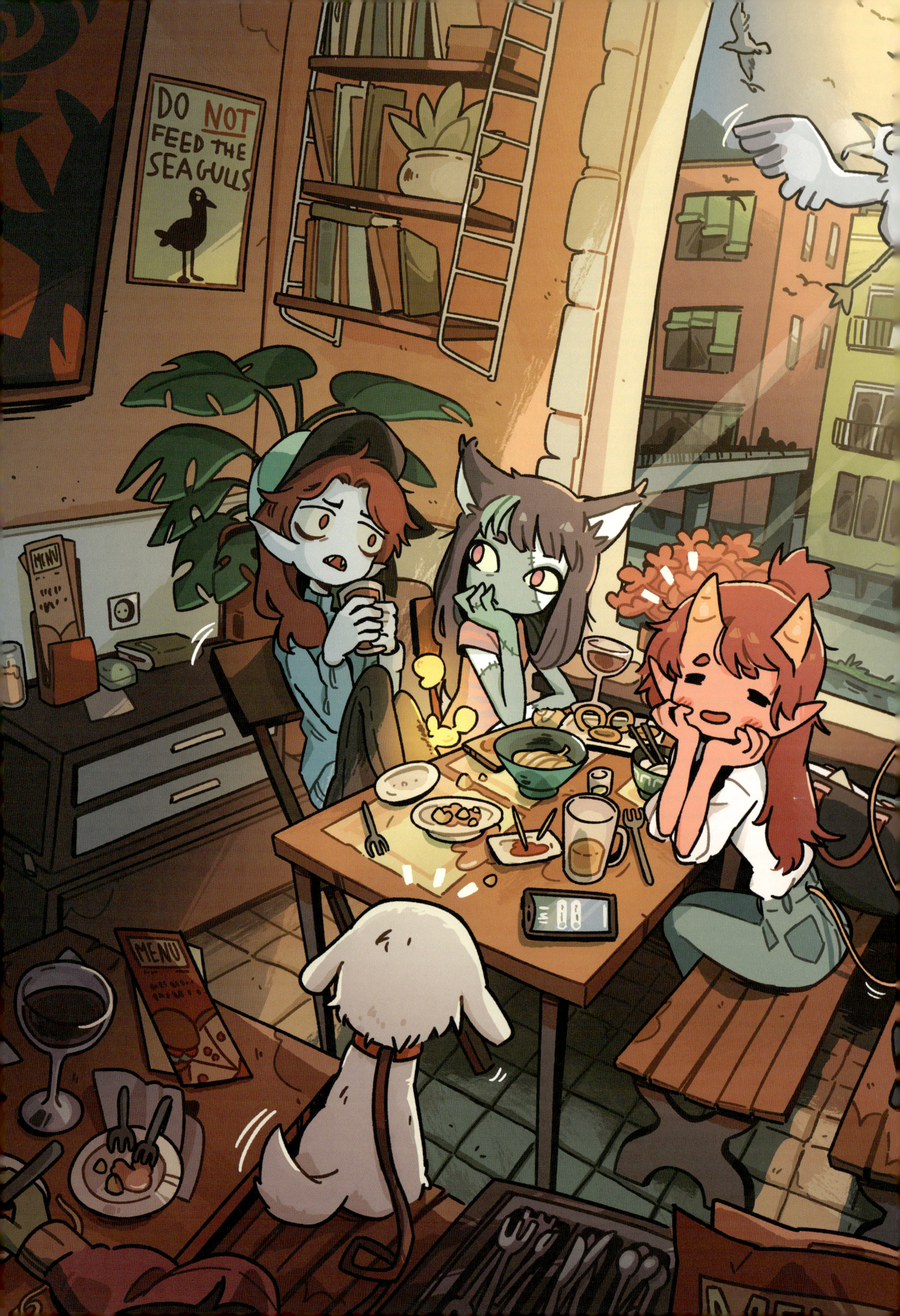
DO NOT FEED THE SEAGULLS
MENU
MENU

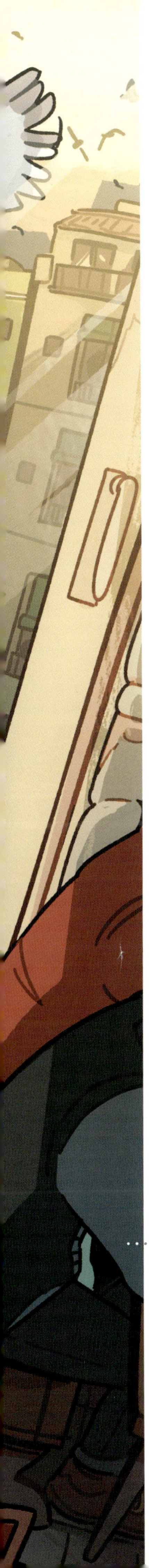

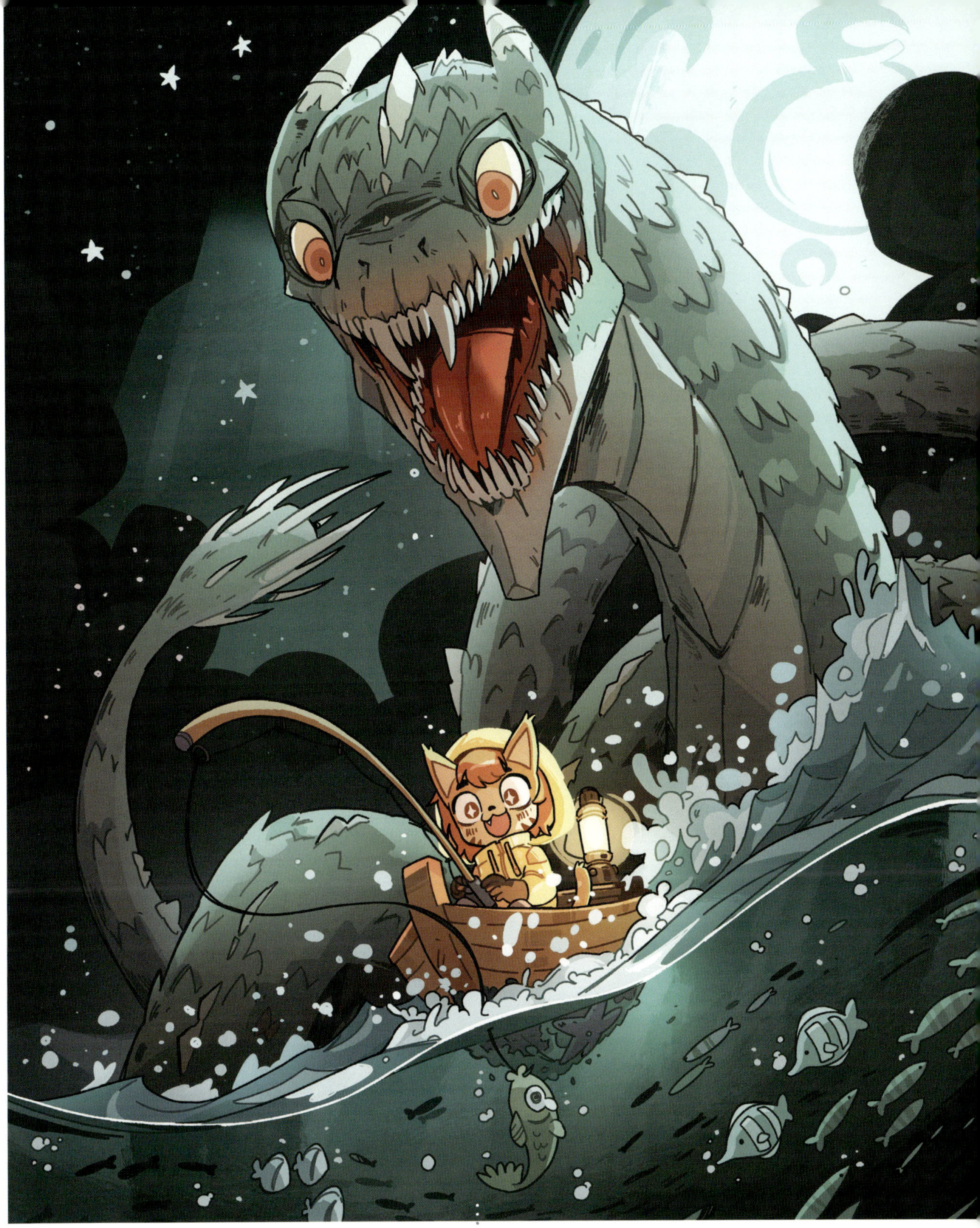

*Seagull Bar*, 2020

Up until this point I used bigger brushes because I was scared of drawing all the little details. My intention with this artwork was to use a smaller brush to clean up the line art. I loved the finished result and still use the same method while inking to this day.

*Sea Monster*, 2021

I wasn't confident drawing monsters and non-humanoid characters, so I created this drawing for practice. It allowed me to improve my workflow for capturing fantasy creatures going forward.

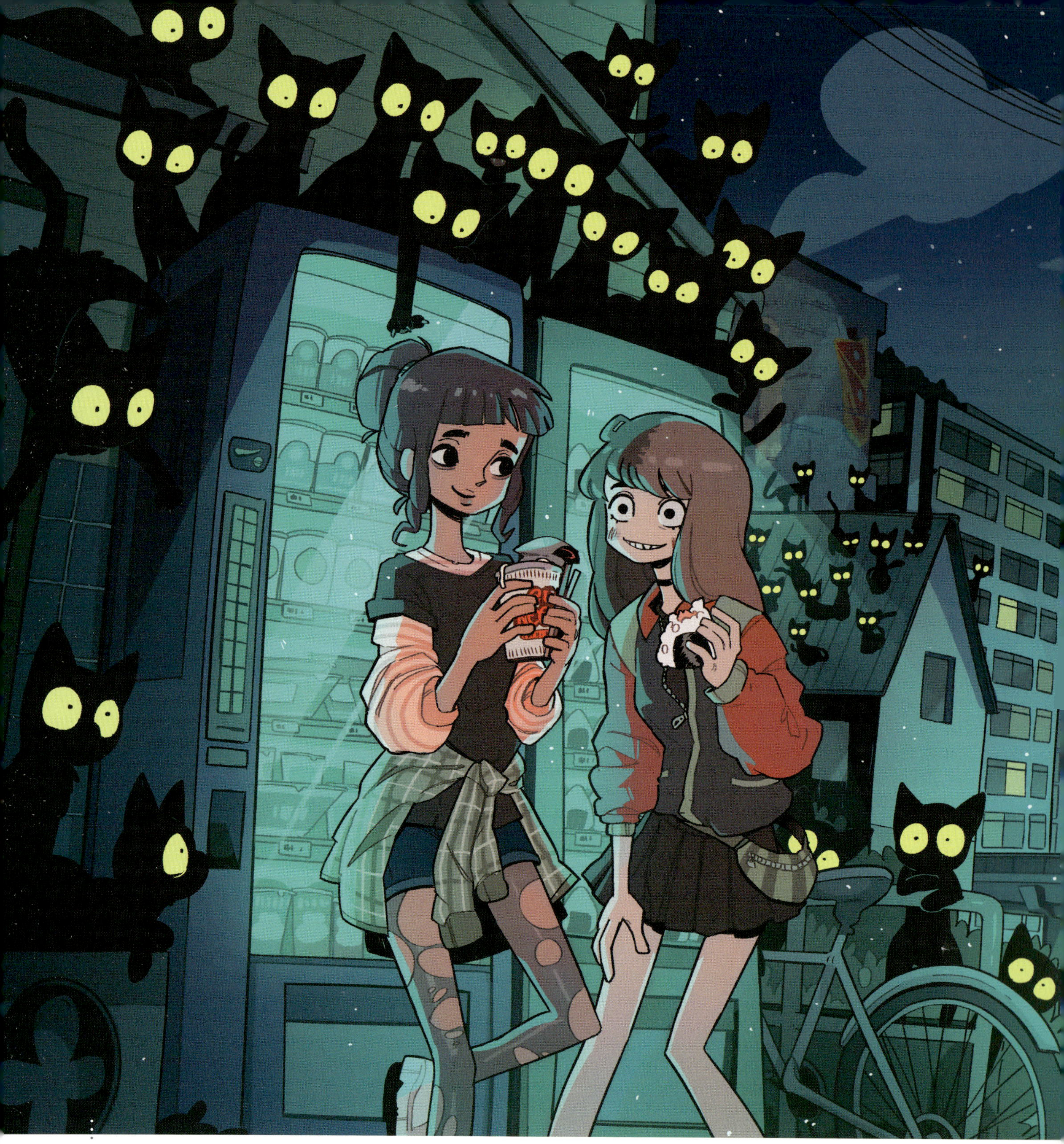

*Cat Night*, 2021

I used to use a lot of color correction filters in Photoshop to clean up and finish my artworks, but worried I was becoming too reliant on them. For this artwork I limited myself to one tone and didn't use any filters. This helped me overcome my fear of sharing artwork that didn't utilize such effects.

*Forest Monster*, 2021

It took me a while to work out how to paint characters without illuminating them with a light source. For this artwork I decided to draw the characters in the shadows, illuminating the background instead. The process helped me understand how to do this and improved my technique.

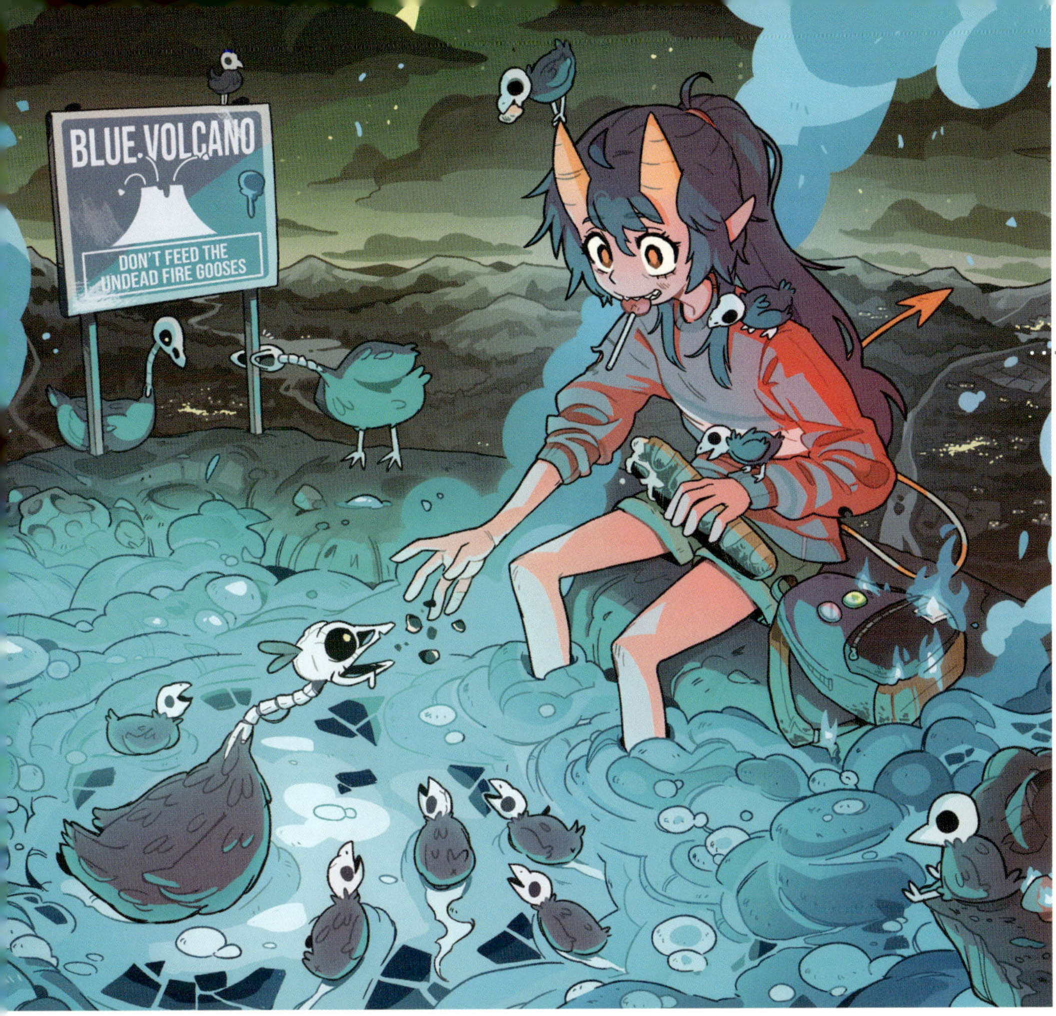


*Mei Volcano*, 2021

I always struggled to paint backgrounds with a lot of detail, while keeping them simple enough not to eclipse the main elements of the image. I practiced this a lot until I figured out how to create an interesting background that didn't overshadow the character and foreground. This skill is useful when working on comics.

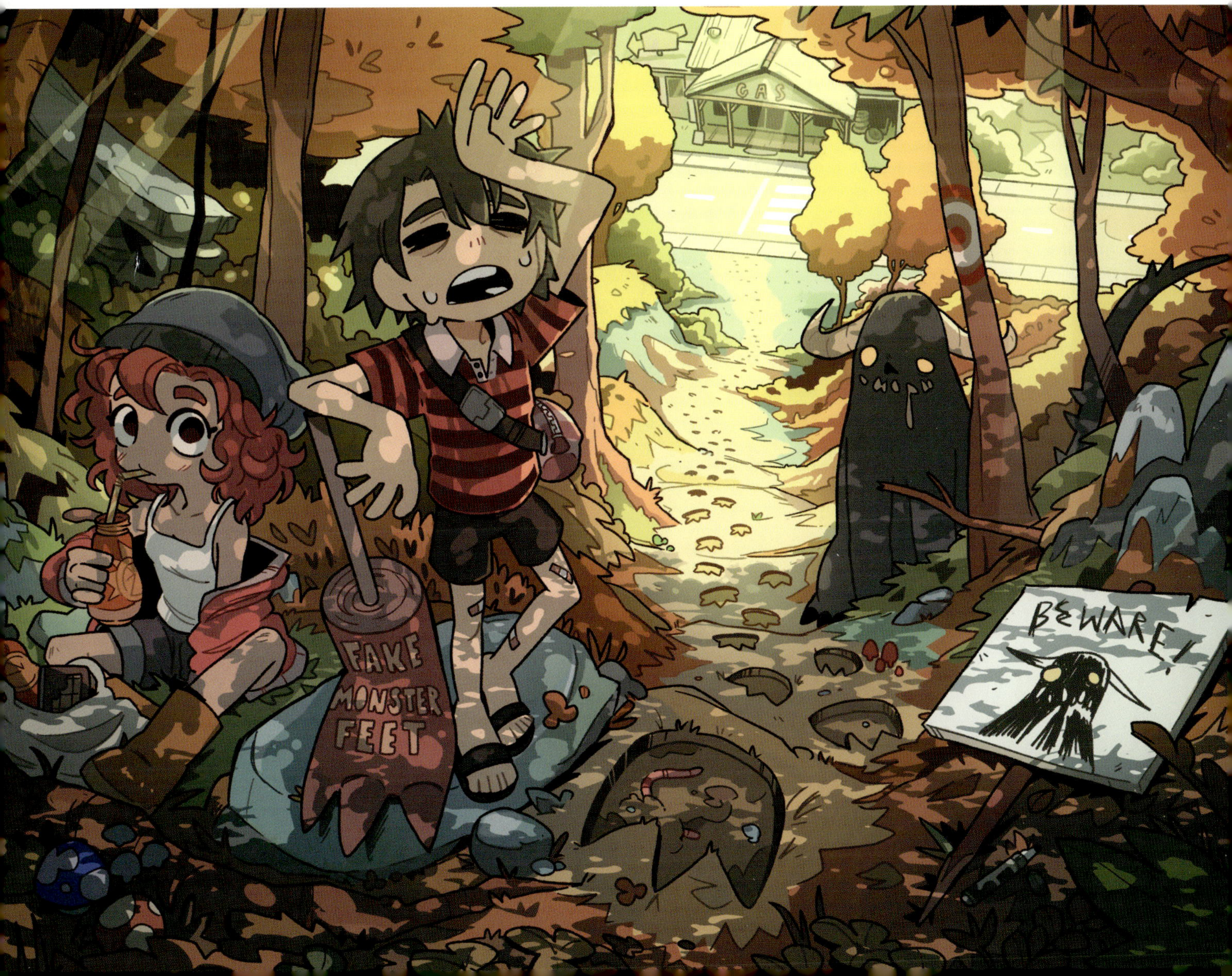

# TUTORIAL

This tutorial will demonstrate my typical workflow for creating one of my anime-style illustrations. It will depict a witch flying over a New York-inspired city, startled as she fends off the pesky seagulls trying to steal her sandwich. When coming up with ideas for my artwork, I often choose random elements – such as a young witch and a swarm of seagulls – then mesh them together to create a story. I focus on what I want to draw, rather than considering a predetermined audience or genre. If working for a company, however, I will always adhere to the audience and theme detailed in the brief provided.

What makes my artwork stand out is its unique combination of simplicity and detail. While people often think my illustrations look complicated, at their core they are very simple. The trick is to stay organized by following methodical steps from start to finish. My signature style comes naturally to me, but it's also the result of many hours of practice. Though my line work is not as clean or neat as it could be, this is what makes my illustrations more personal. When developing your own anime style, find a workflow and style that works for you.

I have used Clip Studio Paint for the line art and Photoshop for coloring, but you can follow along using any digital software or media.

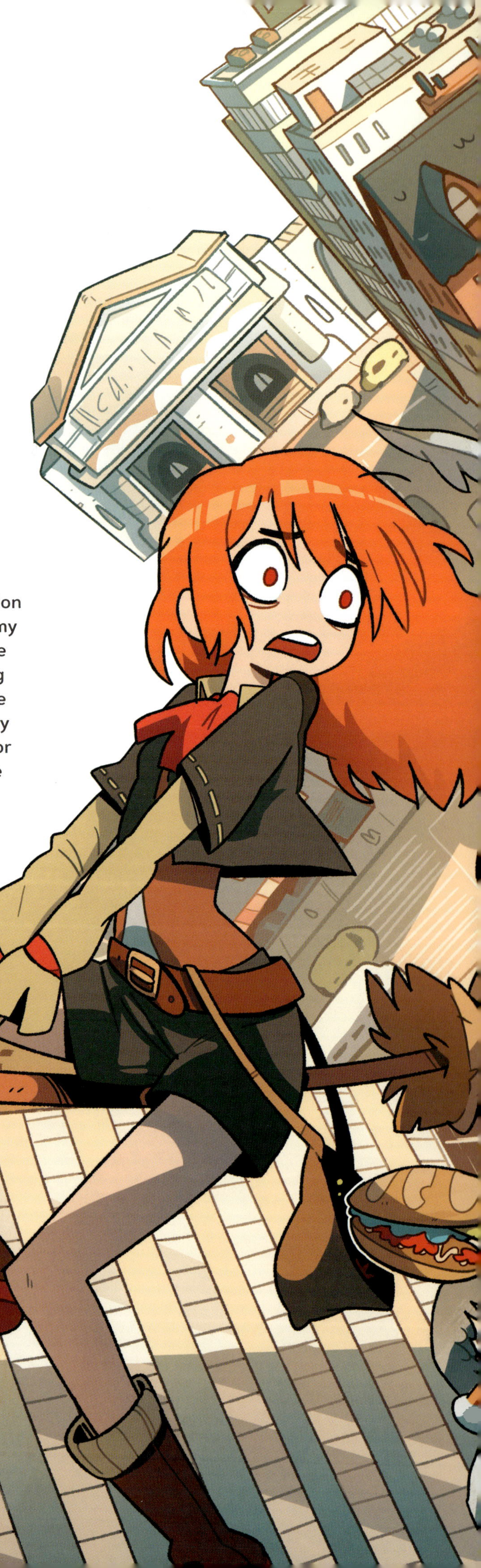

**01** Start by drawing loose doodles that begin to express your concept. When you are happy with this rough sketch, draw a border around it and add a few more details to sketch out the character and background. Focus on the overall idea rather than creating a perfect drawing. At this stage there is no need to consider format, size, or smaller details.

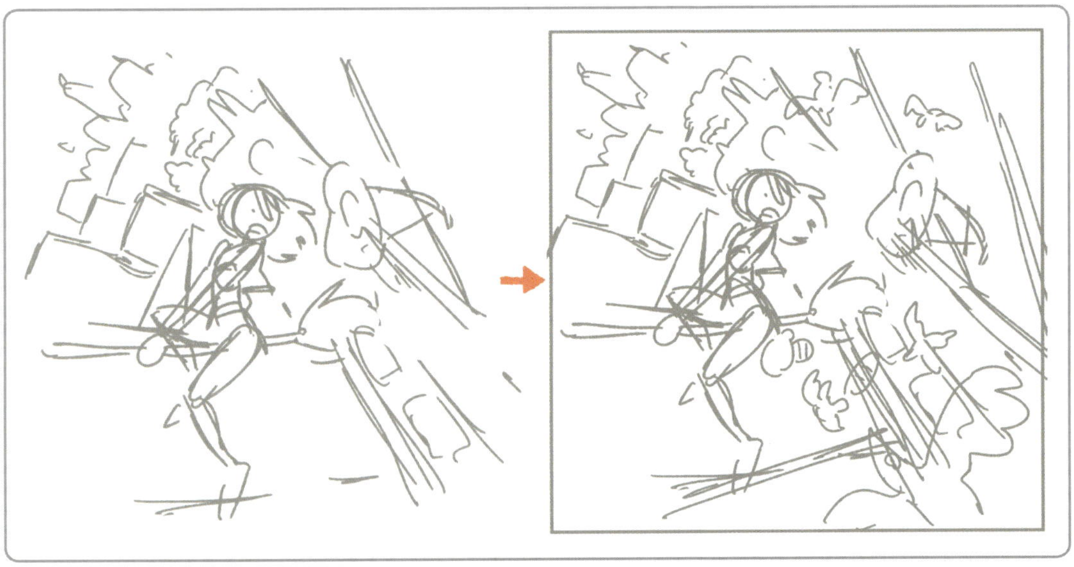

Create an initial rough sketch to explore the concept, before adding more details and margins

### ARTIST TIP

To create a sense of depth in your sketch, try to think in terms of layers that will create the illusion of three-dimensional space. You don't necessarily have to use perspective to make your drawings three-dimensional.

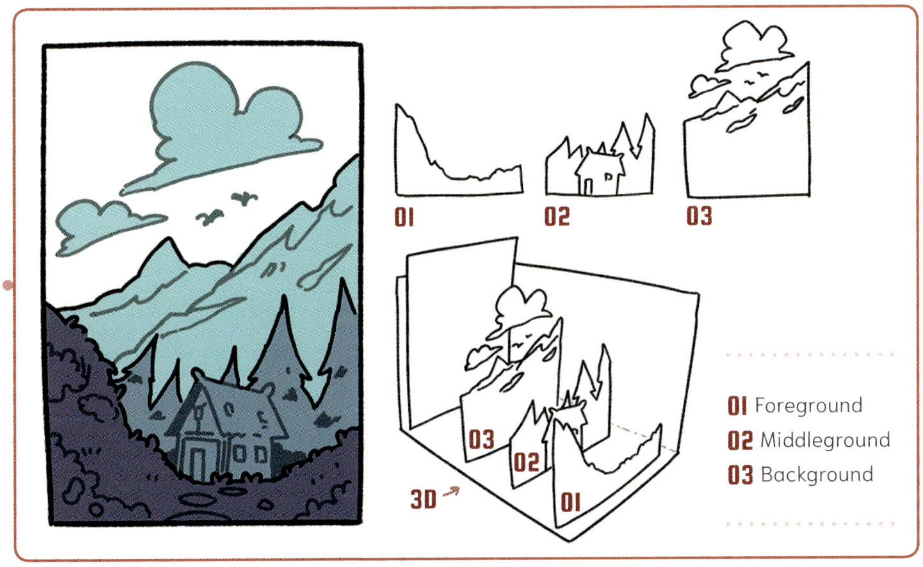

**02** Sketch out the foreground of your image in a little more detail, starting to suggest movement and emotion. I like to position my characters facing the audience, as this makes it much easier for the viewer to understand the moment of action. You can experiment with wackier compositions when working on comics, as you use multiple images to convey a scene, rather than only one. Add small details that begin to tell the story, such as the sandwich and hungry seagulls. Look at references if you don't know how to draw something. Next, if working digitally, fill the first layer with a plain color; here I use white. This will make it much easier to draw the background.

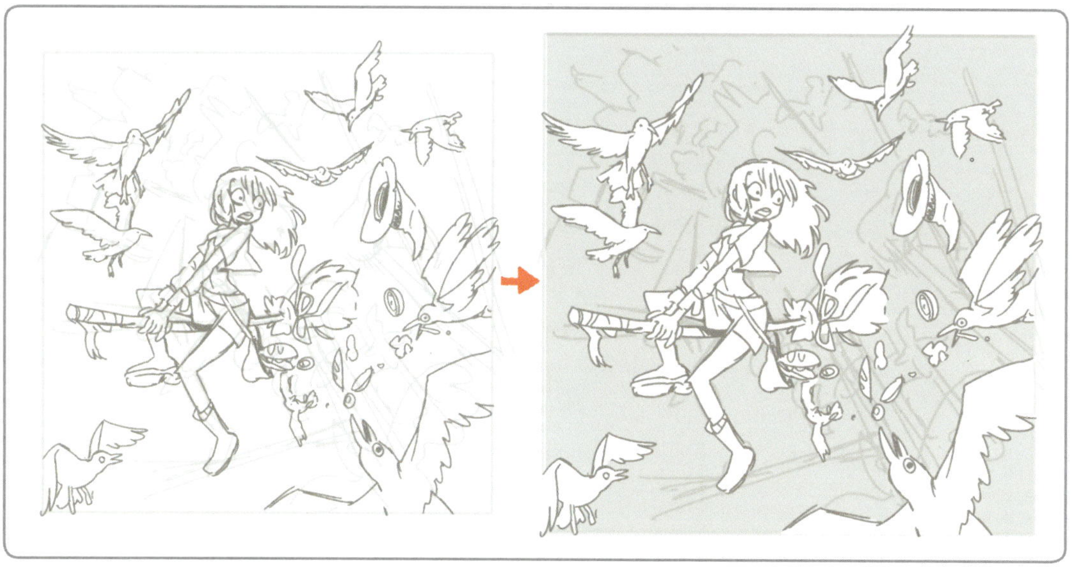

Create a final sketch of the foreground with more detail, before adding the first layer and filling with a plain color, such as white

## ARTIST TIP

When drawing complex backgrounds, such as a city, learn how to simplify the different elements. Think of each part as a basic geometrical form, such as a cube, cylinder, pyramid, or sphere. If you imagine you are drawing a field of boxes with windows, rather than a complex cityscape, the process will become a lot less daunting. A good exercise is to practice drawing geometric forms in perspective, without using any perspective guidelines.

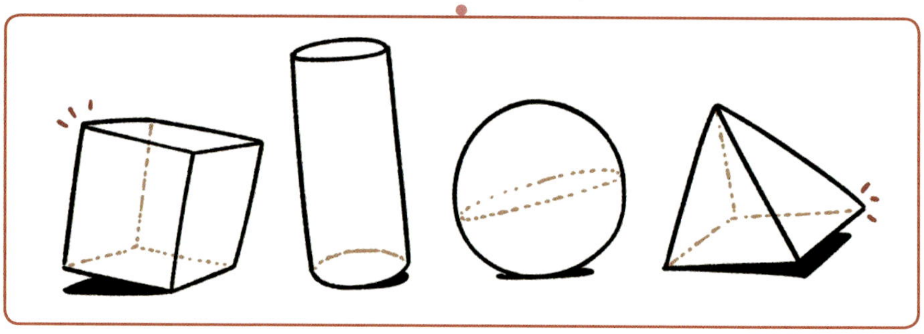

**03** Next, finish your background sketch. While it may seem complex at first glance, if you look closely you can see how the skyscrapers are simply big cuboids with smaller details, such as windows and ceilings, roughly sketched on top. At this stage, it's important to know how to draw shapes in perspective, along with how to use multiple layers to suggest depth. In this case, the first layer is made up of the witch and seagulls, with an additional five layers containing the buildings toward the front of the image, the buildings further back, the museum, the park, and finally the buildings in the distance. Use references to avoid creating buildings that are repetitive and boring.

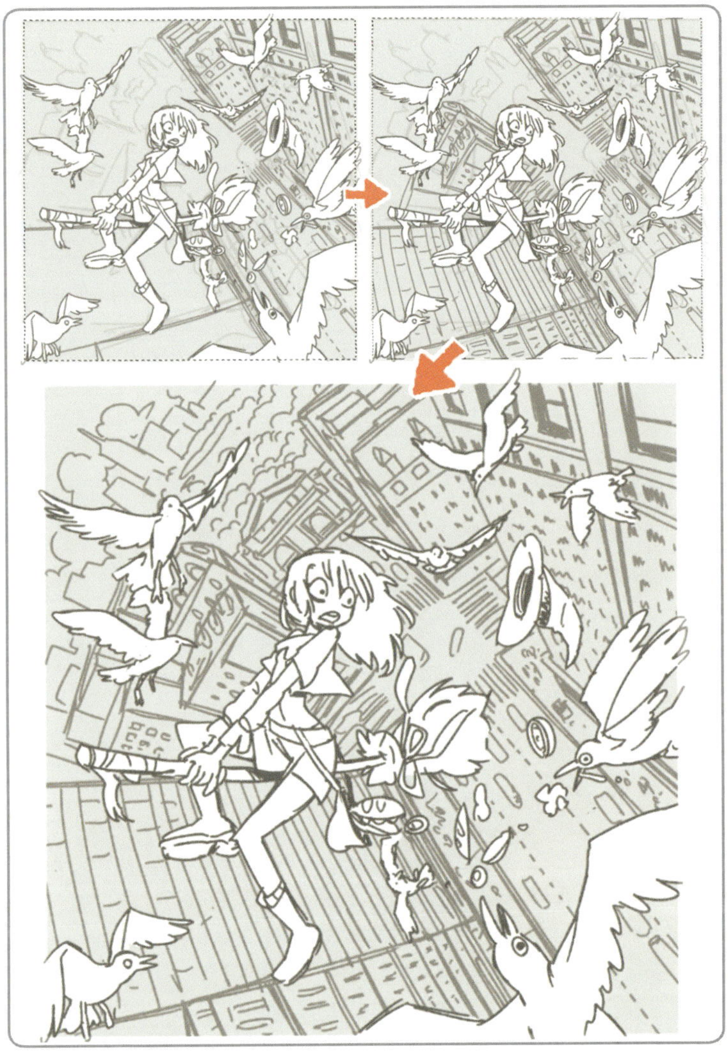

Use a methodical process to create the background, focusing on sketching in the main shapes before adding detail

**04** Depending on your sketching style, you may require a third sketch layer with neater lines. Once you have completed your final sketch, start to draw the line art for the foreground. I like to use Clip Studio Paint's default textured brush for this and have two copies of the same brush; one is the original and the second has the stabilizer set to the maximum. Found in most digital drawing software, the stabilizer creates smoother lines and is helpful when drawing long lines, such as a leg, street, or broomstick. When working on smaller, detailed parts of the illustration – such as the face, hands, or other details – I use the same brush with no stabilizer to achieve more control over the line work. It's important to make the line art as clear as possible to ensure the viewer knows what they are seeing.

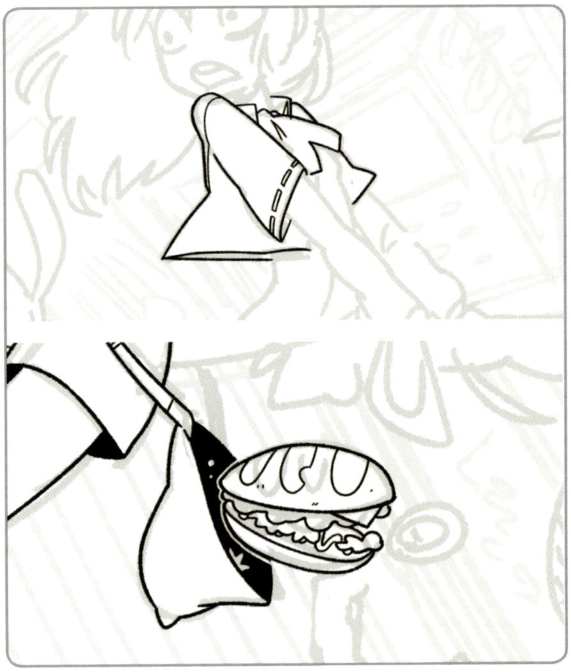

Aim to make your line art as neat as possible

**05** Once you have finished the foreground line art, take a step back and view the image as a whole to spot if there are any errors. I prefer to use a consistent brush size and like to add additional detail to elements that appear closer to the "camera." The farther away elements are, the more I simplify them. Next, on a new layer beneath the others, fill the foreground with one flat color. This will make it easier to paint the character and draw the background later.

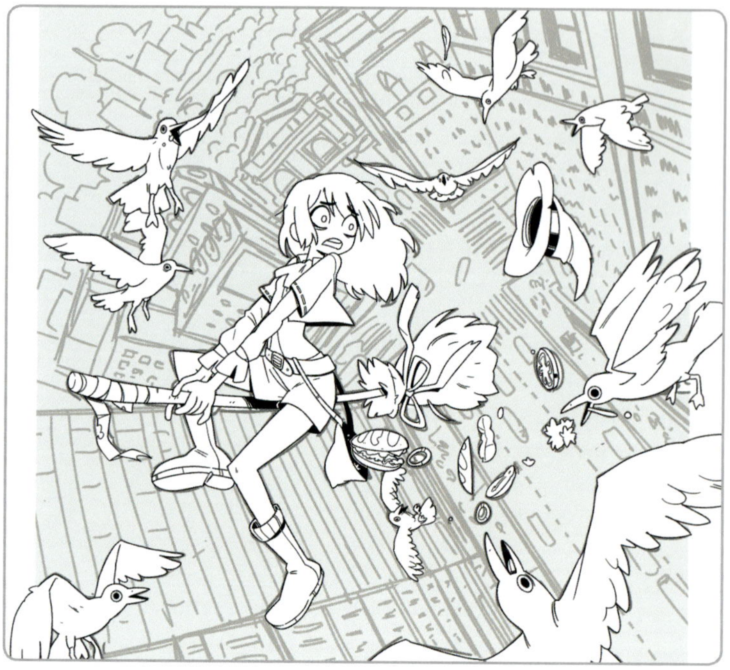

After creating the final line art for the foreground, fill it with a flat color

**06** Draw large rectangles for the shape of the buildings. I like to draw these manually using the smoother brush. On a new layer beneath, use a red color to draw small squares on the front of the building for the windows. Next, use the transformation tool to move this red drawing onto the buildings, transformed into the correct perspective. Finally, trace these details onto the black line-art layer, making them less neat and adding more details. This method will make the process of drawing details such as windows much easier, as the digital software takes care of the perspective.

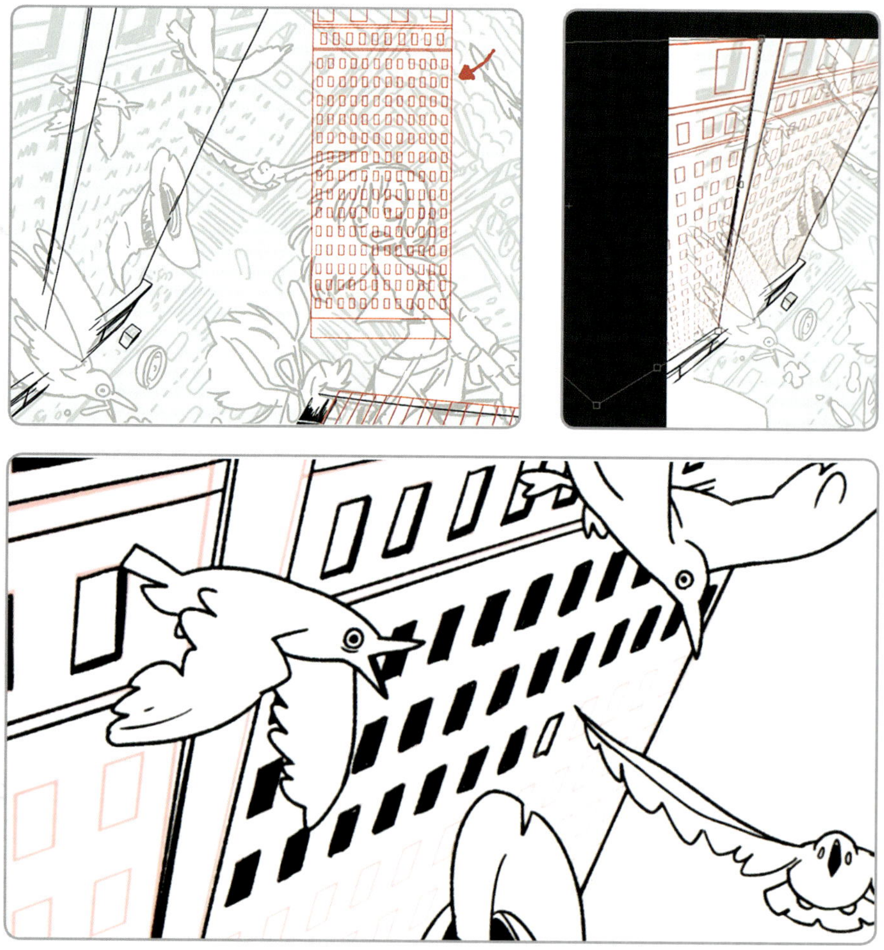

Make use of digital tools to help with drawing small or repetitive details in perspective

**07** Repeating the process used to create the buildings in the foreground, draw the basic geometric shape of the buildings in the background without any detail. You could draw all of the buildings using a one-point perspective if you prefer, but I find this approach allows me to create my signature cartoonlike style.

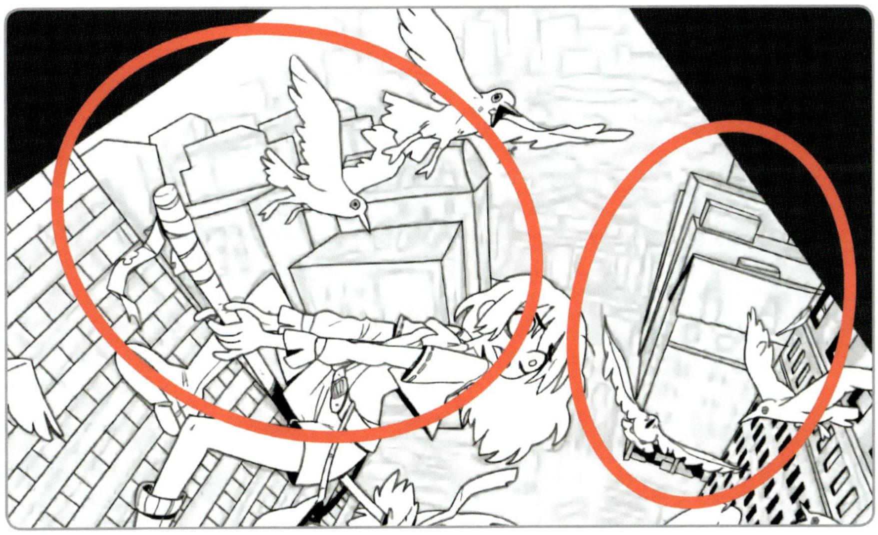

Sketch in geometric shapes to suggest the background buildings

**08** Once you have drawn the basic shapes for the background buildings, lower the opacity and start to draw the details on a separate layer. Sometimes I use the same process as used for the foreground buildings, while at other times I prefer to draw in the details in a more freehand style. This is not an exact science – experiment with both methods to find which feels most comfortable for you.

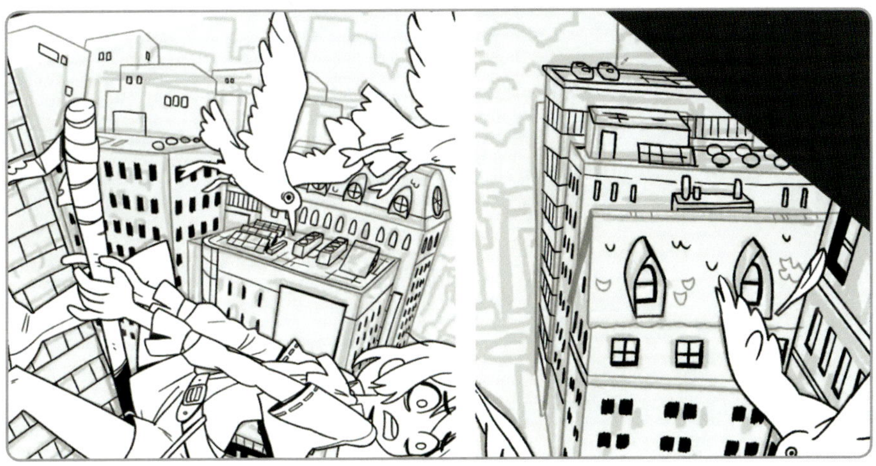

Add details to the background buildings

**09** Follow the same process until you have finished inking all of the line art. Focus on adding more detail in the foreground, while simplifying elements that are farther away in the background. This will make the background elements much easier to draw. If you look closely, the cars are weirdly-shaped boxes, people on the street are vague blobs, the park is made up of little cloud-shaped forms, and the buildings on the horizon are big boxes of different sizes.

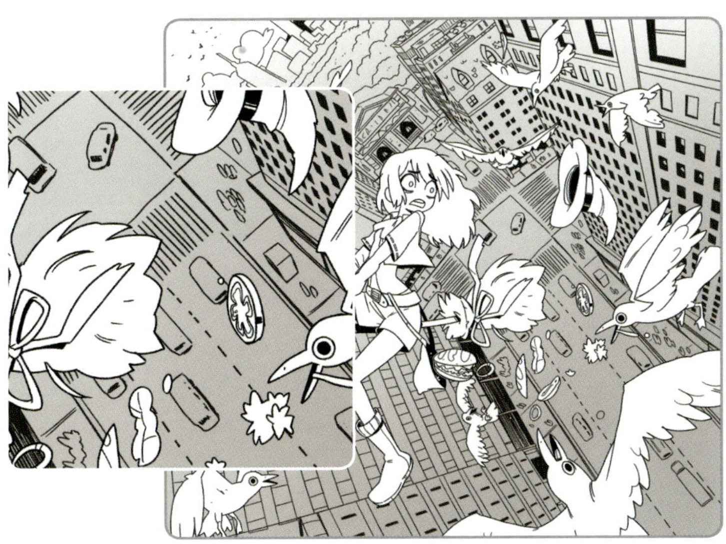

Draw the final line art, with detail in the foreground and simplified shapes in the background

## 10

Now it's time to begin the coloring stage. Select colors for each element of the illustration, starting to block in the foreground without trying to make it look final. I find this to be the most relaxing stage of the drawing, as you don't need to overthink it. Adding an extra layer beneath the background line art and filling the windows with white will make it easier to paint the windows once the background is colored.

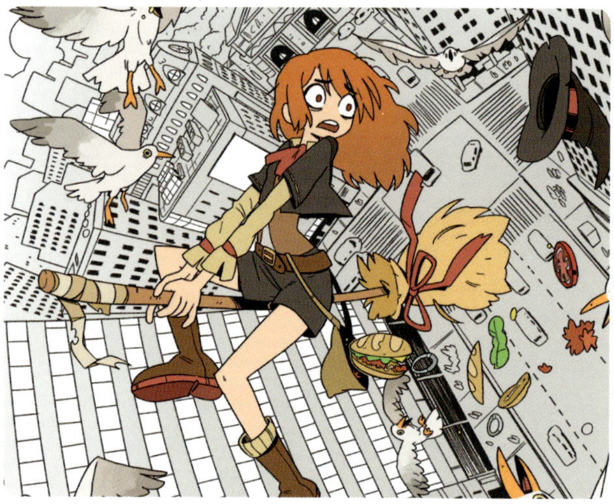

Paint in the base colors

### ARTIST TIP

When painting base colors, I only select tones from inside a limited range. I typically select colors with lower contrast and saturation, as these will always blend together well. Once you have finished the base colors, you can experiment with the other colors in the illustration.

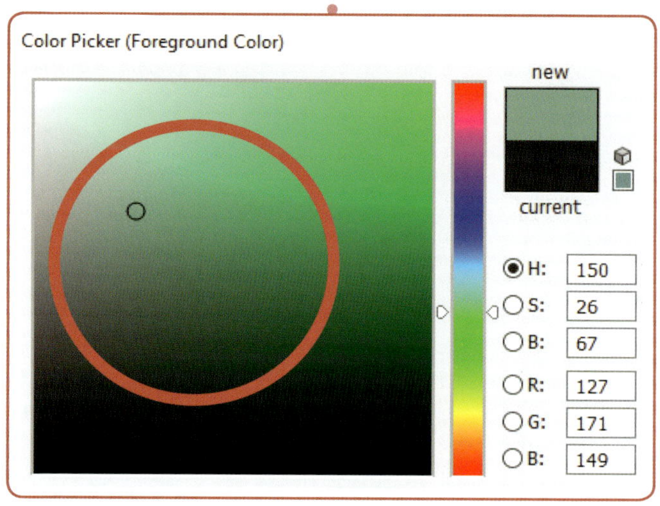


## 11

When coloring the background, it's important to focus on one element at a time. I like to paint each building a random color, which makes it easier to then select each one separately and fill it with the chosen color. Even if you are using low-saturation or low-contrast colors, it's important to make each building look different to provide the illustration with more variation and interest. Using similar tones or complementary colors is a good way to create a harmonious palette.

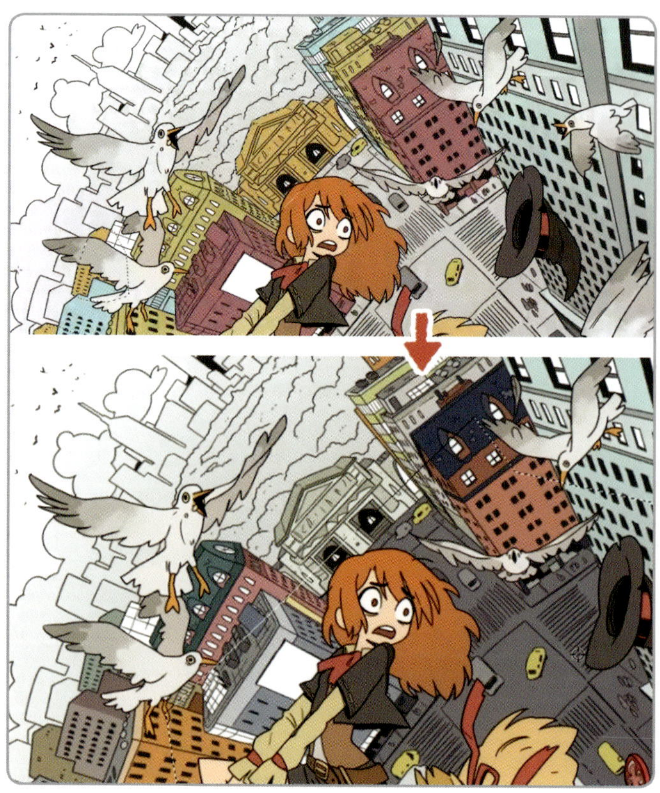

Paint the base colors of the buildings, focusing on one at a time

**12** Once you have finished painting the base colors of the buildings, paint the rest of the background using simple colors, such as green for the vegetation and bluish tones for the buildings and sky. Though the drawing is now fully colored, it still lacks atmosphere, so the next step will explore how to use digital blending modes to enhance shadow and light.

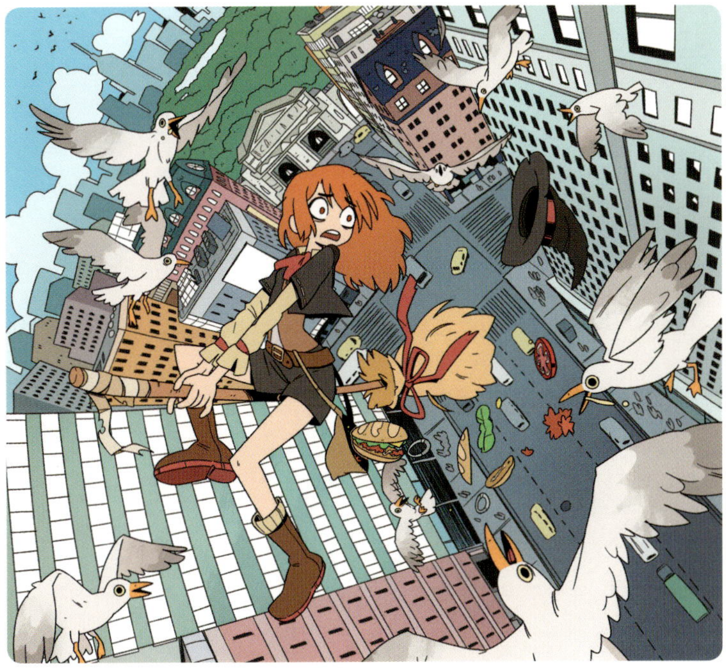

Paint in the base colors for the background

**13** Blending modes, offered by digital painting software such as Photoshop and Procreate, determine how two layers are blended together. Create a new layer for the shadows and another for the highlights. Paint in bright yellow colors on the lights layer and blue tones on the shadows layer. Next, apply the Overlay blending mode to the light layer, and Multiply mode to the shadows layer. These are the two blending modes I use the most when creating my artwork.

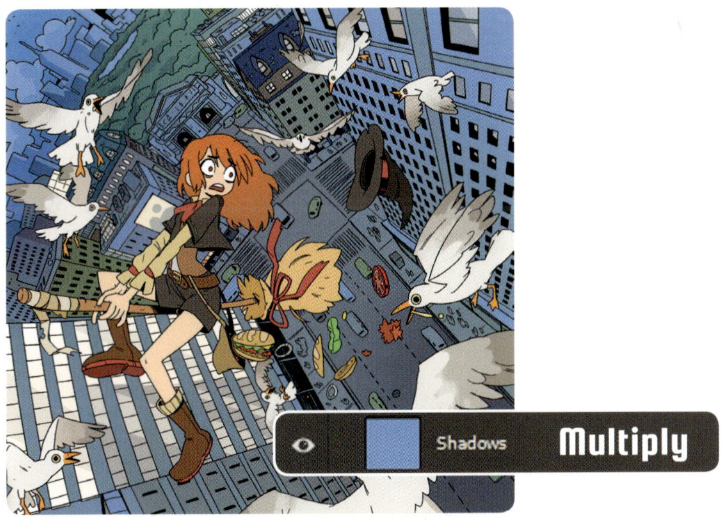


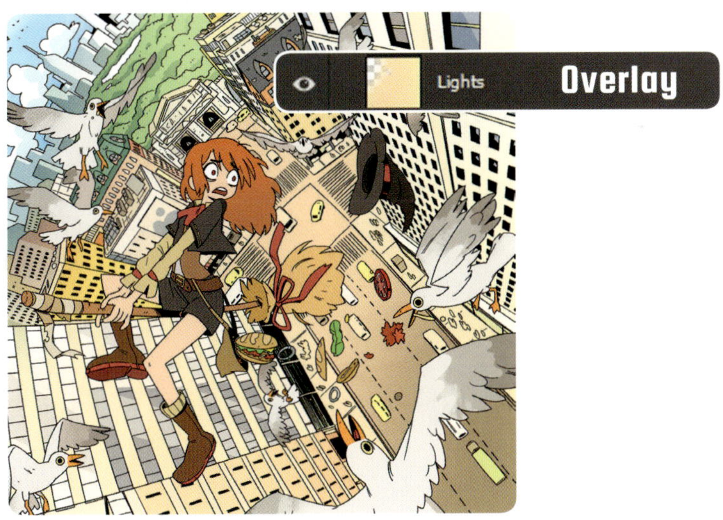


If working digitally, make use of blending modes to adjust the highlights and shadows

**14** Apply a mask on the shadow layer to erase the parts of your illustration that will be in the light. In this case, I determine that the light will be shining from the right. The buildings at the front-right side will therefore cast a large shadow across the scene, which in turn will make the character and seagulls stand out in the final illustration. Understanding how perspective works will help you establish how the light will affect the environment. The trick here is to keep things simple to prevent you from becoming overwhelmed. I do this by only using two layers for the light and the shadows.

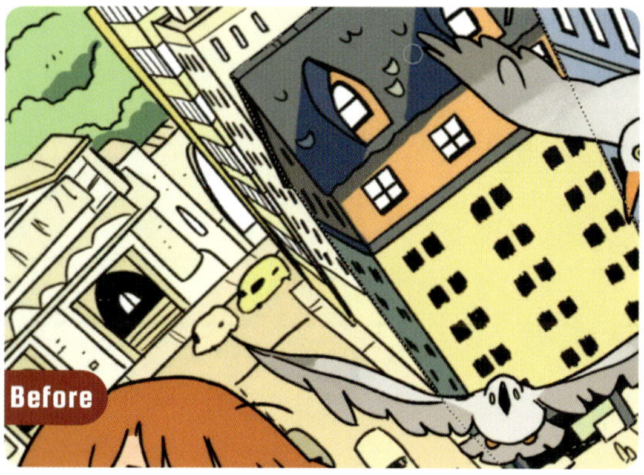


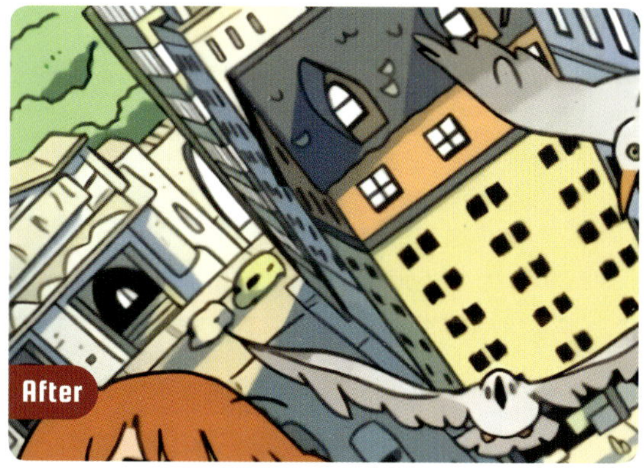


Mask some sections of the shadow layer to create the illusion of light, thanks to the brighter layer below

**15** Though I have finished adding the shadows, the illustration still lacks depth, mainly because the line art is dark black, which makes everything look a little less realistic. This can be fixed by coloring the line art to ensure the background blends in well and has sufficient depth. Do this by blocking all of the line art layers so you can easily paint over them without compromising the line art itself. Use a brush with 50% Opacity and select the color next to the line work you are painting. This will make the colors of the lines blend nicely together. In some cases, such as the road markings, select a different color that makes sense with the element you are working on. Use this step to add some more little details throughout the illustration, such as tiny windows on the skyscrapers in the distance.

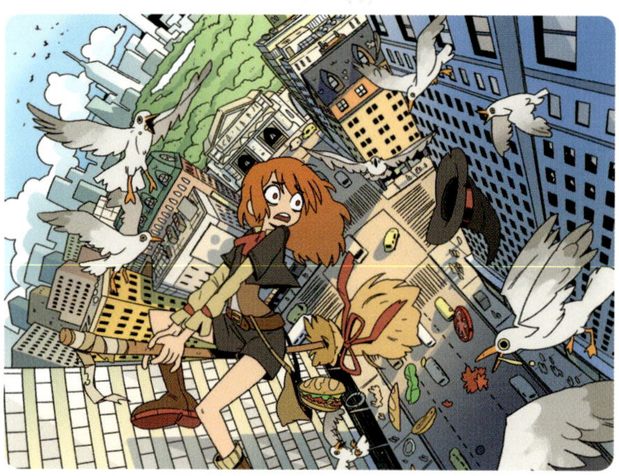

Shadow and light has been added to the background, but it still lacks depth

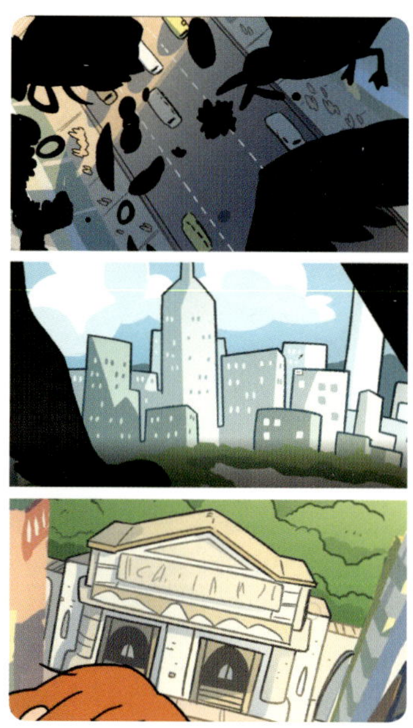

Color the line art and add small details throughout to enhance the illustration

**16** At this stage the illustration is almost finished. The only thing left to do is to merge the witch and the seagulls in the foreground with the scenery in the background. I carry out the final render of the background first, using this as a reference when completing the final render of the foreground character and seagulls. Doing this the opposite way around would make it more difficult to create a cohesive image with the character clearly in the foreground and the cityscape behind.

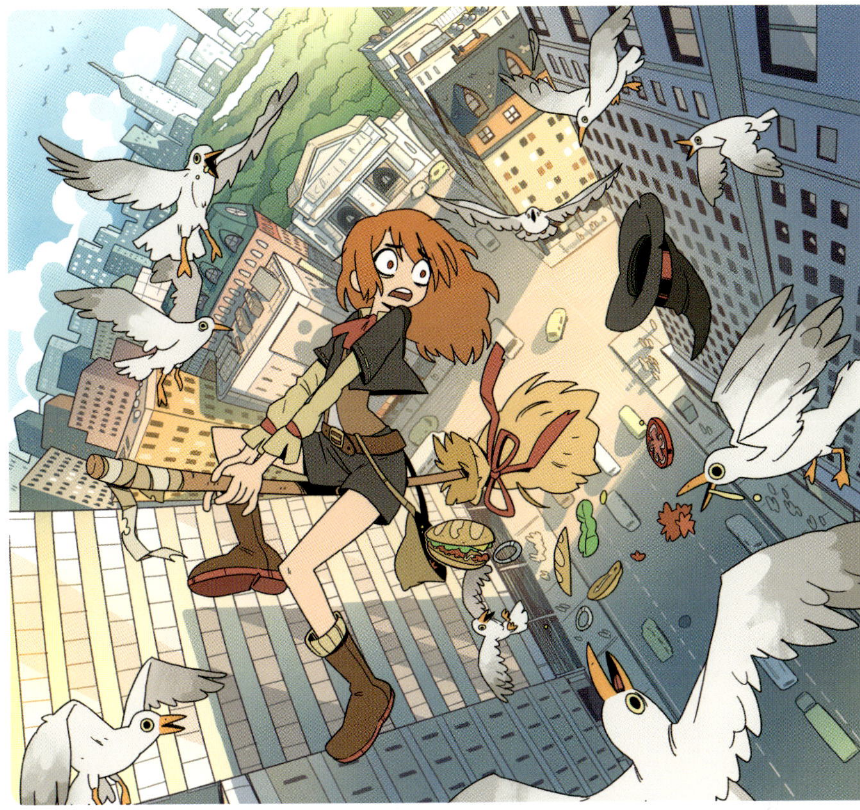

Complete a final render of the background and foreground elements

**17** Once you have finished rendering the shadows, paint the line art of the foreground characters in the same way that you painted the background line work. Try to think of the background scenery and foreground characters as a whole, rather than as separate elements. Using the same workflow for each element of the illustration will help to make the image appear more consistent. I also remove the lighter layer here, as the base colors of the witch and seagulls are already bright enough.

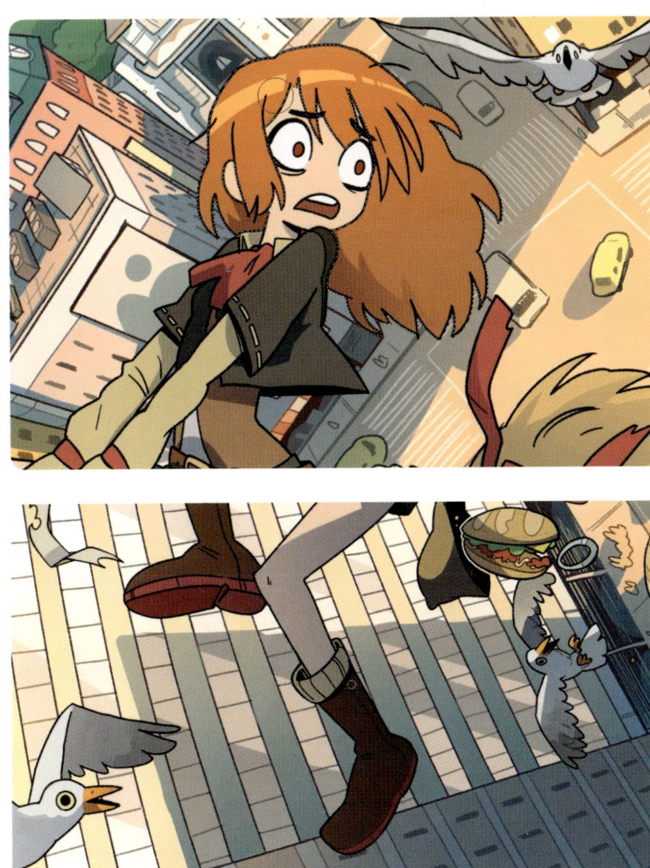

Be consistent when rendering the background and foreground elements, viewing them as a whole rather than separate and unconnected

**18** Take a step back and review the illustration as a whole. Consider how the colors blend together, if there is enough interesting detail, and whether each element is clear. If needed, tweak the colors by experimenting with digital filters and layers set to Multiply or Overlay mode. I increase the saturation of the witch's hair, as the brighter orange color will help to draw the viewer's attention to the center and focal point of the artwork. Little tricks like this can improve the impact of your artwork.

Increase the saturation of the witch's hair to instantly draw the viewer's eye to the character

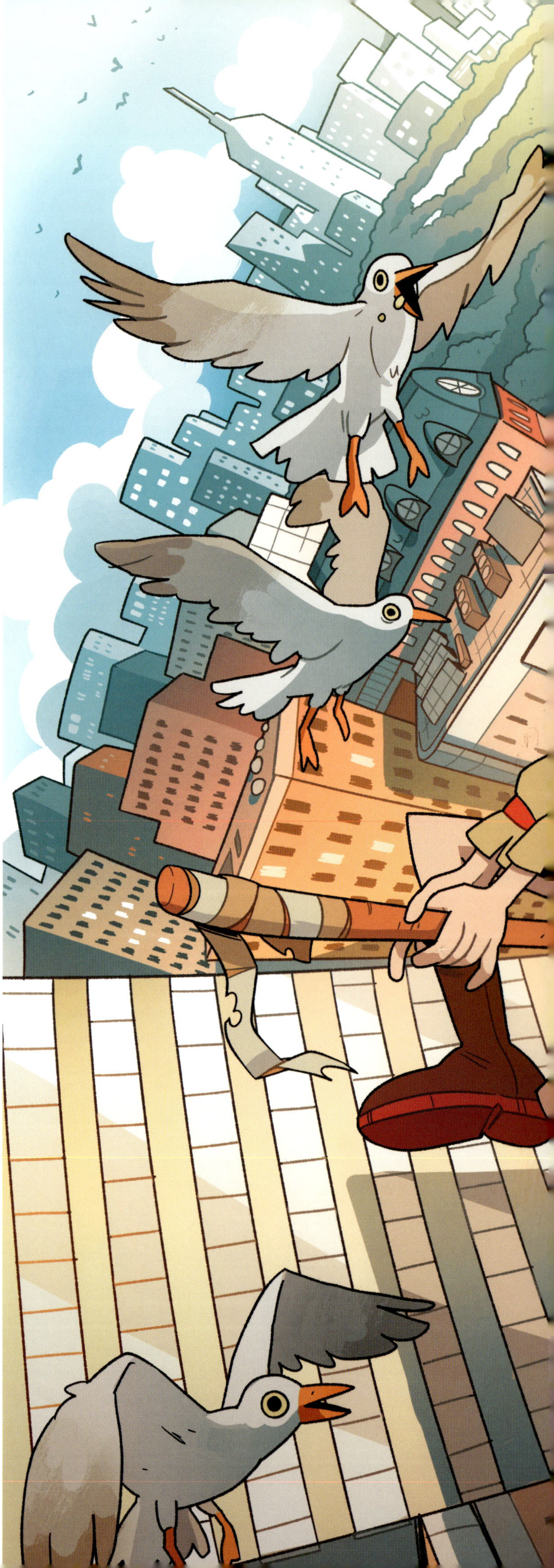

# CONCLUSION

By following this tutorial you will have learned how to create an anime-style character that feels fluid and dynamic, enhanced by bright, playful colors. She has an attractive S-shaped curve to her silhouette, allowing the eyes to travel easily from one side of the design to the other as they take in the detail. The striking purple-yellow complementary color pallete is paired with vibrant pops of red, and overall there is an airy, watercolor feel to the piece, true to my signature style.

The workflow and tips shared here will provide you with the information you need when designing your own character and creating a compelling illustration that you can feel proud of. Consider the importance of reference, composition, and color, as well as how you can imbue the character design with your own unique anime style.

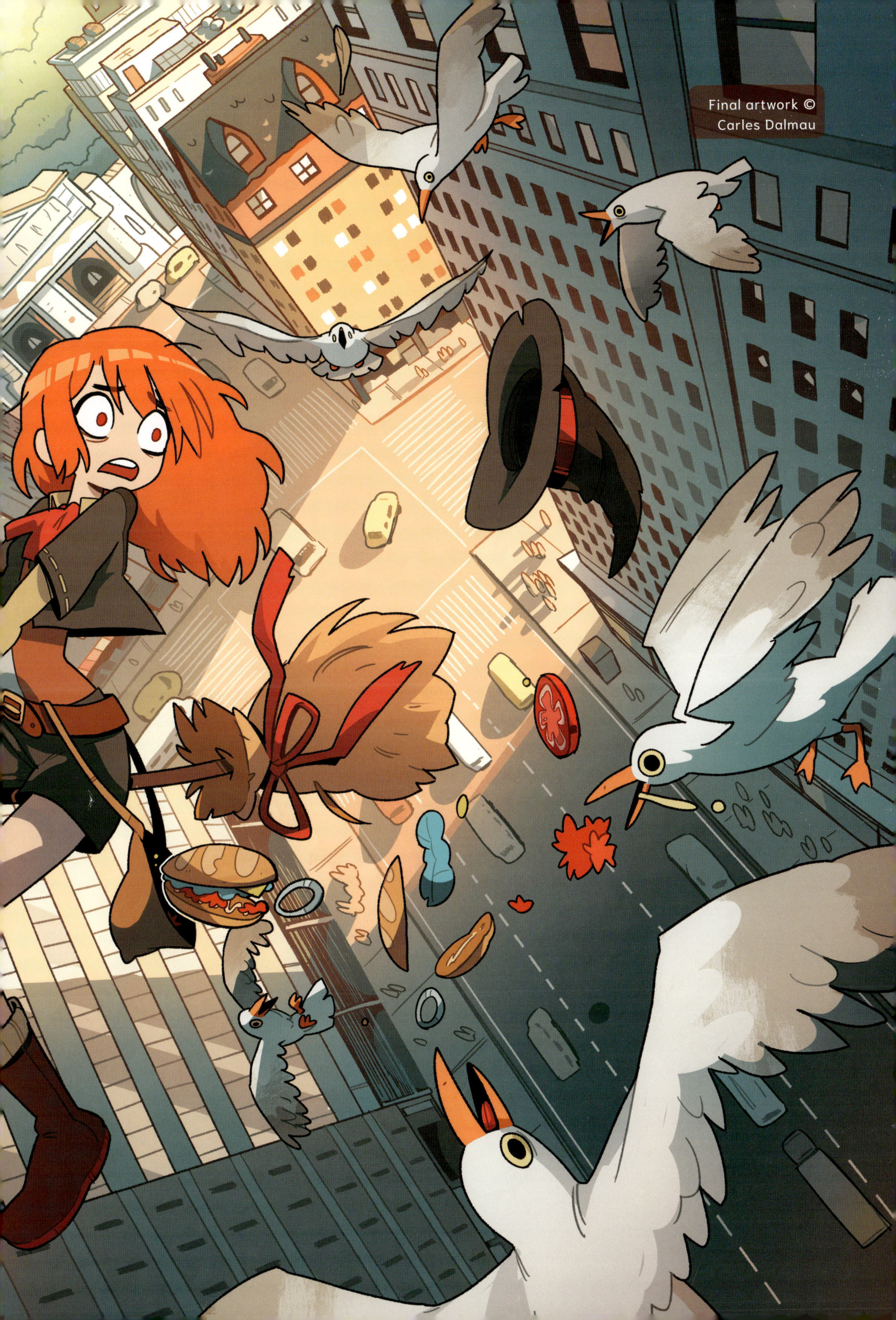

Final artwork © Carles Dalmau

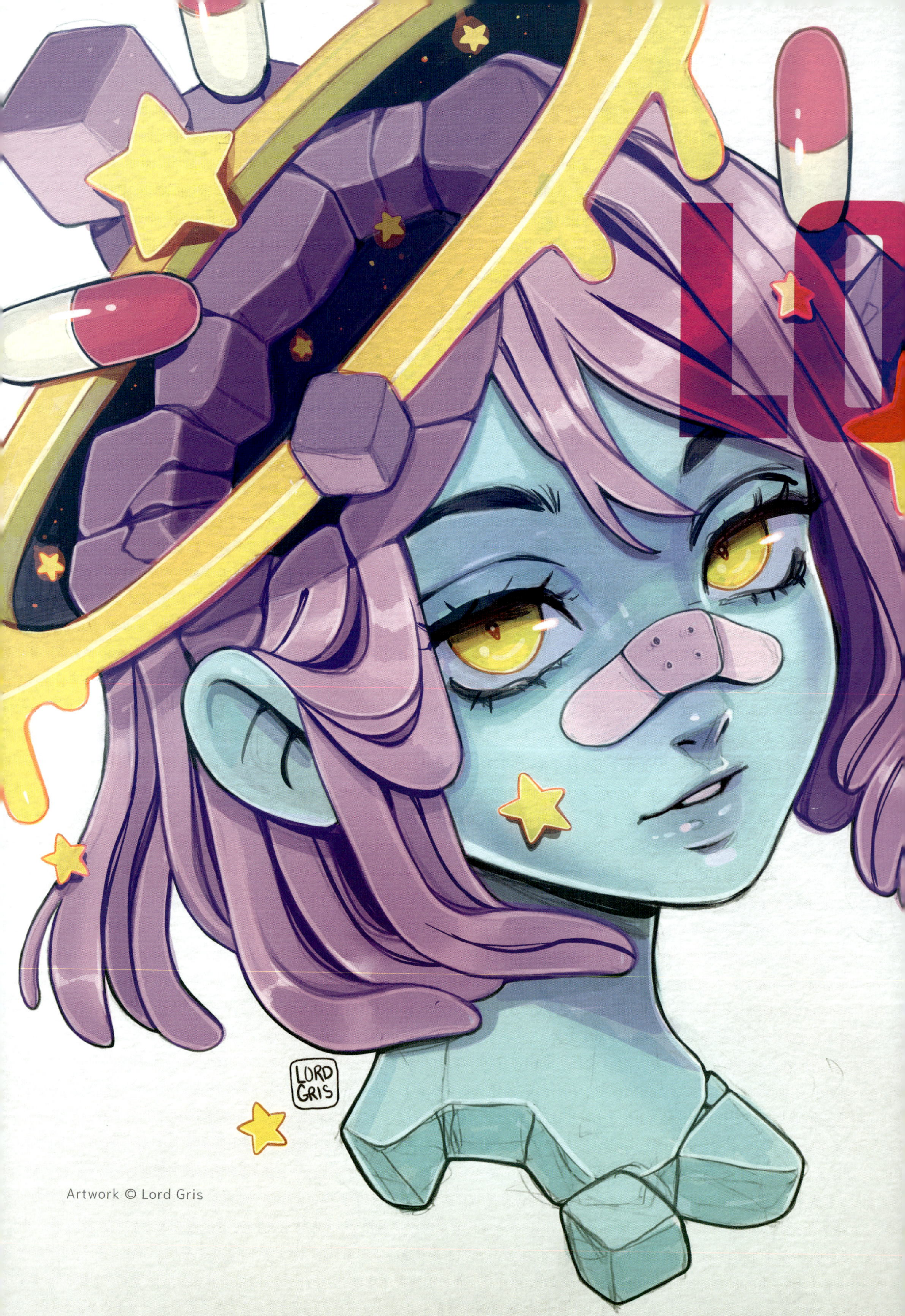


Artwork © Lord Gris

# RD GRIS

## Meet the artist

**Illustrator**

**lordgris.com | instagram.com/lord_gris**

Lord Gris is an anime-style illustrator based in Portland, Oregon. Inspired by the video games and trading cards she encountered growing up, she fell in love with feminine cartoon styles and drew colorful, whimsical characters throughout her childhood. Since finding her niche in online circles, she has gone on to work on video games, design toy concepts, and exhibit paintings in galleries. Her favorite pastime is to design her own unique characters and bring them to life.

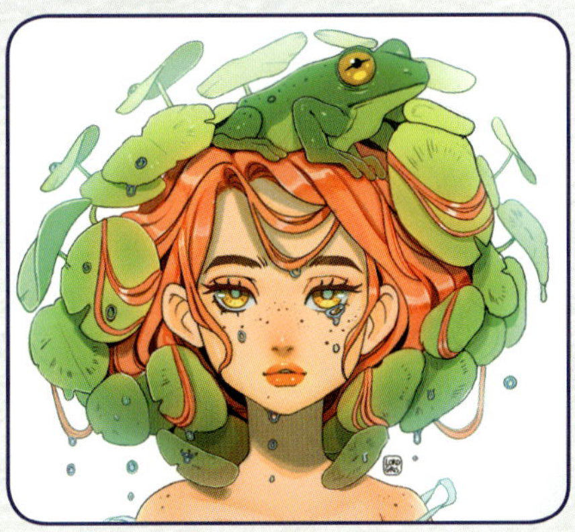

# CASE STUDY



## INFLUENCES, MOTIVATIONS, TRAINING

My journey to becoming an artist was more winding than linear. My brother introduced me to many cartoons and video games when I was young. Though I never heard the words "anime" or "manga," I grew up watching that art style in TV shows, such as *Pokémon* and *Digimon*, and playing video games, such as *Shining Force*, *Phantasy Star*, and *Fire Emblem*. They were cute, fun, colorful, expressive, and often very beautiful. Being surrounded by this media inspired me to create my own colorful characters, especially strong, angelic, warrior women.

Becoming a full-time artist was my only dream for a long time. I spent endless hours doodling characters and vowing that someday I would create artwork for the video games I played, but the older I got, the more out of reach this dream began to look. I became aware of the multitude of talented artists online and how competitive the job market was. I was also told there was no value in the girly, character-centric anime style I'd spent years developing, and social media didn't yet exist to show me otherwise. In my desperation to make my dream of becoming an artist a reality, I tried to change my style to one that was more serious, editorial, and sophisticated, hoping that as long as I was drawing, I would be content with any art career.

I attended art college for three semesters before becoming burned out, depressed, and ultimately dropping out. Not only did I hate the editorial art style, but a teacher I admired told me publicly that I was uncreative and was wasting my time and money being there. This was the nail in the coffin for my confidence in my ability to forge a career as an artist. For many years I wrote off art entirely, instead working in fashion retail and attending eclectic community college classes as I tried to figure out what my "true calling" was.

It wasn't until my mid-twenties, chronically ill and unemployed, that I was given my first tablet and started to dabble in art again. I began exploring social-media sites, such as Instagram, and found a welcoming online world that seemed hungry for exactly the kind of art I was creating. While I'd always been told there was little value in my anime-style character art, I found there was a whole online audience who loved it. It took several years to turn my online following into a means of generating income, with many mistakes along the way, but I'm proud of the journey I took to get me where I am today.

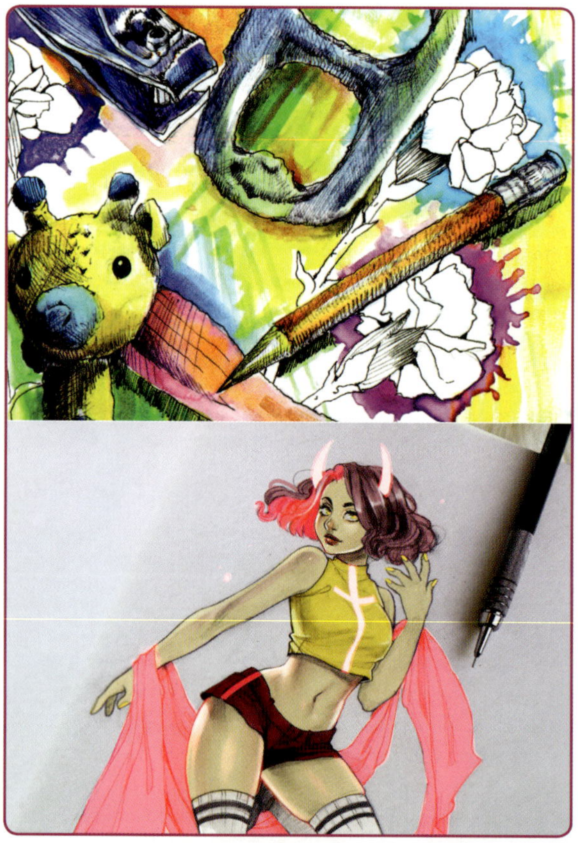

An example of the editorial-style art I made in college versus the anime-style art I make now

## The self-taught path

I studied illustration at a local private art college for a year and a half before quitting. I have mixed feelings about art schools. Some people thrive and feel empowered; it works out for them and I love seeing that. I would never want to discourage someone from attending art college if that's their dream. For others, myself included, it can be an expensive place that extinguishes creativity, teaches little, and leaves you feeling bitter toward art. My verdict is that if you want to go to art college, then go for it, but don't sign up just because you think you have to. Unlike other professions, art school is not a necessity to becoming a successful artist. Much of the information you need is already free and available online, and your portfolio of artwork speaks louder than any qualification. I've never been asked by a company or client hiring me if I had a degree. In fact, the majority of professional artists I know don't have one.

My work is largely self-taught. While I sometimes watched online tutorials and asked an artist friend for tips, my main learning came from studying the art I felt inspired by. I considered how they created the characters and utilized different tools and media to create an effect. I then practiced until I got it right. There were many artists I looked up to when I was younger, such as Loish, whose work I studied and tried to emulate as I gradually developed my own anime style.

Scrolling back to my early days on Instagram, I can see a huge amount of progress in my artistic skill. In a way, I find it comforting that this wasn't the result of an expensive education or some kind of rigorous secret training technique; instead, it was simply down to time and effort. This demonstrates that anyone, anywhere, can improve their artistic skill. Often the only thing holding them back is their own self-doubt. Progressing with art is much like exercise. If you run every day, you're guaranteed to get faster and fitter. Similarly, if you draw regularly, you're guaranteed to improve. The progress won't be quick or immediately obvious. It will be slow and you will hardly notice, until you look back on where you were a year or two ago and realize that techniques or elements that once proved tricky can now be completed with ease.

Created two years apart, the pose is more relaxed and the facial expression more human in the more recent image

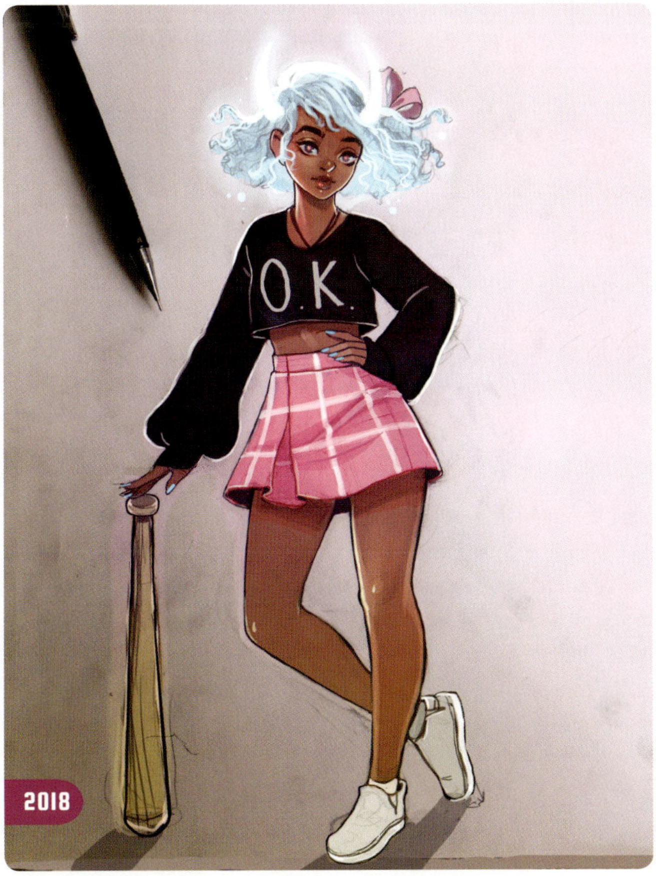


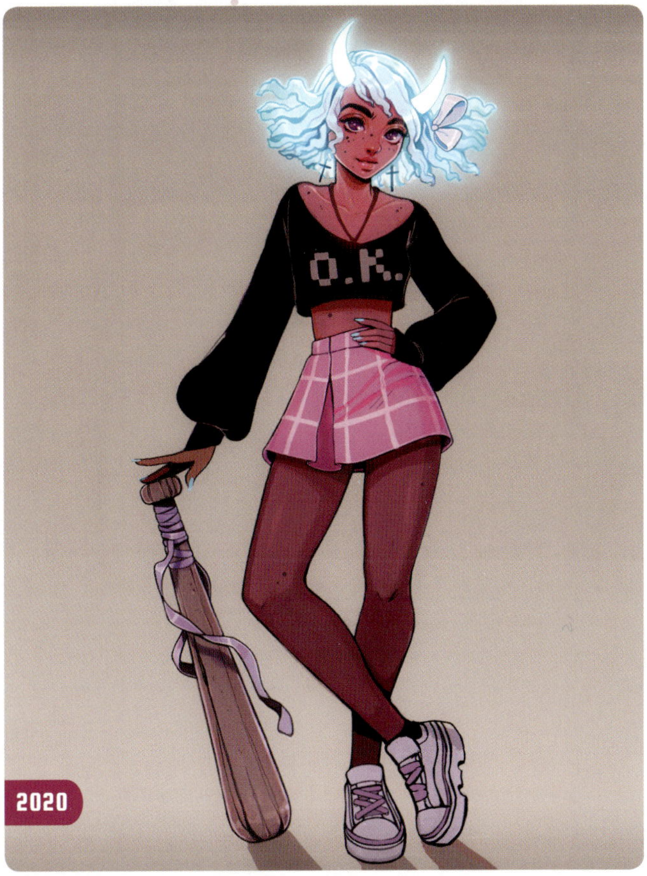

## Tools & media

I create my characters using a "tradigital" method, which involves digital coloring over a hand-drawn sketch. As I wasn't introduced to digital media until later in life, the pencil remains my most comfortable tool, as this was the only media I had access to for a long time. To this day I find sketching on a digital surface slightly weird and uncomfortable, and will always prefer paper. However, as I didn't learn any traditional coloring methods growing up, most of my coloring experience is digital. Being born in the 1990s, I grew up in an analog world that slowly shifted to a digital one, so in a way it feels fitting to have an art style that merges both traditional and digital media.

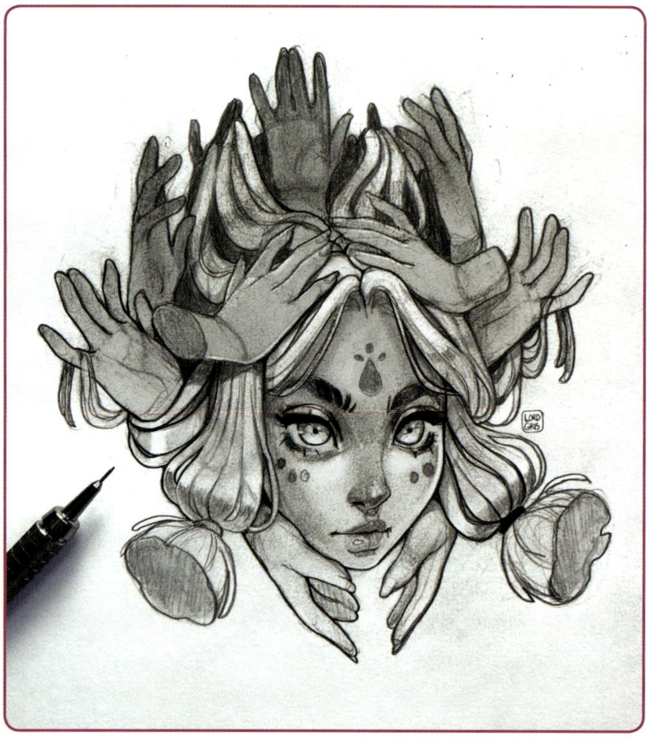

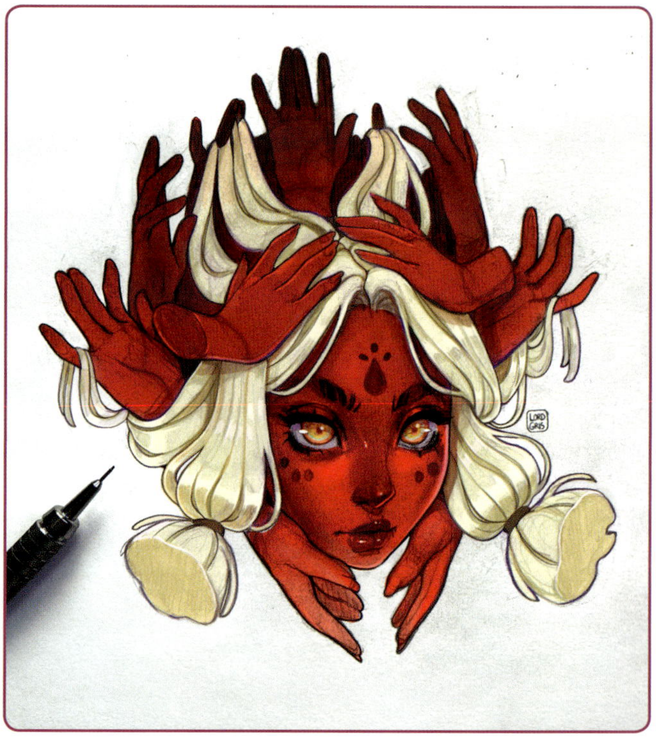

My signature method of coloring digitally over a traditionally drawn sketch

I also enjoy painting and would love to be a painter full time. My first experience with acrylic was in my high school art class, though I didn't learn to paint properly until I started my art career in my twenties. I made friends with a local painter and begged him to teach me his painting techniques. He very kindly let me visit his studio and taught me a few simple tricks that I've been practicing ever since. I later moved into the same studio space and was able to continue gleaning techniques off him every once in a while.

Experimentation is vital. Art is all about trying and failing, again and again, until you find what works. There are so many different ways to create and you never know which tool, media, or technique will resonate until you try it for yourself. I remember the first time I encountered gouache paints in college. I'd never heard of them before and was blown away. They were the perfect middle ground between acrylic and watercolor, allowing me to achieve the thick effects of acrylic with the wonderful blendability of watercolor. As much as I love acrylics, I sometimes feel limited by them, and there are new ways I want to try making art. Recently I have started experimenting with oil paints, which has been thrilling, as well as humbling.

It can be easy to fall into a rut as an artist. When you have built an online following, your followers expect you to create a certain kind of art and often don't want any kind of change. You must always maintain your artistic autonomy, however, giving yourself permission to move in the directions that make you happy and further your growth as an artist. If you begin to feel trapped by your audience and their expectations, your creativity will dry up and you can start to resent art. There's a reason why many famous artists throughout history had different periods in their art, some as dramatic as moving from realism to pure abstraction. Your followers might complain, but you will always be able to build a new audience around the new direction of your artwork. If you're not doing what feels right for you, you will soon burn out.

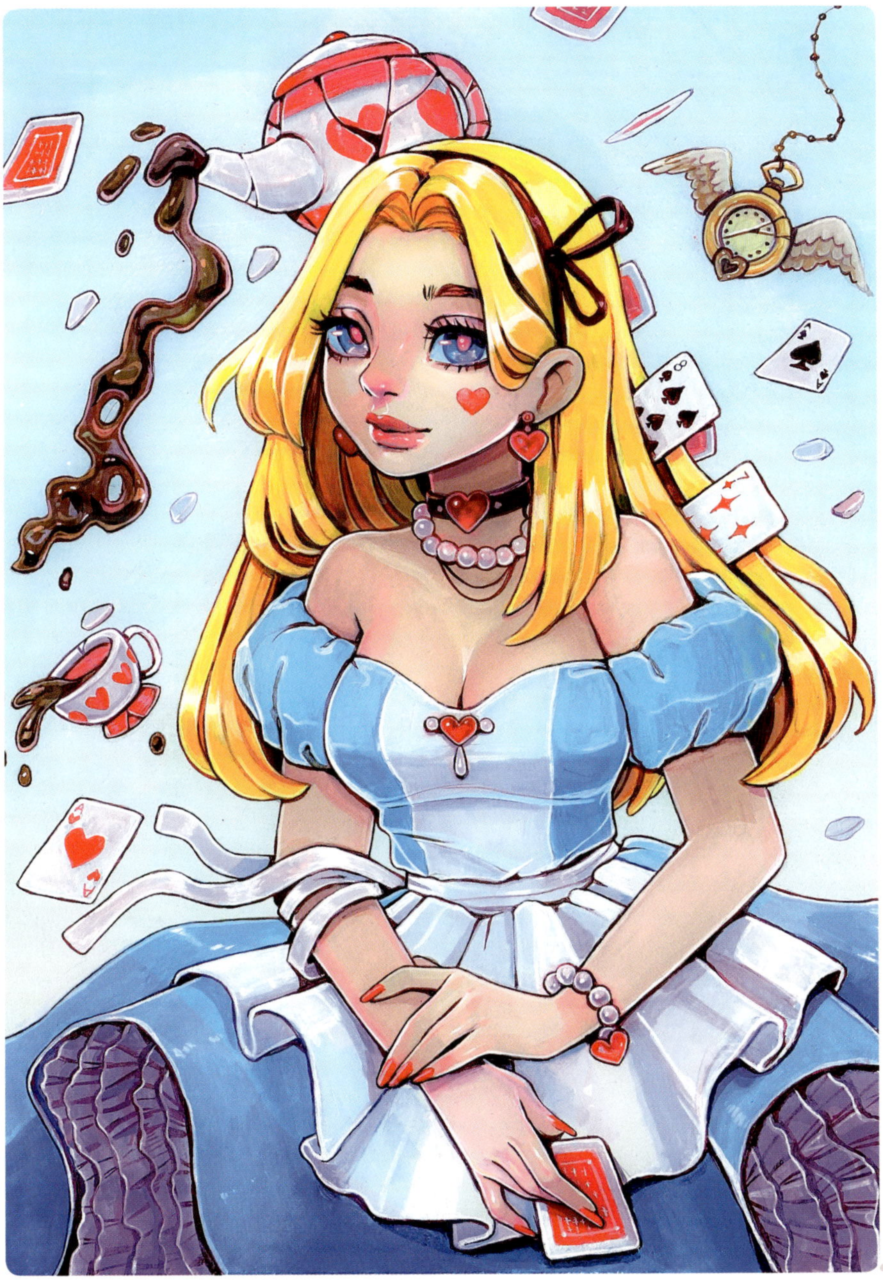

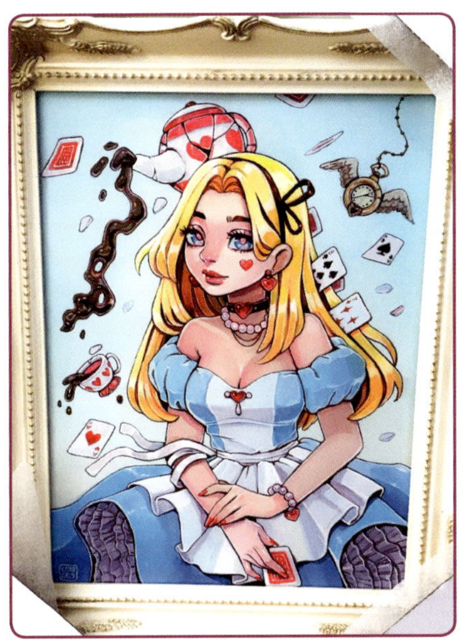

An acrylic painting created for a show in Haven Gallery, New York

# INDUSTRY EXPERIENCE

Just like finding your preferred medium, finding your place in the art world can take time. Some artists love working with clients, so commission work is perfect for them. Others like to create but don't want to engage with clients, meaning they are better suited to exhibiting their artwork in galleries. Some artists love to illustrate long projects, such as story comics, while others prefer to create quick, small drawings and are therefore drawn to social media. Some artists enjoy creating products and apparel, some like to sell originals, others run the convention circuit, and some only sell at local markets.

There are numerous ways to thrive as an artist. Everyone is different and the proverbial "coming of age" journey to finding how you prefer to work can be fairly clunky, as you often don't know until you try. I shuffled through several types of work before landing on what ultimately works best for me.

## Working for companies

I've worked with several companies in the past, including creating a "How to Draw Hair" article for Autodesk and producing doll concepts for a toy company. I worked with Skillshare to create a Skillshare Original video on how to design a stylized portrait, which was filmed in New York City. The biggest project I've worked on was Viz Media's video game *The World Next Door*, which taught me a lot about myself artistically. Initially I was only hired for a weekend's worth of thinktank work – which involved creating character concepts and game ideas to pitch to the company – but when they picked my concept work, I was hired as the full-time character designer. The project lasted about a year and required me to draw all of the characters, including their different poses, expressions, friends, enemies, and props. It was a lot of work and I'm really proud of what I created.

Before working on *The World Next Door*, I was self-employed full time for a few years. It was a big shift to go from making my own schedule and working at my own pace, to suddenly keeping a very tight deadline and organizing projects with a large team of people. I tried to continue with my own work on top of working on the game, but it was difficult to juggle both jobs at once and my personal work did suffer. The hectic nature of a big project was really fun and I loved traveling around with the team and showing off the game, but I did start to miss being able to engage with my audience online, encouraging them and hosting events.

Working on the game was very surreal; I had been hugely inspired by the art I saw in video games when I was growing up and always dreamed of working in the game industry. While I knew my younger self would have been so proud of achieving this dream, I was shocked to realize it was no longer what I wanted to do. I was incredibly grateful for the opportunity to work on *The World Next Door*, but by the time the project ended, I was happy to return to my little niche that I had grown so attached to. I realized that as someone with ADHD, big projects can be overwhelming and I am better suited to working in short bursts. Going forward I became much more selective in the type of projects I agreed to, making sure none interfered with my regular work.

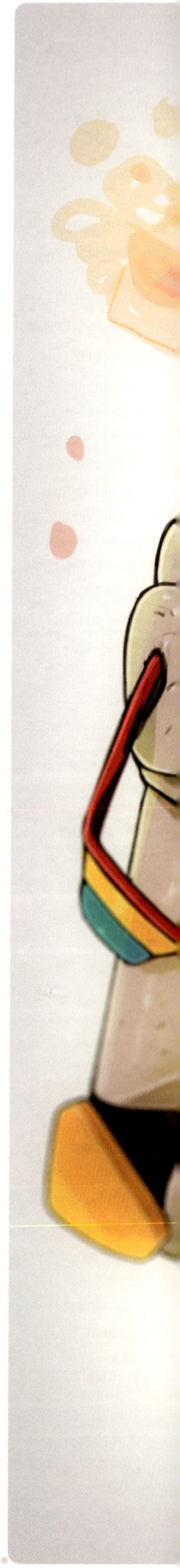

A piece commissioned by Beautiful Glitch for their game *Monster Prom*, featuring the characters Vicky and Calculester

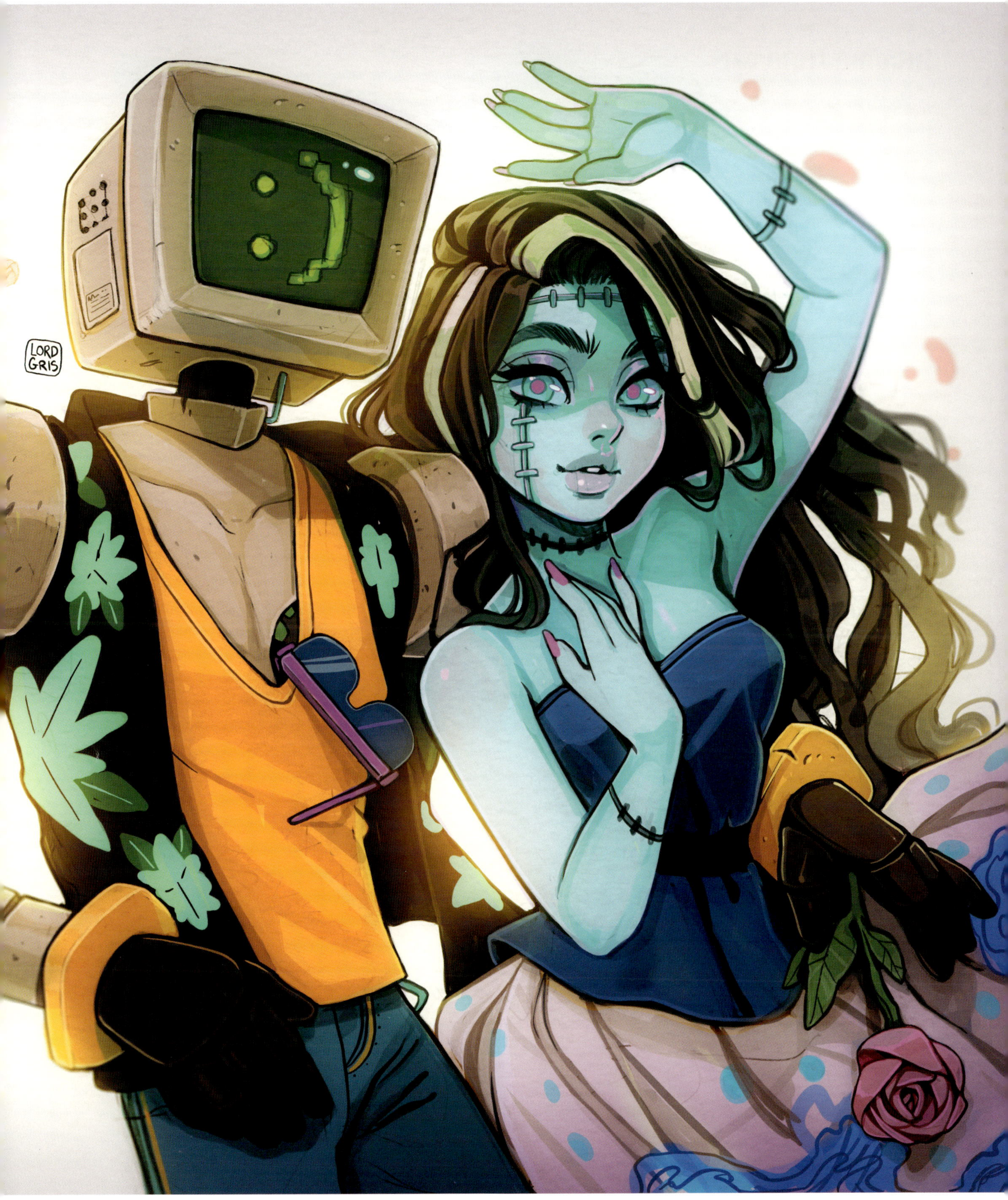
LORD
GRIS

## Income from art

A few years after leaving art school and giving up drawing, I found myself unemployed, behind on rent, chronically ill, and not sure what to do with my life. It was a very low point and I felt a little hopeless about my future. During this time my friend mentioned an incredible painter he knew, Happy D. Artist, who had just left her successful career to become a full-time artist. Over the course of a year, I watched as her following began to explode and felt incredibly inspired. She was sharing exactly the kind of art I wanted to be making: artwork of beautiful fantasy women I had been discouraged from so many years before. This gave me hope that maybe there was room in the world for a style like mine.

Before this I had never heard of a self-made artist. I always thought you had to be hired by a company, or have pre-existing connections to local galleries. Looking online and on Facebook groups, I started researching how to build a career as an anime-style artist, how to generate an income from it, how to design products at home, what manufacturers or online platforms were recommended, and how to apply for conventions. I envisioned that if I could build an Instagram account with 30k followers, I could start a Redbubble store and maybe make money that way. There wasn't much risk for me, as I wasn't quitting a successful career to pursue this dream. I was already at rock bottom... What did I have to lose?

Starting out was immensely fun. I felt giddy when I reached my first 1k followers. Only 29k more to go until I could start earning money! Yet having a big following doesn't always equal income. I only sold one item on Redbubble, which turned out was bought by my friend to make me feel better about the lack of sales. Despite this setback, I kept going. I tried making stickers at home, offering commissions, and designing tattoos. Once in a while a company would pay me a small amount to post about their product. I attended my first convention and made enough to almost cover my rent that month (bills not included).

The real breakthrough moment came when I sold my first original painting for $300 USD. I'd sold a few drawings here and there, but a painting was something big that I'd spent a long time working on. I had been so nervous that no one would buy it, but it sold within half an hour of listing. Someone wanted my art and was willing to pay for it. In that moment I felt like I'd walked through a doorway into a world where I was now a real artist and art was now my career. I haven't looked back.

For the first painting I sold, I custom cut a board to fit the frame

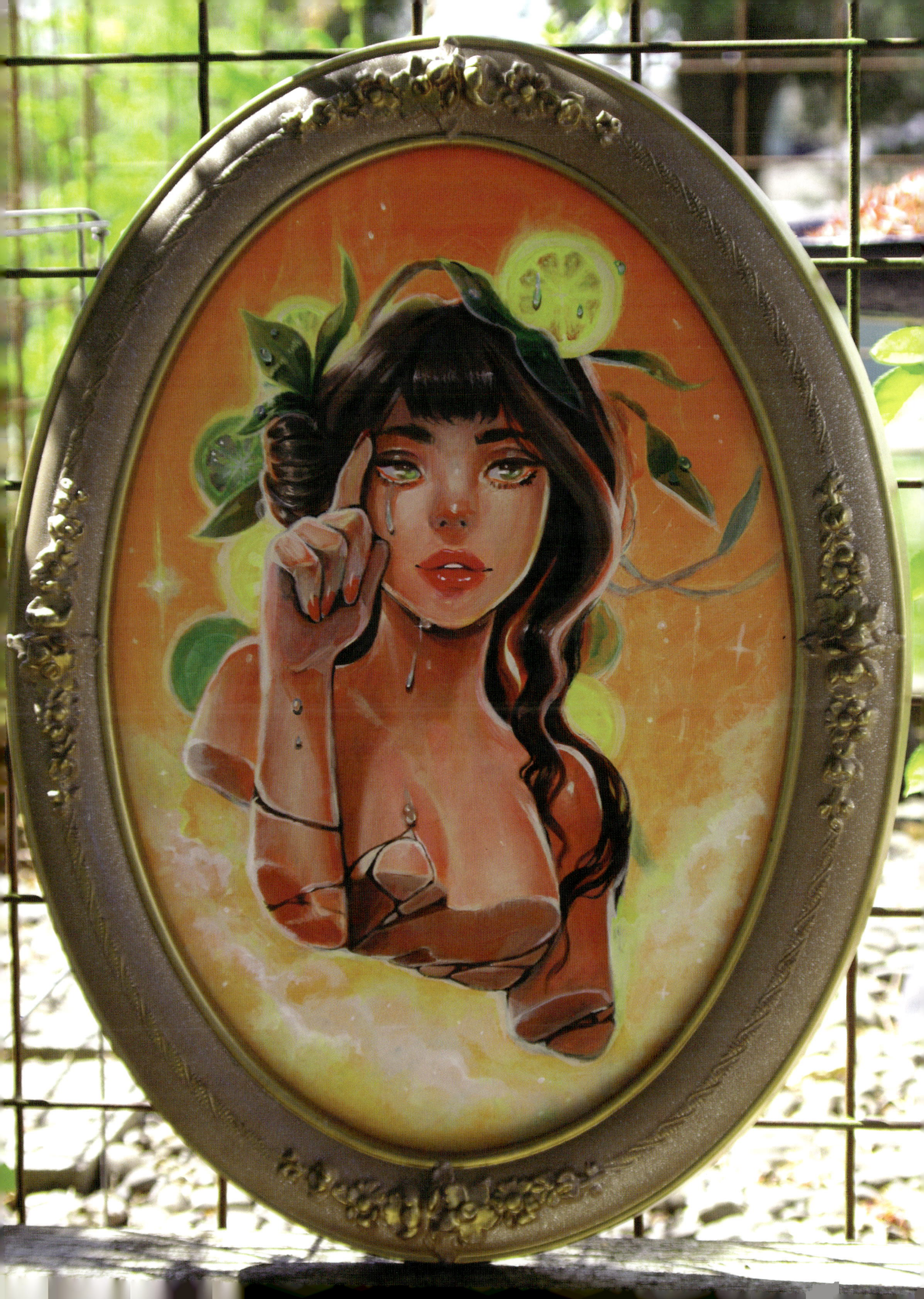

# DEVELOPING YOUR STYLE

Looking back at how my art style has evolved over the years, I can see how it veered off track and has been rerouting ever since.

I don't ever remember a time when I wasn't drawing. My artwork was always very cartoony, as that was the type of art that inspired me when I was young. It became more anime-style when I discovered manga books in middle school, from which I learned many drawing techniques. My artwork was very pure back then, in that it was exactly what I wanted to create. I didn't make it to impress anyone, fit in, or attract an employer. It was simply created out of a love for art.

My mistake was trying to change for an industry that, I didn't realize until later, I didn't even want to be part of. In high school I switched to a more realistic art style to appear more professional. While it wasn't exactly what I was passionate about, I still enjoyed creating it. In college, however, I tried a quirky, stylized line-art style that didn't make me happy. After I'd quit art school and given up making art, every once in a while I would draw a very noodly cartoon character when I was feeling sad, thinking maybe she'd make a good comic someday.

It wasn't until I made the decision to pursue art again that I embraced the old anime style I'd loved back in middle school. I found my favorite sketchbook from that time and redrew an artwork from it, attempting to return to that untainted, authentic style. That redraw was one of my first Instagram posts to attract a high level of engagement and began to grow my account, which felt extremely validating.

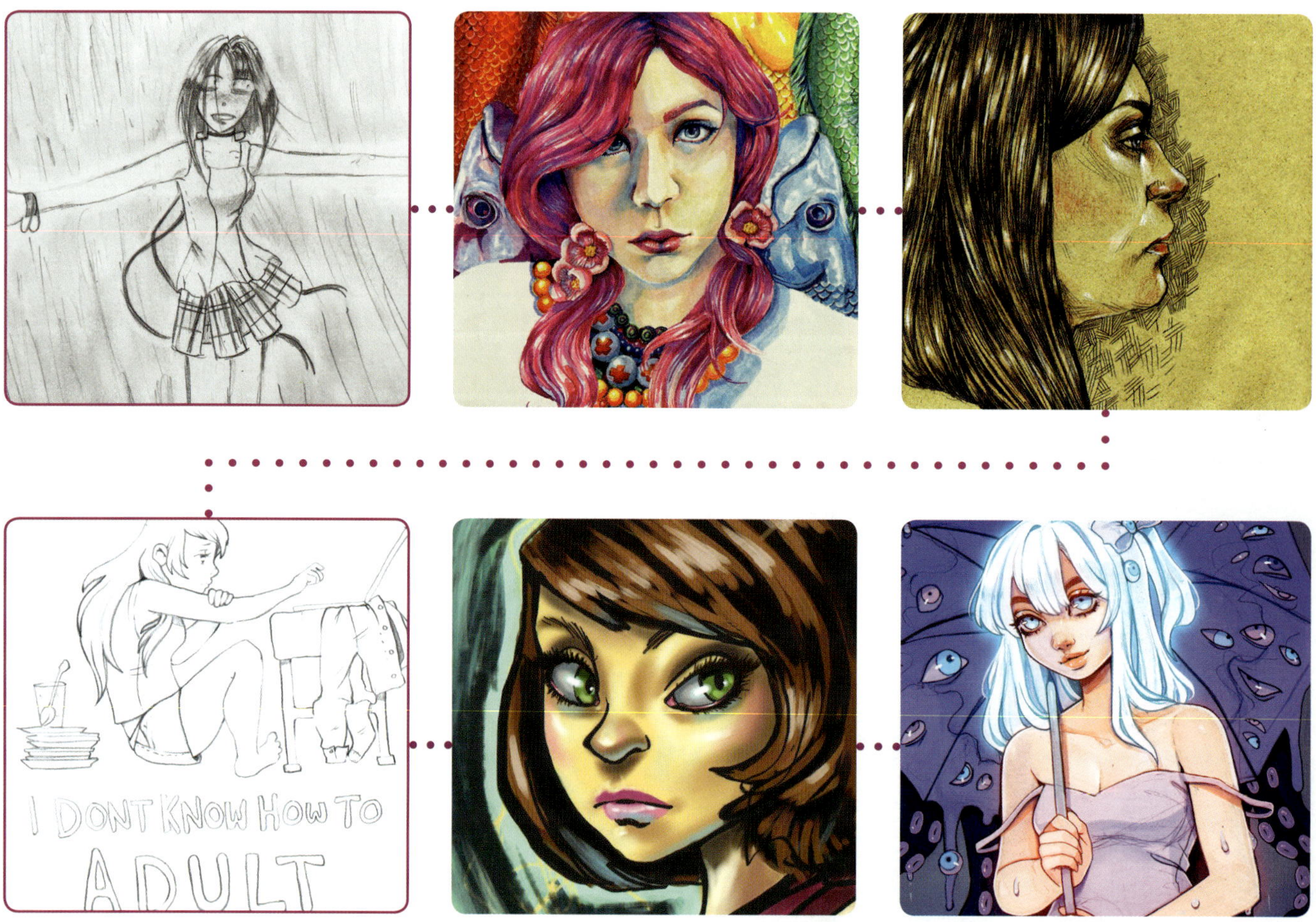


The progression of my style over the years

## Personal style in the commercial world

There is a huge dichotomy between the employed versus the self-employed artist. Before the birth of social media, there were a very select number of art styles that were considered commercially marketable. In order to be hired by a company, you had to adhere to one of those approved styles. As there weren't many job openings available, this would involve forcing yourself to create in a way you didn't like for a lottery shot at employment.

Social media blew the lid off this system. It allowed artists to market themselves and build a following around the kind of work they wanted to produce, proving you can find a fan base for almost any art style. I love seeing the vast range of styles, from detailed hyperrealism to rough sketches and comic doodles that make people laugh. There's an audience for every style of art and room for every type of creator out there. If you love what you're doing and take the time to master your craft, you will find your fan base.

## Working in a bubble versus external influences

Artists who primarily share their artwork and engage with their audience through social media can often find themselves in a bubble. Sometimes the bubble is great; for example, when lots of artists engage with the latest trend or redraw, or simultaneously become obsessed with the same anime show. But sometimes it can start to feel like the same subjects are being drawn on repeat, when you just want to see something new. This is unavoidable, as it's natural to be influenced and inspired by the artists and subjects you see the most. If you're only exposed to the online bubble, this will ultimately affect what you produce.

A common example among Instagram artists, myself included, is the peony flower. While I love peonies, sometimes I look back at my old artwork and notice that, before social media, I used to draw flowers that grow locally to where I live, such as foxgloves, tiger lilies, cherry blossoms, camellia roses, and flowering dogwood. In these I was drawing inspiration from my everyday, personal world, rather than online sources.

Being online can be slightly homogenizing, so it's important to remember to look around and explore your immediate environment. Use all of your senses to interact with it and let it speak to you. Get into the habit of stepping away from your desk at regular intervals to go for a walk, write in a journal, or get away for the weekend; whatever it is that will unplug you from the bubble and allow you to form fresh ideas from your own imagination. The more authentic your voice is in your work, the more you will be able to create a distinct style and fresh subject matter.

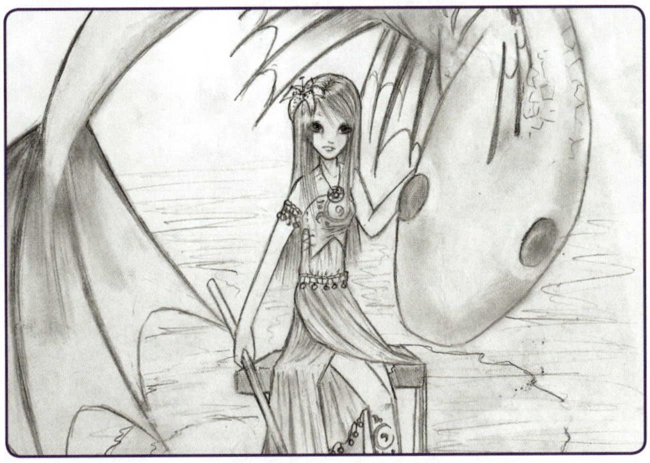

A drawing from middle school featuring tiger lilies, which often grew in my neighbors' yards

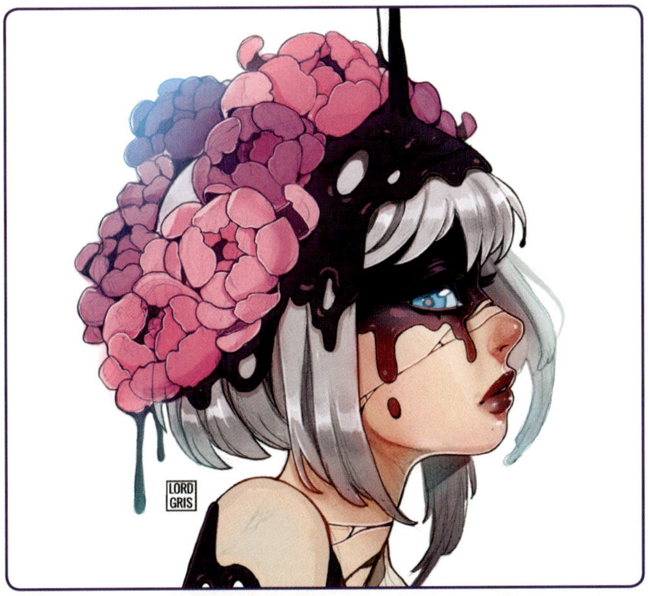


This character is adorned with peonies, typical of anime-style art on Instagram

## Limitations of style

When I was younger I loved to draw in a fairly typical anime style, known for its strong line work and minimal rendering. My characters didn't have noses, their eyes were big and saucerlike, and their mouths were very expressive. As I got older, I began to explore a more sophisticated art style in the hope of finding a place in the art community. Moving toward realism, I created characters that were very stoic and rendered.

My current art style – cartoonlike but still rendered – sits somewhere in between. I miss the full anime style, however, and have slowly been trying to push my art in that direction to create more expressive and less pouty characters, though this has been a very slow transition to avoid an obvious shift.

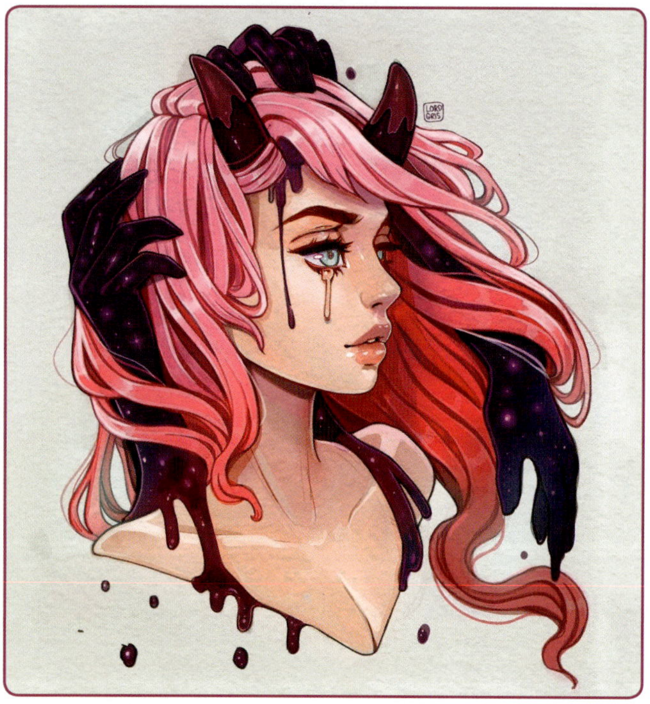

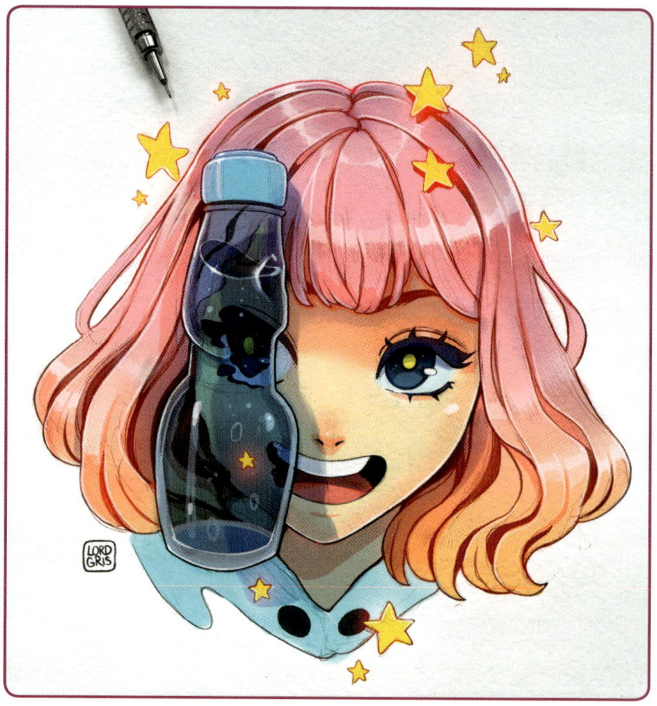

A rendered anime-inspired character versus a more cartoonlike character with typical anime features

# BUILDING YOUR BRAND

I have a brand, but not in the traditional sense of the word, as I don't think my work is overly commercially marketable. While fans of my artwork are likely to buy the products I sell, people who stumble across one of my products online, but aren't familiar with my work, are unlikely to make a purchase. The artwork of some artists will speak to a general audience, but this is a skill I haven't yet mastered.

I do, however, think there is a certain look and vibe associated with my artwork. It's consistently very colorful and feminine, a little strange, and, of course, anime-inspired. If I were to suddenly switch to somber landscape paintings, this would be very off-brand and I would definitely lose my followers. I always try my best to create within my brand boundary, but as this is the type of content I enjoy creating, this comes naturally.

People buy what they are a fan of. It could be they're a fan of your artwork, or perhaps they're a fan of something you're drawing, such as characters from an anime show or video game. This is why, for some artists, fan art can be a good starting point, especially when running the convention circuit; people will walk past your stall and recognize a character they are a fan of. Be careful with fan art, however, because once you enter that world it can be hard to forge a brand outside of it. Don't build a fan base exclusively from fan art, thinking you can then switch to personal art later on, as these followers will often disappear once you make the transition. Feel free to create fan art from time to time, but intersperse it with your own personal work.

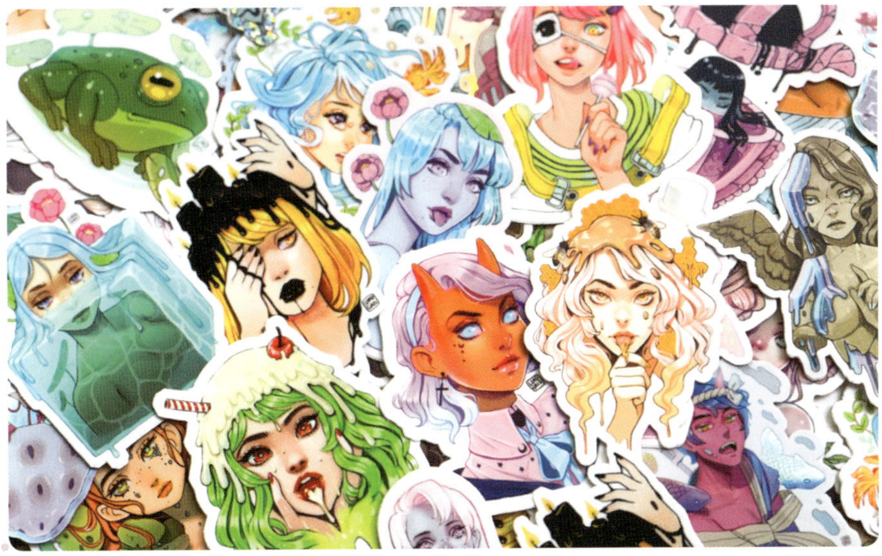

Examples of some of the products I make, including stickers and pins

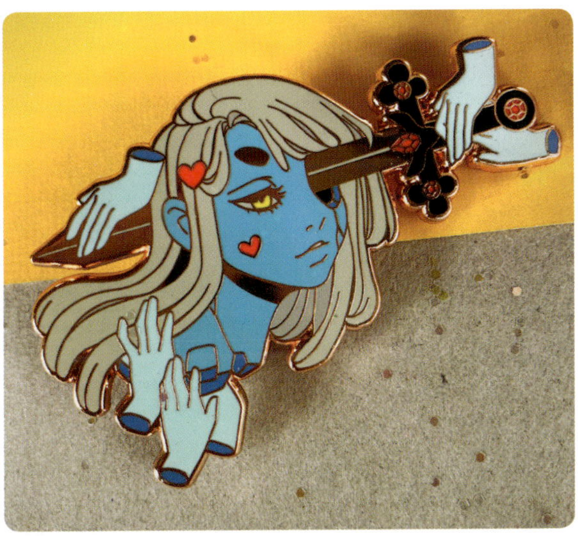

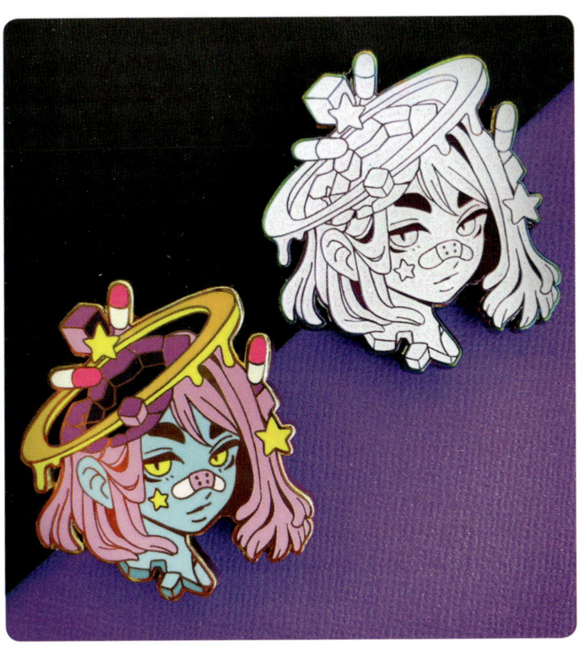

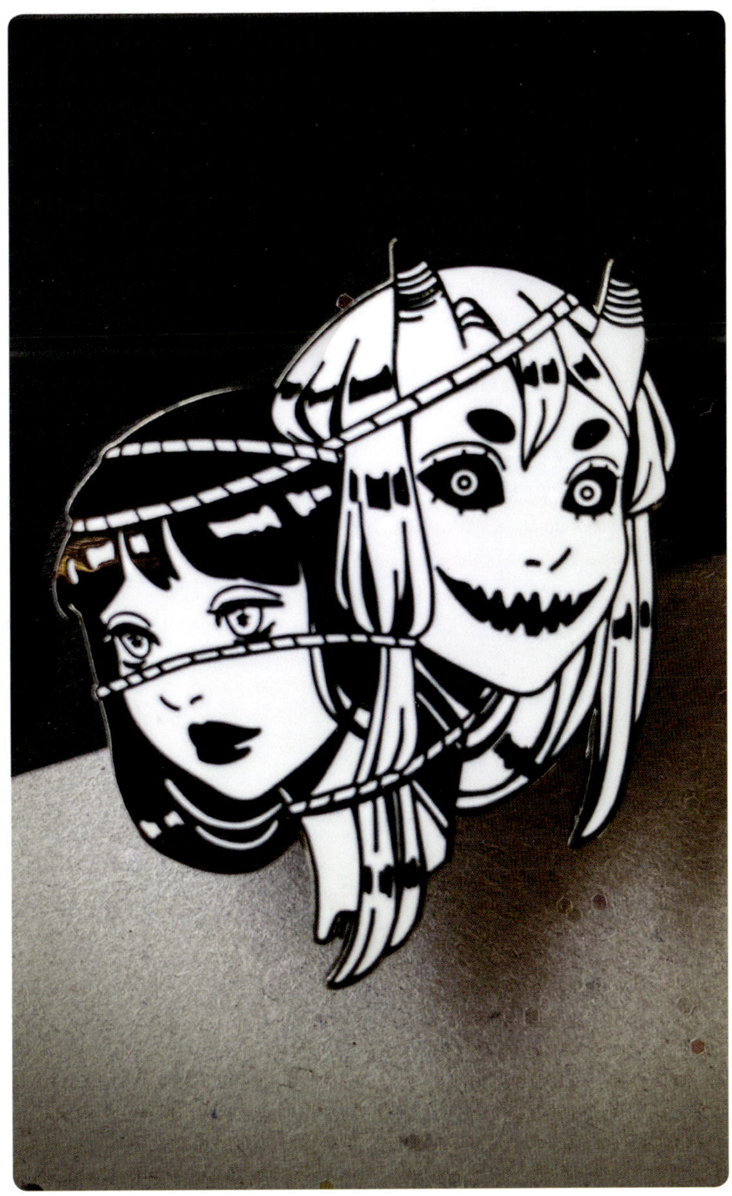

## Memorable & influential brands

Omocat is a popular artist and a prime example of anime-style work that is commercially marketable. Anyone walking past her booth at a convention can feel compelled to buy her products, then and there, without previous knowledge of her work. She was a huge source of inspiration to me when I began creating my own products. Not only does she have a cute, sketchy anime style that I adore, but I admired how she took her signature style and turned it into an amazing apparel brand. While I've not yet delved into clothing production, I've always aspired to make cool shirts and sweatshirts. There's a certain knowledge and nuance to her brand that I hope to master myself someday.

## Choosing an artist name

Lord Gris was a nickname given to me by friends when playing a massively multiplayer online (MMO) game, because my character's name was Griselda, chosen because it seemed like a cool name for a female warrior. It was never a name I expected nor chose to be my lifelong artist name. My friends saw my artwork and encouraged me to create an Instagram account to share my drawings online, something I probably never would have done without their push. I named myself after the silly nickname they had given me to make them laugh. As my art began to grow in popularity online, I realized I was now locked into this nickname and there was no going back, so I embraced it.

Lord Gris is succinct, easy to remember, and makes for a good brand name. There have been countless times I wanted to share an artist I loved, only to realize that I couldn't remember the crazy sequence of letters and numbers used for their name. When people ask me how to come up with their artist name, especially for online profiles, I encourage them to pick one that is easy to spell and remember. This will make it easy for people to find your social media profile or website, and mention or tag you online.

The only downside is that Lord Gris often gets misread as "Lord Girls." I regularly receive messages from followers saying they have been reading my name wrong for years, and I even noticed "Lord Girls" scratched out and replaced with the correct name on the packaging of a product sent to me by a company. I also get messages letting me know "Gris" means pig in Swedish, which makes me laugh. In summary, make sure your artist name can't be misread as something else, especially when multiple words are merged in a hashtag or handle. You could also try translating it into various languages to check what international followers may read it as. Despite this, I wouldn't change my artist name. If I didn't have that small community of friends who gave me that nickname all those years ago, I would never have created the social-media account to share my artwork in the first place.

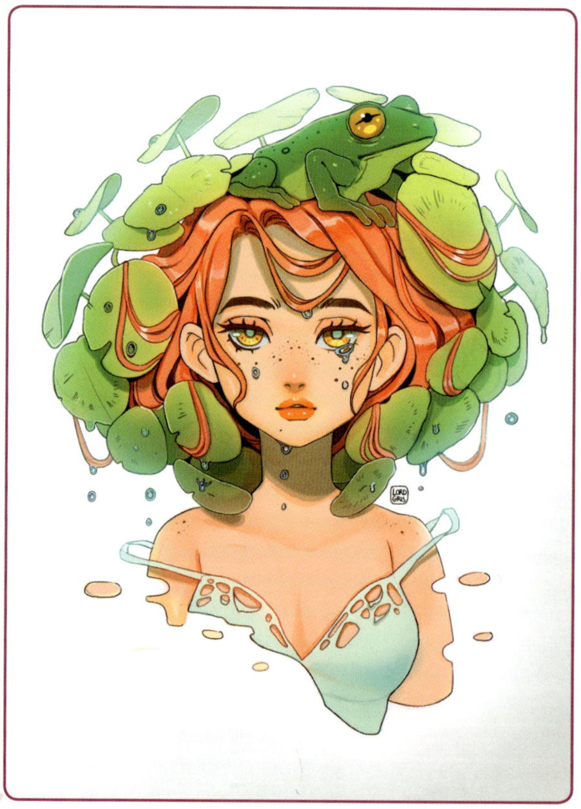

Cement your brand by choosing a memorable artist name and a profile image that is easily recognizable

# Networking & cross promotion

Networking is incredibly valuable for any artist, anime-style or otherwise. While many artists are introverts, preferring to focus on creating their art over talking to people, networking is crucial for creating opportunities for yourself. At the very least, it will lead to making some new artist friends with shared interests. Most likely, you will gain a knowledgeable network of creatives who can share opportunities, expertise, and experiences.

I try to pass opportunities along to other artists. For example, I no longer accept personal commissions, but when an individual does reach out to me with such an opportunity, I recommend artist friends who are well-suited for the project. I also appreciate having more experienced artists to turn to when I have questions. Being a self-employed artist with a large online presence is a fairly new type of career; you can find yourself encountering numerous obstacles when it comes to manufacturing, taxes, producing different types of content, and trusting companies that reach out to you. Having wise artist friends that you can ask for advice – such as what company to use for producing a certain product, or if you should trust a job offer – is an invaluable resource. Similarly, I try my best to answer questions from artists and to be transparent with my brand. I'm a firm believer that you will get back what you put into a community, so be kind, open, and genuine.

I'm often asked how I got into making video games and where I sent my application. In actual fact, it came about because I had been attending a local meet-up group for game-making, which was run by Rose City Games, the company Viz Media hired to make the game. When they needed an artist for concept work, I was one of the people they thought of and reached out to, as they already knew me and my work.

Similarly, I didn't apply for the first gallery I exhibited my artwork in. I had been attending a weekly Drink & Draw event in my city and the host posted my painting on their page. A gallery that followed the Drink & Draw event then got in touch with me. Even the way I learned to paint came from reaching out to a local artist in my area.

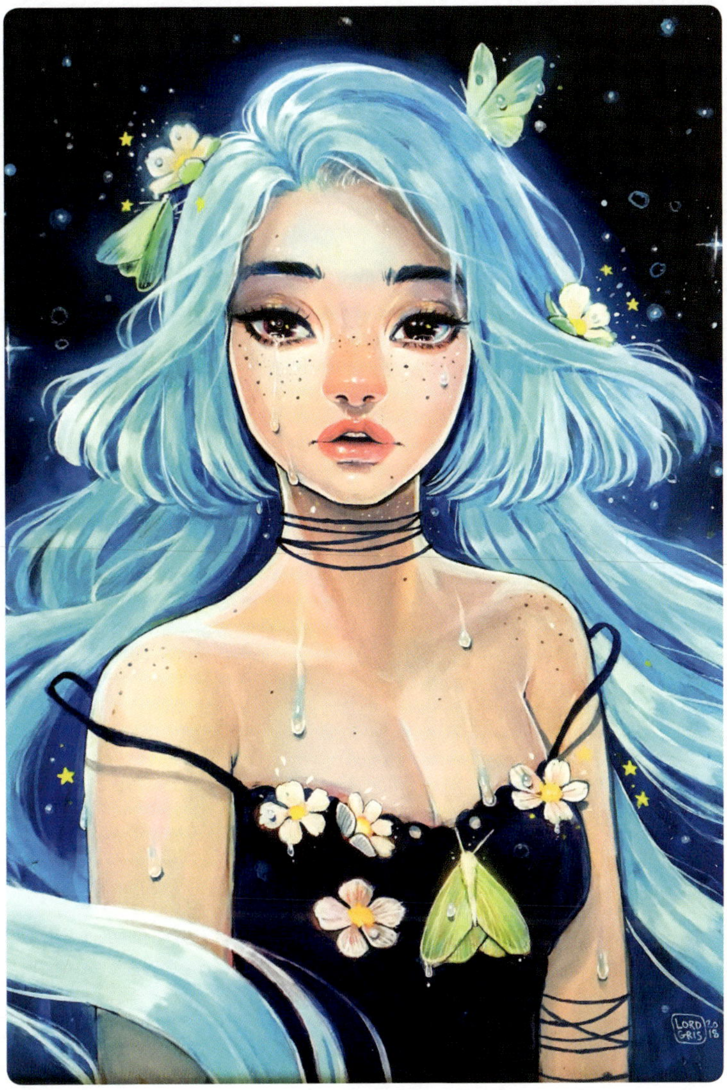

*Water from the Underworld* is the first painting I ever placed in a gallery show

## Ads & marketing

I once paid for an advert as an experiment to see what it could produce, but didn't feel like I got much value out of it. If anything, I felt like it sunk my engagement in an almost predatory manner; I noticed my posts started to perform worse afterward, almost as though the platform was trying to get me to purchase more ads. Ultimately, I aim to create and share content that is engaging and think my followers will like, and hope my platform will grow on its own. In the age of social media, when there are so many ways to share posts, you only need to create something your audience loves and it will promote itself.

Be careful when working with companies who manufacture art materials or similar products. They may reach out to you to offer free art supplies in exchange for your promotion of their products on your social media. This was thrilling to me at first; I felt validated as an artist that a company wanted to work with me! But several years later, I found myself with a closet full of generic brand markers that I never used and still no way to pay my bills, while those companies were making money from my adverts. Don't be scared to ask companies for monetary compensation if they approach you to advertise their products.

The free promotion problem is unfortunately endemic in the art community. Many artists are a little insecure and will say yes to any offer, while companies know they can get away with near-free advertising by sending them products. The current state of affairs means if one artist asks for compensation, the company can easily find another artist who will do it for free. If more artists were firm in their request for payment, the companies would have to change how they treat artists.

## Pricing

Pricing was a learning curve. When beginning to monetize your art, it's easy to get taken advantage of in the desperation to make a sale, especially when dealing with impostor syndrome. When I look at the price I charged for products when I was first starting out, I massively shortchanged myself, though at the time I didn't know any better. There were already so many other successful artists online, I doubted anyone would pay for my products and consequently listed them incredibly cheaply, because that's all I thought they would sell for. I charged $20 USD for commissions, even if the artwork took a week to complete, which was a tiny drop in the ocean of my monthly expenses.

It didn't help that it felt like commissions were so hard to acquire. I found myself talking to thirty potential buyers who all complained about my prices – which were already extremely low – before one agreed to the offer. I would also encounter customers who took the art but never paid. In these early days I didn't know how to use watermarks, write contracts, take payment up front, or be assertive; I was just grateful someone wanted to buy my art at all. Some people will have beautiful originals I sold for only $40 USD. My first stickers sold for $1 USD per sticker, because I thought people would only buy them if I made them really cheap. Over time I learned the cost of paper, adhesive overlays, printer ink, and taxes, and factored in the time it took to cut them out, as well dealing with any errors that lead to binning dozens of pages of stickers, and realized I was starting to lose money.

As the demand for my art increased and my following grew, I started to gain more confidence. After the sale of an original, I learned to sell the next one for more. For commissions, settle on an hourly rate for yourself. You can either charge the buyer based on the exact hours you work, in which case, sign a contract with the buyer prior to starting work, or ask for half of the estimated payment upfront, followed by the remainder on completion. Or more simply, create a flat fee based on your hourly rates for the different kinds of art you make. For example, if on average it takes you around ten hours to complete a portrait, and your rate is $20 USD per hour, then your flat fee is $200 USD, which you should ask for upfront.

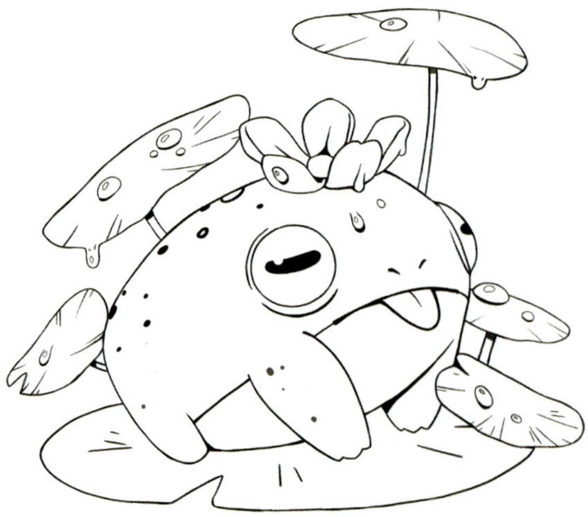

Geoffrey Sugarloaf is the cute frog character that acts as my brand's mascot – he has been turned into a plushie, among other things

Don't start the commission until you receive payment. It's also important to make the rules clear on how many edits or revisions the buyer can ask for.

When selling products, look at the average price successful artists are selling similar items at. For example, small items like pins usually sell for between $12–15 USD. Don't be tempted to charge less, no matter how insecure you may feel. Charge more if you're creating an exclusive item. If you're producing a limited edition pin, for example, demand will be high but supply will be low, so you can afford to raise the price.

Just like everything else in the art world, creating products and attracting customers involves trial and error. Before I started selling products, I looked at the different ways successful anime-style artists made money and thought it seemed fairly simple. I imagined that selling a few prints, stickers, enamel pins, or key chains would be straightforward, but there are so many variables. Do customers want big or small stickers? Do they prefer matte or holographic finishes? Do they favor animal pins or character pins? Colorful or black and white? The designs I thought would be winners didn't sell, while those I deemed a little simple ended up as my top sellers. Over the years I've acquired a better idea of what my audience wants, but there is still an element of guesswork and sometimes you have to take a leap of faith, learning from mistakes along the way.

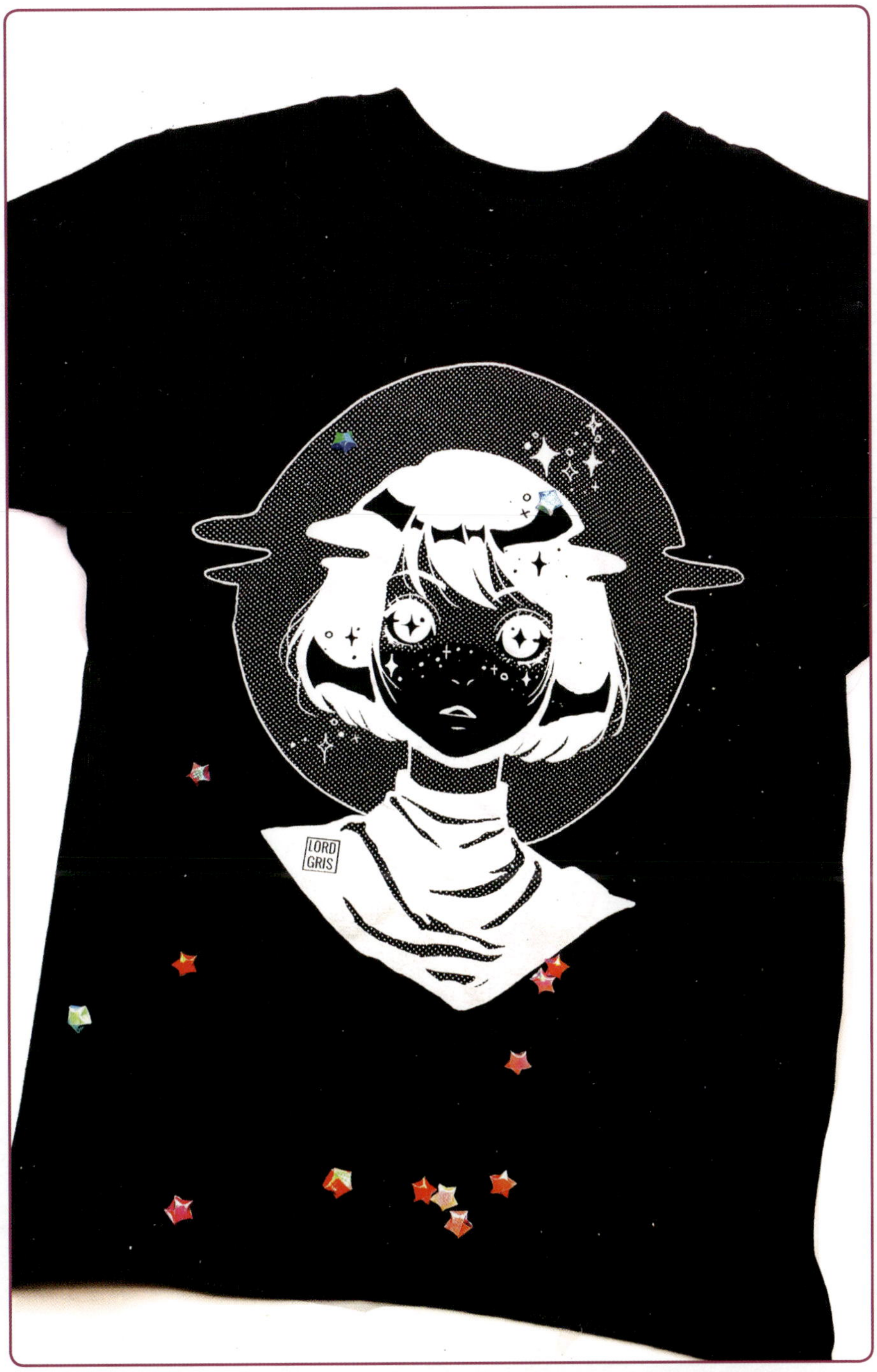


I thought my glitch girl design was a little simplistic, but it has been one of my biggest sellers

## Deciding what to sell

As I create merchandise for my customers, rather than myself, I never feel like I'm compromising creatively. The decision of what to make into merchandise is based entirely on their feedback. If one of my artworks is well received, I will turn it into a sticker, print, pin, or key chain, or similar. If an artwork doesn't receive much interest, I simply don't use it for merchandise. I'm fortunate that while my focus is on creating art, that art can easily be turned into products. Those who exclusively make products, such as enamel pin makers, face more of a challenge in making the product and then hoping it sells. My followers will often comment on an artwork to let me know they wish to see it on a product. If I enough people say they want something, I will make it.

If I'm interested in creating products that are outside the scope of my regular posts – for example, I've been working on creating figurines, which is not something I can repurpose an illustration into – I find it is useful to poll my audience. Discussing ideas with my patrons on Patreon is the most helpful form of feedback, as they are typically my biggest supporters and love to share their opinions on what they would like to see.

The question of knowing specifically what type of product to make is a little broader and can depend on your style of art, as well as your audience. In general, collectible products are a good place to start. For example, I find making enamel pins is more lucrative than making key chains. A person only needs one or two key chains before they reach their key chain limit. Pins, however, can be worn on clothes or stuck onto pin boards, and people love collecting them. There are whole conventions dedicated to pin collection, which makes them much easier to sell. Stickers do better than prints in this regard, as people only have so much wall space on which to hang prints, but they can cover endless sketchbooks, water bottles, computers, bike helmets, and lockers with stickers.

Knowing the age of your audience is also important. If you have a younger audience, they are unlikely to have much money, meaning products with a lower price point will perform better. Conversely, an older audience are more likely to have the income to allow them to buy more expensive giclée prints or limited-edition figurines. Familiarize yourself with the age of your audience and adjust your products accordingly.

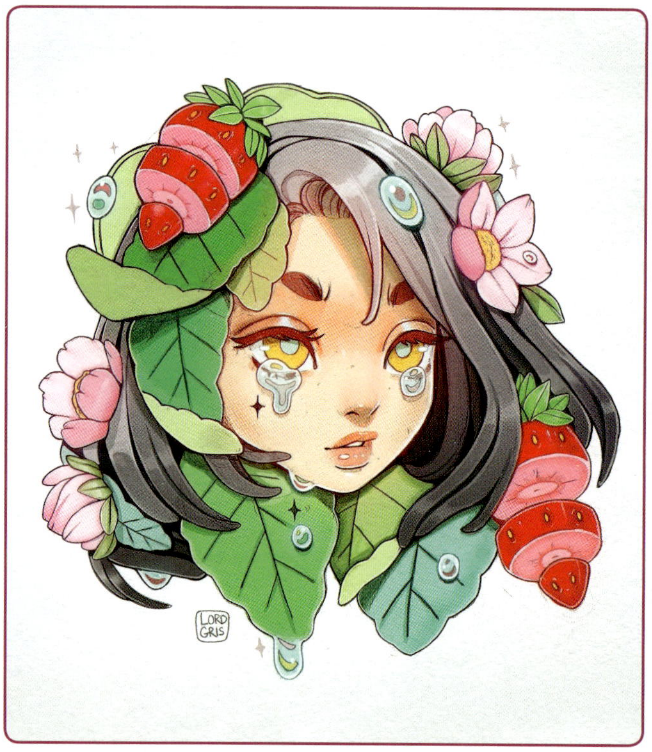


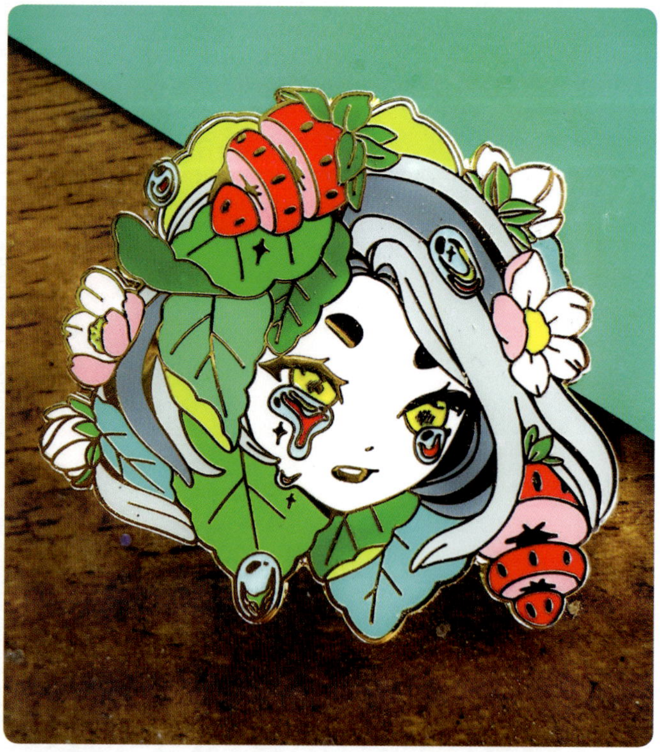

*Vegetation* was a popular design I made into multiple types of product, including tote bags, key chains, and enamel pins

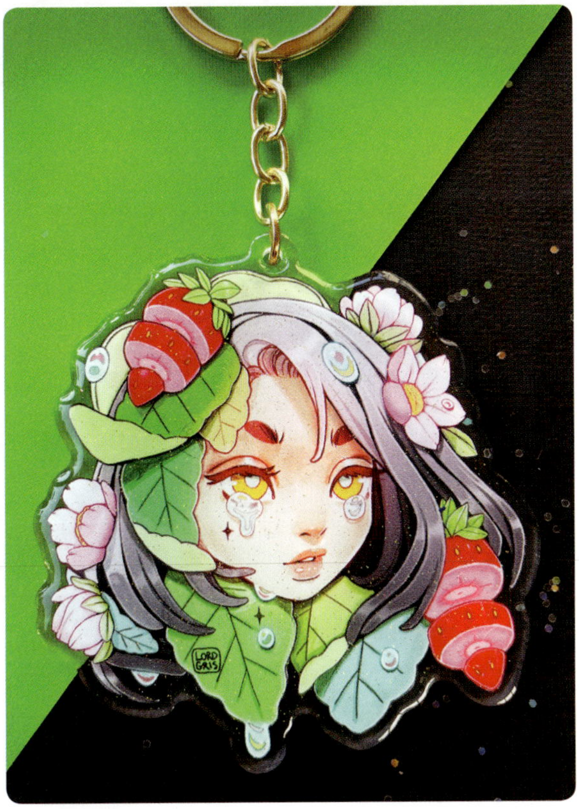

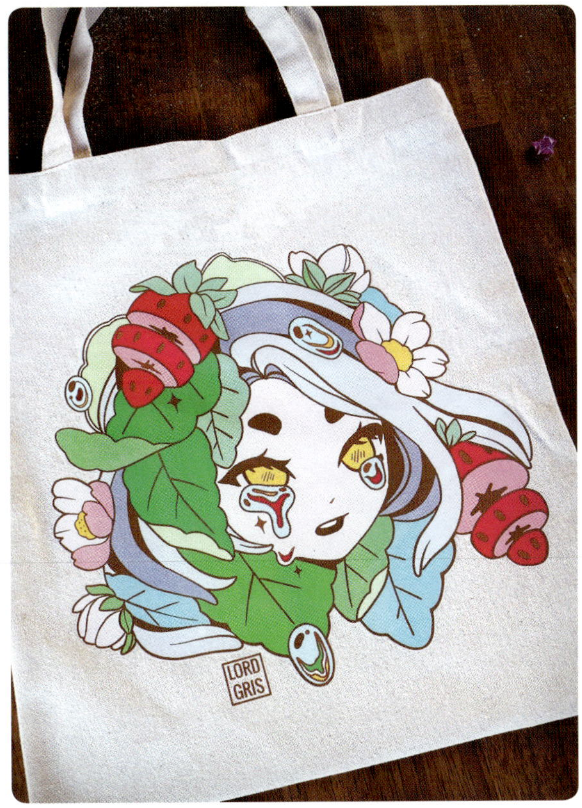


## Making art your job

It's rarely discussed, but monetizing your art can affect the purity of creativity. Making your art your income is a very real threat to how you create as an artist and is something you need to carefully consider before exploring this career path. I wouldn't give up my career as an artist for anything, but I recognize that the way I created when I was a dreamy young kid and the way I create now are very different. Now art is my job, there is a lot more stress involved, as well as a need to appease my followers. Despite your best efforts to maintain autonomy, it can leave you feeling limited or stifled.

The hardest part, especially if you have a large online following, is the sheer volume of artwork you are required to produce. Trying to keep a social media platform alive and thriving requires the constant creation of new artwork to share with your followers. It's very easy to feel like you have run out of ideas, or at worst, burned out completely. To be able to create ideas quickly often means you have to keep your style or ideas fairly simple. I do sometimes feel envious of artists who work solely with galleries to sell their work, as they can almost disappear for a year to create art in a more private, undisturbed space.

I don't agree with the famous saying: "Do what you love and you will never work a day in your life." When you have built a career sharing your artwork online, most days are work days. These can often involve elements of stress and it can be exhausting to summon the motivation to draw when you don't feel creative. You may not have time to pursue the things you feel truly inspired by. For example, I would love to create some giant paintings, but currently don't have the time needed for a project that would require several months of undivided attention, as this just isn't feasible with the way I work.

If you want art to remain a fun hobby or a therapeutic emotional escape, take some time to consider if you truly feel comfortable monetizing this, because it will ultimately become a job, just like anything else.

# FUTURE AMBITIONS

I have all sorts of dreams for my art career, some of which are more realistic than others. In terms of products, I would love to launch a successful clothing line and produce a full run of figurines. Artistically, I would love to expand my painting collection, especially into larger paintings with more background elements and animals, perhaps even exhibiting my own solo show some day. I've never been great at making video content, but I would be interested in creating a YouTube channel. And if the sky's the limit, there are some musicians that I would love to make an album cover or live show asset for. However, none of these are dreams I absolutely must achieve. I already feel so grateful for the incredible opportunity I have to create and share my artwork.

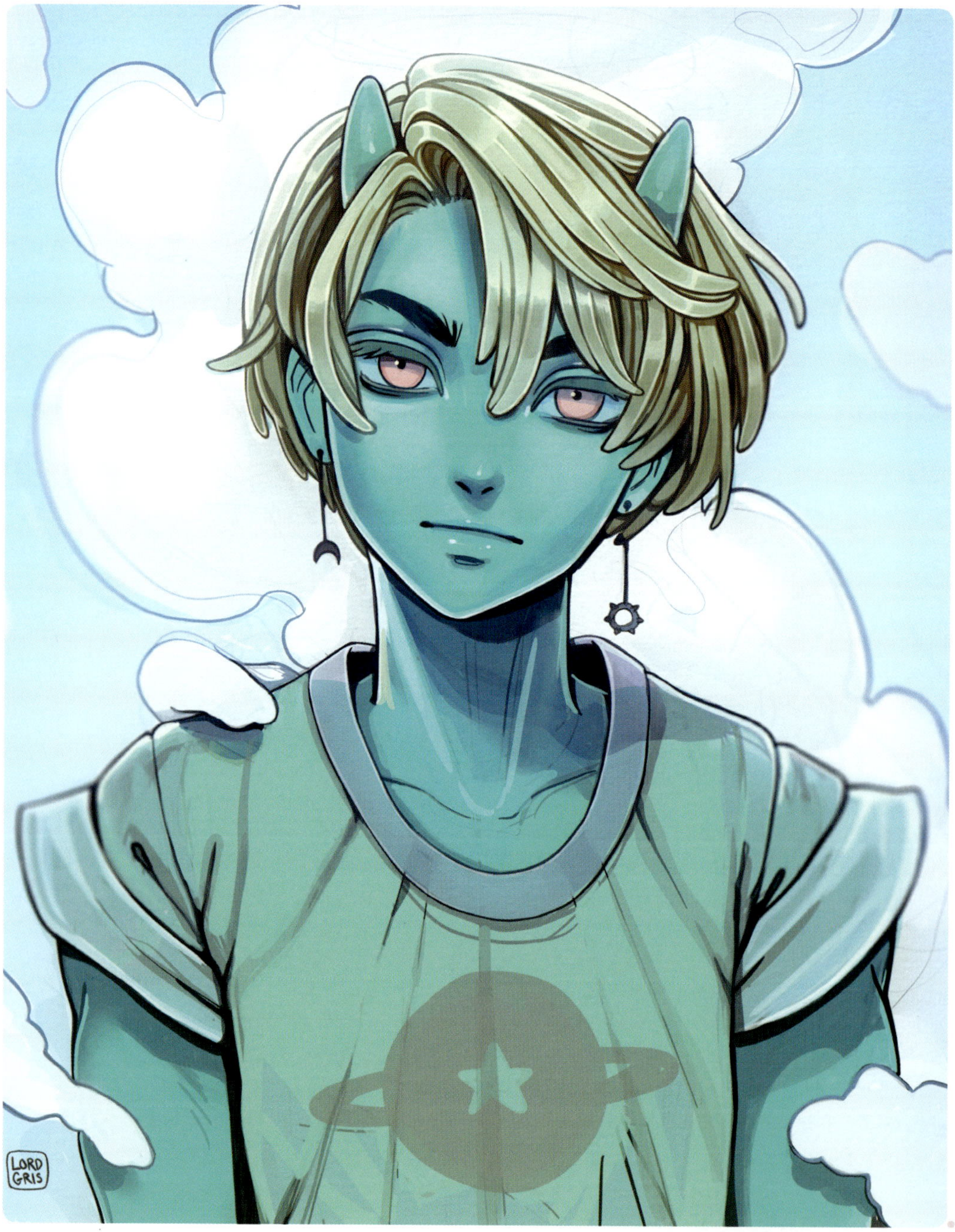


To allow me to keep regularly creating and sharing artwork on my social platforms, I sometimes have to keep my ideas and style fairly simple

# ADVICE

## Self-doubt

When I was younger, I remember seeing artists I admired express insecurity and self-doubt. I couldn't understand how they could be insecure; their artwork was brilliant and they clearly had a successful career. What did they have to worry about? I truly believed that once you were a successful artist, you would automatically be full of confidence, never struggle for ideas, and only have to touch the paper with your pencil to watch as a fully-formed work of art appeared.

I've realized that the insecurity never really goes away. You will always be far more familiar with your flaws than anyone else. Only you know how many tries it took to get that hand right, or how the original image looked in your head versus how it came out on paper. As you grow as an artist you will also grow in confidence and it's important to give yourself credit, especially as there will always be other artists you look up to whose artwork blows you away and reminds you of how far you still have to go. Growth is a lifelong journey and there is no finish line. Everyone's journey is different. You're not behind or ahead; you're exactly where you need to be. Progress is inevitable as long as you keep getting up every time you fall.

## Artist's block

It's normal to experience artist's block from time to time, so try not to sweat it. If I'm struggling for ideas, I will sketch a comfort zone drawing that is super easy and requires zero brain power, such as a cute portrait. I also like to redraw artwork from when I was younger; I don't have to come up with a new idea and instantly feel good when I observe the improvement in my skill level.

Figure drawing warm-ups can also kick-start ideas. If I create a pose I like, I will turn it into a full drawing and call it a new original character. Once I have created something I feel good about, I'm often inspired to start work again.

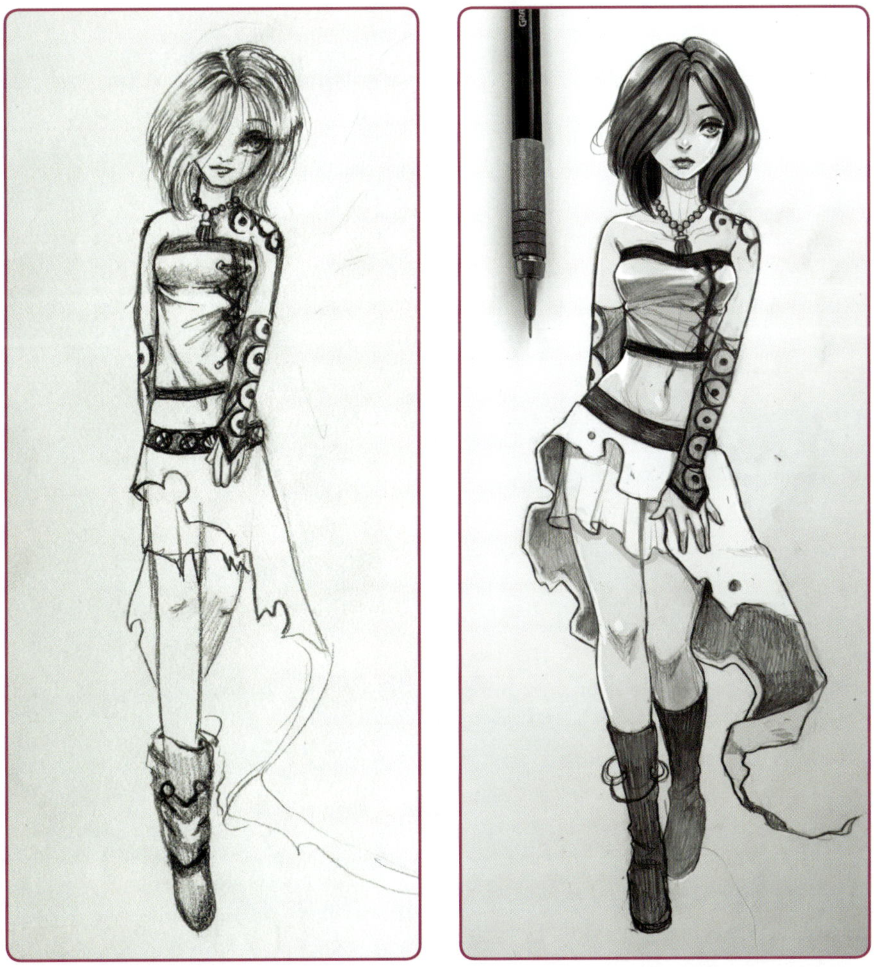

A drawing I did in high school versus when I redrew it a few years ago

# Dealing with criticism

Criticism is a complicated thing and you need to be selective about what you let in and what you block out. Constructive criticism that helps to improve your skill can be very valuable, but if it starts to take away from you, you need to put boundaries in place to protect yourself. When you share your artwork online, it doesn't matter how kind or polite you are, or how perfect the artwork is, there will always be someone who doesn't like it and feels the need to voice their opinion.

Sometimes they will have valid criticism. People used to point out that the noses were wrong when I drew faces from the front. This annoyed me at the time, but now I realize they were right and I can laugh about it. When people point out specific areas of improvement, such as anatomy or lighting mistakes, it can be helpful to consider their comments.

Other people will criticize the type of art you are creating in general. They may say that digital paintings aren't real art and that you should draw traditionally, or should draw less of one thing and more of another. They might criticize you for always drawing in the same anime style, creating the same type of face, or using the same colors. This type of criticism is not valid, as these people are trying to control rather than help. Criticism should always help artists to get where they are going.

My online presence means I've had to develop a thicker skin. I remember the first time I encountered an onslaught of negative comments; I had redrawn one of my old sketches and posted the new and old drawings together. The post got reposted to lots of art-sharing pages, as well as the Autodesk site, and for some reason people didn't believe the first image was genuine. They called me a liar, claiming I had faked my childhood drawing by quickly sketching a poor drawing then pretending I had improved. At the time I was very upset, but if something like this happened now, I would just laugh at how my childhood art was so bad that nobody could believe it was real. I'm now able to sort criticisms into different categories and act on them accordingly.

When you encounter criticism online, ask yourself if it's taking you closer to where you want to go, or if it's just making you feel ashamed of your passions. Never listen to shaming comments. Also, remember that not all advice holds the same weight. Listen very closely to the people who have what you want. There are many people who will tell you how to be an artist, yet they are not artists themselves and have no idea what they're talking about. Listen to the words of artists who have the art styles, success, and careers you want; they will guide you in the right direction.

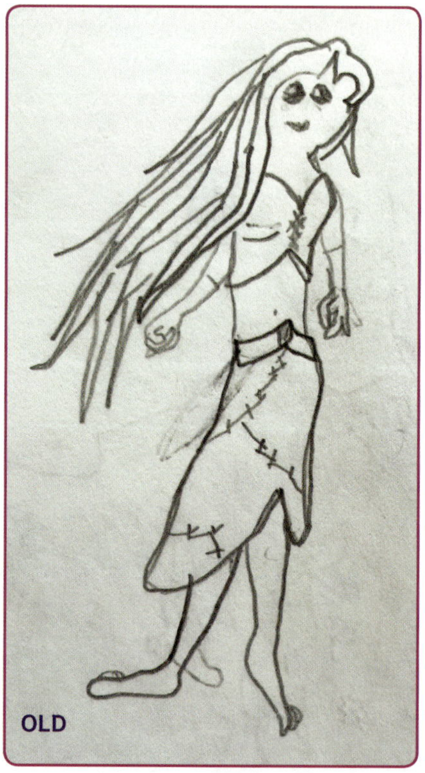


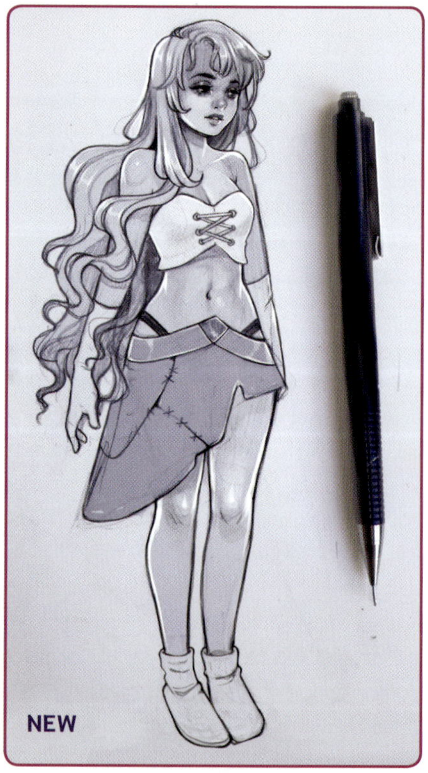


The childhood drawing that no one believed was real

*Borgirl*

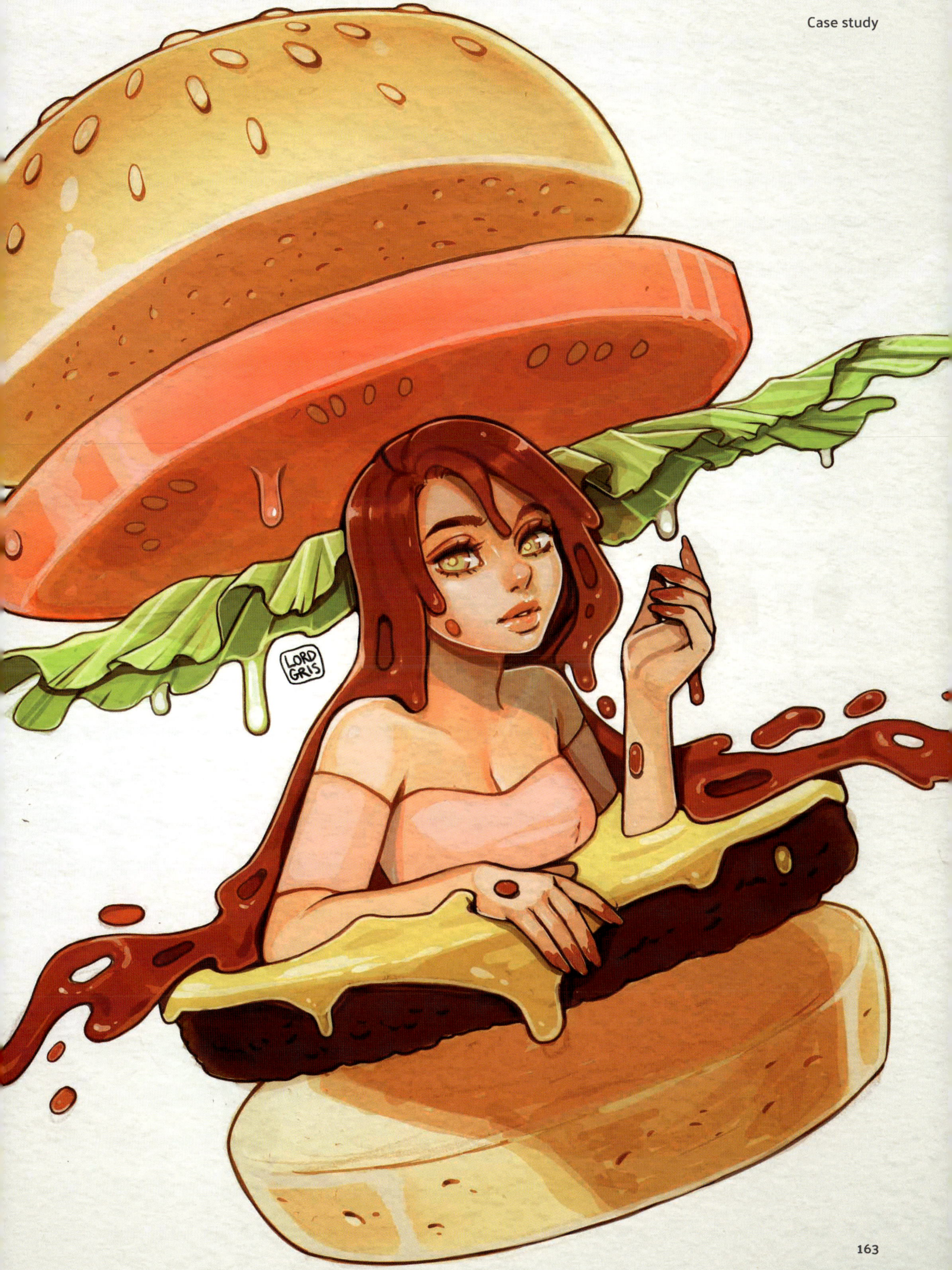
LORD
GRIS

# Final tips

- Be patient; it can take years to develop a recognizable style and build an online following. But just because progress is slow, it doesn't mean you are failing. Stick with it and don't be discouraged.

- If you're just starting out, don't compare your artwork to that of an artist who's had a lifetime of practice. Seeing other artists sharing their work online can be very misleading, as you only see the beautifully polished artwork and never the true, messy, behind-the-scenes process and piles of drawings they have binned. It's also important to remember that just because there are amazing artists online, doesn't mean that you don't get to be an artist too. The existence of other gifted artists with an anime style does not affect your ability to have your own anime-style art career. There is room for everyone for create.

- Create the kind of work you want to create, not what you think other people want to see. When you allow your true voice to shine through, you will enjoy the process more and your audience will sense the authenticity.

- Be an active member of the online art community, leaving comments and connecting with other upcoming artists. Be kind and generous; those connections will prove crucial when you need other artists to turn to for advice and support.

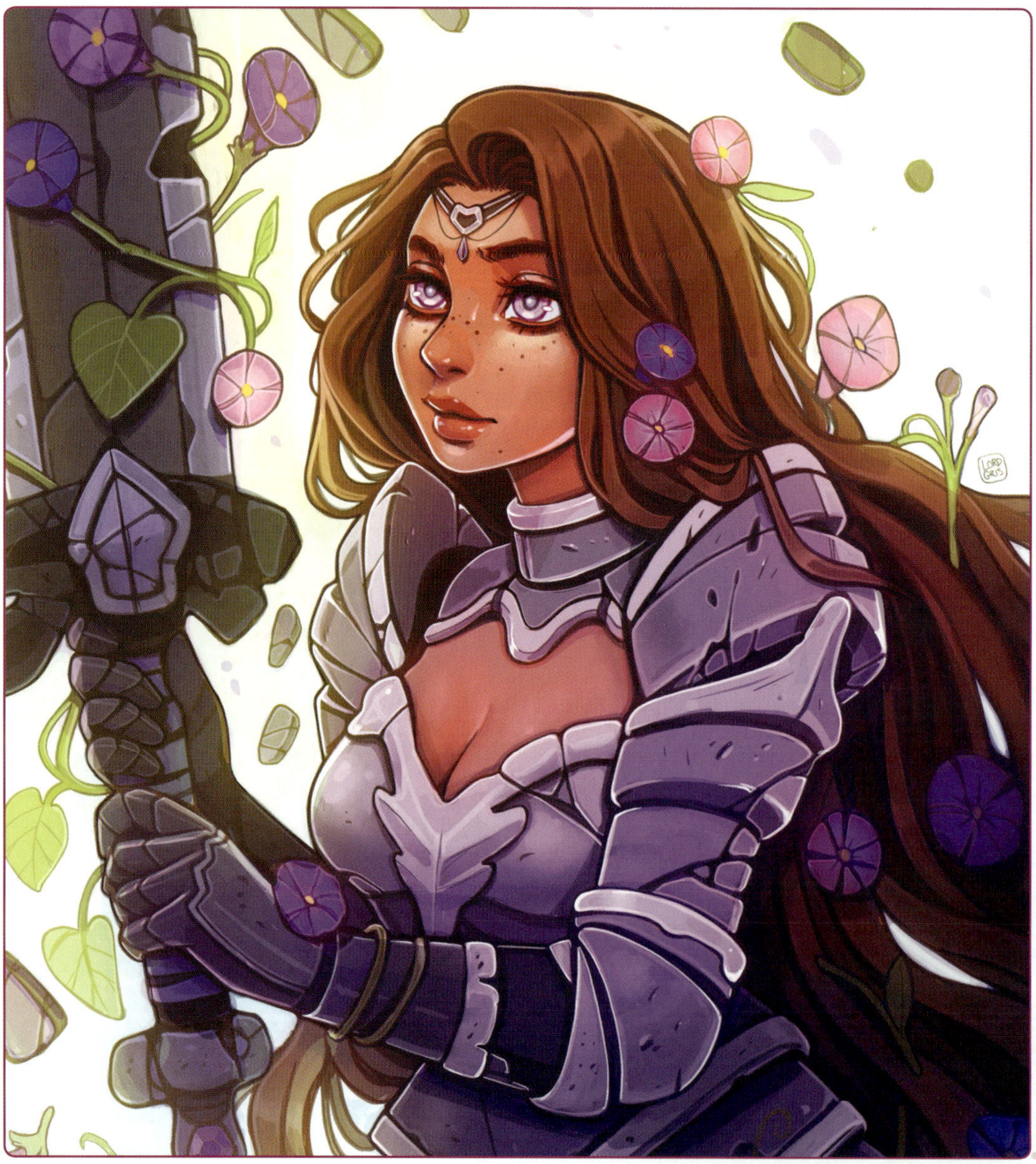

*Ascension*

*Glory*

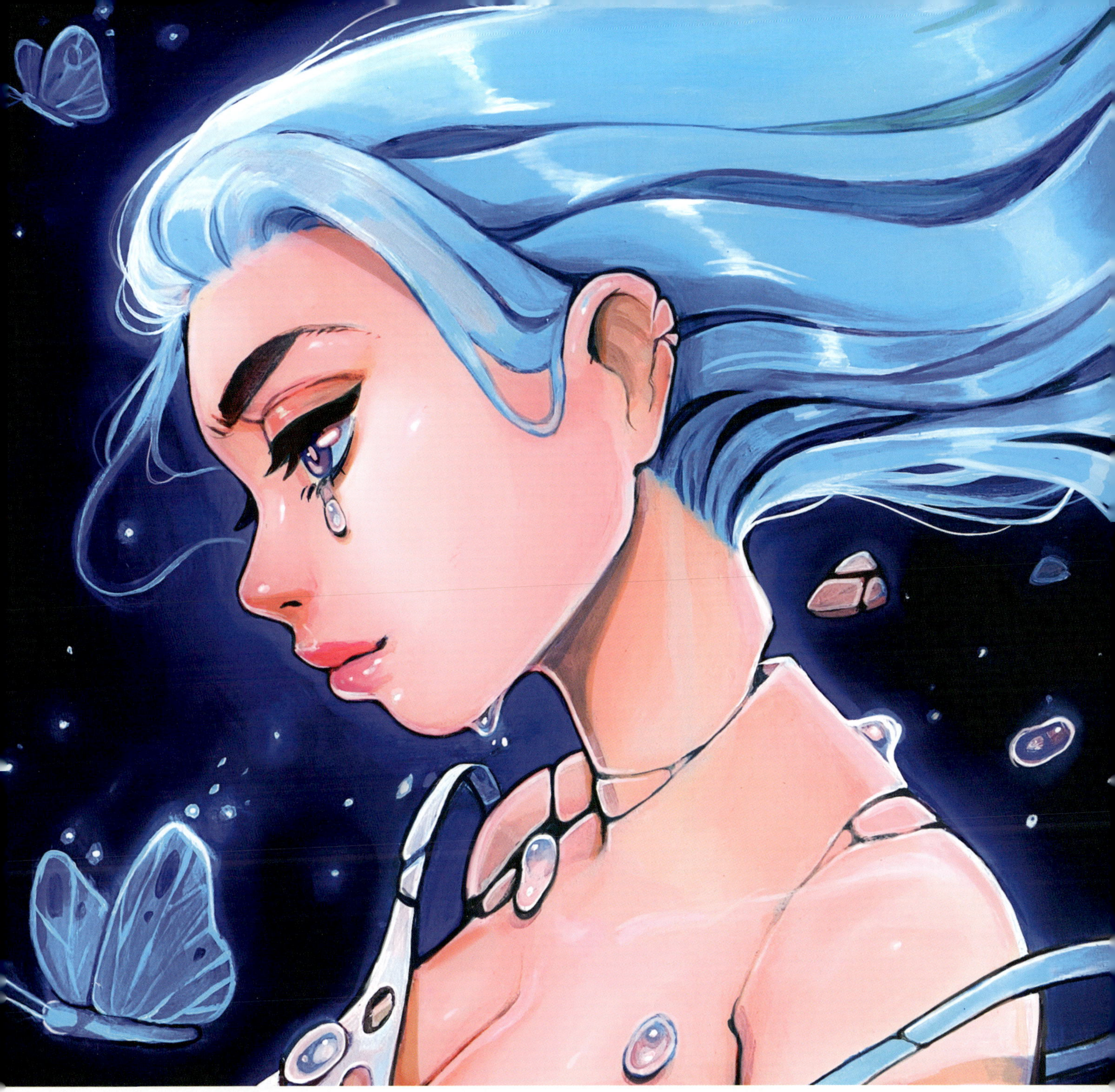

- Join art advice channels. These are full of artists who have a wealth of experience creating art and products, and love to help each other out by answering questions.
- Network with other artists in real life. Visit gallery showings, take part in group art challenges or game jams, attend life-drawing classes or Drink & Draw events. Don't be a salesperson constantly trying to sell your work, and don't use people either. Be kind, be yourself, and make connections.
- Be willing to take chances. It's easy to worry so much about doing something perfectly that you become paralyzed by fear and uncertainty, and don't do it at all. Step out of your comfort zone, make mistakes, laugh about it, learn from it, and try again. This is the only way to grow and improve your craft.
- Consider the strengths of your artwork and how can you utilize the available online platforms to capitalize on that. Every platform has its own algorithm for the content it prefers, meaning different kinds of content will perform differently on each platform. Be mindful of what works for different algorithms and use it to your advantage.

# TIMELINE

**1999**

Discovering early inspirations.

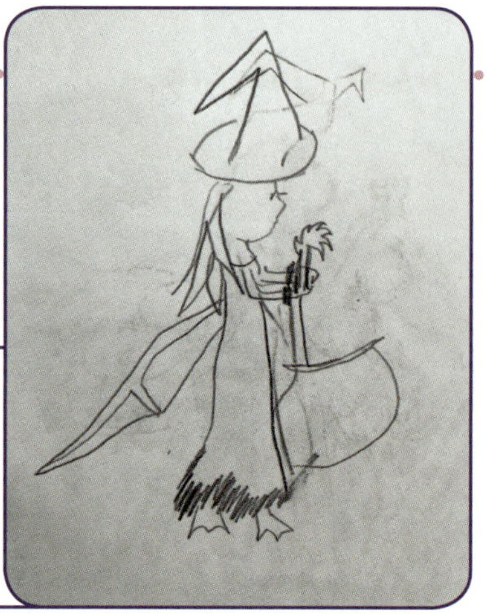

Even when I was a young child, I loved drawing fantasy women. This little witch has duck feet.

**2002**

Finding the anime and manga genre.

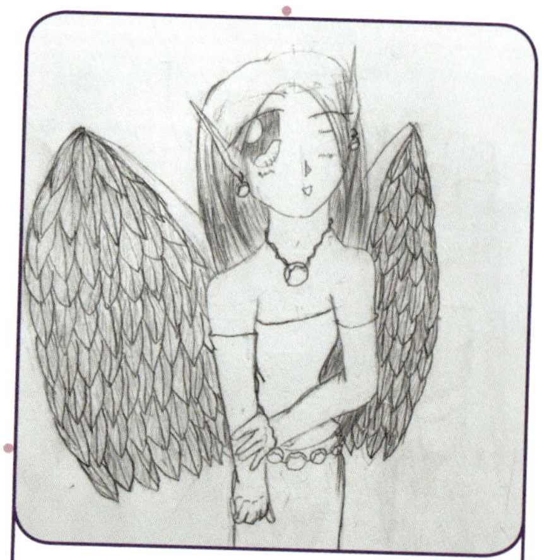

When I was in elementary school, I had a friend who taught me how to draw anime-style characters. I felt drawn to the genre as soon as I saw it.

**2005**

Honing the anime style.

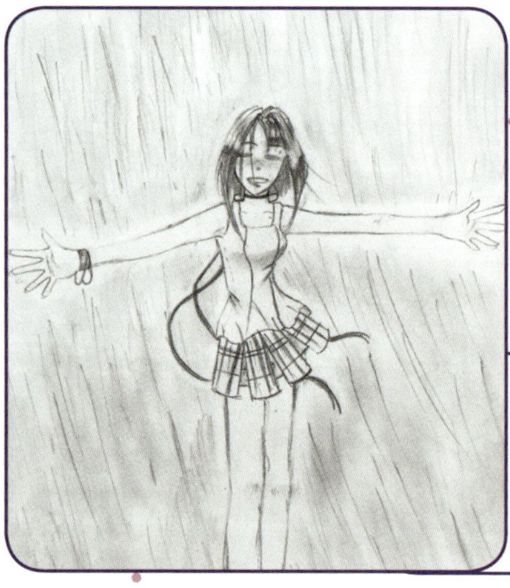

I continued drawing anime-style sketches for several years, inspired by manga books.

**2008**

Delving into realism.

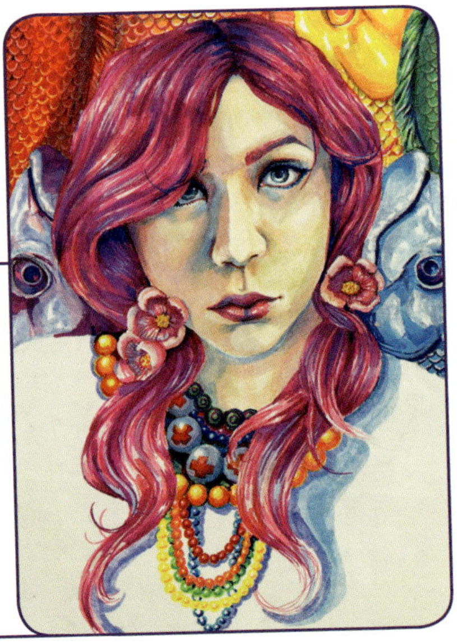

When I started high school, I felt I needed to change my art style to make it seem more sophisticated. I moved into realism, though I still gave my characters bright hair and other fantastical elements.

**2011**

Exploring editorial styles.

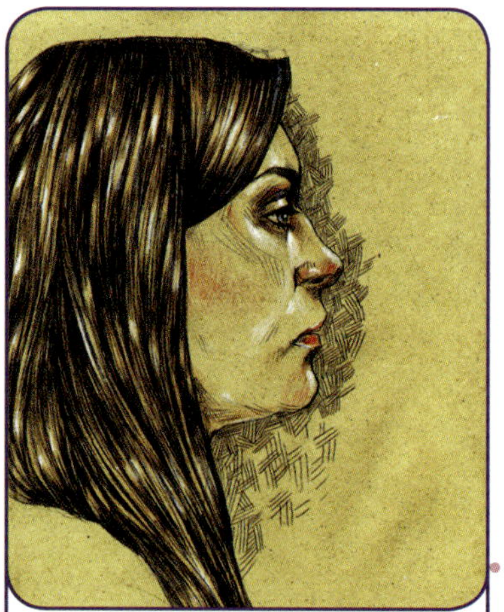

When I attended art college, I was taught that a linework-heavy editorial style was more likely to attract job offers, so I often drew with pen and ink in a cross-hatching style.

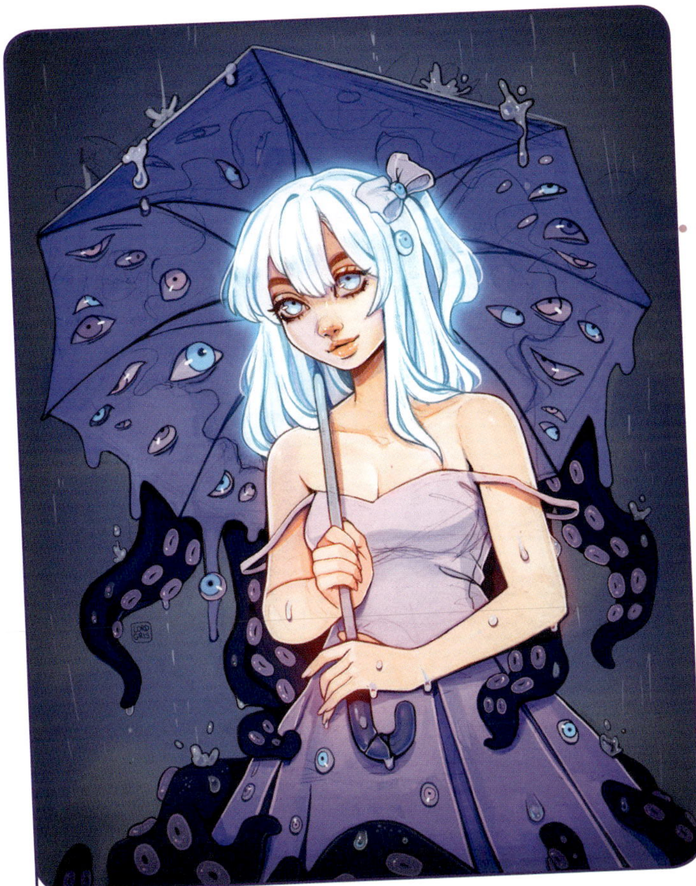

An example of my current art style.

**2020**

Established my current style.

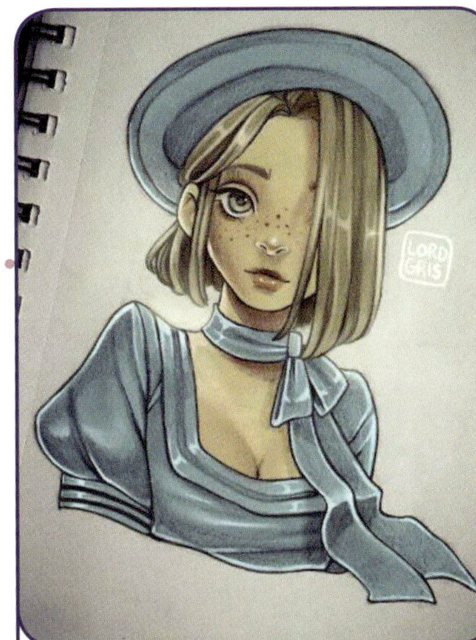

It took about two years of playing around on my tablet before I was able to shift back into a kind of anime style and finally felt like myself again artistically.

**2016**

Returning to the anime style.

**2014**

First digital art.

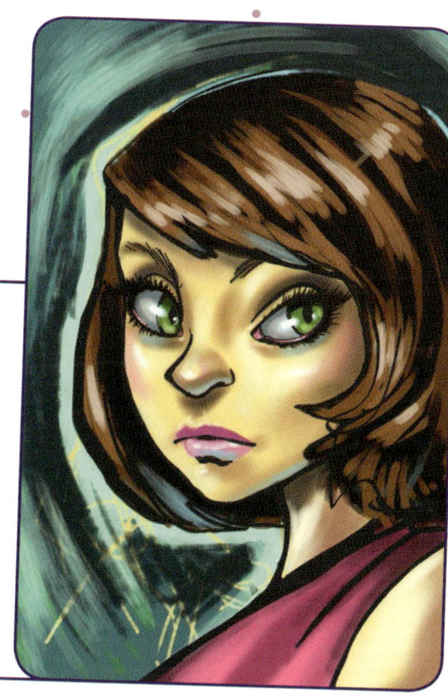

My first digital painting. I wanted to return to my old anime style, but had been drawing realism for so long that I didn't know how to. The result was kind of clunky.

**2013**

Doodling cartoonlike characters.

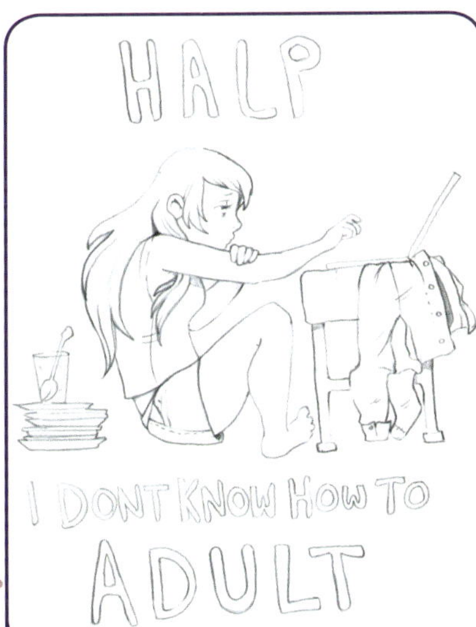


During the years after I quit art, I occasionally drew in a very cartoonlike style, thinking maybe I could hone this and create an online web comic. The comic *Hark! A Vagrant* was a big inspiration at the time.

# GALLERY

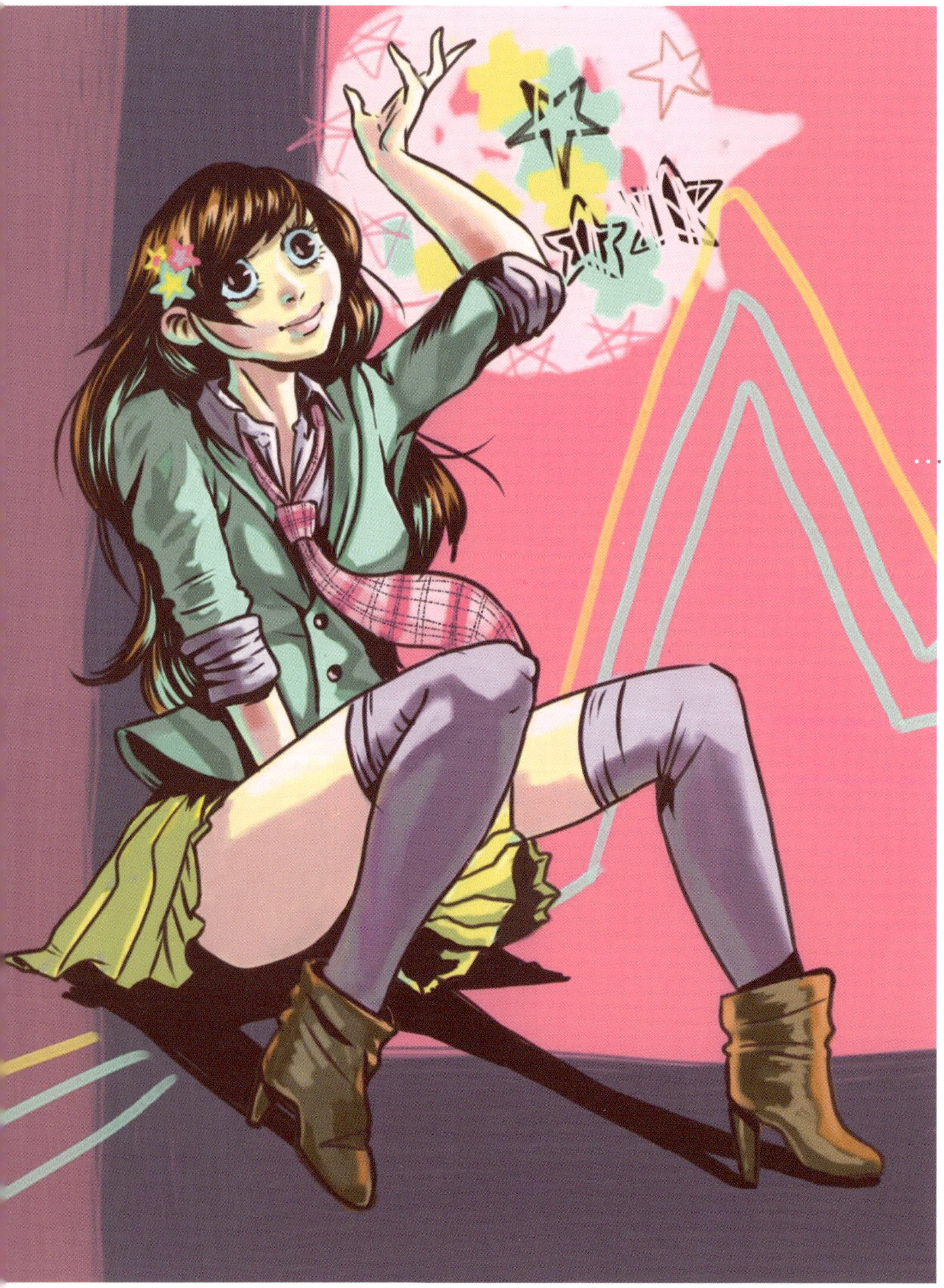

## Early digital art

Digital art was unknown to me for a long time. When my brother gifted me a tablet for my twenty-third birthday, I started creating digital paintings on a little art app. Though it crashed a lot, had no blending tools, and only allowed a maximum of six layers, in many ways it kickstarted my career. I didn't grow up with much more than a pencil and never had money for art supplies, so it was the first time I was able to freely explore color. With digital art I discovered I didn't have to be scared of making mistakes and wasting precious supplies. It opened up boundless possibilities, allowing me to color things in as many different ways as I liked. This is one of the first pieces I created on that tablet, inspired by the pastel imagery in the outro sequence of *Blue Spring Ride*.

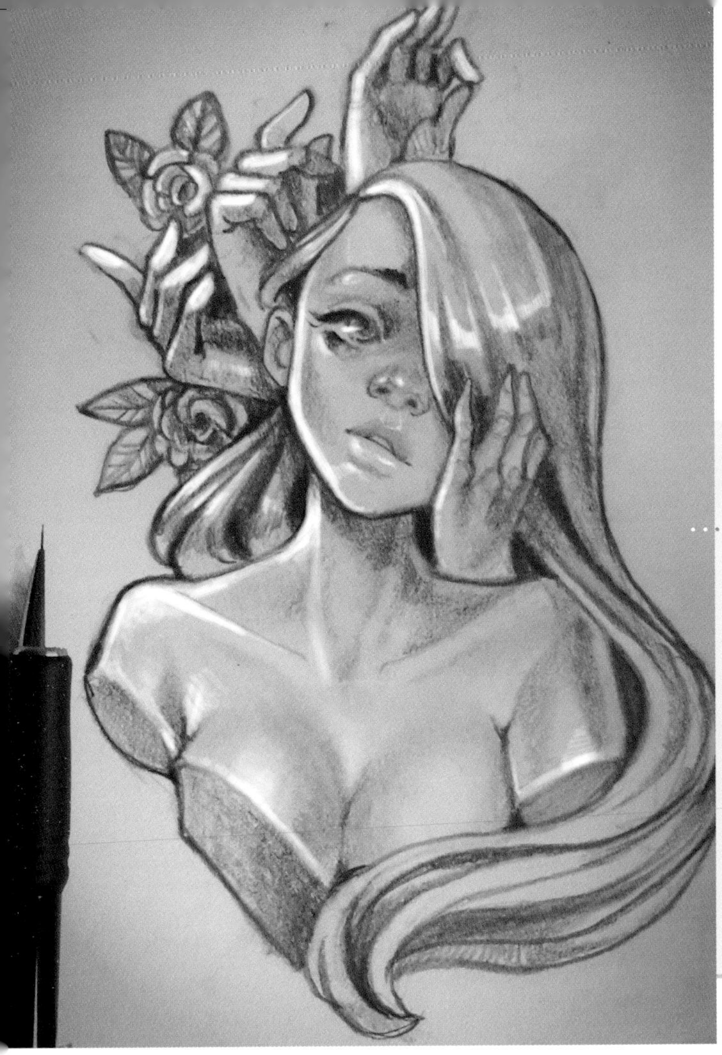

## *Concrete Girl*

When I made the decision to start drawing every day – probably a year or so after I was gifted my art tablet – I decided to return to pencil. I'd seen a few digital artists sharing pencil sketches online and found it refreshing to see their raw work like that, inspiring me to draw something loose and sketchy. While I wanted to include multiple hands, I wished to avoid drawing lots of arms. Cutting off the figure created a stone bust look, which began the "cracked women" characters I often draw. I added cracks and crumbling as time went on, but this was the first in the series.

## My first redraw

This was the first image that really took off online, receiving a lot more attention than my other work. Inspired by artists I admired sharing redraws online, I wanted to redraw some of my favorite art from middle school as a way of revisiting the anime style I'd grown up loving. Looking back, I would redraw the whole design differently now, as I don't feel like the new drawing does the original piece justice. My followers responded positively to the progression, so I started redrawing lots of old artwork, which slowly grew my account over time.

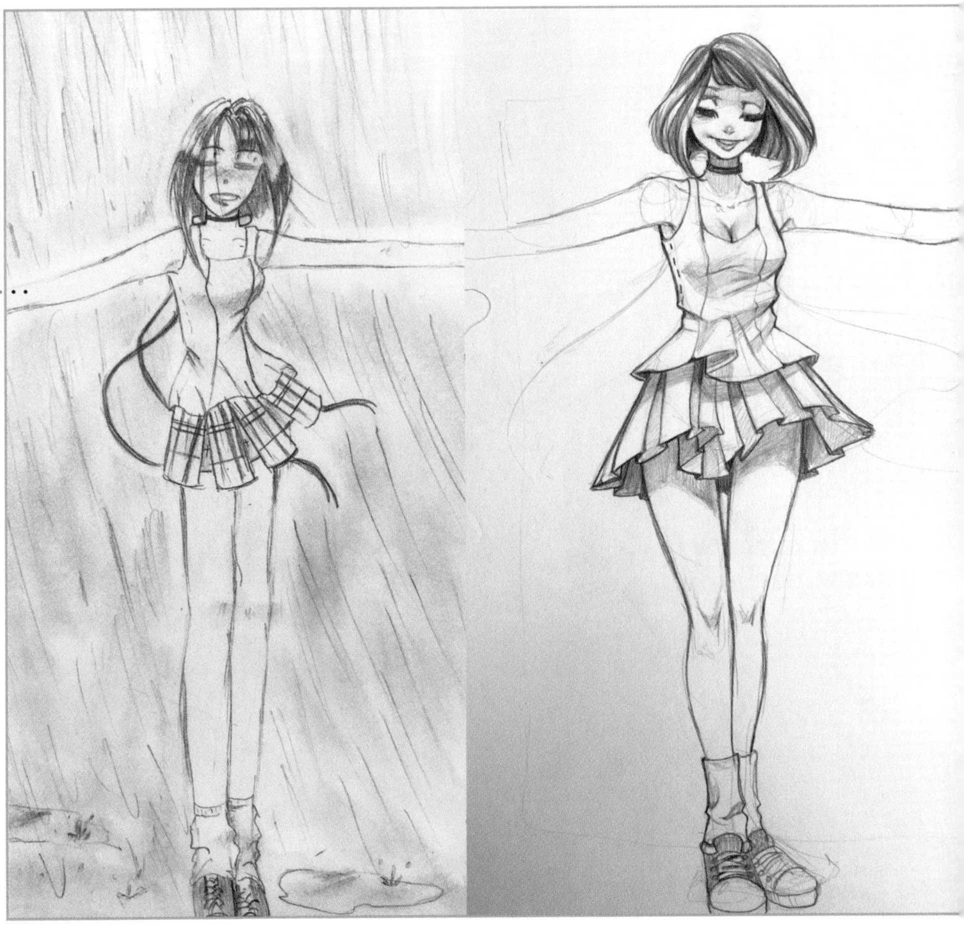

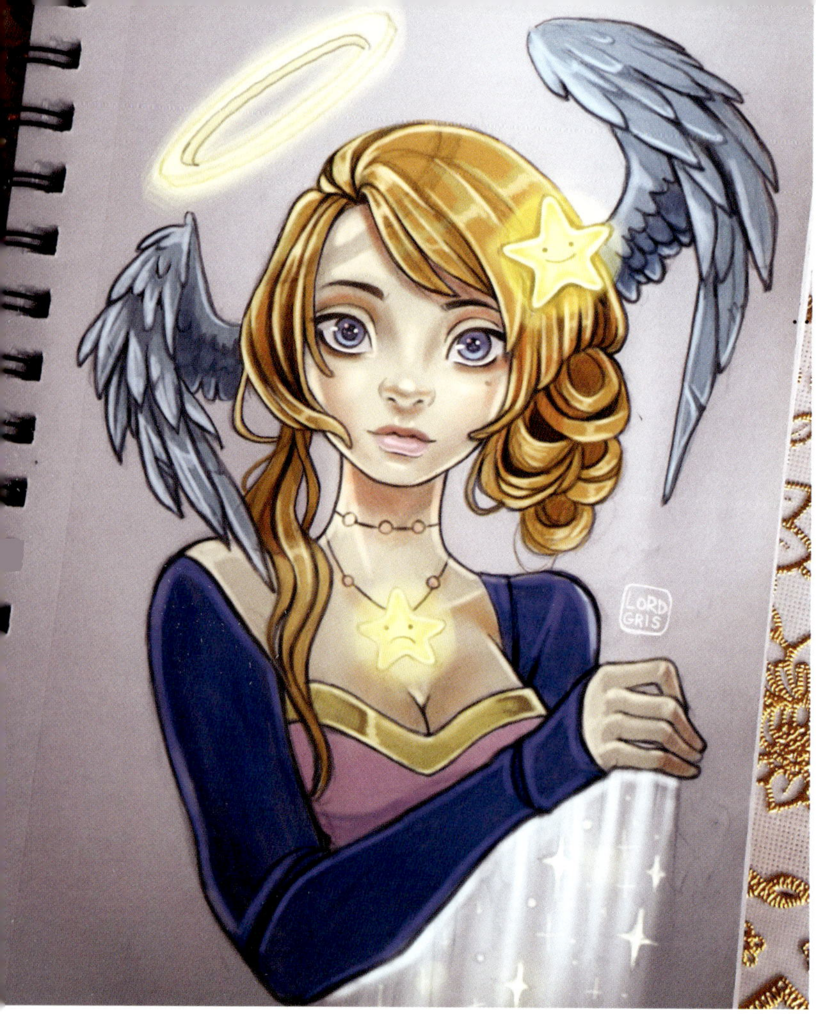


## Tradigital

I first experimented with "tradigital" art (art drawn traditionally and colored digitally) in college. While I had access to a digital painting program, I didn't have an art tablet, so I drew each piece using pencil and paper before using a mouse to color it digitally. Though this was a tedious process, I liked the effect. Most of my early art on Instagram is drawn with pencil; while I wanted to add color, I still didn't have any money for art supplies other than a Crayola watercolor set. Deciding to revisit the tradigital style, I found I loved the ethereal effect of digitally coloring over the pencil marks. It had texture rather than the sleek, smooth look of pure digital art, and it became my signature style from that point on.

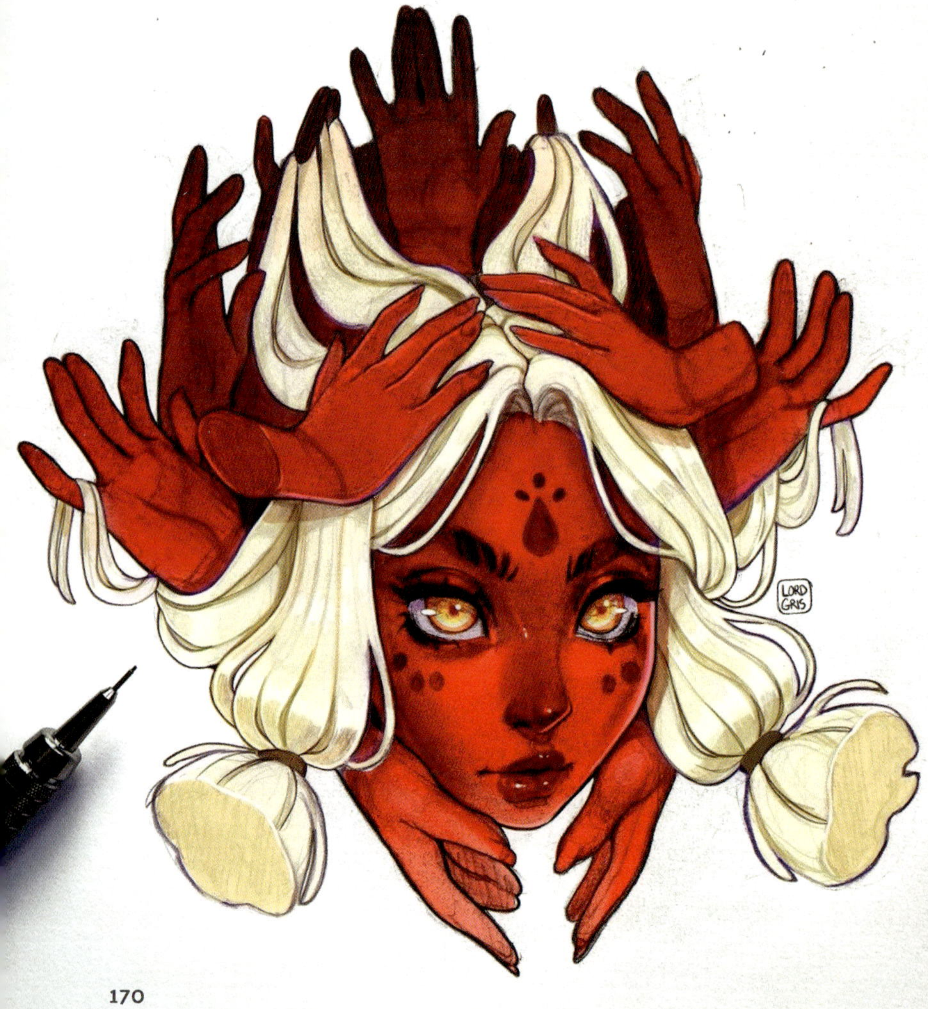


## *Tenacity*

This design was originally a "comfort zone" sketch in my sketchbook that I later colored. It went on to become hugely popular. Making art can be strange and unpredictable. There will be designs you spend hours on that hardly generate any engagement, and others that you whip out super fast, without much thought, that go viral. It's a reminder not to overthink it. It's easy to believe you should always be pushing yourself to make new, intensely detailed, "out of the box" artwork, but in reality, people have followed you for a reason. They like what you create, so if you just let yourself make that artwork, often you will find it is well-received. I return to this piece when I feel like I've been overdoing it and remind myself to make a comfort doodle every now and then.

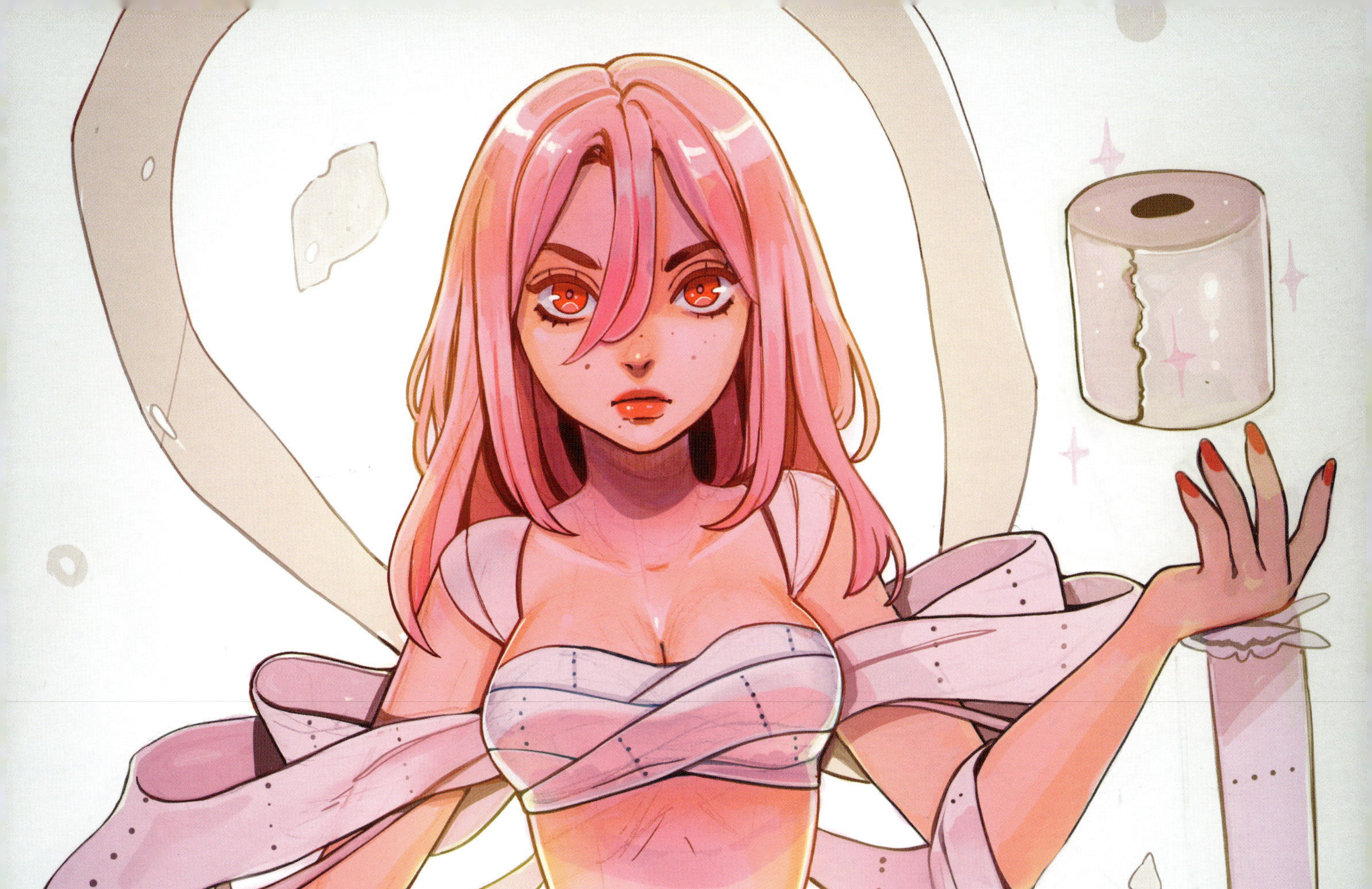


## *TP Chan*

When the Covid-19 lockdowns began in 2020 and people were confined indoors, I hosted a thirty-day drawing challenge to keep my followers occupied. Most of the prompts were fairly standard, but one was "toilet paper" in response to it being hoarded. This led me to create TP Chan, a warrior who punishes those who hoard, inspired by Angewomon from *Digimon*. Up until this point my art had been fairly serious, but TP Chan was much more of a joke character and people had fun with her. She got redrawn, cosplayed, 3D modeled, and even turned into a body pillow. She reminded me to have more fun with my art and not to be afraid to make a joke sometimes.

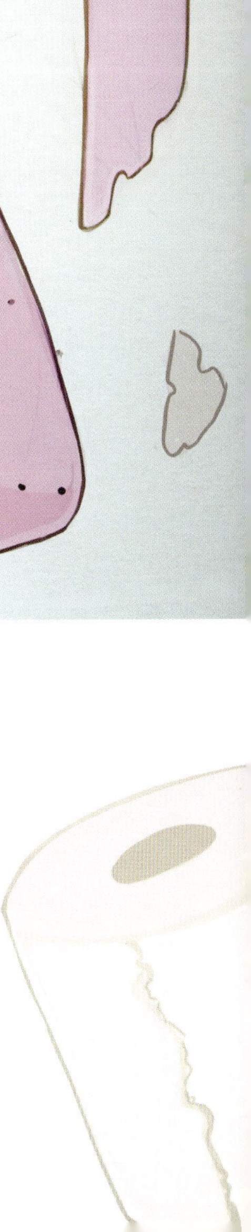

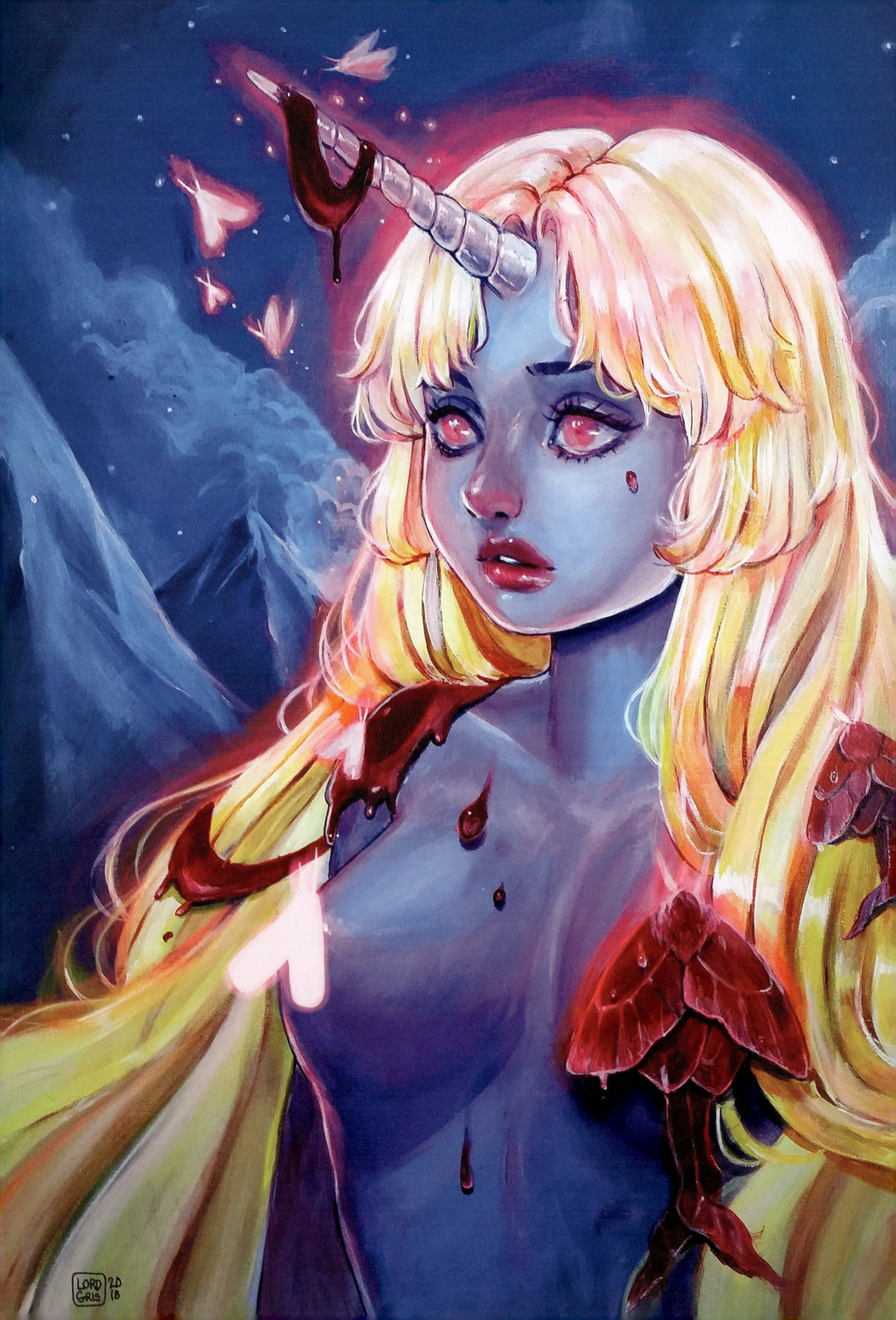
LORD GRIS
2018

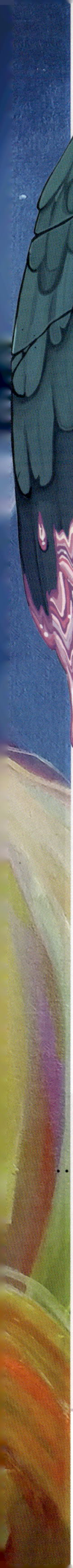

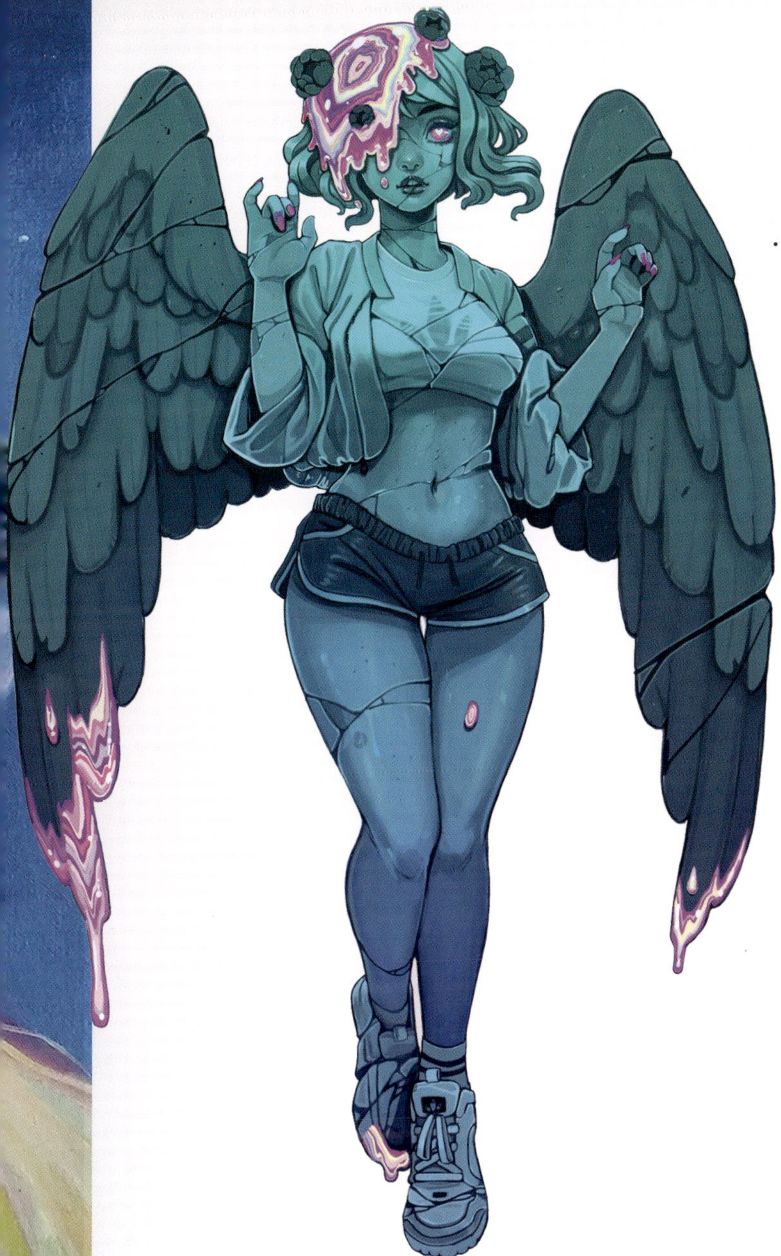

## *Concrete Angel*

This is my favorite of my "concrete girls" series. On securing a deal to create acrylic standees, I decided I needed a design that was really striking, which led to the creation of my first full-body concrete girl. I learned a lot in the process, such as how to create attractive gradients to guide the viewer's eyes around the piece. She ended up being a very popular design, especially as a holographic sticker.

## Early Inktober art

Every October, artists challenge themselves to draw a pen-and-ink drawing every day for thirty-one days. I've never followed the official prompt list or committed to the full month, but I do my best to share a few weird black-and-white pen-and-ink drawings. These end up being some of my most popular designs. They are used for tattoos more than any of my other designs and people love the products I make with them. I always look forward to October for the chance to create more eerie artwork.

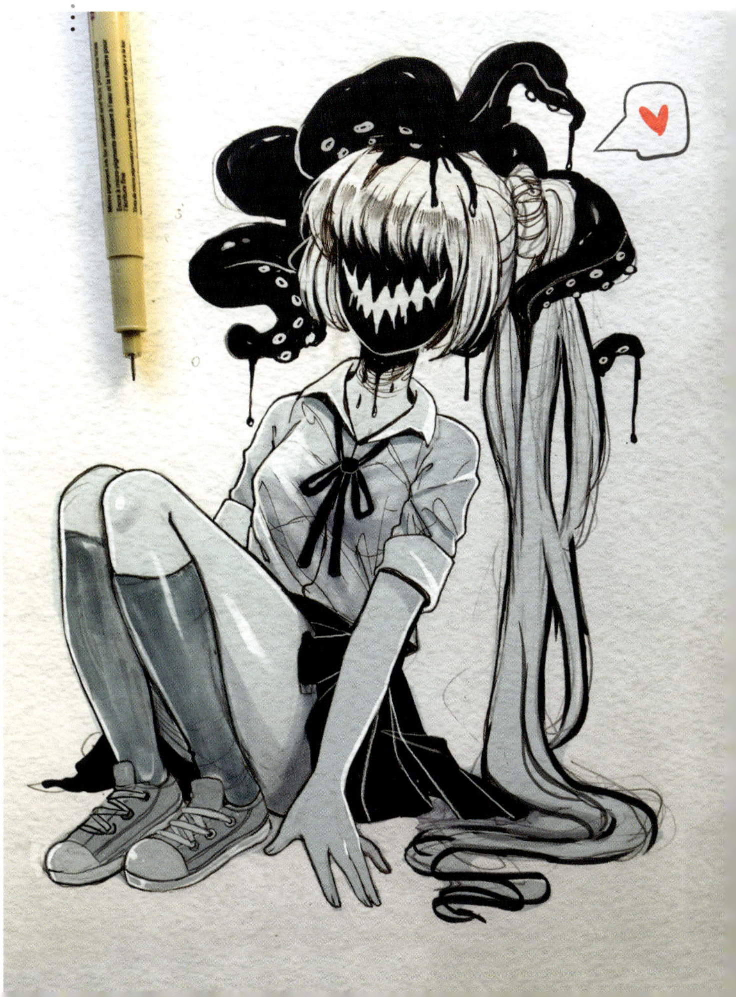

## *The Pride of the Wise*

This is the first acrylic painting of which I felt really proud. I worked on it intermittently in my free time before taking it along to a Drink & Draw event in the city to work on. The event organizers showcased it on their Instagram page, which led to a gallery reaching out to me and ultimately my first gallery show. I was thrilled to display my work in a gallery, as I didn't think it was something that would ever happen.

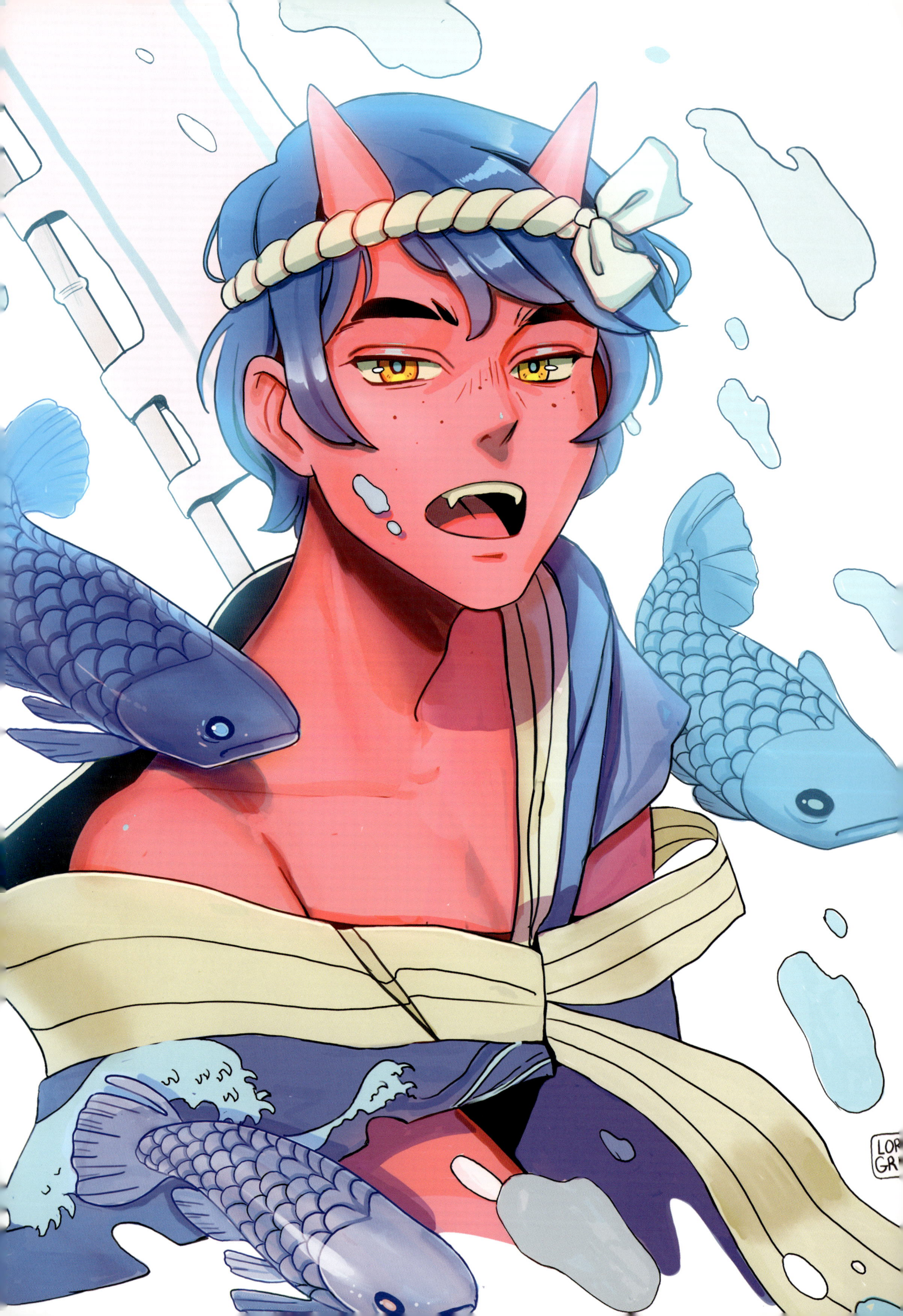

## *Koi Boy*

By this point I'd drawn a lot of female characters, but hadn't succeeded in drawing many men. I'd tried and failed a few times, but at the start of 2020 I made a new year's resolution to practice drawing more male characters. *Koi Boy* was one of the first male designs I deemed a success. While I rarely draw male subjects, I now feel a lot more comfortable with it and they are great fun to paint.

## *Summer Senpai*

As my artwork began as pencil drawings on paper, I didn't have much practice in how to create interesting backgrounds. Once I had access to digital software, I started to explore the use of strong backlighting to create an illuminated effect around my characters, making it appear as if they were outside in bright light. I achieved this luminescence in *Summer Senpai* by tinting the background slightly blue and using a green hue as a shadow overlay on the character, creating a strange, backlit, summery feel. I love introducing this effect and now use it in almost all of my artwork, even if only very subtly.

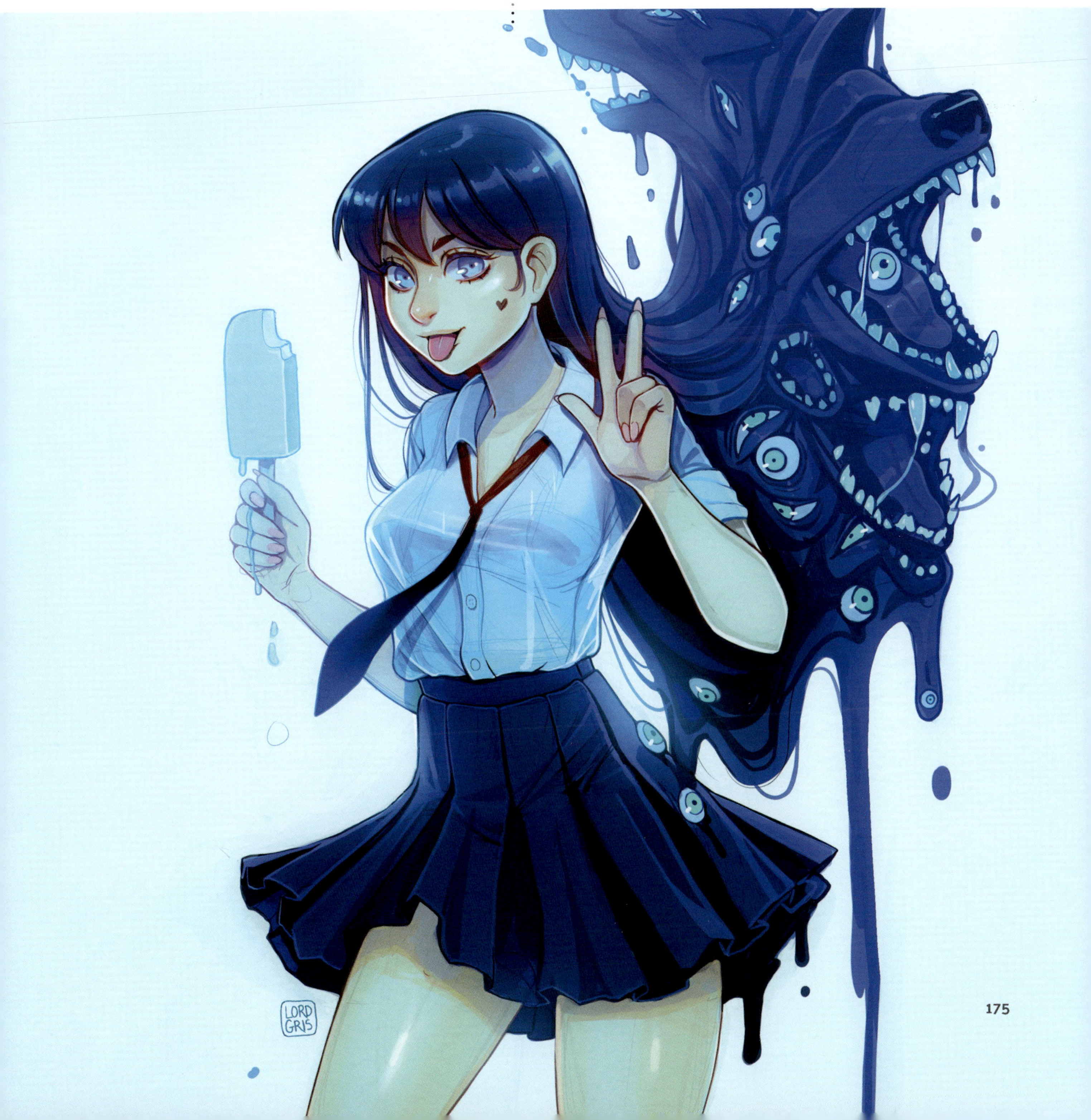

# TUTORIAL

When I was growing up I loved looking at anime character concept art, especially for video games such as *Fire Emblem*. These designs were hugely inspirational to me and had a notable influence on my style of character design. I loved the fluidity of the poses, the cool character outfits, and the fun, bright colors. My time working on various art projects, including video games, has taught me a few tricks for how to approach anime-style character design.

This tutorial will guide you through my step-by-step process of designing an eye-catching character, starting with creating a dynamic pose, sketching, and adding character elements that flow with the design, to recommended color strategies to maximize the focal point. I also share tips for how to make the design your own, whatever your preferred medium or individual style.

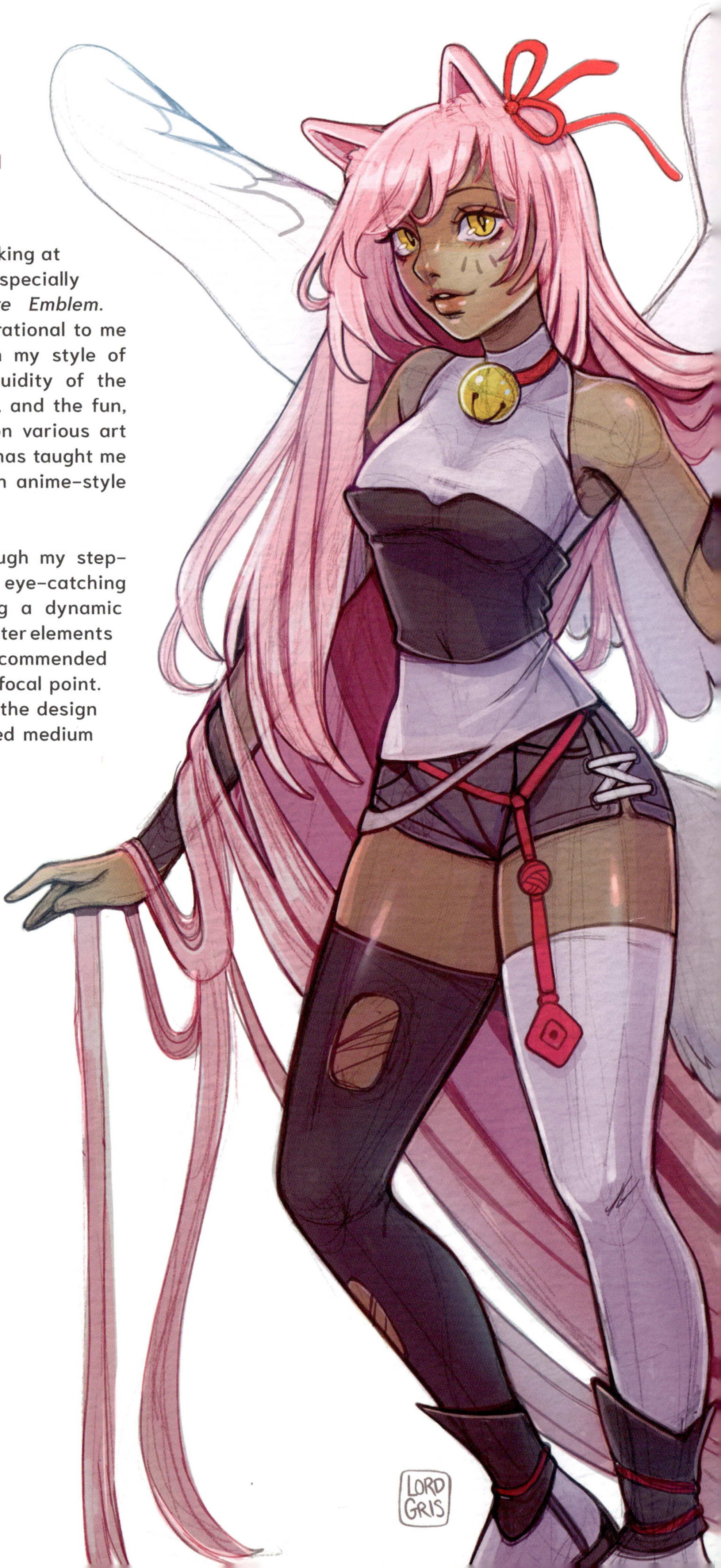

**01** Before choosing a definite design for your character, start by sketching a number of thumbnails to explore different directions. These should be small, quick sketches of concept ideas. An idea in your head can often turn out very differently on paper, and it can be frustrating to find yourself halfway through a fully rendered line art before realizing the idea isn't going to work. Drawing thumbnails will therefore save you precious time in the long run. It will also help you to lock in your idea and feel confident moving forward. Though this character design will be created digitally, I still do all of my initial sketching on paper, as this will always be my most comfortable medium.

Allow your early ideas to change and evolve; this initial thumbnail sketch contains a halo and a staff, though I don't proceed with these accessories

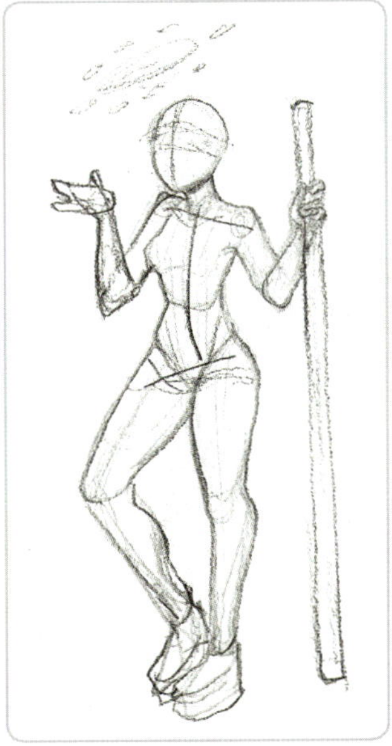

**02** Before starting work on a character pose, it's important to find a reference. The human body is a complex shape and the way its intricate parts interact can be difficult to master, even when using references. Make use of any resources you can find to help you accurately capture the intended pose for your character. There are numerous places to find reference material. You could take a photo of yourself or a friend, pose anatomy figurines, find stock photos, or look for free online resources such as 3D poseable figures. You don't need to copy the reference exactly; you may wish to exaggerate, simplify, or stylize elements to fit with your anime style. Simply use it as a guide to make the pose anatomically believable.

I sometimes use a figurine to help me sketch authentic poses for my characters

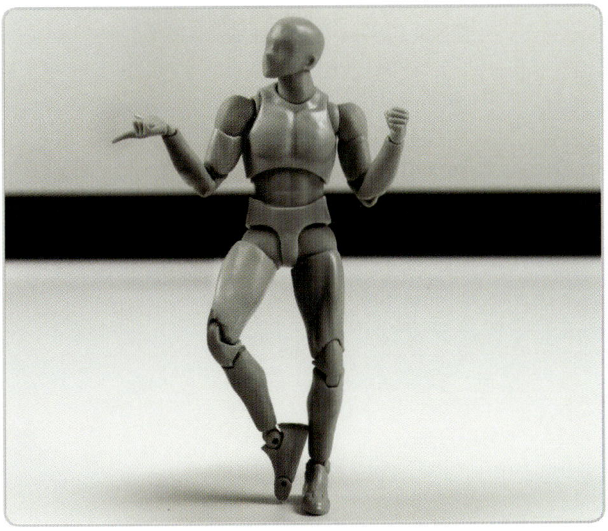

**03** Sketching a pose with movement will enhance your character design. Even if the character isn't actually moving, you can create fluidity in the movement of the image as a whole. The human eye is drawn to serpentine shapes; they create the impression of motion and help to guide the eye around a design. Whenever I'm choosing a pose for an anime-style character, I aim for an S-shape within the movement of the figure.

The S-shape created from the tilt of the head and the curve of the spine into the leg creates movement and fluidity in these designs

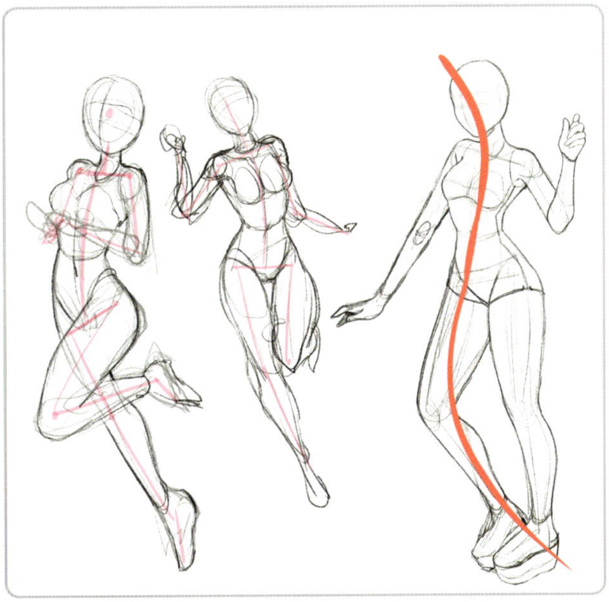

**04** To produce a natural-looking pose, the character's hips and shoulders should tilt in opposite directions. If the left shoulder is raised, the left hip will be lowered, and vice versa. This can create an elegant bend in the torso. I often look for this kind of movement when searching for reference photos.

Note how the shoulders and hips tilt in opposite directions in this sketch, creating slight movement in the body

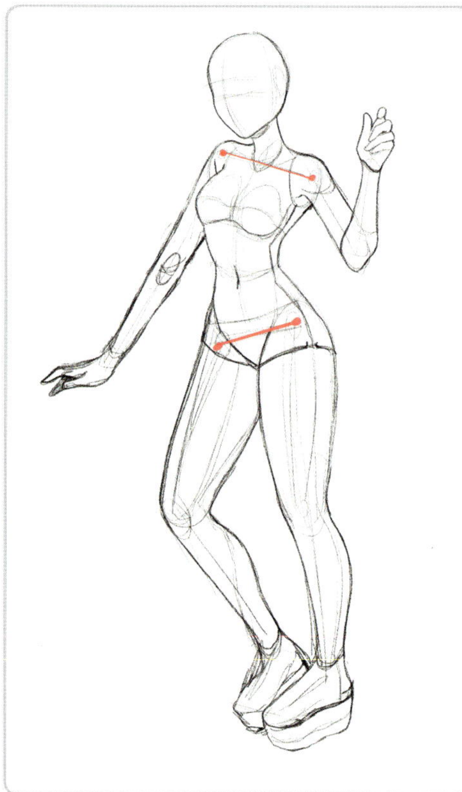

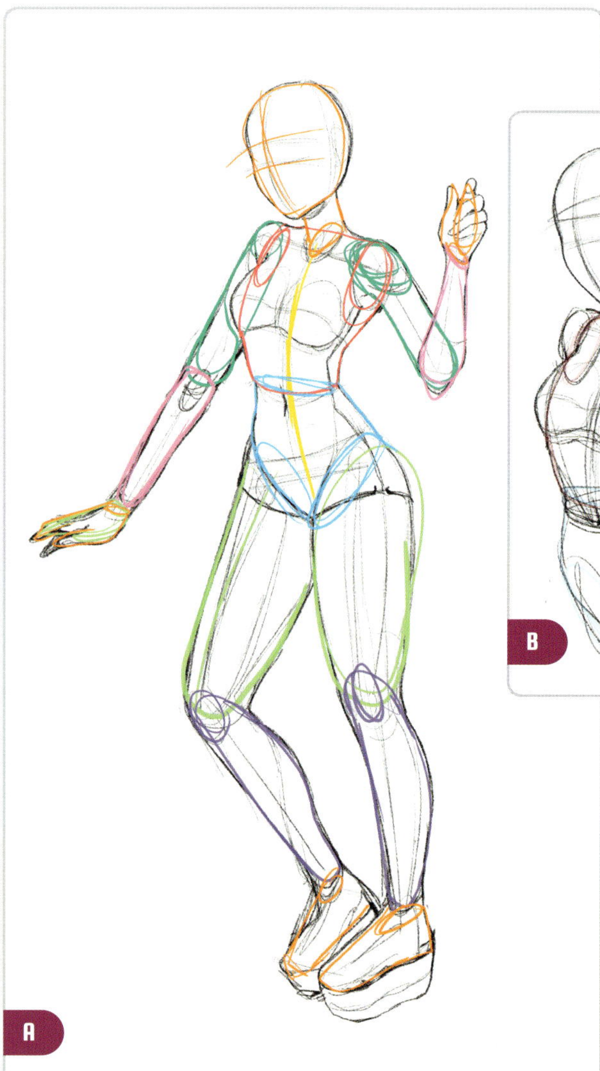


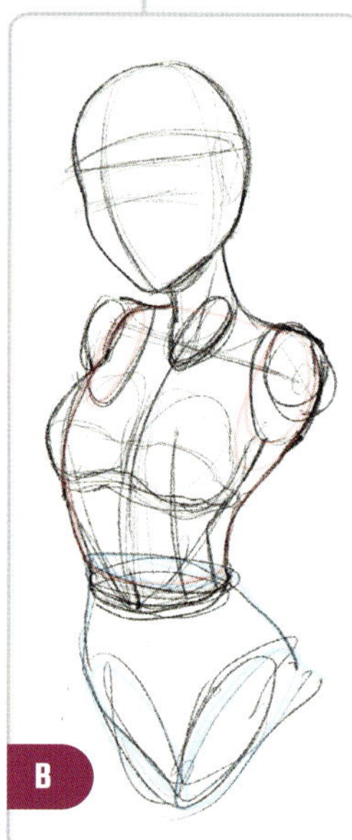


**05** Rather than drawing a stiff, precise outline, start by sketching the basic shapes quickly and lightly. You don't need the exact shape of the neck; try sketching a simple cylinder shape instead. The more you can draw shapes in quick motions like this, the more life your character will have. Before drawing clothes or other elements, focus on sketching the body. Dividing the figure up into smaller segments will help to build the overall shape. Identify where all of the different joints are, as well as the spine. Where does the upper body meet the lower body? Where does the neck meet the torso? Where does the forearm meet the palm? Knowing where these joints are will not only help you to create a more fluid figure, but it can also be useful later on when designing the character's outfit.

A: I love using pencil brushes when sketching digitally and almost never use them on full opacity, preferring to build up the density using brushstrokes instead

B: Sketch basic shapes for each body part, dividing it up into smaller sections and joints

**06** As you begin to add clothing to the character, consider the shape of the design as a whole. For example, wide skirts or billowy shirts can add interest and flare to the composition. However, if you like the shape of the figure you have already sketched out and don't want to obscure it, try using the joints as a starting point for designing a more figure-hugging outfit. Here I use her waistline as the base of her crop top and the joints where her arms meet her wrists for the gloves.

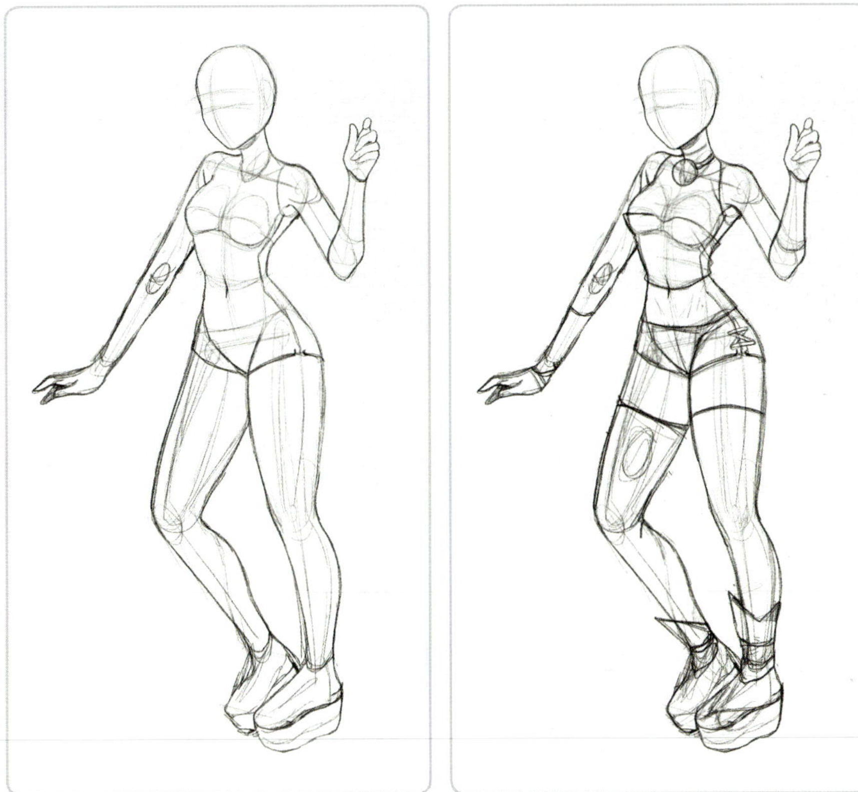

As I already like the character's body shape, I sketch close-fitting clothing so as not to disrupt the form

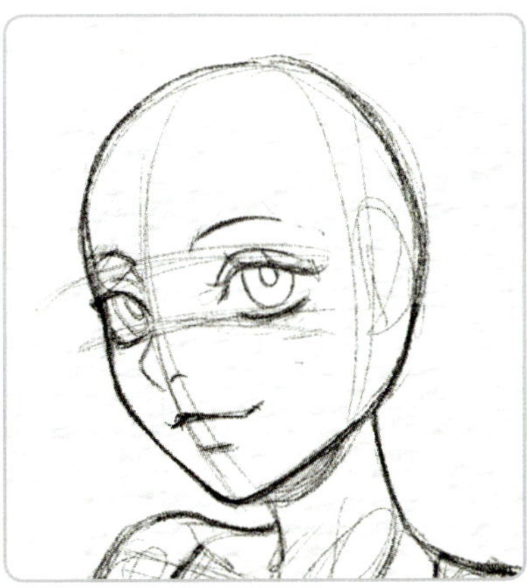

Rather than fully drawing the mouth, I sketch the central crease that separates the lips and the shadow beneath the bottom lip

**07** Keeping in mind the direction in which the face is tilting, map out the facial features using rough guidelines. When in doubt, consider average facial proportions: the eyes are one eye width apart, the corners of the nose line up with the tear ducts, and the corners of the mouth line up with the middle of the eyes. If something about your face sketch appears incorrect, return to these guidelines to figure out what is wrong. This doesn't mean you have to draw characters with typical facial proportions. Knowing these proportions will allow you to create faces that are outside of these guidelines as well. For example, you may wish to sketch large, anime-style eyes. In addition, you don't need to draw an outline for every facial feature. When drawing the mouth, for example, you only need to sketch the central crease, as the lips will be filled in later with shading.

### ARTIST TIP

Flow is the number one thing I consider when creating my anime-style character illustrations. Things that disrupt the flow of the image are called tangents. These distract the eye in a disjointed direction, or cut off forms too early. Try to identify any tangents that show up in your sketch and eliminate them.

**08** Hair can have a huge power over composition. It can be sketched in large, solid chunks, or thin strands that fly in different directions. Consider what you want to say about your character with their hairstyle. A shorter hairstyle may be cuter, edgier, or more practical, whereas longer hair can appear more elegant, feminine, and ethereal. Try to maintain the flow of your design when adding the hair. For example, this character design flows from the upper left-hand corner to the bottom right, so I try to align her long, Rapunzel-like hair in the same direction.

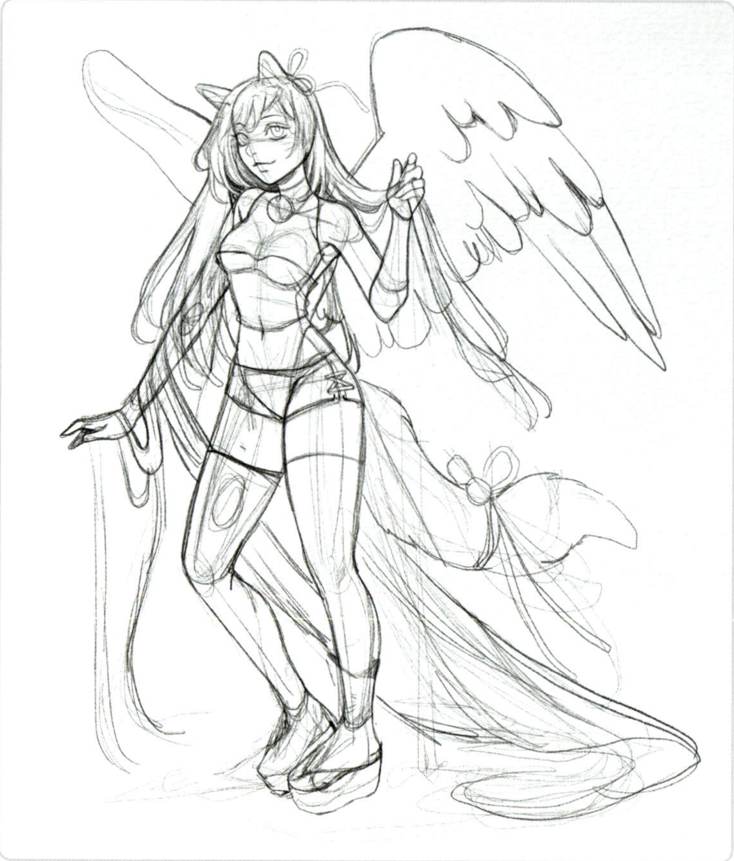

All new elements added to the sketch maintain the S-shape established earlier

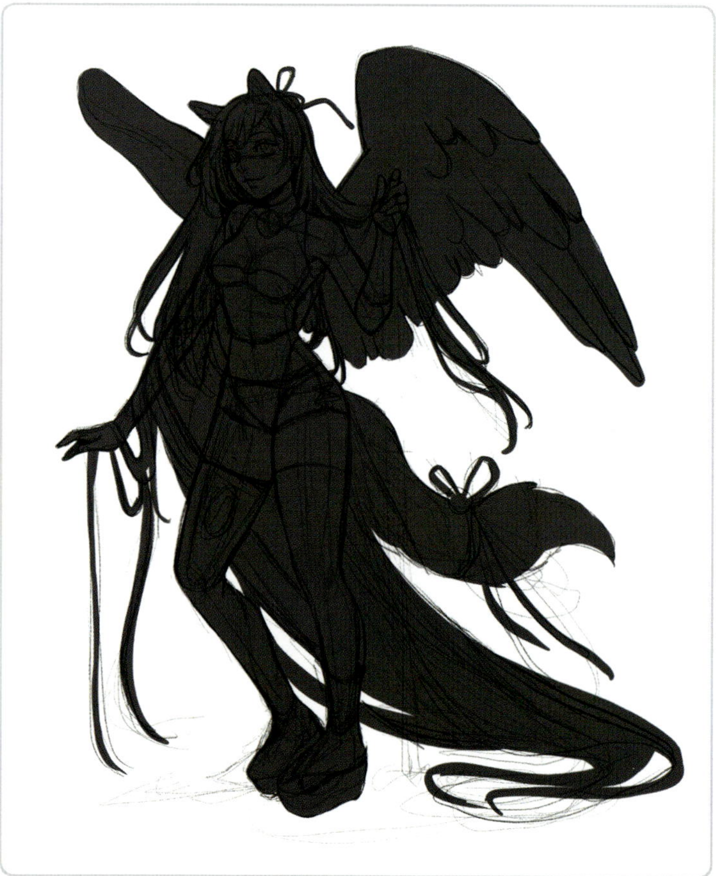

**09** Consider the silhouette as you add new elements to the character's figure. How does the overall design read? Is it still a distinct shape? I study my character's silhouette to see if the design still maintains the S-shaped flow. This is also a good time to consider negative space; that is, the empty parts of the design. Negative space can be a valuable tool for creating a visually interesting image, as leaving empty spaces will help to direct the viewer's attention to focal points in design. Take a moment to black out your image. Do you like the shape you have created so far? If not, make some tweaks.

When viewing the silhouette, I look for a mix of large and small elements – hair and accessories, such as jewelry or props, are a great way to create delicate additions to the silhouette

**10** There is life within a sketch that can add to the design. For this reason I never truly get rid of my undersketch when creating outlines, but simply reduce the opacity instead. When outlining the line art, I don't outline every single line from my sketch either, as I like the look that's created when some are left a little fainter. I try to vary line thickness and often use a thicker outline for the areas on the outside of the figure, while leaving the lines that create small details thinner. I then map out the darkest areas and fill them entirely with black, such as under the chin and sections of the character's hair.

If you are drawing the line art digitally and feel like your pen is becoming too jittery, try editing the brush's smoothness or spacing settings

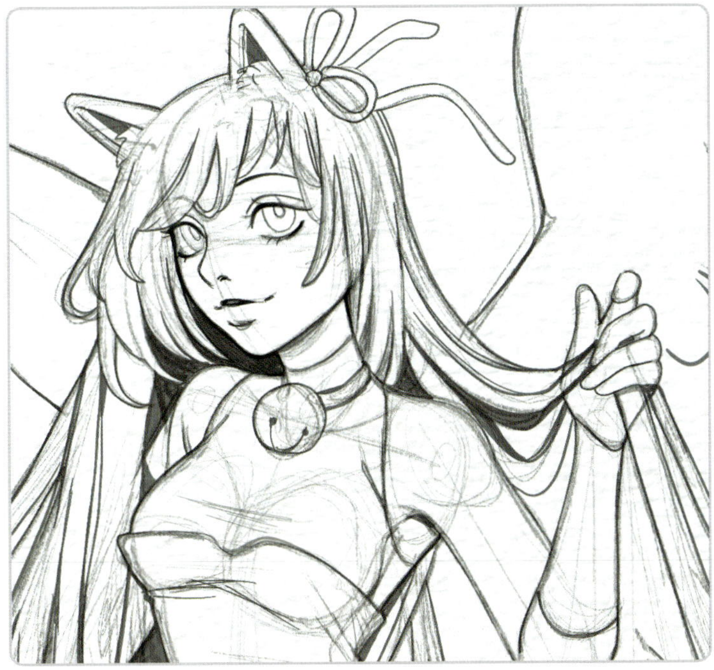

**11** Consider complementary colors when choosing colors for your character, as well as how warm and cool tones blend together. Complementary colors sit opposite each other on the color wheel and pairing them can create a strong color palette. Opting for warm tones and a yellow-purple complementary color set for the overall palette, I paint her eyes and bells yellow to contrast against her purple outfit and hair. When you want to create a striking character composition, another factor to consider is value. If working digitally, switch your character to black and white and observe if there are distinctly different tones of gray, or if everything blends together as the same value. Aim to distinguish each part of the character with different values.

Notice how the different sections of the design have various shades of gray, some darker and some lighter

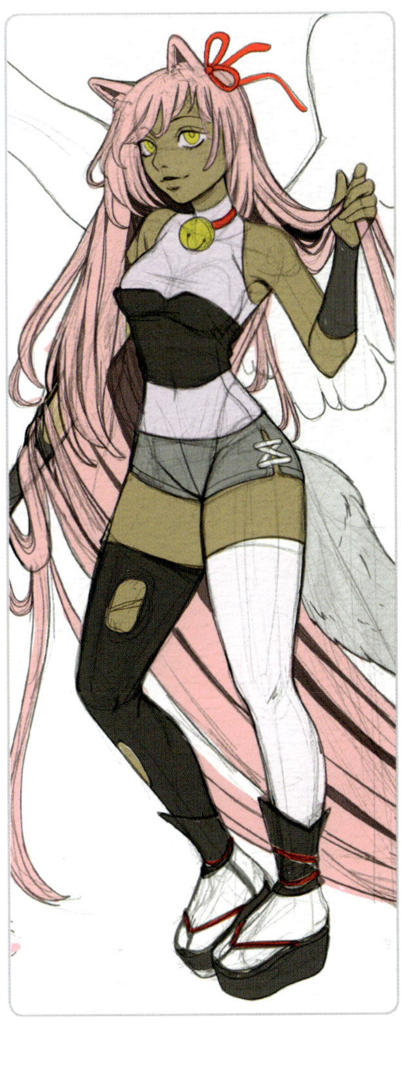

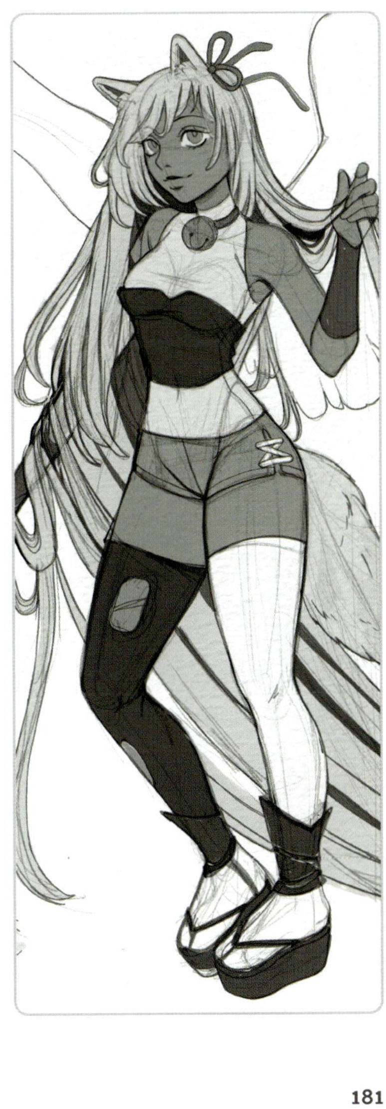

**12** As you begin to render the design, start with soft shadows. These are not the same as harsh cast shadows and will help to add roundness to your character. When adding soft shadows, I tend to use a warm color, such as a light red or purple, with a blending brush. Identify the areas you want to appear round – such as the legs, face, and arms – then contour with a soft blend to help round out the shape.

Applying soft shadows with a blending brush will give your character a more three-dimensional roundness

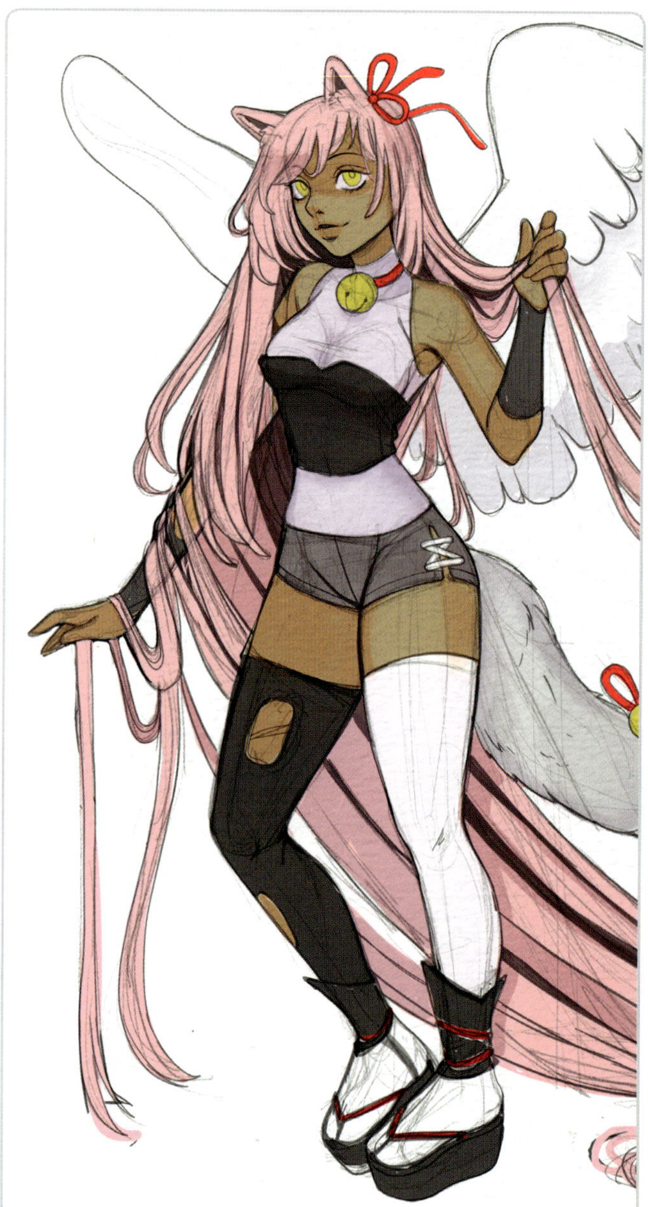

**13** Around this point in the process I like to push the image back with an overall shadow layer. I often choose purple for overall shadows on characters, as it pairs well with other colors. If I'm aiming for a moodier piece, I will select a green or blue, but I never use warm colors – such as red, yellow, or orange – for the push-back shadows. Here I choose a light purple, which helps to create a more cohesive color palette now that the whole image shares a similar purple color. This can also make your character's highlights pop more when added later. When creating a shadow layer, I like to choose a strong color and then lower its opacity until it's very subtle.

The purple color I choose, alongside how it looks once the opacity is lowered

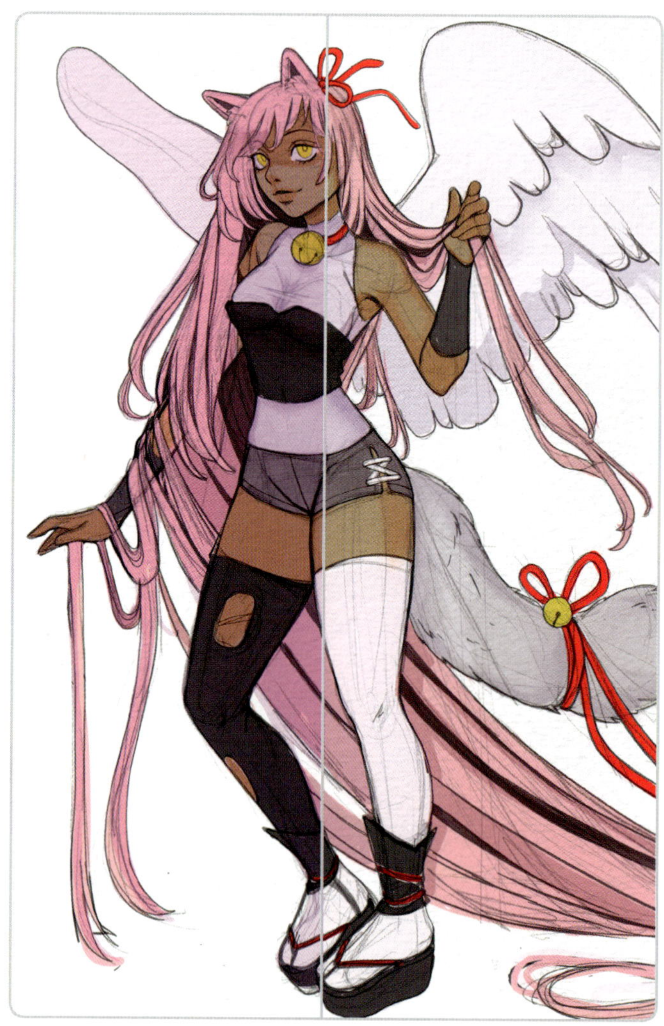

**14** The next step is to add the hard-edged shadows, which are the shadows that are cast over the figure. I select a cooler color, such as a blue or green, and then start looking at the body parts or items that could be casting a shadow on the character. These include the nose, chin, chest, strands of hair, and accessories. You can also darken any areas of the image that look as though they need to be darker at this stage too.

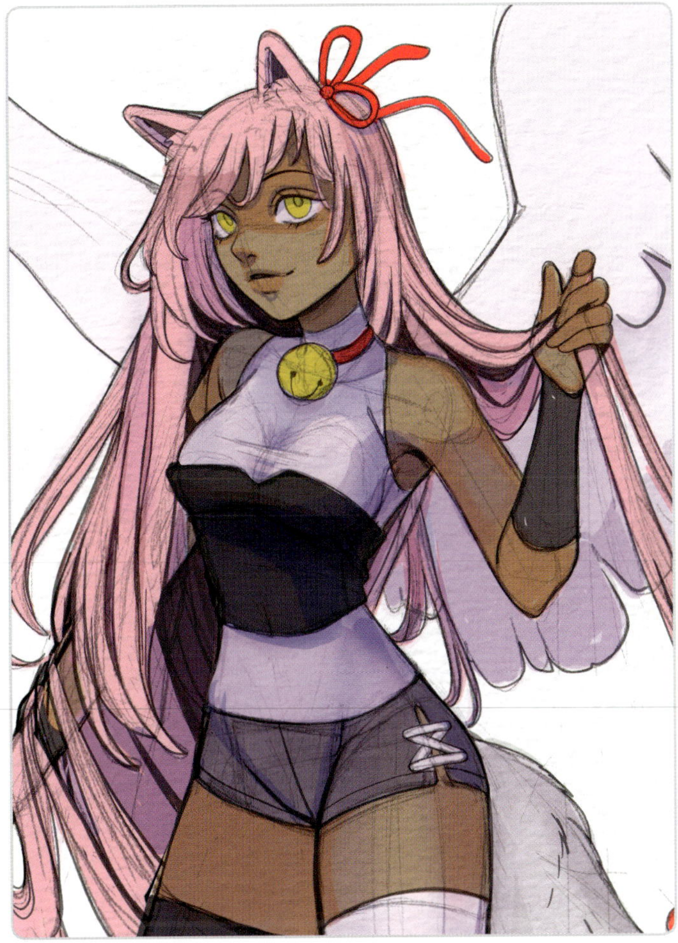

I use a bluish-purple to shade the character, applying it under the nose, bust, hairline, and layers on the wings

**15** After mapping out the values of the character's hair by adding in thick black chunks in step 10, now it is time to soften the hair so it feels more cohesive. I do this using a Screen layer, selecting the most saturated version of the color I want the hair to be, before painting the entirety of the hair with that color. As I want this character's hair to be light pink, I select a vivid pink, before lowering the opacity of the layer until it looks right. This is one of my favorite steps, as it starts to make the design appear much softer.

Before and after lowering the opacity of the saturated pink color for the hair

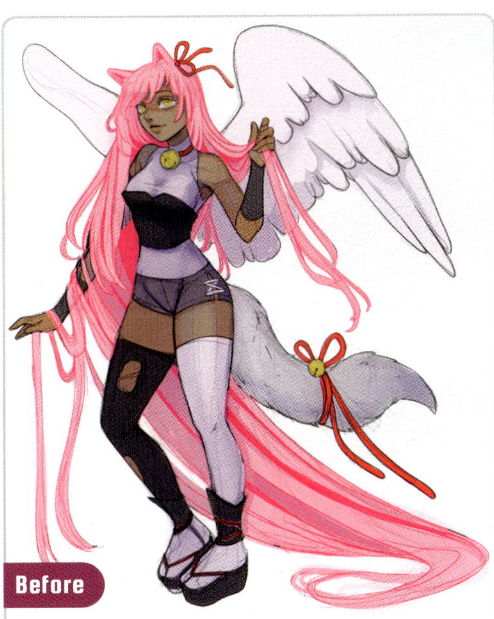


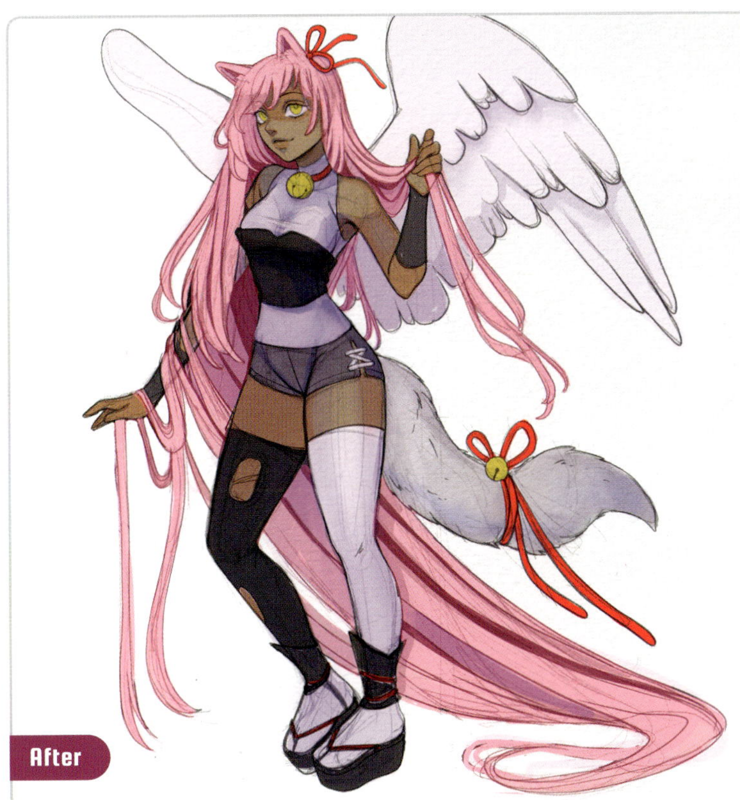

**16** Avoid using white to highlight the character's hair, choosing a lighter version of the current hair color instead. Here I select a very pale pink. You could also use other colors for the highlights if you want to create the impression of reflected light. Selecting a teal color as a highlight, for example, can be an attractive addition to most hair colors. I look for curved or waved strands of hair and highlight the curve, making use of blending tools to blend the edges of the highlights, as I don't like to use overly harsh highlights in my character designs.

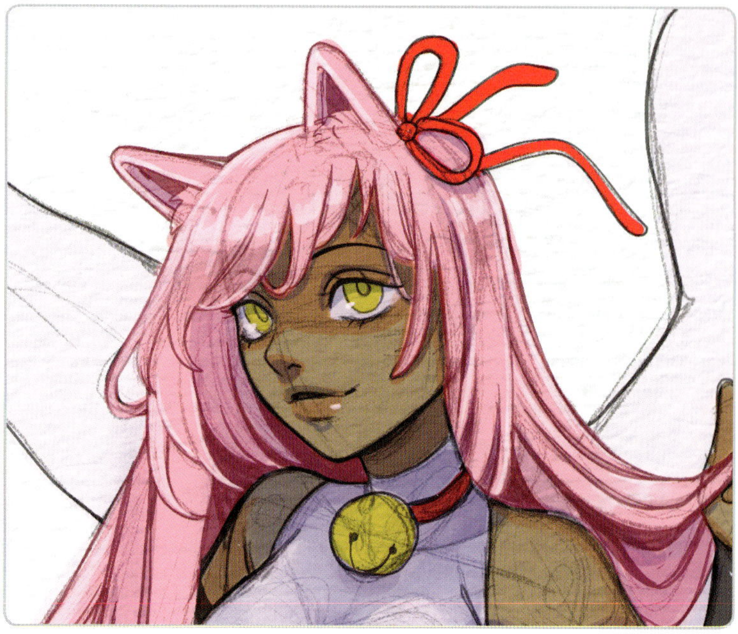

To avoid intense highlights, I use a blending tool to blend the pale pink highlights to create a more subtle look

**17** By this stage you will have locked in the basics of the character, including outlines, lights, and darks. Before moving on to more detailed work, add a new layer on top so that any blacks or grays are removed from the image, allowing you to work with a much softer palette. Similar to how I softened the hair, I add a Screen layer and apply a color over the image, then lower the opacity until I am happy with how it looks. While in this case the hair color and overall image color match, this is not always the case with my character designs. I often use blue for the character's hair and a red color for the rest of the image.

How the Screen layer looks before and after I lower the opacity of the pink

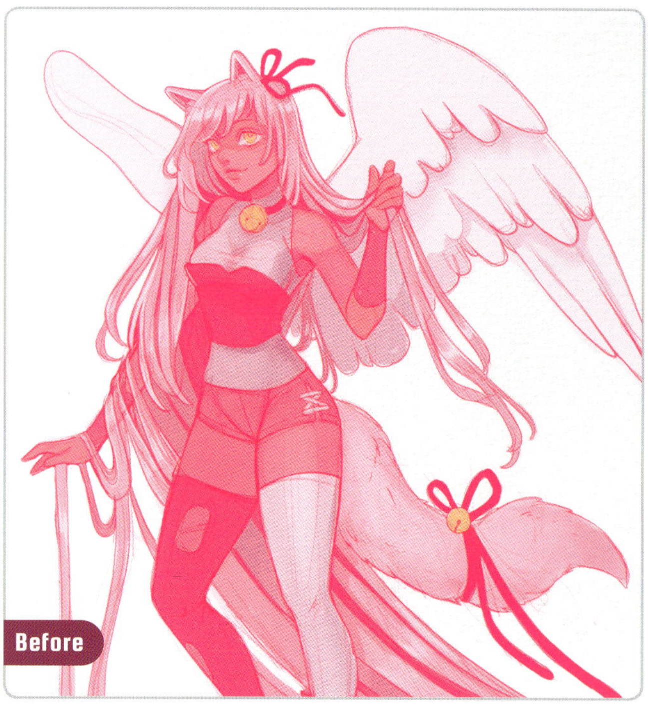


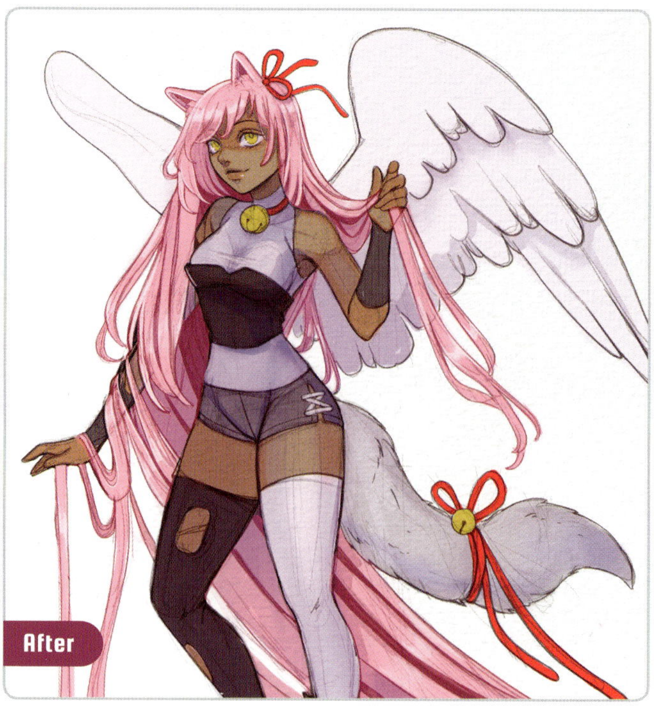

**18** After the alterations added in the previous steps, you may feel like you have lost some of the dark values, or that the design is now missing something. This is a good stage to pause and study the character design as a whole to evaluate what it lacks. Here I notice that I need to introduce some important dark areas and detail to her face. I also decide that I want her big anime-style eyes to be more foxlike, plus I wish to add a belt.

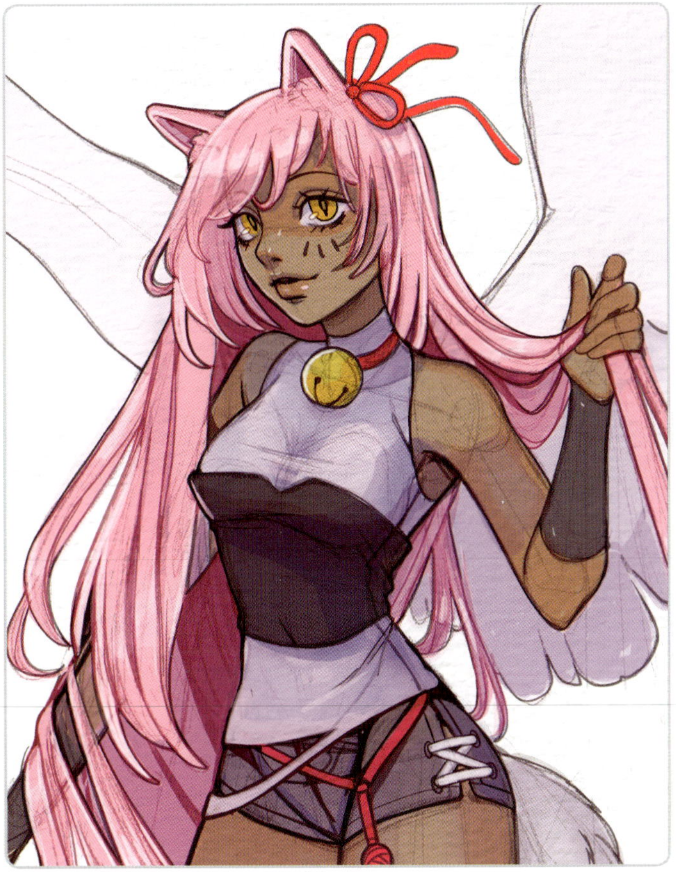

No character design is perfect from the start; I often find that my ideas evolve as the design progresses, so make sure to check in often to determine what is missing

**19** I almost never use white when adding highlights, but instead opt for either a bright or pastel shade, depending on the color I'm painting it onto. I like to add a rim lighting effect to my character designs, where the edges of the figure are lit up. Typically I highlight areas such as the cheekbones, the curve on the bridge of the nose, the collarbones, and the contours of the legs. I also like to outline the seams of clothes to help them stand out a little more.

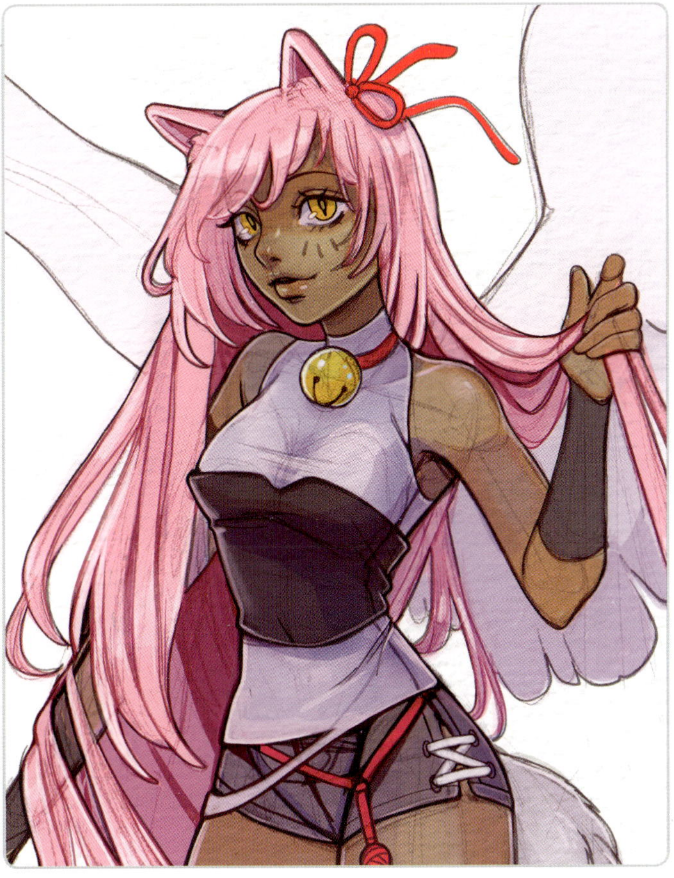

Note how the edges of the clothes have been highlighted so they are more distinct

## ARTIST TIP

When adding highlights, the darker the color you are working on, the brighter the highlight color should be. Here the highlights on the light colored hair are a pale pink, while on the darker legs and tights they are a brighter pink. Using a bright color to highlight will illuminate the rich color beneath it.

**20** Your character's face may require a little more attention than the rest of the design, especially if you want the face to be the focal point of the image. At this stage I introduce "makeup" elements, adding more color to the lips, cheeks, and eyelids, usually using a red color and a Multiply layer.

Adding makeup-like elements, such as rouged cheeks and lips, can draw more attention to the face

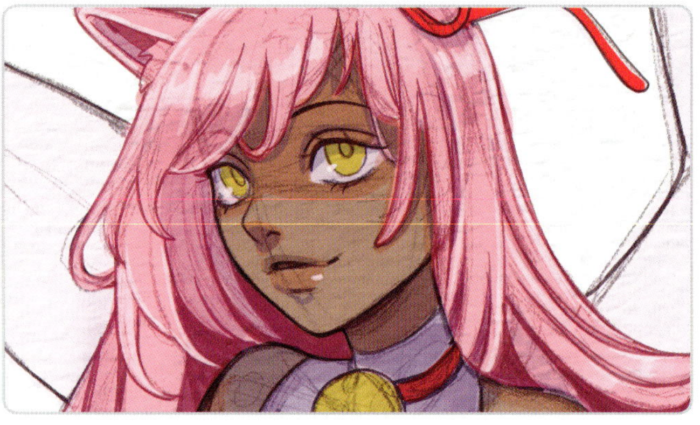

**21** I like adding gradients to my artwork. Because the eye is drawn to the brightest part of an image, a gradient can help to create flow, allowing the eye to focus on the focal point first, before moving on to other areas. To create a gradient digitally, color your entire image with one color, lock the layer's transparency, and design a rough gradient out of varying shades of gray. The whitest part of the gradient should be your focal point. You can use the Gaussian Blur tool to blur the gray tones together to create a smooth transition across your character. As with all my overlays, I then lower the opacity to create the desired effect. Sometimes, instead of gray, I will use a color gradient moving from pink to purple, or from green to blue, across the character. Try experimenting with how color affects your image in this way.

How the gradient looks before and after I lower the opacity

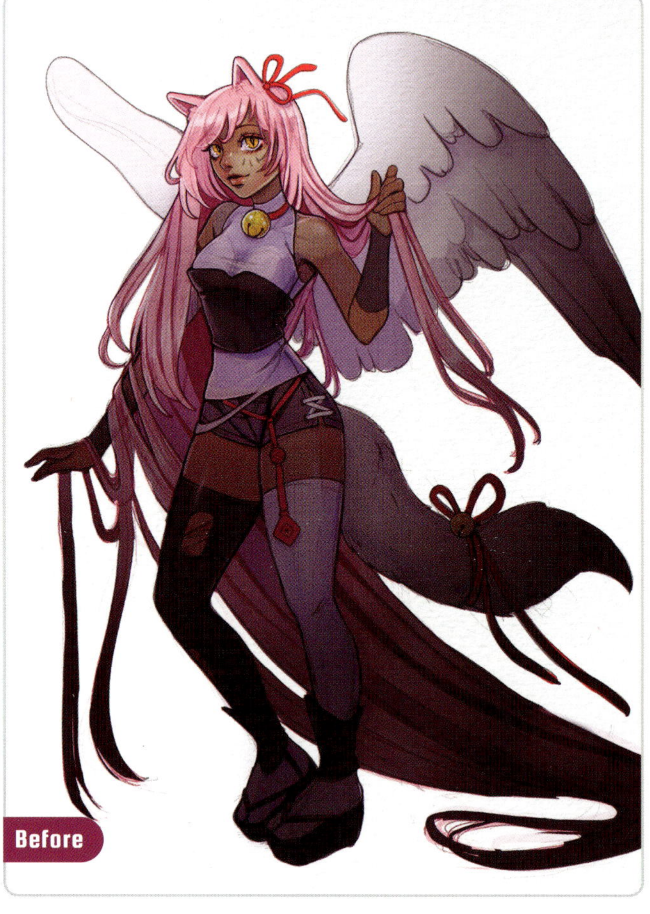

Before

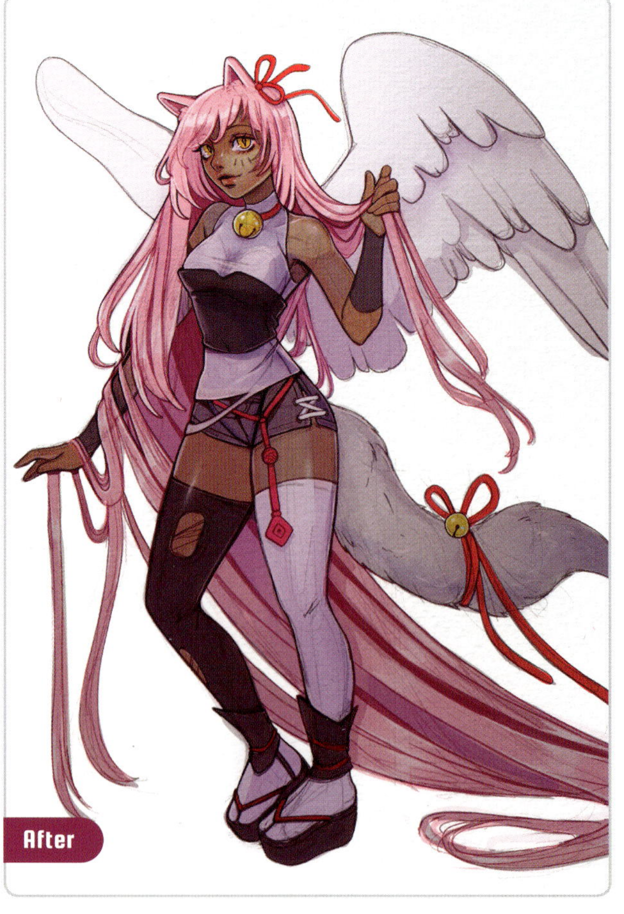

After

**22** View your image as a whole. Here I notice that my design has become too dark for the light, airy aesthetic I'm aiming for, so I apply a white overlay to lighten it. This isn't a necessary step, but one I sometimes use when the numerous Multiply layers and gradients make the piece start to appear darker than intended, especially in the outlines. True to my signature style, I like the outlines to feel soft and subtle to give the piece an attractive watercolor effect.

To lighten the design, I apply a white Screen layer over the entire image, then lower the opacity

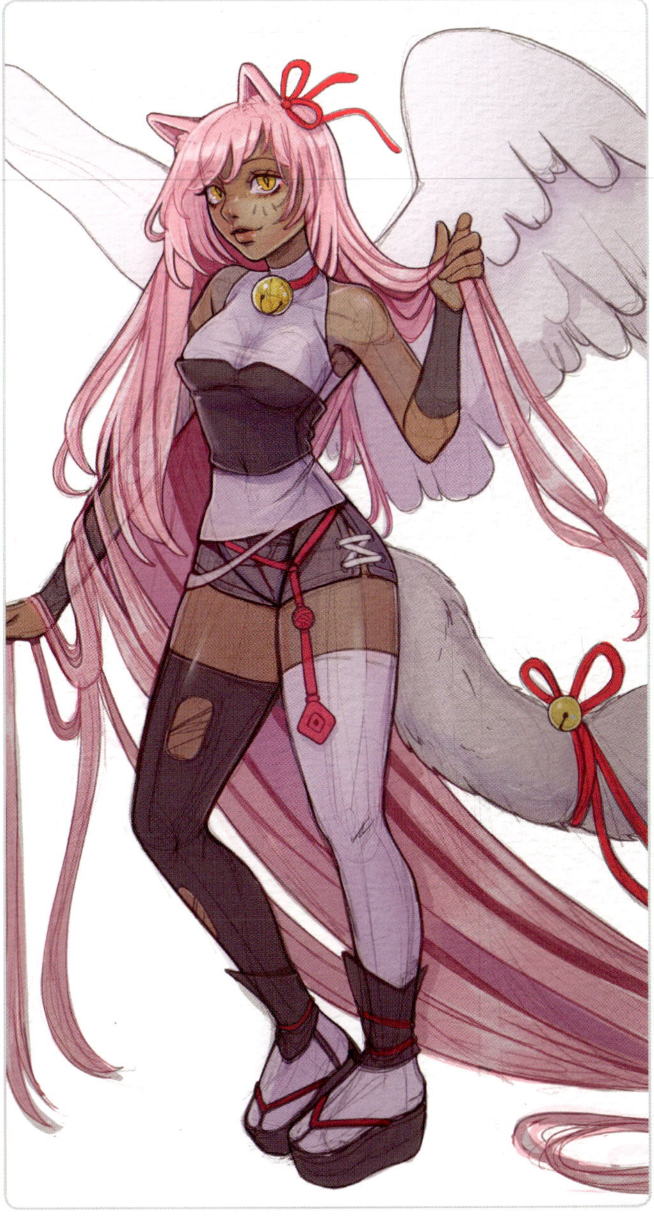

**23** To make a character look as though they are surrounded by light, I often encircle the form with a bright color, either blue or yellow, depending on the look I wish to create. A warm yellow makes the character look as though they are bathed in warm sunlight, like a sunset or sunrise. Conversely, a blue light can produce more midsummer vibes. I use blue for this image, which creates a subtle watercolor effect in the wings. Notice where I lay down the blue color, then switch the layer to a Screen layer, producing the intended atmospheric effect.

Imagining a bright light shining from behind my character, I consider where it would peek through, then paint color in those areas

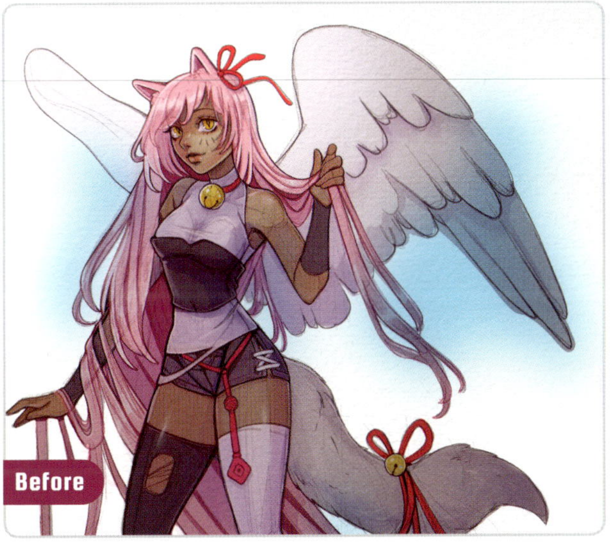


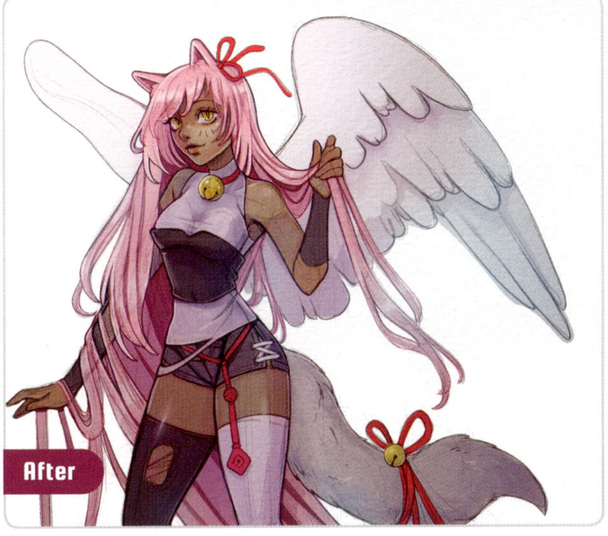

**24** View your design as a whole and make any final tweaks, such as to areas you want to make brighter or darker. At this stage I will often apply a few adjustment layers to tweak the saturation or contrast of the image. Return to adjustments covered in previous steps until you feel like your character design meets your original concept for the piece. Here I paint a more vibrant shine on the legs, bells, and lower hair to make them pop, plus draw in the feather detail on the left wing and stray hairs on the tail. Next, I remove some of my original sketch lines that I feel are disrupting the piece and readjust some outlines. I also adjust the contrast and saturation until I'm happy.

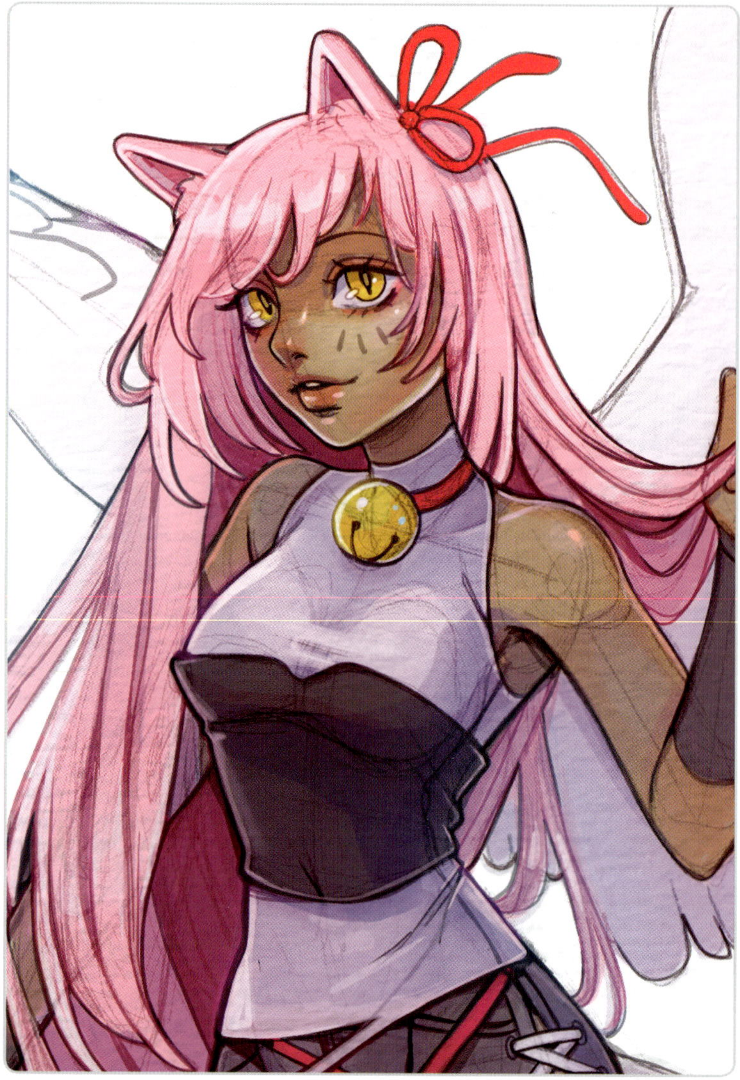

Apply any final adjustments to your image, including highlights, shadows, and additional details

# CONCLUSION

By following this tutorial you will have learned how to create an anime-style character that feels fluid and dynamic, enhanced by bright, playful colors. She has an attractive S-shaped curve to her silhouette, allowing the eyes to travel easily from one side of the design to the other as they take in the detail. The striking purple-yellow complementary color pallette is paired with vibrant pops of red, and overall there is an airy, watercolor feel to the piece, true to my signature anime style.

The workflow and tips shared here will provide you with the information you need when designing your own character and creating a compelling illustration of which you can feel proud. Consider the importance of reference, composition, and color, as well as how you can imbue the character design with your own unique style.

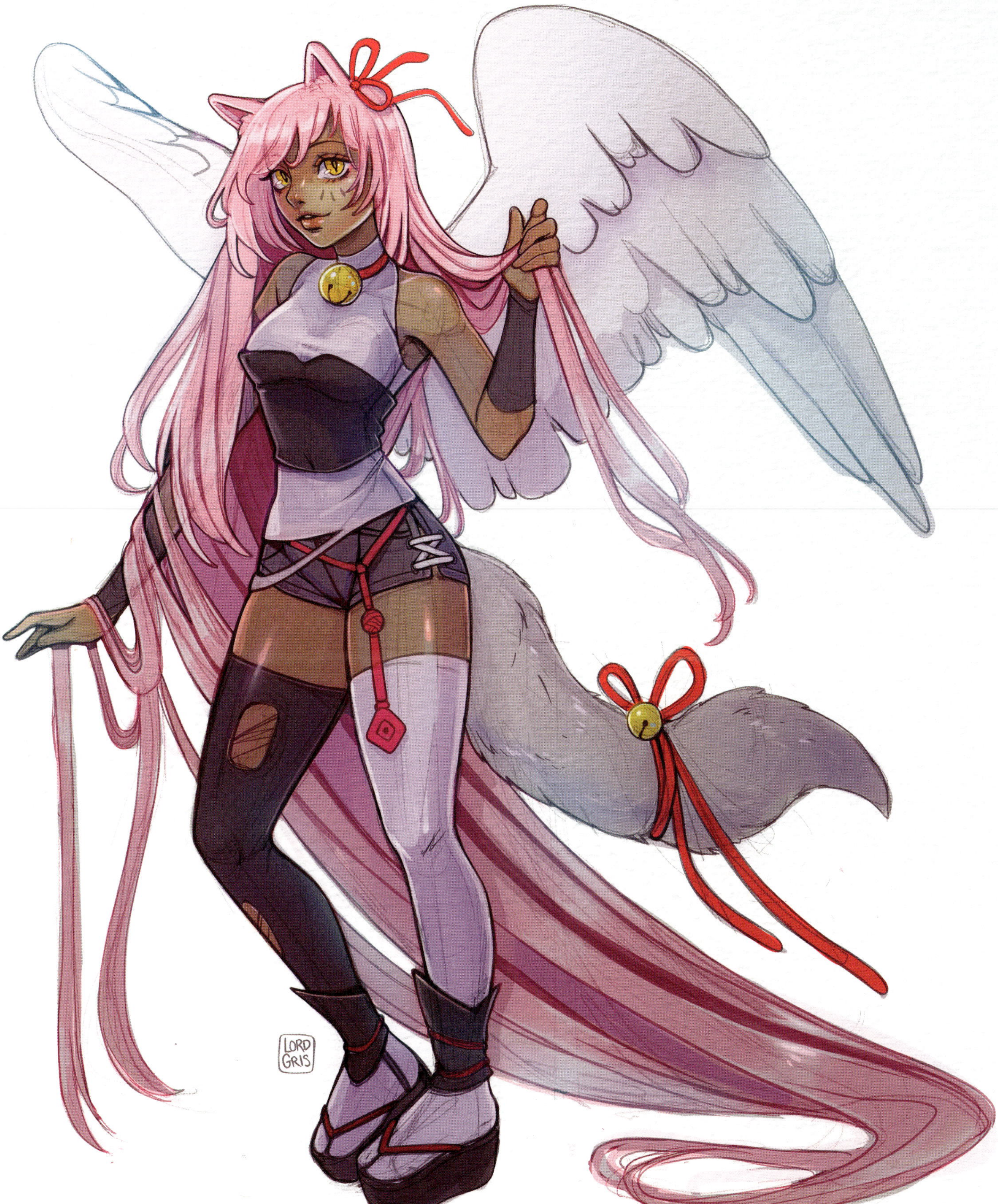


Final artwork © Lord Gris

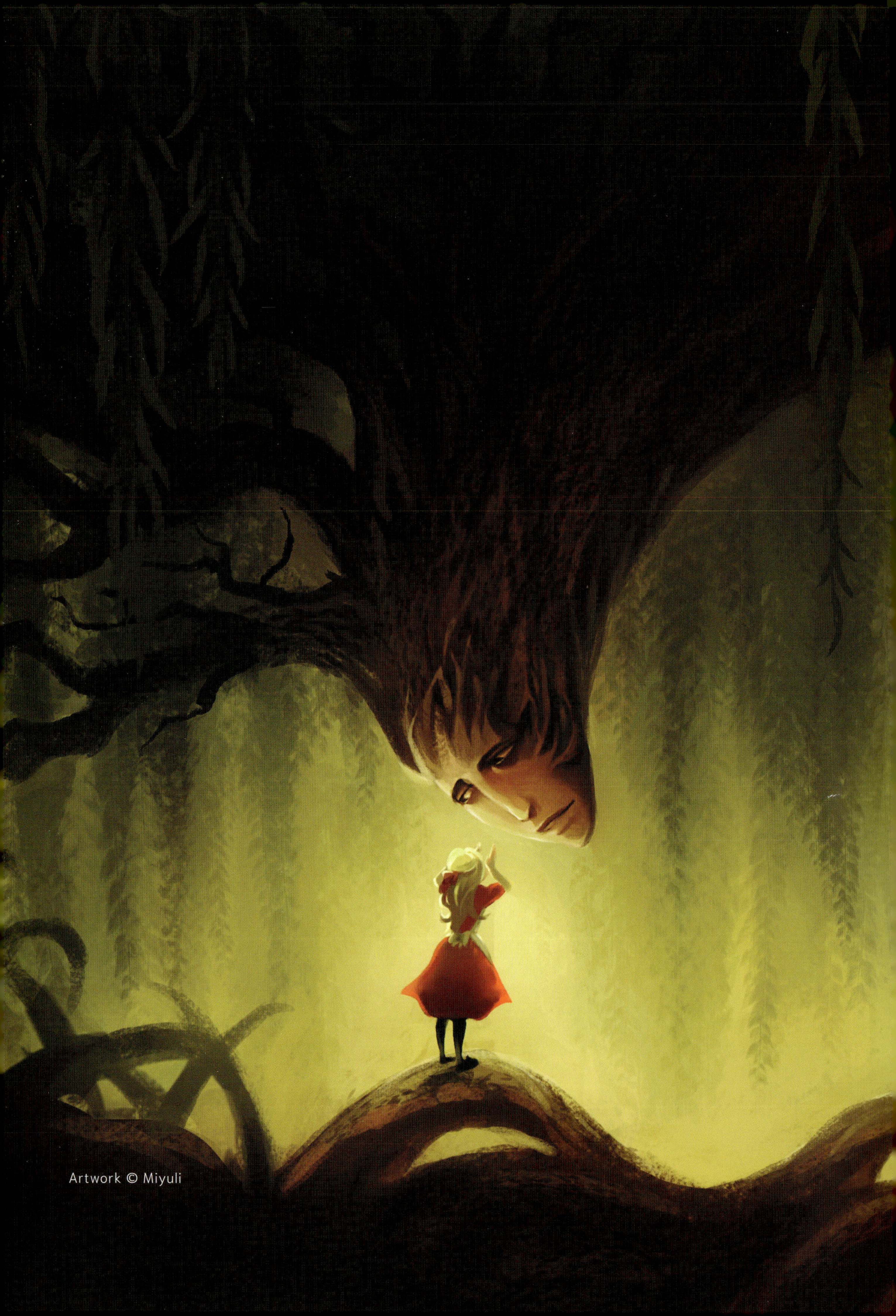

# MIYULI

## Meet the artist

**Comic artist & illustrator**

**instagram.com/miyuliart | miyuliart.com**

Miyuli is a comic creator who likes to draw and write stories. She studied animation in film school, while creating anime-style comics as an independent artist. After posting numerous art studies online, she published a tutorial book in several languages. Her current work includes the popular webtoon *Morgana and Oz*.

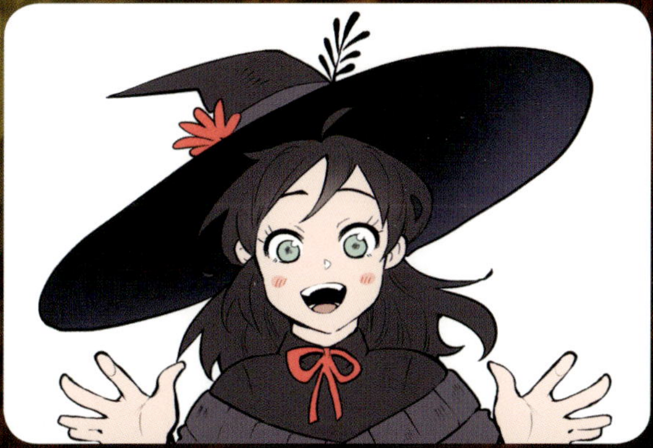

# CASE STUDY



## INFLUENCES, MOTIVATIONS, TRAINING

My interest in art began in childhood. I have always been creatively minded and was a big fan of Soviet cartoons and animated Disney movies. Eager to learn, I sought out older children who were better at drawing so I could try and copy them. When my family moved to Germany, I discovered Japanese animation, such as *Sailor Moon*, and my imagination was ignited. I longed to create my own original characters within that universe. Soon after, I began collecting manga, such as *Magic Knights Rayearth* by Clamp and *Oh My Goddess!* by Kosuke Fujishima. The only European comic I was interested in as a child was the Italian fantasy series, *Witch*.

Inspired by the genre, I spent most of my time thinking up my own characters and started to create stories with friends using my limited art supplies. This took up all of my free time and I began to seriously consider the possibility of an art career, but I worried about whether it was a financially smart choice, so I put a lot of effort into school to keep my options open. While my family supported me in pursuing art as long as my grades were good, art teachers were often not encouraging of my anime style. This motivated me to prove what I could do.

I won a couple of art competitions in my teenage years and participated in local and national comic contests with encouraging results. This inspired me to keep drawing and pursue anime-style art as a career. Around 2008, I bought my first drawing tablet and started experimenting with digital art. I gradually upgraded my equipment and eventually switched from traditional media to an entirely digital workflow.

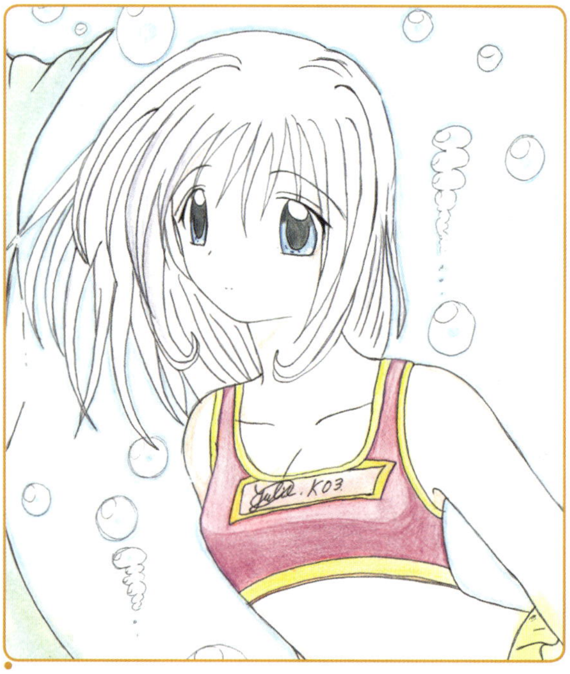

2003 – the first illustration I shared online, colored using discarded chalk from school

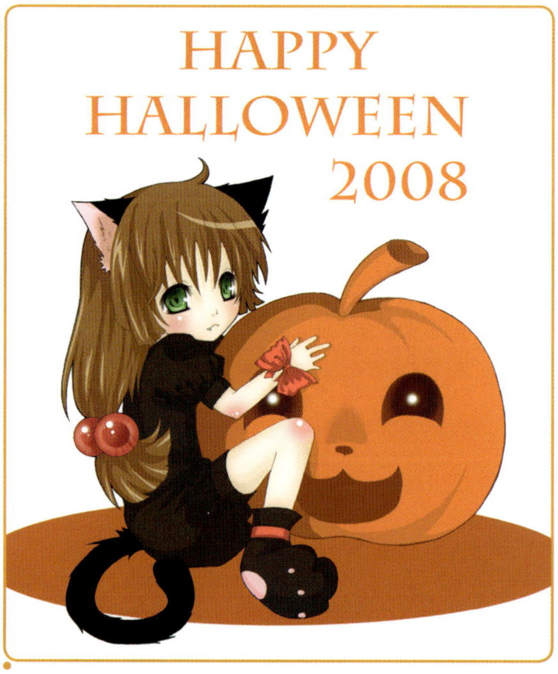


An early attempt to create digital art, drawn in Adobe Photoshop CS3

## Studies

When I graduated from high school, I had to decide whether I wanted to pursue a career in art or follow my other interests in language studies. While I studied hard to graduate with good grades, I realized I was lacking time to draw. I eventually decided to study art so I could practice drawing and polishing my skills full time.

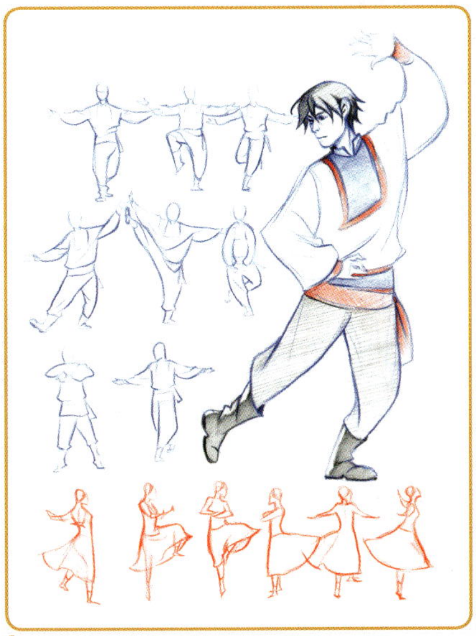

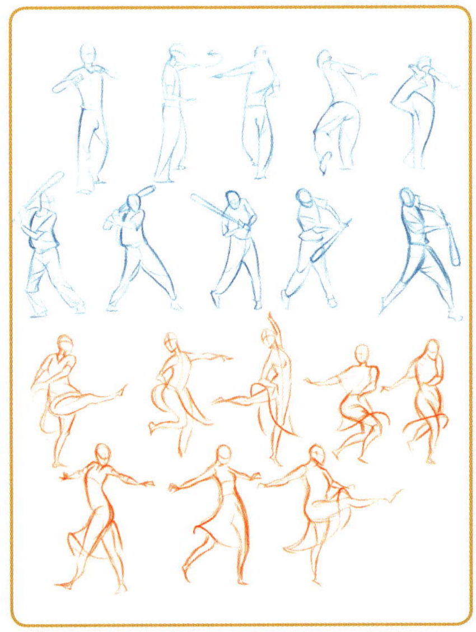

I really enjoy studying and drawing movement, which is what drew me to animation

I began a course in time-based media, which involved everything from graphic and website design to animation. While I thought it would be good to develop a broad skill set, I soon realized the course was more technical than artistic, so I transferred to a film school to study animation instead. Though I considered applying to animation school in the USA, I decided the student debt wasn't worth it, and instead enrolled at the Konrad Wolf Film University of Babelsberg. The program involved many facets of animation, providing me with the opportunity to dive into 2D paper animation, digital animation in Maya and After Effects, clay and sand animation, and stop-motion.

I enjoyed life drawing the most, learning a lot from the course tutor who was a professor in sculpting. While he was never very impressed with my skills, I've always preferred stricter teachers who share constructive criticism. I also learned 3D modeling and animation, but realized it wasn't for me. Though I was able to try experimental animation with sand and clay, the preparation and clean-up took a considerable amount of time, when all I wanted to do was put pen to paper. I did enjoy 2D animation and loved seeing my characters move, but didn't possess the patience it required. I also learned that I prefer to work on my own, rather than in the big teams required for animation. Instead of doing my homework, I ended up drawing my own comics and self-publishing them, and soon realized that comics were where my artistic interests lay.

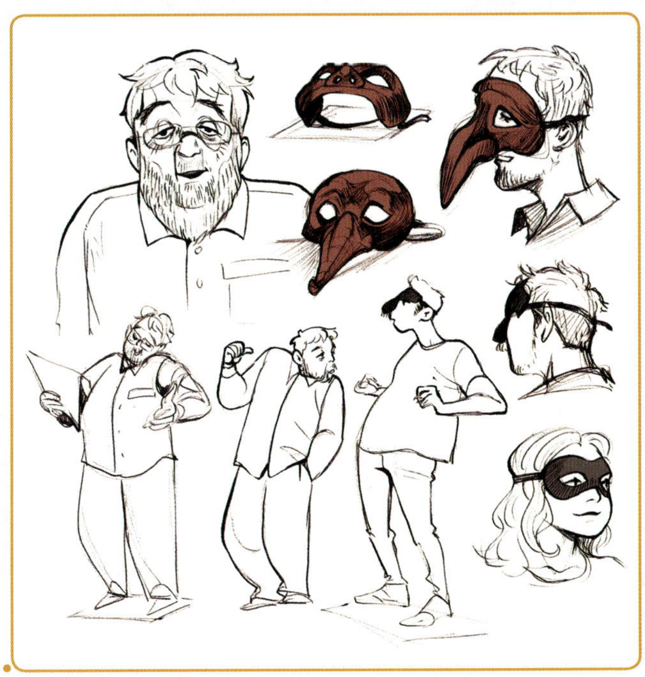

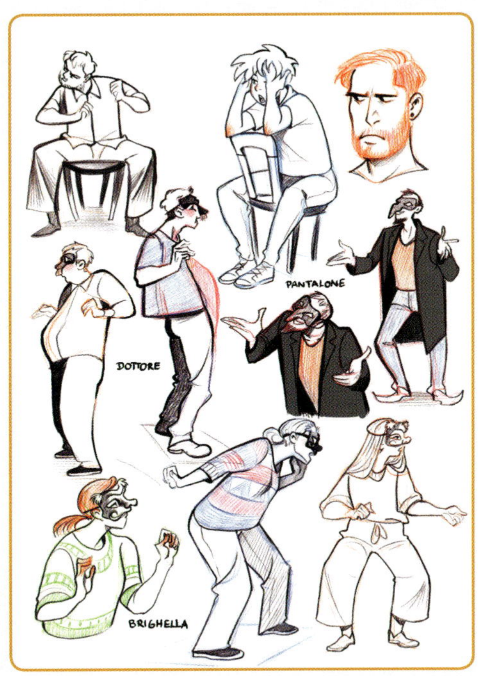


Sketches from a *commedia dell'arte* class I attended at university

I am grateful to have learned basic 2D animation, as I still love the craft of it. I also feel lucky to have been able to attend classes on film music, film history, and acting. All of this greatly informed my artistic decisions. Comics and the anime style in general were not well regarded in any of my university classes, however, so I studied these in my own time. While attending university, I also signed up to a couple of online classes with instructors who work in the industry. After saving up, I was able to take Schoolism and CGMA courses in color and light, perspective, and storyboarding. Receiving feedback from professionals was really encouraging and I realized there was a lot I still had to learn.

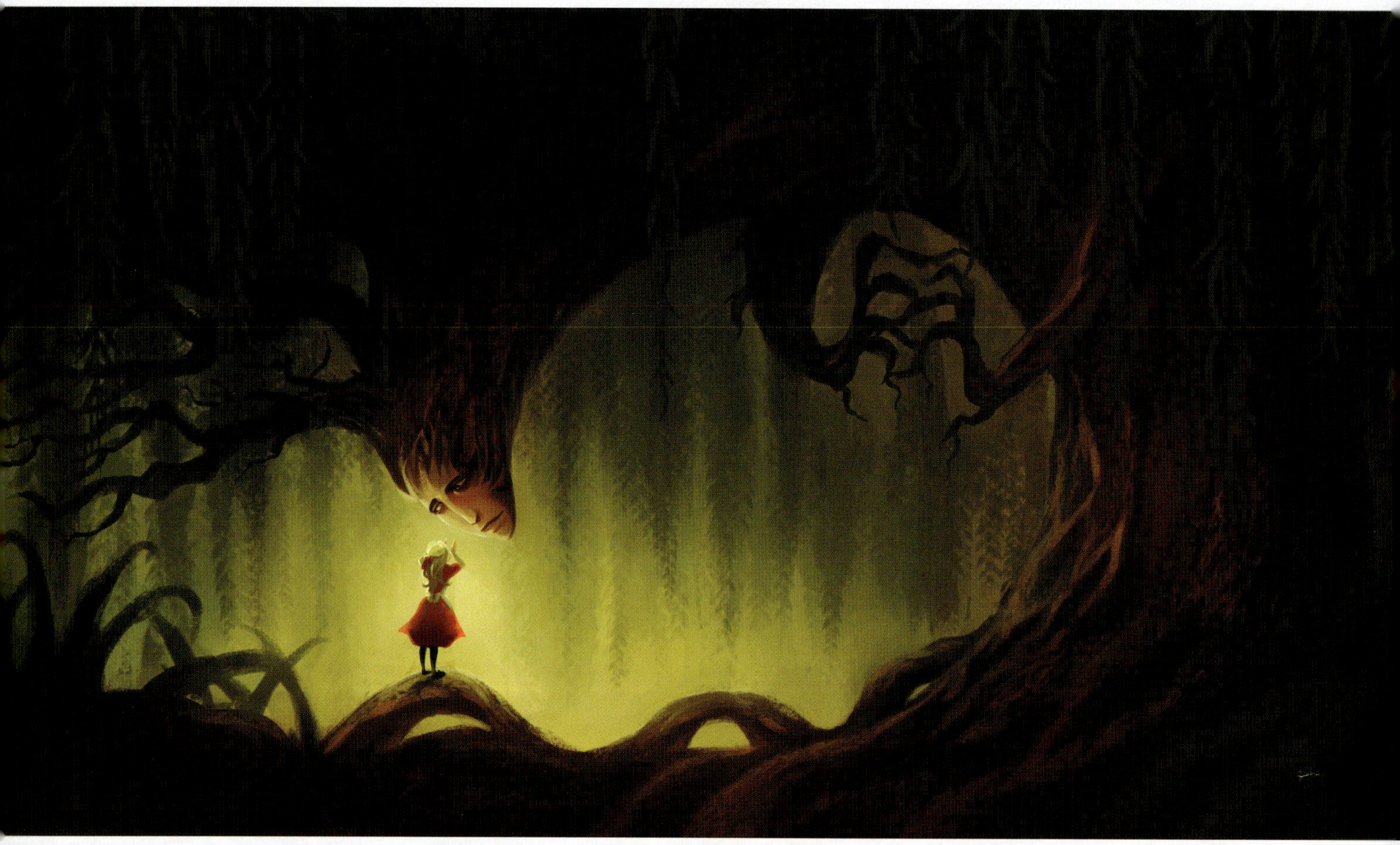

My final illustration from the CGMA course, The Art of Color and Light, in 2014

## Finding inspiration

I have several sources of inspiration that I return to regularly. I love to travel and visit museums, castles, cathedrals, temples, shrines, and other culturally significant places. As a history enthusiast, I enjoy researching the stories or folklore of each place. Europe has many interesting castles and medieval festivals, markets, and museums, and I have explored lots of fascinating places in the Czech Republic, Germany, France, England, and Finland. I have also visited castles, temples, and museums in Taiwan, Hong Kong, and Japan, all of which have provided boundless ideas. There are many countries I still wish to visit. Studying the language and literature of each nation provides an endless supply of inspiration and intriguing discoveries. As the tourist experience can be somewhat artificial in big, popular destinations, I enjoy traveling to small, lesser known places or exploring local festivals.

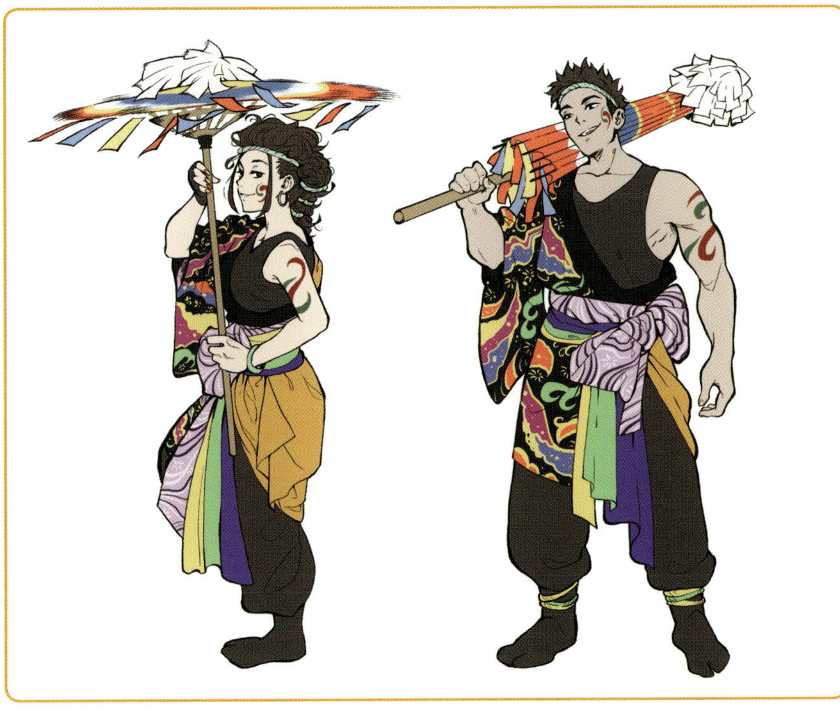

An illustration based on costumes I saw during the Shanshan Festival in Tottori, Japan

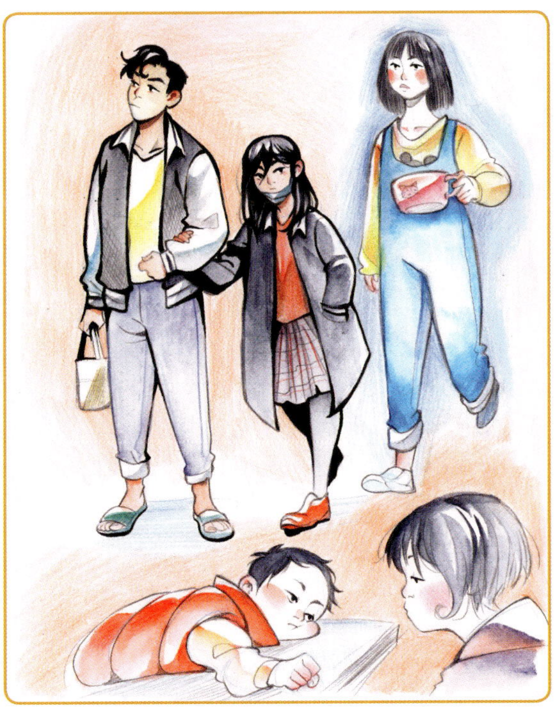

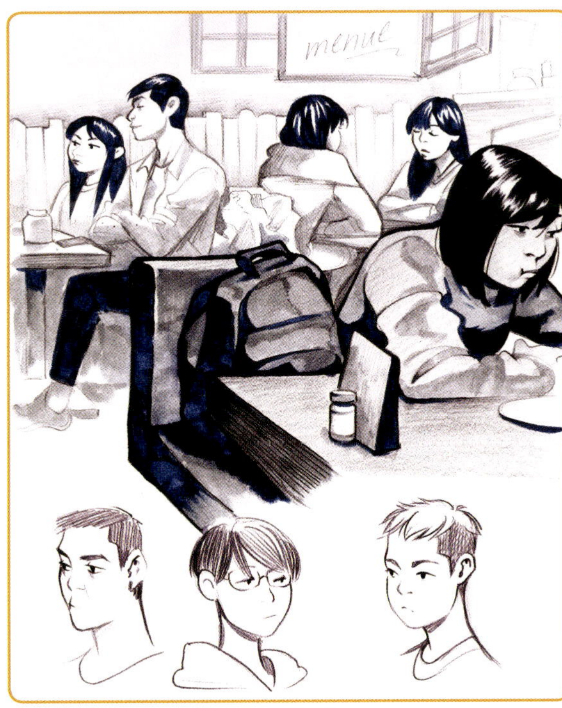

Sketches made while people-watching in Taiwan

Music is a big inspiration and I get many ideas from attending concerts, musicals, and the theater. I also like to attend art events, such as the Dr. Sketchy's Anti-Art School, a burlesque cabaret and life-drawing event, and regularly sit and sketch people in cafés or parks too.

Whether at home or traveling, I read many non-fiction books about the craft of storytelling and drawing. Not everything I read necessarily appeals to my workflow, but it's enlightening to get a glimpse into other artists' thought processes. The more input you have, the more you can begin to adapt new ideas and practices into your own art. If you don't have time to read, there are plenty of podcasts, interviews, and YouTube videos from which you can draw inspiration.

Ultimately, the reason I create stems from my love of fiction. I read a lot of comics, along with watching television shows and playing games. As well as simply enjoying them, there is also great value in analyzing exactly what it is that I enjoy, determining the elements that affect, interest, or inspire me. The more I understand, the more I can try to carry over into my own work.

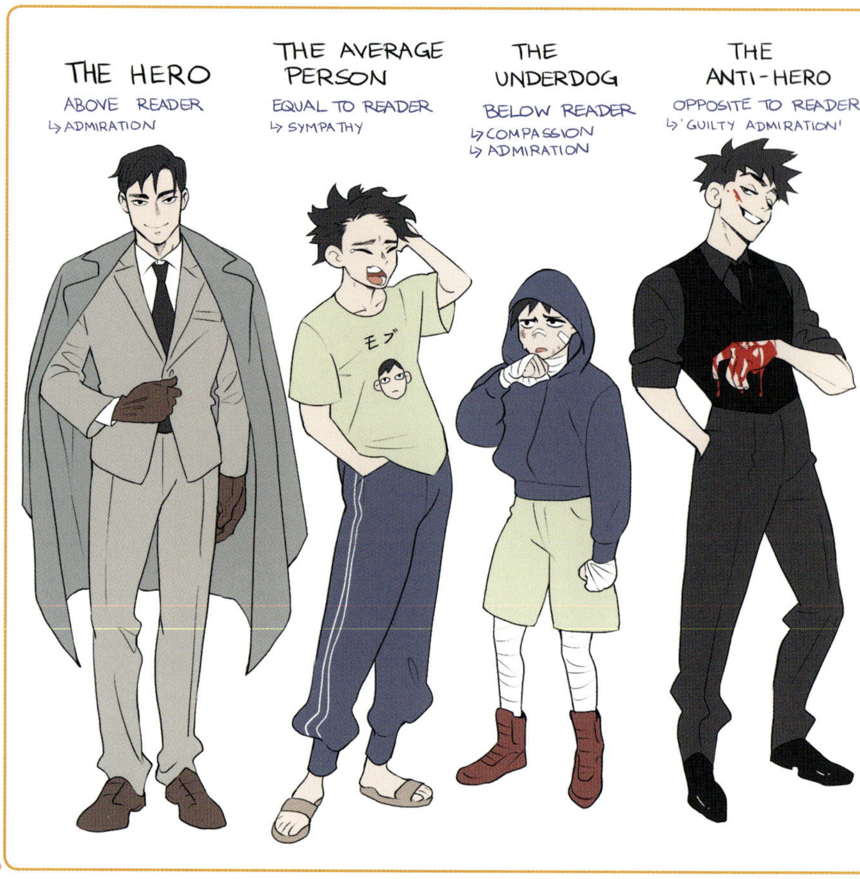


Character studies created after reading about the four types of protagonists in Karl Iglesias' book *Writing for Emotional Impact*

## Art as expression

The subject matter behind my art is often quite self-indulgent. I'm now at a place where I receive monetary support to realize my visions, but it's been a long process to recognize what those visions are. At first I believed that just drawing would be enough and concentrated on polishing my artistic skills. After working with some authors, however, I realized that I wanted more control over my own storytelling. I now see art as a form of communication through which I can connect with my audience.

For a while I thought art didn't always need to say something and that it was enough for a story or illustration to simply be entertaining. Eventually I realized that I gain a lot more value from artwork that invites me to ponder the issues it presents. I aim to create a good middle ground where my art and stories are entertaining, but also offer something to digest. As an artist you get to experiment with how far you wish to push your personal expression.

I no longer think too hard about what represents me. I simply draw what I enjoy and representation follows naturally. If I get bored or realize I wouldn't read what I'm working on, that's when I know it's not a true representation of who I am. I prefer to let my audience decide what my work represents, with the understanding that every individual will experience it differently.

While I sometimes struggle to verbalize my ideas, I'm able to express them through my art instead. My thoughts and opinions are constantly evolving in response to the new information I digest on a daily basis. I will never have full control over how my art is interpreted by its audience, but unless something is taken out of context or misused for an unintended purpose, this is all part of the fun. All I can do is hone my skills.

## Tools & media

My current favorite tools are Clip Studio Paint and the Wacom Cintiq. I enjoy working digitally as it is efficient, there is no cleaning up, and as I rarely have to refill or replace anything, it pays off financially. Before this I tried a hybrid approach, sketching and inking line work traditionally before scanning the illustration and coloring it digitally. This took much longer, but the illustrations had a more organic look. While I decided to sacrifice this look for speed, I might return to it someday.

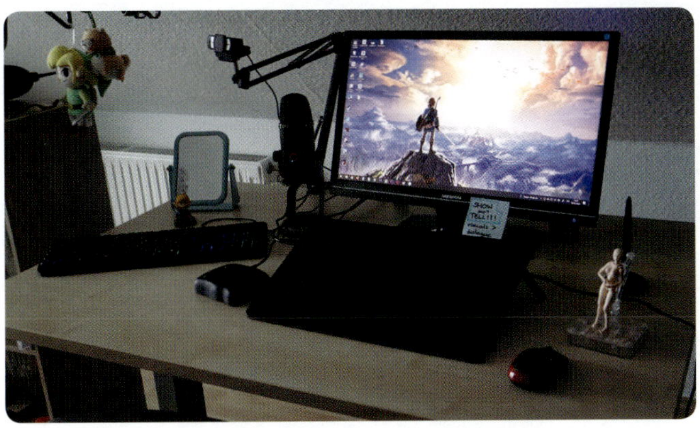

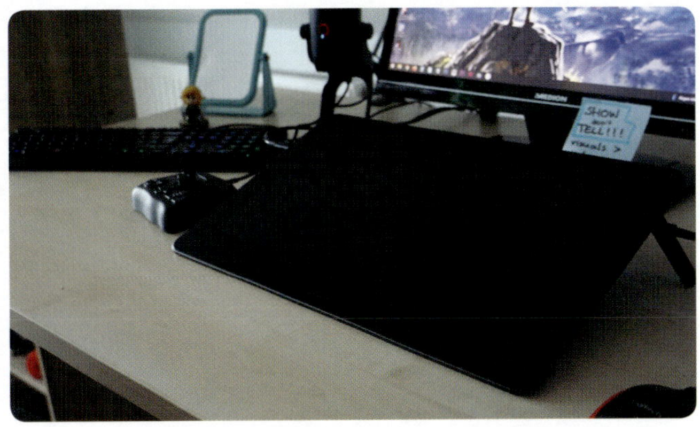

My current workspace

Though I seldom use them now, gouache paints and watercolors are firm favorites. I love the feeling of a soft brush and used to experiment with the effects I could create, until I realized that paints are more suited to illustrations than comics. As my main work is creating anime-style comics, I don't use traditional media very often.

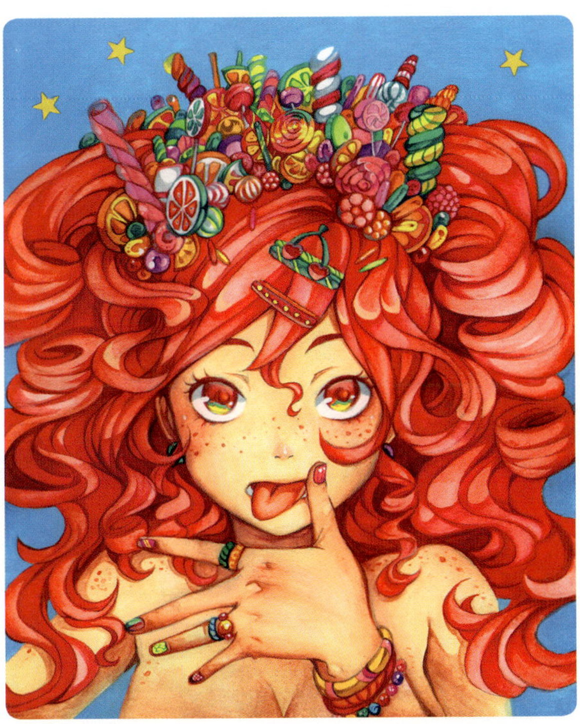

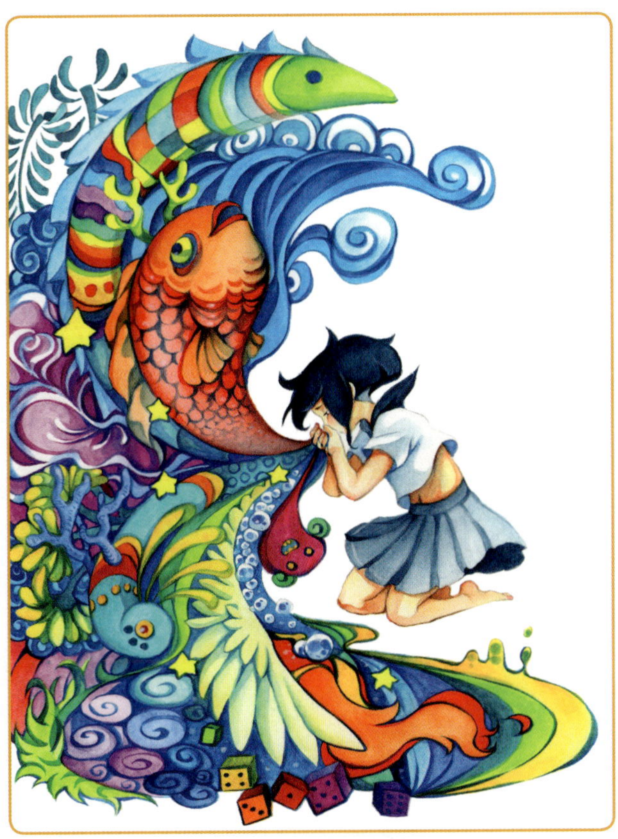

Traditionally drawn experiments using Shinhan poster colors, which are similar to gouache (very opaque, but can become translucent when mixed with water)

# INDUSTRY EXPERIENCE

I have taken numerous freelance jobs over the years and, for the most part, they went well. Due to time constraints, I now have to be more selective about the freelance work I accept. Companies that find me through my social-media platforms often want to commission something in a style that has already proven popular. This is why it's important to share the work you enjoy creating on your social-media platforms; you will become well known for that style of work and there is greater chance you to will be hired to create more of it.

Several companies have also commissioned me to create art tips resources. For instance, in 2021 I was commissioned to create live webinars focusing on how to draw characters in perspective. This was a great opportunity to get paid to learn and polish my drawing skills, and using my voice as part of a commission was a completely new experience. I have also had the pleasure of being commissioned by publishers to work with authors. This experience helped me realize that I wanted to write my own stories, rather than solely create artwork for other people's stories. Though it is harder and requires more work, I enjoy working on my own ideas the most.

While I feel more pressure undertaking work for a company, it is also more secure financially. I can create whatever I like when making art for my social media, but that does not necessarily translate into new Patreon supporters, followers, or customers.

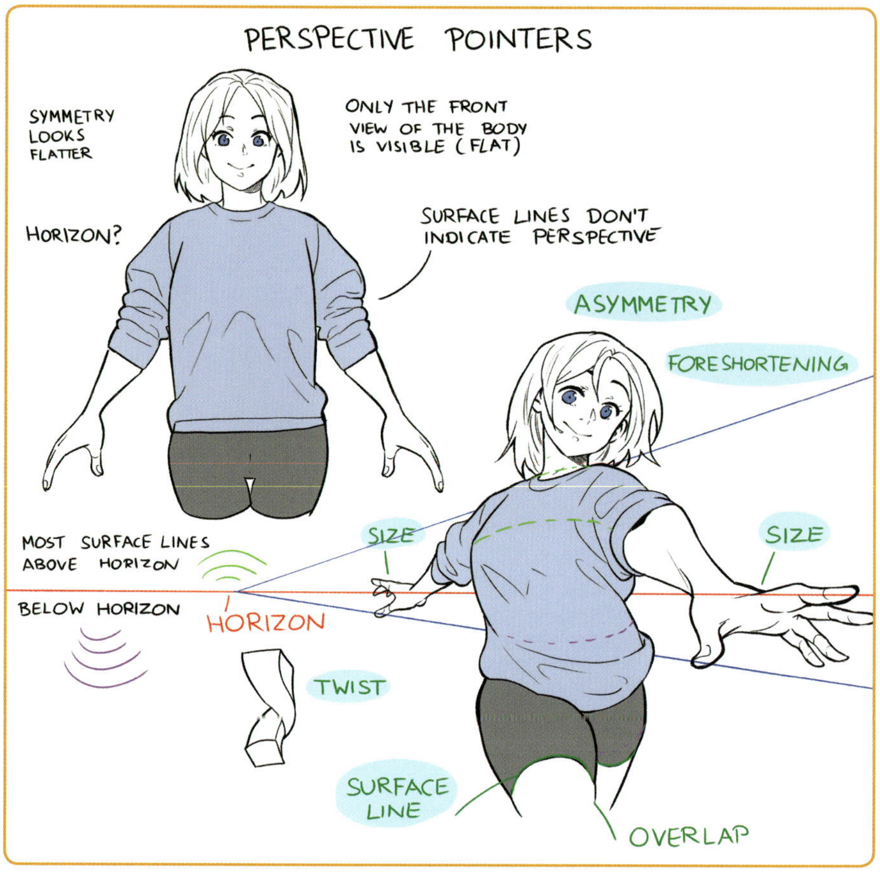


Part of the webinar I created on drawing characters in perspective

## Income from art

While I have always known my dream was to become an artist, my artistic journey has taken me in many directions. The idea that I could actually generate an income from my art was a gradual realization. At university I didn't worry too much about finances, as I took on a lot of freelance and independent work. Having saved up a good amount during that time, I took a leap of faith and became a full-time artist after graduating. With a few smaller comic projects already lined up, I had to quickly learn about all of the paperwork required when self-employed.

The monthly financial support from my Patreon supporters is especially useful when my freelance work or other projects have gone quiet. Nowadays, I work closely with various publishers while still maintaining my independence, which feels like a comfortable place to be in my career.

## Recognition

The first time I felt real recognition as an artist was on the success of my self-published short comic, *Hearts for Sale*. This received hugely positive feedback from both readers and other industry professionals. Not only was it an incredibly fun and rewarding project, but its success opened numerous doors for me.

Another moment of real success was when my art tips resources were published in several languages, receiving a positive reception in Japan. I hope to publish more books of art tips in the future.

At the time of writing, I'm working on my webtoon *Morgana and Oz*, which I'm hoping will mark another successful milestone in my career. Once the comic is complete, I plan to explore writing different genres to see where else my art and storytelling can take me.

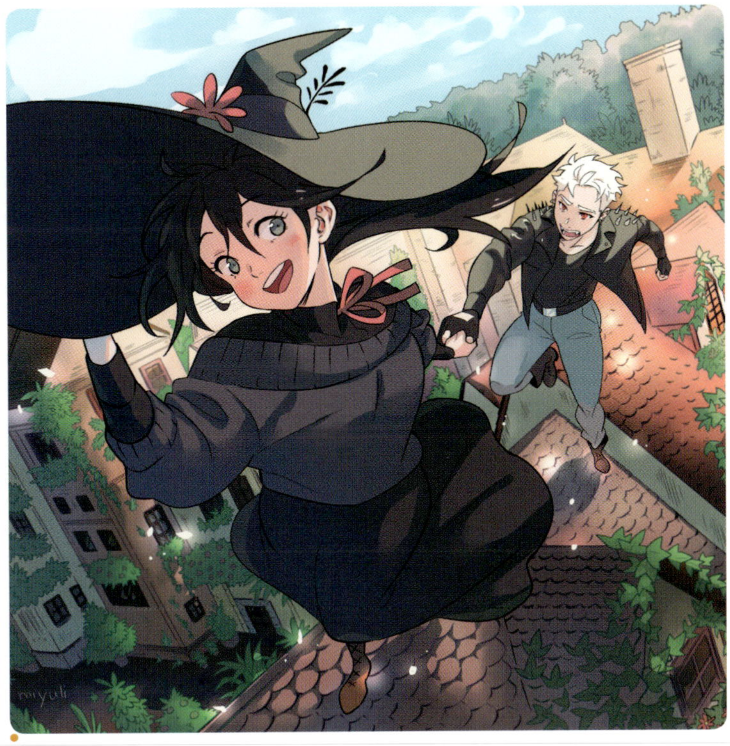

The characters Morgana and Oz, from my webtoon of the same title

# DEVELOPING YOUR STYLE

The stories and manga I read have always provided inspiration when I'm exploring ideas for my own characters and worlds. It started when I first discovered *Sailor Moon* and immediately wanted to create my own Sailor Senshi. Nowadays, I keep an inspiration folder in which I save inspirational imagery, stories, music, and other interesting articles I stumble across online. This proves especially useful when I need to summon ideas quickly.

I find it useful to watch other artists' Pixiv and Instagram pages to gauge what viewers respond well to. As I am mostly a reader, however, I find the majority of my inspiration in stories. I stay up to date with new releases on Webtoon and check what appears on Shōnen Jump+, an online manga magazine. When a new game I like is released, I look up the artists and designers to see if they have *Art of...* books. Early discarded and behind-the-scenes designs can provide a great deal of insight into a designer's thought process.

When I am inspired by something – whether an illustration or a comic – I try to analyze which elements are speaking to me and which differ from my own work. It can be useful to examine different art styles to explore how stories and characters function in different contexts. It's notoriously hard to break out of your own comfort zone, and this exercise helps me to see things a little differently.

Style is sometimes determined by how much time and assistance you have, along with which platforms you operate on. As not all art styles are suitable for all platforms or situations, there are always decisions to be made. It took me a while to realize that you don't necessarily need to have a fixed art style, but can choose to be much more flexible in your approach. I'm now more conscious and attentive to changes in my anime style, noticing areas where I could improve. This awareness helps me to grow as an artist. The only thing I believe is innate is the perseverance and passion to create. The rest is hard work. Even though the speed of improvement can fluctuate, it will always move forward if you put in the time and practice.

I used to spend a lot of time on social media, but as I grow older I have found it to be more exhausting than inspirational. While I use it to share my artwork and promote my webtoon, I avoid it the rest of the time and prefer to talk to my artist friends in person. Social media can be a good way to observe what is happening in the industry, but more often than not it can be a distraction. Though there is so much that demands your attention, try to focus instead on what you find inspiring and what you want to create.

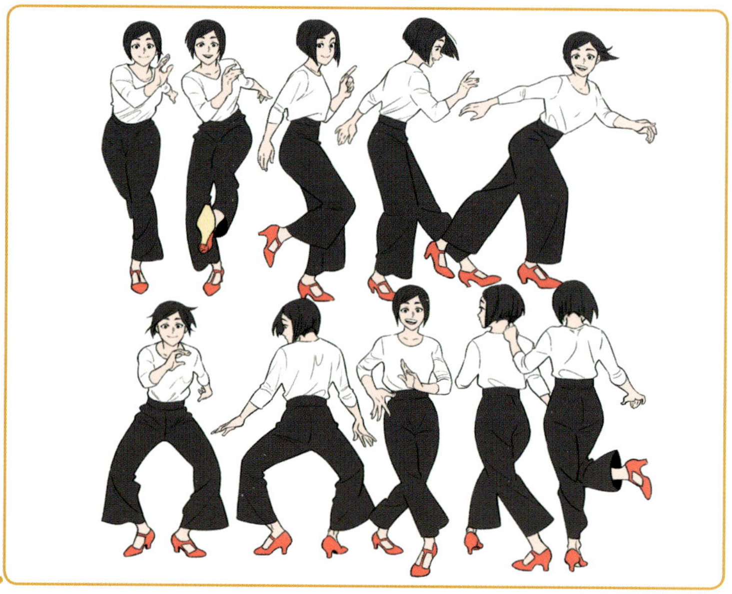

Analysis of the Charleston dance

## Evolution of style

My style of anime art has undergone many changes throughout my commercial work and is determined by the industry for which I am working. I used to enjoy detailed illustration work, which differs massively in style to my comic work, which necessitates a quicker and less detailed workflow.

I enjoy experimenting with new techniques. Sometimes these experiments are quite short-lived and are only used for one project, or even just one illustration. If I like the results and think they could fit into my main work, I may choose to merge them with my usual style. While I often make small changes in my work, good constructive criticism can be hard to come by and I am reliant on engagement from my followers. If an artwork is well received online, I count that as a success and consider keeping the new technique. If an artwork is ignored, I know this is either because it didn't reach the right audience or it simply was not very good.

In 2015 I often used gouache and watercolors. I painted and sold original illustrations and even tried to create a whole comic using poster colors. Though this took a great deal of time and effort, it wasn't hugely popular with my following, so I didn't attempt to make another comic in this style again.

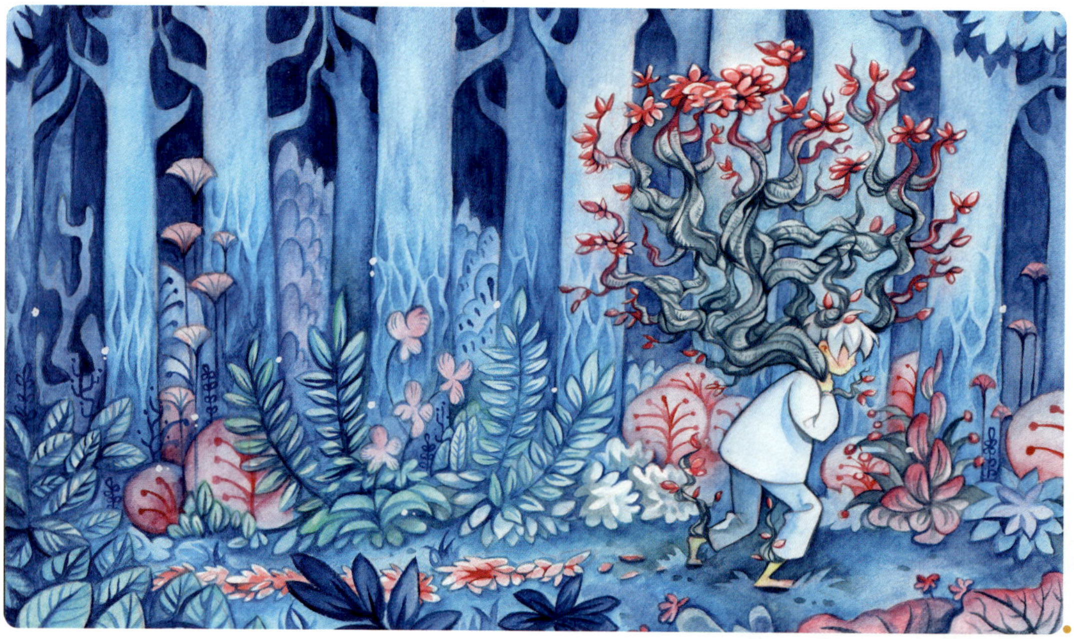

2015 – a short comic drawn entirely with poster colors and without words

When first starting out, I was inspired by Western animated movies and wanted my work to appeal to a Western market. Over time my consumption changed to more mature media, which I mostly found in Japanese and Korean stories. My style has always been heavily influenced by what I'm reading, but over the past few years it has started to become more consistent. I still like to experiment with different coloring and rendering techniques from time to time, but my workflow needs to be quick and efficient enough that I can rely on it for commercial work.

While the fantasy genre has been my biggest inspiration throughout my career, I have long been interested in exploring science fiction and horror. I try to widen my inspirations as much as possible by watching movies and playing video games, though my schedule does not always permit for too much of that.

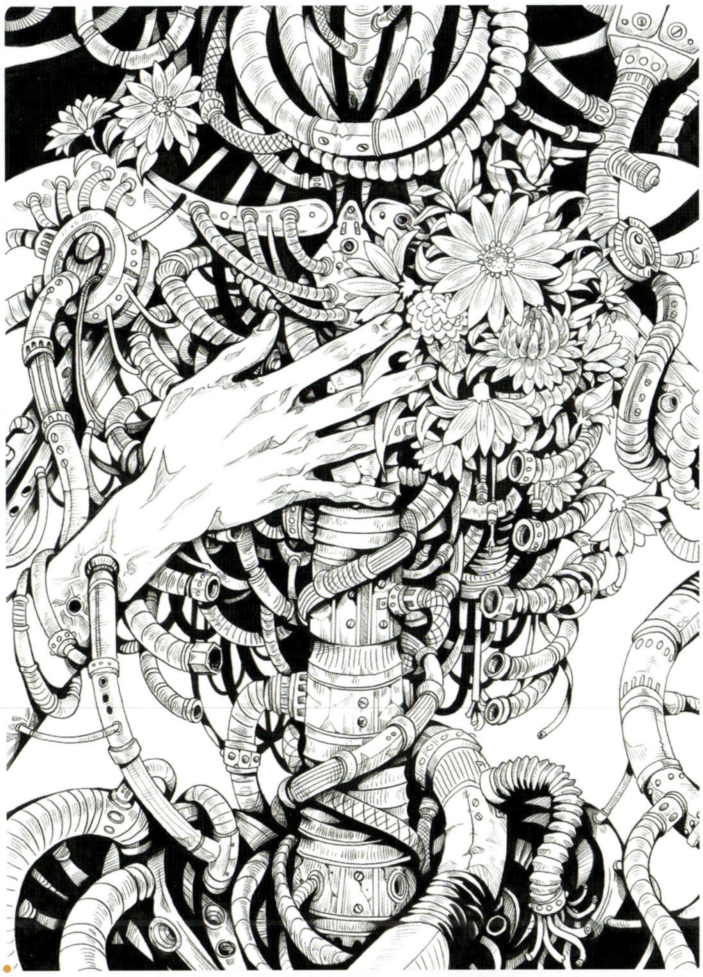

2016 – a page from my cyberpunk-inspired sci-fi comic

There are many artists who are known for their unique style of anime art and get hired specifically for this. If you have commercial aspirations, you have to prove to potential employers that your work will stand out, while also fulfilling the brief. Ultimately, there is no one way to go about developing your personal anime style.

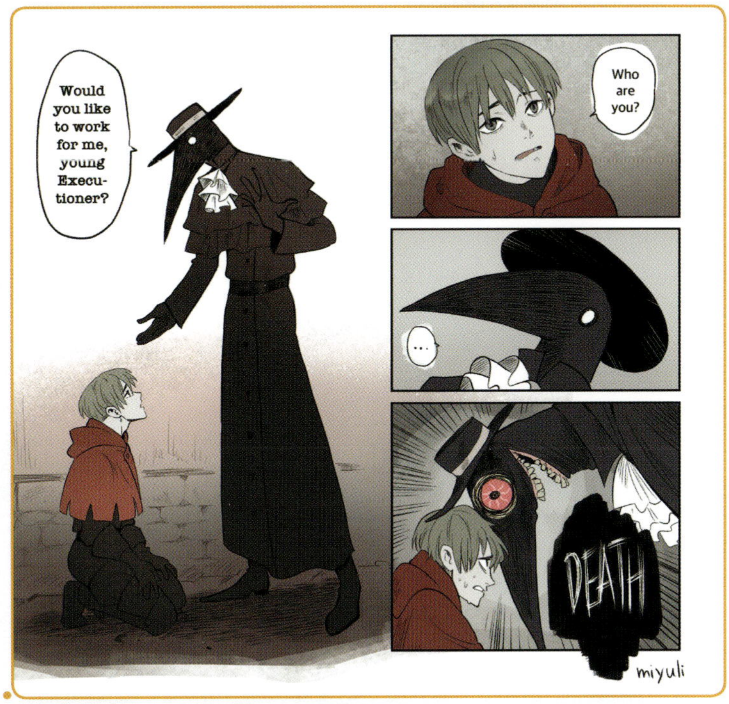


2016 – an experiment into the horror genre, which I would like to pursue in the future

## Personal style vs. commercial success

Your personal art style develops naturally with experience and practice. Many artists start out by copying other artists they admire, but as they begin to follow their individual interests and preferences and learn to draw on personal experiences, their own unique anime style will begin to emerge. I don't feel too much pressure to be unique, working with the assumption that no artist has the exact same background experiences as I do, so what I create will always be unique to me.

Of course, it's also wise to research current trends and what is already successful in the industry. It may be that your style doesn't quite fit with commercially successful industry titles, meaning you might want to consider aiming for a more niche market instead. It can be useful to analyze what distinguishes your work from the so-called "mainstream" and ask yourself if you're willing to adjust your artwork to fit this style, or if this shift would compromise what you truly enjoy making. Some artists have two completely separate art styles for their commercial and personal work, allowing them to find work that pays, while creating their personal work on the side.

## Working in a bubble vs. external influences

Try to find a balance between working in your own creative bubble and actively seeking out external influences. When in "research mode," I explore fresh, exciting ideas and cultivate a healthy curiosity for anything new and interesting. In "work mode," however, I prefer to isolate myself from external influences, as I have already made my decisions and need to finish the current artwork or chapter before I can begin research for the next one. How you choose to balance these two modes depends on your preferred workflow and current projects. While I find that entering research mode every other day brings fresh ideas to my work, drawing from too many influences can risk reshaping your work entirely and distracting from decisions already made.

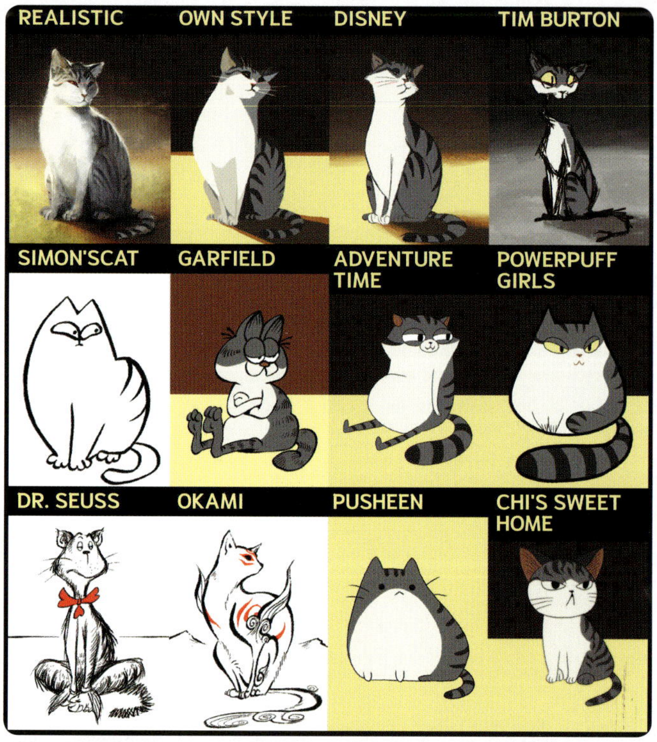


An exploration of different art styles, based on my cat

## Limitations of style

Whenever I feel limited by my anime art style, I try to evolve my work and take any frustrations I have as a sign that I need to spend more time practicing my skills. If you find that you no longer like your style, push out of your comfort zone and experiment. However, if you are working on a project for a client or company, you must be professional and push through your frustrations to fulfill the work in the required style.

Drawing art studies increases my confidence and reminds me of the freedom and flexibility I have to experiment with style. This prevents me from becoming so comfortable that I'm no longer able to see my mistakes. Another helpful practice is to create "art style" grids, imagining what decisions other artists make when they draw. This will allow you to see if you could benefit from similar stylistic choices.

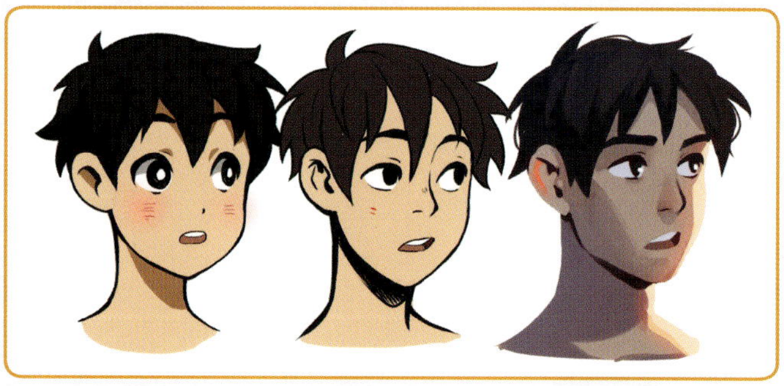

The different anime styles I used for various clients in 2018

# BUILDING YOUR BRAND

While not every artist needs a brand, having one will make marketing easier. A recognizable brand can help you get noticed and respected, which in turn will lead to more offers of work.

There are several different approaches you can take when creating your anime-style brand. Many artists build a brand based on their personality, which, as long as you're sincere, can be a good way to find like-minded people and naturally share your work with charisma. This approach requires a specific confident personality type, however, and I am far too shy to showcase myself in front of a group of strangers. Additionally, I would rather people interact with my artwork than with me directly. For this reason, I made the conscious decision to keep my personal comments to a minimum, as I don't want my followers to get distracted from my work.

As I am a very private person, this second approach comes more naturally to me. Distancing who you are as a person from your artistic brand may not be fully possible, but mentally it helps me to compartmentalize the two. One way of doing this is to choose an artist name that is different from your real name. I came up with the name Miyuli in fifth grade, based on stories I was reading at the time. While it does share similarities to my real name, it gives me an element of privacy as well as a consistent and memorable brand. When people voice their criticisms, I know it's because they simply don't connect with my work and is not any kind of commentary on me as a person.

## How much to share

How I share my artwork online has changed over the years. When I was younger, I made a big effort to connect with my followers and other artists. While this is not a bad approach, I have now realized that I prefer to channel my time and focus into creating artwork instead. Many artists I admire hardly ever post anything personal, and some don't have social media at all. Inspired by these artists, I have been removing any irrelevant posts from my social-media platforms to ensure my work is the focus.

This tactic may not succeed for everyone. When you are starting out, it's good to connect with other artists to network, build your following, and show your humanity. Unfortunately, quite often the more popular an artist becomes, the less people regard them as human. I try to avoid this conundrum by keeping my personal life private, though you can only influence your reputation so much.

## Influential brands

There are many Japanese storytellers I admire. The way Akira Kurosawa uses visuals so intentionally in his movies is very inspiring. His insightful commentaries on human behavior are fascinating and I am drawn to the characters he depicts. There are also countless mangaka who inspire me, such as the creator of *Demon Slayer*, known as Koyoharu Gotouge. Her series became a huge worldwide hit, yet there is very little personal information available about her online. Another is Eiichiro Oda, who has been creating *One Piece* since 1997. I admire his stamina, creativity, and ability to craft a story with so much care and foresight.

I fell in love with the work of Naoki Urasawa after experiencing *Monster*, which floored me with its depth of research into West Germany and its different subcultures. I was also deeply impressed and inspired by his documentary series, *Manben*, in which he interviews other mangaka about their work and processes. I admire his knowledge and the amount of research he does in creating his series.

In contrast, I also love the video-game work of Yoko Taro, who is a little more eccentric. His *Nier* series is incredibly thought-provoking and melancholic, revealing his passion for experimentation and hunger to discuss deep philosophical issues. Though he wears a mask in interviews – I can relate to his desire for privacy – they provide a small window into his intentions. I am also inspired by the *Legend of Zelda* series due to the sense of adventure and exploration the games create for the player. The design work that goes into the world and game mechanics is extremely well thought-out and the series has a dedicated fan base that enjoys the gameplay, puzzles, and characters.

## Marketing & publicity

I don't have a fixed marketing budget or schedule, but spend one or two hours a day focused on promoting my work online. However, when I was revamping my anime-style brand and removing anything irrelevant from my online platforms, I did set aside a few days for it. While I have listened to a few social-media marketing seminars, their relevance changes with the changing algorithm, which makes it challenging to find a suitable strategy.

Up until now I have not felt the need for a marketing team and have been able to manage on my own. In the future, however, I would like to hire a marketing professional to handle all of my social media, as I find it somewhat distracting. I don't do much research into the optimal uploading times or best filters or cropping angles, so I would appreciate someone to manage that side of my brand.

While I work for Webtoon, my current series, *Morgana and Oz*, is promoted by their team. It's interesting to see someone else's approach when publicizing it. I often feel too embarrassed to market my own work in a loud manner and always hoped it would speak for itself, but with so much competition online, it's not that simple. While you may not wish to appear self-centered and pushy, if there is no one else employed to shout about your work, it's up to you to make sure the world knows about it.

## Online platforms

I have never invested in paid-for marketing on my social-media platforms. I don't know how to use it wisely, nor do I currently have the motivation to find out. Instead I take note of how other artists present themselves online. For example, they may add their email address to their bio to give potential clients a way to contact them directly. I also use my personal website to keep all of my links, contact details, and portfolio of work in one place.

Social media allows you to share your work with a wider audience. I rarely use it for conversation and don't have private messaging enabled as I simply don't have time to check it. Instagram is a useful platform for allowing new people to see my work and to grow my following. If I share an interesting post, there is a good chance people will want to find out more about the content. Twitter is useful for sharing links that allow people to buy my work, and I have recently seen some success on Facebook. Many people who read my comics say they come across my art on Pinterest, though I hardly use it.

While video platforms, such as YouTube and Twitch, are great for marketing, creating videos can be quite time-consuming. If you are interested in these platforms but don't have the time, you may want to consider hiring a video editor. TikTok is also proving increasingly popular, especially with a younger audience.

Patreon is the most important site for me as an artist, as it provides direct financial support that allows me to continue my work. Though I rarely advertise it, as I dislike asking for money, it can be an invaluable source of income for any artist and you will likely find that your followers want to support your creative endeavors.

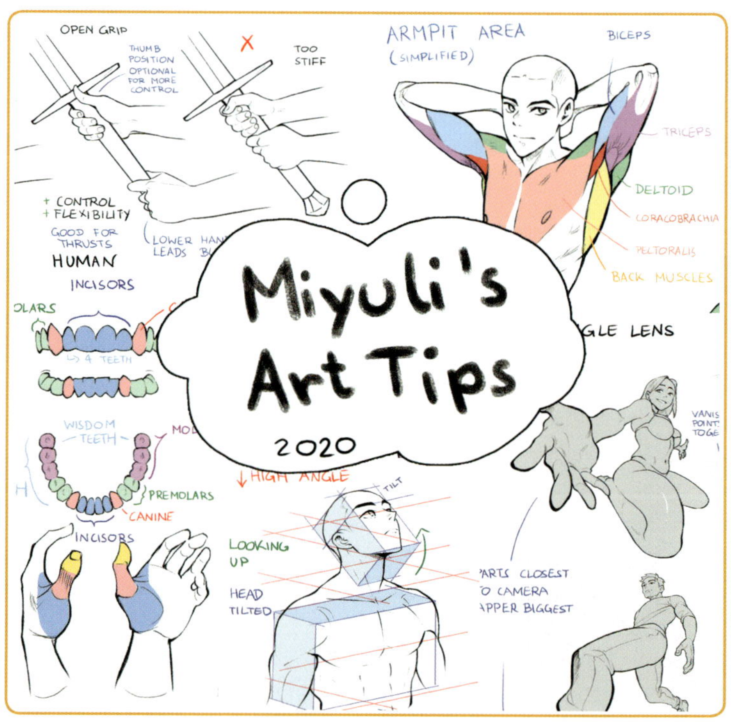


Self-published PDFs of my art tips and tutorials, previously sold on Gumroad, but now only available for my patrons

# Networking

I'm not overly experienced at networking online, preferring to connect with other artists in real life instead. This type of communication was much more common when I was younger, but the digital age has brought innovative new ways to converse and collaborate with artists all around the world. Look out for daily or monthly art challenges, as well as fun social-media hashtags such as #drawthisinyourstyle. Support other artists by taking part in their challenges, but don't expect anything in return. While you may get your artwork noticed and gain more followers, it may simply be a way of cheering on the wider art community.

However you approach networking, be sincere, support artists whose work you admire, and create what you truly enjoy. You may find that opportunities present themselves as you make new connections.

# Selling work online

When deciding what artwork to make and sell, I sometimes ask my followers what they would like to see. Tutorials are useful for helping people master skills they are struggling with, and I occasionally post polls to help me decide on topics and themes. With prints, I usually sell artwork that has proven popular or of which I'm proud. While you can never predict what will sell well, the reception after posting it online can provide a general guideline.

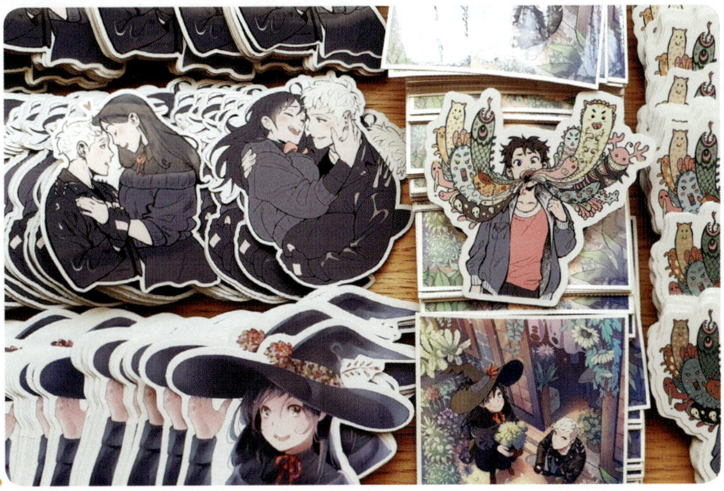

Stickers of my artwork, created with StickerApp

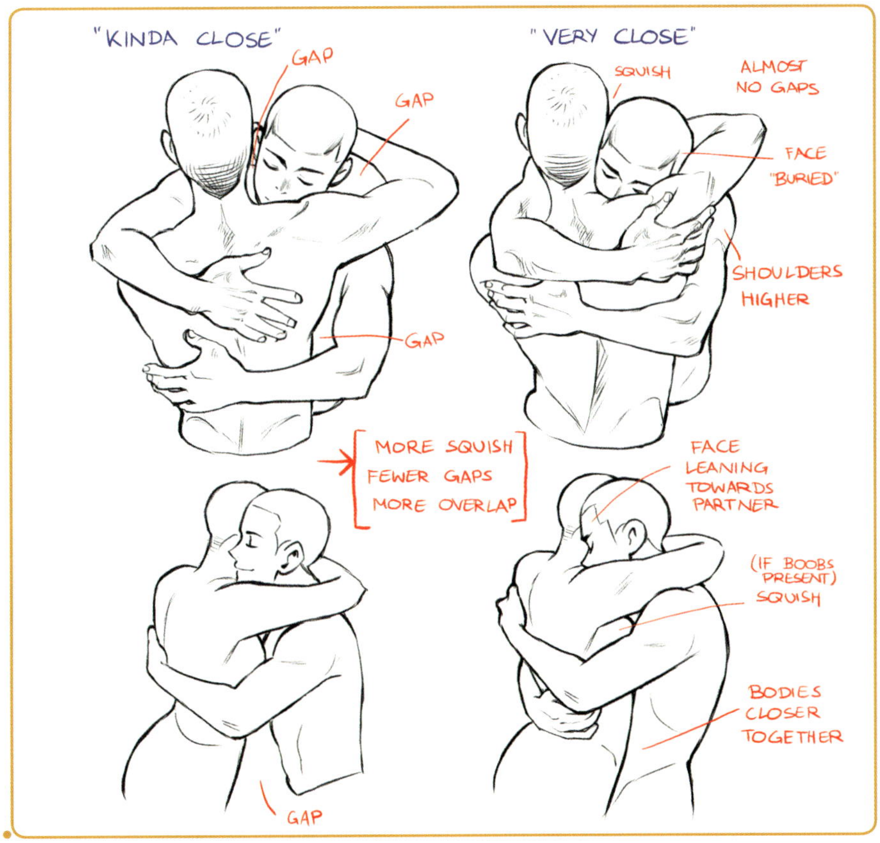


Highly requested art studies on how to draw two characters hugging

## Pricing

My aim is to create resources that fellow artists will find useful. I try to offer as much tutorial content as I can for free, but do sell digital or physical compilations as well as exclusive Patreon access. Similarly, I like to give as many people as possible the opportunity to read my comics. I don't like to hide my work behind paywalls, unless it's not suitable for children. As many people like to own physical copies of digital comics, there is a market for these as well.

When deciding on pricing for commissions and freelance work, I consider how many hours of work are required for the job and charge accordingly. Though I try to work as quickly and efficiently as I can, as a perfectionist I often spend too much time on assignments. I rarely take commissions because of this and hope my followers will purchase my personal work instead. I plan to work on more of my own projects and ideas in the future, though it can be hard to know how much to charge for resources I would create anyway, such as my art studies. It helps to establish an hourly rate, then consider how many hours it takes to make an artwork or resource.

Your income can fluctuate a great deal when working as a freelance artist, so you need to be prepared to be flexible. There have been instances when a project has only paid off when the artwork has sold well, as I received a percentage of the profit. In other cases, I sell royalties for the usage of my existing work.

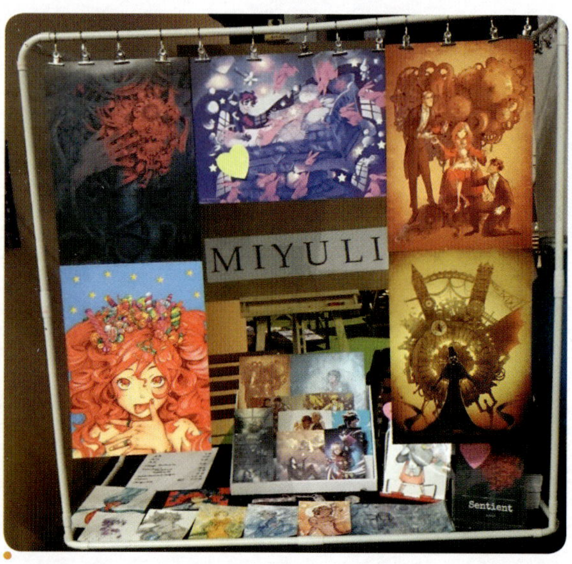


One of my first attempts at selling my artwork at various anime conventions

## Curating a portfolio

As my website and social-media platforms function as my online portfolios, I only post relevant work and delete anything that could distract potential clients. While social-media galleries are unfortunately not always suited to sharing all types of artwork, they are a good way to get your work noticed by employers.

Create specific portfolios for different kinds of jobs. If you want an illustration job, fill your portfolio with illustrations. If you wish to work in comics, find online platforms that allow you to present sequential art in an optimal way. I only put less emphasis on curating my portfolio when I'm not looking for work.

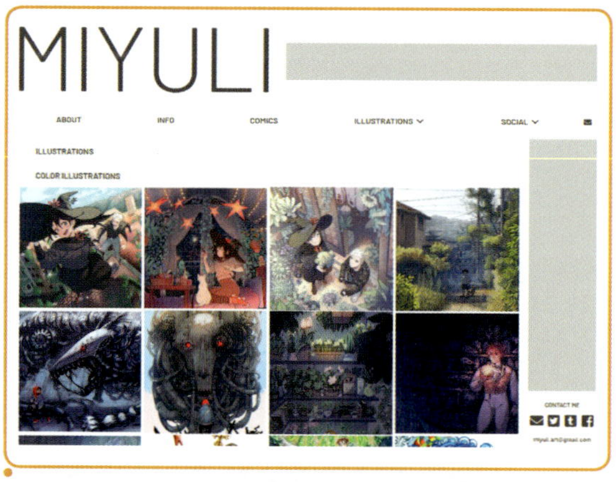


**miyuliart.com**
My current website has an emphasis on illustration and comic work

## Running a business

It's important to remember that an art brand is also a business, and the business side of it can take up a substantial part of your day. I aim to clear my email inbox at least every other day and post on social media as frequently as possible. I spend time talking to my editors or assistants, and once or twice a month I take a good look at my accounting and finances. While it can be overwhelming at first, it's wise to keep track of the money coming in and out. Hiring an accountant has helped with managing this paperwork.

Experience has given me the knowledge I need to read contracts through carefully before signing, but in the future I hope to hire someone to help with this. Writing invoices is another essential skill for every freelancer or business owner. While the business side of your work may take up a lot of time in the beginning, it will get easier with time and practice. Start small before moving on to bigger tasks. While I would like to outsource every part of my work except for the actual creation of artwork, I still want to maintain control of my business.

# FUTURE AMBITIONS

I still have a keen interest in animation and one day hope to see my stories brought to life on screen. I would also love to create a video game. The immediate goal, however, is to continue to create more stories. At the time of writing, I am still working on my webtoon, *Morgana and Oz*, which is a fantasy story with romance elements aimed at a teenage and young adult audience. Looking ahead, I would also like to write for an older audience and experiment with different genres I enjoy, such as action, horror, and dark fantasy. Though I have considered writing a book, this endeavor has proven difficult so far because I enjoy drawing too much. My goal is to keep polishing my skills and improve at storytelling through my art.

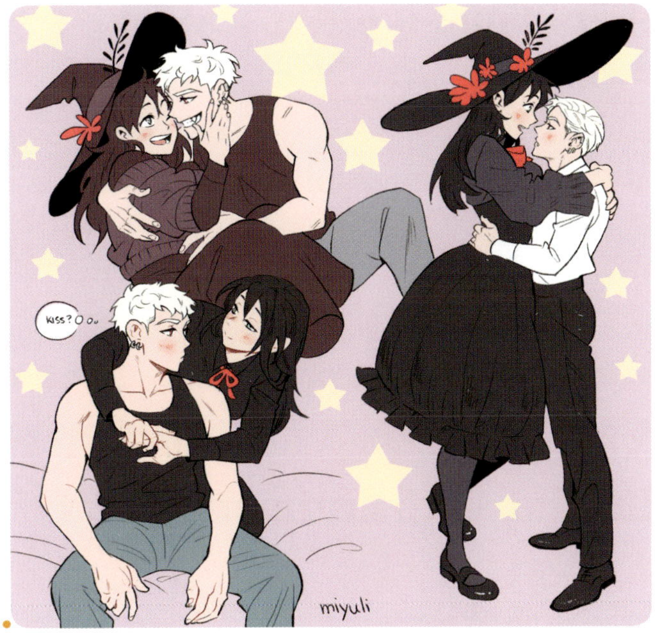


The characters Morgana and Oz from my webtoon

## Areas of development

There are always aspects of my art that I wish to improve on and develop; one of which is learning how to implement a three-dimensional quality more gracefully in my artwork. I make a habit of studying anatomy models when drawing difficult poses, which is a huge help with environmental work. Speed is a desirable skill when drawing comics, so I would also like to get better at drawing three-dimensional volume to create a faster comic-drawing workflow.

In a more abstract manner, I would like to develop my intuition to better understand what makes my readers excited about certain characters and stories. Once or twice a year I draw a character or scene I know will be well received, but the rest of the time it's difficult to anticipate the engagement a post will generate. I'm still in the process of analyzing exactly what captures my attention as a reader; I hope to one day provide my readers with the same excitement I find in the fiction I love.

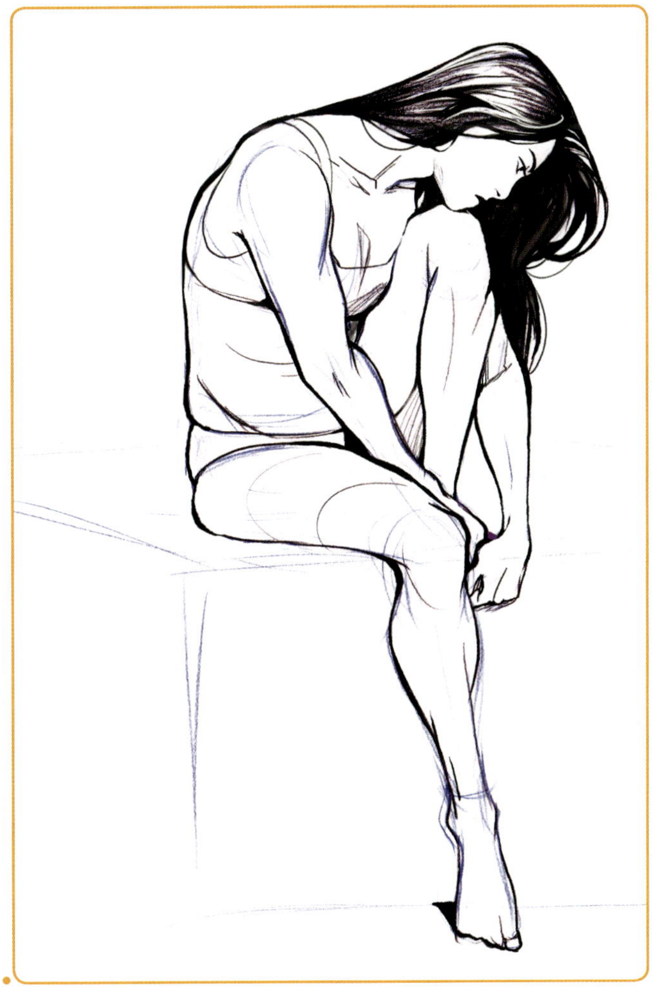

Life drawing has helped me to view the body in a three-dimensional way – a skill I carry into my anime-style characters

# ADVICE

## Self-doubt & artist's block

Every artist suffers from self-doubt and artist's block. There will always be other anime-style artists who are better at what you want to do and it's easy to compare your skill to theirs. I use this as a motivation to study and practice my drawing and storytelling. Sketching anatomy or drapery studies usually lifts an art block, as does trying a new medium such as different brushes and paper, or a different coloring style. Experimenting with a new process or workflow can provide a fresh look at your art.

Another approach to overcoming art block is to take a break to enjoy what inspires you. Even with my tight schedule of making comics, I try to dedicate a few hours each day to reading or gaming. This resets my vision and I return refreshed and able to tackle my own art with new ideas. Setting down your tools to get out of the house, move your body, and experience nature can also have a very healing effect, as can spending time with loved ones.

## Dealing with criticism

While a piece of myself will always naturally sink into my work, I have started to think more carefully about how I can accomplish this more intentionally. I try to be aware of what is important to me and what ideas, values, or stories I would like my followers to cherish. This doesn't always align with what others think is important, however, and sometimes I get critical comments from people with different values, which I usually ignore. It's important to protect your mental health and put boundaries in place that prevent you from getting drawn into other people's negativity.

When you share your work online, there will always be people who don't like it. Make your peace with this and concentrate on your target audience, listening to what they have to say. While artists can sometimes be blind to the flaws in their own art, lashing out defensively, I try to welcome criticism from my target audience, as it directs me to my weaknesses and what I need to work on. This can be motivating, but I need to be in the right headspace to properly analyze the criticism to determine what I can take away from it.

## Taking your hobby to a professional level

When you first start drawing, the most important thing is to have fun. You will encounter many influences over the years, so take the time to experiment before making intentional choices and pursuing a specific style, medium, or method. Don't be afraid to draw what you enjoy and don't let other people's opinions make you feel bad about your taste in media.

Once you are ready to turn your hobby into a full-time career, begin by analyzing other anime-style art. Analyze the work of artists you admire, analyze what is clearly successful, and analyze what you dislike or disagree with, then use your knowledge to improve your own work. Share the type of artwork you want to be best known for and that encapsulates the direction you wish your career to take.

When I was first starting out, I thought anime-style art was not very popular, but I was simply not looking in the right places. Whatever type of art you like to create, there is likely already an audience for it. Seek them out. At the same time, it's a good idea to be flexible and experiment with new approaches and styles of art. Learn as much as you can from realism, then implement your knowledge into the anime style you're aiming for. Take the time to study anatomy and nature, as well as studying other artists and types of stylization.

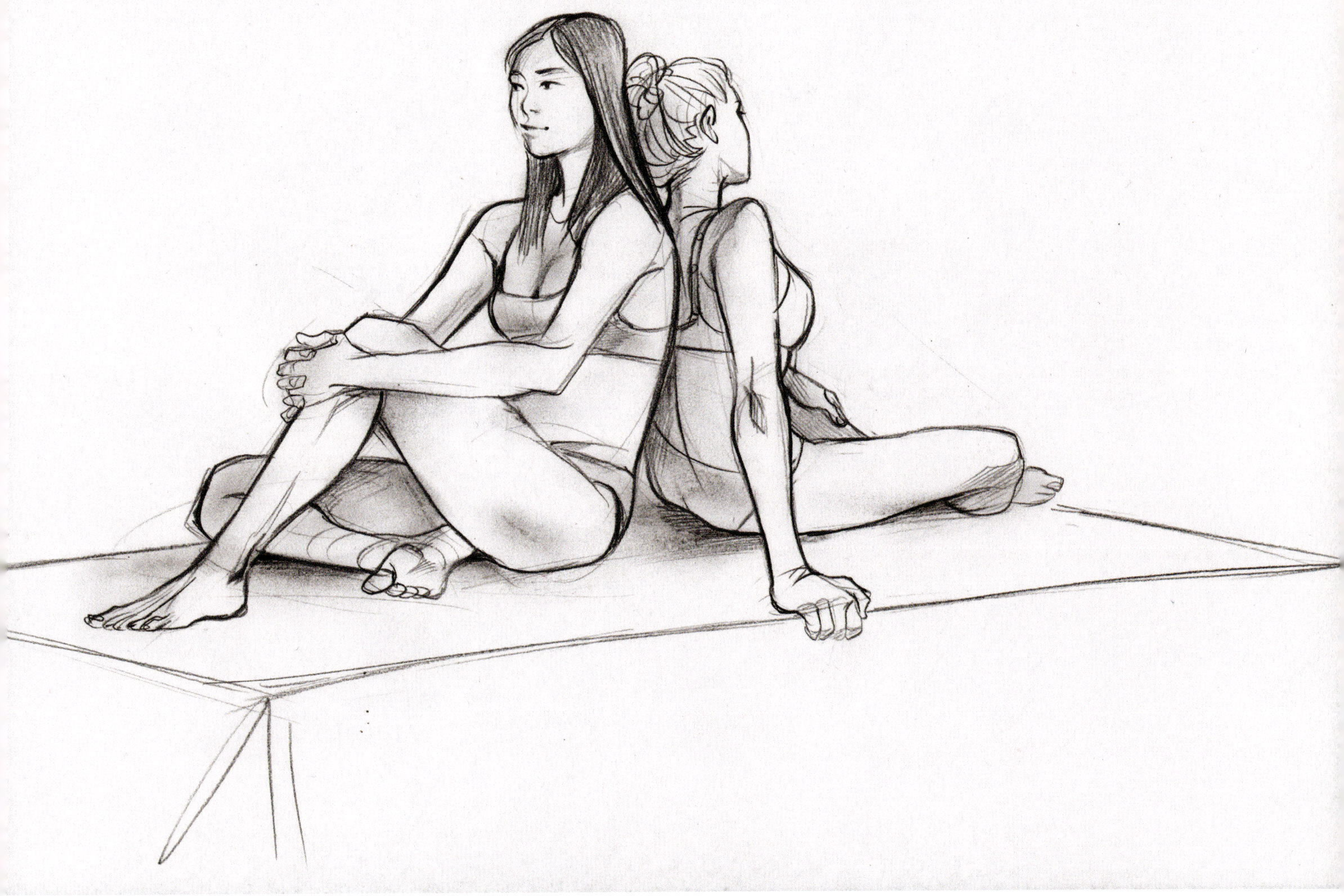

Learn how to accurately capture human anatomy, then stylize this to fit your anime-style characters

## Final tips

- Before you begin accepting jobs, try to acquire as much knowledge and experience as you can. This will allow you to negotiate for better terms and conditions in a contract.
- Your time is incredibly valuable. Keep track of how much time you work on each project, print, or job, so you know how much to charge for it.
- Don't be afraid to say "no" sometimes. Freelance artists often don't have much choice when first starting out, and you may find yourself needing to accept all kinds of work to pay the bills. Where possible, try to seek out the anime-style work you truly want to do.
- Forging a career as an artist is a marathon, not a sprint. Take care of your body and make staying healthy a priority. Don't underestimate the dangers of sitting still for long periods of time. Drink water, get enough sleep, take breaks, and find a stretching routine that will prevent back pain and allow you to concentrate on making your art.

# TIMELINE

**2000s**

Posting silly art and web comics online while in middle and high school.

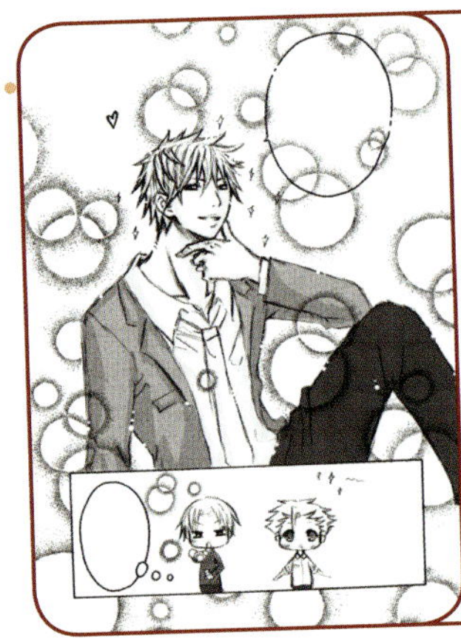

When I first learned English, I uploaded my artwork and comics on websites such as SmackJeeves and DeviantArt.

**2007**

First short story published.

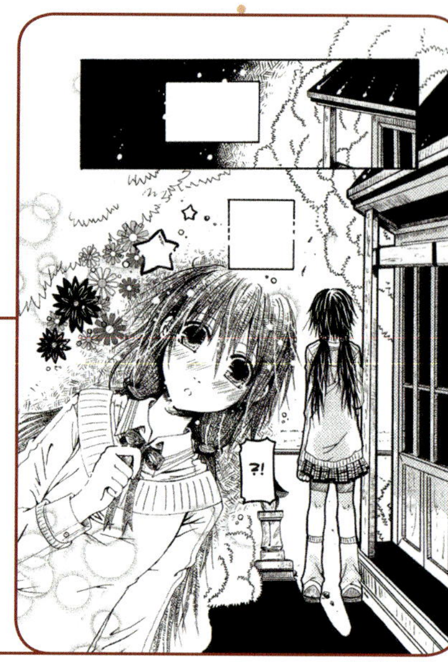


My short story, *Ami no Magical Adventure*, was published in a German shojo anthology by the small indie publisher Schwarzer Turm.

**2010s**

Attended my first life-drawing class.

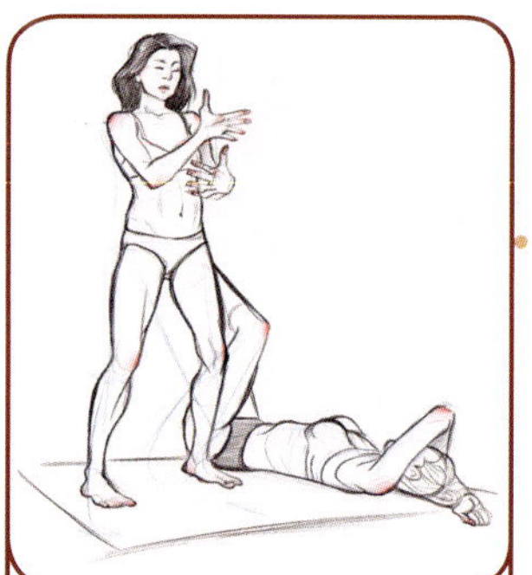

A life-drawing sketch of two models.

**2013–2017**

Accepted into film school to study animation.

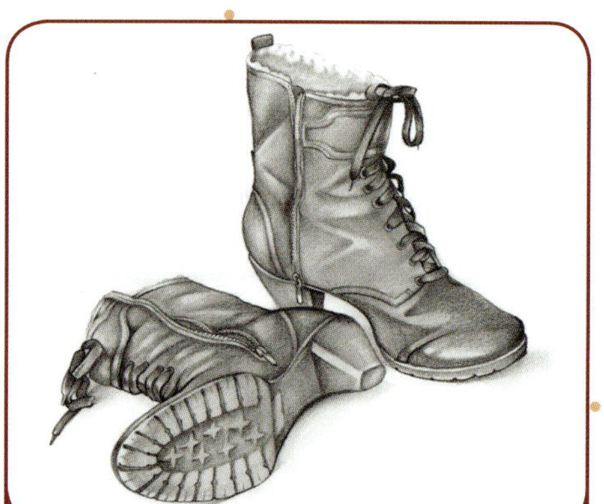

A still-life study of my shoes that I included in my portfolio, one of the requirements for the application.

**2014**

Self-published *Hearts for Sale*.

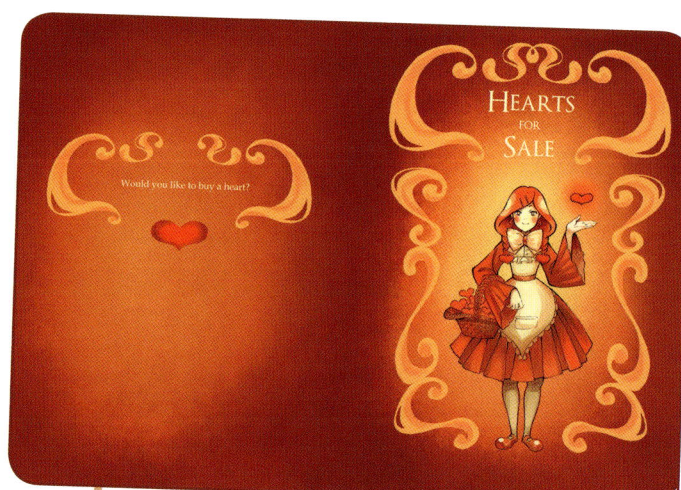


I learned a lot from self-publishing and printing my own comic.

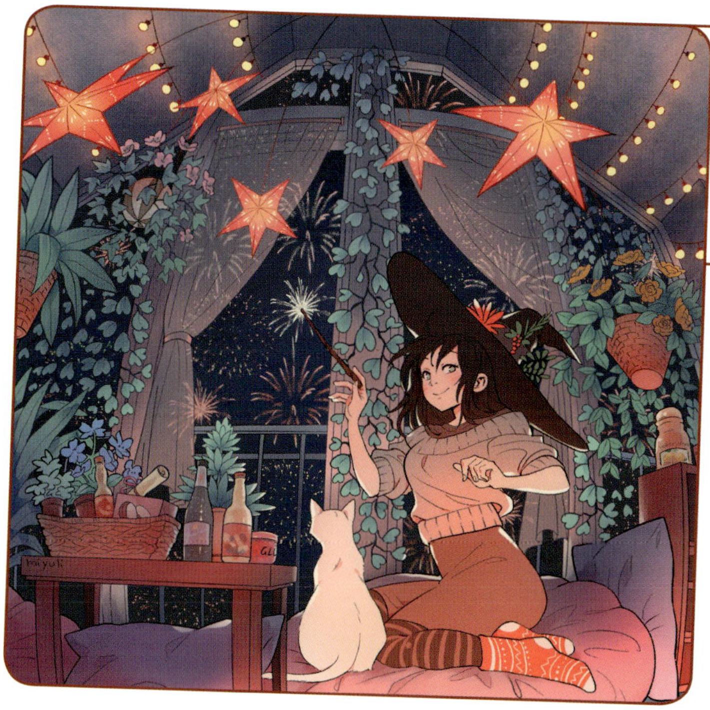

In December 2021 I launched my Webtoon Original series, *Morgana and Oz*. I had been noticed by Webtoon after participating in their 2020 short story contest with my entry *Leona the Werewolf*, which received an honorable mention.

**2021**

Publishing on Webtoon.

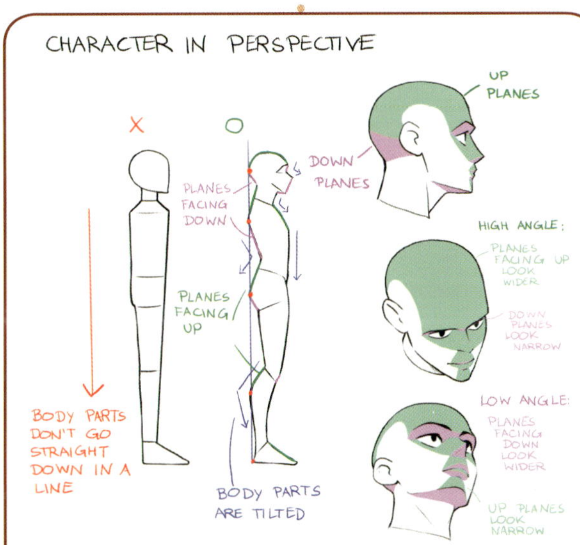


This image is part of a webinar I created about how to draw a character in perspective using Clip Studio Paint.

**2015**

Participated in CGMA courses about color and light, perspective, and storyboarding.

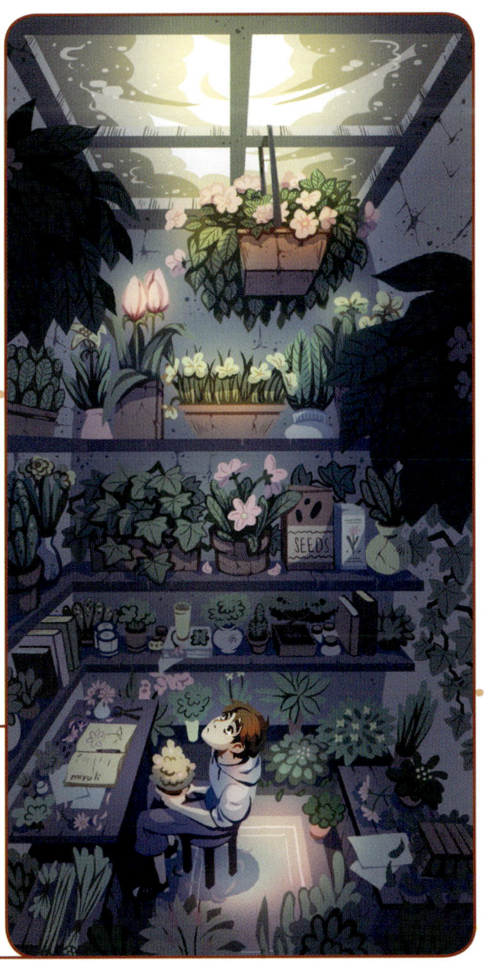

These courses taught me vital skills, including learning how to draw in angled perspective.

**2019**

Took commissions and did interviews for CELSYS, Wacom, and XP-Pen.

# GALLERY

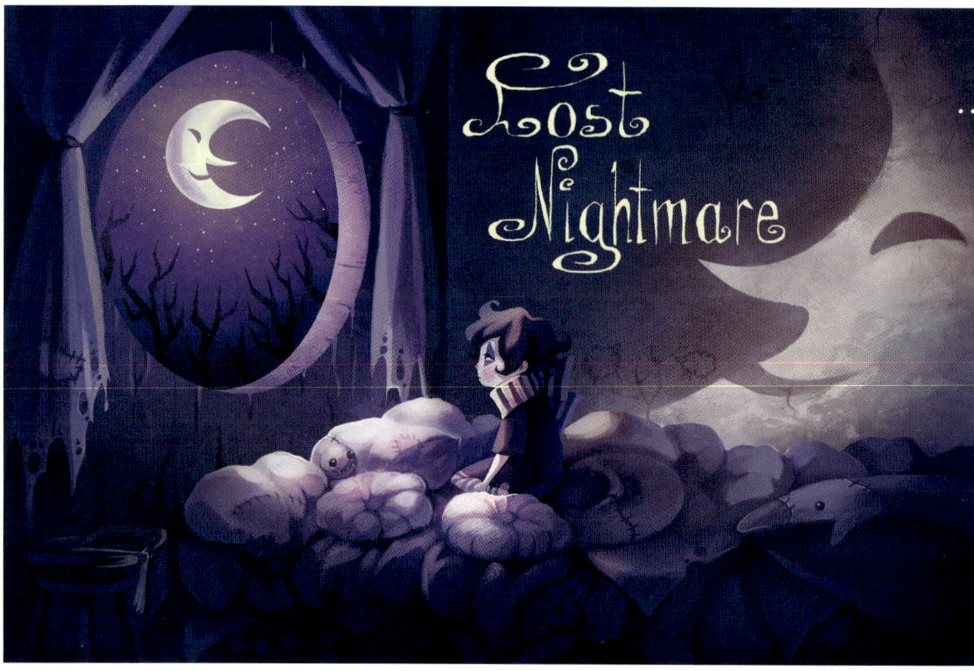


## *Lost Nightmare*, 2012–2017

Inspired by dark animated movies, *Lost Nightmare* is a comic I began drawing after graduating from high school. I wanted to create a melancholic children's story that could be enjoyed by both young and old readers. While there were breaks between uploads at the start, it eventually got picked up by the online publisher Hiveworks and given a weekly uploading schedule.

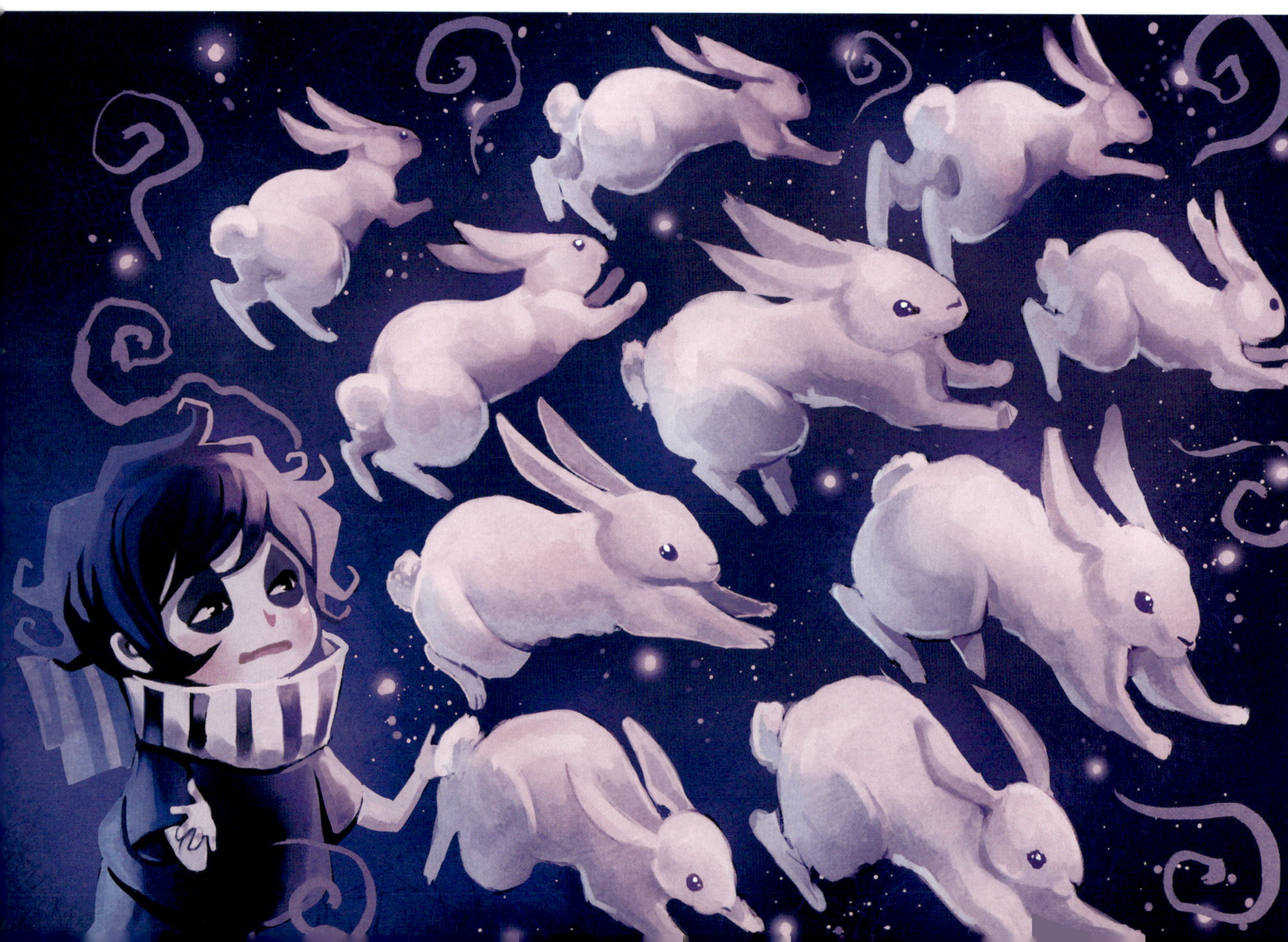

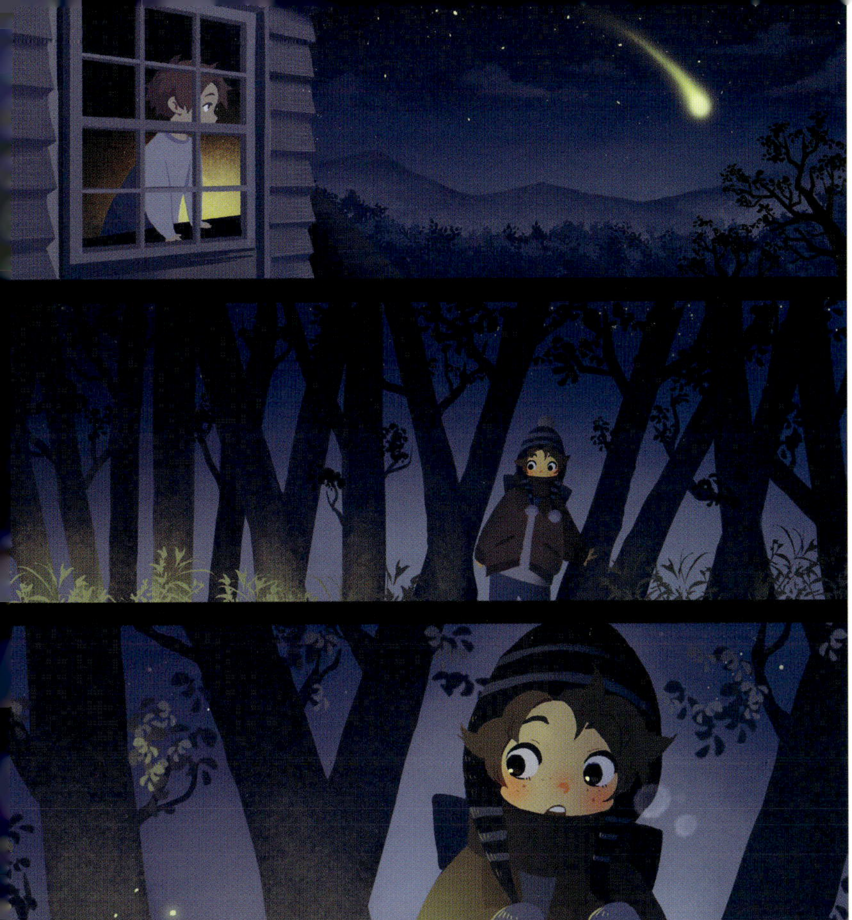

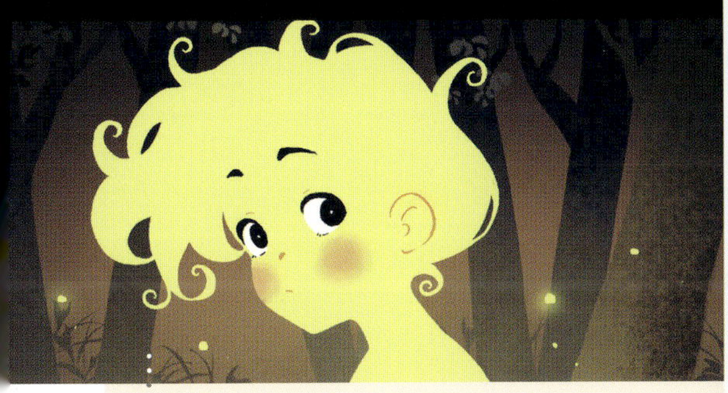

*Falling Star*, 2013

Inspired by the pre-production work of American animated movies, this short sequential piece helped me acquire a place at animation school in 2013. I wanted to create something simultaneously cold and warm. Though I would choose different colors if I were creating it now, I still remember it fondly.

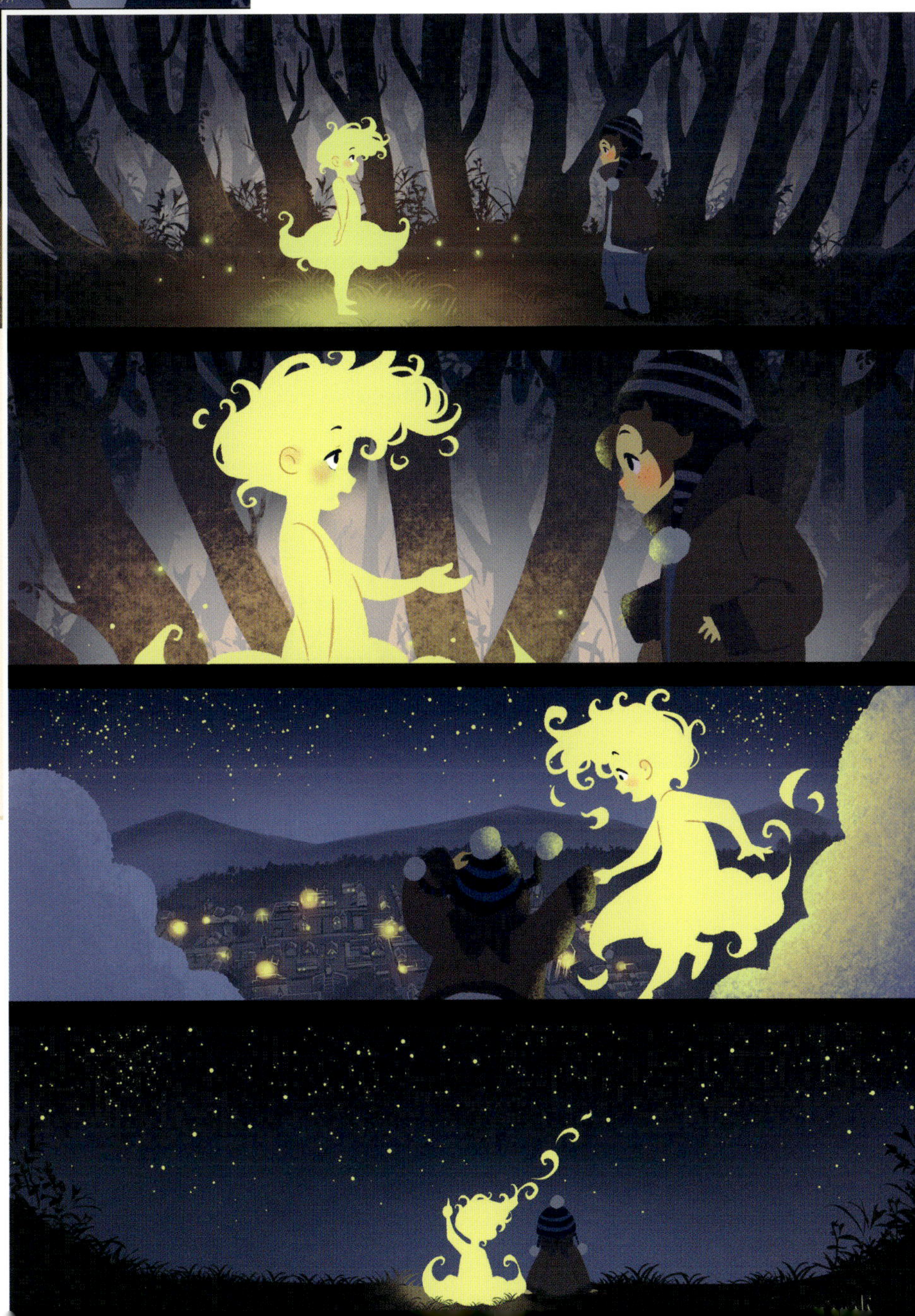

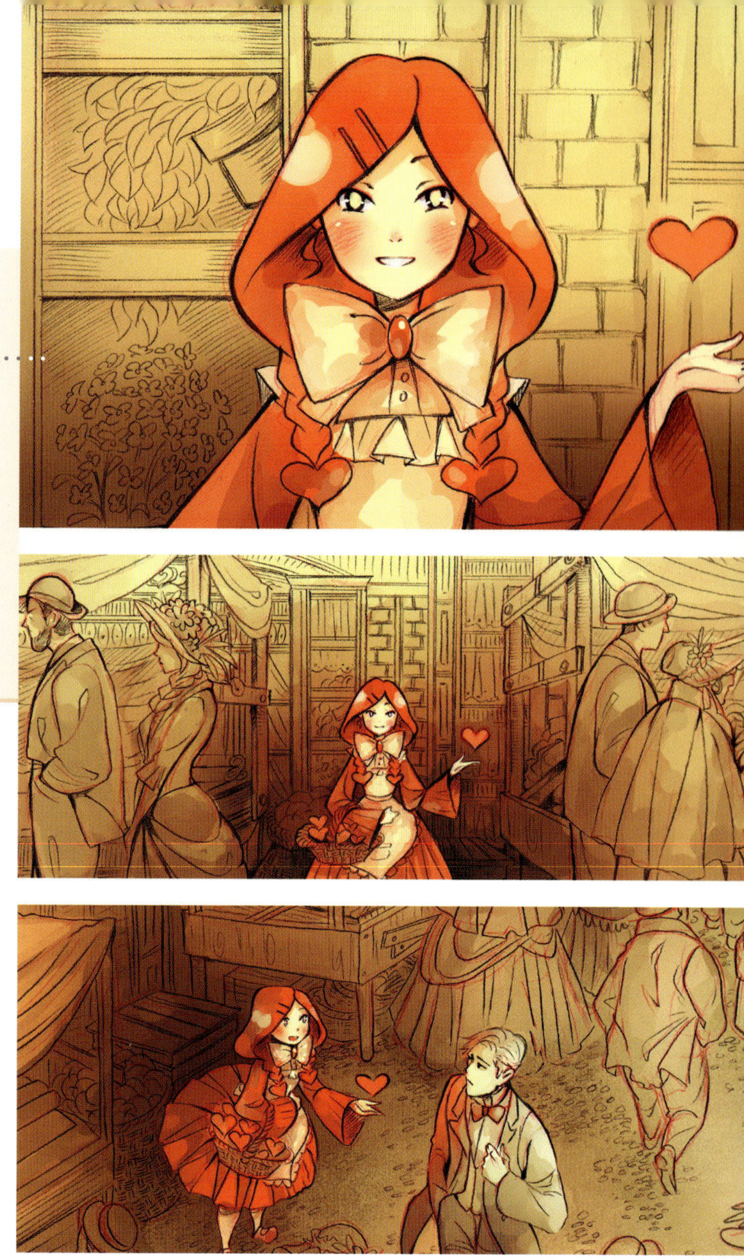

## *Hearts for Sale*, 2014

*Hearts for Sale* is a short self-published comic I created while studying animation. Wanting as many people to see it as possible, I posted it online and it received a high level of engagement. While nobody knew who I was, they had somehow heard of this comic. I was happy the comic became so popular, but was also quite intimidated by how fast it went viral, and was never able to draw a sequel.

## *Couple*, 2017

When I was in my final year of university and considering what direction I wanted my art career to take, I saw a young couple at the train station playing some sort of kissing tag. I attempted to sketch their interaction from memory when I got home and the resulting drawings resonated with many of my followers on social media. While the drawing was only an experiment, it was fun to capture these intimate moments and, going forward, my character artwork changed to depict more interactions like these.

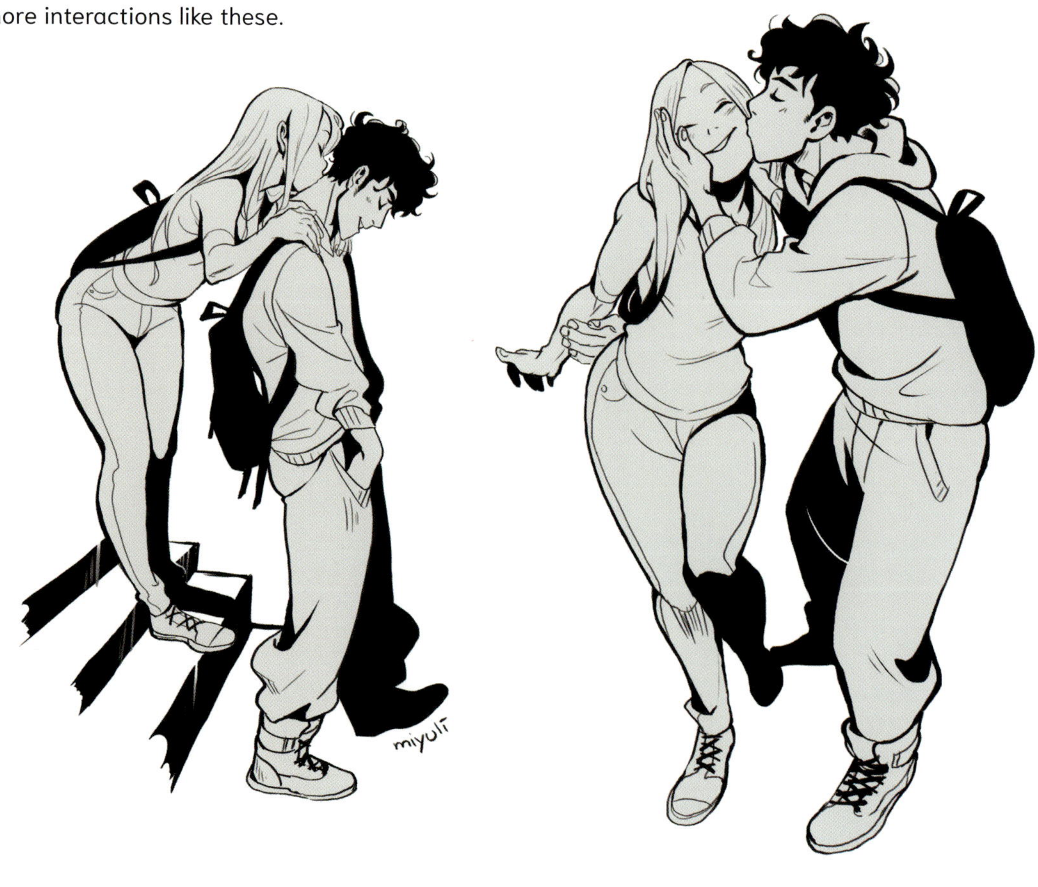

## *Little Red Riding Hood*, 2017

After graduating from animation school, I prepared an animation portfolio based on a cyberpunk retelling of *Little Red Riding Hood*. Adapting the fairy tale and creating the characters was a lot of fun. In the end I felt the story wasn't strong enough, and as I'd just started work on other comic projects, I didn't submit the portfolio anywhere. I did use these two images in small exhibitions, however, as I'm still proud of the final artwork.

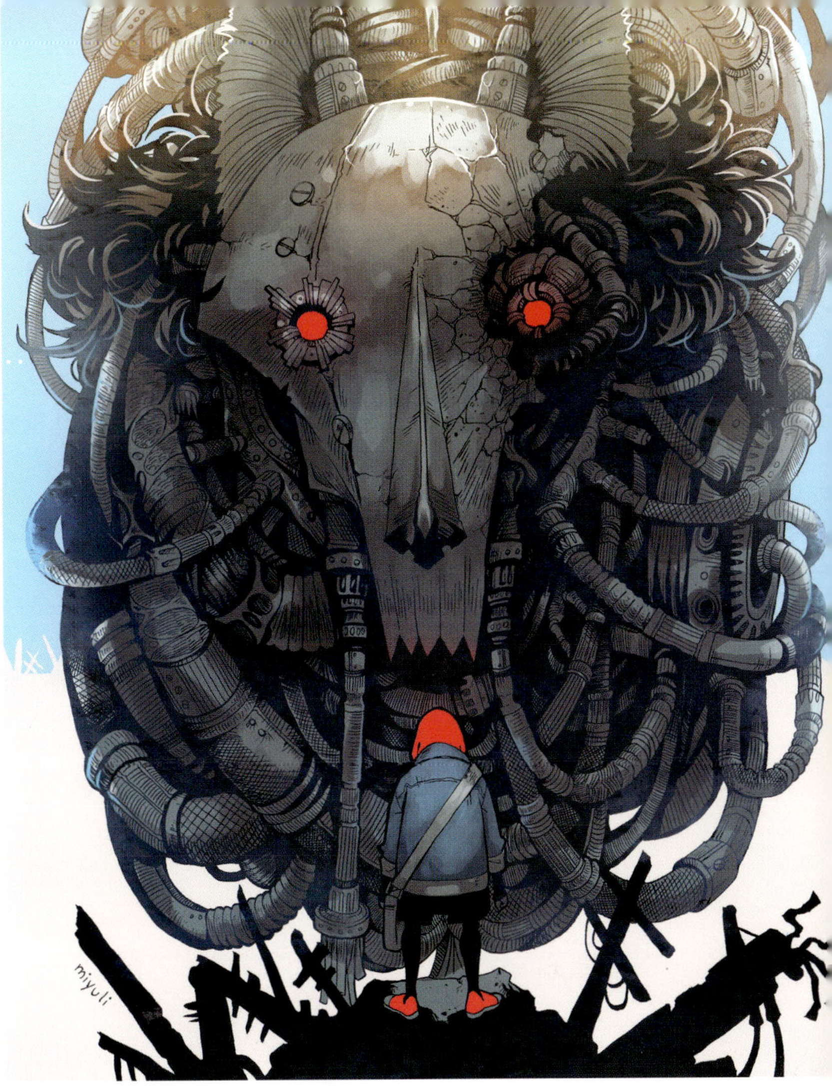


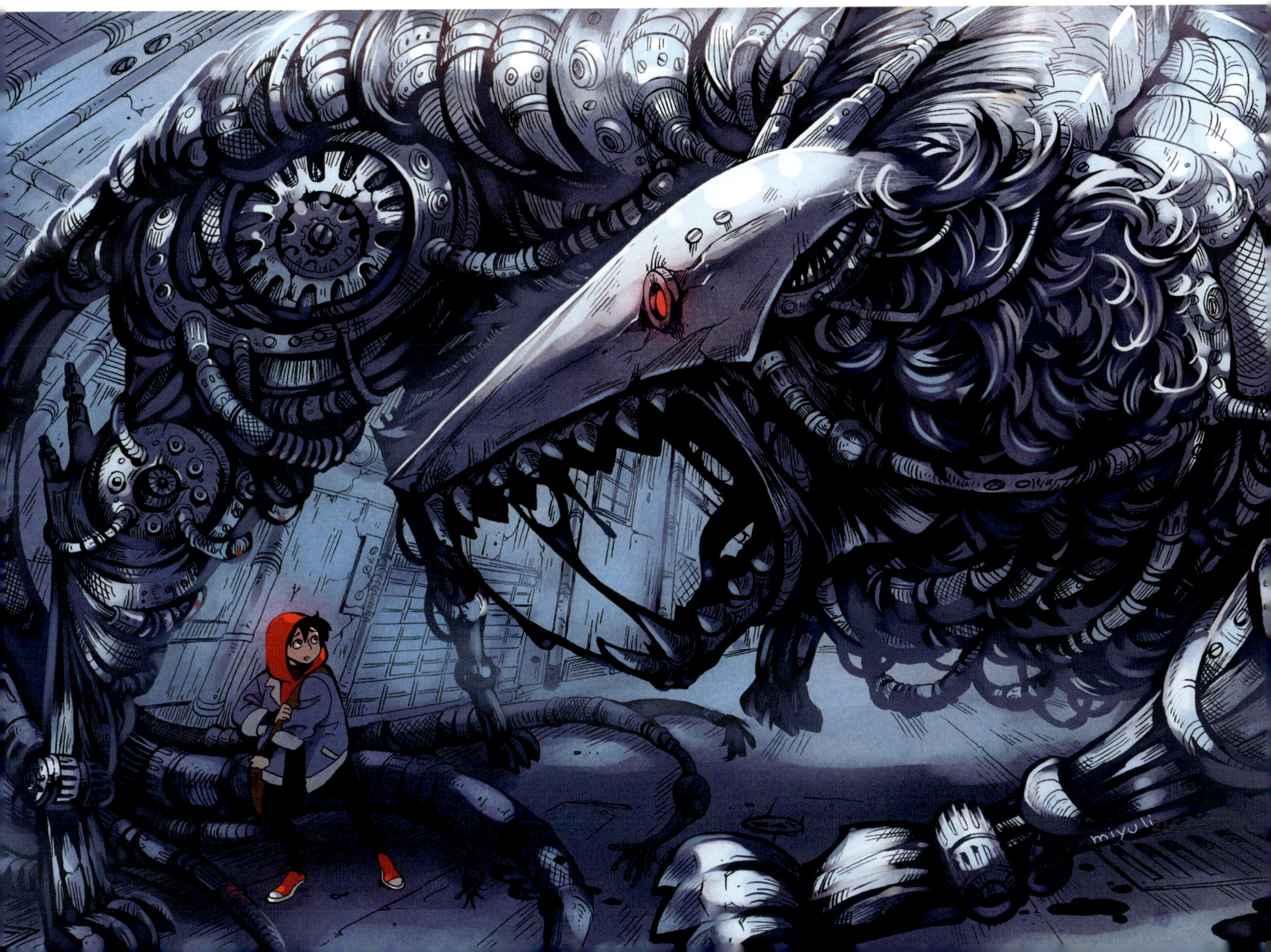

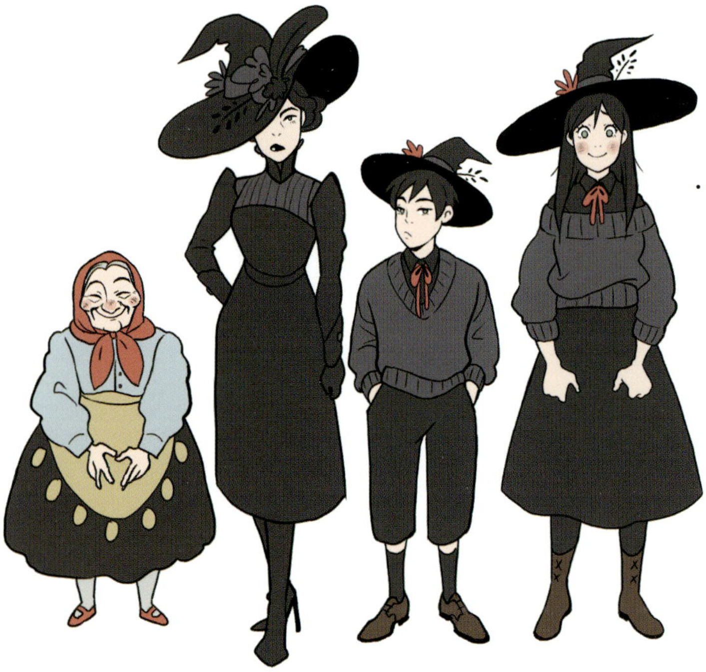

*Families*, 2018

In 2018, I came up with the characters of a tall witch named Morgana and her vampire boyfriend, Oz. Wondering what their families would be like, I created these line-ups. Morgana's family are witches, while Oz was adopted by a werewolf-human family. As these ideas were so well received, I developed their stories further, which led to the launch of my comic *Morgana and Oz* on Webtoon in 2021.

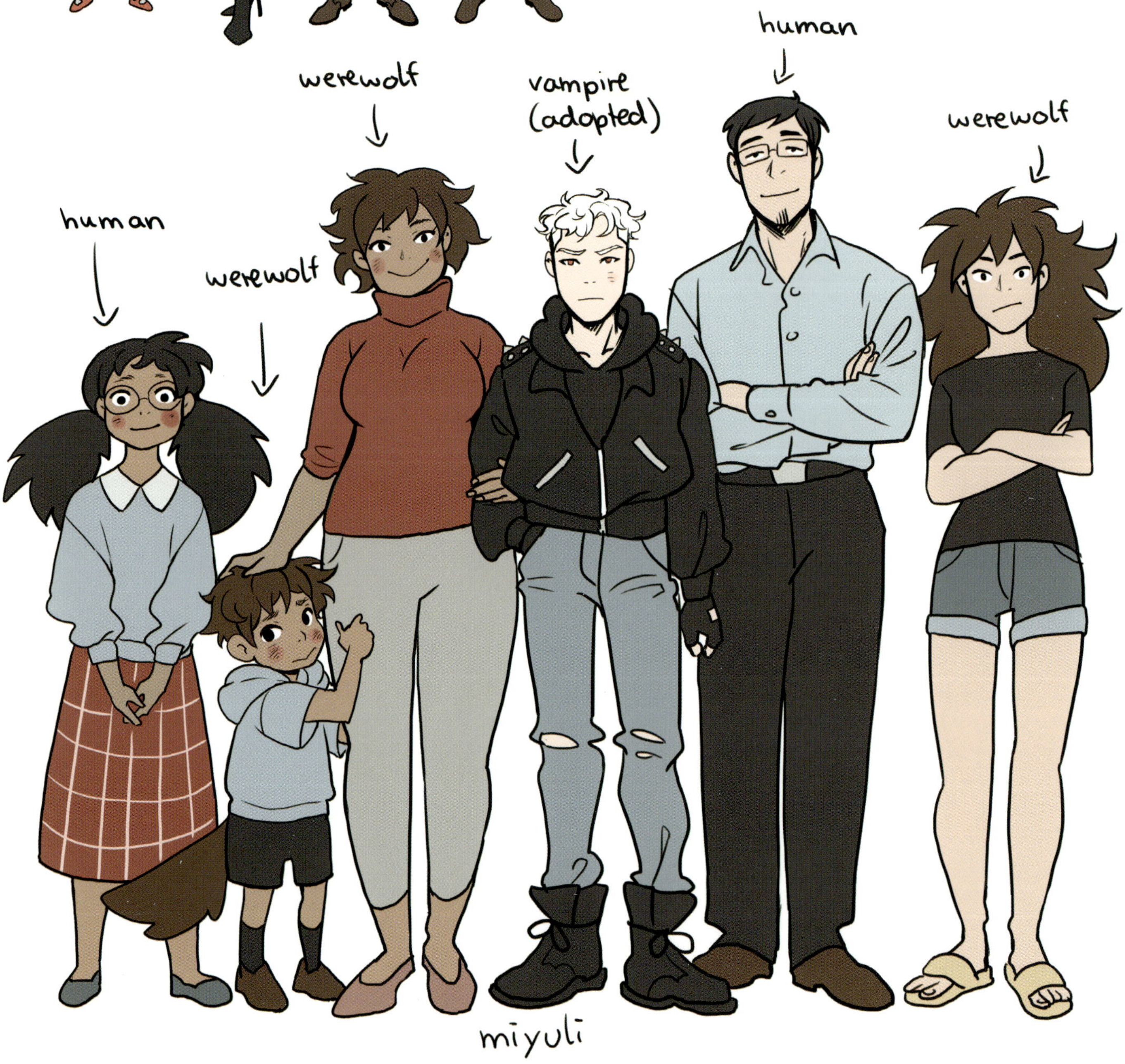

## *Studies*, 2018 & 2020

While I've always drawn small art studies to help me improve my skills, I decided to make them more coherent to encourage me to remember the principles more easily. Many of my followers seemed to benefit from these studies and notes, and as a result of the high engagement, a couple of publishers approached me with offers to turn them into books.

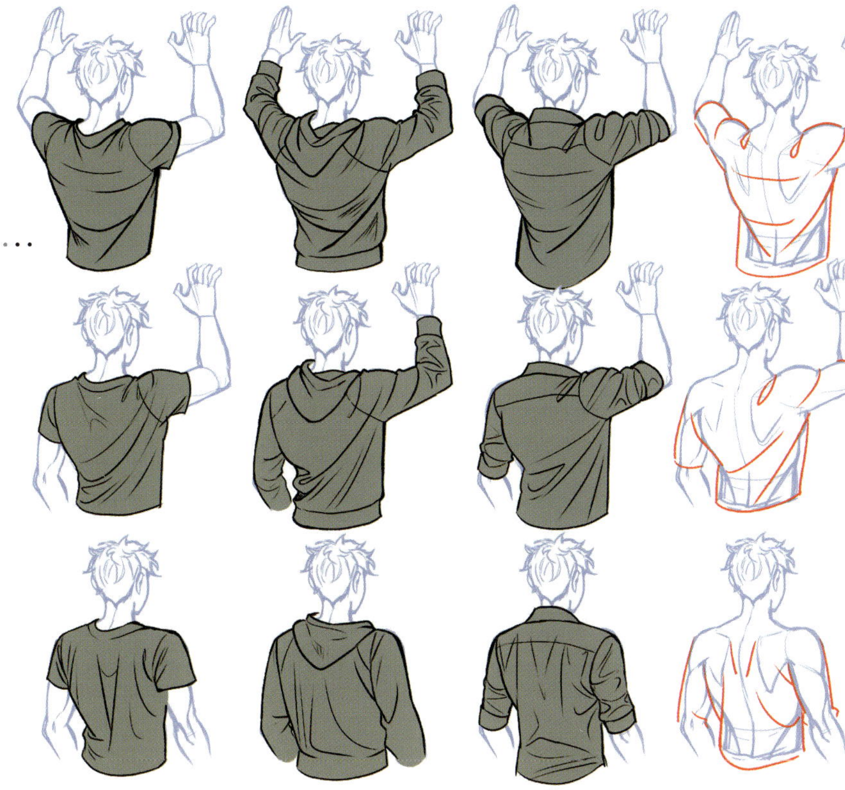

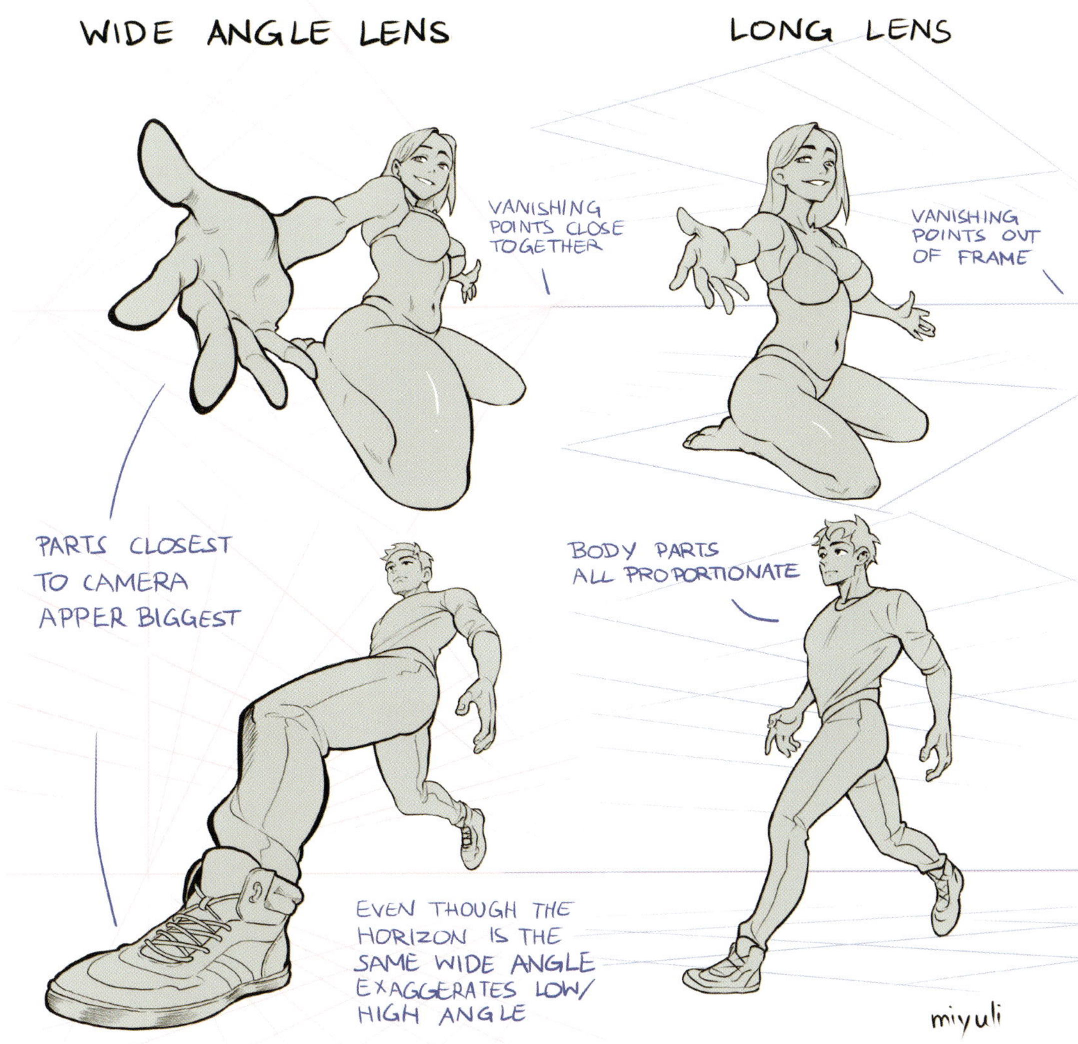

*Frisk*, 2021

While creating new characters and exploring their interactions, I also wanted to lean more toward the fantasy genre I love. I began drawing mermen, and this character was especially well received. I would like to draw a comic that involves merfolk or other similar fantasy elements.

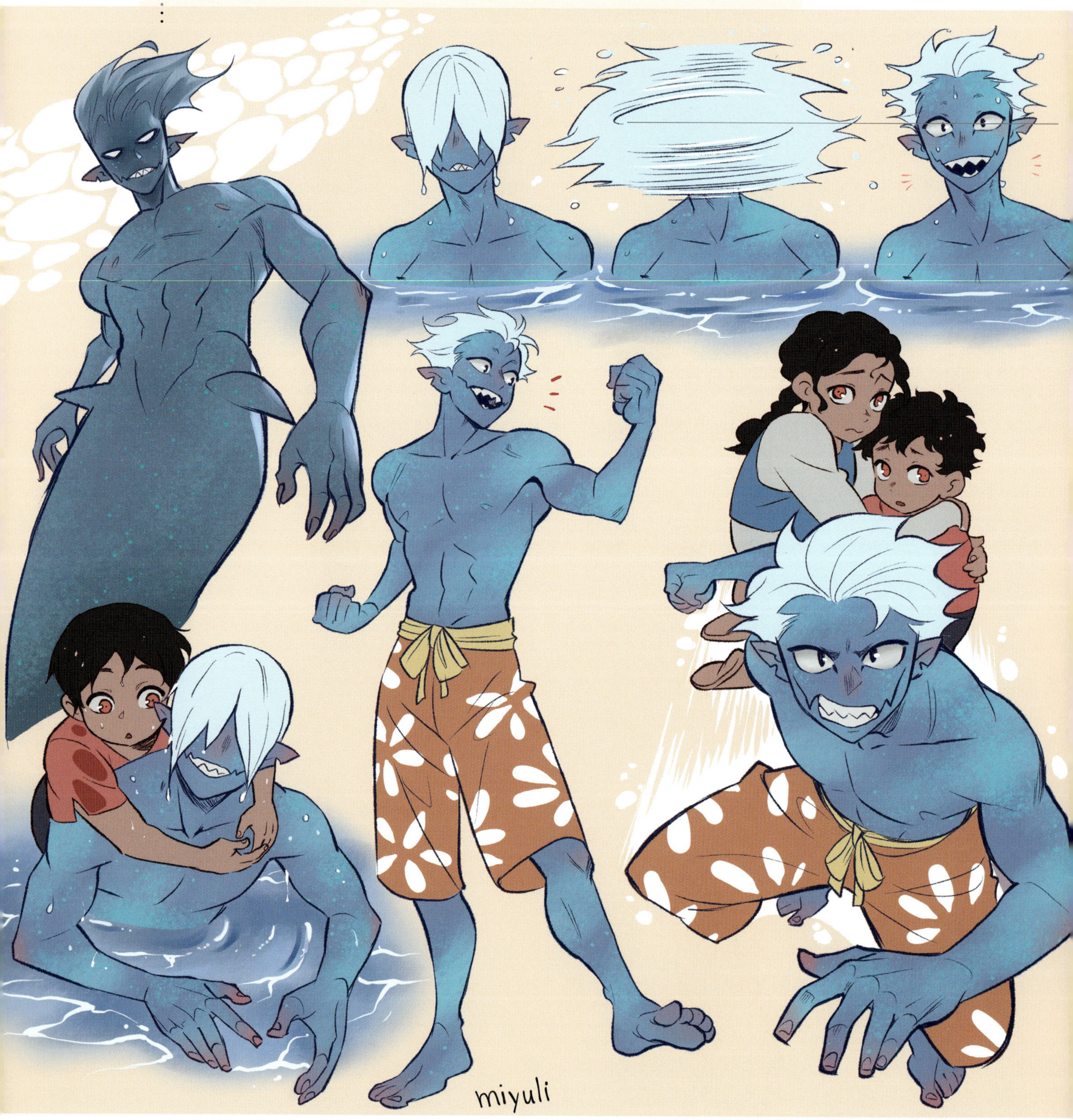

## *My Brother is a Goth*, 2021

Enjoying creating intimate interactions between characters, I had the idea for two young children whose older brother is a goth. While he may look intimidating, he has a softer side, too. This artwork gained a tremendous amount of attention online and many of my followers seemed to connect to the concept.

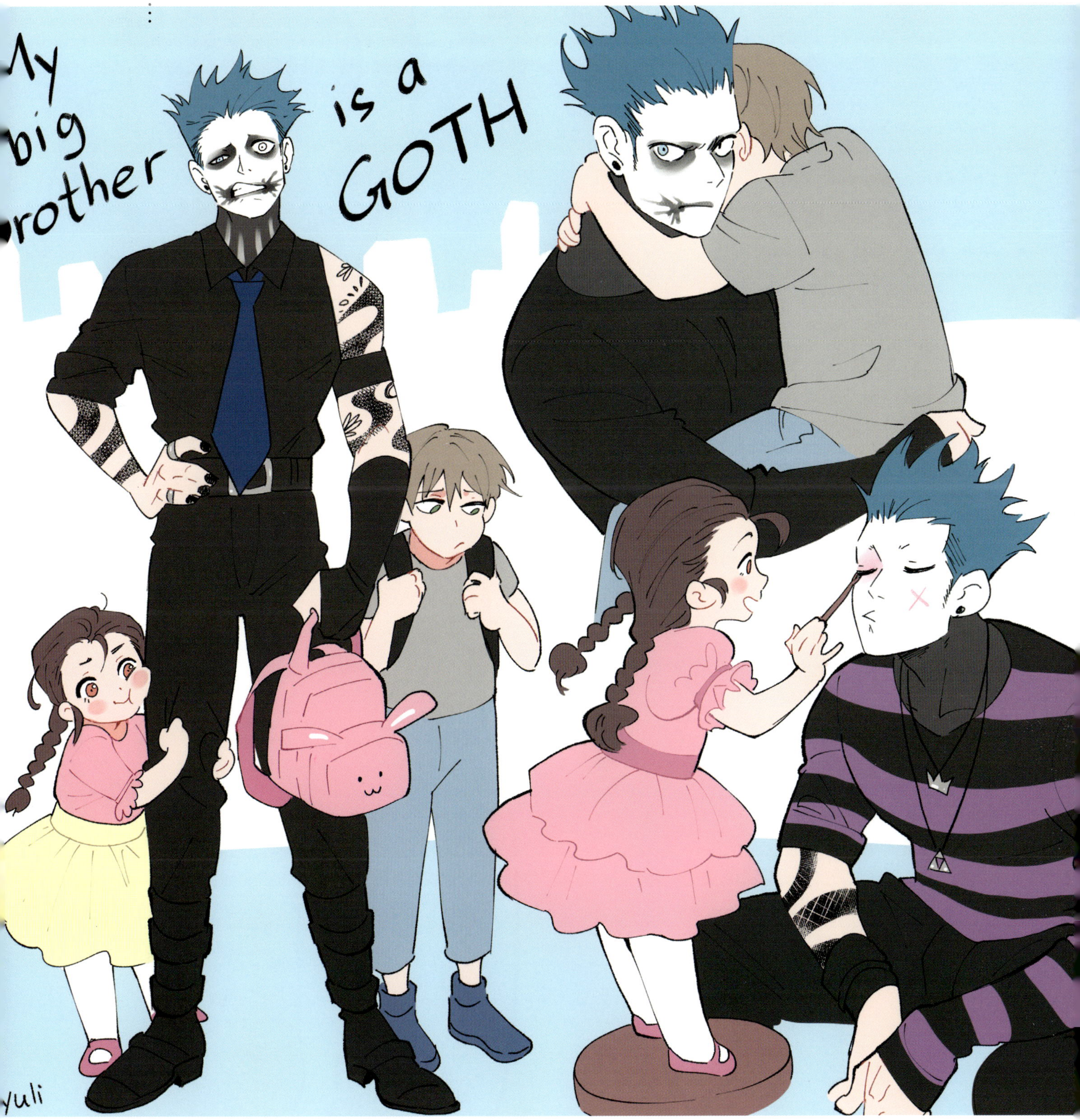

# TUTORIAL

This tutorial will show you how to create an anime-style illustration of three handsome gentlemen with their cute cats, each of whom subtly mirrors the appearance of their owner. Not only is this subject matter one that I enjoy drawing, but it will also appeal to my social-media following, who enjoy seeing my character designs.

Overlaid in a collage-style composition, the characters will provide the focus of the illustration. The background will therefore be simple, showing a bit of the environment of each character without proving a distraction.

Before beginning a new piece of art, it is important to consider its audience and purpose. Even if I am only drawing an illustration to share online with my followers, I always make sure the image is at least 300dpi, in case I later decide to print it. A square is the default shape for Instagram posts and tends to look good on other social-media platforms, too. For prints, I often opt for A5 or B5, which are popular sizes for independent comics in Europe and Japan.

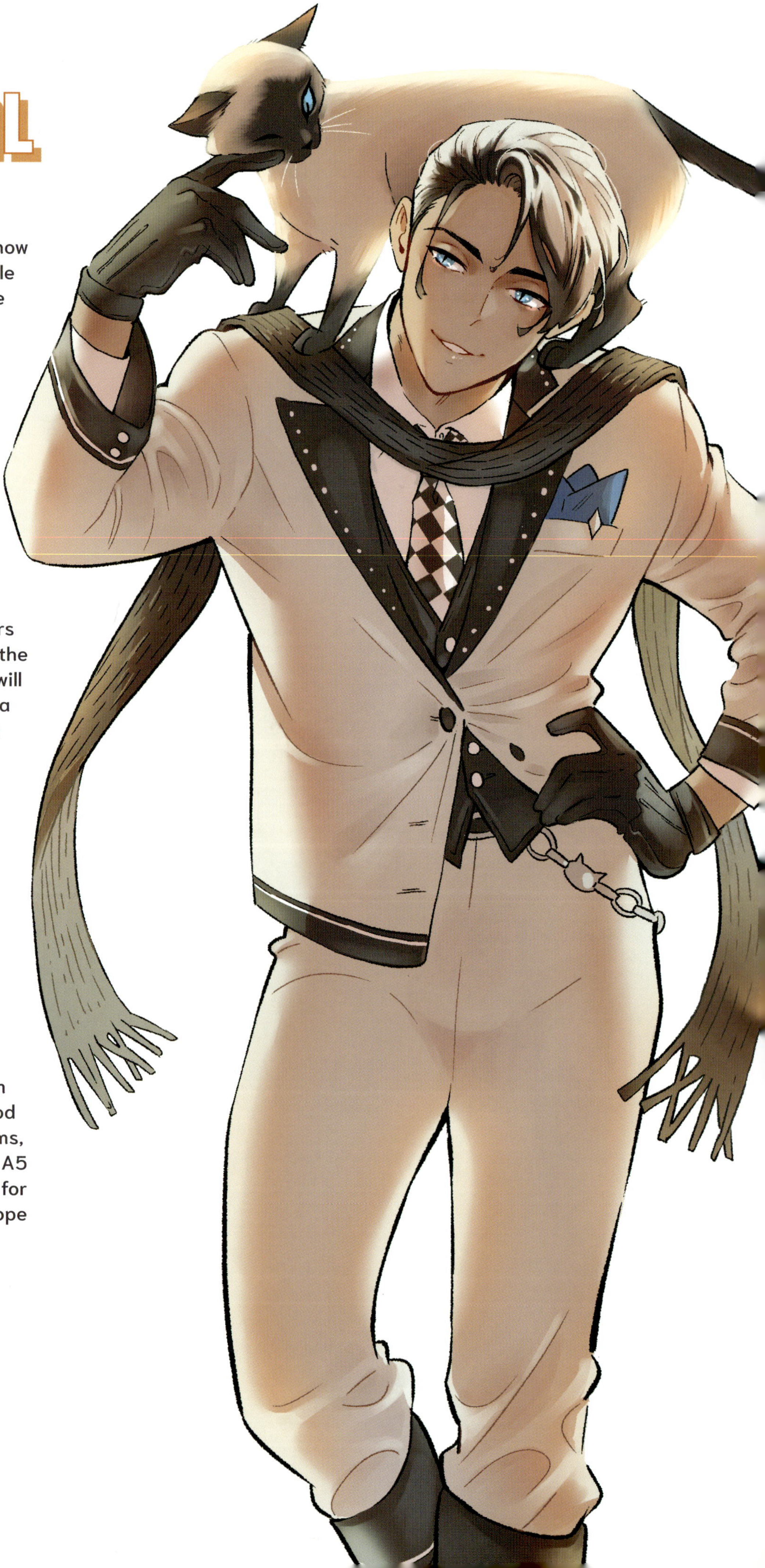

**01** When designing a character, it's useful to begin with research. I look up photos of cats online, researching the different breeds and their characteristics. Choosing a Siamese cat, Norwegian Forest cat, and Scottish Fold cat, I explore these breeds further and consider how I can use them as inspiration for three human characters. When undertaking commercial work, I often compile extensive notes to ensure my thought process and intentions are clear and can be explained to the client. For personal work, photo research can sometimes be enough. The deeper the research, the more interesting and believable the final result will be.

## SIAMESE CAT

**ORIGIN:**
Thailand

**APPEARANCE:**
Muscular body
Triangular head
Light blue, almond-shaped eyes
Long neck
Short, glossy fur
Light fur color, darker on extremities

**TEMPERAMENT:**
Intelligent
Affectionate
Social & extroverted
Active & playful
Low-pitched voice
Suffers from separation anxiety

- Black gloves & boots
- Light suit
- Light-blue eyes
- Short hair
- Muscular

## NORWEGIAN FOREST CAT

**ORIGIN:**
Norway

**APPEARANCE:**
Strong build
Large body & long legs
Bushy tail
Long, thick, water-resistant fur
Long head
Strong chin
Almond-shaped eyes
Large ears
Good climber

**TEMPERAMENT:**
Friendly
Intelligent
Highly active

- Lumberjack
- Earthy tones

## SCOTTISH FOLD

**ORIGIN:**
Scotland

**APPEARANCE:**
Folded ears
Owl-like
Medium-sized
Rounded body, especially head & face
Large, round eyes
Medium-short legs
Short neck
Sweet expression
Any hair length & color

**TEMPERAMENT:**
Loving & affectionate
Good-natured
Playful
Clean
Intelligent
Stubborn

Initial research on cats, including their appearance and characteristics

**02** Explore early ideas for your characters, sketching whatever comes to mind. Look online for references if you lack inspiration for poses. It's much easier to search for pose references if you have a specific direction in mind. I look up images of men holding cats, or for more unique results, "man in suit holding cat." You can also try posing in front of the mirror or arranging 3D anatomy figures to capture different positions and body language.

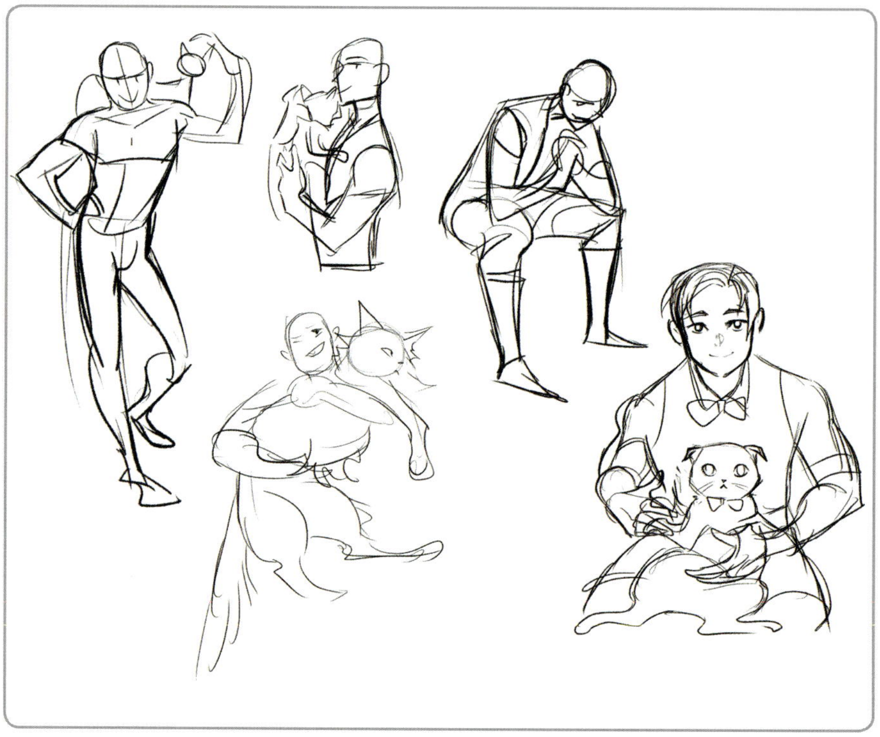

The first rough sketch is loose and experimental, exploring ideas for the characters

**03** Select your favorite poses from your rough sketches and arrange them on the canvas. As I have chosen three attractive cats, I decide to pair them with handsome, muscular men. For the Norwegian Forest cat, I sketch an outdoorsy, rugged-looking man with an axe. The Scottish Fold is round and cute, with flat owl-like ears, so its owner has rounded shoulders and a gentle expression. The final character is stylish and confident, mirroring the intelligent, graceful Siamese cat that perches on his shoulders. Be intentional with your design choices and experiment with different variations until you are satisfied. The more you sketch, the more ideas you will generate.

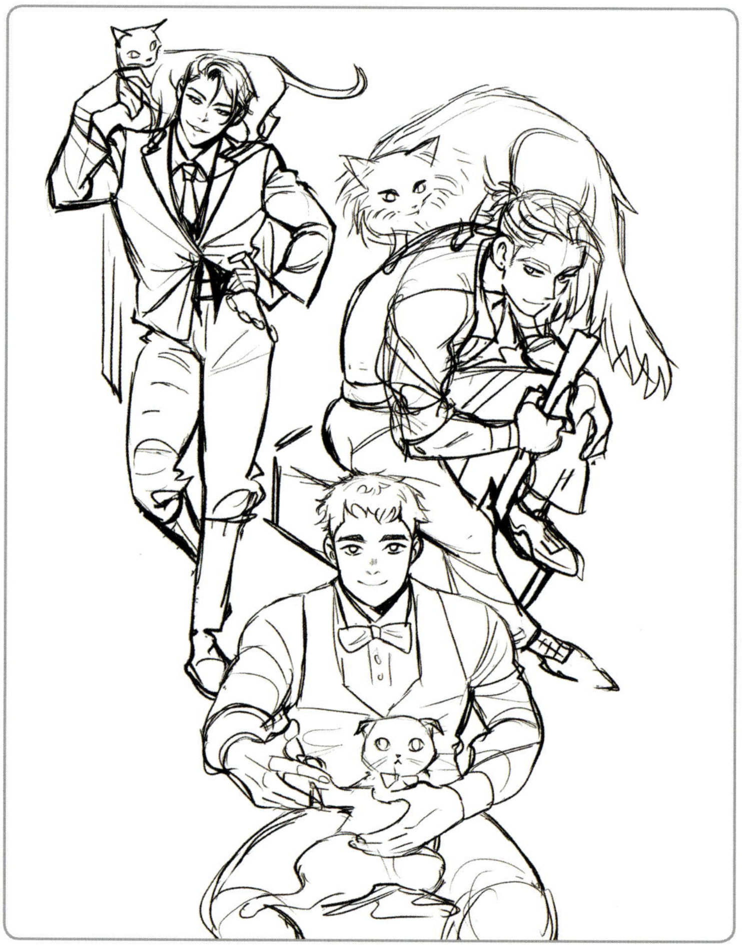

Focus in on the visual characteristics of your characters, using pose to convey their personality

**04** When drawing anime-style characters, begin by looking at average human facial proportions before deciding which elements to stylize. Anime styles can vary in different ways from these standard proportions. The space above the eyes is typically larger than the space below the eyes, and the above section is then extended further with the addition of hair. The lower the eyes, the younger and cuter the character will look. You can also experiment with how tilted you make the sides of the character's head. The more triangular the tilt, the more feminine the face will appear. Analyze the facial proportions of your favorite anime styles and consider which you find most appealing.

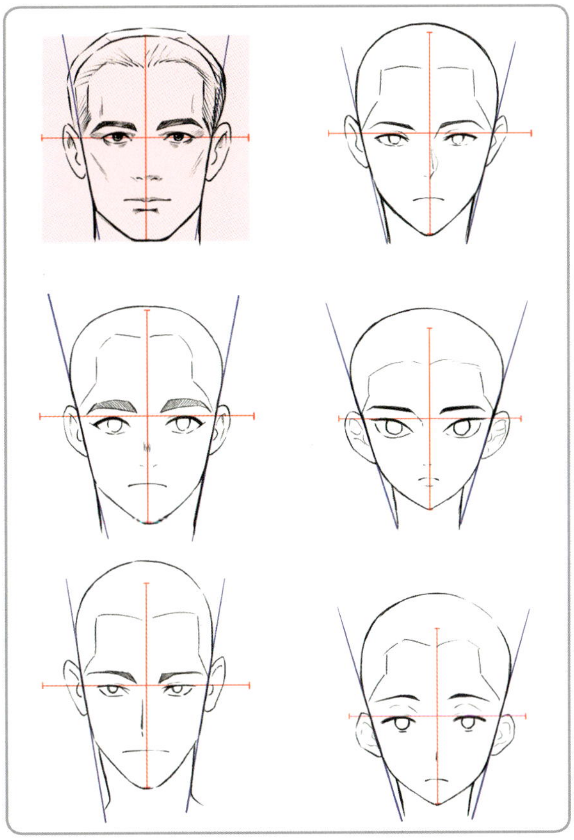

Explore different anime facial styles and proportions to determine which will work best for your characters

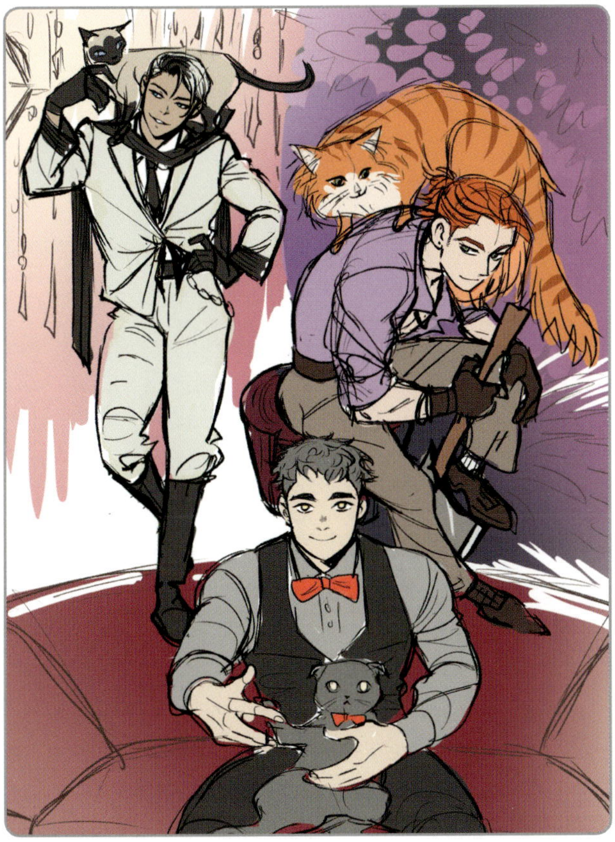

**05** Consider your color palette early on in the character design process. As I have limited myself by basing the three characters on their representative cats, the Siamese character wears a pale suit with black gloves and boots. His hair is cropped short and mirrors the cat's bicolored fur, and I add a black a scarf to represent the tail. Siamese cats are known for their striking blue eyes, which the character also has. I make a note to research and add more intricate details later. While the Norwegian Forest character needs longer hair and more earthy tones, to reflect his feline companion, I also give him a violet shirt for visual contrast. For the playful Scottish Fold character, I experiment with the idea of a casino dealer with dark clothes and statement bowtie. I also sketch in some quick background experiments, though these may change later.

Decide on the colors and general composition of the characters and their cats

**06** Our brains will often try to straighten our sketches out, which can make them appear static and boring. While static designs can work well when designing clothes and art for 3D modeling, my intention is to design characters with personalities and to capture this in their gestures. Try to offset the axis of the hips, shoulders, eyes, and any other body parts that appear too flat and level. Tilting body parts toward the viewer can create a greater sense of space and perspective. To avoid distortion, imagine taking a photograph of your character using a long lens where the vanishing points are far apart. Train your brain to imagine your characters in a three-dimensional space.

Use your character's pose, body language, and gesture to convey their personality, while also creating a three-dimensional effect

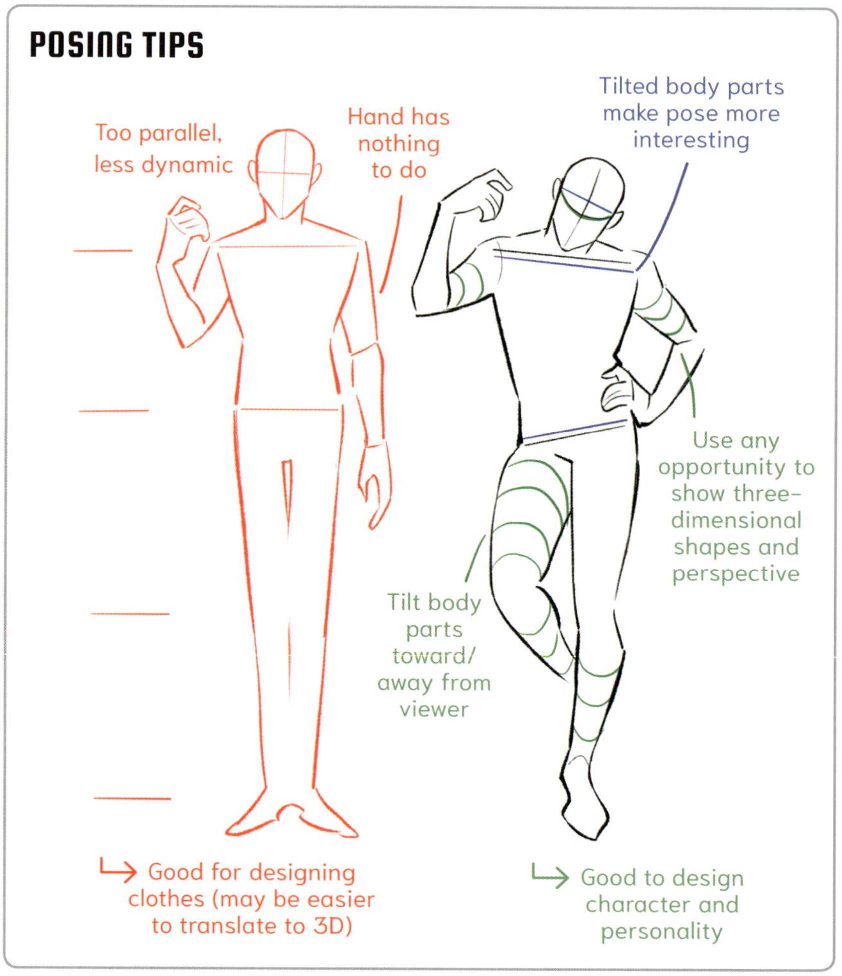


**07** Sitting poses can be useful for showing a character's personality through how they are balancing their body. Are they leaning back, or sitting up straight and alert? I need to sketch the Norwegian Forest character leaning forward to allow space for the cat to perch on his back. Any pose can look pretty boring if captured from the wrong angle, so I place my "camera" at a high angle to create more overlap and a more interesting perspective. When drawing a high or low angle, take extra care with the perspective. Here I introduce a chair to help establish the angle. I consider creating more distortion by pulling the vanishing points together and making the head bigger and legs smaller, but this will look a little jarring compared to the other characters. Even though I sketch him from a high angle, I still use a fairly long lens.

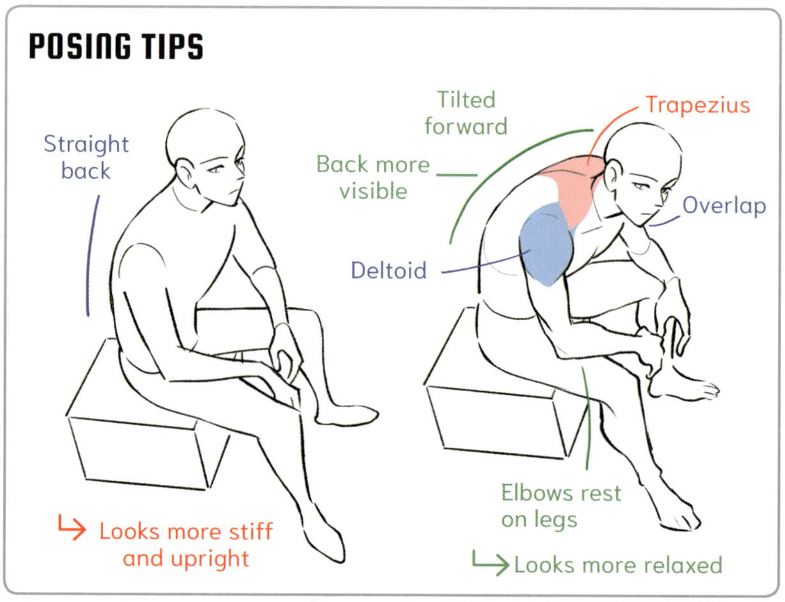


Pay attention to angle and perspective when sketching a character's seated position, ensuring it doesn't distract from the rest of the composition

**08** Make use of references when drawing clothing, such as the Siamese character's suit. Details such as folds will depend on the material and texture of the fabric. Suit jackets often have padded shoulders that may not react to movement as you would expect from softer materials. Suits are also fashioned to minimize folds to make them appear smart, but with enough movement, folds will pull at the seams. Be mindful of where the folds squash the overall form and where stretches create smooth arcs. Since the arms are rounded forms, spiral folds will encircle them. The amount of folds drawn on a character's outfit will also depend on your personal style. For animation or a simple comic style, I would recommend only including the most essential folds. Illustrations or detailed comic styles allow you to add numerous folds, however, as long as they follow the general rules of the form and material.

### NOTES ON FOLDS

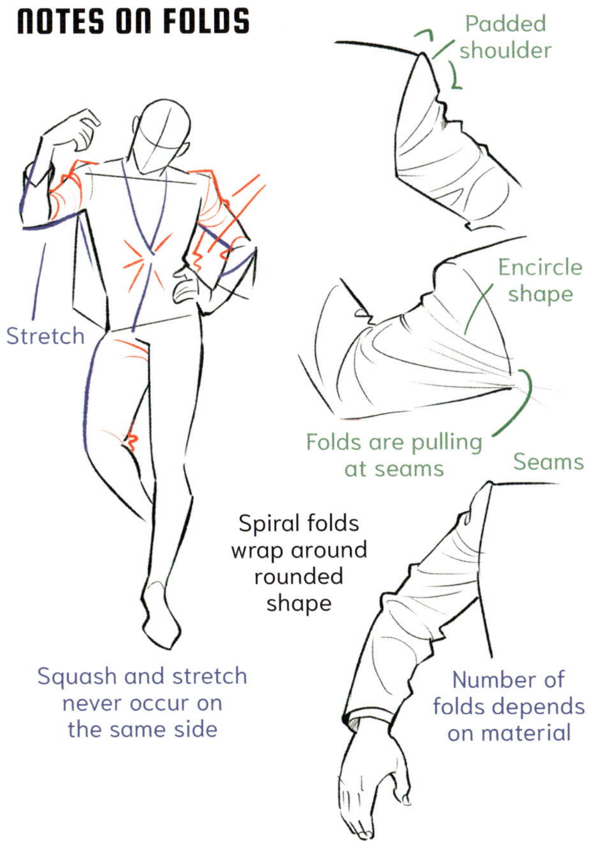


The simplicity or detail of your anime style will dictate the amount of detail, such as folds in clothing, you can add

**09** Study the characters' hands in your initial sketch. If they require some work, try taking photos of your own hands to analyze how they could be improved. Avoid simply copying what you see, but try to understand how your initial attempt fell short. I realize I have misjudged the angle of the hands in my initial sketch. The Siamese character should tilt his hand toward the cat, rather than away from it. Meanwhile, the Scottish Fold character's hand should face the viewer more as it wraps around the cat's form. Acting out the characters' poses and gestures will allow you to recognize any mistakes.

### HANDS

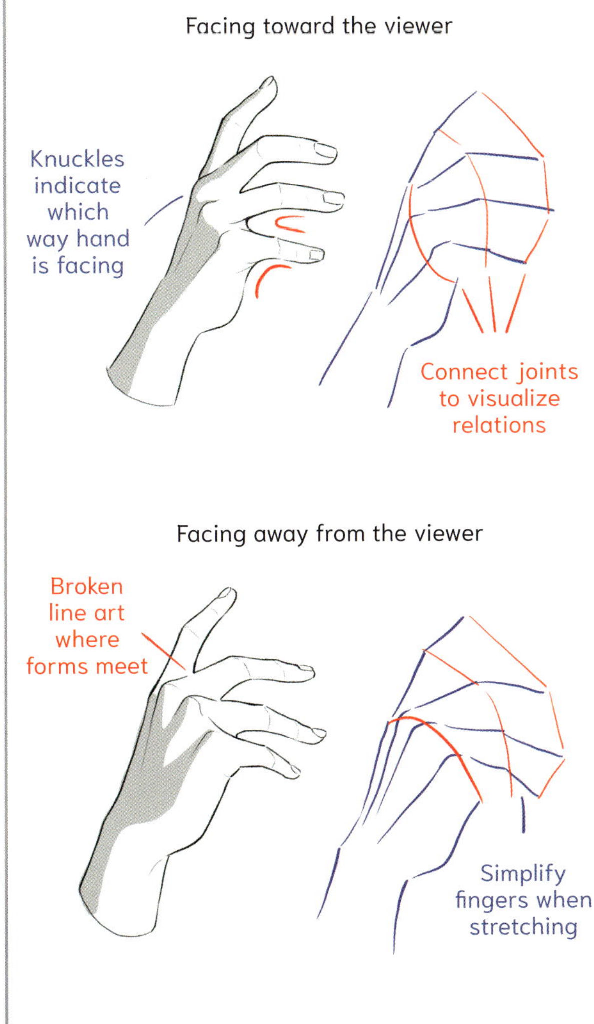


Tips for drawing hands

**10** When drawing hands, it's important to understand the relation of the joints to one another. Don't draw each part independently, but view them in relation to each other. Sketching in the fingertips will allow you to see if the length is correct. The thumb moves in a slightly different direction to the other fingers, so this may require extra practice. When drawing arcs in my characters' hands, I like to exaggerate them a little by juxtaposing the soft arcs from the fat pads and muscles with the hard edges of bone. This adds visual interest.

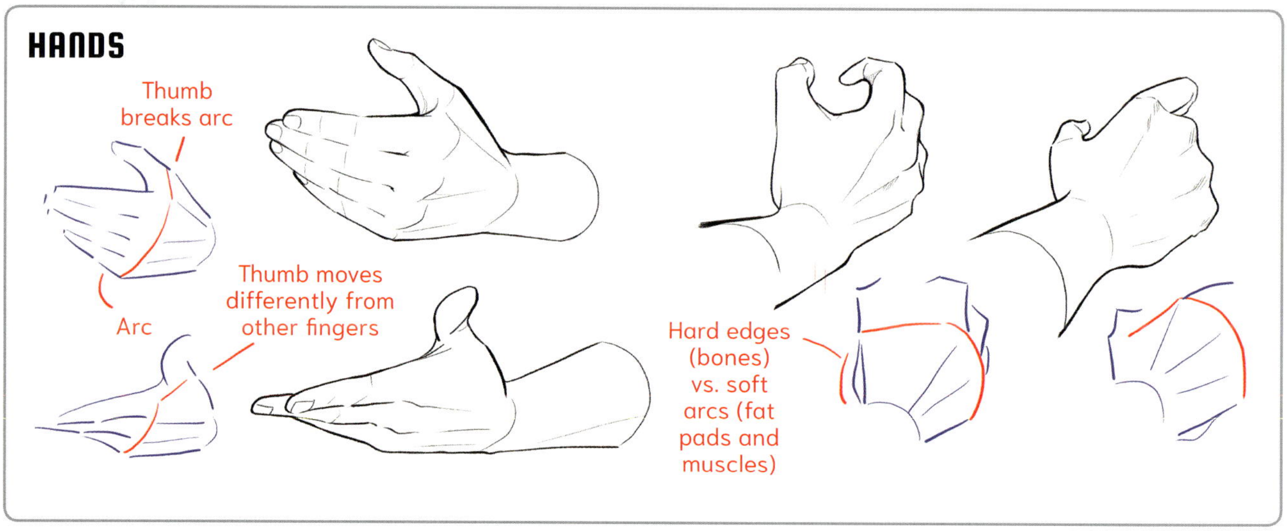


Explore how your characters' simplified hands can be anatomically realistic, while also somewhat stylized

**11** Draw the line work, adding smaller details and using references as needed. I left these details out of the initial sketch to allow myself more freedom and spontaneity at this stage. Anime-style artwork is typically known for fairly thin lines, but introducing slight variation in line width can add interest. For example, you may wish to use thicker lines for the outline of the forms, then thinner lines to describe anything within. You can also simulate soft edges, such as the cats' fur, by breaking the line work or using soft hatching. I use the Real G-Pen in Clip Studio Paint for my line work.

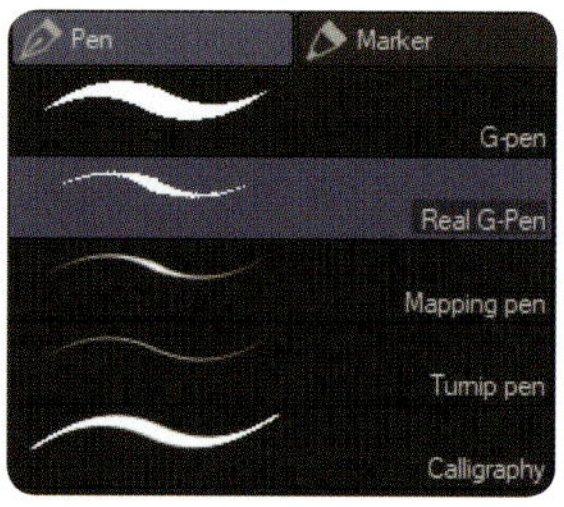


Introduce smaller details when drawing the line work, paying attention to line width

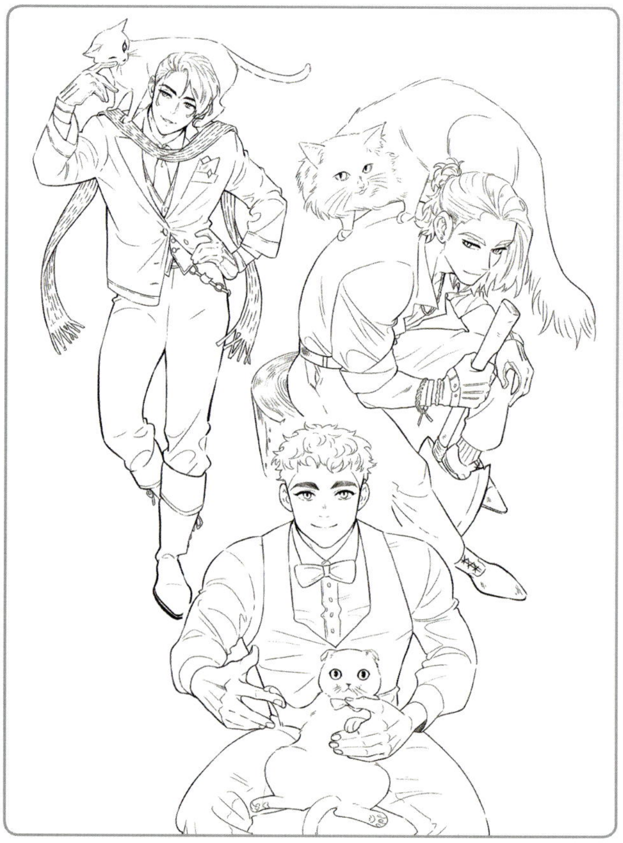

## ARTIST TIP

Choose line weight and speed according to your preferences and the purpose of the artwork. Comics often need to be drawn quickly, so lines will be fast and loose. Quickly drawn lines contain more energy and tend to be easier on the wrist. Practice drawing different types of line work with various brushes to see which results you like best. Additionally, study the line work of artists you admire and try to figure out the intentions behind their decisions.

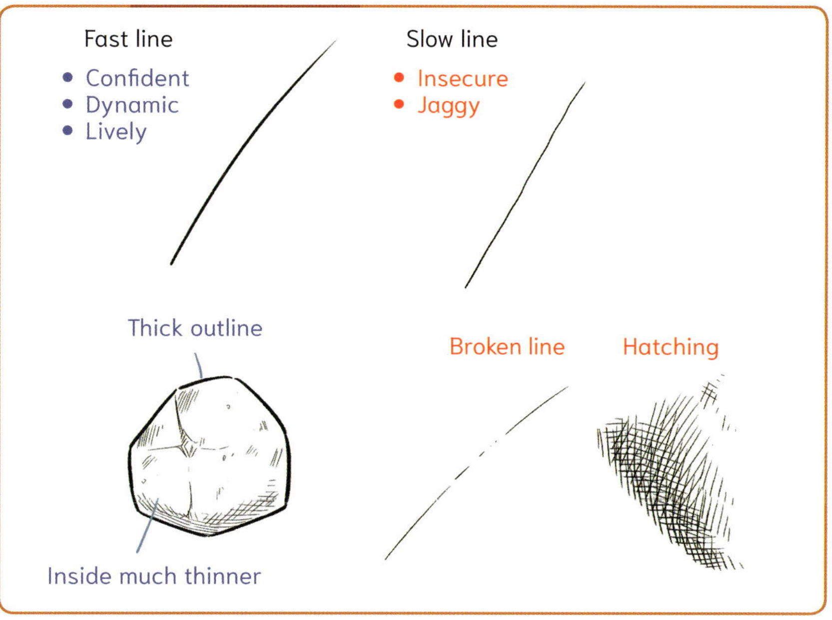


**12** Working digitally allows you to separate individual elements of your illustration onto designated layers. I create six layers: one for each character and each cat. While you can further separate elements out onto different layers – such as hair, clothing, and accessories – I am sometimes overwhelmed by too many layers and prefer to keep it simple. Use this stage to move the elements around the illustration, if needed.

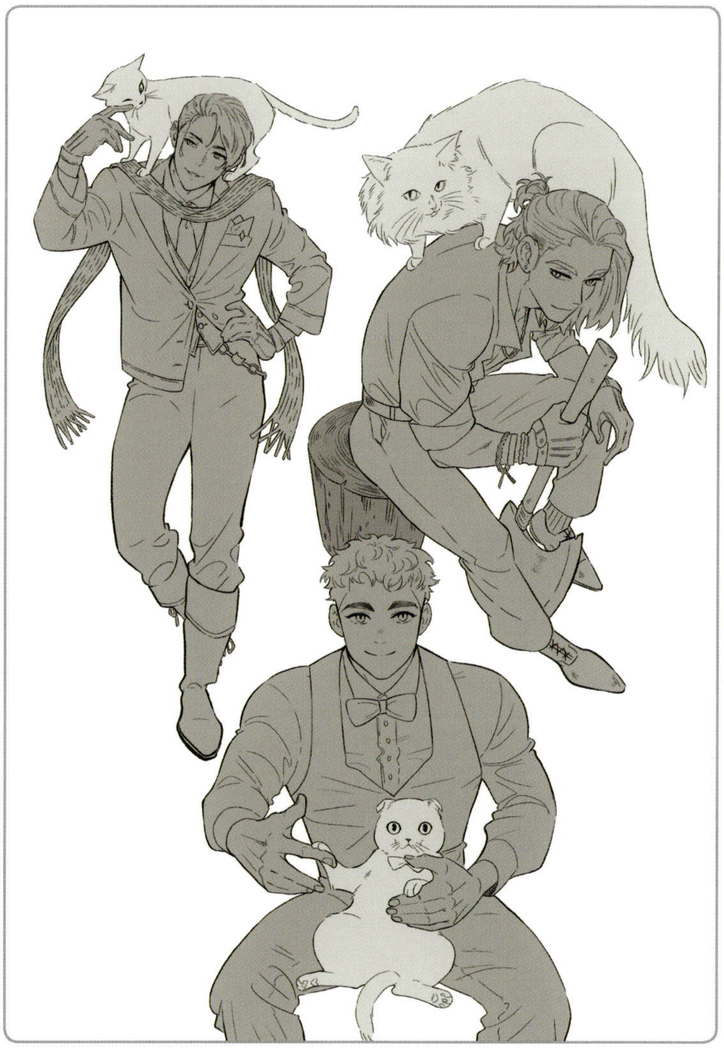

Create a layer for each character and cat, allowing you to work on them separately

**13** Choosing the right colors can be a daunting task. If you feel at a loss, take some time to study color theory and explore the different color harmonies that can be created. It's wise to limit yourself to a few colors per character, rather than overloading the audience with too many. Select a dominant color and make everything else subordinate to it. Also note that desaturated colors will often work better together than lots of saturated colors. Don't be afraid of experimenting with grays. I often opt for desaturated, grayer colors in my artwork.

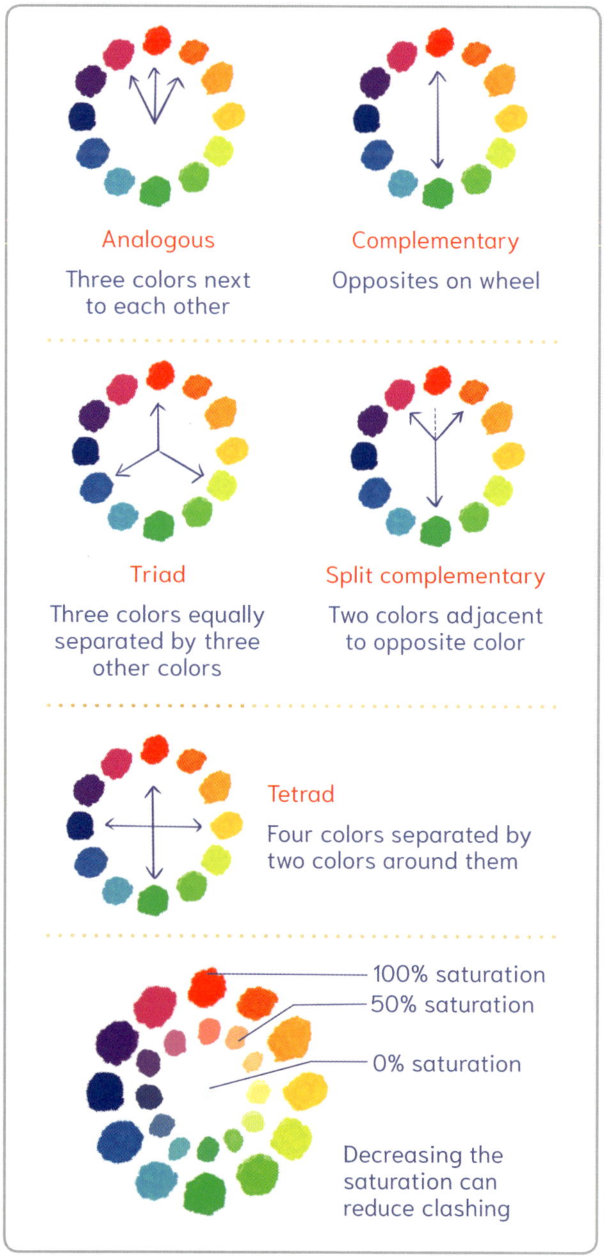


Notes on color harmony and choosing colors for your illustration

**14** I experiment with four different color palettes, each of which has a distinct look. The monochromatic palette consists of one color taken through different hues. This can look unique and subtle when done well, but can appear boring and monotone if it fails. Another approach is to consider the temperature of colors. A balance of warm and cool can create a harmonious appearance. As cool colors often seem to recede, I use them here for areas further away from the viewer. Alternatively, choosing a monochromatic color palette and adding one saturated color accent is a technique I love, as the accent always attracts interest. Finally, I explore a tetradic palette. Though this is the most vibrant, it's not one I would typically use in my own art style.

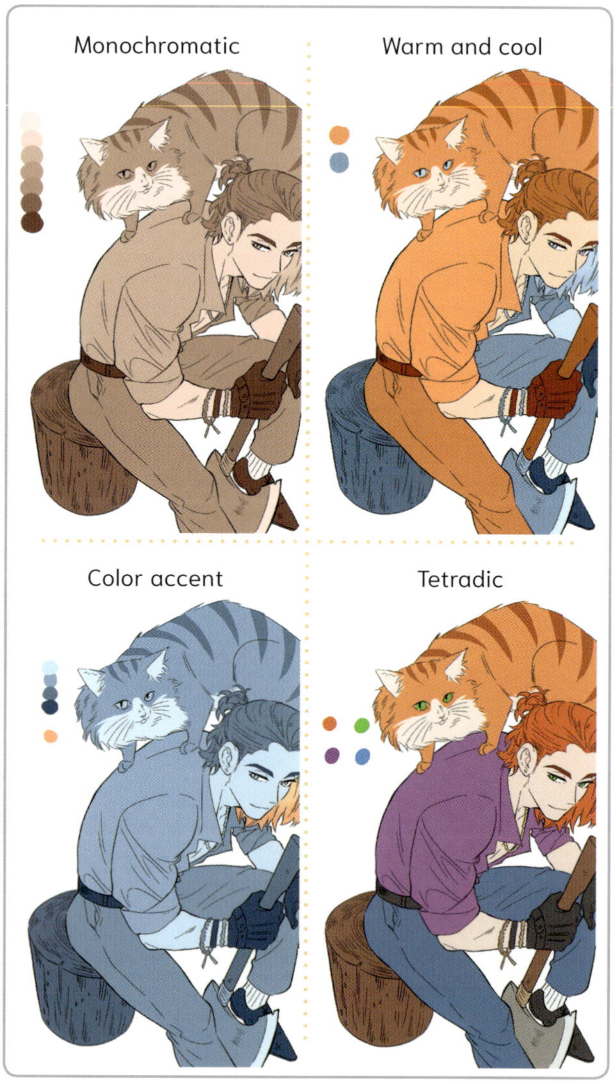


Use color theory to limit your palette as you explore colors for each character

**15** Next, explore the following color schemes for the three characters – each a personification of their cat. The suited character's design encompasses both dark and light, with a blue accent. As his base is rather colorless, I use a bold, saturated blue for his eyes and decorative handkerchief. Selecting a striking orange for the Norwegian Forest cat, I then take a triadic approach for the man and his axe. I choose a saturated green for the eyes, pairing this with a cooler violet for the shirt. The brown tones sit well with the warm orange of the cat and the character's hair, and don't interfere with the rest of the design. I saw many gray Scottish Folds in my research, so use an almost grayscale approach for the cat and casino dealer character, with warm, saturated accents of red and yellow.

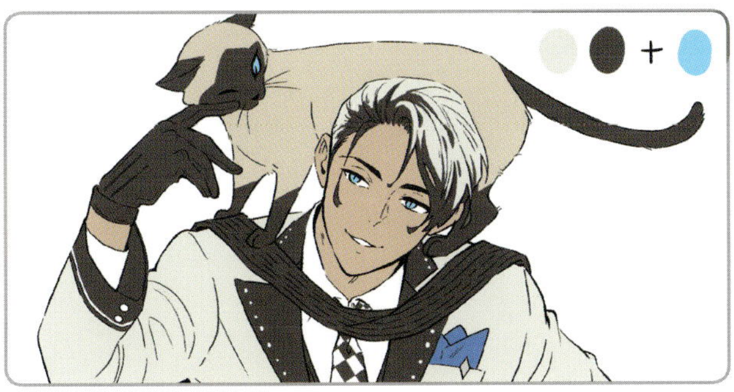

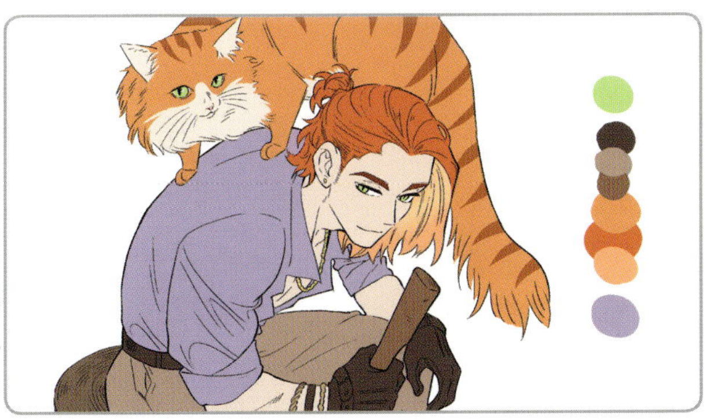

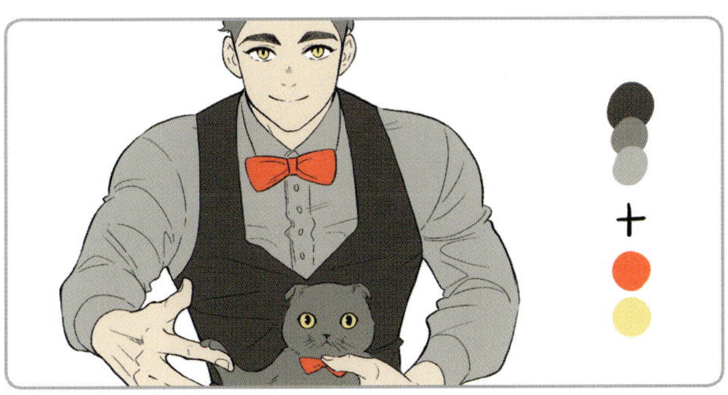

Add in the base colors, letting each cat's coloring inform the colors of their human counterpart

**16** Adding a light color on a Multiply layer will create a quick cel-shading look, one of the most popular looks for anime-style artwork. This is often used in animation, as it's much quicker than other approaches. The color of your shadow will depend on the color of your secondary light (or what is reflected from the primary light). Here I start with a warmer shadow color, before deciding to opt for warm light and a cooler shadow instead. At this stage, your base color is the lit area.

This is where I stop if posting the artwork to Instagram. My final paintings don't perform well on Instagram, so I now only post very simply colored characters there. If posting to Twitter, however, I will continue working on the illustration. Try posting different looks on different platforms and see what your followers engage with most.

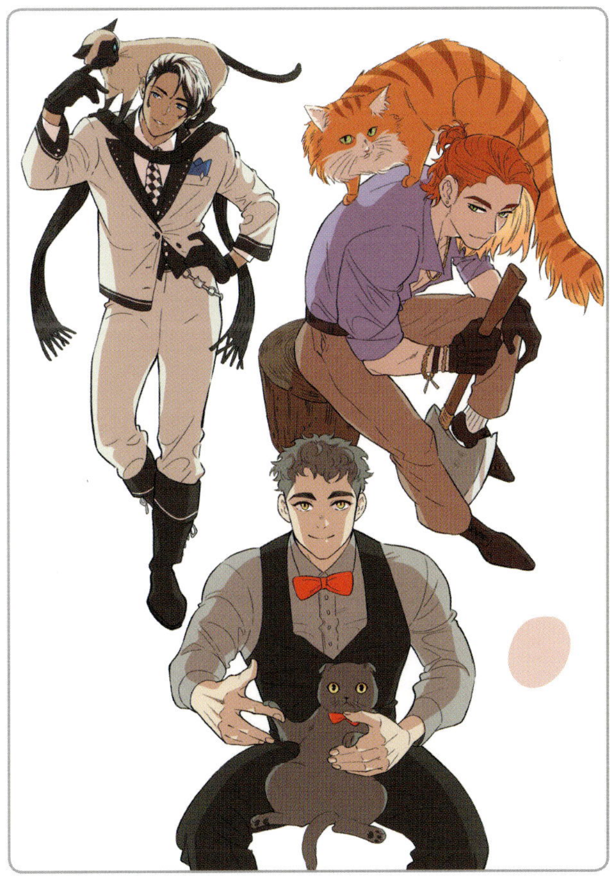

Cel shading is a simple but classic option for creating an animelike look

**17** When adding shadows to your illustration, consider the direction of your light source. The simplest approach is to opt for a front light in a generally well-lit scene. When everything is bright, we feel calmer. If the light is coming from the side or behind, this can look more dramatic. Take care if introducing a light source from below, however, as this will create unusual shadows on a character's face that can look unnerving or mysterious. As with everything else, make a plan and use light and shadow with intention. You might also want to consider using several light sources for balance. I decide to use a backlight, which will make the illustration more interesting.

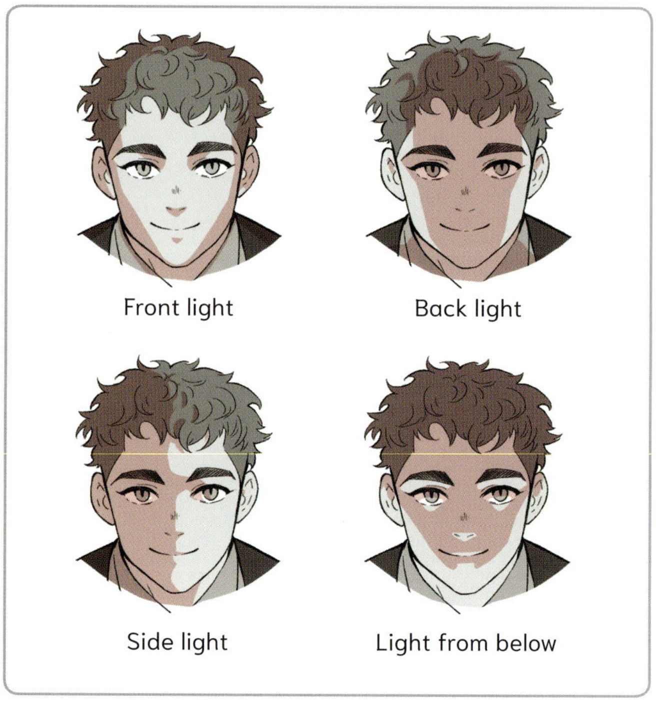


Different light directions create different effects, so be intentional with which you choose

**18** Study light and shadow in real life, implementing what you observe in your artwork. It's important to learn how to control the edges in detailed paintings. For example, notice how soft edges wrap around rounder shapes, creating a halftone.

Limiting your values will create a clearer image. Shadows might not be as dark as you think once you add the reflected light. Also, take care not to make the shadow area brighter than the light area.

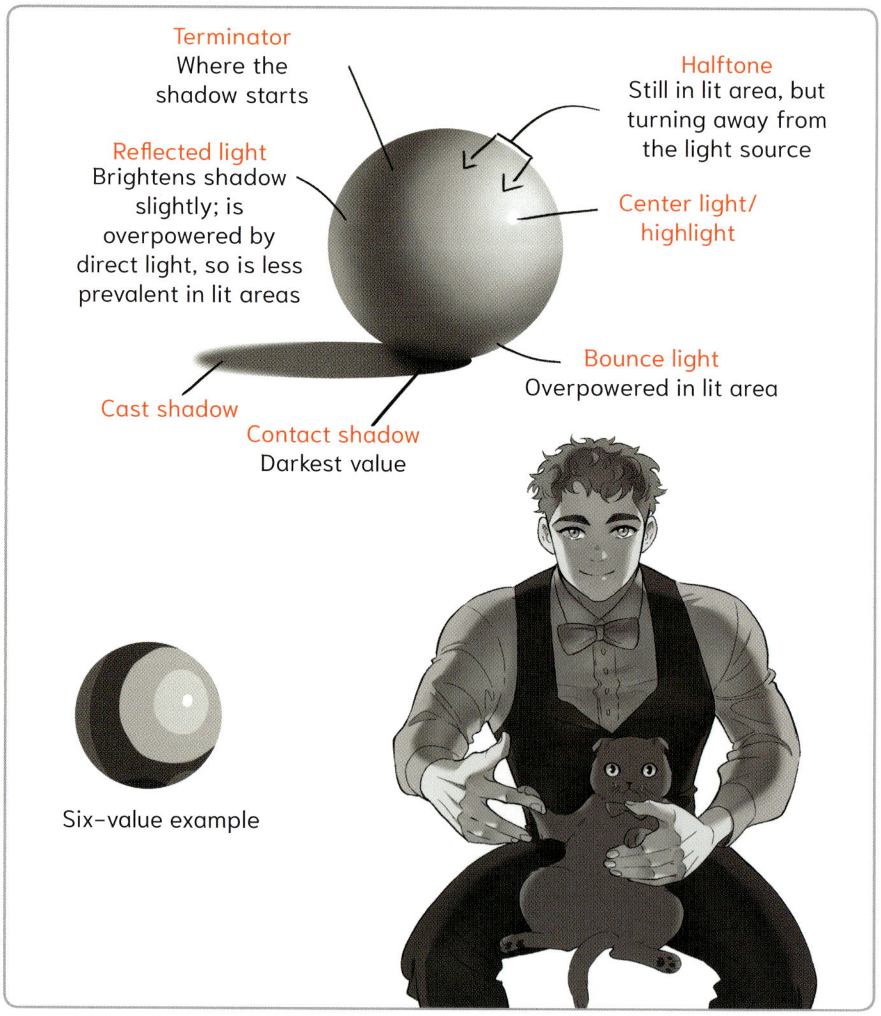


Refined shading can be achieved by controlling hard and soft edges

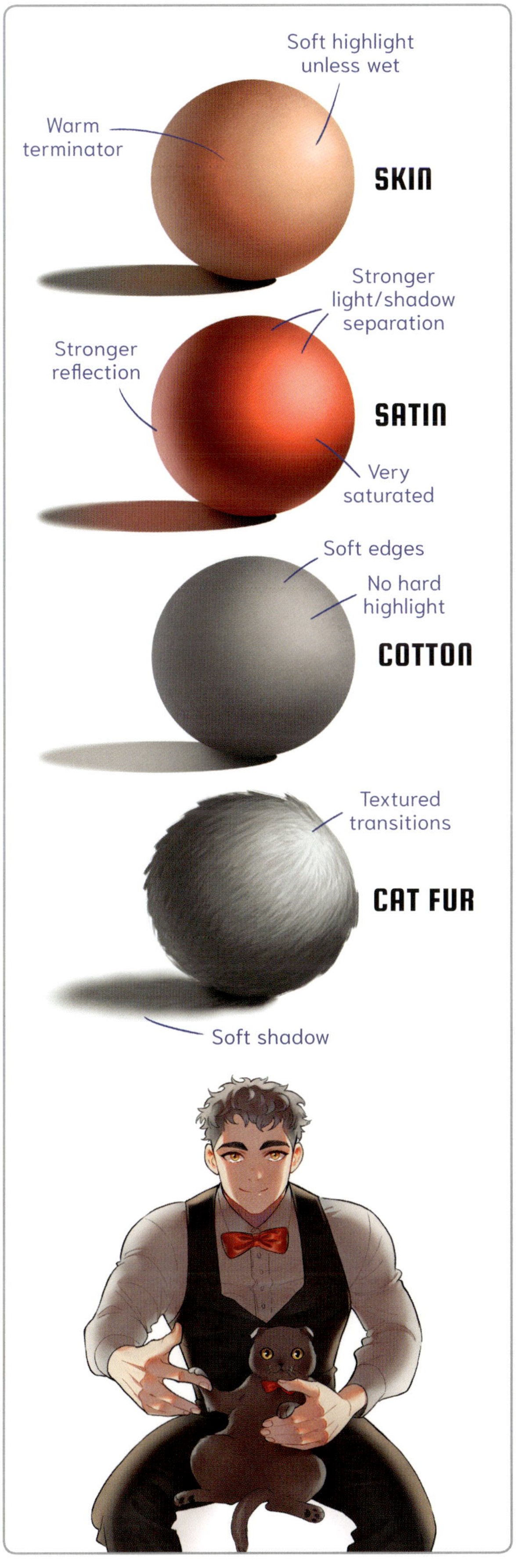


**19** Different materials reflect light in different ways. Hard and glossy surfaces appear much shinier than matte materials that absorb the light more. When painting skin, you can add a warmer tone to liven up the character. While hair and fur can prove more challenging, as they consist of numerous strands, they still follow the core principles introduced in step 18. Simplifying the hair of each character and fur of each cat into main shapes will allow you to represent them more easily.

Note how different materials reflect or absorb light, then implement this in your illustration

**20** Though there are many core principles regarding color and light, there is still room for stylization and experimentation. While the colors you choose don't need to be realistic, it does help if they're believable. I typically use a simple coloring process when painting eyes, as I prefer to spend my time working on the characters' gestures instead. There are simple tricks for making a character's eyes pop, which are often used in animation. Think of eyes like gemstones and add lots of saturated reflections. If painting a close-up shot of the eyes, devoting more time to rendering them will add intensity to the character. Experiment to find what style best suits the character and the intended purpose of the illustration.

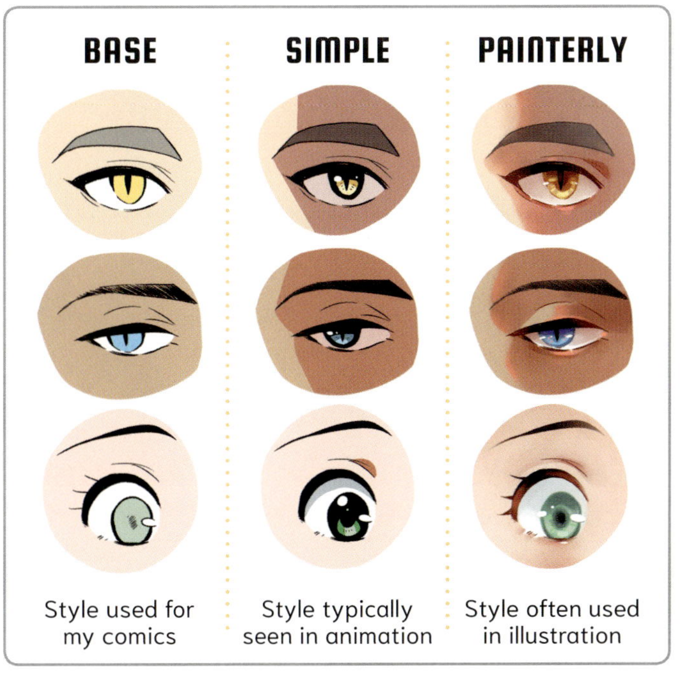


Explore different ways to color the eyes until you find your preferred style

**21** Starting out with my cel-shaded approach, I soften the edges on rounder forms and paint in a few reflections. As the area between light and shadow is often quite saturated, I manipulate the colors in those spaces slightly. Typically, I like to leave all of my line work black, as I like the look this creates. Black or bold line work can often look jarring against painterly and soft edges, however, so you may wish to take a different approach. For example, you could color the lines using a similar color to that of the form they outline. Here I've done a mix of the two.

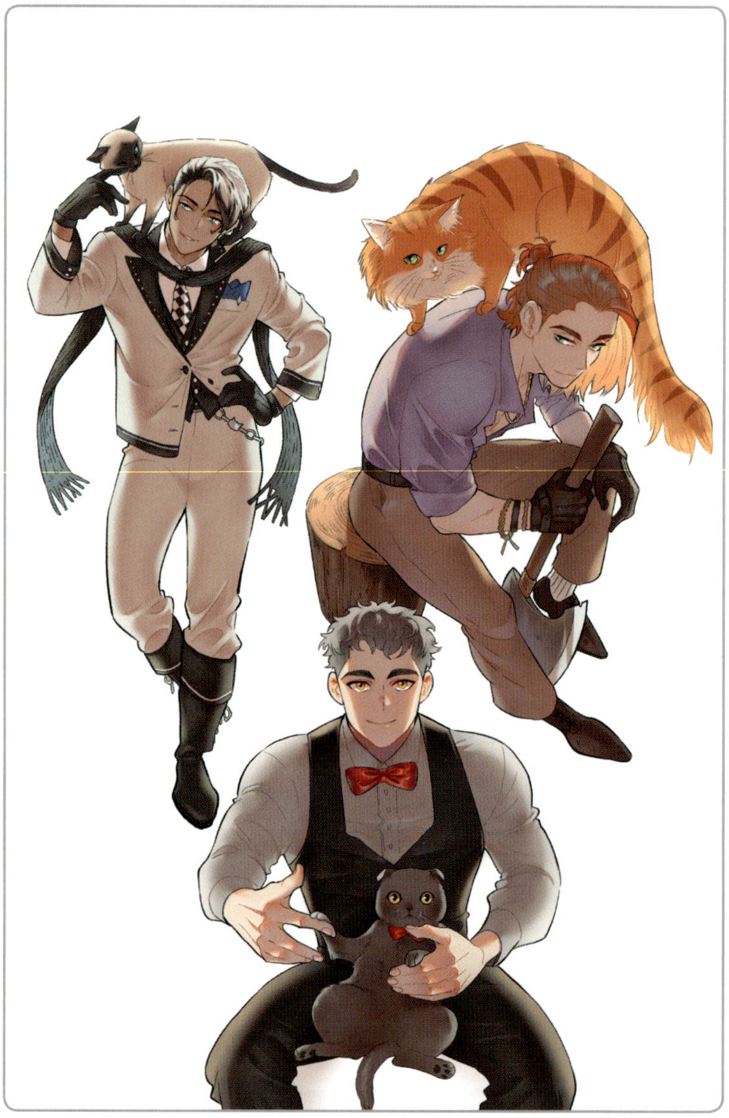

Paint in reflections, soften forms, and color in the line work

## ARTIST TIP

There are many different approaches you can take when coloring and rendering. My artwork receives much more engagement on Instagram when I leave it as simple base-colored drawings with line work, so this is what I post. However, there is no rule stating that you need keep the line work when creating an anime-style character. Experiment to see which approach and style you prefer.

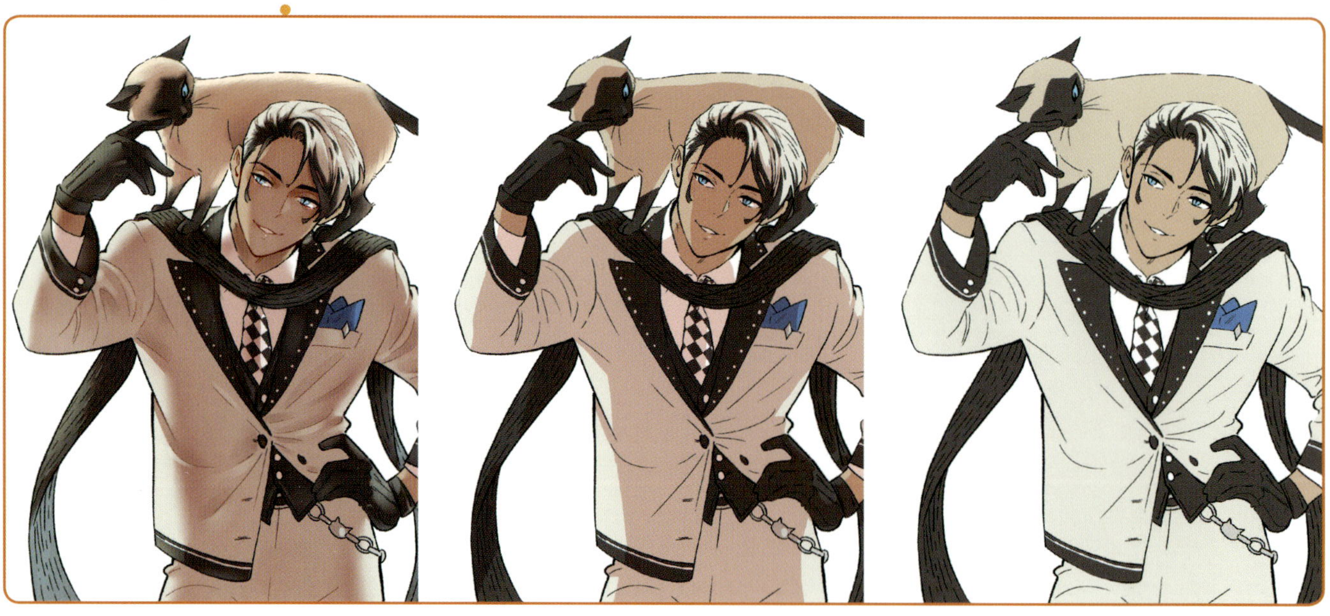

**22** Though it's fine to leave the background plain when creating simple character collages, I usually add uncomplicated colors and shapes to create visual interest. Here I wish to add some elements that fit with each character and their cat. I sketch opulent chandeliers for the Siamese cat and a forest scene for the Norwegian Forest cat. For the Scottish Fold I draw a blackjack table to support the casino concept. As the backlight is warm and bright, I use yellow for the background of all three characters, which helps to unify the illustration. The green of the blackjack table and forest adds slight contrast and feels more interesting than the violet tones I often use.

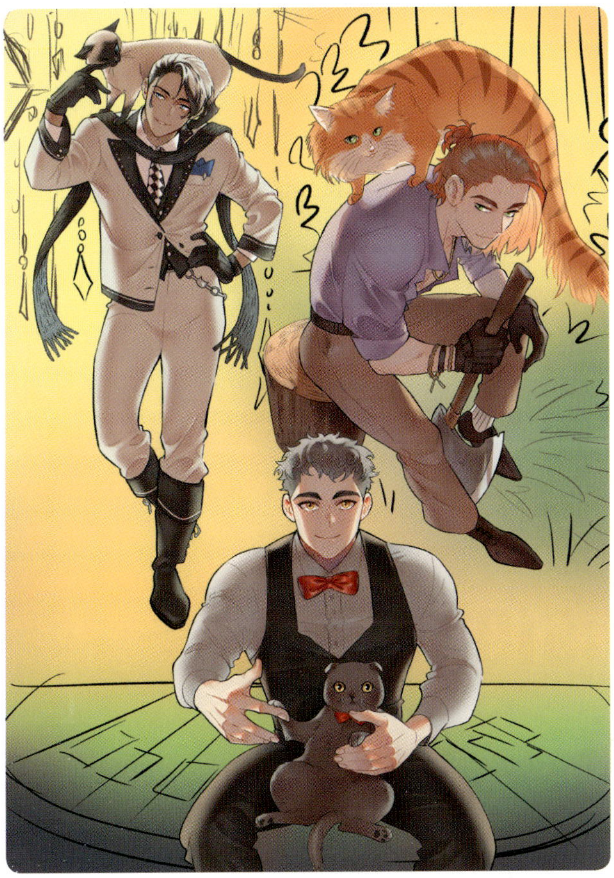

Consider adding a background to further tell your characters' stories

**23** Make good use of references when drawing and rendering your background. Don't be afraid to search out visual information that will enrich your illustration. I look up images of blackjack tables, as I've never seen one in real life, and research forest sunsets to help me choose colors for the Norwegian Forest cat's environment. On noticing that the perspectives of each character don't quite match, I add a checkered floor to help unify the image. While it would have been better to have spotted this error earlier in the process, there is often a way to fix such oversights.

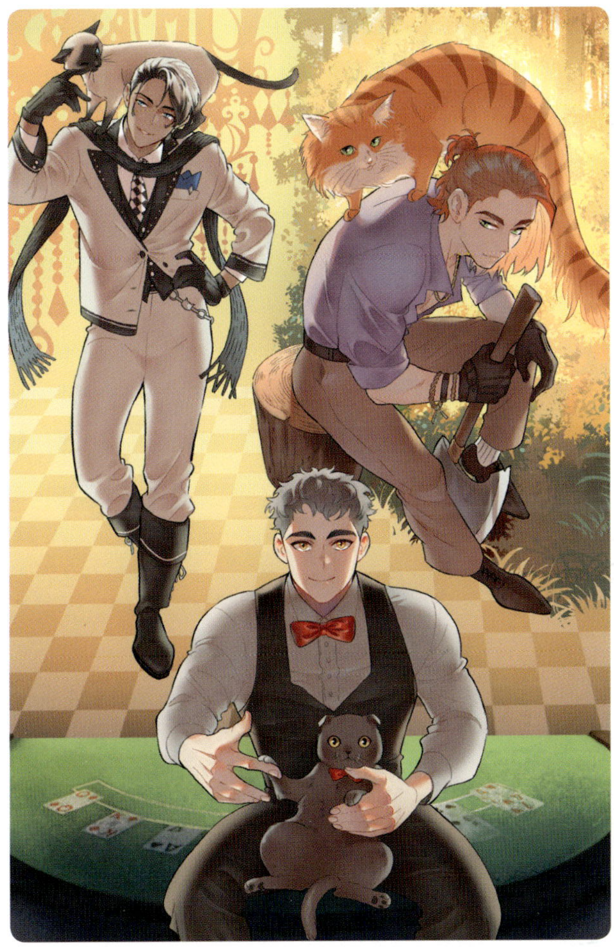

Use references to create an engaging background for your characters

**24** Take a step back and view your illustration as a whole to work out what final touches are needed. I add some highlights, color in more of the line work, and strengthen the light. I also add Overlay layers to create more warmth and saturation around the characters' outlines, which makes them stand out from the background. Avoid introducing too many details that will distract from your focal point. Though this illustration has numerous points of interest, which does make it look quite busy, the characters' faces and the cats are strong enough to capture the viewer's attention. Artists often make their character's face the focal point in an illustration, as humans are wired to automatically search out faces, but it can also be interesting to choose a completely different focal point for your artwork.

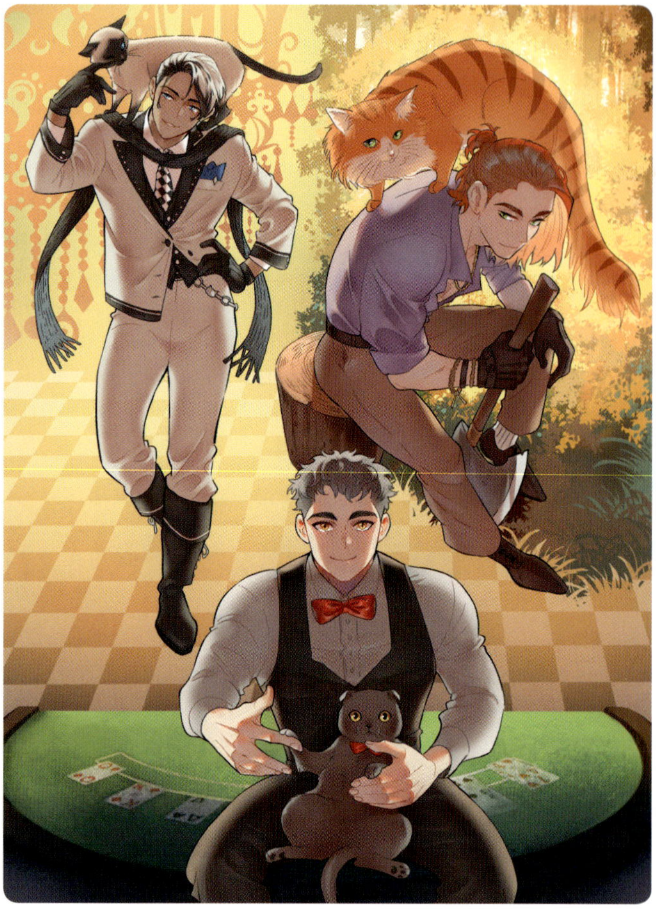

Adding final touches, such as highlights and digital effects, to make the characters "pop"

# CONCLUSION

The process of creating this illustration has taught me many new things. Using references as a guide, I learned how to render and shade suits, including how to create realistic folds in the fabric. Spotting a small mistake with the perspective has inspired me to use a single perspective grid for my next character collage to more effectively unify the illustration as a whole. And I now know why my neighbor's Norwegian Forest cat can go outside in any weather... waterproof fur!

Don't worry if this rendered way of painting is not your style. Try the simpler cel-shading approach popular in a lot of anime-inspired art, or simply finish at the base colors. This will allow you to spend more time fine-tuning the anatomy and gesture of the characters instead. While I am known for drawing very clean line art, you can experiment with messier lines, or even lineless drawings as well. There are many stylistic paths open to you; feel free to explore until you find the one that's right for you. View every illustration and character design as a learning experience toward finding your own style and preferred way of working.

I hope these gentlemen and their cats will pique my followers' interest. If the illustration receives a good amount of engagement on social media, I may choose to expand these characters and create a story for them. Developing stories is central to my artwork and brand as an anime-style artist.

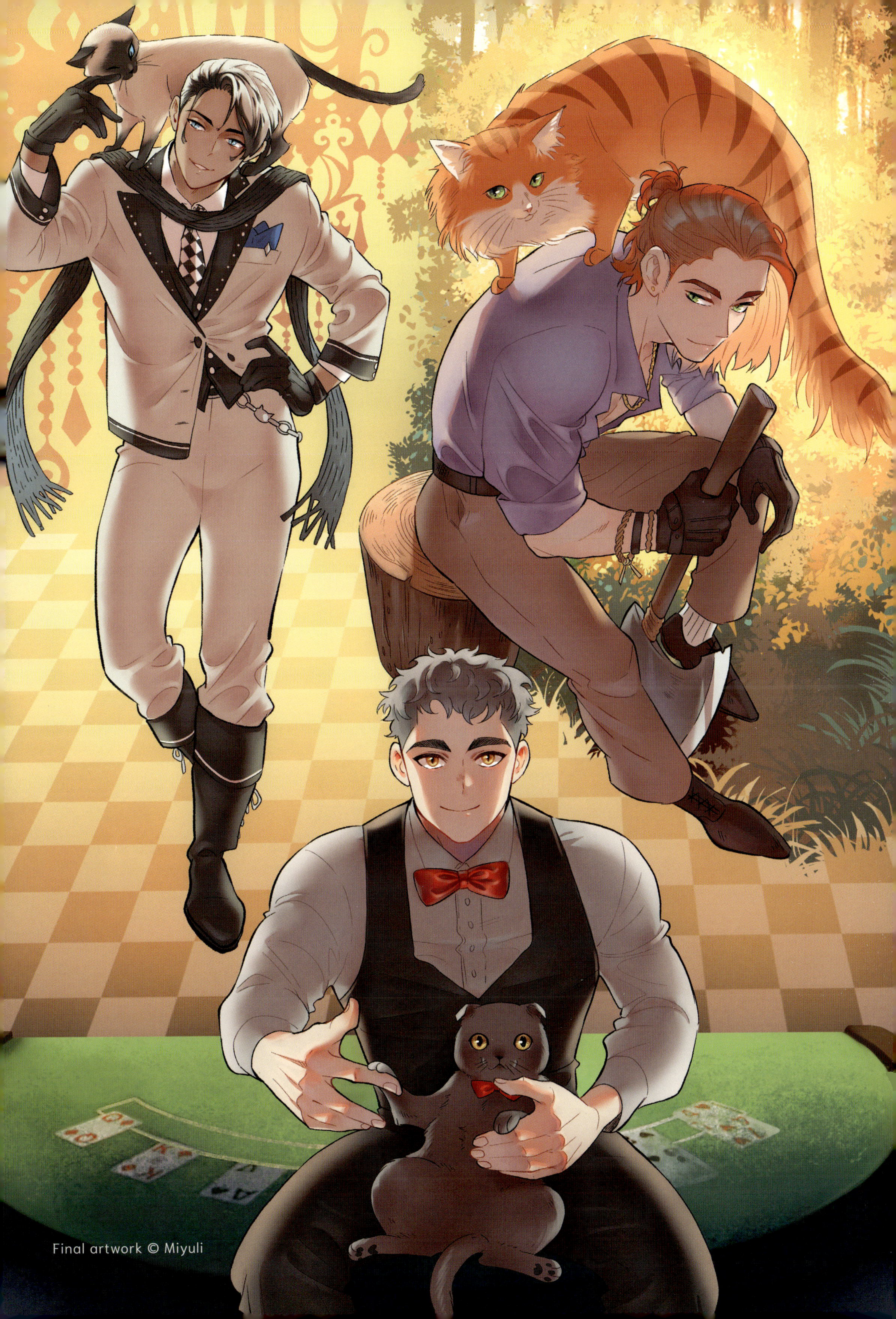

Final artwork © Miyuli

# SIMONE FERRI

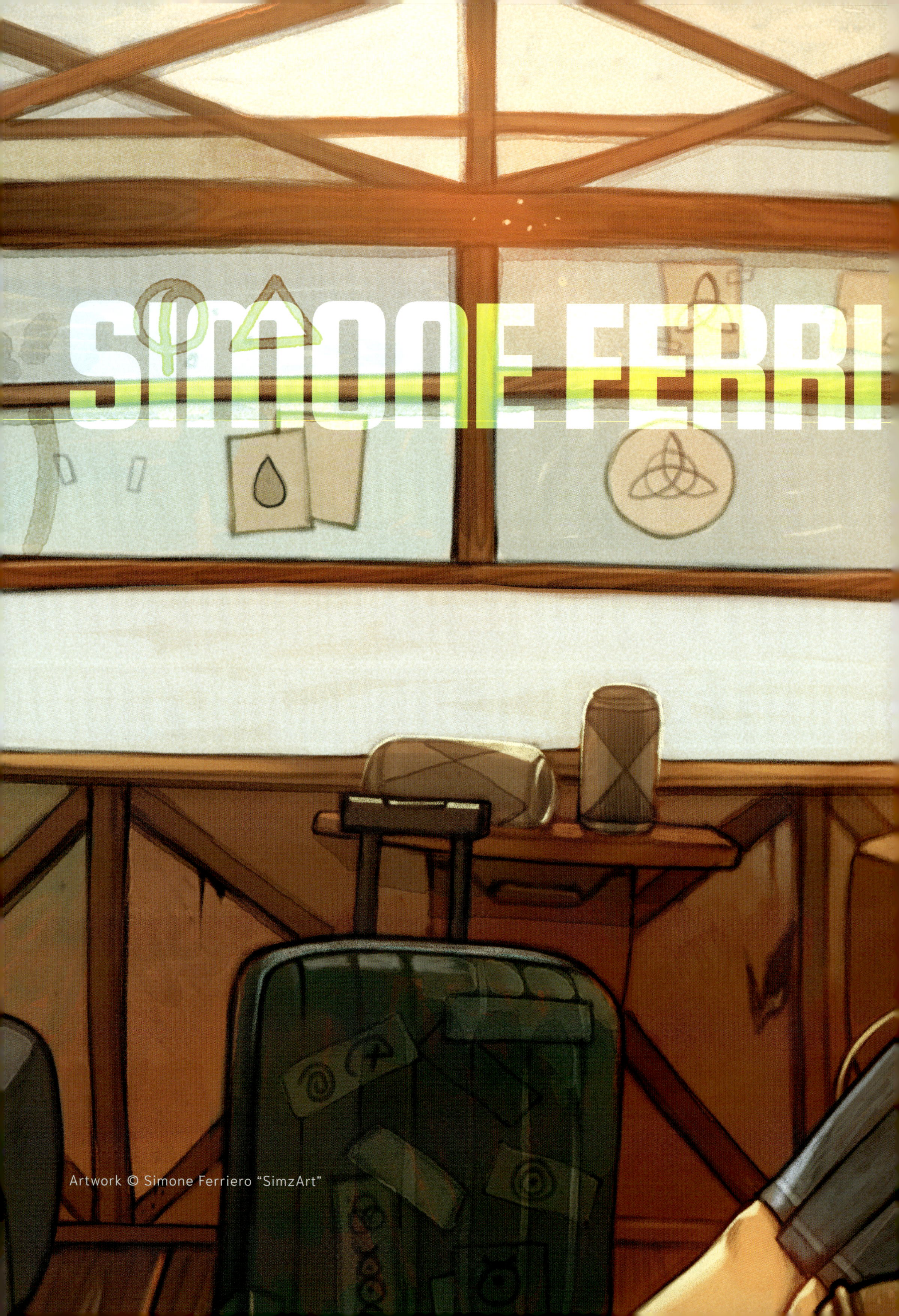

Artwork © Simone Ferriero "SimzArt"

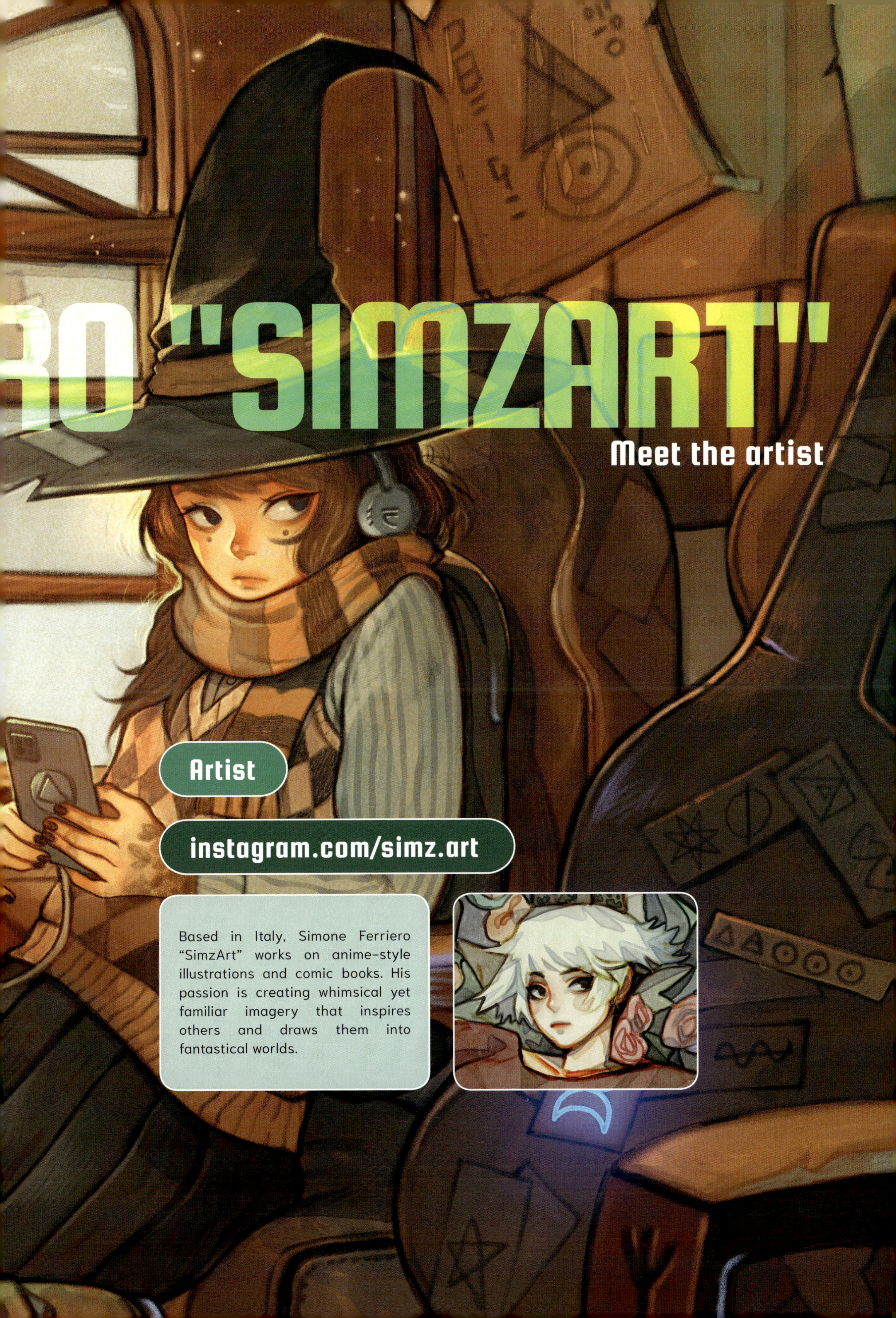

# RO "SIMZART"

## Meet the artist

**Artist**

**instagram.com/simz.art**

Based in Italy, Simone Ferriero "SimzArt" works on anime-style illustrations and comic books. His passion is creating whimsical yet familiar imagery that inspires others and draws them into fantastical worlds.

# CASE STUDY



## INFLUENCES, MOTIVATIONS, TRAINING

I've loved drawing since I was very young and spent the entirety of my childhood making artwork. Over the years I have been influenced by many art styles, with anime and manga having a great impact on my sense of aesthetic, especially during my teenage years. Some of my biggest anime and manga influences include Kentaro Miura, Eiichiro Oda, Akira Toriyama, and Masashi Kishimoto. The idea of working on a project to create stories and images that touch millions of people has always been a great leitmotif, or recurring theme or motif, for me.

While I have always been naturally inclined toward creative work, after high school I was unsure which path to follow. Though I went on to study engineering for a few years, I dreamed of pursuing a career in the creative industries and finally decided to follow my ambitions and enroll at an art school. I graduated from Accademia delle Belle Arti (fine art school) and began my anime-style art career in my mid-twenties. Though I began by undertaking work for companies and private customers, I soon realized I would prefer to work on my own projects where I would be free from following someone else's rules and artistic guidelines. It was at this point that I decided to embark on my freelance career.

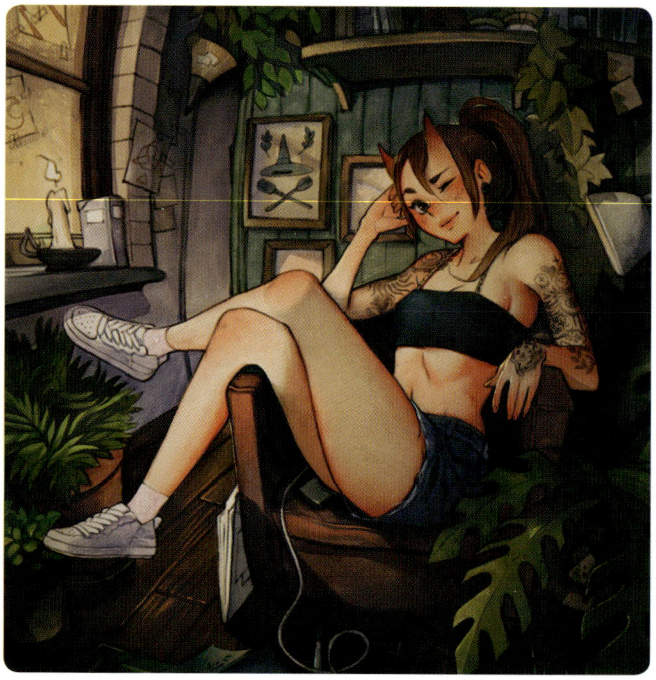

*Wink* – I have always enjoyed drawing characters in cozy, relaxing environments

### Studies

I enrolled in art school in Italy during my twenties, studying new technologies applied to art. Before that, I had mostly worked in graphic design, digital photography, digital video, and interactive art installation. The Accademia delle Belle Arti had a more formal and classical footprint, allowing me to study modern and contemporary art history. Throughout the course I had several mentors (local artists and professors) who opened my mind to the different approaches to making art. While this knowledge was not oriented toward illustration in particular, it helped me to develop the right mindset for when I began my career.

The internet has also provided an invaluable source of knowledge. I'm always impressed by the array of creative opportunities it provides, both in terms of learning and of reaching out to fellow artists. I continue to use it as a tool to fuel my studies and growth as an artist.

### Finding inspiration

I draw inspiration from my surroundings and everyday occurrences. With a love of photography, I often take photographs or sketch subjects that inspire me. My current artwork depicts calm, slice-of-life situations in my illustrative anime style. I love the idea of inviting the viewer to dive into a scene and experience a taste of a different life.

I also enjoy going to museums, galleries, and exhibitions where I can admire the work of historical and contemporary artists and try to learn from them. The internet is another big source of inspiration. My aim is to try to draw from these sources in an unconventional way, always trying to break the rules without being constrained by canonical techniques.

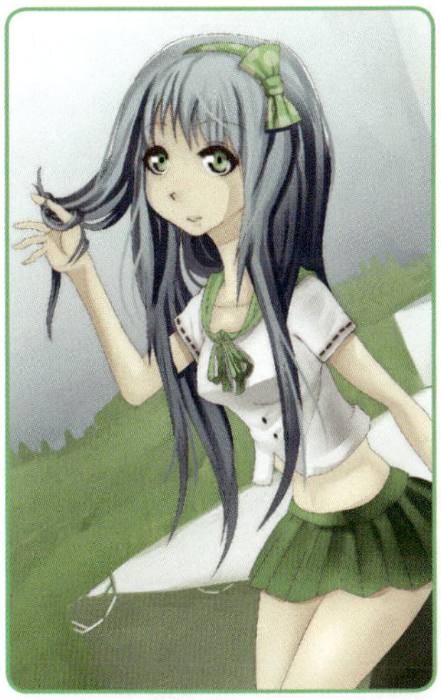

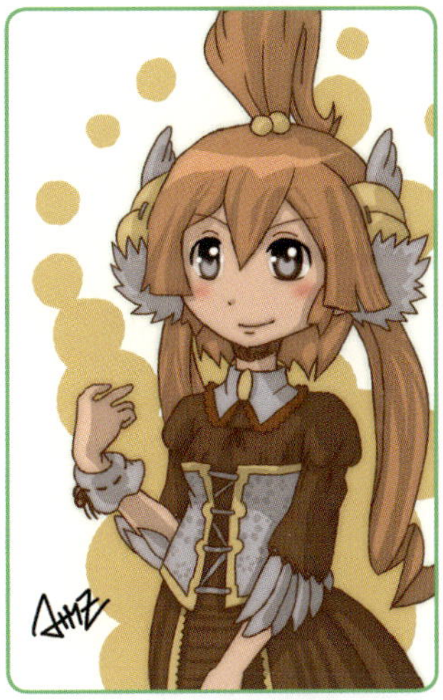

Early artwork created in 2011 when I was in art college and attempting digital painting for the first time

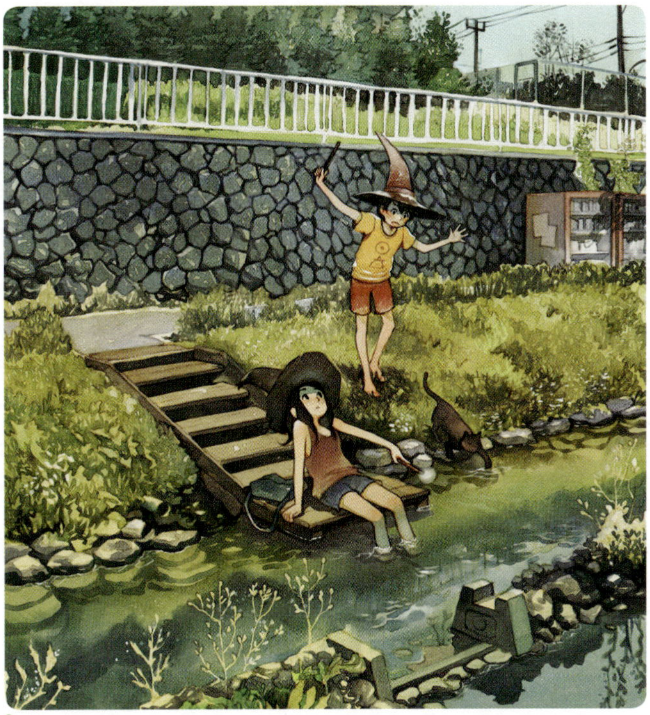

*River* – I developed custom brushes and textures in order to achieve this watercolor-inspired look

## Chosen imagery

Creating is an intrinsic part of life. I draw whenever I get the chance, and I feel like something is missing when I don't engage in this practice. The imagery I create and subjects I bring to life stem from what inspires me in the moment.

Recently I have been developing a series of illustrations featuring young witches, as I have always been fascinated by the lore and imagery surrounding witchcraft. It also fits with my love of capturing everyday situations with a slight twist, giving my illustrations a *punctum* (a sensory and subjective effect on the viewer), to quote Roland Barthes. I'm interested in pairing the sense of belonging created by a realistic or recognizable scene with an unsettling and slightly uncomfortable magical element that disturbs the perfection. My goal is to provide the viewer with a glimpse into a magical life that could be theirs and, in some way, already is.

To create work that stays true to my vision, I try to block out the background noise of everyday life to allow me to channel what's on the inside. While it's easy to create an image that follows a set formula or technique, you can always tell when the soul is missing from a piece of artwork. I'm happy to explore any subject or point of view, but the core of every illustration must remain raw and simple to allow the viewer the opportunity to interpret and inhabit it in their own way.

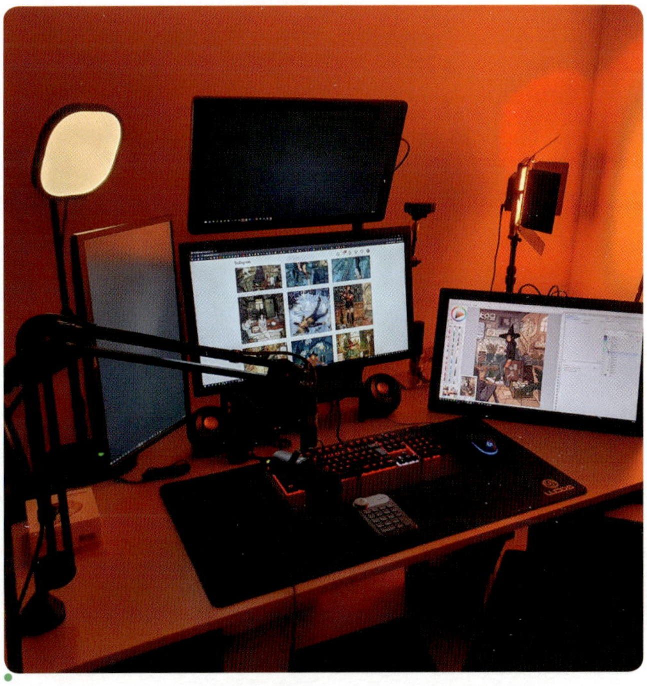

My current workspace

## Tools & media

A simple pencil and paper are my favorite tools. It's where my journey as an artist began and allows me to do what I love. Drawing lines and shapes is my favorite part of every illustration. Even when working digitally on a graphic tablet, I always try to instill my illustrations with a feeling of pencil and paper. I have also used watercolors and ink in the past, both of which still influence my digital work today. While it took me a long time to learn how to emulate traditional media using digital software, over the past couple of years I have been developing a digital painting technique that is strongly inspired by watercolors.

Experimentation is really important. I never settle! Even when I feel like the tools I've created in a graphics program are good, I will keep improving them to give myself more options. While I don't have a formula for success, thinking outside of the box as much as possible will always produce creative results.

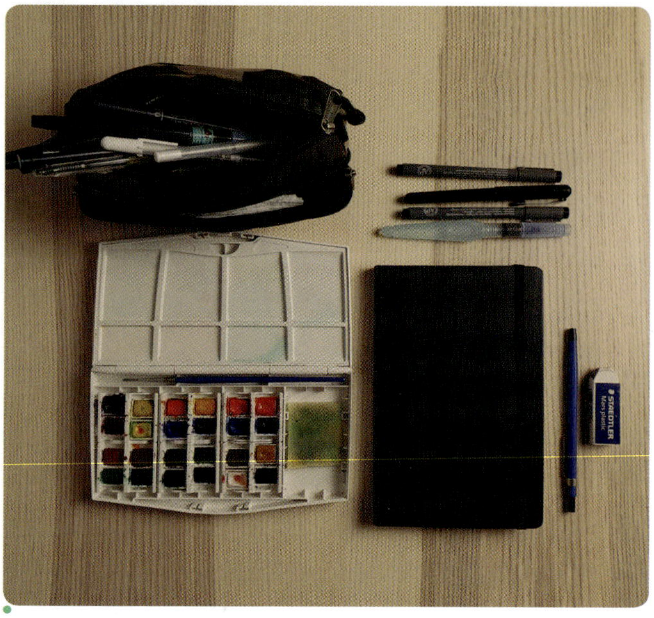

I like to take my go-to toolkit of watercolors, ink, and pencils everywhere I go

# INDUSTRY EXPERIENCE

The process of turning my artistic practice into a business has been one of the most complicated aspects of the job, but this is not the same for every artist. While I have always loved making art, I never had a solid plan for exactly how to turn this passion into a source of income. I knew that in order to keep working solely on my art, I needed to turn it into a profitable business and reach as many people as possible with it.

I made the decision not to restrict myself to small commissioning circles whose projects would take up all of my time and prevent me from creating work for my own personal portfolio. Instead I chose to focus on building an online presence and networking with as many creative communities as possible. The growth of my social media has provided exponentially more opportunities to create an income, and I have been able to work on my own content at the same time.

## Freelance work

Since I launched my freelance art career and created my social-media accounts, I have had the chance to collaborate with several different brands and companies. I intend to keep this work freelance, rather than become an employee, as this allows me the freedom to adapt different jobs to my personal needs and projects. I try to avoid commissions that push me toward aspects of the job that I'm not interested in. Even when working on a commission, I like to make the type of content I would create myself anyway.

Balancing commissioned and personal work is not always easy, but I will usually accept commissions that give me the opportunity to network with new communities, as that ultimately leads to new followers and helps my own content creation.

# Recognition

There have been many moments over the past few years that have made me feel proud of what I have achieved so far. For example, when popular artists or brands have followed me online, contacted me in private, or featured my work on their platforms. While none of these moments dramatically changed my life, each gave me an enormous boost in popularity and the exposure I needed to keep my art business going.

There are several illustrations that I class as milestones. These are the ones that went viral to the point that I received thousands of comments across my different social platforms, as well as countless job offers. One such illustration was featured at the top of Reddit's "/r/all" feed of popular posts. Holding prime position on such a popular website for hours is no easy feat. It made me realize that whatever I was doing was not just good enough, but was proving popular with a huge number of people.

My piece *Final Touches* received great recognition across multiple online platforms, with over 200,000 likes and 35,000 retweets in the space of a few hours, and over seven million impressions alone. Another illustration that went viral is *Morning Coffee*, which received 282,000 likes, 40,000 retweets, and over ten million impressions overall. When I consider what made these two illustrations so popular, I've concluded that it's the attention to detail in the relatable slice-of-life scenes, along with the presence of my signature ghost cats. Many people have had beloved pets that have passed away, and based on the comments and messages I received, they find the concept comforting.

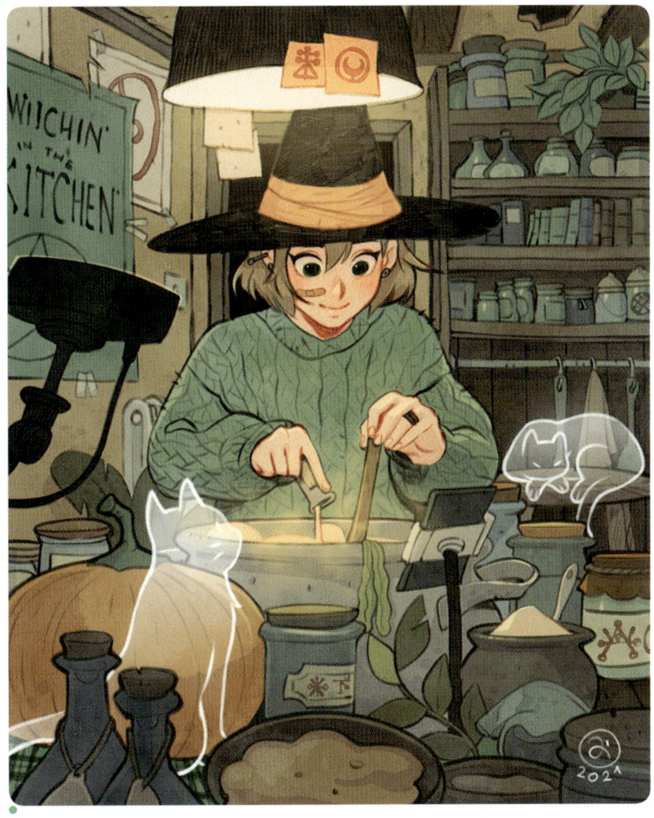

*Final Touches* – a witch brewing a potion while streaming the process is a classic concept reinterpretation

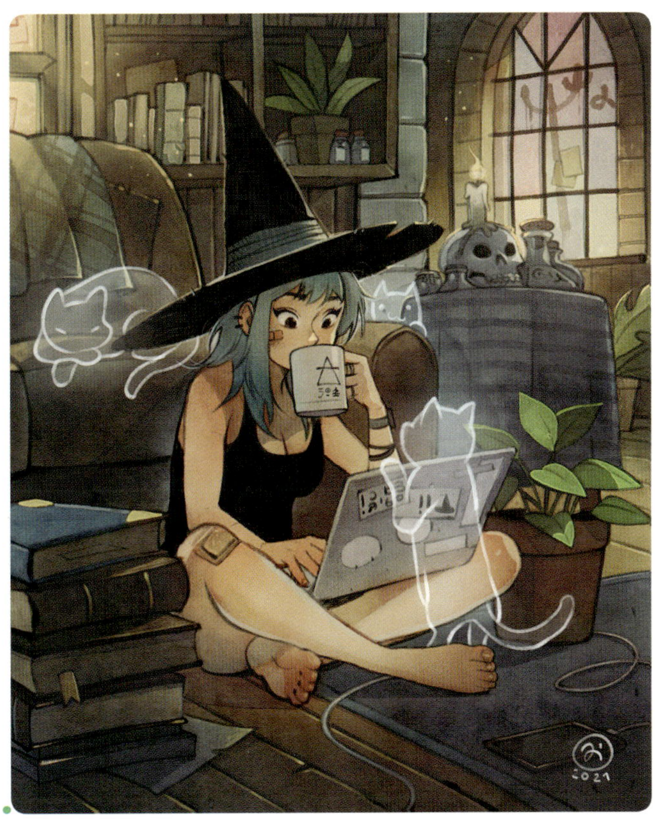

*Morning Coffee* – slice-of-life scenes with a magical twist often prove popular with my followers

Another memorable moment was the creation of my Webtoon Original comic, *Falling in the Blue*. The comic was a natural evolution of a series of illustrations that I created between 2018 and 2019, including a trio of characters called Lake, Willow, and Memi, a giant Kiwi bird. The theme was travel and the characters were always finding themselves in different situations and locations as they traveled across the universe.

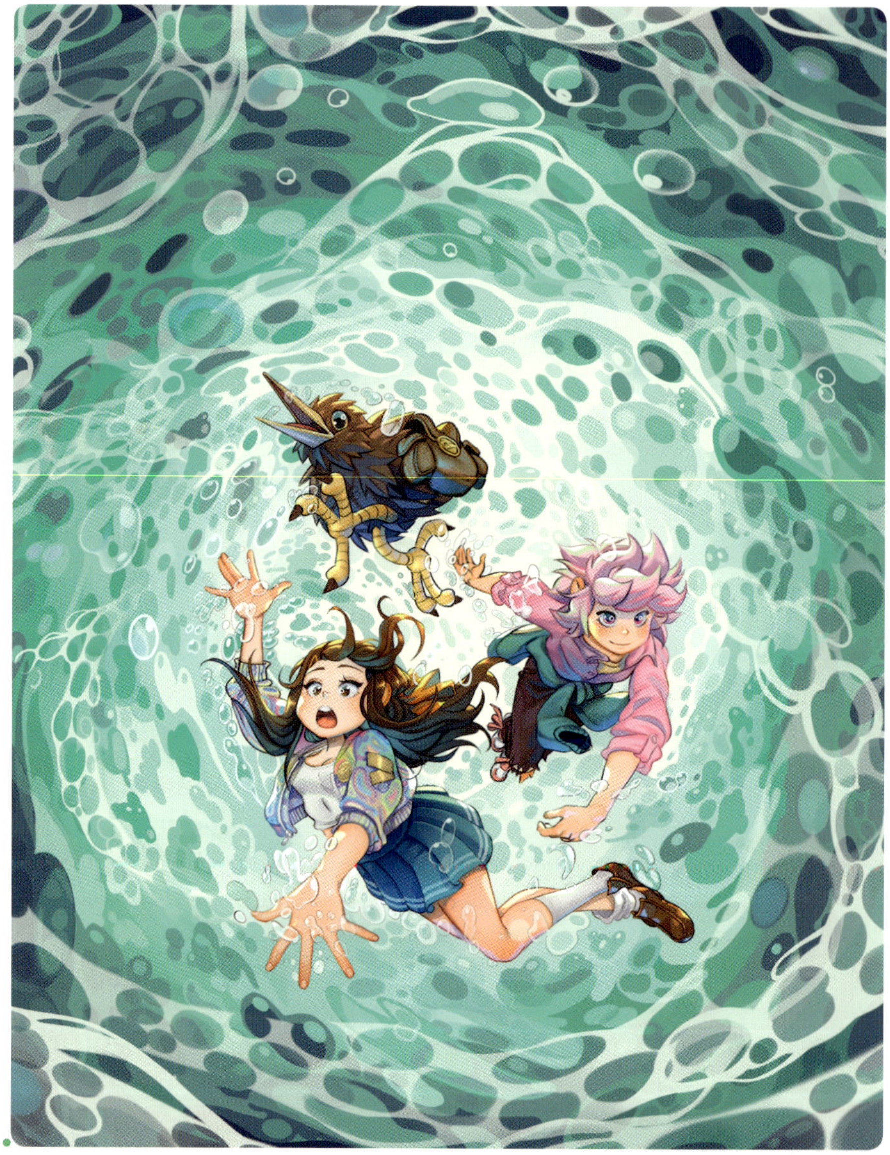

*Falling in the Blue*, 2019 – this is the cover image used for the pilot episode of my Webtoon Original, which I presented to different publishers

# DEVELOPING YOUR STYLE

Drawing has always come naturally to me. I've never tried to force a certain style, though when I was younger I tried to learn by imitating other artists. I worked on portraiture and human figures when I first started my social-media accounts, as well as creating fan art. I experimented with many different styles and techniques, and consequently my artwork has been through many phases, all of which still influence the content I create today.

It's impossible for me to say what my biggest influence or inspiration has been, or how much is innate or acquired taste. I'm inspired by countless visual inputs and ideas from different fields, including anime and manga. I love looking at the work of fellow anime-style artists and feeling inspired by their ideas. I try not to compare my work to that of other artists, however, and strive to avoid trends and industry standards where possible.

## The anime & manga style

I'm a big fan of the anime and manga masters known for creating some of the most iconic imagery in the world. I find their work hugely inspirational, but much of the art made by Japanese and Korean artists and mangakas is influenced by their culture and traditions, which means there may be elements to which viewers living in Western countries cannot easily relate. What we can do is look at the way these masters take inspiration from their surroundings, and apply that to our own style to create very personal artwork.

When beginning your journey into anime art style, it can also help to study the practical information, such as how anime and manga art simplifies anatomy and other elements. But be wary, because although this will help you to recreate classic cartoonlike characters, starting from this point could potentially affect your ability to draw the basics. Take the time to study a real-life, realistic approach to drawing before diving into the more stylized anime look, which will prove much easier to achieve once you have mastered a more complex representation of reality.

## Evolution of style

I am best known for my digital watercolor anime-style artwork. This has become my signature style over the years and it has been enjoyable yet challenging to continue developing it. I have moved further and further away from preconceived rules and constructs to allow my personality to emerge through my artwork. I try to embrace imperfections, transforming them instead of hiding them away.

My style changes constantly. If you were to compare my current illustrations to my early work, you would notice significant differences. I enjoy experimenting with varying styles and techniques, while staying within my comfort zone. When approaching a new project, I enjoy exploring a specific style and pushing its limits, but also try to avoid reinventing the wheel. I like the idea of using the tools and techniques I've learned over the years as notes to compose a different melody, or style, every time.

*Checking Socials* is a good example of my current style, as it includes several of my trademark stylistic elements. The young witch character is depicted in a moment of relaxation in a slice-of-life scene, surrounding by my signature ghost cats. The background shows a relatable modern environment, combined with more traditional architectural elements, such as the tall arched window with the stained glass. This contrast between modern and traditional is the epitome of the style I am currently developing.

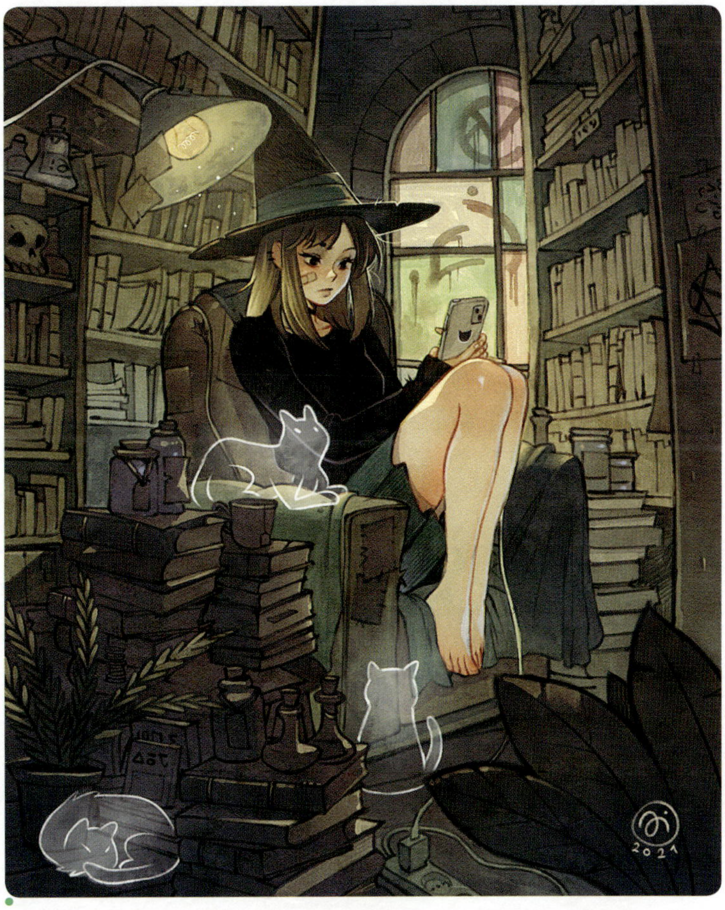

*Checking Socials* – as well as the signature young witch and ghost cats, my current style can be recognized through the juxtaposition of modern and traditional elements

## Personal style in the commercial world

I often hear artists complaining that the artwork they are required to make for their job is completely different from what they create in their free time. I experienced this frustration until I made the decision to stop accepting jobs that didn't fit with the style of artwork I enjoy creating. This was challenging to begin with, as I had to refuse many commercial opportunities, but long-term it has meant I have never had to worry about maintaining a particular style – I simply have to be myself. While this decision came with some risk and may not be feasible for every artist, I found it allowed me to achieve inner peace between my commercial and personal work.

## Pivotal stylistic moments

There have been several instances where my style has evolved due to changes I have made to my artistic process. The three most important developments have been the use of backgrounds, a more traditional-looking painting technique (digital watercolors), and finally, the introduction of ghost animals and witches. The introduction of these elements has enabled me to create a signature anime style that is easily recognizable and relatable.

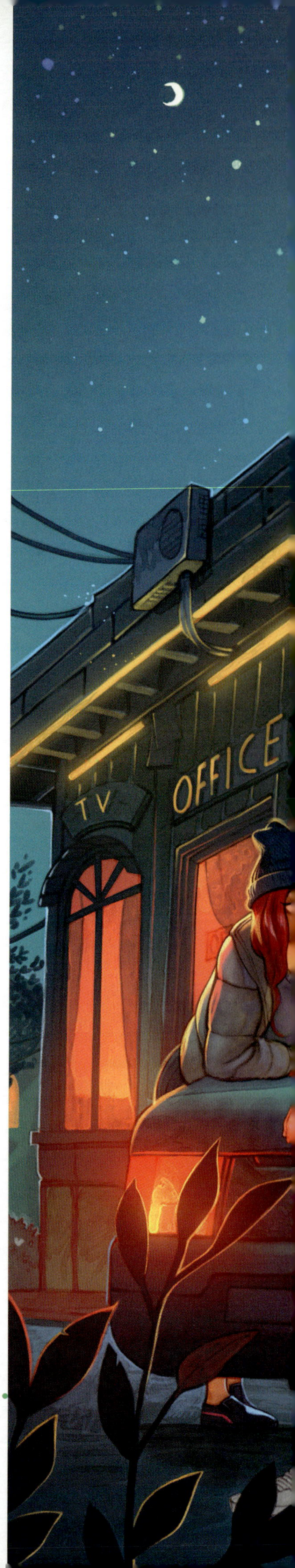


*Motel* – a group of witches traveling across the country stop for the night in a motel

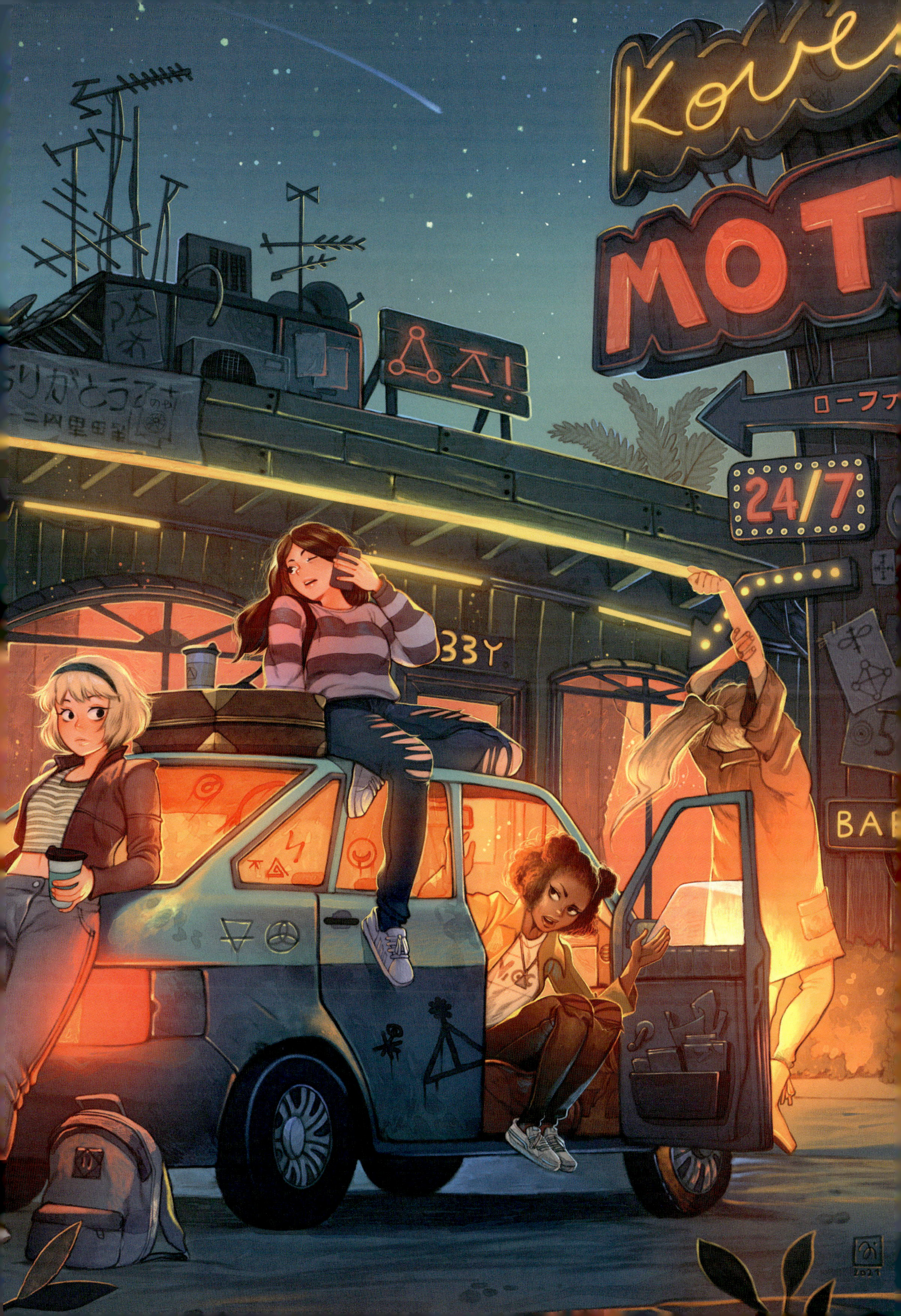

Kove
MOT
ローファ
24/7
33Y
BA
2021

## Stylistic evolution

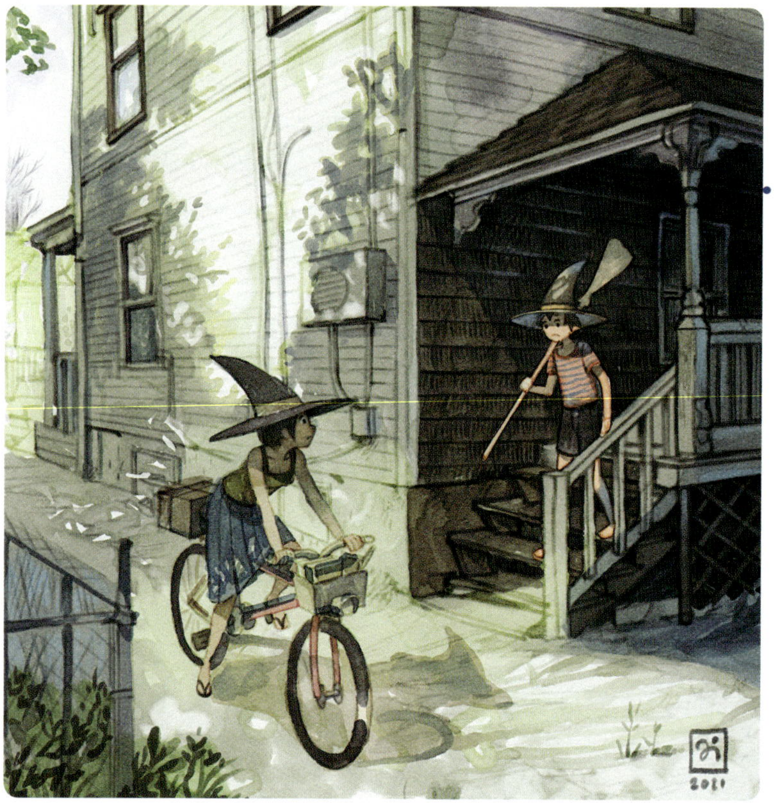

*Summer Adventures*, May 2021

On a hot summer's day, two characters are ready for an adventure. The challenge with this image was to create a watercolor look using digital software. I also experimented with a high-key light, a change from my usual indoor scenes. I make it a priority to create a set of tools and techniques that allow me to depict any type of situation.

*Swamp*, June 2021

This piece continues the previous theme, but experiments with different textures and surfaces. I wanted to paint water, which can prove challenging to capture realistically. Painting two characters in a swamp on a rainy day seemed like the ultimate test for the style I'm developing.

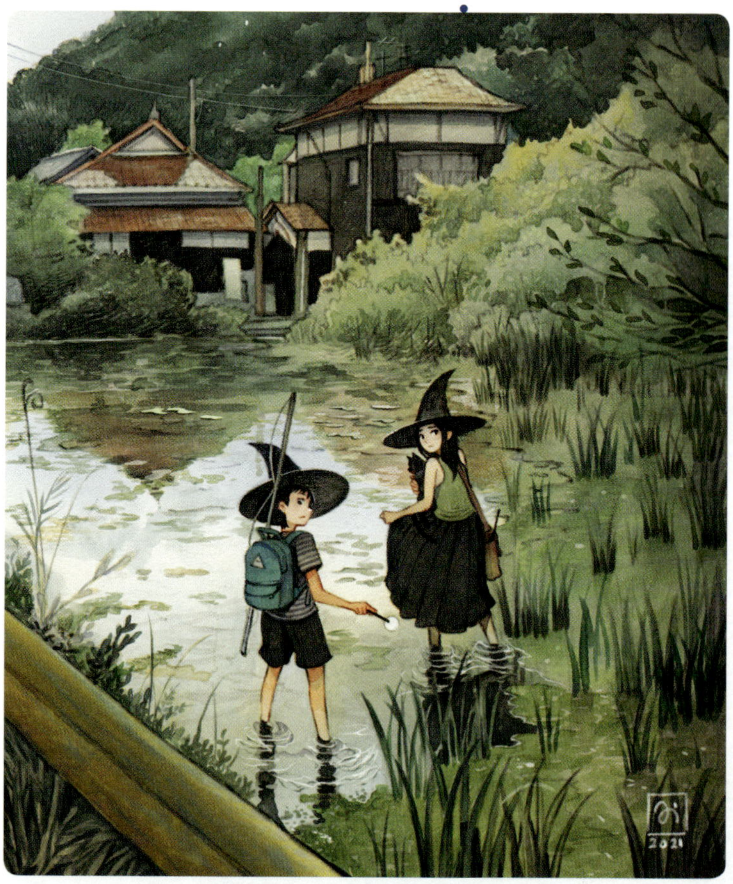

*Cats*, September 2021

A witch reads a book on the stairs, surrounded by her ghost cats. I wanted to investigate what would happen if I replaced realistic colors with a more creative monochrome look. This illustration also represents a milestone, as it was the first time I added my ghost cats, whose presence have brought a new fuel to my creative process.

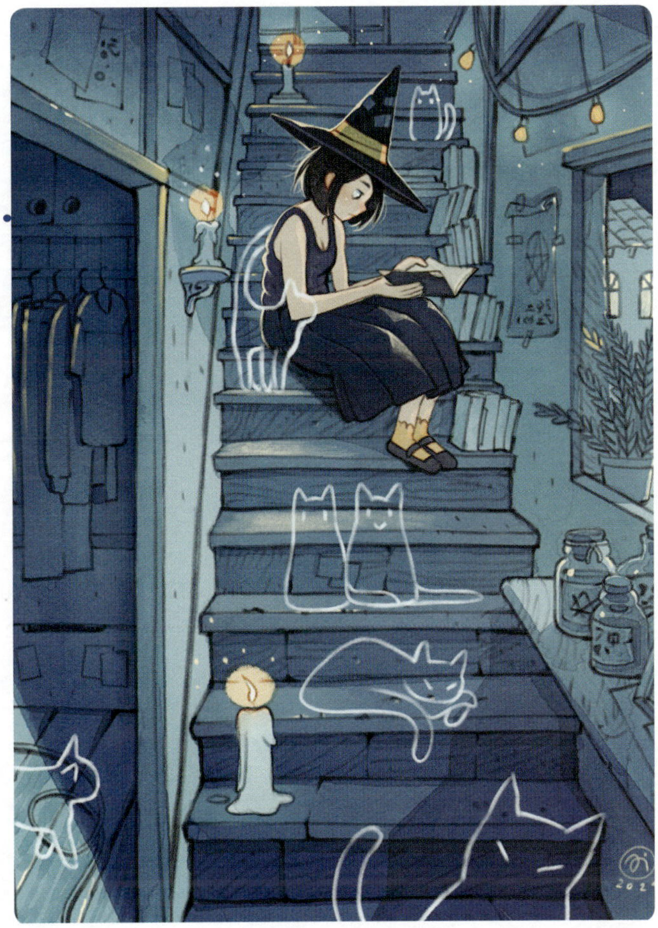

*Building Furniture*, November 2021

This represents an episode from my daily life that I was able to translate into the fantastical world of my artwork. I was able to combine everything I'd learned into one illustration, as well as introducing a different line art approach that is a slightly more dynamic and cartoonlike. Aside from the technical aspect of illustration, having a wide creative range is one of the most important skills for an artist to have.

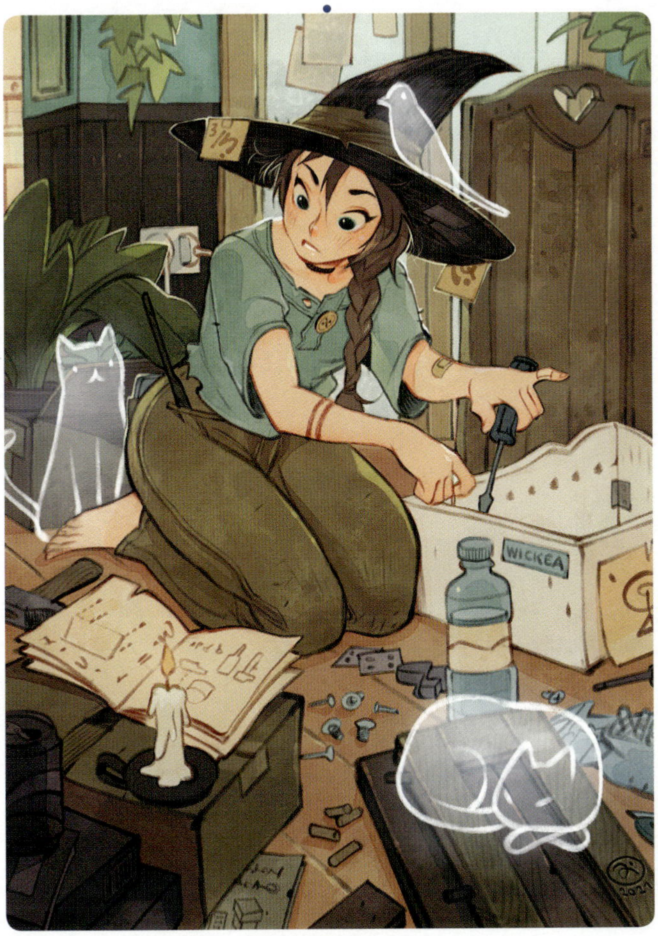


## External influences on style

I create my artwork using the tools, processes, and style I find most comfortable. I try to avoid obsessing over a certain topic for too long, however, especially when it comes to visual art. From time to time I like to look at what other artists are creating to gather new ideas and inspiration. Though finding a new artist or a style that I particularly enjoy can provide a huge boost in creativity, it can also polarize ideas for future work, so I try to keep moving forward to ensure I focus on my own content. While I accept that my style has its limits, the way that I express myself through my art is genuine and I've never felt limited by it. I am always seeking to improve and am not afraid to push out of my comfort zone.

Artists are often compared to one another. In order to make sense of what they see, people will associate certain elements of my work with something they already know. However, the majority of my followers like my style because they find it unique and personal to me.

# BUILDING YOUR BRAND

In one way or another, every artist whose work is identifiable is their own brand. When I first started my social-media accounts, I was aware that my content needed to be consistent in order for my artwork to be recognizable. My style has organically fluctuated and evolved over the years, however, in line with my changing beliefs and ambitions. Consistency of style is connected to self-discovery; the process of looking inward to determine who I am and what I want to create has had a huge impact on my creative decision-making. When I have a goal and direction, being consistent comes naturally.

Each of the illustrations I share on my social-media platforms tells a story. While this story can contain any number of fantastical possibilities, my priority is to keep it as close as possible to my real self, as I wish to avoid distancing my brand from the human behind it. I came up with the nickname "Simz" when I was younger, as an easy way to shorten my full name, Simone. Some friends started to call me by it, and so when I began posting on social media, I added Art at the end to create "SimzArt". Not only is it short and memorable, but this personal name was important in connecting me to my brand.

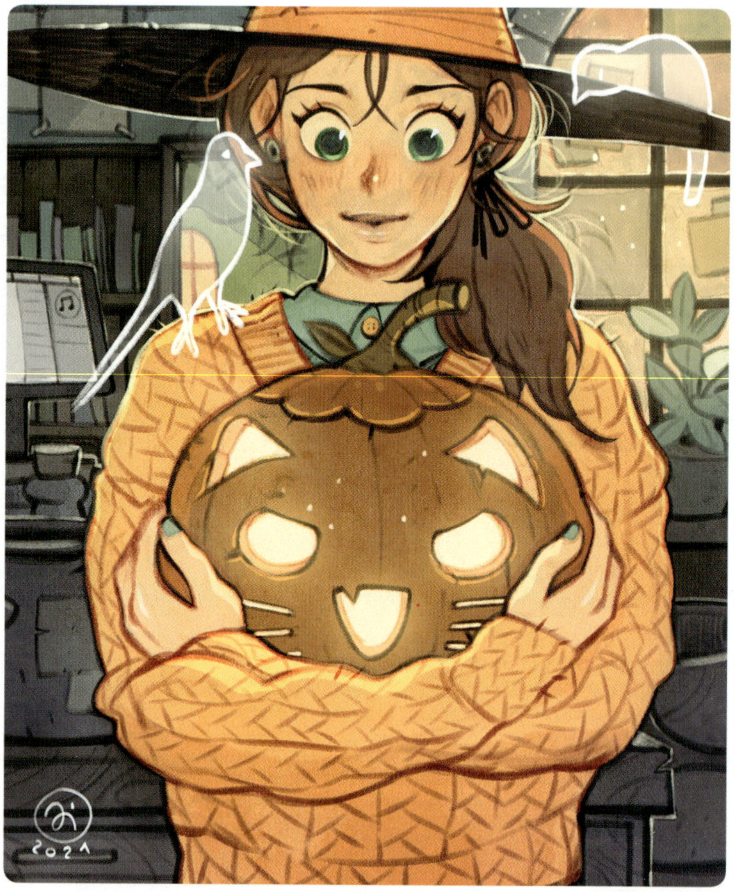

*Pumpkin Season* – the young witch character and ghost animals (in this case, birds) have become recognizable as my brand

## Memorable brands

There are many anime artists I admire, one of whom is Claire Belton, the creator of Pusheen. Through her simple yet iconic designs, she has created a brand that is extremely recognizable and unique. It's often thought that art production needs to be grand and complex in order to achieve success. Studying the success of Pusheen, however, has taught me that the core idea and heart we put into our artwork can have greater influence.

## Third-party assistance

Building my artistic brand by myself has required me to have a strict work ethic and to manage my time well. Whether working on commissions, collaborating with other brands, or building my online platform, I keep a list of all of my tasks to ensure I deliver them on time. I have considered consulting a third party to assist with my branding in the future, as this would likely provide more opportunities, but I am happy with how I have managed my brand so far.

## Online presence

I don't have a website and, thanks to my large following on social media, I haven't had an issue without one so far. I mostly use Instagram, Twitter, Tumblr, DeviantArt, Facebook, Patreon, Reddit, YouTube, and Twitch. I have also worked in partnership with Ko-fi and currently sell prints on Redbubble. I have found Instagram, Reddit, Twitter, and Facebook to be the most effective for reaching large audiences, while DeviantArt, Twitch, and Tumblr are useful for finding niche communities. Patreon, Ko-fi, and Redbubble provide helpful routes to creating an income, as well as ways to reward customers for their support. In addition, I have a YouTube channel, which I use to review art supplies. I plan to use it to post other content in the future and am curious to see how it will evolve.

I view my social-media platforms as an online portfolio, so I don't post content unrelated to my brand. This ensures they remain clean, focused, and professional. What people see is what they get. I try to stay as human as possible and I like the idea that anyone, individuals and companies alike, can easily contact me. Where possible, I prefer to create content that can be shared with my followers on social media. For this reason, I tend not to accept too much exclusive work that will prevent me from posting publicly for too long. As my online platforms are the way I grew my brand, it would not feel right to turn my back on them to focus on corporate work instead.

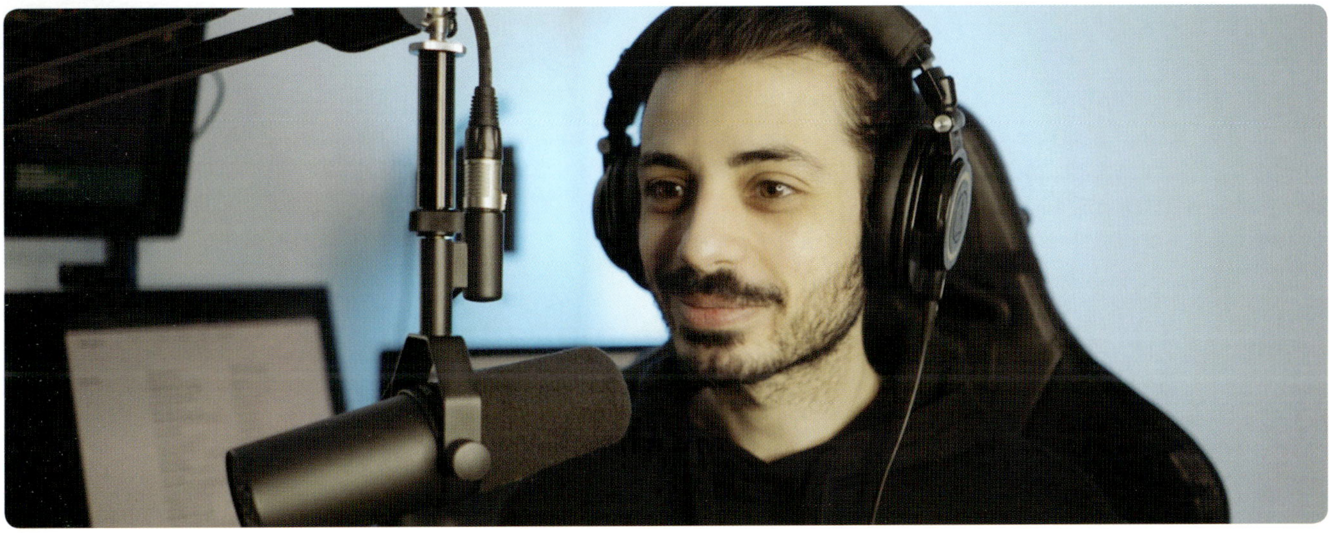

A screenshot from a video in which I am reviewing a pen tablet brand called Xencelabs on my YouTube channel

## Networking & cross-promotion

Networking has been incredibly important for my brand. While the priority is creating interesting artwork, coming up with good ideas, and having fun while doing it, possessing the right contacts has given me the opportunity to show the world that the anime-style content I create is a serious business. When one of my illustrations is associated with an important or professional company, brand, or platform, this has been beneficial for my brand, allowing me to network with even more companies, brands, and platforms.

## Marketing budget

I have never had a budget for marketing. While I tried paying for growth once when I was first starting out, and used a very small budget to promote an illustration, I soon realized that the audience I was able to reach was not even close to what was possible through people naturally sharing my work. I concluded that paying for views was not a viable solution for the growth of my brand. My process is very organic; my growth is a result of producing a high volume of artwork and people sharing it. Since the beginning I have relied heavily on word of mouth and this hasn't failed me yet. There is a certain joy in discovering an artist through word of mouth rather than being bombarded by adverts for their work, and this approach has been very important for my brand.

## Pricing & selling merchandise

Choosing which artwork to make into prints or products is usually fairly easy, as my followers let me know what they want to see. I often receive comments asking if I will sell a certain illustration as a print, if I would offer a tutorial, or turn it into a jigsaw puzzle. The number of requests and overall engagement determines which artwork I select. Working on such commercial choices requires a sacrifice of my creative time, so I try not to break from my personal work for more than a week at a time.

I currently sell my artwork on Redbubble, as I prefer to use a website that manages the selling and shipping process, even if this means they take a cut on the final earnings. In exchange, I only have to upload the artwork in high resolution and let them know how I want it to be printed. I currently sell my illustrations as a variety of different merchandise, including mouse mats, posters, art prints, stickers, photographic prints, jigsaw puzzles, phone covers, tote bags, and t-shirts.

How I price a print, product, freelance project, or commission typically depends on the client, the type of work involved, and the time taken to complete it. I have never been aggressive with self-promotion in order to sell my art, but hope that if someone likes what I'm creating, they will choose to support me. I created a Patreon account with different tiers for people who want a behind-the-scenes look at my creative process, a Ko-fi account for those who want to show their support through a direct donation or buying a commission, and Redbubble for fans who want to buy a print or merchandise.

If an artist wishes to turn their artwork into merchandise, I would recommend focusing on building a substantial portfolio first. After viewing your work, your audience will let you know which illustrations they would like to see as merchandise. Expecting people to buy your products before they are familiar with your artwork, solely based on advertising or other marketing tricks, is unlikely to prove as successful. From my experience, if you rush into selling merchandise you risk being underwhelmed by the uptake. This can affect your morale as you create new artwork, which should always be the priority. Be patient and wait until your followers ask you for products to buy.

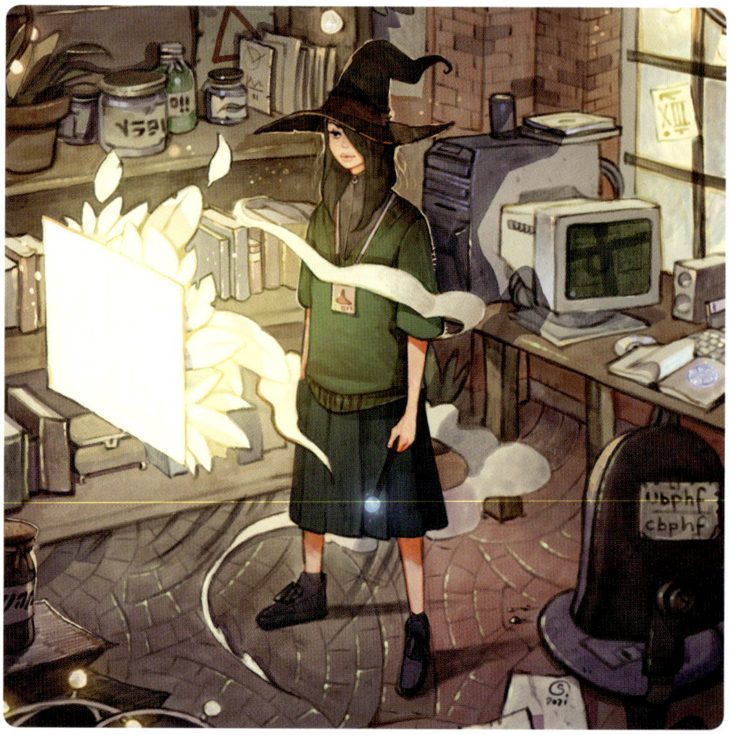

*Overgrowth* – a surreal box of light shines in the middle of the room

## Time management

Turning your art hobby into a business can be time-consuming. I am still working on the balance between time spent building my brand and time spent creating new artwork. I try not to accept too many commissions and business inquiries at the same time, even if it means losing some opportunities. I also make sure to set aside time to draw. Maintaining this equilibrium has allowed me to grow my business to where it is today.

While often overlooked by artists seeking to grow their business, it's important to schedule in time to work on your personal content, as well as to rest and switch off. Ensuring your mental health is in a good place should be a priority. Art should always be inspired, surprising, and creative, and nothing stifles the creative process more than being stressed, overworked, and forced to produce work to an overly strict deadline. It doesn't matter how many opportunities you're given; if your mind is not well-rested or in a healthy place, your artwork will suffer. Taking time to rest, get outside, pursue hobbies, and doodle is just as important as promptly replying to emails and messages.

Try splitting your time equally between working on your business and creating new content. Whether you can turn what has been created into business opportunities, or it was simply produced for fun, no time has been wasted.

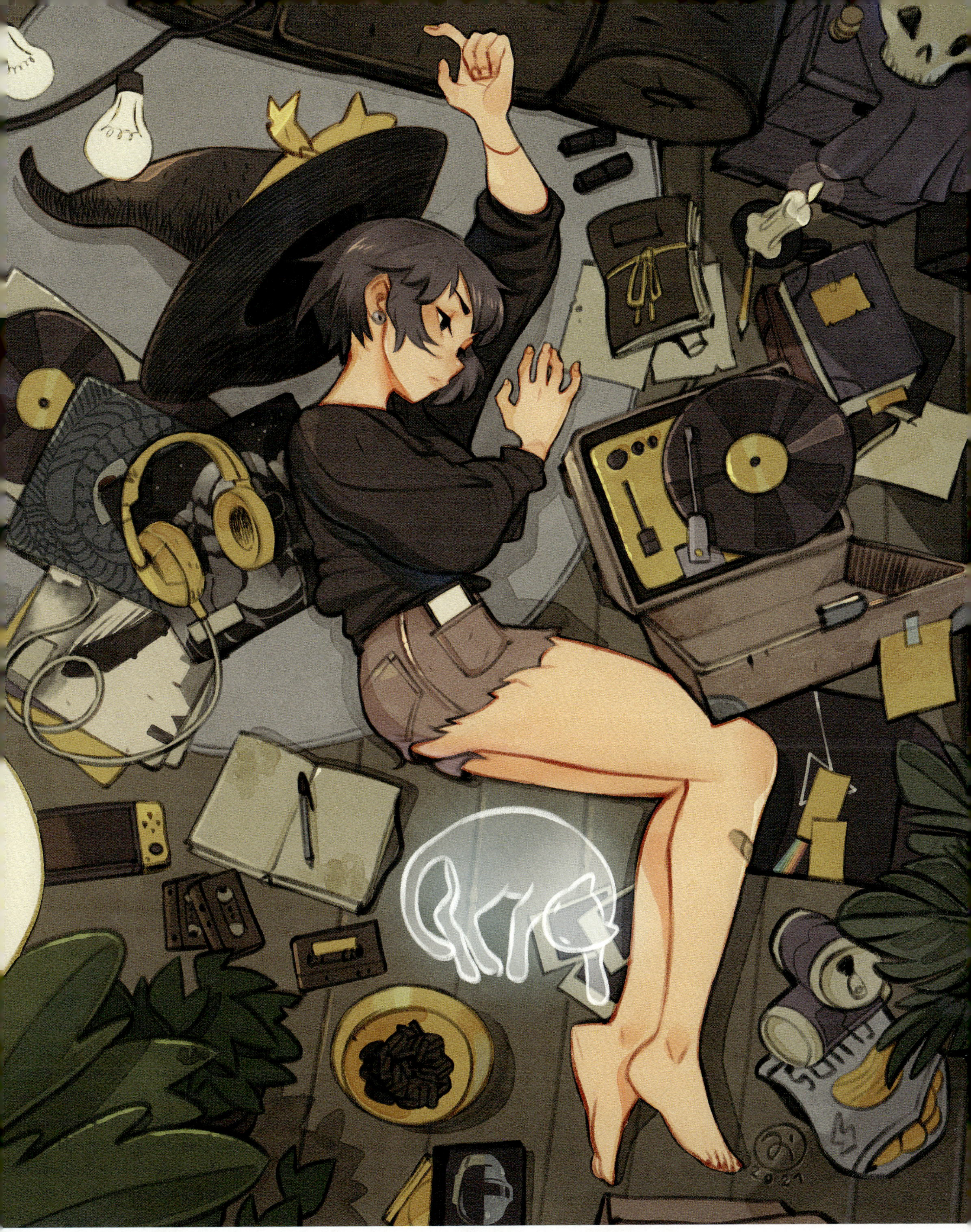

*Vinyl* – this illustration captures a relatable moment of relaxation as the character curls up, surrounded by her belongings

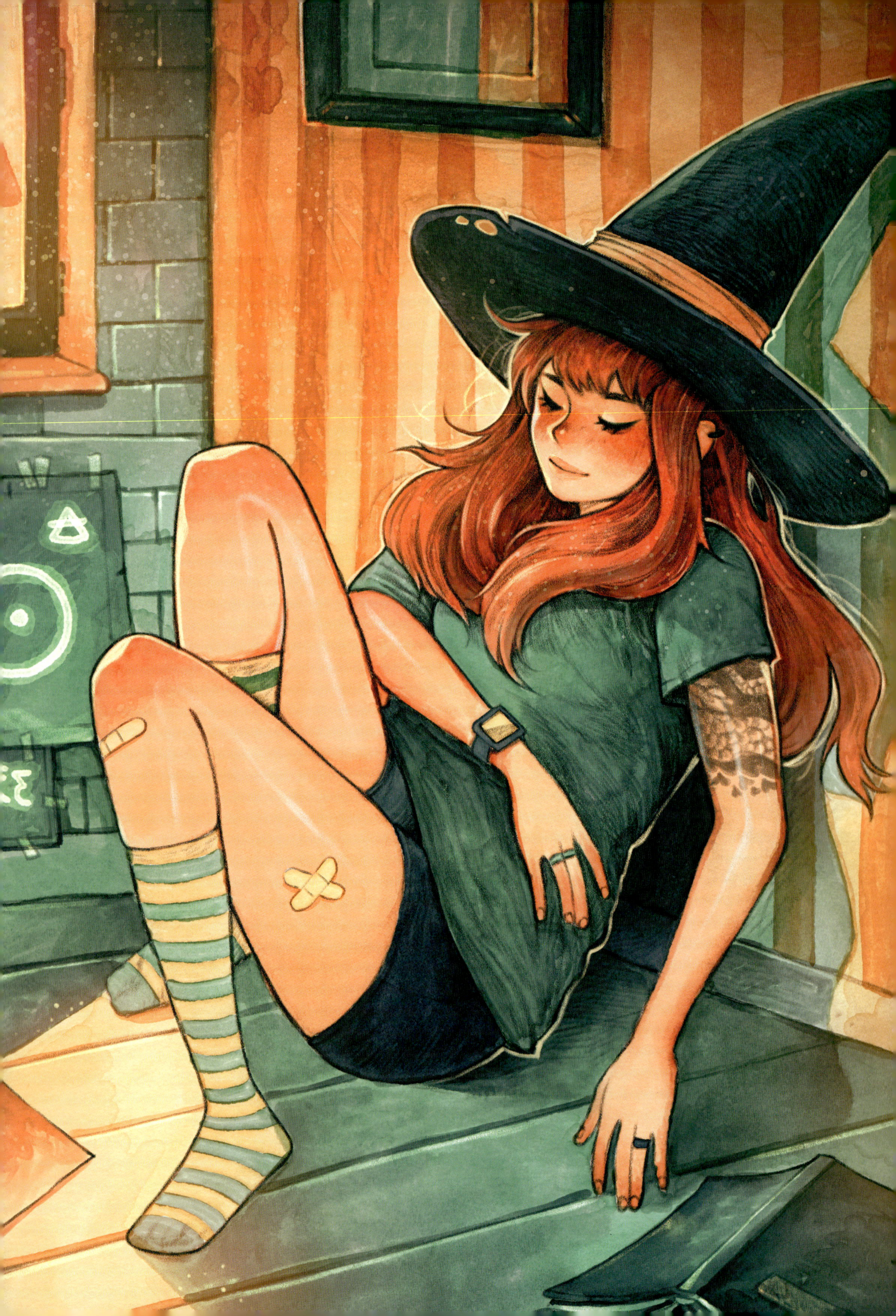

*Resting* – a limited color palette illustration of a character resting in the afternoon sun

# FUTURE AMBITIONS

At the time of writing, I'm working on the pre-production phase of a new comic. As well as world-building, I'm also writing some of the story and have started to define the characters. While I don't have any definitive comic illustrations yet, I have created some concept art and character design. My experience of working on a comic project in collaboration with Webtoon has given me a solid understanding of what is required. I'm now trying to apply the lessons I learned from that project to my new comic, ensuring I establish a clear idea, direction, and overall story arc before diving into the drawing.

Looking to the future, I would one day like to create art for a video game, animated film production, or comic. Commercially, I'm happy where I am and plan to continue what I'm doing. However, I'm also aware there are many opportunities I haven't even thought of yet, so I remain open to learning and trying new things.

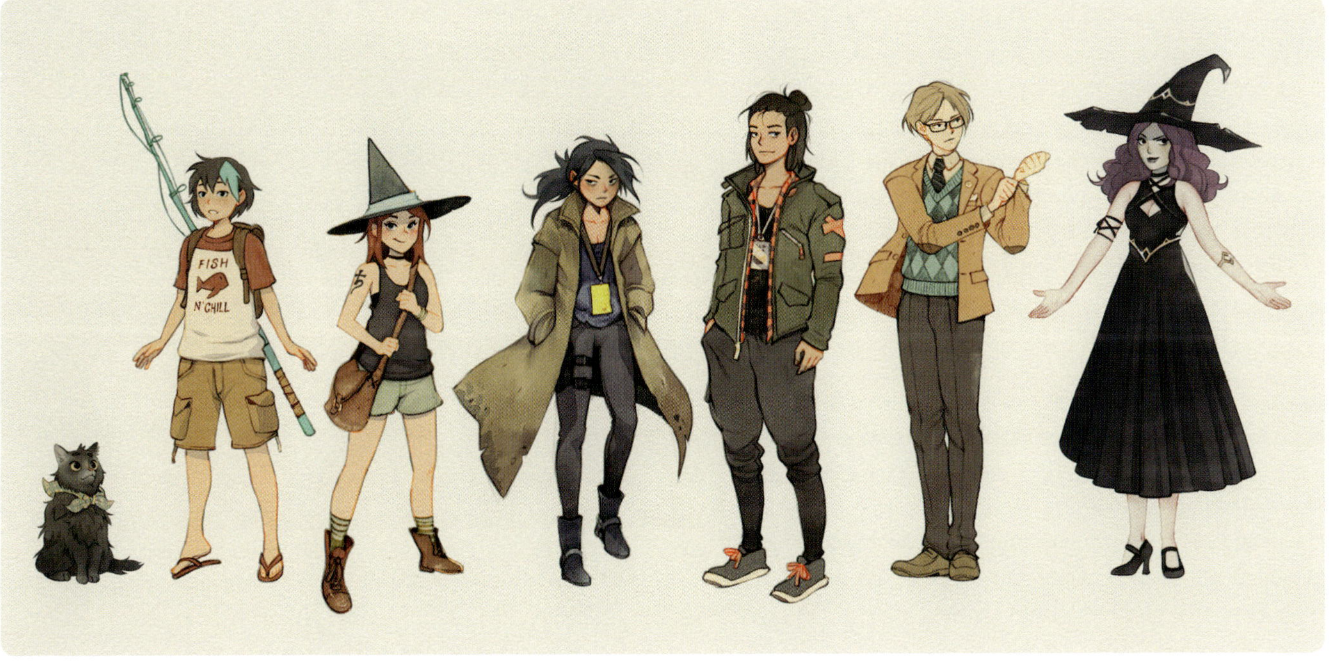

Character design ideas for my upcoming comic

## Areas to improve

I strive for freedom when creating my artwork. My goal is to get rid of anything that slows me down or is unnecessary for my creative process, until I am left with only what I need to create. The benefit of this would not only be stronger imagery, but also fewer problems and less back-and-forth during the drawing process. The more streamlined and faithful to my personality my artwork becomes, the more confident I feel while creating it, and ultimately, the better the viewer experience.

# ADVICE

## Self-doubt & artist's block

Like all artists, I have experienced periods of self-doubt and artist's block. Going back to basics can be an effective way to break free of these issues. When I'm stuck drawing a complex illustration, I set the project aside and take some time to simply draw what I see around me. This restores my confidence and helps me to find my rhythm again, ready to return to the more complex drawing.

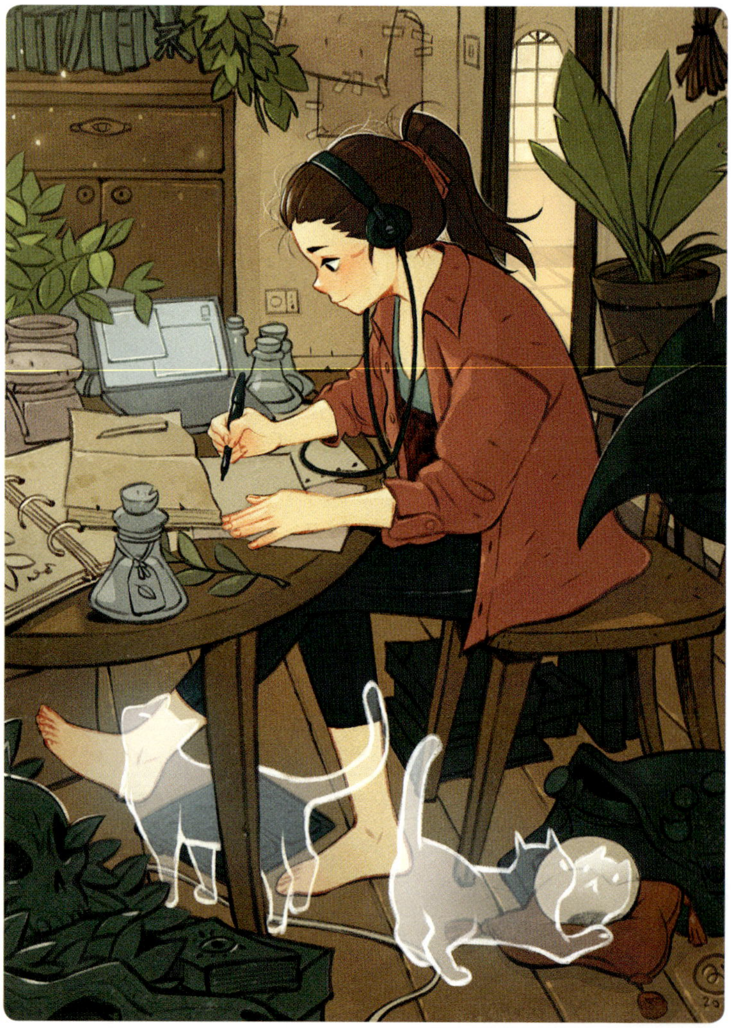

*Taking Notes* – a character takes notes while listening to music, with ghost cats at her feet

## Dealing with criticism

My artwork has been criticized for many different reasons, which is an inevitable part of sharing your work online. A long time ago I accepted that while I can't control what people think of my artwork, I can control how I react to their comments. This is one of the first lessons you need to learn when launching a career in the art industry. It's important to be able to distinguish good criticism from bad criticism, acquiring the ability to filter out what comments are relevant, helpful, and can be learned from.

As each of my illustrations represents a certain aspect of my personality or life in one way or another, it's crucial that I don't take negative comments to heart. As long as I'm doing my best, creating artwork I'm proud of, and enjoying my work, no amount of criticism will change who I am as an artist and the type of anime-style content I create.

## Final tips

- Becoming a successful anime-style artist is not without its challenges. Growing your brand to ensure you stand out among thousands of other online content creators can be a tough assignment. It's normal to feel daunted, stressed, or overwhelmed along the way. *Mens sana in corpore sano* is a Latin saying that translates as "a healthy mind in a healthy body." While it can be all too easy to focus exclusively on making a name for yourself in the industry, scheduling time to enjoy hobbies, catch up with friends, and take care of your health is essential for long-term success.
- Being honest with yourself and as transparent as possible with your followers are two notable ways to stand out as an artist.
- Make creating amazing artwork your priority, setting aside time to seek out inspiration to fuel your creativity and motivation.
- Art should never just be a profession; it should be something you love doing.

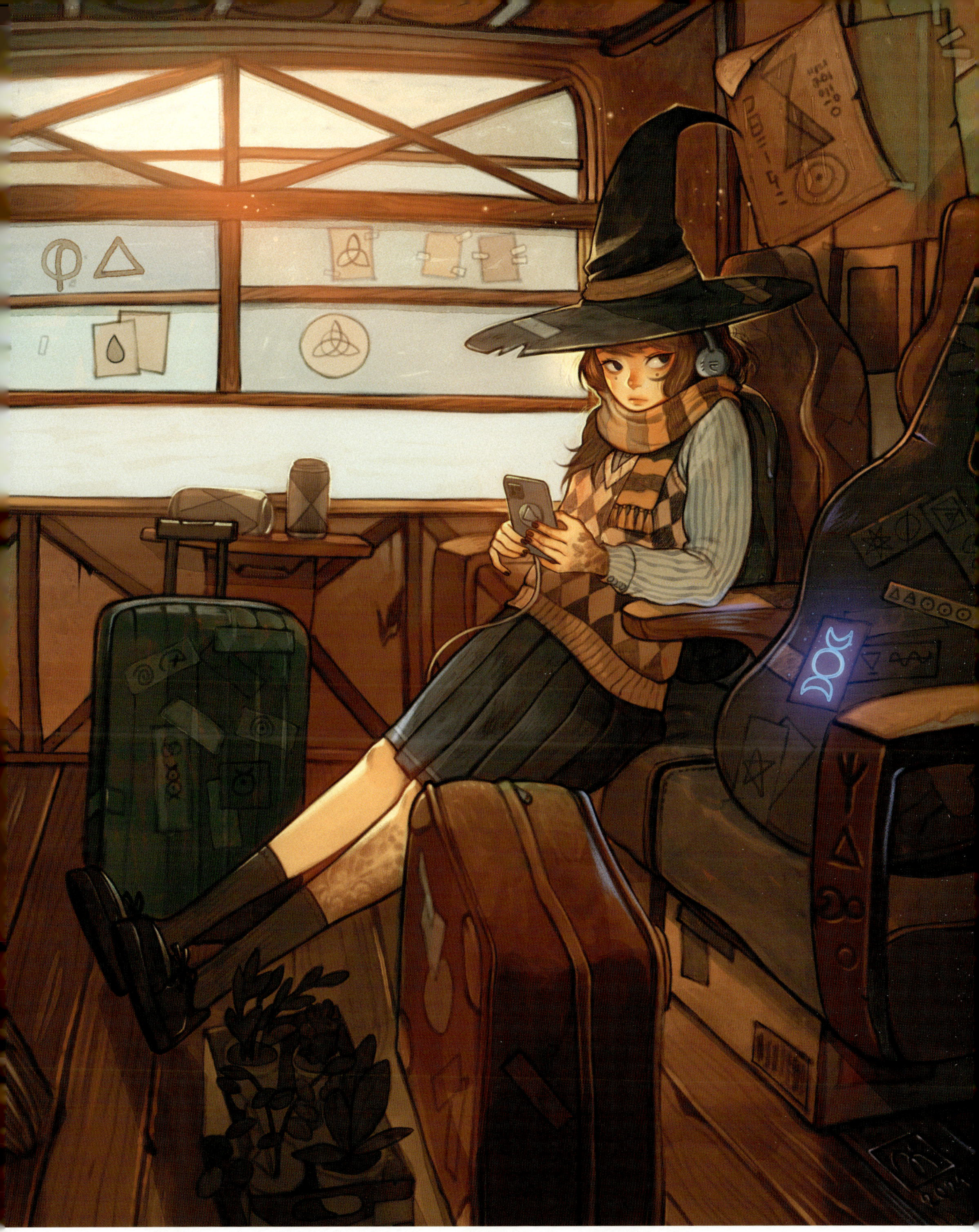

*Train Travel* – this slice-of-life scene shows a witch caught in a moment of relaxation on a train journey

# TIMELINE

**2015**

Graduated from the Fine Art Academy.

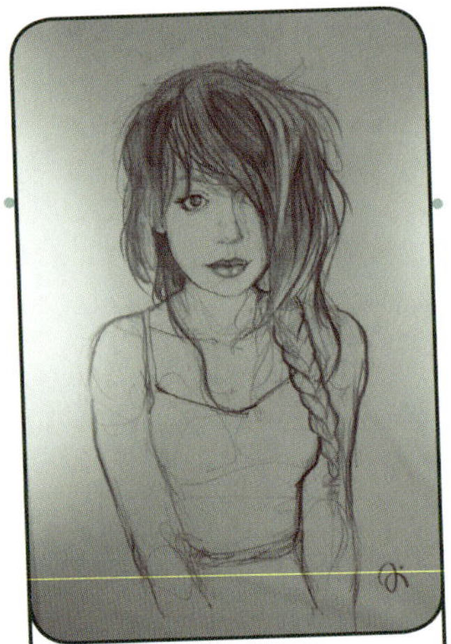

One of the many sketches I created during college.

**2017**

Created my social-media accounts.

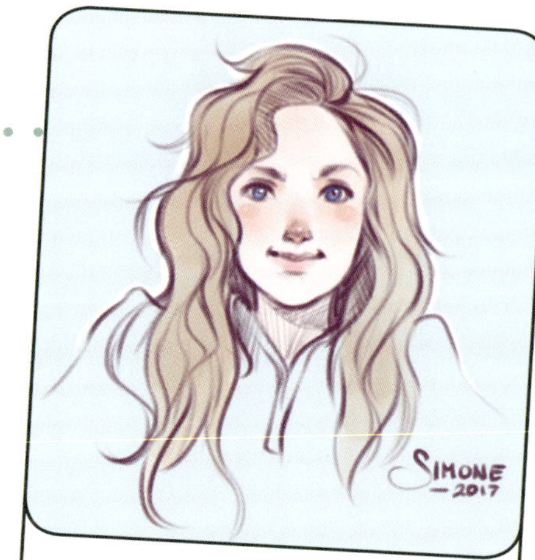


I worked on hundreds of portrait commissions during this time.

**2017**

Started streaming on Twitch.

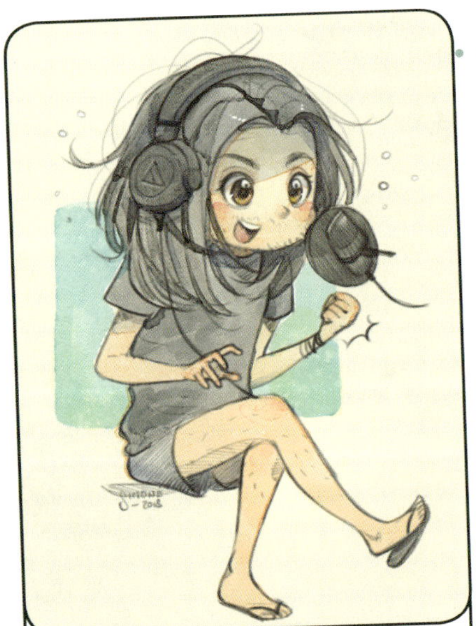

My streaming career helped to shape who I am today.

**2019**

Created a Webtoon Original comic called *Falling In the Blue.*

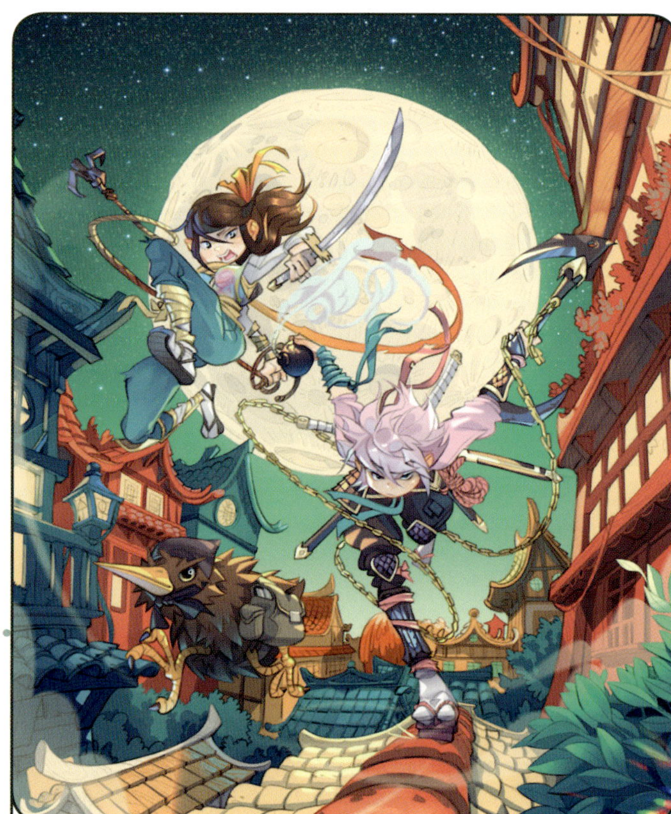

The characters Willow, Lake, and Memi in ninja outfits.

**2022**

Became a Partnered Twitch Streamer.

I created this artwork around the time that I became Partnered.

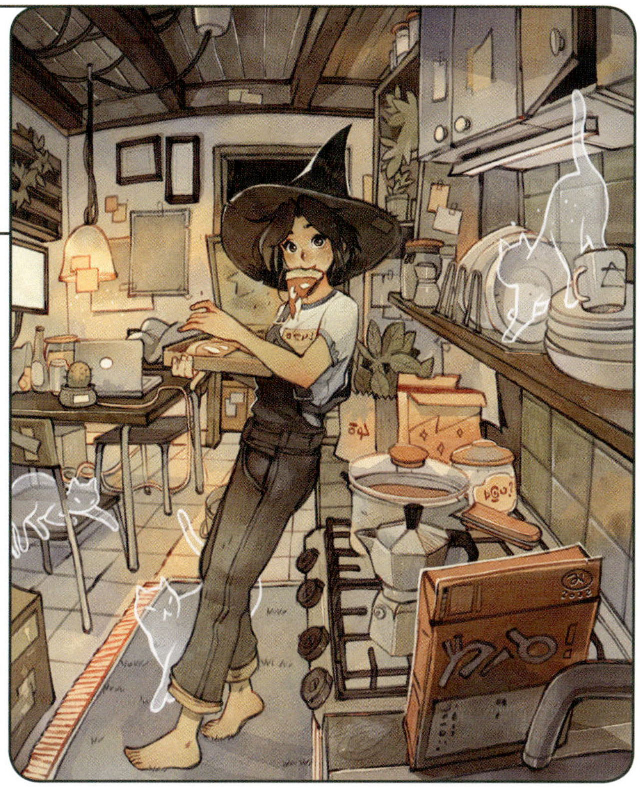

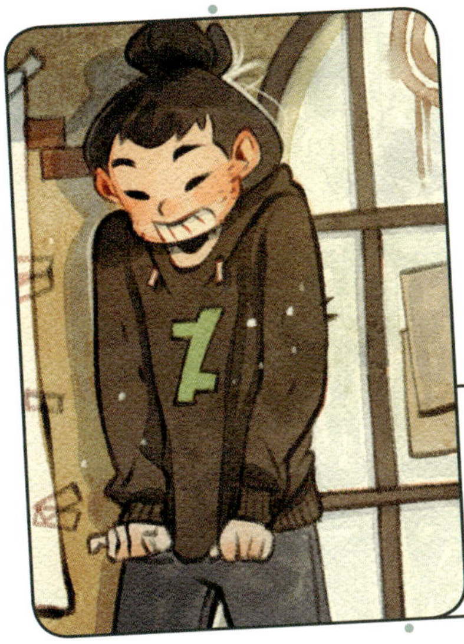

One of the doodles I created for the DeviantArt Collective social posts.

**2021**

Became part of the DeviantArt Collective.

One of my artworks that received attention from a large audience.

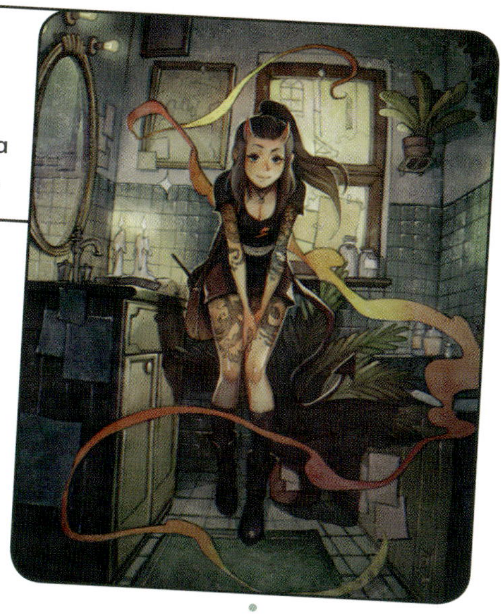

This was the illustration I used for the webinar – I love the combination of yellow and purple.

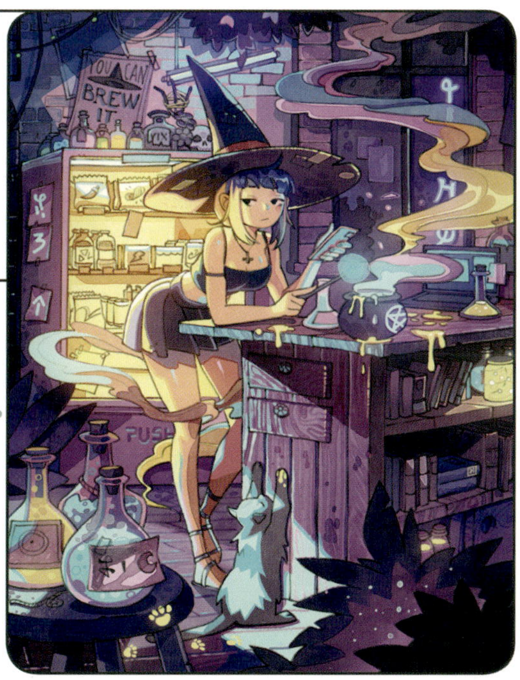


**2020**

Created my first webinar with Graphixly about Clip Studio Paint.

**2021**

Reached 100,000 followers on Instagram.

# GALLERY

OPEN

*Stargazing*, 2018

This was one of the first artworks in which I focused on cozy, relaxing themes. The color palette served as inspiration for *Falling In The Blue*, a web comic I went on to create.

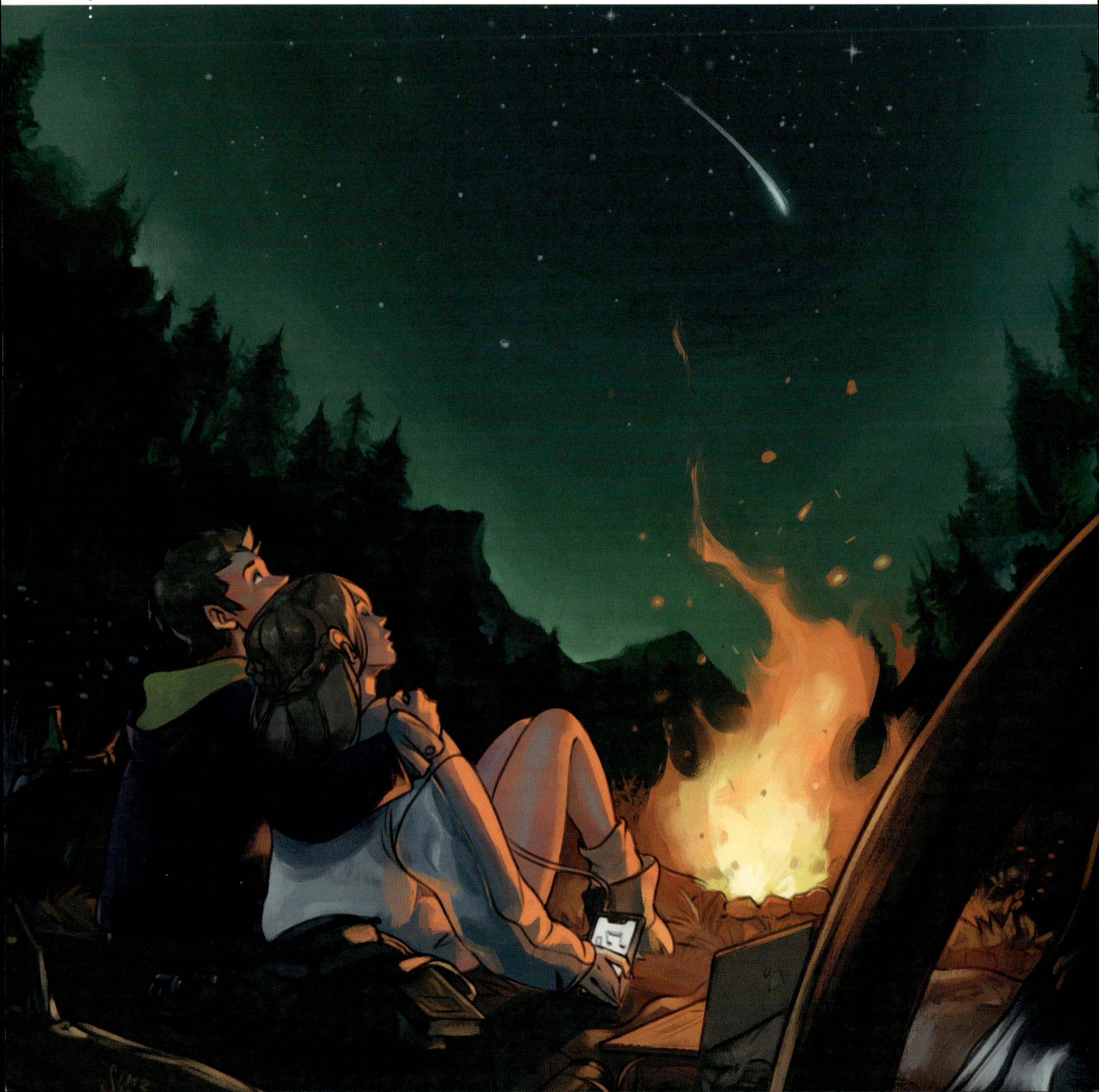

## *Portrait*, 2017

I worked on many portrait commissions when I first launched my art career online. It proved an important step, allowing me to practice and improve my skills while interacting with the people I drew.

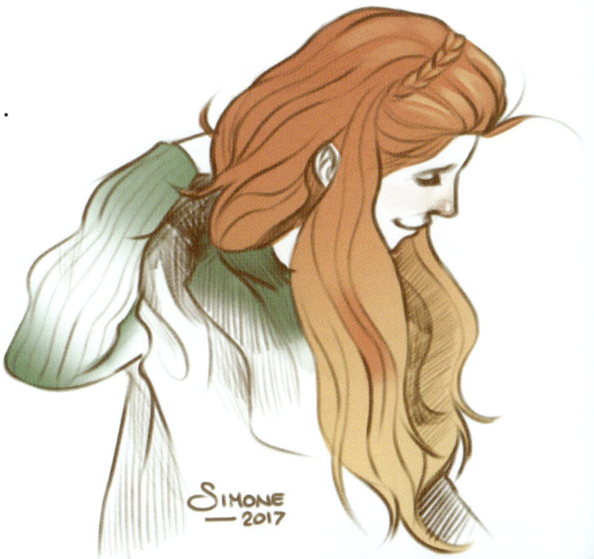


## *Airport*, 2018

This was the first artwork that included these three characters. I went on to use this trio in many other illustrations after this one, leading to the creation of my web comic, *Falling In The Blue*.

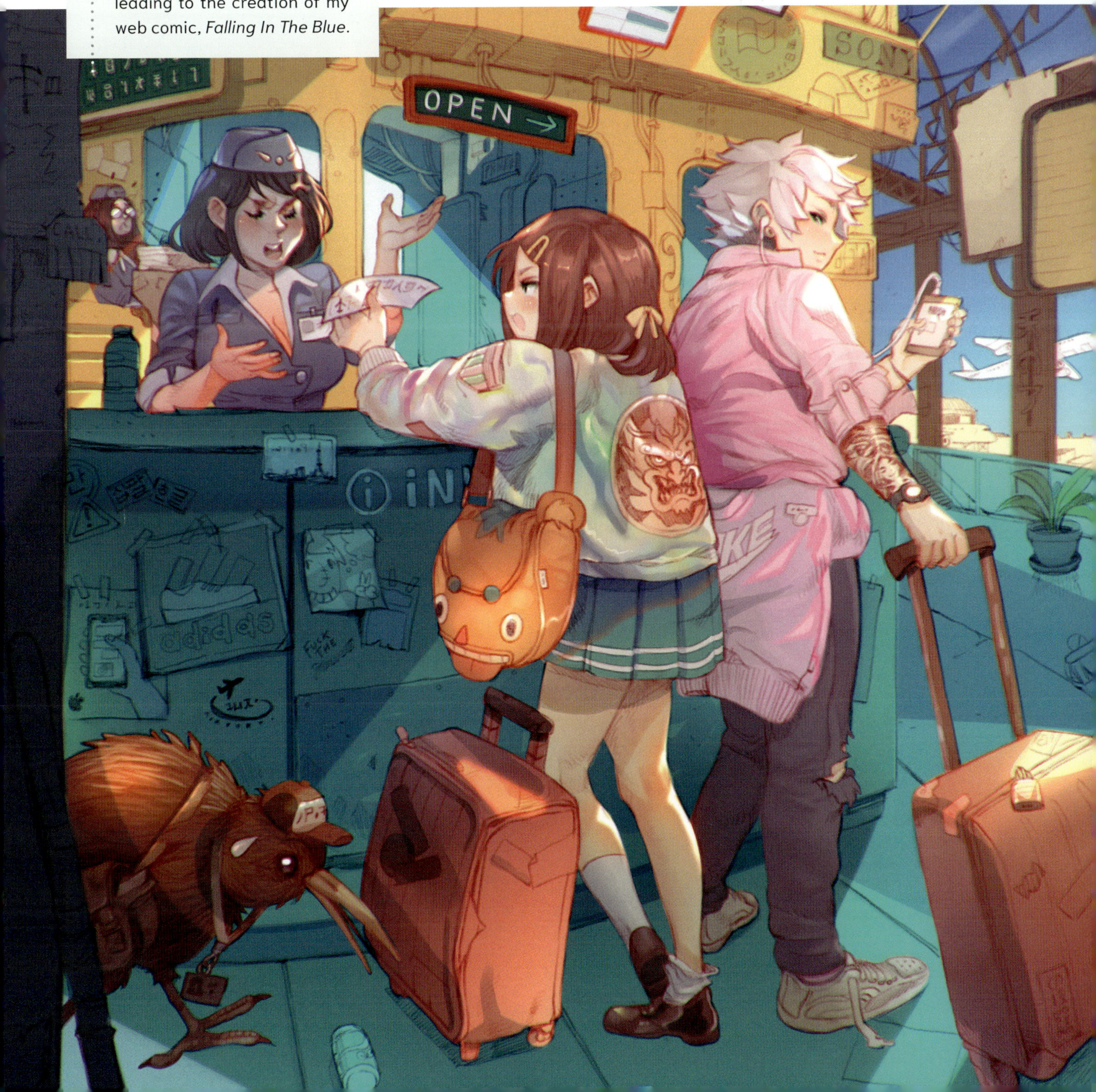

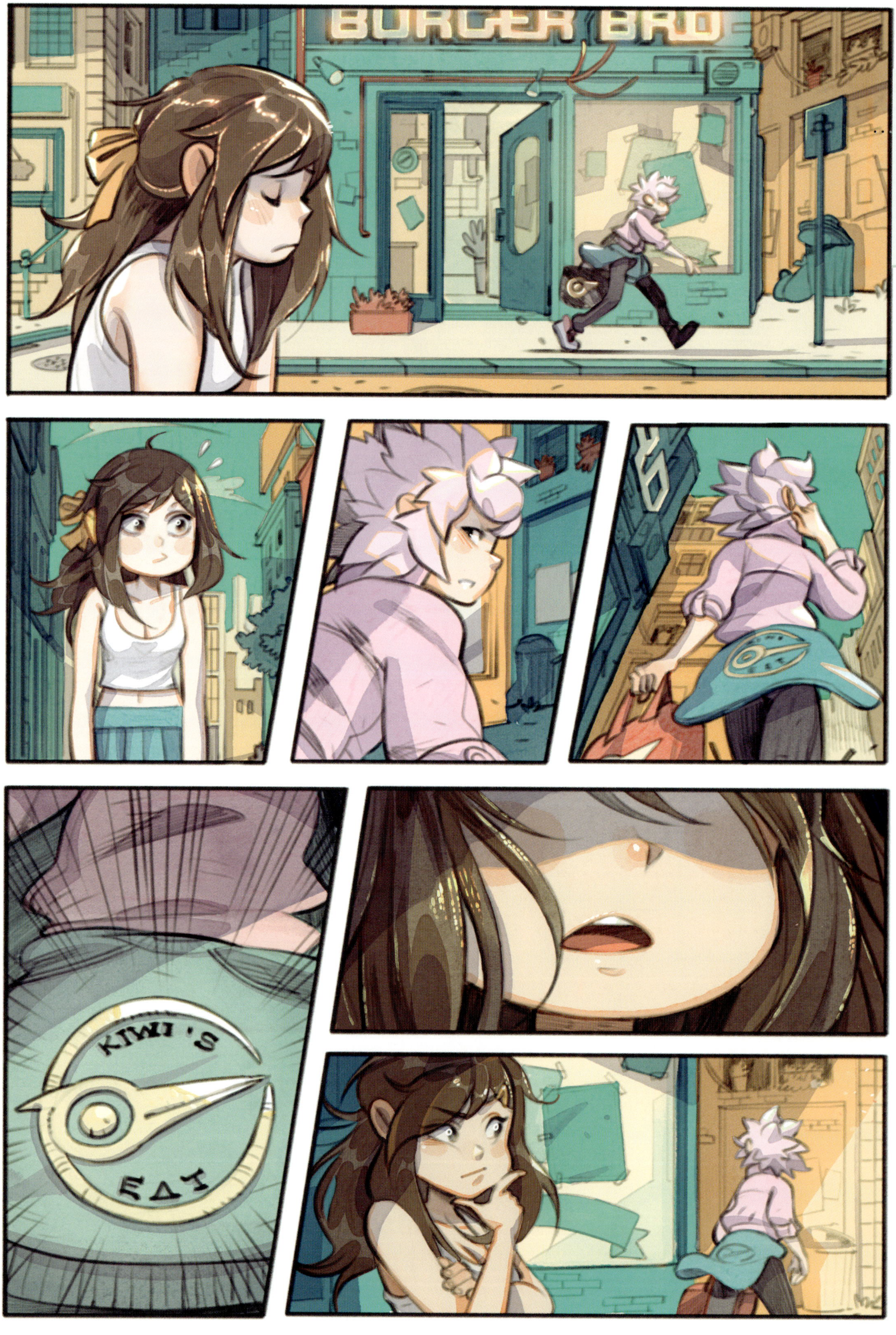
BURGER BRO
KIWI'S
EAT

## *Falling In The Blue*, 2019

A page from the pilot episode of *Falling In The Blue*, based on the series of illustrations I made of the three characters. This was my first official publication.

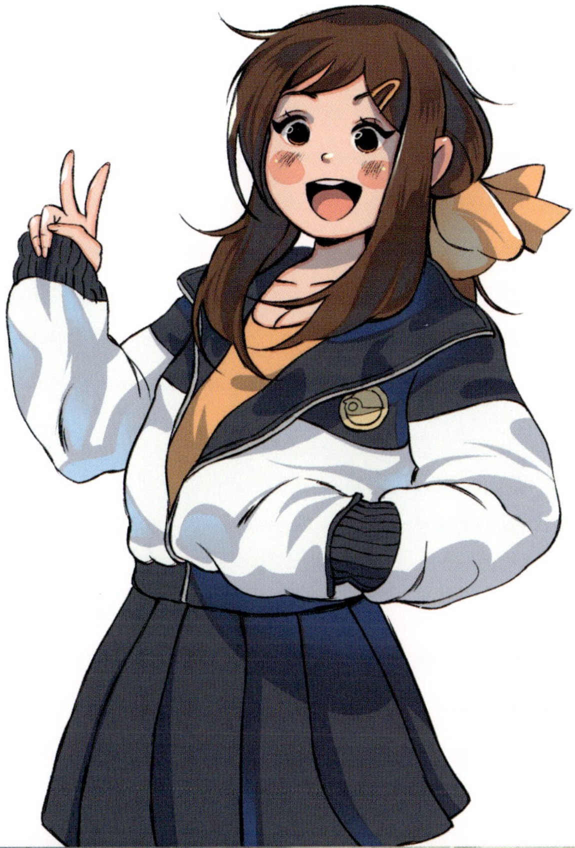

## *Willow*, 2019

I spent nearly two years working on my Webtoon Original, *Falling in the Blue*. This was challenging, as the deadlines for publishing one episode per week were very tight. There was a lot of work involved in writing the story, sketching, drawing, and coloring, and I learned many lessons from the experience.

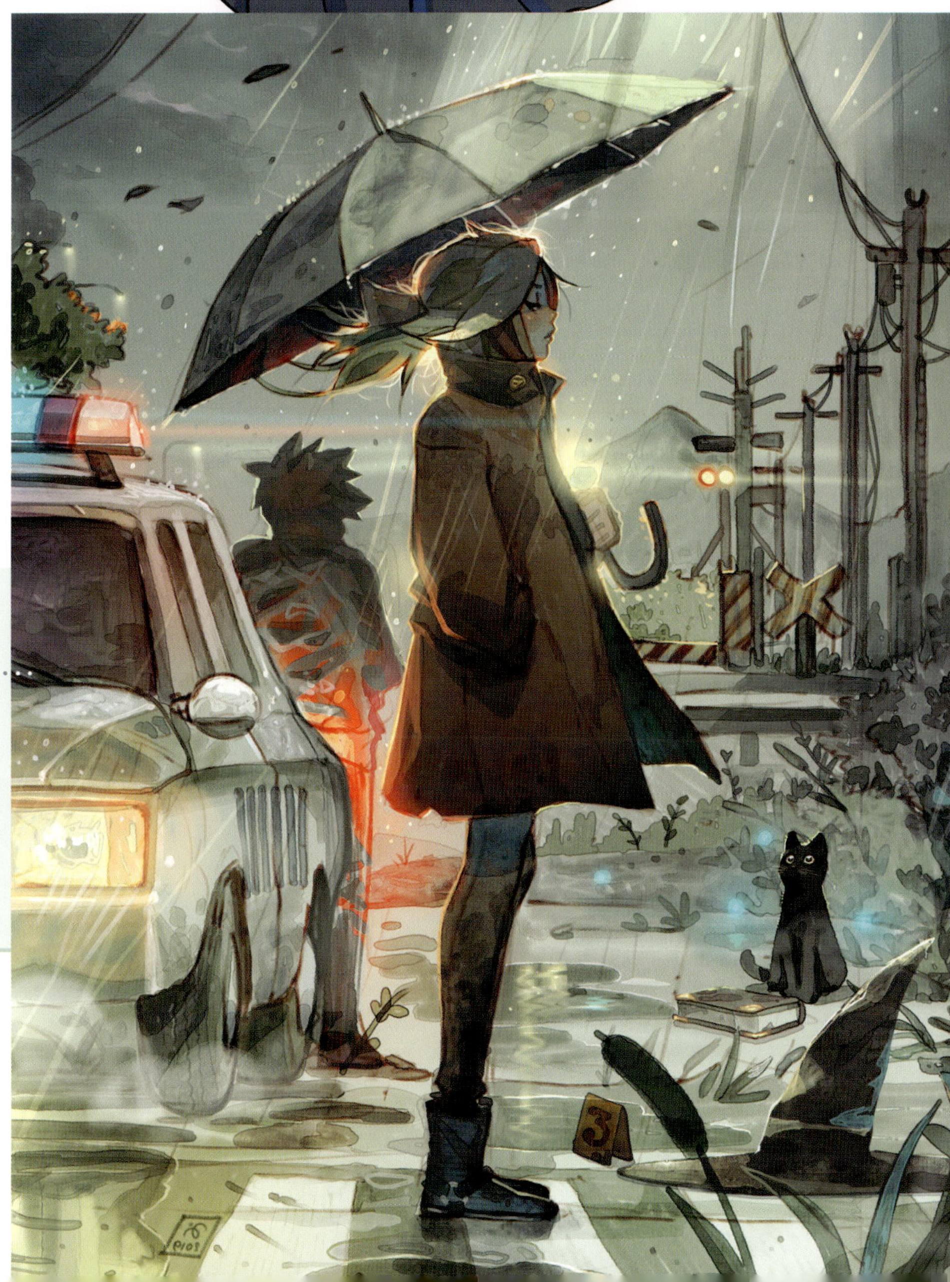

## *Witch Hunt*, 2019

I created this artwork inspired by some of the elements I was using in *Falling in the Blue*. Realizing that I liked the mood of the illustration, I started working on more concept art using this aesthetic.

## *Me Time*, 2021

This artwork was chosen by Tumblr for their Tumblr Radar and received a high level of engagement across my platforms. I learned that a simple drawing, created from my imagination, could contain more personality than when I purposefully tried to create a piece I thought would be popular. This helped set the tone for my artwork going forward. It also allowed me to experience the positive feedback and growth in followers that happens when an artwork is popular.

## *Building Furniture*, 2021

This is one of my more recent artworks in which I'm developing the aesthetic and style for a new series based on modern-day witches. The illustration features cute ghost cats, which have become a theme I continue to explore in my artwork.

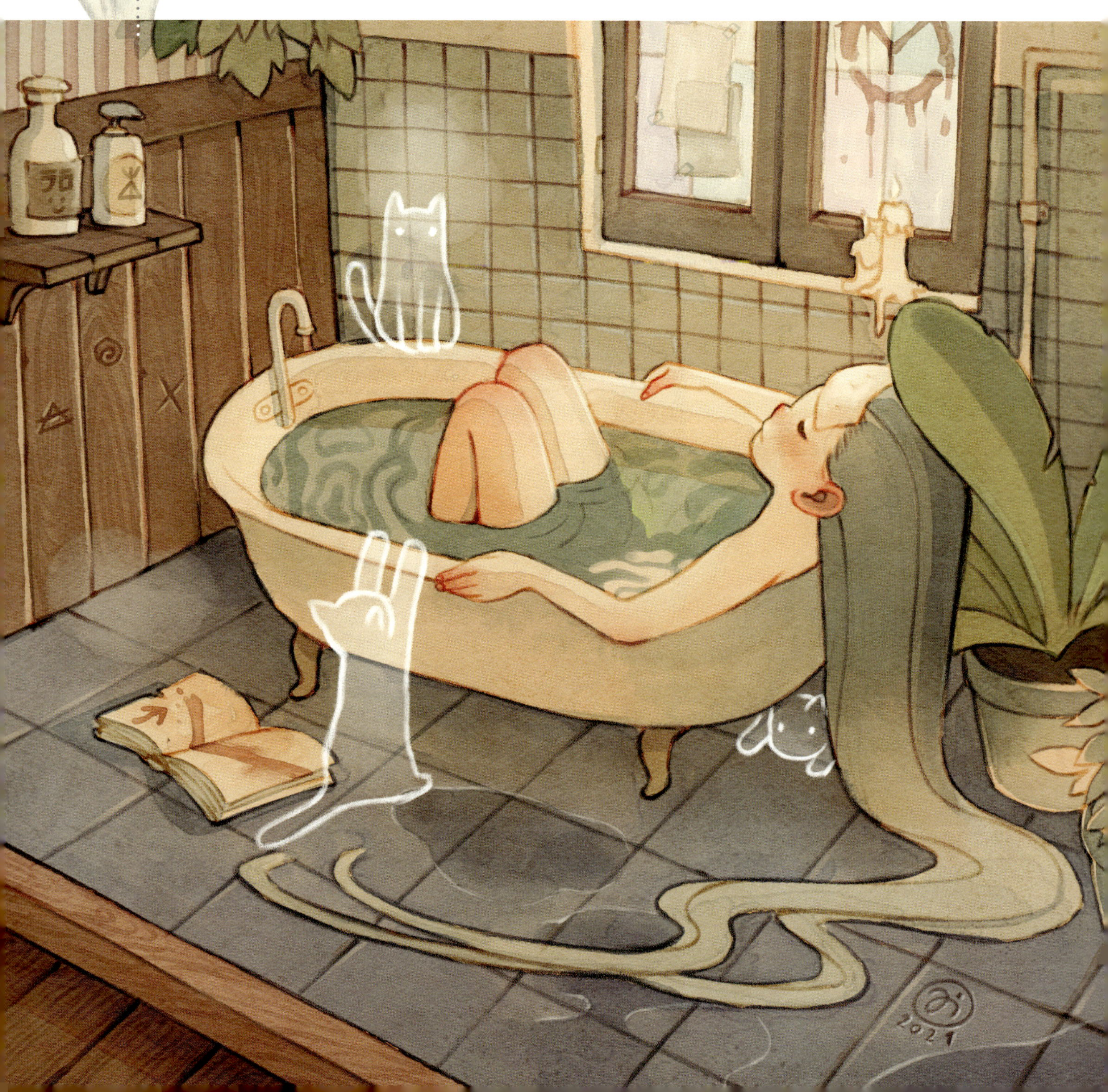

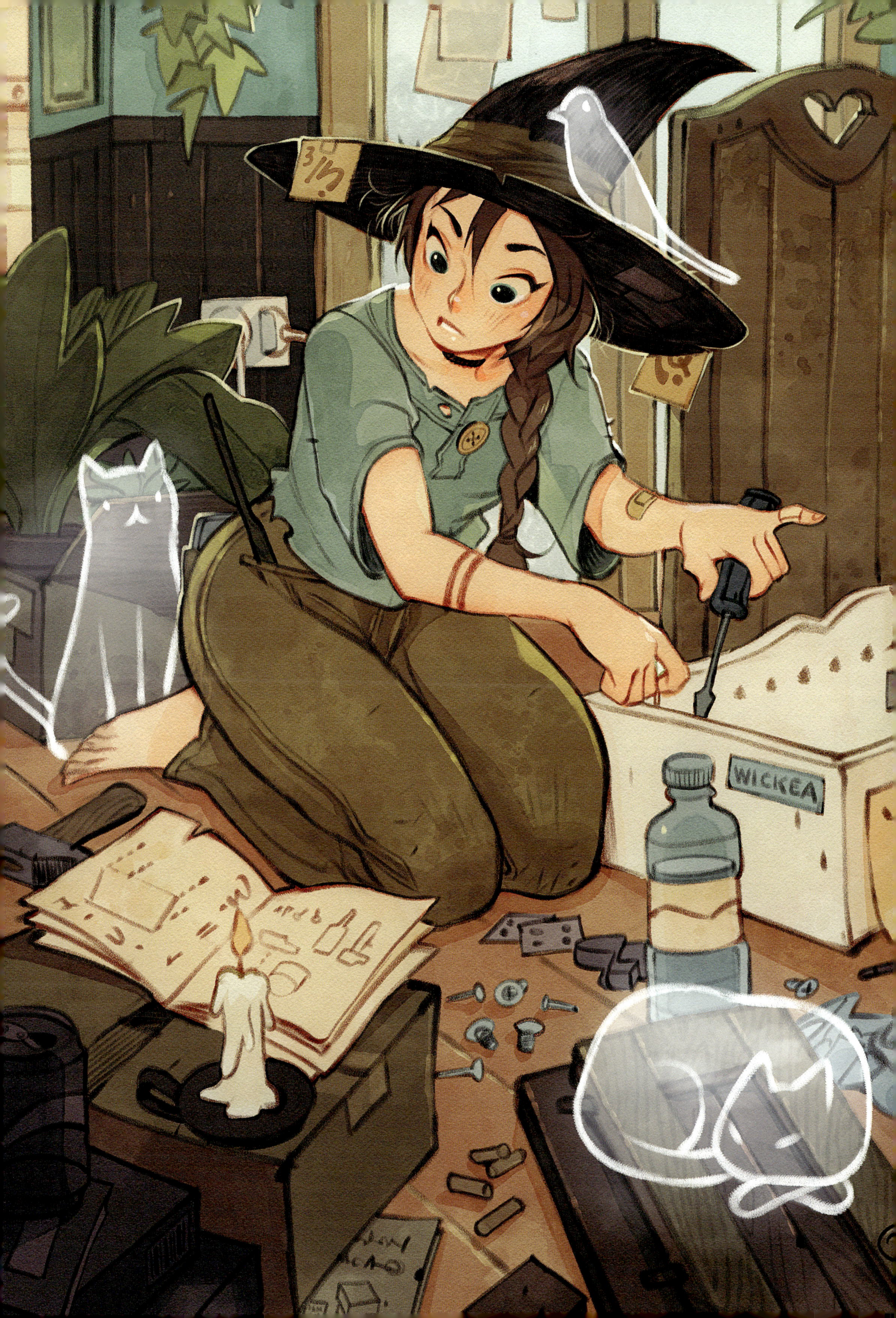
WICKEA

# TUTORIAL

This tutorial will guide you through how to create an anime-style illustration that represents the barely noticeable elements of travel. I like to put my characters in a context that audiences will recognize, but at the same time depicts a magical world where things don't work exactly as we expect. I experiment with subtle elements to communicate this idea, fusing magic with the relatable everyday. As it can be challenging to make the environment feel alive when creating such scenes, I will demonstrate how to introduce details to create a sense of it being lived-in.

Though I rarely have a specific audience or genre in mind when creating my illustrations, my artwork tends to fall into the slice-of-life category, with an added touch of magic and mystery. This inevitably attracts an audience that is drawn to this kind of imagery. Rather than creating work for a particular audience, I stay true to my ideas and let the right audience discover my work. I often find myself returning to specific themes, such as a character experiencing a moment of rest while drinking coffee, reading a book, or checking their phone. I like my artwork to feel relatable, while also having a fantastical element.

When creating an illustration in my anime-inspired signature style, introducing a subtle texture that evokes a paperlike rather than overly digital look is crucial. Line thickness is also key. I have spent years developing control of my line work so it can stand on its own as an uncolored version of the final image.

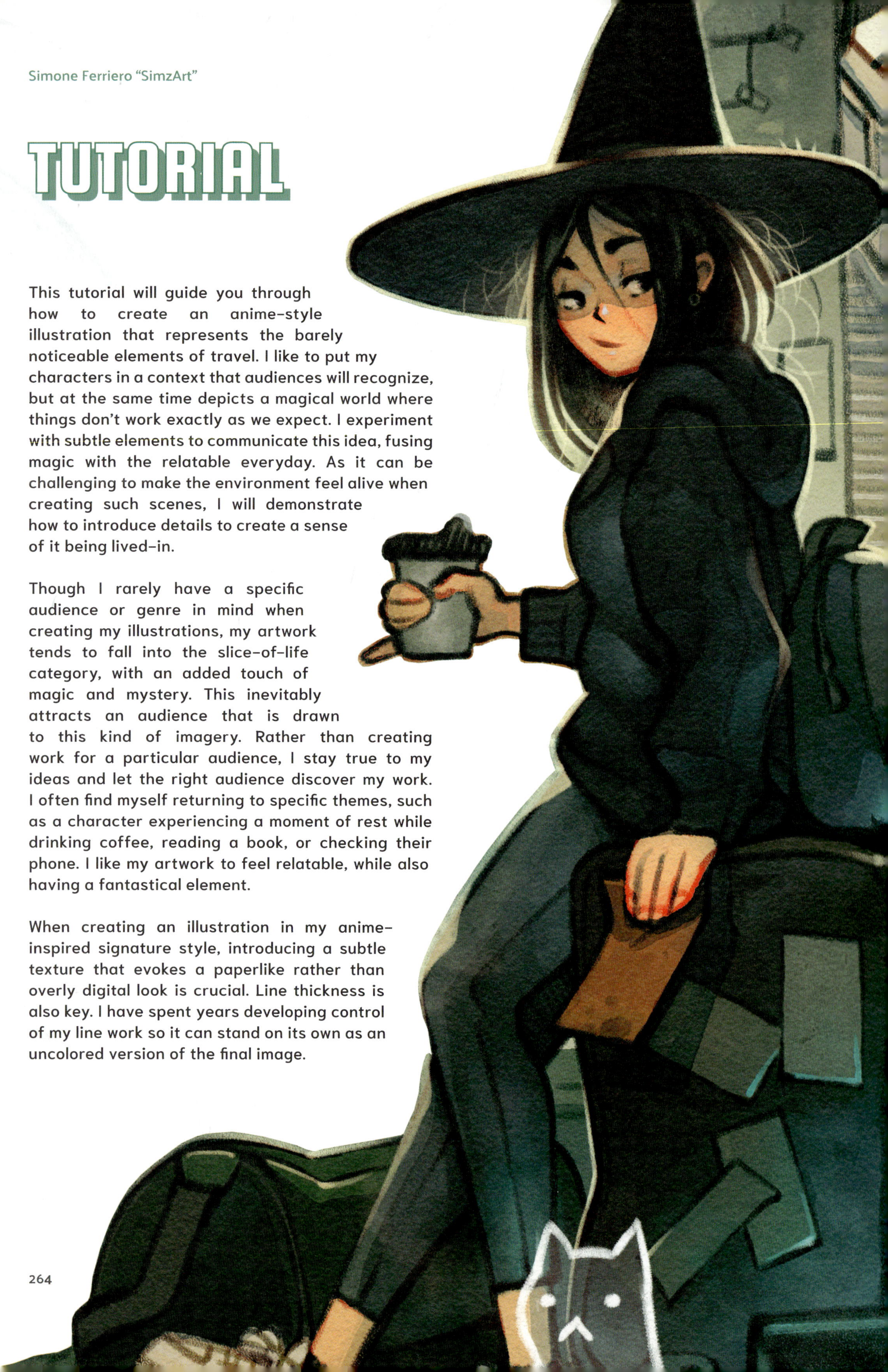

**01** Begin with a sketch, focusing on the basic shapes and overall flow of the image. Avoid overly detailed under-sketches and construction lines. The goal at this early stage is simply to provide indications about the space that suggest a three-dimensional environment, without exaggerating it too much through rigid grids and perspective lines.

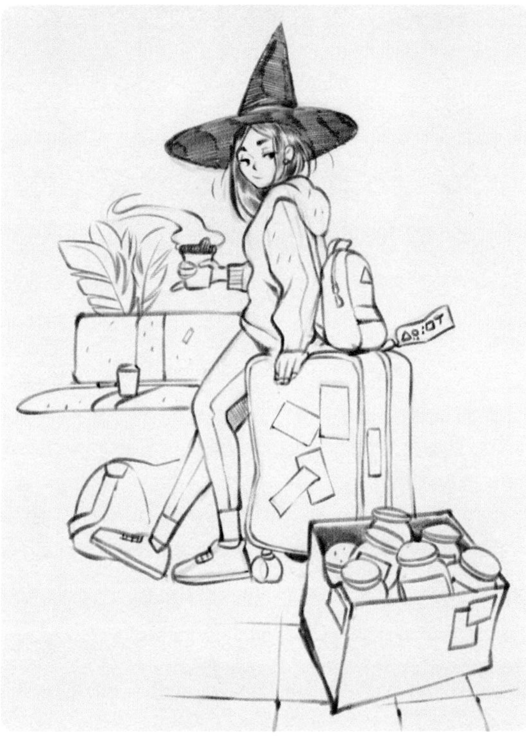

The initial sketch is one of the most important parts of the illustration process

**02** Continue to add detail to the composition, while keeping the individual elements balanced. Overlapping various objects can be a good way to create layering and a sense of depth, but ensure it remains readable. Avoid altering the size of your lines too often, as this can create a very scattered look. Instead, focus on selecting the correct line weight for the different parts of the illustration. Objects in the foreground, for example, require a thicker line, while distant or smaller objects in the background will need a slightly thinner line.

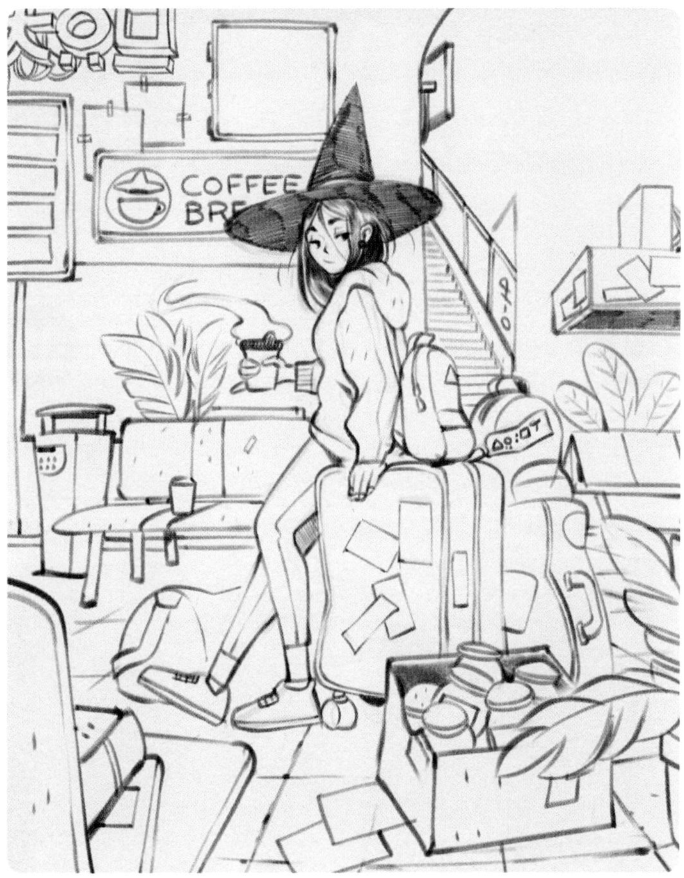


Adding too much detail can easily create too much clutter

**03** Add weight to your line work and slight shadows to any areas of the composition where light would fail to reach. The combination of line weight and occlusion shadows will help to create weight and rhythm. Draw lines with dynamic strokes, instead of a flat one-dimensional line. A line that changes size throughout the brushstroke will create more visual interest.

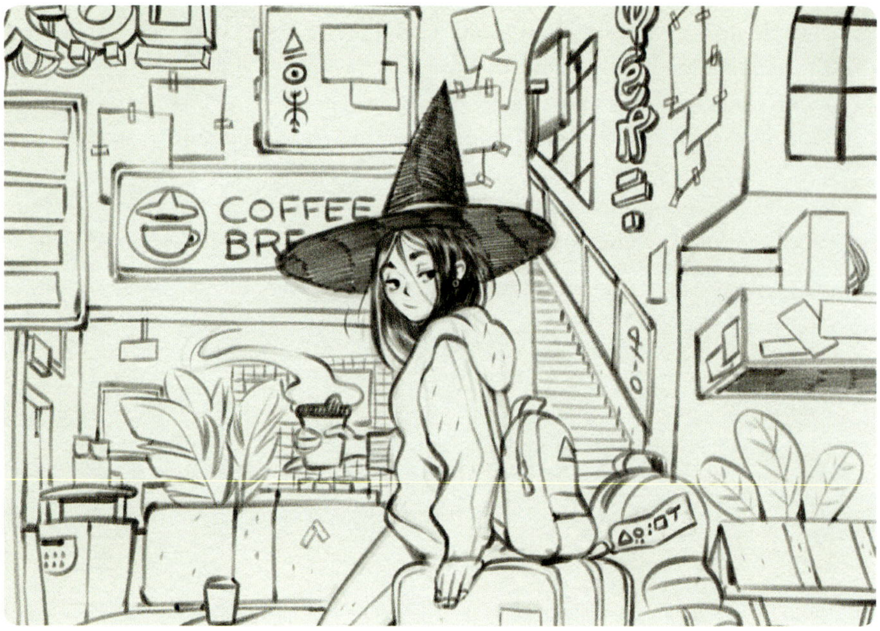


Lines don’t only describe an area, but can provide important information about the volume of an object

**04** Once the line art is complete, it’s time to start coloring the illustration. If working digitally, create a new layer and fill it with a flat tone that will act as the undertone of the whole image. The undertone color will influence the whole coloring process, from start to finish, so consider what mood and atmosphere you want to suggest. Here I select a warm tone that will capture the peaceful afternoon moment.

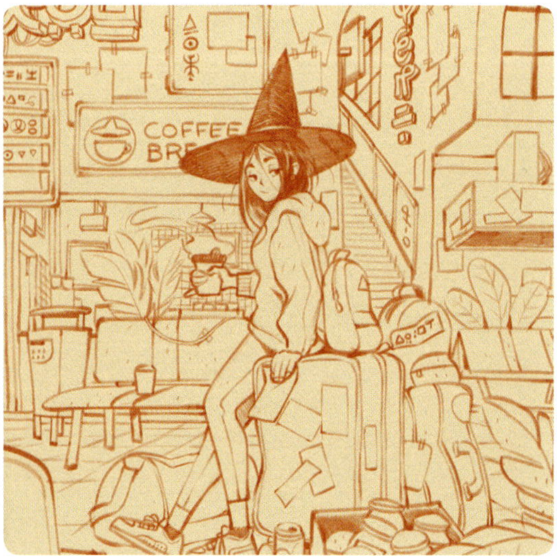


The warm undertone will act as a base for the colors painted on top

**05** Before continuing with the coloring process, use a solid brush to select the larger areas of the illustration, avoiding elements that are too small. This will minimize the visual clutter. Place each area on a separate layer, painting each one a different color. Group all of the layers in a folder named “Selections”. Ultimately you will hide this folder, recalling it only when selections are necessary.

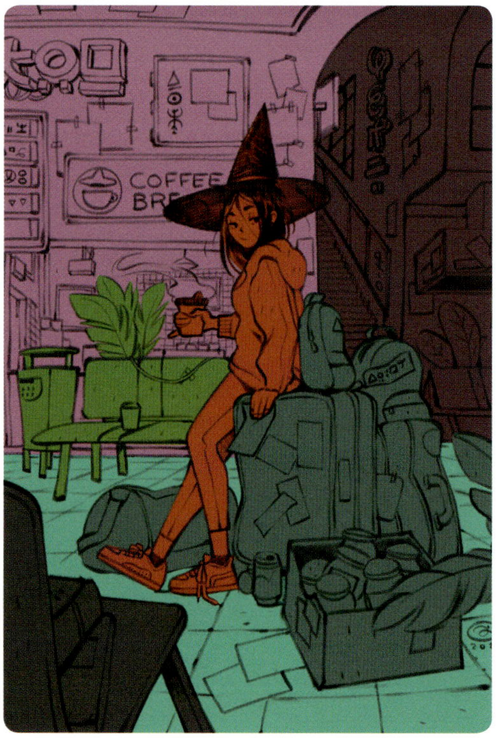


Filling the selection layers with different colors makes them easily identifiable

**06** With the selection layers grouped in the folder, fill each area with a color that works with the warm undertone color already established in step 04. As I chose a warm undertone, I select other largely warm tones in the shades of green, brown, and orange. Select increasingly warmer colors for the brighter elements and cooler colors for the darkest. This will create a visual hierarchy between the different areas of the composition.

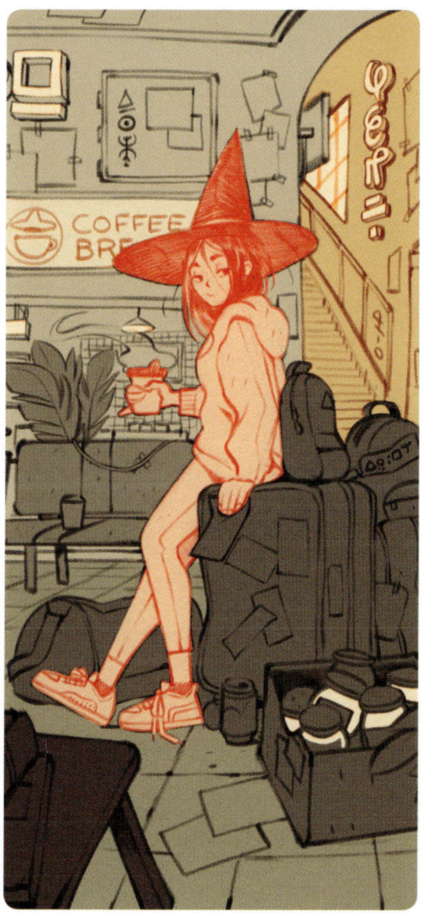


Choosing the initial color palette is a pivotal moment in determining the color scheme of the illustration

**07** After filling in the main areas, it's time to color each one individually. Start with the character, as this is the primary element and first part the viewer will look at. Color the character with values that are in tune with the rest of the image. Here I use muted tones, starting from the undertone chosen in step 04. Adding a slight red to the undertone of the skin will brighten it slightly. For the pants, introducing cooler colors to the original undertone will darken them.

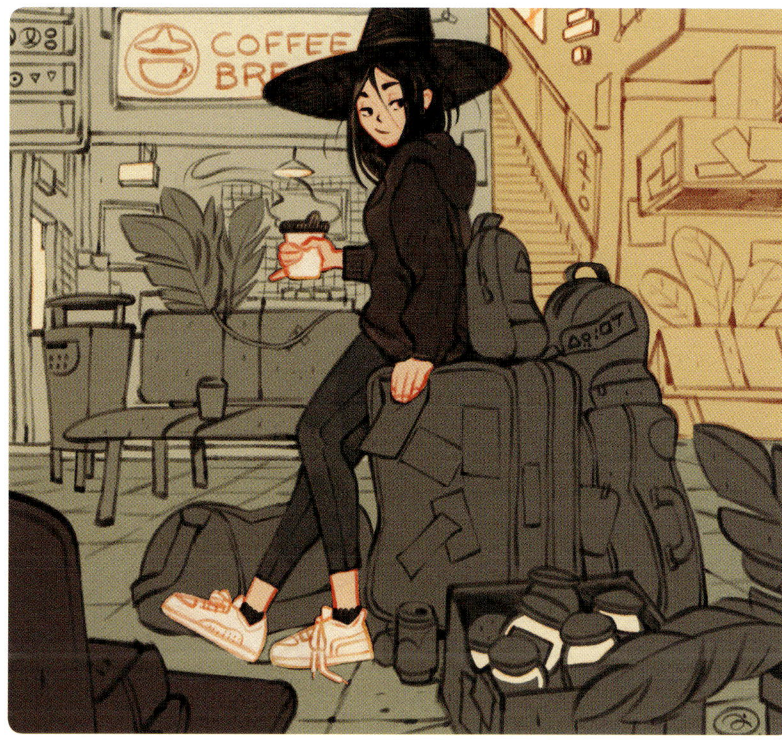


Ensure the flat colors of the main character complement the surrounding color palette to create a unified look

**08** Pay attention to skin color. Painted skin can take on an unnatural appearance that an audience will easily notice. There are no set colors that work well consistently for skin; the trick is to start from a base tone and slowly add subtle hues. Don't introduce colors that abruptly change the skin tone, as in most cases this will look unnatural. Here I select a reddish tone that will provide a little life and color to the edges of the character.

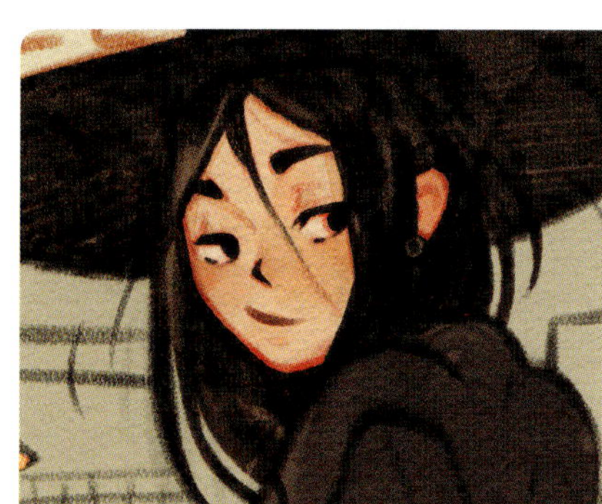

Take a subtle approach when building up skin tones

**09** Next, add shadows using a cooler tone. These will create a sense of depth and volume in the illustration. Introduce them slowly, starting from a very light shadow, and progress into increasingly darker values. There is no limit to how many shadows can be added; it all depends on how rich and dramatic you want the final image to appear. Begin to add shadows around and on the main character, before moving on to the other elements.

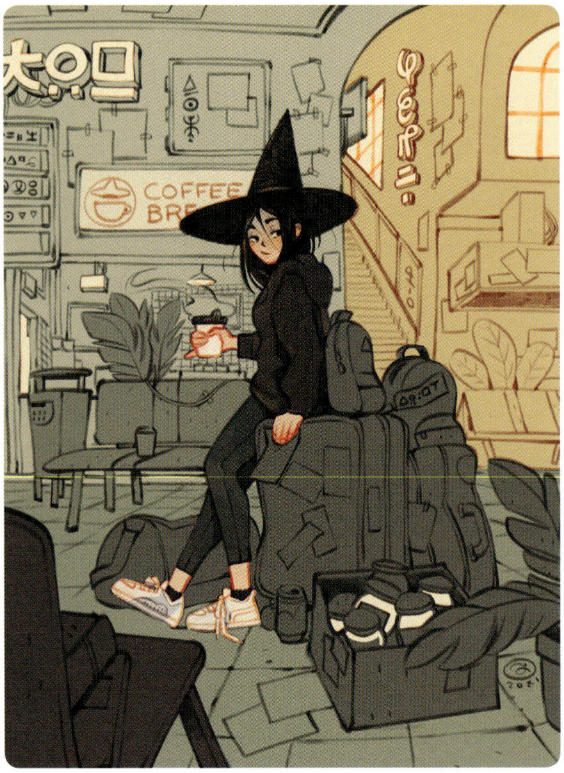


Use a cooler tone to paint in shadows, gradually increasing the intensity

**10** Slowly and carefully, paint large gradients onto the main areas. This will instantly push certain areas back, while pulling others forward, increasing the readability of the image as a whole. Take regular breaks throughout the painting process. This is a critical stage and should be taken seriously, as the later steps will build on top of it.

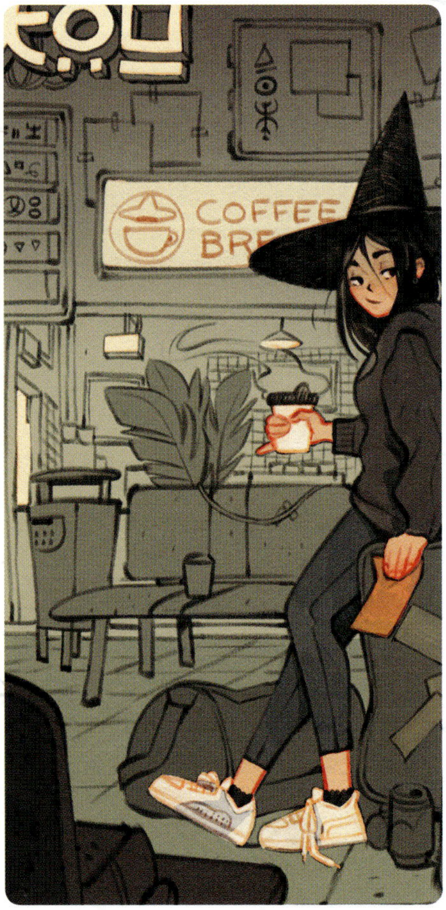


Gradients can act as a great visual aid to help define complex environments

## ARTIST TIP

Using strong, saturated colors, paint in small accents to make your image "pop." Choose carefully which elements to highlight, as this will make them more visible than the objects that surround them. Don't overdo this step; if too many elements are highlighted, the purpose is lost, and nothing will really stand out.

**11** On a new layer, carefully paint in shadows over the rest of the image. These shadows should start from light values, before getting slowly darker. It's possible that some undertone colors will need to be fine-tuned during this process. This is a work in progress and nothing has to stay the way it is. Make use of the advantages of working digitally, such as the ability to correct and rethink your illustration.

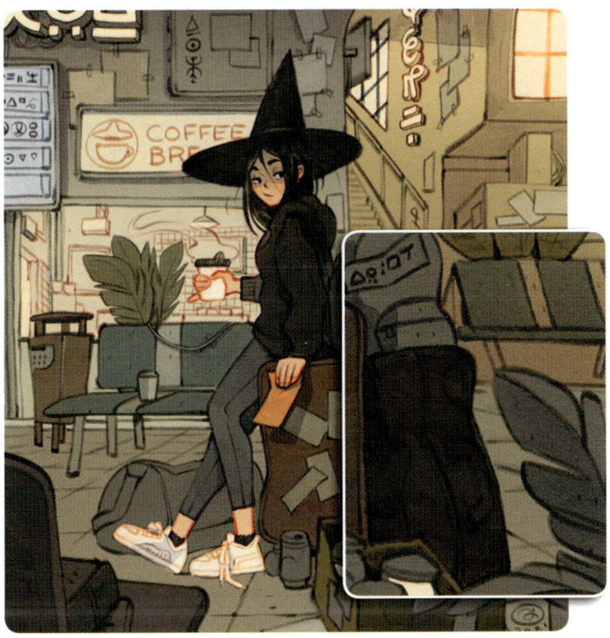

Adding shadows to the background elements creates depth and pushes the foreground objects forward

**12** Fine-tune each element by adding further shadows, always working from big to small. This will make for more linear progress, as well as providing your final image with a more balanced look. Avoid focusing on smaller details at this stage, even if they seem important. Take a step back at regular intervals to view the image as a whole, as well as looking at the small preview thumbnail if working digitally. This preview image provides an overall look of the artwork, without showing the smaller details.

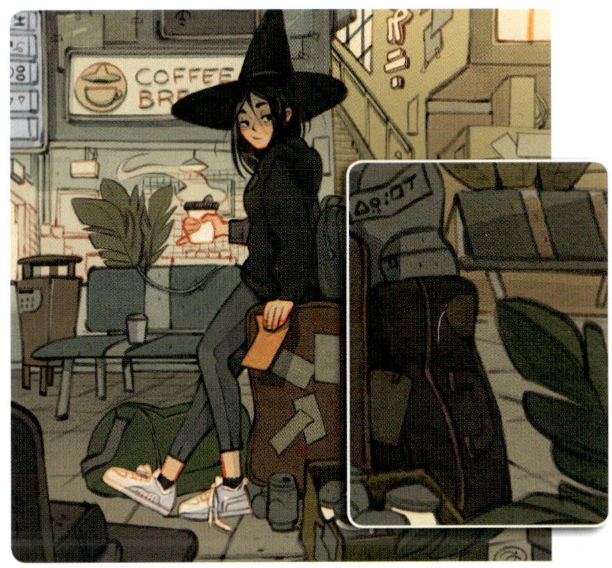

Smaller shadows can be painted in only once the main masses have been defined

**13** Paint cold reflections into the shadowed areas to create a more three-dimensional look. Cool tones painted over warm areas will also add more vibrancy to the color palette. Don't overdo this, however, or this will create a camouflage-like appearance and remove too many of the darker areas, making the final image appear flatter.

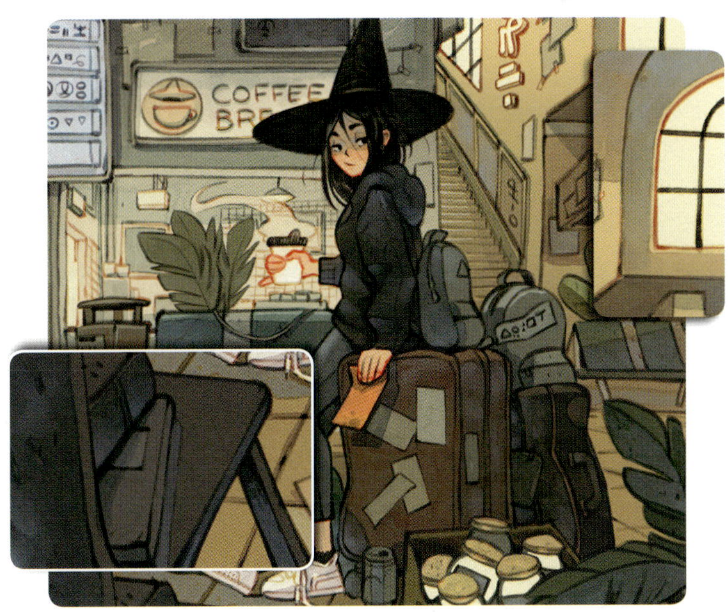

Reflections are a great way to suggest a sense of volume

**14** Keep adding reflections and shadows, while monitoring the overall values of the image. Ensure any overlapping elements have a high enough difference in value that they remain easily readable. The selection layers created in step 05 at the beginning of the coloring process will make editing the values of each area simple. Don't be afraid to return to or combine your selections if you wish to change the values of a problematic area of the illustration.

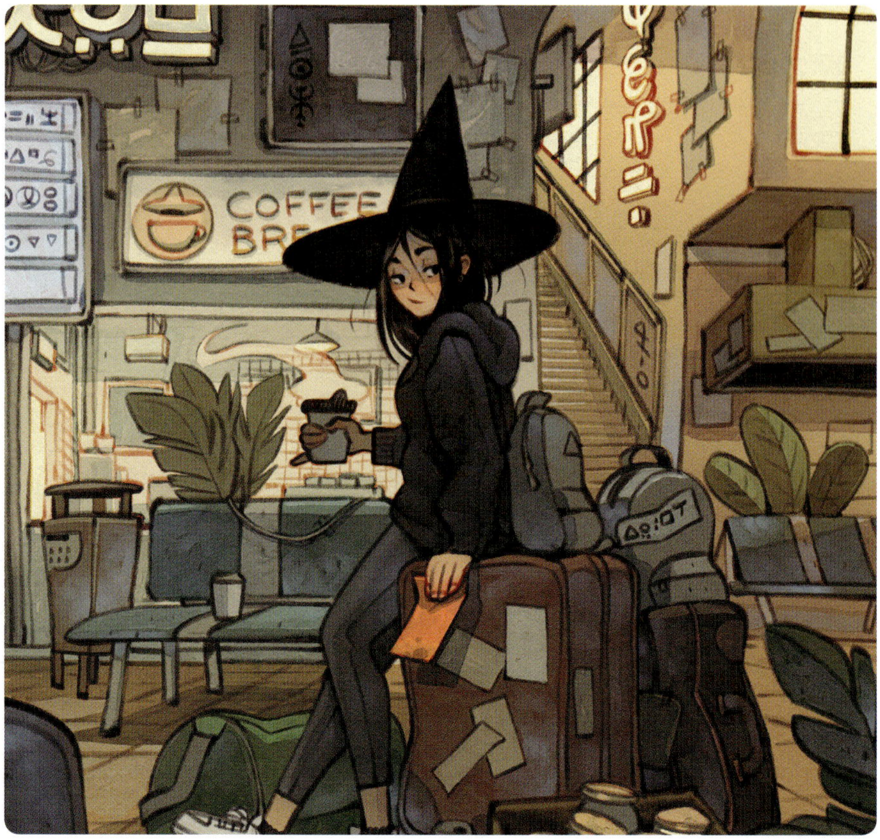

Keep an eye on the values and correct them using the pre-established selections

**15** Introduce gradients, fog, or lighting effects to create more separation between the different elements in the illustration. Not only will it make the environment more interesting, but it will also create a stronger silhouette for the foreground objects. Again, don't overdo these effects or they will overwhelm and ruin the design. To add a subtle fog effect on a new layer, decrease the opacity to zero before slowly increasing it until the effect is just strong enough.

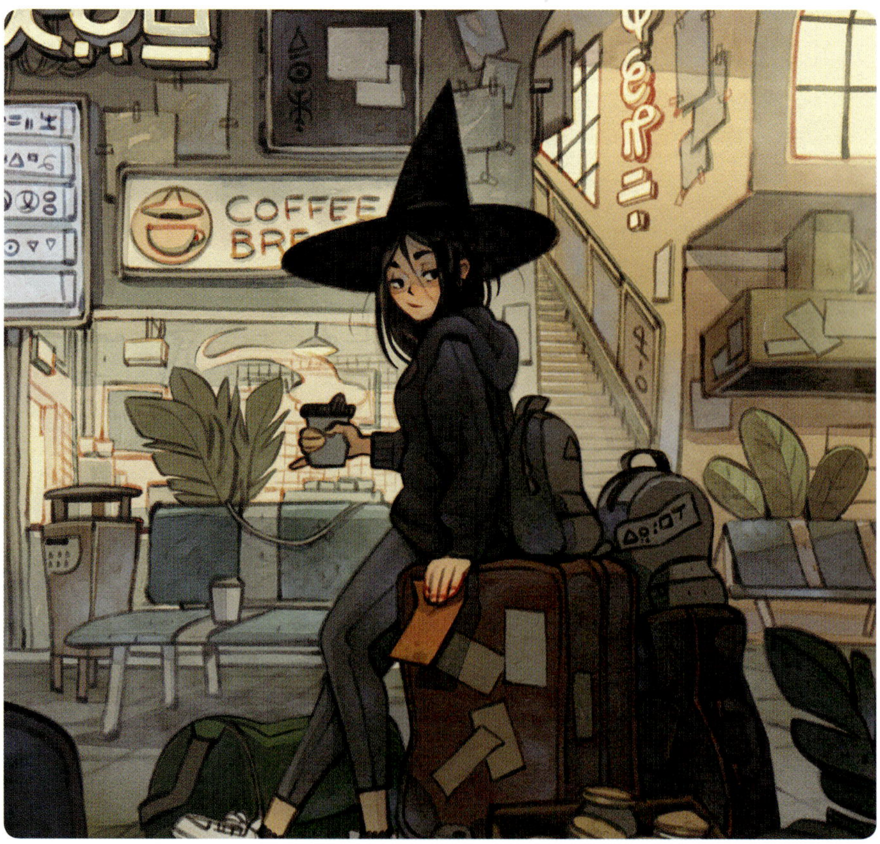

Fog and mist can provide the illustration with more depth and visual interest

**16** Paint in more reflections and highlights to push the more important elements forward. Focus on the character initially, before moving slowly toward the outer regions in a radial motion. Continue to adjust the values of the different areas of the image, creating contrast and enhancing the readability of the piece. The key word here is "subtlety." Always lower the opacity of the layer, or at the very least, evaluate if the amount of paint or contrast added is too much. It's very easy to get carried away with such visual effects, especially in the final stages of the painting process.

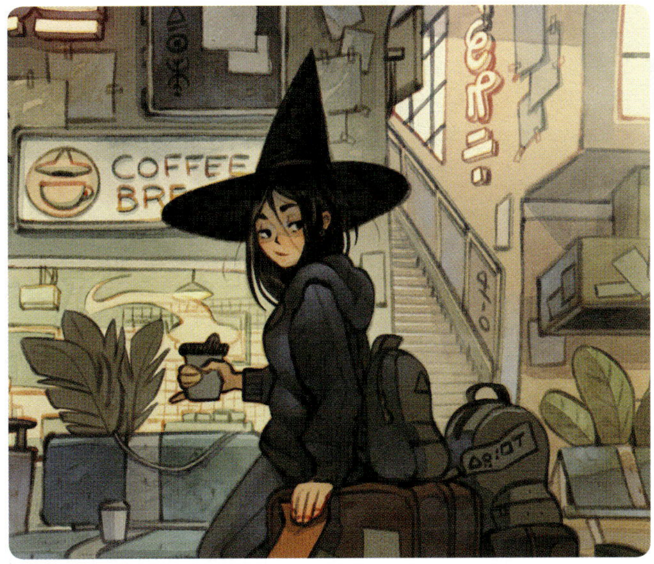


Introducing glow and reflections will create areas of visual interest

**17** The next stage is to create a sense of magic, a signature of my anime-style witch illustrations. Create a new layer set to Hard Light, which is a strong blending mode that will color over any hue beneath it. Next, select your desired color. Here I choose blue, which is perfect for creating a mystical glow emanating from the box of jars. Use different brushes, such as a cloud brush or a smoke brush, to create a glowing area with an interesting textured look. Ensure you add the glowing effect in a radial way, so it is strongest in the center and fainter as it moves outward. Also consider how the glow will cast light on surrounding elements, such as the floor, other objects, or characters.

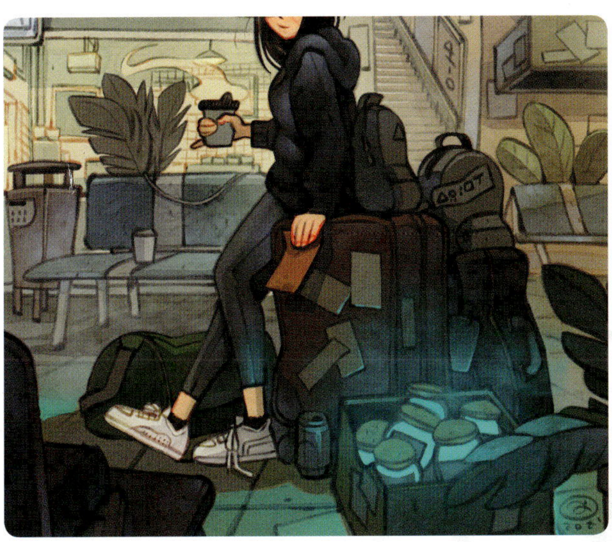

A glow effect will create a feeling of magic and mystery

**18** Create the impression of air or atmosphere by adding a new layer set to Hard Light and filling it with a light tone. Lower the opacity until the image has an overall light haze, then increase or decrease the opacity depending on the look you wish to create. Keep your layers separate as much as possible, only merging them when you are completely sure you do not need to make further edits. I prefer to keep the layer count low to help with performance, as well as when fixing issues that crop up throughout the process. Too many layers can make it difficult to adjust the image in the long run.

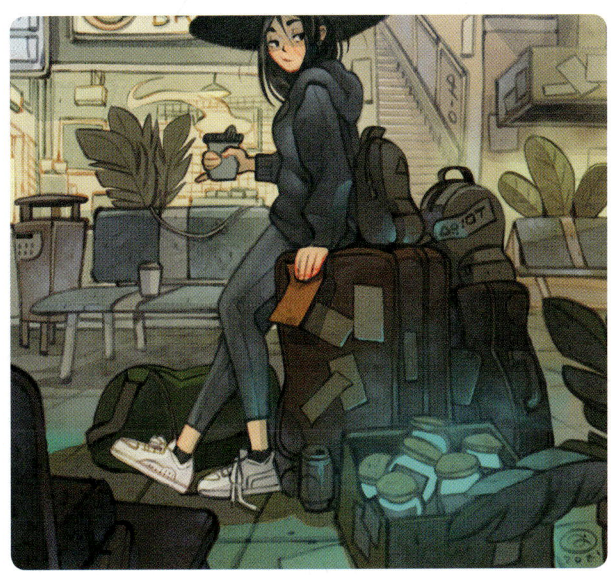

Adding a light haze over the illustration is a great way to blend colors together

**19** Create a correction layer to fine-tune the brightness and contrast of the illustration. This will be useful when editing the image as a whole, as well as when boosting or reducing the contrast in smaller areas. As you work, continue to add small adjustment layers using the selections made earlier in step 05. This will help you to create a perfect balance of values across the entire image.

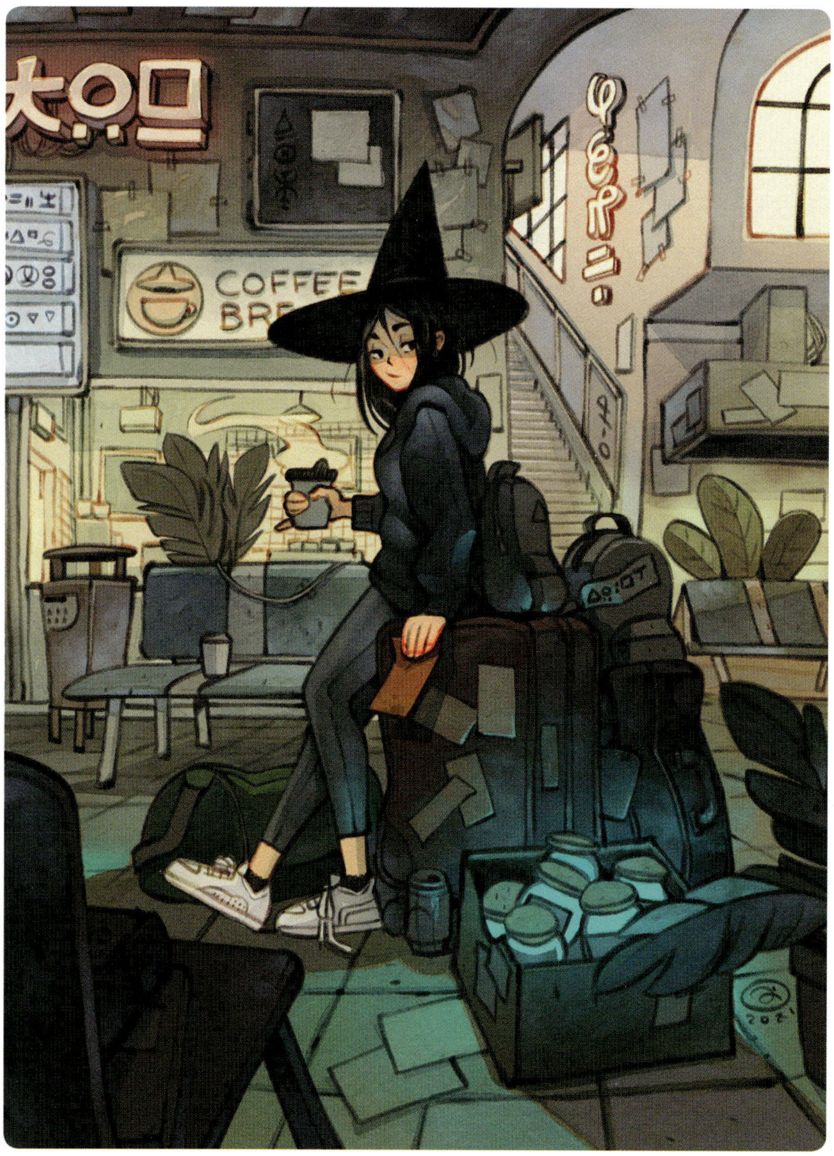


Adjustment layers can fix problematic areas of the illustration, both on a macro and micro level

**20** In step 04 the line art was placed on top of the colored undertone layer. In the final stages, it's important to paint colors and highlights over the line art to instill the illustration with an even more captivating look. Use light colors to shape specific elements, such as under the brim of the hat or on top of the plants. This will create a stronger sense of volume in the final image.

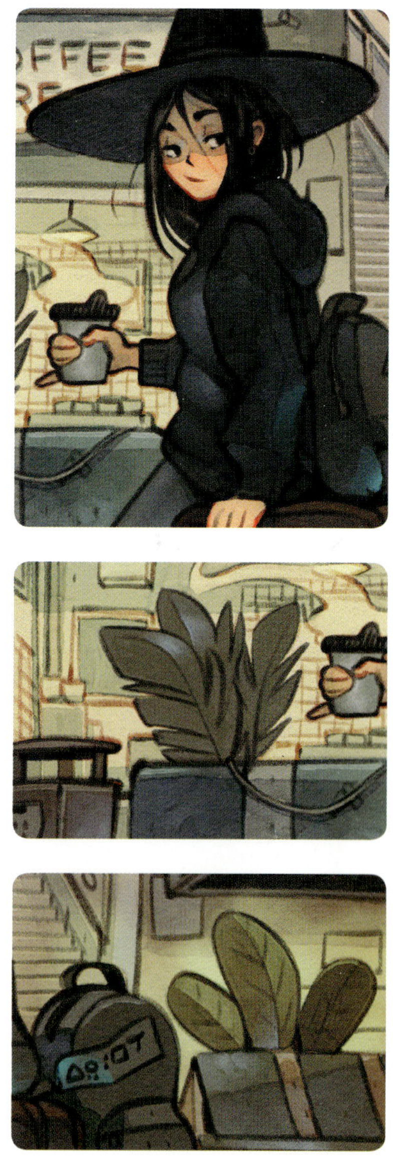

Painting over the line art will create a more three-dimensional look

## ARTIST TIP

Add a new layer over the top of the entire artwork. Fill it with a solid black or white, then change the blend mode to Color. This will instantly change the whole image to black and white. Turning this layer on will allow you to evaluate the values in the entire illustration, without getting distracted by the individual colors. Keep the layer turned off while coloring, only turning it on to check the values as needed.

**21** Use Color Balance correction layers to subtly alter the colors as you work. Next, paint in fine details on an Overlay layer, adding rim light to important areas, such as the character. Focus the final details on the focal points and ignore areas of lesser importance. This will help to guide the viewer's eyes around the illustration. These final highlights can easily make or break the image, so take some time to map out where these should fall before committing.

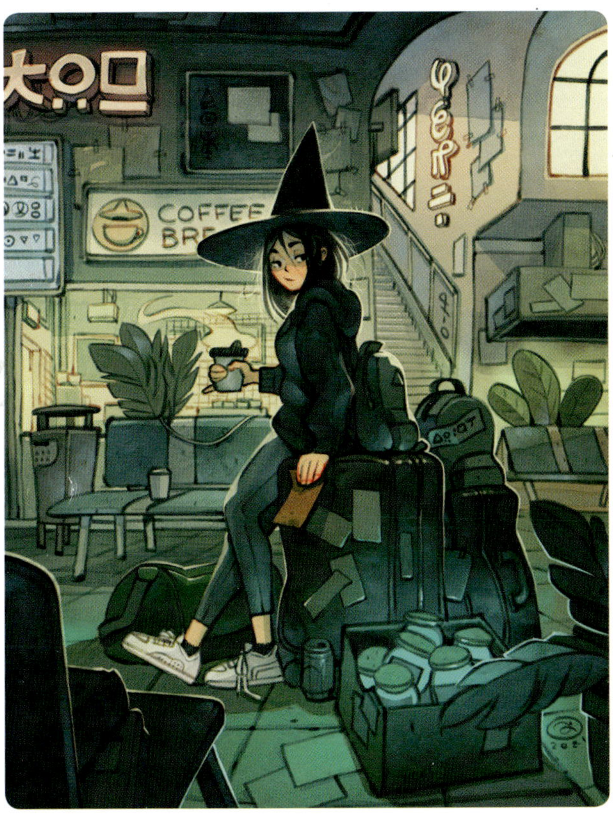


Rim lighting will highlight the character and other focal elements of the illustration

**22** Using the selections and a few Hard Light layers, add flat tones to make the colors more homogeneous. Select red tones for the character and green for the background, before decreasing these tones until they are barely visible. Putting complementary colors next to each other will emphasize the difference between the elements of the illustration, giving them a more dramatic contrast. Use strong color accents for the neon lights and any other illuminated elements of the illustration.

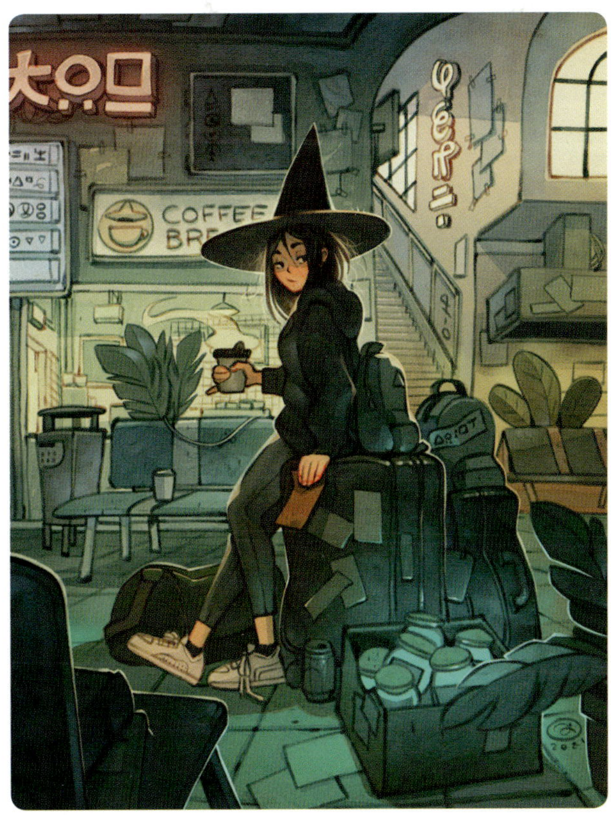


Using large areas of complementary color in low opacity will enhance the palette

**23** The next step is to add the smallest details in the illustration: the illuminated dust specks that float on the air near the light sources. Every new layer and effect must be fine-tuned and its opacity controlled. Don't add too many special effects, or viewers will not be able to understand what they're looking at or where to look.

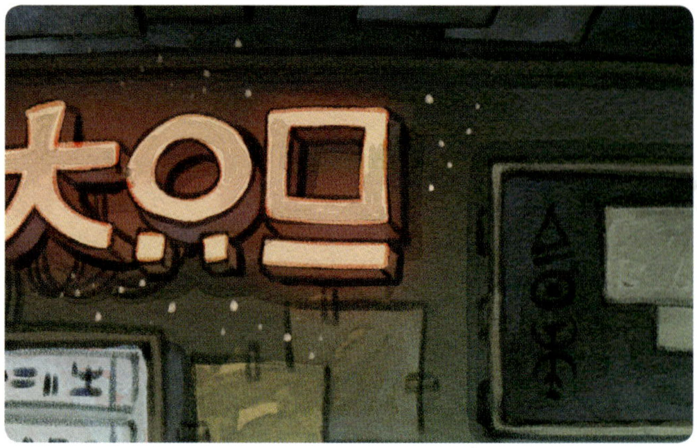

Small details like shimmering dust specks give the illustration a sense of movement

**24** The final step is to add the ghost cats that often appear in my witch artwork. Use a strong white value to paint them on a new layer, giving them a soft ethereal glow. Ensure they are pale and ghostly, rather than overly bright or luminous. Additionally, take care to space them throughout the illustration, as grouping them all in one corner could easily unbalance the composition of the entire image.

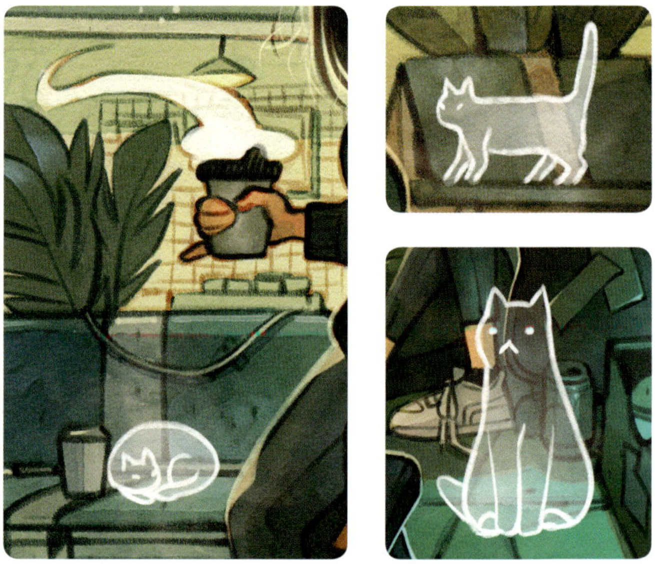

Ghost cats are a signature of my illustrations; I use them to add a sense of magic to a scene

# CONCLUSION

Congratulations! You have now completed an illustration with a familiar, detailed environment, as well as a mysterious fantasy theme. The final image contains many of my signature elements, such as the cute ghost cats, as well as a strong anime influence. The color combinations create an urban atmosphere, while the character's pose and mannerisms provide the viewer with a relatable anchor. While this tutorial walks you through my process of creating an anime-style illustration, it is now up to you to tailor the workflow to suit your preferred media and style of working.

When developing your personal style, it can be helpful to look at the work of other artists with an anime or manga style, as well as watching anime films and television shows. Keep in mind, however, that your art style should be unique to you, influenced by your life, personality, and interests. Imposing another artist's style on your work can be detrimental to your natural way of creating art. Your personal style will emerge over time and is not something that can be forced. All you can do is put in the practice, using tutorials such as this one to inspire you.

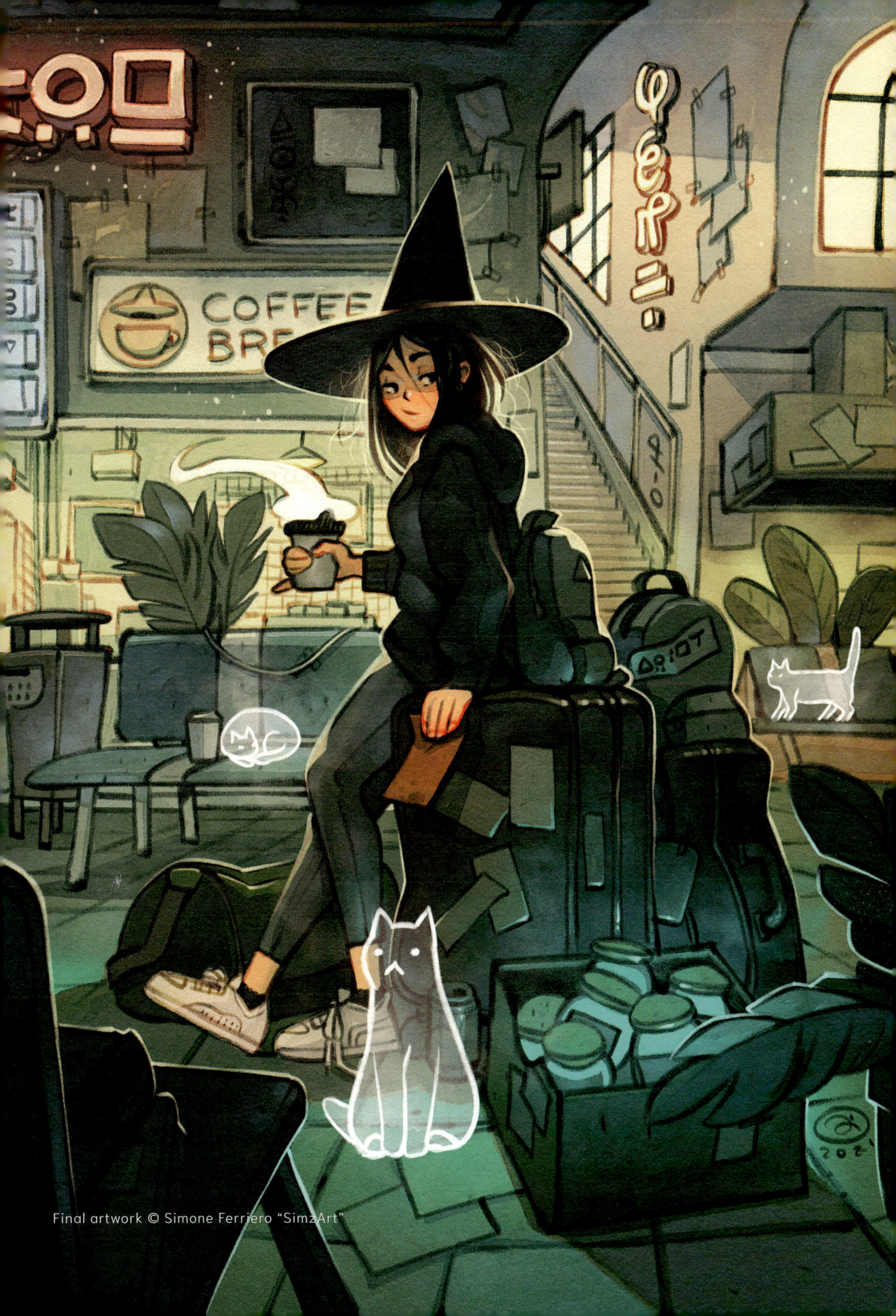


Final artwork © Simone Ferriero "SimzArt"

# GLOSSARY

By Anny "Yoai"

**Adoptables/Adopts**
Character designs for sale, typically in the form of reference sheets.

**Animation**
In the context of anime and manga, this involves creating a series of graphics or illustrations for the purpose of creating a moving "animated" image. In traditional animation, this is achieved by running the graphics together sequentially. With digital animation, an animation is created by programming a 2D or 3D model or object to move.

**Anime**
Japanese cartoons and animation spanning a variety of media, namely television and movies. The term is often used to refer to the art style itself.

**Art trade**
When an artist trades artwork with another artist, typically agreeing to draw each other's characters.

**Audience**
Individuals who follow an artist's work, also known as followers, subscribers, or a following on social-media platforms such as Twitter and Instagram.

**Brand**
A set of characteristics and factors of an artist's work, business, and who they are as an artist that uniquely identifies their work. The image they portray to the world, it is what their work is known for and recognized by; what sets them apart from other artists.

**Character design**
The design of a character, made up of various elements that make it recognizable and unique, such as the species, color palette, style, or theme (such as an ocean or space). To design a character is to focus on several important factors, such as shape language, line work, color palette, and intended audience.

**Comic**
Sequential drawings that tell a story, illustrate a situation or conversation, or convey a message. The artwork is typically accompanied by text in the form of narration or dialogue.

**Commercial success**
While this is a subjective term based on an artist's individual goals and objectives, it is typically defined as the means to be able to make money from a product or business. Exactly how much money is made, and what methods and resources are employed to make it, can determine the level of success.

**Commercial use**
In reference to commissions, this is commissioned artwork that the artist is allowed to use to make money for themselves, such as using the artwork for merchandise or as an album cover.

**Commission**
Creating artwork to a brief or specifications set by the commissioner, in exchange for a fee.

**Copyright**
Ownership and the rights to use, distribute, or modify intellectual property, including creations such as artwork. Put simply, who owns the artwork. In the United States and many other countries, the creator of the artwork is automatically given copyright of their creation, unless they sign it over to another party.

**Crowdfunding**
When a project is funded by a large number of individual people (sometimes several thousand or more), each investing small amounts of money (sometimes only a few dollars), in exchange for early access to the completed project's product or other rewards, such as discounts or merchandise. This is an increasingly popular alternative to sourcing investment from multiple big companies. When in the process of gathering funds, a crowdfunded project is typically called a "campaign" and is usually hosted on platforms such as Kickstarter or GoFundMe.

**Engagement**
When an artist's followers, or other social-media users, interact with their content, such as sharing, "liking," or commenting on a post.

**Genre**
The general categorization or grouping for something, within which there may be subgenres. For example, shojo is a genre of anime and manga aimed at young girls, within which is the subgenre of mahou shojo, which is still aimed at young girls, but has a specific "magical girl" theme.

**Josei**
A genre of anime and manga intended for young women, aged eighteen and above, that contains serious or mature themes, such as romance or crime. The word itself means "women."

**Kodomomuke**
A genre of anime and manga intended for very young children, aged three and above, of all genders. Light-hearted and fun, it is typically drawn in a simpler and more cartoonlike style than other anime genres. The word itself means "for children."

**Manga**
Japanese comics, or comics created in a style reminiscent of these. Manga precedes anime, and many anime shows are based on manga series.

**Marketing**
The act of promoting a product or service that is for sale, with the aim of convincing people to buy it.

**OC**
"Original Character." The opposite of fan art, this is a character an artist has designed themselves.

**Online presence**
How active an artist is online and how many different social platforms they use to promote their work. For example, do they post artwork on their social-media channels daily, weekly, or only a few times a year? It can also refer to how well known they are in an online community, though this is nuanced as there are thousands of different communities online. Even in the anime-style art community, there are multiple subdivisions; some provide a space for artists who draw mainly fan art, while others focus on artists who create their own original characters.

**Personal use**
Used in reference to commissions, this is commissioned artwork that can only be used for personal purposes, such as decoration, collecting, and referencing. The artist is not permitted to sell or use the artwork in any way to make money.

**PFP**
Profile picture.

**Portfolio**
Almost like a resume, a portfolio is a carefully curated selection of artwork that best represents an artist's skill level, style, abilities, and flexibility (showing the range of what they can draw), as well as any notable work they have created in the past.

**Reference sheet**
The visual reference for a character, (often an original character or "OC") usually in the form of a drawing, where the character's pose and overall composition is for the purpose of showing the design's details and accurate colors.

**Seinen**
A genre of anime and manga intended for young men, aged eighteen or older, that usually contains mature themes, such as violence or horror. The word itself means "young men."

**Shojo**
A genre of anime and manga aimed at young girls, typically aged ten to seventeen years. The word itself means "young girl."

**Shonen**
A genre of anime and manga geared toward young boys aged ten to seventeen years. The word itself means "young boy."

**Storyboarding**
Quick sequential sketches and captions that map out the different scenes of an animation, including major movements, scene changes, events, and dialogue, to let the animators know what to draw.

**Style**
In the context of creating art, this is the various aspects of each individual artist's work and creative quirks that are specific to them. For example, this can include their specific way of drawing characters, what media they use, their unique brushstroke techniques, and many other factors.

**Trends**
Practices, imagery, themes, or ideas that are currently popular with the online art community. What artists like to create, engage with, adopt as part of their own work, or employ as a marketing strategy.

**WIP**
Work-in-progress, used when referring to unfinished artwork.

**YCH/YCH commission**
"Your Character Here." This is a type of commission where an artist draws a quick concept sketch of a composition, with only a simple stick-figure or blank base for the character, and offers to draw the commissioner's OC in that spot.

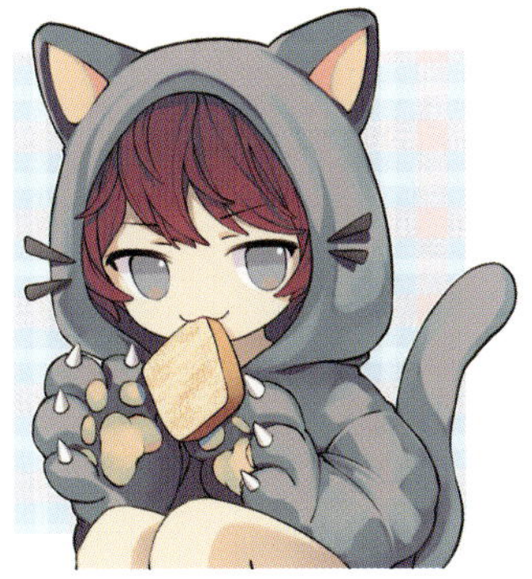

Artwork by Anny "Yoai"

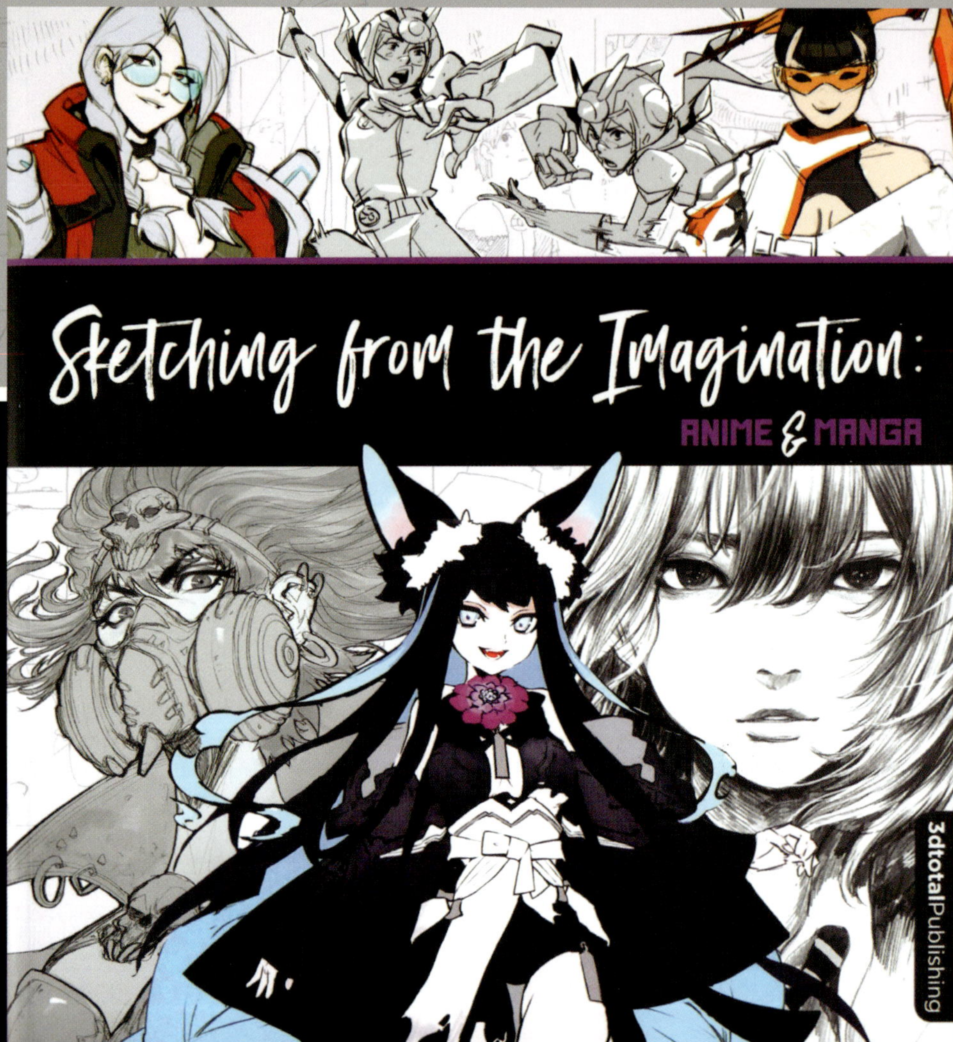


Following on from the success of previous titles in this popular series, *Sketching from the Imagination: Anime & Manga* presents a wide array of interpretations of the Japanese art forms. You will have an access-all-areas pass to the sketchbooks of 50 accomplished artists from various fields as they share their inspiration, favorite tools, and techniques. Discover hundreds of sketches accompanied by the insightful narratives and advice of these illustrators, concept artists, and 3D artists alike. From action and adventure to the paranormal, horror, science fiction, and more, every corner of the anime genre is reimagined for artists of all disciplines and skill levels. Whether you're a beginner, an experienced artist, or just a lover of this genre of art so synonymous with Japan, you're sure

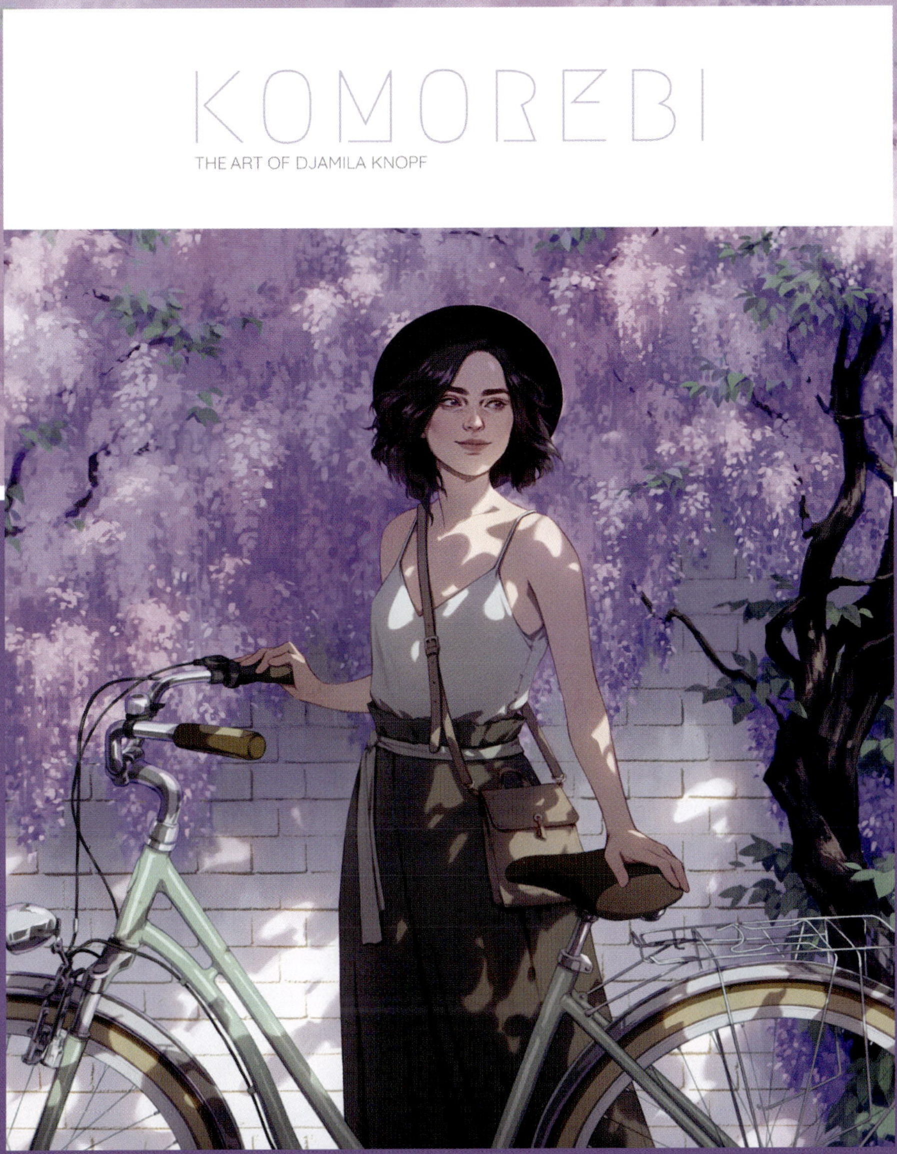
KOMOREBI
THE ART OF DJAMILA KNOPF

# **3dtotal**Publishing

**3dtotal Publishing is a trailblazing, creative publisher specializing in inspirational and educational resources for artists.**

Our titles feature top industry professionals from around the globe who share their experience in skillfully written step-by-step tutorials and fascinating, detailed guides. Illustrated throughout with stunning artwork, these best-selling publications offer creative insight, expert advice, and essential motivation. Fans of digital art will enjoy our comprehensive volumes covering Adobe Photoshop, Procreate, and Blender, as well as our superb titles based around character design, including *Fundamentals of Character Design* and *Creating Characters for the Entertainment Industry*. The dedicated, high-quality blend of instruction and inspiration also extends to traditional art. Titles covering a range of techniques, genres, and abilities allow your creativity to flourish while building essential skills.

Well-established within the industry, we now offer over 100 titles and counting, many of which have been translated into multiple languages around the world. With something for every artist, we are proud to say that our books offer the 3dtotal package:

LEARN • CREATE • SHARE

---

**Visit us at 3dtotalpublishing.com**

**3dtotal Publishing is part of 3dtotal.com, a leading website for CG artists founded by Tom Greenway in 1999.**

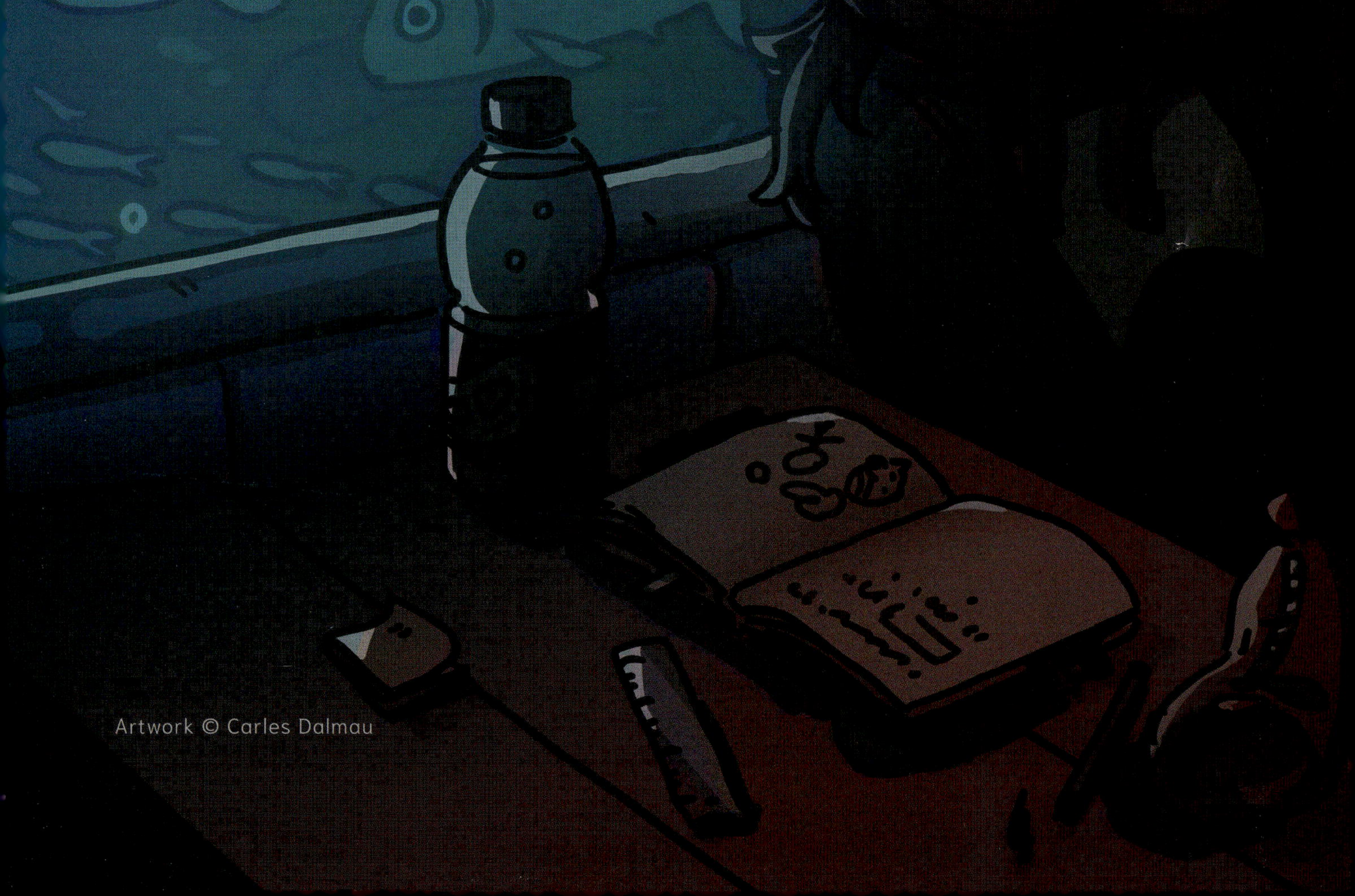

Artwork © Carles Dalmau